Feminist Television Criticism

Feminist Television Criticism

A READER

Second edition

Edited by Charlotte Brunsdon and Lynn Spigel

Open University Press

Open University Press
McGraw-Hill Education
McGraw-Hill House
Shoppenhangers Road
Maidenhead
Berkshire
England
SL6 2QL

email: enquiries@openup.co.uk
world wide web: www.openup.co.uk

and Two Penn Plaza, New York, NY 10121–2289, USA

First published by Oxford University Press, 1997
Second edition published by Open University Press, 2008.

A catalogue record of this book is available from the British Library

ISBN-13: 978 0335 22545 3 (pb)   978 0335 22544 6 (hb)

Library of Congress Cataloging-in-Publication Data
CIP data applied for

Typeset by RefineCatch Limited, Bungay, Suffolk
Printed in Great Britain by Bell and Bain Ltd, Glasgow

The **McGraw·Hill** Companies

Contents

Acknowledgements

Thanks to the authors and publishers for permission to reprint the work included in this book. Many thanks also to the friends, colleagues and institutions that helped with this second edition. We are particularly grateful to Julie D'Acci who co-edited the first volume of *Feminist Television Criticism* with us in the 1990s, and whose contributions and ideas still help shape this second edition. Max Dawson, Abigail Derecho, Elizabeth Nathanson, Kirsten Pike and Linda Robinson (at Northwestern) and Amy Holdsworth, Sarah Thomas, and Jennifer Twyford (at Warwick) helped with additional research. We also want to thank Northwestern University and the University of Warwick which supported the project financially, including an undergraduate research studentship for Jennifer Twyford at Warwick.

Note on the text

Television is studied in both the humanities and social sciences, and the articles we have selected for this reader come from journals and books which use different scholarly conventions. In all cases, the conventions used on first publication have been retained, as have spellings of word such as 'programme/program' and the hyphenation (or not) of 'post-feminism'. The chapters by Kimberly Springer and Beretta Smith-Shomade, which come from books with integrated bibliographies, have had lists of references provided by the editors for this volume.

Introduction to the Second Edition

A decade has passed since the first edition of *Feminist Television Criticism*. What's on television has changed, as have ideas of what television is, and how it might be watched. Television studies, first formed between film studies and mass communications and the sociology of the media, now finds itself paired with 'new media' and a range of digital platforms, even as television gains recognition as a legitimate object of study in disciplines as diverse as history, anthropology and urban studies. And feminism too is paradoxically both more and less present in relation to television: there are new journals, new television programmes, new debates, new attitudes to, and practices of, gender. There are new feminists, while at the same time there is less memory of feminism as a series of nineteenth- and twentieth-century movements. Apparently we now live, as many of the chapters in this book suggest, in 'post-feminist times'. In 1997, we did not imagine that these would take the form of programmes like the British/US Reality show *Wife Swap* (which first aired in Britain in 2003), the US drama *Desperate Housewives* (2004–present), the Colombian telenovela *Yo soy Betty la fea* (1999–2001), or the US pay cable drama *the L Word* (2004–present), each of which works over the terrain of gender in ways which both assume and ignore feminist ideas.[1] This new edition reflects on the many changes that have taken place in that decade within the television industries, within the academic field of television studies, and within the culture and politics of feminist movements. We haven't tried to be inclusive – how could we be, in a book this size? – but we have tried to trace, systematically, key directions and developments in feminist television criticism.

Feminist television criticism was partly formed in the 1970s and 1980s in the encounter between the young, often privileged US and European women who were drawn to second wave feminism and the destiny of 'the housewife' that they were determined to avoid. It was the energy of this encounter that fuelled the early repudiation, investigation and defence of the defining women's genre of twentieth-century television, the soap opera, as well as the investigation of the performance of the housewife and her liberated 'other', the new woman/working girl in sitcoms and dramas set in domestic and/or workplace locales. Feminist critics returned repeatedly to questions of everyday life, the home, and the repetitive structure of time in both the housewife's daily tasks and in television narratives aimed at her. In addition, critics (particularly those in the US) investigated television as a suburban medium. This work, which was represented in the first edition of this book, persists as a key structure in this edition, but here the house-wife and the new woman are joined by the more recent figures of the post-feminist girl, the 'out' lesbian, and the female entrepreneur. Today's scholarly TV line-up includes media moguls such as Oprah Winfrey and Martha Stewart and police officers like Jane Tennison, as well as such fashionable TV heroines as Buffy Summers, Carrie Bradshaw, Nigella Lawson, *the L Word*'s sexy lesbians, and the desperate housewives of Wisteria Lane – a group of women who are notably contradictory in their appeal as powerful action heroines, CEOs (Chief Executive Officers), working girls, school girl 'vamps', and above all, women fully at home in consumer culture.

This cast of female characters appears at a time when television as an institution, industry, and everyday practice has itself undergone major transformations. New forms of cable and satellite narrowcasting to niche audiences, new modes of convergence between the television and the Internet, new developments in digital television and digital video recorders (DVRs), new modes of globalization and conglomerate business structures, and new forms of regulation (or deregulation) have taken hold in a number of national contexts. Although these transitions have been afoot since the 1980s, by the millennium the television systems in many parts of the world had changed considerably. As terrestrial broadcasting was supplemented and in many cases supplanted by private cable and satellite systems, the older state-run, public, and private/network broadcast stations increasingly became just one among many choices, so that audiences now gather as 'niche' publics rather than 'national' publics *per se*. So too, digital con-vergence has meant that those parts of the world population equipped with DVRs, computer Internet connections, or (most recently) cell phones can watch programmes in their own space and according to their own clocks. This means that women's 'rhythms of reception' are no longer necessarily bound to the temporal flows of TV schedules in the ways that they were when Tania Modleksi first coined that phrase in the 1980s.[2] Time-shifting (which began, of course, with the video cassette recorder (VCR)) correlates with the changing conception (both in the industry and in feminist criticism) of the TV audience as a family unit and the woman viewer as a housewife *per se*. Rather than family viewing, television's contemporary audiences often gather according to social formations of taste. Among these, categories of youth, gender, and sexual preference have been a salient feature, if only because the global marketers for television particu-larly want to engage these demographic groups as consumers. In this context, programmes like *Ally McBeal* (1997–2002), *Sex and the City* (1998–2004), and *Queer Eye for the Straight Guy* (2003–present) have especially appealed to young women and gay men as 'cross-over' niche consumer publics presumably interested in cosmopolitan lifestyles, fashion, and international design.

Nevertheless, these global media flows have not erased local 'situated' habits of producing and viewing television. As Ien Ang suggests, the global popularity of *Dallas* (1978–91) has never been replicated (at least at such an extreme level). So too, despite critics' fears of homogenization, worldwide dramas did not exactly replicate American productions; instead, serial dramas often express local meanings and con-cerns. Considering the transnational East Asian success of the (post-) trendy Japanese drama *Tokyo Love Story* (which aired in the early 1990s), Ang argues that rather than thinking about globalization as a worldwide phenomenon with uniform effects, it is more useful to think of the ways in which 'cultural proximity' among audience formations accounts for both programme popularity and the transnational flow of meanings across national boundaries.[3] In this volume, in Chapter 15, Elizabeth MacLachlan and Geok-lian Chua take up this issue of cultural proximity in relation to Chinese viewers of Japanese dramas in Singapore, while in Chapter 16 Ksenija Vidmar-Horvat explores how her 'post-socialist' Slovenian students understand the politics of US-inspired postfeminist ideals in *Ally McBeal*. Such research suggests that even if postfeminist TV dramas circulate on a global market, the meanings of postfeminism depend on the wider social and political context in which the programmes are viewed.

The new configurations of the 'post-network/post-public service' television systems have also provided a context for the emergence of new programme types – among which docu-soaps, reality television and 'lifestyle' programming have proved especially genera-tive on a global scale. Despite their popularity in markets ranging from Japan to Sweden to India to New Zealand to Canada and the US, these genres are prime examples of 'glocal' production as format rights are sold across nations and the format is repro-duced with local/national 'accents'. For example, the original first season of the British *Wife Swap* was shot and edited with a documentary look that echoes the realist look of historical British documentary formats, while the US version has much faster editing, gimmicky digital effects, upbeat music, and an overall glitzy look and feel. Meanwhile, India's 2002 Reality marriage broker show *Kahin naa kahin koi hai* (*There's Someone, Somewhere*) presented its own version of heterosexual coupling (and is also somewhat of a prototype for the short-lived 2003 US Reality show *Married By America*).

In addition to the Reality format's glocal appeal, its putative claims to represent ordinary people living 'real' lives have made these formats interesting to television critics who have explored them in relation to how different national versions of ordinari-ness are constructed, and to the regimes of appropriate behaviour and appearance that they present in relation to gender, sexuality, race, ethnicity and class. Programmes ranging from Reality makeover shows like *What Not to Wear* [2003–present] and *Extreme Makeover* [2002–06] to court shows like *Judge Judy* (1996–present) and *Judge Hatchett* (2000–present) to cooking shows (with hosts like Nigella Lawson and Martha Stewart) to home decoration programmes like *Changing Rooms* (1996–2004) and *Trading Spaces* (2000–present) are met with an ambivalent mix of moral outrage and enjoyment. While some critics see these shows as the ultimate forms of degradation and humiliation, others argue that the programmes make visible previously undervalued skills and invisible publics (for example, several of the home decorating shows feature gay and lesbian couples).[4] The lifestyle shows have also spawned a new contradictory figure – the corporate housewife exemplified by media mavens Martha Stewart, Delia Smith, Rachel Ray and more. With huge fandoms, these women wield power across media platforms and turn homemaking skills into media empires, making them in some critics' views postfeminist figures *par excellence* (a subject Joanne Hollows explores in her essay on Nigella Lawson reprinted in this volume, Chapter 8).[5]

Indeed, many of the popular programmes and heroines that critics now choose to discuss offer different forms of attraction than did earlier programmes that depicted disgruntled housewives (like Britain's *Butterflies* [1978–83]) or liberated 'new women' (like *The Mary Tyler Moore Show* [1970–77] in the US). Even while the classic 'new woman' working girl shows sometimes presented fashionable heroines (Mary Richards of *The Mary Tyler Moore Show* is a case in point), the narrative trajectory in programmes like *Sex and the City* or *Desperate Housewives* (2004–present) – or aspirant British programmes like *Gold-Plated* (2006) – is more concerned with the *mise-en-scène* of a fabulous feminine 'lifestyle' than with the narrative dilemmas they pose regarding marriage vs. career, babies vs. clubbing, or suburbs vs. cities. These narrative dilemmas – once pivotal to second wave feminist and feminist TV plots – are now in some sense in 'quotes' (intended either as residual cultural knowledge and/or straight out parody of the 1960s/1970s women's lib) while the glamour of lifestyle – fashion, upscale décor, food, restaurants, and diegetic shopping sprees – are often the focus of the shows.[6] Given this focus on *mise-en-scène* over plot and narrative denouement, it seems fitting that theories of performativity (as inspired by Judith Butler) have supplemented the hermeneutics of textual analysis and close textual/ideological readings in feminist TV scholarship.[7] Reality and lifestyle TV are, of course, ripe for this kind of analysis because, while scripted, they are primarily about the performance of self.

The performance of sexuality has also become a concern in studies of television that focus on queer subjectivities and gay and lesbian characters. When we edited the first edition of this book, lesbian kisses on the British soap opera *Brookside* (1982–2003) and the US drama *L.A. Law* (1986–94) were among the few appearances of lesbian love on television. The turn of the century has seen what some regard as a 'queering' of Anglo-American television, so much so that Ron Becker refers to this period in the US as the 'gay nineties'.[8] In Britain there has been a little more visible lesbianism, including, for example, the 2002 quality lesbian drama, *Tipping the Velvet* (based on Sarah Waters' novel), while gay men populated the screen in Russell. T. Davies' sexually explicit series, *Queer as Folk* (aired in Britain in 1999 and adapted in 2000 on the premium US cable channel Showtime). Showtime also features *the L Word*, a drama set in a lesbian and bisexual community in Los Angeles, while US broadcast networks present gay sitcoms like *Will and Grace* (1998–2006). However, as Bonnie Dow details in Chapter 5, the period has also seen the cancellation of the sitcom *Ellen* (1994–98), after both the character Ellen Morgan and the star Ellen DeGeneres came out. The concerns of queer theory and transgender studies, while they cannot easily be equated with feminism or the pursuits of the feminist TV critic as she was formulated in the past, nevertheless do have shared concerns with the production of gendered subjectivities. In the literature we can discern a movement from hegemony models and censorship to issues of queer visibility and post-lesbian identity.

The history of feminist television criticism reveals both continuities and discontinuities over time as scholars have struggled to make sense of why media matter and what women want the media to do. The history of feminist television criticism also parallels struggles within feminism – struggles over who exactly counts as a 'woman', who belongs, who is excluded, and increasingly who even wants to be a feminist at all.

Feminist television criticism was formed initially through two quite different agendas, one directed at the medium itself and the other at the existing traditions of critical scholarship about television. In the first case, as with other 1960s political movements, feminists took the media to task for their demeaning and stereotypical images of women. The feminist critical engagement with television can be traced to media workers, and in particular to women who wrote for women's magazines. The advice column (which itself grew out of nineteenth-century domestic manuals) is associated with women's everyday life (cooking, cleaning, childrearing), but in the postwar period, women's magazines also included nascent critiques of the housewife role and 'woman's place'. In 1962, Helen Gurley Brown published one of the most famous examples of this mode – *Sex and the Single Girl* – a book that (vaguely) used the insights of 1950s sexology to advise women on how to extend their girlhood into their thirties and take advantage of the pleasures of being a career girl bachelorette.

Brown was not known as a political feminist or a media critic – but she was certainly a powerful woman media worker who came to have a special voice in women's culture via *Cosmopolitan*. In *Sex and the Single Girl*, Brown advises women, 'Have a TV set for quiet little evenings at home and shows of major importance but not too great a TV set or you'll never get out of your apartment. One of the impressive-income girls I mentioned . . . is still viewing on a 9-inch set for this reason.'[9] Yet, despite her parsimony, Brown also advises women that television is a great career path to success (her models are Madelyn Martin, co-writer of *I Love Lucy*, and film/TV producer Joan Harrison, a graduate of Oxford who produced the TV show *Alfred Hitchcock Presents* [1955–62]).[10]

This advice mode persists today in numerous popular media forms. Magazines aimed at girls and women are still associated with powerful women media workers, such as Martha Stewart (*Martha Stewart Living*), Delia Smith (who had a long association with the British supermarket chain, Sainsbury's) and especially Oprah Winfrey, who advises us what to watch and read on her TV show, in her magazine and, of course, in her book club. Advice discourse is also common to Grrrl Power's investment in cultural styles and is used in 'handbooks' like Carla Sinclair's *Net Chick: Smart Girl Guide to the Wired World* (1996).[11] And the advice mode is embroiled in feminist media scholarship if only because the feminist often thinks she knows how other women *should* do something. That is, she thinks she knows how women should 'read' cultural texts, and she tries to transform women into feminist readers by giving them interpretive tips. Notably in this respect even while the 'thirdwaver' often identifies herself in distinction to the more moral 'schoomarmishness' of the second wave feminist, and even while she often embraces popular culture, third wave feminists and postfeminists (who sometimes but not always categorize themselves in the same vein) also take up this pedagogic advice mode. Jennifer Baumgardner and Amy Richards (both young media workers at Gloria Steinem's magazine *Ms.*) appropriated this form for their book *Manifesta: Young Women, Feminism, and the Future* (2000). *Manifesta* is an account of third wave feminism, which begins with a homage to pioneers of second wave feminism, especially Steinem. However, as self-declared thirdwavers, Baumgardner and Richards also distinguish themselves from their predecessors and such distinctions are largely achieved through their more immersive relation to popular media of all sorts, which they consider coextensive with (opposed to antithetical to) feminist activism.[12] The historical persistence of the advice made across media forms addressed to women has often been associated with product promotions and tie-ins. These cross-media relationships have proliferated in the recent period, with merchandising and branding becoming a more significant aspect of television production. In this volume, in Chapter 2, Jane Arthurs considers how a reigning example of postfeminist television – *Sex and the City* – incorporates this women's magazine/advice column function into its narrative through the main character Carrie Bradshaw (who writes an advice column on relationships) as well as the Internet and ancillary 'advisory' discourses surrounding the show. Also in this volume, in Chapter 7, Laurie Ouellette discusses how the US Reality court show, *Judge Judy* (1996–present) articulates traditions of advice-giving within neo-liberal assumptions about how society works, and the obligations of individuals in the post-welfare state.

Given the fact that women's magazines and magazine writers developed feminist criticism in the context of advice discourse, it is fitting that when Betty Friedan wrote her bestseller book *The Feminine Mystique* (1963), she marshalled her critique of patri-archal oppression not only at social and political structures but also at the media. Like Brown, Friedan had worked for women's magazines. But, *The Feminine Mystique* turns the magazine discourse of advice inside out through the rhetoric of criticism. Friedan's second chapter is in effect an early example of feminist media criticism as it traces female heroines in women's magazines from their career girl adventure roles in the late 1930s to the 'happy housewife heroine' of the postwar world (the woman who sacrifices career for marriage).[13] Friedan's book was so widely read that in 1964 she even went on to write a two-part article for *TV Guide* critiquing the 'feminine mystique' on television.[14] Germaine Greer, Sheila Rowbotham and Juliet Mitchell, in the inaugural books of British Women's Liberation, also devoted significant space to media critique, because tele-vision, part of the media and image-making industries, was seen as instrumental in *misrepresenting* women.[15] In this early period of second wave feminism, feminist deal-ings with television were often calls to action growing out of a conviction that women's oppression was very much related to mass media representations and that change was not only urgent, but possible. The famous iconic moments of this are the protests against the 1968 Miss America contest in the US and the 1970 Miss World pageant in London.

By the 1970s, feminist film criticism was developing into its own discursive practice – particularly with the 1974 trade book publication of Molly Haskell's *From Reverence to Rape: The Treatment of Women in the Movies*.[16] Like Brown and Friedan, Haskell was a media worker (she wrote film reviews for the *Village Voice*, but also wrote for *Vogue* and *Mademoiselle*). Throughout the 1970s, feminist media criticism also developed within university contexts. Writing from a social scientific perspective, some scholars explored images of women via content analysis and image criticism.[17] In this period there was also a thriving, only partly institutionalized radical culture, from which emerged journals such as *Jump-Cut, Radical America, Women and Film*, and *Camera Obscura* in the US, and in Britain, the film journal, *Screen* as well as the feminist 'women's magazine', *Spare Rib*. First published in *Screen* in 1975, Laura Mulvey's influential essay 'Visual Pleasure in Narrative Cinema' opened up a still ongoing debate about the degree to which mainstream media (in her case classic Hollywood films) pre-sent women as visual objects of male pleasure (organized around voyeurism, fetishism of the woman's body, and sadism at the level of narrative from a male hero's point of view).[18] Feminists writing about both film and television have, ever since, debated whether or not this theorization of visual pleasure leaves any modes of pleasure (aside from masochism) available to women, and, if so, in what way women (as Christine Gledhill put it) make 'pleasurable negotiations' with mainstream film and media texts.[19] In response to this debate, early television scholars from humanities-based perspec-tives of feminist theory investigated genres aimed at women. With regard to television,

Carole Lopate's (1977) and Tania Modleksi's (1979) work on daytime TV moved away from image analysis *per se* toward issues of women's everyday life, female experience, and pleasures.[20] Meanwhile, over the course of the 1970s Michèle Mattelart wrote about the role of the media and women in Chile in the period surrounding the coup against the elected president Salvatore Allende.[21]

Feminist television critics aimed not just to disclose the myths behind television 'images' of women or even just to rethink the dynamics of visual pleasure; they also sought to critique the 'two sphere' mythos that private and public life were somehow divided, with the housewife in the private space of the home and politics as a public and male domain. In other words, like other feminists of the time, feminist TV critics proceeded on the more general second wave premise that the 'personal is political'. Feminists took issue (often implicitly) with the existing critical work on television that disregarded femininity, gender, and sexuality in discussions of the 'political'. Here, the political was interpreted in very narrow terms of government, the market and public policy (arenas that were mostly populated by male executives, producers, and policy-makers). As in other disciplines, feminist critics argued for a broadening of the meaning of the term 'political' to include a general interest in everyday life, especially the female-associated spheres of domesticity and consumerism.

Given this, it is no surprise that one of the first subjects to which feminist television critics turned was daytime programming and soap opera in particular. In the inaugural work on soap opera, it is possible to discern both ambivalence towards the object of study (which is characteristic of much feminist criticism of popular culture) and the desire for the institutional legitimation of the feminist television critic within the academy. The ambivalence is often manifest through the invocation of 'guilty pleasures', most frequently, the guilty pleasures associated with conventional femininities. However, the desire for legitimation was often central and explicit, and demanded a reconfiguration of what should be seen as the proper objects of study for media scholars. In this regard, it was also very much an attempt – like the early women's movement itself – to render visible the invisible (and often culturally disregarded), everyday conditions of women's lives in the home.[22] This is clear, for example, in the work of Dorothy Hobson, whose 1970s research in Birmingham (from which she developed the *Crossroads* project) was about the ways young mothers at home with their children used both television and radio in their daily routines, or the subsequent work of Ellen Seiter, who has conducted long-term participant observation in the use and regulation of television in contexts such as parent/toddler groups.[23]

The early feminist scholarship branched out toward a number of methodological pursuits that have had considerable longevity. There has been a large body of work that employs textual analysis (or the close reading of programmes for their narrative structures, iconography, symbolic codes, themes, and their solicitation of pleasure, identification and subjectivity). This focus on the text and its relation to female subjectivity and women's pleasure persists from the early 1970s/1980s literature (in this volume Tania Modleski, Ien Ang, and Annette Kuhn) to the present (in this volume, Jane Arthurs, Deborah Jermyn, and Susan J. Wolfe and Lee Ann Roripaugh). Since the 1980s, textual criticism has augmented its focus on soap opera and family melodrama with an account of a broader range of genres with action heroines in a number of national production contexts.[24]

The preoccupation with textual analysis stems partly from its more general methodological prominence in critical writing in the humanities. However, with the transformation of access to television programming engendered by the introduction of the domestic VCR in the 1970s, there is evident, retrospectively, a certain shared chronology between early feminist textual analysis of television and the new abilities to view programmes more than once. In these days of ritual viewing and reviewing of favourite programmes available in DVD box sets or through one's personal DVR 'archive', it is worth emphasizing how significant the video-recorder was in first permitting re-viewing, and also prompting fan productions and 'Slash' tapes (or tapes that use a cut-up aesthetic to re-edit popular television series). For example, as Constance Penley, Henry Jenkins, and Camille Bacon Smith first demonstrated, *Star Trek* fans cut up scenes in *Trek* to foreground what they saw as the homoerotic relation between the characters Spock and Kirk, a practice that paralleled homoerotic fanzines on the series and which today continues with digital fan art now circulated on fan websites and more widely on YouTube.[25] In this sense, textual analysis is not just a critical mode but is also related to the production of art and the cultures surrounding women's investments in television series more generally.

In addition to the interest in television as a textual form and the strategic rewriting and redaction of texts associated with fandom, feminist critics have also developed a strong interest in relating television to its wider discursive, social, institutional, and historical contexts. Julie D'Acci's groundbreaking work on *Cagney and Lacey* (1982–88) explored how female authors and producers worked within the mainstream and often heterosexist structures of Hollywood, and she showed, for example, that network censors required script changes and demanded that the more butch-looking Meg Foster be replaced with a more eye-candy, man-pleasing actress Sharon Gless in the role of Cagney.[26] This approach continues and develops in feminist institutional analysis of programmes (often written or produced by women) including Deborah Jermyn's work on Lynda La Plante, Beretta Smith-Shomade's analysis of Oprah Winfrey, and Bonnie Dow's essay on Ellen DeGeneres, all of which we have reprinted here.[27] However, as several of these scholars have observed, there is still surprisingly little scholarship on women as creators and producers of television. To take just British cases, there is very little on figures such as Debbie Horsfield (*Making Out* [1989–91]), Victoria Wood, Dawn French and Jennifer Saunders (best known for *Absolutely Fabulous* [1992–2004]), Meera Syall (co-creator of *Goodness Gracious Me* [1998–2000] and *The Kumars at No. 42* [2001–present]), Kay Mellor (*Band of Gold* [1995–97]), and the influential producer, Verity Lambert.[28]

In addition to work on authors and institutions, feminist television scholars have explored the relationship between text and context by looking at the broader social history of spectatorship and/or audiences. Some of the inaugural work here was especially interested in the context of reception inside and outside the home. David Morley's audience ethnography *Family Television* (1985) looked at the way gender and class structured family viewing patterns; Ann Gray's *Video Playtime* (1986) did the same for the then new VCR households; while Anna MacCarthy's more recent *Ambient Television* (2001) shows how gender and class dynamics pervade the way we use television screens as part of the everyday environment from shopping malls to restaurants to bars.[29]

Historical work on the domestic reception context has similarly examined how gender, class, ethnicity and national identities relate to modes of reception. Beginning in the late 1980s, historians like Mary Beth Haralovich, George Lipsitz, Shaun Moores, Ella Taylor, Lynn Spigel, Nina Liebman, and Marie-Françoise Levy rethought the terms of television (and also radio) history by opening up traditional broadcast histories – usually concerned with industry and policy – to focus on the social history of television with regard to gender, consumerism, and the home.[30] Conceptualizing television as part of a broader history of everyday life, this work draws on a range of sources associated with women's culture – including women's magazines, books on interior décor and architecture, advertisements aimed at women and their families, and television programmes (like soaps or sitcoms) associated with female audiences. Typically based on archival research methods, it treats these sources as primary historical documents that shed light on women's culture rather than treating them (as does much traditional history) as mere anecdotes. Moreover, this scholarship (either implicitly or explicitly) argues that these 'feminized' sources are just as useful as the more 'masculinized' and so-called 'official' sources such as network files and policy reports that were usually recorded by men in male-dominated institutions. Nevertheless, historians do also analyse official institutional sources through feminist interpretative strategies as Janet Thumim does in her scrutiny of BBC production files and Marsha Cassidy does in her history of 1950s daytime TV.[31] In other words, as with feminist history in general, these kinds of feminist television histories are interested in finding women's voices, or the conditions under which femininity is produced, and this means either looking in places that are not conventionally regarded as 'legitimate' or revisiting and re-visioning traditional sites and sources. Whether via a historical, sociological, and/or textual analysis, the focus on media in (or about) the home continues today in work on both television and digital media.[32] In this volume, in Chapter 18, Marsha Cassidy engages these interests with her study of the studio audiences for It Could Be You and Strike it Rich – two early 'makeover' programmes which she claims had special appeal to housewives living in the new consumer suburbs of postwar America.

Ever since Raymond Williams coined the term 'mobile privatization', television scholars have been interested not just in domesticity per se, but in the way television serves to negotiate the contradictions in industrial societies between the emphasis on the private family home and modern forms of mobility in the city. Like transportation systems, communication systems help to bridge the inside to the outside. But, rather than literal transport, broadcasting provides a fantasy of being in touch with the world while safely cloistered in the living room. Television, as Williams suggested, epitomized this fantasy by offering people imaginary forms of travel to distant locales.[33] Expanding on this concept, numerous feminist critics show how television's placement in the home is never simply just about the home but also part of a wider cultural fantasy of mobility and connectivity to the world outside (a point which David Morley made most explicitly in his article 'Notes from the Sitting Room' and his subsequent books) but which continues in much of the work on commercial satellites in, for example, Lisa Parks's Cultures in Orbit (which shows how satellites redefine ways of looking at the world).[34]

This interest in mobility and connectivity is often also present in work on media, citizenship, and/or diasporic populations. Marie Gillespie's Television, Ethnicity and

Cultural Change (1995) explores British Asian youth cultures in Southall (a London district), looking, for example, at teenagers' use of soap operas as a means of gossip and of differentiating themselves from their parents. Purnima Mankekar's *Screening Culture* (1999), from which her essay in our book is derived, explores how Indian women use commercial television, especially soaps and advertisements, in the context of their daily lives. Rathiba Hadj-Moussa explores how satellite television has affected the gendered structures of private and public space in Algeria. Lisa B. Rofel's work on the Chinese serial *Yearnings* (a big success in the early 1990s) investigates the programme's relationship to national and gender identity. Vicky Mayer examines how Mexican American girls use telenovelas with regard to their hybrid national identities across the US-Mexico border. Lee-Dong Ho explores how young women in Korea appropriate Japanese TV dramas and negotiate their cultural and gender identity through transnational TV consumption. Lila Abu-Lughod explores the contradictions at stake in the modernization projects forged by Egyptian television producers who create serial programming aimed at rural populations, and she shows, for example, how rural audiences often reject the modernization ethos in the serials.[35] As is evident, this scholarship on audiences spans a diverse set of subjects, not least of which is self-reflection on the complexities involved in doing ethnographic and/or qualitative audience research, particularly with regard to the social relations between the researcher and her subjects.

Inaugural studies, such as Ien Ang's *Watching Dallas* (1985) and Janice Radway's *Reading the Romance* (1984) presented the voices of women fans while offering feminist critique. Not only did the studies generate new knowledge about how women make sense of and find pleasure in popular texts, they also foregrounded the complex relations between the feminist and her interview subjects (who were often housewives and/ or less privileged, at least in terms of their educational capital, than the feminist critic). Indeed, a central problem for feminist television criticism, which has recurred throughout its history, is the relation between the feminist critic and 'women' in general.[36] Within ethnographic projects, the intersubjective relation of 'self–other' has become most explicit. Interview-based studies such as Constance Penley's work on *Star Trek* fans, Ellen Seiter's work on Christian parents, Dorothy Hobson's work on young Birmingham mothers, Seiter and Jacqueline Bobo's essay on viewers of the 1989 miniseries *The Women of Brewster Place*, Andrea Press's research on female viewers in the US, and, in Britain, Lyn Thomas's research on *Inspector Morse* fans, all display considerable self-consciousness about the role of the researcher, as well as, in some cases, questioning the degree to which 'feminism' is a relevant term for the participants in the research.[37] This has been particularly important in terms of questions of social class and critiques of racism. Bobo and Seiter's essay, included in the first edition of this Reader, demonstrated the institutional and methodological bias of ethnographic research, which, they suggest, has typically excluded the voices of women of colour. In addition, they argue, the whole field of feminist television criticism has been preoccupied with notions of 'woman' that are decidedly white and middle class, and has marginalized issues of civil rights and public life that centrally touch the lives of women of colour. As Kimberly Springer suggests in Chapter 4 in this volume, the term 'postfeminism' too does not signify a liberatory politics, particularly because of feminism's legacy of exclusions and its lack of attention to the lives and concerns of women of colour.

In feminist television criticism, the object of study bears its own legacy of racism. This has different historical and institutional inflections in different national contexts and broadcasting systems, and shapes employment, output and audience address. However, since the 1980s, there have been perceptible shifts in the regulated whiteness of most televisual output in the USA and the UK, and a range of genres, including talk shows, comedy and music video have increasingly addressed more diverse audiences and provided more representations of black (and in the US, Latina) women and in some cases more opportunities in the field of television production, which have in turn been addressed by scholars. The increased scholarship on Oprah Winfrey by critics such as Beretta Smith-Shomade, which we include in this volume, is an example of newer critical interventions, while the notable success of the British Asian comedy, Goodness Gracious Me (1998–2000) signalled a shift in the generic repertoires available to British Asian writers and performers.[38]

Nevertheless, the industry's practices of regulated inclusion are just as complex as is their historical legacy of exclusion. Although the multichannel systems and new consumer demographics have created some more choices, the issues are by no means resolved just because there are more media outlets. While this is a complex problem, it is clear that the current multichannel landscape is not a world of infinite diversity but rather a sophisticated marketplace that aims to attract demographic groups with spending power. Even minority networks like Black Entertainment Television (BET) or the Hispanic network, Telemundo, are first and foremost concerned to reach a consumer constituency so as to attract advertisers (and note that both are owned by huge media conglomerates: BET is owned by Viacom while Telemundo is owned by Sony Pictures Entertainment in conjunction with other corporate shareholders). As scholars such as Herman Gray and Beretta E. Smith-Shomade argue, television tends to level differences and address racialized groups as homogeneous consumer types (i.e. the African-American audience is imagined as one block rather than a group composed of different social, political and class interests).[39] In the multi-channel universe, this kind of homogenization of various publics has become a way to turn the smaller niche audiences of cable into a marketable brand (e.g., Lifetime or Oxygen are the 'woman's' channel; BET is the 'black network'). In this sense when scholars write about television in relation to issues of gender and sexuality, their emphasis is often on the imbrication of gender and sexuality with determinants of race and ethnicity, and the tendency in much of the work is to consider television within a wider frame of media practices, as does Kimberly Springer in the essay (Chapter 4) included here.[40]

Although we have been separating out various approaches and topics of concern in the literature, there is actually a much more fluid interaction among these areas of study. As various articles in this volume demonstrate, television scholarship has become an increasingly interdisciplinary endeavour, and feminist-inspired work on the medium has encouraged methodological elasticity as scholars search for ways to understand television's numerous (and rapidly changing) cultural forms. In this respect, while we have laid out a series of discrete pursuits, the field is actually more dynamic and the categories of analysis tend to overlap and intersect. Textual/spectator analysis, institutional/historical 'context' analysis, and audience research are often intertwined in television criticism.

In this respect, Stuart Hall's essay 'Encoding/Decoding' (1980) was enormously influential in setting an agenda for critics. Using insights from semiotics and Antonio Gramsci's theory of hegemony, Hall argued that media producers draw on taken-for-granted cultural understandings and working practices to create textual meanings, but that audiences (depending on their own social formations) do not always 'decode' the text in line with the intentions of its producers.[41] Some critics interpreted Hall's nuanced model as a call to search for 'resistant' readings of popular texts, and transformed, rather over-enthusiastically, much viewing of popular television to a subversive act. However, his theorization of the necessity for media scholars to pay attention to multiple determinations (including, production contexts, text, and audience) has inspired scholars to bring together numerous methods and modes of inquiry. Media critics now often explore an object from numerous perspectives, showing, for example, how a single television programme is a product of the political economy of production; its social and cultural context; its relation to broader narrative, genre, and aesthetic conventions; and its reception by audiences. Although not all authors can 'do it all', much of feminist television criticism is an attempt to understand the multiple pressures put on texts by the industry, by writers and producers, by the people who interpret them, by censorship or regulation, and by the larger discursive and social context in which programmes circulate.

Conclusion

Assessing the field as it appears today, since the first edition ten years ago, there has been a proliferation of sites in which feminist television criticism is practised. These range from new print journals such as *Feminist Media Studies* to e-journals and websites. Our first draft of our selected bibliography ran to more than seventy pages. Publishers will commission work that can be used in courses in a number of fields that increasingly take gender and popular culture as a serious topic of concern, and they also commission books likely to gain a crossover readership with television fans, many of whom have an interest in gender and sexuality on TV. Nevertheless, the increasing economic pressure on academic publishing means that it is actually more and more difficult to secure publication for scholarship on media forms produced outside the Anglo-American, and, increasingly, East Asian axis. In other words, there is more, but not necessarily greater diversity.

So too, although there is certainly increased interest in gender, sexuality and television, since the first edition of this book there really has not been a major paradigm shift within the scholarship *per se*. Textual analysis, ethnographic audience research, fan studies, institutional analysis, narrative analysis and ideological analysis still form the major approaches to the object. Rather than new methodological procedures, in more recent scholarship, it is attitudes towards and tastes for both TV and feminism that have changed. It is this observation that has led us to structure the book with considerable attention to the debates about post-feminism and its heroines, and the articles in this volume represent a set of shifting perspectives towards the objects – TV and feminism – that reflects the scholarship at large.

As stated at the outset, the most noticeable shift in feminist television criticism over the past ten years has been formed in response to the appearance of the post-feminist girl character and her embrace of consumer lifestyles, girliness, and popular culture. When we published this book in 1997, the idea of post-feminism was not yet really prevalent – at least in television studies. Elspeth Probyn's essay, 'New Traditionalism and Post-Feminism' which appeared in our first volume was one of the very first essays to theorize this change as it became manifest in television programmes.[42] Today, scholars writing about these issues – for example, Susan Douglas, Natasha Walter, Imelda Whelehan, Sarah Projansky, Angela McRobbie, Kimberly Springer, Amanda Lotz, Diane Negra and Yvonne Tasker – often consider the meaning and politics of post-feminism in relation to feminism, particularly with regard to issues of generational politics between the 'waves', the backlash against feminism, the problems of race, sexuality and class that traditionally haunted feminist movements, and the general question of global justice and citizenship in patriarchal social structures.[43] In this volume, Karen Boyle provides a compelling account of these issues, using the figure of Buffy Summers as a nexus for discussing not just the differences among second wave feminists and third wave 'girlness' that Buffy embodies but also the problems of male violence against women which that programme could make us rethink.

The richness and variety of the scholarship are captured, we hope, in this second edition. The book is organized into two sections, each with their own introductions. The first, 'Programmes and Heroines' collects together articles which have as their focus textual readings of television programmes, while the second, 'Audiences, Reception Contexts and Spectatorship', explores the viewing of television programmes in a range of contexts, and the ways in which this has been theorized. As a whole the book explores the new personae of feminist television criticism – the post-feminist girl, the corporate housewife, the 'out' lesbian, and the action heroine – and it also investigates the complex modes of transnational delivery and reception among viewers living in different parts of the world. Mostly written since the late 1990s, the essays revolve around a paradox regarding television and feminism that was not yet entirely apparent when we published the first edition in 1997. Today, it is clear that the terms 'television' and 'feminism' are productive poles around which debate circles in the academy and popular culture, and we reproduce some of the most interesting work in this book. Yet, at the same time, it is also clear that each term, 'feminism' and 'television', is marked by greater uncertainty than ten years ago. Feminism has become both old-fashioned and younger, local and global in different and changing ways, while television's place in domestic and national imaginaries is being transformed as we write, and increasingly it is uncertain what TV will be, and how people will watch it and on what technological platforms/screens. These essays chart both these developments and these uncertainties.

Notes

1 The dates for *Wife Swap* are for the British version; the US version ran from 2004–present. The telenovela *Yo soy Betty la fea* was adapted for the US as the primetime drama *Ugly Betty* (2006–present).

2 Tania Modleski, "The rythms of reception: daytime television and women's work', in *Regarding Television: Critical Approaches – An Anthology*, ed. E. Ann Kaplan (Frederick, MD: University Publications of America, 1983), 67–75.

3 Ien Ang, 'The cultural intimacy of TV drama', in *Feeling Asian Modernities: Transnational*

Consumption of Japanese TV Dramas, ed. Koichi Iwabuchi (Hong Kong: Hong Kong University Press, 2004), 303–10.

4   See, for example, Rachel Moseley, 'Make-over takeover on British television', *Screen* 41:3 (Autumn 2000): 299–314; Andy Medhurst, 'Day for night', *Sight and Sound* 9:6 (1999): 26–7; Lisa Taylor, 'From ways of life to lifestyle: the "ordinary-ization" of British gardening lifestyle television', *European Journal of Communication* 17:4 (2002): 479–93; Frances Bonner, *Ordinary Television: Analysing Popular TV* (London: Sage, 2003); David Bell and Joanne Hollows, eds, *Ordinary Lifestyles: Popular Media, Consumption and Taste* (Maidenhead: Open University Press, 2005); Dana Heller, ed., *The Great American Makeover: Television, History and Nations* (New York: Palgrave Macmillan, 2006); Chris Straayer and Tom Waugh, eds, 'Queer TV style', dossier in *GLQ* 11:1 (2005): 95–117; Anna Everett, 'Trading private and public spaces @ HGTV and TLC: on new genre formations in transformation TV', *Journal of Visual Culture* 3:2 (2004): 157–81; Angela McRobbie, 'Notes on *What Not to Wear* and post-feminist symbolic violence', in *Feminism After Bourdieu*, ed. L. Adkins and B. Skeggs (Oxford: Blackwell, 2004): 99–109.

5   On the female television cook/housewife, see, for example, Niki Strange, 'Perform, educate, entertain: ingredients of the cookery programme genre', in *The Television Studies Book,* ed. Christine Geraghty and David Lusted (London: Arnold, 1998), 301–14; Ann Mason and Marian Meyers, 'Living with Martha Stewart: chosen domesticity in the experience of fans', *Journal of Communication* 51:4 (December 2001): 801–23; Carole A. Stabile, 'Getting what she deserved: the news media, Martha Stewart, and masculine domination', *Feminist Media Studies* 4:3 (2004): 315–32. Margaret Talbot, 'Les très riches heures de Martha Stewart', *New Republic* 214: 20 (1996): 30–3; Charlotte Brunsdon, 'The feminist in the kitchen: Martha, Martha and Nigella', in *Feminism in Popular Culture*, ed. Joanne Hollows and Rachel Moseley (Oxford: Berg, 2006), 41–56; Melissa Click, 'Untidy: fan response to the soiling of Martha Stewart's spotless image', in *Fandom: Identities and Communities in a Mediated World*, ed. Jonathan Gray, Cornel Sandvoss and C. Lee Harrington (New York: New York University Press, 2007), 301–15.

6   Television's own most vivid parody of the 'new woman' plot is found in Jennifer Saunders' British sitcom, *Absolutely Fabulous* (1992–2004) which, pokes fun at the bohemian lifestyle, sexual freedoms, and milieux of fashionable female consumption.

7   Judith Butler, *Gender Trouble: Feminism and the Subversion of Identity* (New York: Routledge, 1990).

8   Ron Becker, 'Prime-Time TV in the gay nineties: network television, quality audiences, and gay politics', in *The Television Studies Reader*, ed. Robert C. Allen and Annette Hill (London: Routledge, 2004), 389–403. Also see Ron Becker, *Gay TV and Straight America* (New Brunswick: NJ: Rutgers University Press, 2006).

9   Helen Gurley Brown, *Sex and the Single Girl* (New York: Bernard Geis Associates, 1962), 135–6.

10   Ibid., 92.

11   Carla Sinclair, *Net Chick: Smart Girl Guide to the Wired World* (New York: Henry Holt and Company, 1996).

12   Jennifer Baumgardner and Amy Richards, *Manifesta: Young Women, Feminism, and the Future* (New York: Farrar, Straus, and Giroux, 2000), 21. Note that the authors do at times critique media, but they do so in the context of their own immersion in media culture. This insistence is also shared by Joanne Hollows and Rachel Moseley in *Feminism in Popular Culture* (Oxford: Berg, 2006), where they discuss, in their Introduction, the significance of their choice of 'in', rather than 'and' popular culture in their title (see pp. 1–3).

13   Betty Friedan, *The Feminine Mystique* (New York: Dell, 1963).

14   Betty Friedan, 'Television and the feminine mystique', Part 1, *TV Guide*, 24 January 1964,

6–24; and 'Television and the feminine mystique', Part 2, *TV Guide*, 1 February 1964, 19–24.

15 Germaine Greer, *The Female Eunuch* (London: Paladin, 1971); Juliet Mitchell, *Women's Estate* (Harmondsworth: Penguin, 1971); Sheila Rowbotham *Women's Consciousness, Man's World* (Harmondsworth: Penguin, 1973). See also Josephine King and Mary Stott, *Is This Your Life?* (London: Virago, 1997), again mainly written by media workers.

16 Molly Haskell, *From Reverence to Rape: The Treatment of Women in the Movies* (New York: Penguin, 1974).

17 Notable examples are Gaye Tuchman, Arlene Kaplan Daniels and James Benét, eds, *Hearth and Home: Images of Women in the Mass Media* (New York: Oxford University Press, 1978), 3–38; Muriel Cantor, 'Daytime serial drama: our days and nights on TV', *Journal of Communication* 29:4 (1979): 66–72; Muriel Cantor and Suzanne Pingree, *The Soap Opera* (Beverly Hills, CA: Sage, 1983).

18 Laura Mulvey, 'Visual pleasure in narrative cinema', *Screen* 16:3 (1975): 6–18.

19 Christine Gledhill, 'Pleasurable negotiations', in *Female Spectators: Looking at Film and Television*, ed. E. Deidre Pribram (London: Verso, 1988), 64–89.

20 Carole Lopate, 'Daytime television: you'll never want to leave home', *Radical America* 11/1 (1977): 32–51; Tania Modleski, 'The search for tomorrow in today's soap operas: notes on a feminine narrative form', *Film Quarterly* 33:1 (1979): 12–21.

21 Her work during this period is partially available and collected in Michèle Mattelart, *Women, Media and Crisis: Femininity and Disorder* (London: Comedia, 1986).

22 Charlotte Brunsdon, *The Feminist, the Housewife and the Soap Opera* (Oxford: Clarendon Press, 2000).

23 Dorothy Hobson, *Crossroads: The Drama of a Soap Opera* (London: Methuen, 1982); Ellen Seiter, *Television and New Media Audiences* (Oxford: Oxford University Press, 1999); Ellen Seiter, *The Internet Playground: Children's Access, Entertainment and Mis-Education* (New York: Peter Lang, 2005).

24 For examples of work on crime series and action heroines, see Joke Hermes, *Re-Reading Popular Culture* (Oxford: Blackwell, 2005); Sue Thornham, ' "A good body": the case of/for feminist media studies', *European Journal of Cultural Studies* 6:1 (2003): 75–94; Geneviève Sellier, 'Construction de identités de sexe dans les séries policières françaises', in *Les Séries Policières,* ed. Pierre Beylot and Geneviève Sellier (Paris: L'Harmattan, 2004), 259–72; Sherrie A. Inness, *Tough Girls: Women Warriors and Wonder Women in Popular Culture* (Philadelphia, PA: University of Pennsylvania Press, 1998); Sherrie A. Inness, ed., *Action Chicks: New Images of Tough Women in Popular Culture* (New York: Palgrave Macmillan, 2004); Bill Osgerby and Anna Gough-Yates, eds, *Action TV: Tough Guys, Smooth Operators and Foxy Chicks* (London: Routledge, 2001); Amanda Lotz *Redesigning Women: Television After the Network Era* (Urbana, IL: University of Illinois Press, 2006. See also the many essays on the Buffy website, www.Slayage.tv.

25 Constance Penley, *NASA/Trek: Popular Science and Sex in America* (London: Verso, 1997); Henry Jenkins III, *Textual Poachers: Television Fans and Participatory Culture* (New York: Routledge, 1992); Camille Bacon Smith, *Enterprising Women: Television Fandom and the Creation of Popular Myth* (Philadelphia, PA: University of Pennsylvania Press, 1992). See also studies of fan culture on digital platforms including Henry Jenkins III, *Convergence Culture: Where Old and New Media Collide* (New York: New York University Press, 2006); Henry Jenkins III, *Fans, Bloggers, and Gamers: Media Consumers in a Digital Age* (New York: New York University Press, 2006); June Deery, 'TV.com: participatory viewing on the web', *Journal of Popular Culture* 37:2 (2003): 161–83; Nancy K. Baym, 'Talking about soaps: communicative practices in a computer-mediated fan culture', in *Theorizing Fandom, Subculture, and Identity*, ed. Cheryl Harris and Alison Alexander

(Cresskill, NJ: Hampton, 1998), 111–29; Sarah R. Wakefield, 'Your sister in St. Scully: An electronic community of female fans of *The X Files*', *Journal of Popular Film and Television* 28 (Fall 2001): 130–7; Susan Clerc, 'DDEB, GATB, MPPB, and Ratboy: *The X Files* media fandom, online and off', in *Reading the X Files*, ed. David Lavery, Angela Hague, and Marla Cartwright (Syracuse, NY: Syracuse University Press, 1996), 73–97; Susan Murray, 'Saving our so-called lives: girl fandom, adolescent subjectivity, and *My So-Called Life*', in *Kids, Media, Culture*, ed. Marsha Kinder (Durham, NC: Duke University Press, 1999), 221–35.

26   Julie D'Acci, *Defining Woman: The Case of Cagney and Lacey* (Chapel Hill, NC: University of North Carolina Press, 1994).

27   Work on women as programme makers includes Madeleine Macmurraugh-Kavanagh's studies of BBC drama such as 'Boys on top: gender and authorship on the BBC *Wednesday Play*, 1964–70', *Media, Culture & Society* 21: 3 (May 1999): 409–25; Julia Hallam, *Lynda La Plante* (Manchester: Manchester University Press, 2005); Kathleen Rowe Karlyn, *The Unruly Woman: Gender and the Genres of Laughter* (Austin, TX: University of Texas Press, 1995); Claire Tylee, 'The Black explorer: female identity in black feminist drama on British television in 1992', in *Frames and Fiction on Television: The Politics of Identity Within Drama,* ed. Bruce Carson and Margaret Llewellyn-Jones (Exeter: Intellect Books, 2000), 100–12; Mary Desjardins, "Lucy and Desi: sexuality, ethnicity, and TV's first family', in *Television, History, and American Culture: Feminist Critical Essays*, ed. Mary Beth Haralovich and Lauren Rabinovitz (Durham, NC: Duke University Press), 56–74; and Janet Thumim, *Inventing Television Culture: Men, Women, and the Box* (Oxford: Oxford University Press, 2005. There is significant feminist scholarship devoted to the study of news programming, often including work on print journalism. See, for example, Liesbet van Zoonen, 'One of the girls: the changing gender of journalism', in *News, Gender and Power,* ed. Cynthia Carter, Gill Branston, and Stuart Allen (London: Routledge, 1998): 33–46; Patricia Holland, 'When a woman reads the news', in *Boxed In: Women and Television*, ed. Helen Baehr and Gillian Dyer (London: Pandora, 1987): 133–49; Mary Douglas Vavrus, 'Opting out moms in the news: selling new traditionalism in the new millennium', *Feminist Media Studies* 7:1 (2007): 47–63; Shawn J. Parry-Giles, 'Mediating Hillary Rodham Clinton: television news practices and image-making in the postmodern age', *Critical Studies in Media Communication* 17:2 (2000): 205–26; Carolyn M. Byerly, 'After September 11: the formation of an oppositional discourse', *Feminist Media Studies* 5:3 (2005): 281–96. Finally, in the United States, niche television networks aimed at women have also attracted scholars to undertake institutional histories, such as Julie D'Acci's special issue of *Camera Obscura* on Lifetime, Constance Penley, Lisa Parks and Anna Everett's work on Oxygen. See Julie D'Acci, ed., 'Lifetime: a cable network "for women"' (Special Issue) *Camera Obscura* 33–4 (1994–5); Constance Penley, Lisa Parks and Anna Everett, 'Log on: the Oxygen media research project', in *New Media: Theories and Practices of Digitextuality*, ed. Anna Everett and John Caldwell (New York: Routledge, 2003): 225–42. Also concerned with new cable networks and gender, are Heather Hendershot ed., *Nickelodeon Nation: The History, Politics, and Economics of America's Only TV Channel for Kids* (New York: New York University Press, 2004) and Sarah Banet-Weiser, *Kids Rule! Nickelodeon and Consumer Citizenship* (Durham, NC: Duke University Press, 2007).

28   However, Victoria Wood is discussed in Andy Medhurst's forthcoming book on British comedy, *A National Joke: Popular Comedy and English Cultural Identities* (London: Routledge, 2007). On Dawn French and Jennifer Saunders, see Pat Kirkham and Beverley Skeggs, '*Absolutely Fabulous*, absolutely feminist?' in Geraghty and Lusted, (eds) *The Television Studies Book*, 287–300; Anne Hole, 'Performing identity: Dawn French and the funny fat female body', *Feminist Media Studies* 3: 3 (2003): 315–28. On female-authored

ensemble dramas on British television in the 1990s, see Charlotte Brunsdon, 'Not having it all', in *Cinema of the 90s*, ed. Robert Murphy (London: British Film Institute, 2000): 167–77. On *Goodness, Gracious Me*, see Sarita Malik, *Representing Black Britain: Black and Asian Images on Television* (London: Sage, 2001): 101–03; Moya Luckett, 'Postnational television: *Goodness, Gracious Me* and the Britasian diaspora', in *Planet TV: A Global Television Reader*, ed. Lisa Parks and Shanti Kumar (New York: New York University Press, 2003): 402–22; Marie Gillespie, 'From comic Asians to Asian comics: *Goodness, Gracious Me*, British television comedy and representations of ethnicity', in *Group Identities on French and British Television*, ed. Michael Scrivens and Emily Roberts (New York: Berghahn, 2003), 93–107. Scholarship on Syall concentrates on her writing, rather than her television work. See, for example, Graeme Dunphy, 'Meera's mockingbird: from Harper Lee to Meera Syall', *Neophilogus* 88 (2004): 637–59.

29 David Morley, *Family Television: Cultural Power and Domestic Leisure* (London: Routledge, 1986); Ann Gray, *Video Playtime: The Gendering of a Leisure Technology* (London: Routledge, 1992); Anna McCarthy, *Ambient Television: Visual Culture and Public Space* (Durham, NC: Duke University Press, 2001).

30 Mary Beth Haralovich, 'Suburban family sitcoms and consumer product design: addressing the social subjectivity of homemakers in the 50s', in *Television and Its Audience*, ed. Phillip Drummond and Richard Paterson (London: British Film Institute, 1988): 38–60; Mary Beth Haralovich, 'Sitcoms and suburbs: positioning the 1950s homemaker', *Quarterly Review of Film and Video* 11:1 (1989): 61–83; George Lipsitz, 'The meaning of memory: family, class and ethnicity in early network television programs', in *Private Screenings: Television and the Female Consumer*, ed. Lynn Spigel and Denise Mann (Minneapolis: University of Minnesota Press, 1992), 71–109; Shaun Moores, ' "The box on the dresser": memories of early radio and everyday life', *Media, Culture and Society* 12: 1 (1988): 23–40; Ella Taylor, *Primetime Families: Television Culture in Postwar America* (Berkeley, CA: University of California Press, 1989); Lynn Spigel, *Make Room for TV: Television and the Family Ideal in Postwar America* (Chicago: University of Chicago Press, 1992); Nina Liebman, *Living Room Lectures: The Fifties Family in Film and Television* (Austin, TX: University of Texas Press, 1995); Marie-Françoise Levy, 'Television, family and society in France 1949–1968', *Historical Journal of Film, Radio and Television* 18: 2 (June 1998): 199–203.

31 Thumim, *Inventing Television Culture*; Marsha F. Cassidy, *What Women Watched: Daytime Television in the 1950s* (Austin, TX: University of Texas Press, 2005). See also Michelle Hilmes, 'Desired and feared: women's voices in radio history', in *Television, History, and American Culture: Feminist Critical Essays*, ed. Mary Beth Haralovich and Lauren Rabinovitz (Durham, NC: Duke University Press, 1999), 17–35; Spigel, *Make Room for TV*; Susan Murray, *Hitch Your Antenna to the Stars: Early Television and Broadcast Stardom* (New York: Routledge, 2005); Elana Levine, *Wallowing in Sex: The New Sexual Culture of 1970s American Television* (Durham, NC: Duke University Press, 2007); Michael Kackman, *Citizen Spy: Television, Espionage and Cold War Culture* (Minneapolis: University of Minnesota Press, 2005).

32 See, for example, Lisa Parks, 'Cracking open the set: television repair and tinkering with gender, 1949–1955', *Television and New Media* 1:3 (August 2000): 257–78; Shunya Yoshimi, 'Television and nationalism: historical change in the national domestic TV formation of postwar Japan', *European Journal of Cultural Studies* 6 (November 2003): 459–87; Usha Zacharias, 'The smile of Mona Lisa: postcolonial desires, nationalist families, and the birth of consumer television in India', *Critical Studies in Media Communication* 20:4 (December 2003): 388–406; William Boddy, *New Media and Popular Imagination* (Oxford: Oxford University Press, 2004); Lynn Spigel, 'Designing the smart house:

posthuman domesticity and conspicuous production', *European Journal of Cultural Studies* 8:4 (2005): 403–26; David Morley, *Media, Modernity and Technology: The Geography of the New* (London: Routledge, 2006); Shanti Kumar, *Ghandi Meets Primetime: Globalization and Nationalism in Indian Television* (Urbana, IL: University of Illinois Press, 2005); Fiona Allon, 'An ontology of everyday control: space, media flows, and "smart" living in the absolute present', in *Mediaspace: Place, Scale, and Culture in a Media Age*, ed. Nick Cauldry and Anna McCarthy (London: Routledge, 2004), 253–75; Barbara Klinger, *Beyond the Multiplex: Cinema, New Technologies, and the Home* (Berkeley, CA: University of California Press, 2006).

33   Raymond Williams, *Television, Technology and Cultural Form* (London: Fontana, 1974).

34   David Morley, 'Where the global meets the local: notes from the sitting room', in his *Television, Audiences and Cultural Studies* (London: Routledge, 1993), *Home Territories: Media, Mobility and Identity* (London: Routledge, 2000), *Media, Modernity and Technology: The Geography of the New* (London: Routledge, 2006); Lisa Parks, *Cultures in Orbit: Satellites and the Televisual* (Durham, NC: Duke University Press, 2005).

35   Marie Gillespie, *Television, Ethnicity and Cultural Change* (London: Routledge, 1995); Purnima Mankekar, *Screening Culture, Viewing Politics: An Ethnography of Television, Womanhood, and Nation in Postcolonial India* (Durham, NC: Duke University Press, 1999); Rathiba Hadj-Moussa, 'The slippery road: the Maghreb and the new media', in *Electronic Elsewheres: Media and Social Space*, ed. Chris Berry, Soyoung Kim, and Lynn Spigel (Minneapolis: University of Minnesota Press, forthcoming 2008); Lisa B. Rofel, 'Yearnings: televisual love and melodramatic politics in contemporary China', *American Ethnologist* 21:4 (1994): 700–22; Vicky Mayer, 'Living telenovelas/telenovelizing life: Mexican American girls' identities and transnational telenovelas', *Journal of Communication* 53:3 (September 2003), 479–95; Lee-Dong Ho, 'Transnational media consumption and cultural identity: young Korean women's cultural appropriation of Japanese TV dramas', *Asian Journal of Women's Studies* 12:2 (2006): 64–87; Lila Abu-Lughod, *Dramas of Nationhood: The Politics of Television in Egypt* (Chicago: University of Chicago Press, 2005).

36   Brunsdon, 'Identity in feminist television criticism', *Media, Culture and Society* 15:2 (1993): 309–20.

37   Constance Penley, *NASA/Trek: Popular Science and Sex in America* (London: Verso, 1997); Ellen Seiter, *Television and New Media Audiences* (Oxford: Oxford University Press, 1999); Andrea Press, *Women Watching Television: Gender, Class and Generation in the American Television Experience* (Philadelphia, PA: University of Pennsylvania Press, 1991); Jacqueline Bobo and Ellen Seiter, 'Black feminism and media criticism: *The Women of Brewster Place*', *Screen* 32:3 (1991): 286–302; Lyn Thomas, *Fans, Feminisms, and "Quality" Media* (London: Routledge, 2002). There is a long list of literature on this subject, which we cannot hope to reference here, but for some additional important studies see Trinh T. Minh-ha. *Woman, Native, Other* (Bloomington and Indianapolis: Indiana University Press, 1989); Valerie Walkerdine, *Daddy's Girl: Young Girls and Popular Culture* (Cambridge, MA: Harvard University Press, 1997); Ien Ang and Joke Hermes, 'Gender and/in media consumption', in *Mass Media and Society*, ed. James Curran and Michael Gurevitch (Sevenoaks: Edward Arnold, 1991), 307–28; Julia Hallam and Margaret Marshment, 'Framing experience: case studies in the reception of *Oranges Are Not the Only Fruit*', *Screen* 36:1 (1995): 1–15; Beverly Skeggs, ed., *Feminist Cultural Theory*, (Manchester: Manchester University Press, 1995); Ellen Seiter, 'Making distinctions: case study of a troubling interview', *Cultural Studies* 4:1 (1990): 61–84; Jacqueline Bobo, *Black Women as Cultural Readers* (New York: Columbia University Press, 1995).

38 Smith-Shomade is in this volume; also on Oprah, see Eva Illouz. *Oprah Winfrey and the Glamour of Misery: An Essay on Popular Culture* (New York: Columbia University Press, 2003); and Sherryl Wilson, *Oprah Winfrey, Celebrity and Formations of Self* (London: Palgrave Macmillan, 2004). On *Goodness, Gracious Me*, see Malik, *Representing Black Britain* 101–3; Luckett, 'Postnational television', Gillespie, 'From comic Asians to Asian comics'.

39 Herman Gray, *Cultural Moves: African Americans and the Politics of Representation* (Berkeley, CA: University of California Press, 2005); Beretta E. Smith-Shomade, *Shaded Lives: African American Women and Television* (New Brunswick, NJ: Rutgers University Press, 2002). On the creation of demographic 'ghettos' in multichannel TV, also see John Caldwell, 'Convergence television: aggregating form and repurposing content in the culture of conglomeration', in *Television after TV: Essays on a Medium in Transition*, ed. Lynn Spigel and Jan Olsson (Durham, NC: Duke University Press, 2004), 41–74. On issues of diversity in US network programming, also see Kristal Brent Zook, *Color By Fox: The Fox Network and the Revolution in Black Television* (New York: Oxford University Press, 1999).

40 See, for example, Gray, *Watching Race*; Gray, *Cultural Moves*; Smith-Shomade, *Shaded Lives*; Chon A. Noriega, *Shot in America: Television, the State, and the Rise of Chicano Cinema* (Minneapolis: University of Minnesota Press, 2000); Bambi L.Haggins, *Laughing Mad: The Black Comic Persona in Post-Soul America* (New Brunswick: NJ: Rutgers University Press, 2007); Sasha Torres, ed., *Living Color, Race and Television in the United States* (Durham, NC: Duke University Press, 1998); Sarita Malik, *Representing Black Britain: Black and Asian Images on Television* (London: Sage, 2001); Jim Pines, ed., *Black and White in Colour: Black People on British Television since 1936* (London: BFI, 1992).

41 Stuart Hall, 'Encoding/Decoding', in *Culture, Media Language*, ed. Stuart Hall, Dorothy Hobson, Andy Lowe and Paul Willis (London: Hutchinson, 1980), 128–38.

42 Elspeth Probyn, 'New traditionalism and post-feminism: TV does the home', *Screen* 31 (1988): 147–59.

43 Susan J. Douglas, *Where the Girls Are: Growing Up Female with the Mass Media* (New York, Crown, 1994); Natasha Walter, *The New Feminism* (London: Virago Press, 1999), Imelda Whelehan, *Overloaded: Popular Culture and the Future of Feminism* (London: The Women's Press, 2000); Sarah Projansky, *Watching Rape: Film and Television in Postfeminist Culture* (New York: New York University Press, 2001); Angela McRobbie, 'Post-feminism and Popular Culture', *Feminist Media Studies* 4:3 (November 2004): 255–64; Kimberly Springer (in this volume); Amanda Lotz, *Redesigning Women: Television After the Network Era* (Urbana, IL: University of Illinois Press, 2006); Yvonne Tasker and Diane Negra, eds, *Interrogating Postfeminism: Gender and the Politics of Popular Culture* (Durham, NC: Duke University Press, 2007); Joanne Hollows and Rachel Moseley, *Feminism in Popular Culture* (Oxford: Berg, 2006).

Part 1

PROGRAMMES AND HEROINES

The essays in the first part of this collection are selected from what comprises by far the dominant mode of feminist television scholarship, the critical readings of television programmes. The emphases of these readings differ, and they can be grouped and regrouped in different ways. Some, like Tania Modleski's analysis of US daytime soaps and Deborah Jermyn's discussion of the British crime drama *Prime Suspect*, examine the generic qualities of fictional programmes and consider the articulation and construction of gender through generic repetition and innovation. Some concentrate on the constitution of star personae, 'Oprah', 'Ellen', 'Judge Judy' and 'Nigella', through televisual performance, while in each case attending to the manner in which these personae are augmented, and sometimes ruptured, by publicity materials, tabloid gossip and other 'extra-televisual' accounts of the star. If early feminist television criticism, here represented by Modleski, was preoccupied with the figure of the woman viewer, often conceived as 'the housewife', more recent work has responded to the proliferation of 'the girl'. Sarah Banet-Weiser discusses programmes aimed at the girl-child watching television. Karen Boyle analyses Buffy, the high-school girl warrior, while Jane Arthurs, in an analysis of the consumer cultures associated with *Sex and the City*, engages with the extended girlhood of Carrie Fisher and her New York girlfriends. It is in the context of this 'extended girlhood' that we refer readers to some of the historical essays we have been unable to include such as Moya Luckett's essay on the 1960s girls of *The Avengers* and *Peyton Place,* in order to give some historical contextualization to the much celebrated mobilities of these 'post-feminist' girls.[1]

The 'post' question haunts any attempt to collect together feminist television scholarship in the twenty-first century, and several of these essays address this question directly, drawing on different resources and coming to different conclusions. Together, the essays have been selected to demonstrate that 'post-feminism' is a term which is in contestation, a contestation which we would argue is part of a feminist political and critical project. Karen Boyle outlines some of the key political debates here, while Jane Arthurs considers the creation of a successful 'post-feminist' brand for a commercially attractive post-network audience: 'independent' consuming (white) women. The post-feminism which permits Nigella's semi-ironic kitchen commentary works in a different way for the black women on television analysed by Kimberly Springer who argues for the importance of another 'post', 'post-Civil Rights' in determining some of the ways in which African-American women figure on US television. But it is not just political movements like feminism and civil rights, as well as network television, which are being refigured as 'post'. Susan J. Wolfe and Lee Ann Roripaugh argue for the significance of Showtime's the L Word to 'post-lesbian' identities, suggesting that the new visibilities of lesbian women may permit new forms of being and not being defined through sexual orientation.

Paradigms of visibility have been an organizing element of feminist television criticism from its earliest days. Initially, the focus was on the over-visibility of certain categories of women (white women as wives/mothers and 'sex-objects'), and the invisibility of other categories of women, most notably women of colour. Springer surveys the continuing limited ways in which black women figure on television – pointing, for example, to the paradoxical excess of African-American women judges – while Smith-Shomade argues, in relation to Oprah Winfrey, that Oprah can be seen as both too present – over-visible – and somehow also absent. Other figures too have changed relations to visibility. Sarah Banet-Weiser analyses some of the programmes addressed to girls on the cable network Nickelodeon to examine the paradoxes of the new televisual visibility of girls with the popular cultural phenomenon of 'girl power'. Bonnie Dow directly addresses the visibility of lesbian women in her discussion of the history of lesbian and gay representation on television, while Wolfe and Roripaugh also organize their discussion of the L Word in these terms. There is also, though, the persistent question of the visibility of women and scholarship outside the Anglo-American axis, which has haunted our choices as we have found ourselves reproducing the international dominance of US television as this is the television which so many viewers will have seen.

This part starts with the earliest essay in the book, Tania Modleski's 'The Search for Tomorrow in Today's Soap Opera'. Modleski's 1979 article, later incorporated into her influential book, Loving with a Vengeance, is, along with the work of Michèle Mattelart, Carole Lopate, Ellen Seiter, Dorothy Hobson, and Charlotte Brunsdon, one of the first feminist articles on television soap opera, here in its US daytime serial form. Modleski's approach to the genre, often seen in the period as one of television's most despised forms, considers the way in which daytime soap opera addresses its female audience in contrast to Hollywood cinema. The article is an example of feminist television scholarship's hybrid origins, as this early work was formed in dialogue with film studies and literary studies, as well as notions of avant-garde practice and political activism. Modleski argues that soap opera offers forms of pleasure and identification different from those encouraged by Hollywood cinema (which at this point in feminist film theory was largely seen as privileging masculine desire). She maintains, for example, that soaps even provide female revenge fantasies by presenting beloved villainesses who manipulate femininity in ways which defy male power and privilege. Writing in dialogue with early feminist film theory, Modleski concludes that television soaps' narrative form might serve as a model for a popular women's cinema. While this did not happen, Modleski's analysis, as well as other early feminist soap opera criticism, has been generative for scholarship on female audiences all over the world, as some of the essays in the second part of the book attest.

We move directly from the characteristic concerns of early feminist television criticism with everyday life in the home to a discussion of one of the defining shows of 'post-feminism', *Sex and the City*, which places its 'girl' characters in the public spaces of the city. Jane Arthurs's '*Sex and the City* and Consumer Culture: Remediating post-feminist drama' explores the popularity of this programme in the context of the new multichannel 'niche' television system and the rise of what she calls a 'bourgeois bohemian' post-feminist women's culture directed particularly at the educated and economically privileged woman. In the first case, Arthurs argues that as a multichannel programming phenomenon *Sex* bears a strong relation to the woman's magazine – especially *Cosmopolitan* – in its niche market appeal and liberal sexual content (possible now on cable). Different from the 1970s–1980s era 'new woman' workplace comedies and dramas (which drew on the discourses of second wave feminism), and also different from the workplace dramas like *Ally McBeal, Sex* is less concerned with its heroines' careers than with their female friendships and commodity lifestyles (often connected through their mutual love of shopping or dining out in New York). As an oxymoron of sorts, the term 'bourgeois bohemian' is used by Arthurs to indicate the contradictions and ambivalence at stake in the kind of post-feminist subjectivity the programme inspires. Although the programme promotes extended girlhood and women's sexual agency (as exemplified in its main character Carrie who writes a relationship advice column), its four heroines are nevertheless all looking for long-lasting love with a man. And while it also presents its heroines as sexual entrepreneurs, it nevertheless encourages self-objectification by asking women to think of their bodies in relation to commodities (Carrie's fetish for stiletto heels is a prime example). Moreover, Arthurs argues, the programme's bourgeois bohemianism is further complicated by the ironic and even 'campy' pose (borrowed from gay culture) that *Sex* promotes.[2] In the end, Arthurs presents *Sex and the City* as a prime example of the shifting dynamics of both post-network television and post-feminism, and she shows us the interrelationships between these two 'posts' as they relate to contemporary (upmarket and class-aspirant) women's culture.

In 'Women with a Mission', Deborah Jermyn returns to the case of *Prime Suspect* (1991) more than ten years after it was first broadcast on British television to examine both Lynda La Plante, one of the most successful and prolific writers on British television, and the programme's role in refiguring the place of women in television crime drama.[3] As Jermyn points out, in comparison with *Cagney and Lacey* (1982–98) and earlier British programmes such as *Juliet Bravo* (1980–85), which to some extent feminized the genre, *Prime Suspect* placed a central female protagonist within a recognizably 'masculine' format. Jermyn contextualizes *Prime Suspect* in relation to La Plante's œuvre and women in British television crime fiction. However, her main concern is with the aesthetics of the text, in particular, the use of camera work, framing and editing to explore and construct a narrative of the gendered detection of gendered crimes. Jermyn's essay thus offers detailed textual analysis of how the text works to produce Jane Tennison (Helen Mirren) as a new kind of female protagonist on television, the necessary precursor, she argues, of central female investigators in shows like *The X-Files* (1993–2002), *Silent Witness* (1996–present) and *Crime Scene Investigation* (2000–present). Her essay also, though, hints at homologies between the discrimination faced by Tennison within a mainly male police force and the institutional pressures on a female television writer like La Plante.

Kimberly Springer's essay, 'Divas, Evil Black Bitches and Bitter Black Women:

African-American women in postfeminist and post-civil rights popular culture', is concerned with the contemporary stereotypes of African-American women circulating in the culture of the 'posts' which she names in her title, drawing attention to the retrenchments of 'post-civil rights' US culture. She observes that although much scholarship on post-feminism notes the whiteness of its televisual protagonists, it fails to comprehend the way in which 'race is *always* present', suggesting that women of colour are the counterpart against which white female characters are 'defined and refined'. Springer explores the extent to which the notion of 'having it all' as an option extends across racial categories, arguing that black women have always had to manage homes, children and work, and quite often, other people's homes and children as well. Using the example of Diana Ross, Springer shows how the figure of the 'diva' has changed genres, moving from opera to popular culture, and, through its deployment in relation to figures such as Ross, Jennifer Lopez and Mariah Carey, Springer argues that the 'talented but difficult' stereotype is most commonly associated with women of colour. Springer's next case study is of class differentiation of 'the black lady' (such as Condoleeza Rice) with the mouthy, promiscuous, over-fertile working-class woman. It is in this context that she discusses reality shows, and appearances of 'the Sista with Attitude', 'the angry black woman' whom, she suggests, has become a recognized member of the cast repertoire of these programmes in the US. Here, she is concerned to investigate the extent to which it is possible for 'real people' to appear on these shows in ways which do not confirm already existing scripts and stereotypes. The final case study moves away from television to films such as *Waiting to Exhale* (1995) and *Diary of a Mad Black Woman* (2005) to explore whether there are any other narratives for black women here, and she concludes that the choices of 'post-feminism' for black women remain prescribed.

The next four essays engage in different ways with the production of the persona of the powerful woman on television. The television genres analysed are different: sitcom, talk show, reality court show and cookery programme, but in each, there are questions of the authorship and performance of the self as a television icon – and also, in Oprah's case, a huge empire of enterprise.

In '*Ellen*, Television, and the Politics of Gay and Lesbian Visibility', Bonnie Dow explores the media frenzy surrounding the coming out episodes on Ellen Degeneres's hit US series *Ellen*. The episodes, which aired in 1997, were generally greeted as a 'first' in the history of primetime television, and the media publicity surrounding the episodes typically conflated Ellen Morgan's (the character's) coming out with the star's own self-disclosure on talk shows, news shows, and in magazines. The programme even spawned a website, AfterEllen.com, a media site that presents commentary on the representation of lesbians and bisexual women in entertainment and the media, as well as several journal essays.[4]

Dow's essay places *Ellen* in the context of a history of one-off 'lesbian' episodes (for example, in the 1970s *All in the Family* ran a lesbian episode as did *The Golden Girls* in the 1980s). More generally, Dow considers *Ellen* in terms of television's hegemonic practices of inclusion, practices that entail appealing to new consumer groups while at the same time not offending the more conservative and in many cases homophobic audiences nationwide. In this case, despite its 'open closet' policies, the programme was heavily regulated by ABC and once Ellen Morgan was out, the series could not sustain a presentation of lesbian love and was rather quickly axed from the network line-up. Via textual readings, Dow shows how *Ellen* followed the logic of 'confessional narratives' which Michel Foucault famously argued are central to Western discourses and power regarding sex, an idea that has previously been utilized in relation to talk shows.[5] Dow concludes that the confessional mode is integral to the politics of neo-liberalism, in which individuals are made to feel responsible for themselves. *Ellen* (both the programme and the star publicity surrounding it) suggested that lesbianism was a matter of self-disclosure and private politics rather than having any relation to the state (for example, the programme did not analyse the state's role in job discrimination or equal justice for gay marriage or health care). In this regard, while a case study, Dow's essay raises more general concerns about the ways in which sexualities are tied to a concept of the neo-liberal self and the privatization of justice in contemporary media culture (a topic which Laurie Ouellette takes up later in this part).

The next essay is a chapter taken from Beretta E. Smith-Shomade's book on African-American women and television, *Shaded Lives* (2002). This book is one of the first to deal exclusively with this topic, and focuses on the genres of situation comedy, music video, national news and talk shows. The chapter on talk shows, reproduced here, concentrates on Oprah Winfrey as a complex and contradictory cultural icon. Winfrey's pre-eminence as a talk show host is contextualized within a wide range of material, including the historical role of Black women in US culture; Christianity and the tropes of confession, testimony and salvation; the American ethos of hard work; the narratives of Oprah's body; and her media empire and her role as an entrepreneur of images of African-American culture through productions like *The Women of Brewster Place*. Smith-Shomade argues that Winfrey both performs herself and is (as Smith-Shomade puts it) 'played upon', and that she exemplifies what Smith-Shomade calls 'the psychosis of American society in the latter part of the twentieth century'. In particular, she suggests that Winfrey's enormous success with mainly white women as the audiences for her talk show is achieved at the cost of her own 'colorized and gendered form', and that she is 'absent in her own presence'. Talk shows like *The Oprah Winfrey Show* dominated the modes of appearance of 'real people' on the television screen before the rise of 'docu-soaps' and reality formats at the end of the twentieth century. The promise of redemption which Smith-Shomade demonstrates to be a dominant tone of *Oprah* can usefully be contrasted with the castigatory tone with which real people are handled by 'Judge Judy' in one of the later reality formats discussed by Laurie Ouellette in the next selection. The promise of redemption has been replaced by the reprimand for making the wrong choices.

As noted in the general Introduction, Ouellette's ' "Take Responsibility for Yourself": *Judge Judy* and the neoliberal citizen', situates the programme in relation to the idea that television plays a significant role in the inculcation of neo-liberal attitudes and practices in the contemporary US. The format is a US reality court show in which 'ordinary people' bring their law cases to the court of a former New York family court judge, Judith Sheindlin. Litigants are offered travel costs and court fees to present their cases on national television at the cost of dropping out of the public court system and accepting Sheindlin's judgement. Sheindlin, like other television performers discussed in this part, has produced herself as a media property across more than one site, also writing the best-selling book, *Don't Pee on My Leg and Tell Me It's Raining*. Ouellette argues that the 'tough love' that Sheindlin dispenses and her constant stigmatizing of dependency make no allowances for the structural differences in the positions of some of the appellants. Ouellette also shows how the look of the programme establishes it as distinct from 'tabloid television', lending authority to the Sheindlin persona and supporting industry claims that the show is educational. But, Ouellette argues, the main lesson in *Judge Judy* is that of the new modes of subjectivity required of the 'neo-liberal citizen', in which the destiny of individuals is determined by their own choices without the support of any kind of safety net provided by the state. Although *Judge Judy* provides a particularly unmediated form of this neo-liberal discourse, Ouellette's argument is that these attitudes, and the emphasis on individual choice and self-improvement, structure the new wave of reality programmes.

The persona of 'Nigella' explored by Joanne Hollows in 'Feeling like a Domestic Goddess: Postfeminism and cooking' could hardly be more different. The harsh contrasts and dark colours of the courtroom are here replaced by the soft, warm colours of a sensuous, upper-middle-class domesticity in a series of cooking programmes presented by a woman who wrote a best-selling cookbook called *How to Be a Domestic Goddess*. Hollows demonstrates, though, that Nigella too can be understood in relation to the contemporary refiguring of women's position through notions of 'choice', as if choice were equally available to all. She uses critical and popular responses to Nigella's programmes and books, as well as detailed analysis of the programmes to analyse the way in which Nigella embodies a post-feminist identity in a domestic context. Her study is thus usefully set alongside the discussions of the post-feminist girls included in this book. The fantasy here though, rather than shopping and hanging out in Manhattan bars, is of escaping the time constraints on the modern woman who must 'do it all'. Hollows suggests that the allure of the new domesticity of figures such as Nigella Lawson and Martha Stewart lies precisely in how very time-consuming their labours of domesticity are, and explores theorizations of fantasy to understand their attraction for the harried contemporary woman. She suggests that the attractions of the figure of the domestic goddess, the yearning for a feminine identity which appears more stable, allow women to retreat from some of the pressures of managing and ordering both everyday life and feminine selves.

Karen Boyle takes as her texts *Buffy the Vampire Slayer* and the debates about post-feminism in 'Feminism Without Men: Feminist media studies in a post-feminist age'. *Buffy* has inspired a huge fan literature, and is perhaps the privileged heroine of what is often called third wave feminism. She embodies the post-feminist girl-heroine, and her switches between high-school student (in the early series) and scourge of vampires have delighted her fans, keen to argue that the opposition between feminism and femininity is transcended in this blonde girl from the West Coast of the USA. Boyle first provides an exposition of the theoretical and political definitions and arguments about post-feminism. She suggests that the paradoxical consequences of the destabilizing of the category 'woman' in these debates has in practice led to a narrow focus on individual women in feminist media studies. However, her point is not to fix the meanings of post-feminism, but to suggest that much work in feminist media studies seems to be at war with itself, with the focus repeatedly on women, feminism and femininity as the problem, rather than men and masculinity. It is in this context that she moves to an analysis of *Buffy*, which she discusses in relation to ideas of gendered violence, arguing that it is essential for feminist media scholars to keep in mind the purpose of their study.

The questions of the relationships between television, female subjectivity and ideas of feminism are approached in response to a different group of texts in the next essay,

'Girls Rule!: Gender, feminism and Nickelodeon'. Sarah Banet-Weiser's study of girls' programming on the US cable network Nickelodeon, examines this output in the context of the 1990s phenomenon of 'Girl Power' and 'third wave' feminism. Banet-Weiser points to the way in which Nickelodeon's programming for girls has overturned received industry wisdom about the use of girls as lead characters, and has received both professional and scholarly recognition for its strong, intelligent lead characters. She approaches Nickelodeon as a key producer of girl power culture within a context in which girl power practices and commodities are proliferating in a range of sites. Her interest lies in theorizing the way in which these often contradictory media representations function as a kind of feminist politics, and to do this she looks in detail at two programmes, *Clarissa Explains it All* and *As Told by Ginger*, as well as at the treatment of girl power themes in the news programme, *Nick News*. Her method combines textual analysis of these programmes with attention to Nickelodeon's institutional strategies, as well as a discussion of some of the contradictions of contemporary feminist attitudes to the media. In arguing against the dismissal of girl power as simply a media-created commercial opportunity which commodifies girls, she points to the changed contexts of feminist politics in the twenty-first century. The collectivist drive that defined the feminist movement of the second wave emerged, she argues, not because of particular qualities of those feminists, but because of the rich context of collective protest on a much broader scale, which included civil rights, gay rights and anti-war movements. The changed contexts of the present, and the increasing significance of commercial culture, mean that the discourses of contemporary feminism materialize in very different ways, and must be addressed on their own terms, and not always in comparison to a nostalgic golden age of feminism in the 1970s.

The part concludes with Susan J. Wolfe and Lee Ann Roripaugh on 'The (In)Visible Lesbian: Anxieties of representation in *The L Word*' (a glossy lifestyle drama set among a group of lesbian and bisexual friends in Los Angeles). With lesbian filmmaker Rose Troche prominently involved in its production, *The L Word* was first aired in the US on the Showtime premium cable channel in January 2004 and was marketed to appeal to the *Sex and the City* demographic with the slogan 'Same Sex, Different City'.[6] Wolfe and Roripaugh argue that the programme 'enacts and critiques' what they characterize as the 'anxieties' of lesbian representation through a series of devices which draw attention to questions of viewing, voyeurism and television representation. They suggest that the repeated formal and thematic concerns with the question of looking at lesbian women is both playful and serious in its reminder of voyeurism in the programme. They conclude that it would be impossible for a programme of this type not to display anxiety about its mode of representation, and for it to attract diverse judgements but they celebrate what they see as *the L Word*'s sophisticated engagement with these issues.

In the US, *The L Word* provoked debates about the representation of its lesbian characters in both the mainstream media and specialist websites. In Britain, its reception has been more muted, and Paula Graham has suggested that one reason for this is the very different social distribution of non-terrestrial television in the two countries.[7] While cable in the USA may mean upmarket viewers, in Britain, its association with Rupert Murdoch's News International and its primary marketing through sports, mean rather the opposite. Satellite pay television, in Britain, has a quite different demographic to cable in the USA. The very women that the programme needs to build a core audience would, in Britain, tend not to be watching pay satellite channels. This limited example of the different national reception of a would-be cult television programme cautions us against extrapolating too much from the television text alone, as well as demonstrating that there are national specificities to the evolving 'post-network' television landscapes of different countries. These issues of global distribution and reception are taken up further in the second part of the book, but we close this first part with an account of the way in which *The L Word*, a show which undeniably breaks new ground in its presentation of more-than-one-lesbian at a time, uses a variety of textual strategies to frame and reflect on its own representational strategies.

Notes

1   Moya Luckett, 'Sensuous women and single girls: reclaiming the female body in 1960s television', in Hilary Radner and Moya Luckett eds, *Swinging Singles: Representing Sexuality in the 1960s* (Minneapolis: University of Minnesota Press, 1999), 277–98. See also Lisa Parks, 'Watching the "Working Gals": Fifties sitcoms and the repositioning of women in postwar American culture', *Critical Matrix* 11:2 (1995): 42–66; Aniko Bodroghkozy, " 'Is this what you mean by color TV?': race, gender, and contested meanings in NBC's *Julia*', in Lynn Spigel and Denise Mann, eds, *Private Screenings: Television and the Female Consumer* (Minneapolis: University of Minnesota Press, 1992), 143–68 and Julia Hallam, 'Remembering *Butterflies*: the comic art of housework', in Jonathan Bignell and Stephen Lacey, eds, *Popular Television Drama: Critical Perspectives* (Manchester: Manchester University Press, 2005), 34–50.
2   On the debt to gay culture, see Mandy Merck, 'Sexuality in the city', in Kim Akass and Janet McCabe, eds, *Reading Sex and the City* (London: I.B. Tauris, 2004), 48–62.
3   Published since Jermyn's article, see Julia Hallam, *Lynda La Plante* (Manchester: Manchester University Press, 2006), Sue Thornham, ' "A good body": the case of/for feminist media studies', *European Journal of Cultural Studies* 6:1 (2003): 75–94 and Susan Sydney-Smith, '*Prime Suspect*: deconstructing realism through the female body', *Feminist Media Studies* 7:2 (2007): 189–202.
4   See, for example, Anna McCarthy, '*Ellen*: making queer television history,' *GLQ* 7:4 (2001): 593–620; Susan J. Herbert, 'What's wrong with this picture? The politics of Ellen's coming out party,' *Journal of Popular Culture* 33:2 (1999): 31–5.
5   Michel Foucault, *The History of Sexuality: An Introduction*, Vol. 1 (New York: Pantheon, 1978). See Mimi White, *Tele-advising: Therapeutic Discourse in American Television* (Chapel Hill, NC: University of North Carolina Press, 1992); Jane M. Shattuc, *The Talking Cure: TV Talk Shows and Women* (New York: Routledge, 1997); Kevin Glynn, *Tabloid Culture: Trash Taste, Popular Power, and the Transformation of American Television* (Durham, NC: Duke University Press, 2000).
6   Showtime has framed its identity as a channel through a willingness to show relatively sexually risqué material. It was on Showtime that the sexually explicit Channel Four (network) British series, *Queer as Folk* was broadcast.
7   Paula Graham, '*The L Word* underwhelms the UK', in Kim Akass and Janet McCabe, eds, *Reading the L Word: Outing Contemporary Television* (London: I.B. Tauris, 2006), 15–26.

1

The Search for Tomorrow in Today's Soap Operas

Notes on a feminine narrative form

Tania Modleski

Originally published in *Film Quarterly*, 33:1 (1979): 12–21.

In soap operas, the hermeneutic code predominates. 'Will Bill find out that his wife's sister's baby is really his by artificial insemination? Will his wife submit to her sister's blackmail attempts, or will she finally let Bill know the truth? If he discovers the truth, will this lead to another nervous breakdown, causing him to go back to Springfield General where his ex-wife and his illegitimate daughter are both doctors and sworn enemies?' Tune in tomorrow, not in order to find out the answers, but to see what further complications will defer the resolutions and introduce new questions. Thus the narrative, by placing ever more complex obstacles between desire and its fulfilment, makes anticipation of an end an end in itself. Soap operas invest exquisite pleasure in the central condition of a woman's life: waiting – whether for her phone to ring, for the baby to take its nap, or for the family to be reunited shortly after the day's final soap opera has left *its* family still struggling against dissolution.

According to Roland Barthes, the hermeneutic code functions by making 'expectation ... the basic condition for truth: truth, these narratives tell us, is what is *at the end* of expectation. This design implies a return to order, for expectation is a disorder.'[1] But, as several critics have observed, soap operas do not end. Consequently, truth for women is seen to lie not 'at the end of expectation', but *in* expectation, not in the 'return to order', but in (familial) disorder.

As one critic of soap opera remarks, 'If ... as Aristotle so reasonably claimed, drama is the imitation of a human action that has a beginning, a middle, and an end, soap opera belongs to a separate genus that is entirely composed of an indefinitely expandable middle.'[2] The importance of this difference between classical drama and soaps cannot be stressed enough. It is not only that successful soap operas do not end, it is also that they cannot end. In *The Complete Soap Opera Book*, an interesting and lively work on the subject, the authors show how a radio serial forced off the air by television tried to wrap up its story.[3] It was an impossible task. Most of the story-line had to be discarded, and only one element could be followed through to its end – an important example of a situation in which what Barthes calls the 'discourse's instinct for preservation'[4] has virtually triumphed over authorial control. Furthermore, it is not simply that the story's completion would have taken too long for the amount of time allotted by the producers. More importantly, I believe it would have been impossible to resolve the contradiction between the imperatives of melodrama – i.e. the good must be rewarded and the wicked punished – and the latent message of soaps – i.e. everyone cannot be happy at the same time. No matter how deserving they are. The claims of any two people, especially in love matters, are often simply mutually exclusive.

John Cawelti defines melodrama as having

> at its center the moral fantasy of showing forth the essential 'rightness' of the world order. . . . Because of this, melodramas are usually rather complicated in plot and character; instead of identifying with a single protagonist through his line of action, the melodrama typically makes us intersect imaginatively with many lives. Subplots multiply, and the point of view continually shifts in order to involve us in a complex of destinies. Through this complex of characters and plots we see not so much the working of individual fates but the underlying moral process of the world.[5]

It is scarcely an accident that this essentially nineteenth-century form continues to appeal strongly to women, whereas the classic (male) narrative film is, as Laura Mulvey points out, structured 'around a main controlling figure with whom the spectator can identify'.[6] Soaps continually insist on the insignificance of the individual life. A viewer might at one moment be asked to identify with a woman finally reunited with her lover, only to have that identification broken in a moment of intensity and attention focused on the sufferings of the woman's rival.

If, as Mulvey claims, the identification of the spectator with 'a main male protagonist' results in the spectator becoming 'the representative of power',[7] the multiple identification which occurs in soap opera results in the spectator being divested of power. For the spectator is never permitted to identify with a character completing an entire action. Instead of giving us one 'powerful ideal ego . . . who can make things happen and control events better than the subject/spectator can',[8] soaps present us with numerous limited egos, each in conflict with one another and continually thwarted in its attempts to 'control events' because of inadequate knowledge of other peoples' plans, motivations, and schemes. Sometimes, indeed, the spectator, frustrated by the sense of powerlessness induced by soaps, will, like an interfering mother, try to control events directly:

> Thousands and thousands of letters [from soap fans to actors] give advice, warn the heroine of impending doom, caution the innocent to beware of the nasties ('Can't you see that your brother-in-law is up to no good?'), inform one character of another's doings, or reprimand a character for unseemly behavior.[9]

Presumably this intervention is ineffectual; and feminine powerlessness is reinforced on yet another level.

The subject/spectator of soaps, it could be said, is constituted as a sort of ideal mother: a person who possesses greater wisdom than all her children, whose sympathy is large enough to encompass the conflicting claims of her family (she identifies

The Soap Formula

Currently, twelve soap operas are shown daily, each half an hour or an hour long. The first goes on the air at about 10 a.m., and they run almost continuously until approximately 3.30 p.m. With the exception of *Ryan's Hope*, which takes place in a big city, the soaps are set in small towns and involve two or three families intimately connected with one another. Families are often composed of several generations, and the proliferation of generations is accelerated by the propensity of soap characters to mature at an incredibly rapid rate; thus, the matriarch on *Days of Our Lives*, who looks to be about 65, has managed over the years to become a great-great-grandmother. Occasionally, one of the families will be fairly well to do, and another will be somewhat lower on the social scale though still, as a rule, identifiably middle class. In any case, since there is so much intermingling and intermarrying, class distinctions quickly become hopelessly blurred. Children figure largely in many of the plots, but they don't appear on the screen all that often; nor do the very old. Blacks and other minorities are almost completely excluded.

Women as well as men frequently work outside the home, usually in professions such as law and medicine, and women are generally on a professional par with men. But most of *everyone's* time is spent experiencing and discussing personal and domestic crises. Kathryn Weibel (see n. 11) lists 'some of the most frequent themes':

the evil woman

the great sacrifice

the winning back of an estranged lover/spouse

marrying her for her money, respectability, etc.

the unwed mother

deceptions about the paternity of children

career vs. housewife

the alcoholic woman (and occasionally man)

(Weibel, p. 56).

Controversial social problems are introduced from time to time: rape was recently an issue on several soap operas and was, for the most part, handled in a sensitive manner. In spite of the fact that soaps contain more references to social problems than do most other forms of mass entertainment, critics tend to fault them heavily for their lack of social realism (on this point, see Edmondson and Rounds (n. 3), pp. 228–47). As for the fans, most insist on soap opera's extreme lifelikeness and claim that the characters have to cope with problems very like their own.

with them all), and who has no demands or claims of her own (she identifies with no one character exclusively). The connection between melodrama and mothers is an old one. Harriet Beecher Stowe, of course, made it explicit in *Uncle Tom's Cabin*, believing that if her book could bring its female readers to see the world as one extended family, the world would be vastly improved. But in Stowe's novel, the frequent shifting of perspective identifies the reader with a variety of characters in order ultimately to ally her with the mother/author and with God who, in their higher wisdom and understanding, can make all the hurts of the world go away, thus insuring the 'essential "rightness" of the world order'. Soap opera, however, denies the 'mother' this extremely flattering illusion of her power. On the one hand, it plays upon the spectator's expectations of the melodramatic form, continually stimulating (by means of the hermeneutic code) the desire for a just conclusion to the story, and, on the other hand, it constantly presents the desire as unrealizable, by showing that conclusions only lead to further tension and suffering. Thus soaps convince women that their highest goal is to see their families united and happy, while consoling them for their inability to bring about familial harmony.

This is reinforced by the image of the good mother on soap operas. In contrast to the manipulating mother who tries to interfere with her children's lives, the good mother must sit helplessly by as her children's lives disintegrate; her advice, which she gives only when asked, is temporarily soothing, but usually ineffectual. Her primary function is to be sympathetic, to tolerate the foibles and errors of others.

It is important to recognize that soap operas serve to affirm the primacy of the family not by presenting an ideal family, but by portraying a family in constant turmoil and appealing to the spectator to be understanding and tolerant of the many evils which go on within that family. The spectator/mother, identifying with each character in turn, is made to see 'the larger picture' and extend her sympathy to both the sinner and the victim. She is thus in a position to forgive most of the crimes against the family: to know all is to forgive all. As a rule, only those issues which can be tolerated and ultimately pardoned are introduced on soaps. The list includes careers for women, abortions, premarital and extramarital sex, alcoholism, divorce, mental and even physical cruelty. An issue like homosexuality which, perhaps, threatens to explode the family structure rather than temporarily disrupt it, is simply ignored. Soaps, contrary to many people's conception of them, are not conservative but liberal, and the mother is the liberal *par excellence*. By constantly presenting her with the many-sidedness of any question, by never reaching a permanent conclusion, soaps undermine her capacity to form unambiguous judgements.

These remarks must be qualified. If soaps refuse to allow us to condemn most characters and actions until all the evidence is in (and of course it never is), there is one character whom we are allowed to hate unreservedly: the villainess,[10] the negative image of the spectator's ideal self. Although much of the suffering on soap operas is presented as unavoidable, the surplus suffering is often the fault of the villainess who tries to 'make things happen and control events better than the subject/spectator can'. The villainess might very possibly be a mother, trying to manipulate her children's lives or ruin their marriages. Or perhaps she is avenging herself on her husband's family because it has never fully accepted her.

This character cannot be dismissed as easily as many critics seem to think.[11] The extreme delight viewers apparently take in despising the villainess[12] testifies to the enormous amount of energy involved in the spectator's repression and to her (albeit unconscious) resentment at being constituted as an egoless receptacle for the suffering of others. This aspect of melodrama can be traced back to the middle of the nineteenth century when *Lady Audley's Secret*, a drama about a governess turned bigamist and murderess, became one of the most popular stage melodramas of all time.[13] Discussing the novel upon which the stage drama was based, Elaine Showalter shows how the author, while paying lip-service to conventional notions about the feminine role, managed to appeal to 'thwarted female energy':

> The brilliance of *Lady Audley's Secret* is that Braddon makes her would-be murderess the fragile blond angel of domestic realism. . . . The dangerous woman is not the rebel or the blue-stocking, but the 'pretty little girl' whose indoctrination in the female role has taught her secrecy and deceitfulness, almost as secondary sex characteristics.[14]

Thus the villainess is able to transform traditional feminine weaknesses into the sources of her strength.

Similarly, on soap operas, the villainess seizes those aspects of a woman's life which normally render her most helpless and tries to turn them into weapons for manipulating other characters. She is, for instance, especially good at manipulating pregnancy, unlike most women, who, as Mary Ellmann wittily points out, tend to feel manipulated by it:

> At the same time, women cannot help observing that conception (their highest virtue, by all reports) simply happens or doesn't. It lacks the style of enterprise. It can be prevented by foresight and device (though success here, as abortion rates show, is exaggerated), but it is accomplished by luck (good or bad). Purpose often seems, if anything, a deterrent. A devious business benefitting by indirection, by pretending not to care, as though the self must trick the body. In the regrettable conception, the body instead tricks the self – much as it does in illness or death.[15]

In contrast to the numerous women on soap operas who are either trying unsuccessfully to become pregnant or have become pregnant as a consequence of a single unguarded moment in their lives, the villainess manages, for a time at least, to make pregnancy work for her. She gives it 'the style of enterprise'. If she decides she wants to marry a man, she will take advantage of him one night when he is feeling especially vulnerable and seduce him. And if she doesn't achieve the hoped-for pregnancy, undaunted, she simply lies about being pregnant. The villainess thus reverses male/female roles: anxiety about conception is transferred to the male. He is the one who had better watch his step and curb any promiscuous desires or he will find himself saddled with an unwanted child.

Moreover, the villainess, far from allowing her children to rule her life, often uses them in order to further her own selfish ambitions. One of her typical ploys is to threaten the father or the woman possessing custody of the child with the deprivation of that child. She is the opposite of the woman at home, who at first is forced to have her children constantly with her, and later is forced to let them go – for a time on a daily recurring basis and then permanently. The villainess enacts for the spectator a kind of reverse *fort-da* game,[16] in which the mother is the one who attempts to send the child away and bring it back at will, striving to overcome feminine passivity in the process of the child's appearance and loss. Into the bargain, she also tries to manipulate the man's disappearance and return by keeping the fate of his child always hanging in the balance. And again, male and female roles tend to get reversed: the male suffers the typically feminine anxiety over the threatened absence of his children.

The villainess thus continually works to make the most out of events which render other characters totally helpless. Literal paralysis turns out, for one villainess, to be an active blessing, since it prevents her husband from carrying out his plans to leave her; when she gets back the use of her legs, therefore, she doesn't tell anyone. And even death doesn't stop another villainess from wreaking havoc; she returns to haunt her husband and convince him to try to kill his new wife.

The popularity of the villainess would seem to be explained in part by the theory of repetition compulsion, which Freud saw as resulting from the individual's attempt to become an active manipulator of her/his own powerlessness.[17] The spectator, it might be thought, continually tunes in to soap operas to watch the villainess as she tries to gain control over her feminine passivity, thereby acting out the spectator's fantasies of power. Of course, most formula stories (like the Western) appeal to the spectator/reader's compulsion to repeat: the spectator constantly returns to the same story in order to identify with the main character and achieve, temporarily, the illusion of mastery denied him in real life. But soap operas refuse the spectator even this temporary illusion of mastery. The villainess's painstaking attempts to turn her powerlessness to her own advantage are always thwarted just when victory seems most assured, and she must begin her machinations all over again. Moreover, the spectator does not comfortably identify with the villainess. Since the spectator despises the villainess as the negative image of her ideal self, she not only watches the villainess act out her own hidden wishes, but simultaneously sides with the forces conspiring against fulfilment of those wishes. As a result of this 'internal contestation', the spectator comes to enjoy repetition for its own sake and takes her adequate pleasure in the building up and tearing down of the plot. In this way, perhaps, soaps help reconcile her to the meaningless, repetitive nature of much of her life and work within the home.

Soap operas, then, while constituting the spectator as a 'good mother' provide in the person of the villainess an outlet for feminine anger: in particular, as we have seen, the spectator has the satisfaction of seeing men suffer the same anxieties and guilt that women usually experience and seeing them receive similar kinds of punishment for their transgressions. But that anger is neutralized at every moment in that it is the special object of the spectator's hatred. The spectator, encouraged to sympathize with almost everyone, can vent her frustration on the one character who refuses to accept her own powerlessness, who is unashamedly self-seeking. Woman's anger is directed at woman's anger, and an eternal cycle is created.

And yet . . . if the villainess never succeeds, if, in accordance with the spectator's conflicting desires, she is doomed to eternal repetition, then she obviously never permanently fails either. When, as occasionally happens, a villainess reforms, a new one immediately supplants her. Generally, however, a popular villainess will remain true to her character for most or all of the soap opera's duration. And if the villainess constantly suffers because she is always foiled, we should remember that she suffers no more than the good characters, who don't even try to interfere with their fates.

Again, this may be contrasted to the usual imperatives of melodrama, which demands an ending to justify the suffering of the good and punish the wicked. While soap operas thrive, they present a continual reminder that woman's anger is alive, if not exactly well.

We must therefore view with ambivalence the fact that soap operas never come to a full conclusion. One critic, Dennis Porter, who is interested in narrative structures and ideology, completely condemns soap operas for their failure to resolve all problems:

> Unlike all traditionally end-oriented fiction and drama, soap opera offers process without progression, not a climax and a resolution, but mini-climaxes and provisional denouements that must never be presented in such a way as to eclipse the suspense experienced for associated plot lines. Thus soap opera is the drama of perepetia without anagnorisis. It deals forever in reversals but never portrays the irreversible change which traditionally marks the passage out of ignorance into true knowledge. For actors and audience alike, no action ever stands revealed in the terrible light of its consequences.[18]

These are strange words indeed, coming from one who purports to be analysing the ideology of narrative form! They are a perfect illustration of how a high-art bias, an eagerness to demonstrate the utter worthlessness of 'low' art, can lead us to make claims for high art which we would ordinarily be wary of professing. Terms like 'progression', 'climax', 'resolution', 'irreversible change', 'true knowledge', and 'consequences' are certainly tied to an ideology; they are 'linked to classical metaphysics', as Barthes observes. 'The hermeneutic narrative, in which truth predicates an incomplete subject, based on expectation and desire for its imminent closure, is . . . linked to the kerygmatic civilization of meaning and truth, appeal and fulfillment.'[19] To criticize classical narrative because, for example, it is based on a suspect notion of progress and then criticize soap opera because it *isn't* will never get us anywhere – certainly not 'out of ignorance into true knowledge'. A different approach is needed.

This approach might also help us to formulate strategies for developing a feminist art. Claire Johnston has suggested that such a strategy should embrace 'both the notion of films as a political tool and film as entertainment':

> For too long these have been regarded as two opposing poles with little common ground. In order to counter our objectification in the cinema, our collective fantasies must be released: women's cinema must embody the working through of desire: such an objective demands the use of the entertainment film. Ideas derived from the entertainment film, then, should inform the political film, and political ideas should inform the entertainment cinema: a two-way process.[20]

Clearly, women find soap operas eminently entertaining, and an analysis of the pleasure that soaps afford can provide clues not only about how feminists can challenge this pleasure, but also how they can incorporate it. For, outrageous as this assertion may at first appear, I would suggest that soap operas are not altogether at odds with a possible feminist aesthetics.

'Deep in the very nature of soaps is the implied promise that they will last for-ever.'[21] This being the case, a great deal of interest necessarily becomes focused upon those events which retard or impede the flow of the narrative. The importance of interruptions on soap operas cannot be overemphasized. A single five-minute sequence on a soap opera will contain numerous interruptions both from within and without the diegesis. To give an example from a recent soap opera: a woman tries to reach her lover by telephone one last time before she elopes with someone else. The call is intercepted by the man's current wife. Meanwhile, he prepares to leave the house to prevent the elopement, but his ex-wife chooses that moment to say she has something crucial to tell him about their son. Immediately there is a cut to another couple embroiled in an entirely different set of problems. The man speaks in an ominous tone: 'Don't you think it's time you told me what's going on?' Cut to a com-mercial. When we return, the woman responds to the man's question in an evasive manner. And so it goes.

If, on the one hand, these constant interruptions and deflections provide consola-tion for the housewife's sense of missed opportunities, by illustrating for her the enormous difficulty of getting from desire to fulfilment, on the other hand, the notion of what Porter contemptuously calls 'process without progression' is one endorsed by many innovative women artists. In praising Nathalie Sarraute, for example, Mary Ellmann observes that she is not

> interested in the explicit speed of which the novel is capable, only in the nuances which must tend to delay it. In her own discussions of the novel, Nathalie Sarraute is entirely antiprogressive. In criticizing ordinary dialogue, she dislikes its haste: there not being 'time' for the person to consider a remark's ramifications, his having to speak and to listen frugally, his having to rush ahead toward his object – which is of course 'to order his own conduct'.[22]

Soap opera is similarly antiprogressive. Just as Sarraute's work is opposed to the traditional novel form, soap opera is opposed to the classic (male) film narrative, which, with maximum action and minimum, always pertinent dialogue, speeds its way to the restoration of order.

In soaps, the important thing is that there always be time for a person to consider a remark's ramifications, time for people to speak and listen lavishly. Actions and climaxes are only of secondary importance. I may be accused of wilfully misrepresent-ing soaps. Certainly they appear to contain a ludicrous number of climaxes and actions: people are always getting blackmailed, having major operations, dying, con-ducting extramarital affairs, being kidnapped, going mad, and losing their memories. The list goes on and on. But just as in real life (one constantly hears it said) it takes a wedding or a funeral to reunite scattered families, so soap opera catastrophes provide convenient occasions for people to come together, confront one another, and explore intense emotions. Thus in direct contrast to the male narrative film, in which the climax functions to resolve difficulties, the 'mini-climaxes' of soap opera function to introduce difficulties and to complicate rather than simplify characters' lives.[23]

Furthermore, as with much women's narrative (such as the fiction of Ivy Compton-Burnett, who strongly influenced Sarraute), dialogue in soap operas is an enormously tricky business. Again, I must take issue with Porter, who says, 'Language here is of a kind that takes itself for granted and assumes it is always possible to mean no more and no less than what one intends.'[24] More accurately, in soaps the gap between what is intended and what is actually spoken is often very wide. Secrets better left buried may be blurted out in moments of intensity, or they are withheld just when a character most desires to tell all. This is very different from night-time television programmes and classic Hollywood films with their particularly naïve belief in the beneficence of communication. The full revelation of a secret on these shows usually begins or proclaims the restoration of order. Marcus Welby can then get his patient to agree to treatment; Perry Mason can exonerate the innocent and punish the guilty. The necessity of confession, the means through which, according to Michel Foucault, we gladly submit to power,[25] is wholeheartedly endorsed. In soap operas, on the other hand, the effects of confession are often ambiguous, providing relief for some of the characters and dreadful complications for others. Moreover, it is remarkable how seldom in soaps a character can talk another into changing his/her ways. Ordinarily, it takes a major disaster to bring about self-awareness – whereas all Marcus Welby has to do is give his stop-feeling-sorry-for-yourself speech and the character undergoes a drastic personality change. Perhaps more than men, women in our society are aware of the pleasures of language – though less sanguine about its potential as an instrument of power.

An analysis of soap operas reveals that 'narrative pleasure' can mean very different things to men and women. This is an important point. Too often feminist criticism implies that there is only one kind of pleasure to be derived from narrative and that it is essentially a masculine one. Hence, it is further implied, feminist artists must first of all challenge this pleasure and then out of nothing begin to construct a feminist aesthetics and a feminist form. This is a mistaken position, in my view, for it keeps us constantly in an adversary role, always on the defensive, always, as it were, complaining about the family but never leaving home. Feminist artists *don't* have to start from nothing; rather, they can look for ways to rechannel and make explicit the criticisms of masculine power and masculine pleasure implied in the narrative form of soap operas.

One further point: feminists must also seek ways, as Johnston puts it, of releasing 'our collective fantasies'. To the dismay of many feminist critics, the most powerful fantasy embodied in soap operas appears to be the fantasy of a fully self-sufficient family. Carol Lopate complains:

> Daytime television . . . promises that the family can be everything, if only one is willing to stay inside it. For the woman confined to her house, day-time television fills out the empty spaces of the long day when she is home alone, channels her fantasies toward love and family dramas, and promises her that the life she is in can fulfill her needs. But it does not call to her attention her aloneness and isol- ation, and it does not suggest to her that it is precisely in her solitude that she has a possibility for gaining a self.[26]

This statement merits close consideration. It implies that the family in soap operas is a mirror-image of the viewer's own family. But for most viewers, this is definitely not the case. What the spectator is looking at and perhaps longing for is a kind of *extended* family, the direct opposite of her own isolated nuclear family. Most soap operas follow the lives of several generations of a large family, all living in the same town and all intimately involved in one another's lives. The fantasy here is truly a 'collective fantasy' – a fantasy of community, but put in terms with which the viewer can be comfortable. Lopate is wrong, I believe, to end her peroration with a call for feminine solitude. For too long women have had too much solitude and, quite rightly, they resent it. In a thought-provoking essay on the family, Barbara Easton persuasively argues the insufficiency of feminist attacks on the family:

> With the geographical mobility and breakdown of communities of the twentieth century, women's support networks outside the family have weakened, and they are likely to turn to their husbands for intimacy that earlier generations would have found elsewhere.[27]

If women are abandoned to solitude by feminists eager to undermine this last support network, they are apt to turn to the right. People like Anita Bryant and Mirabel Morgan, says Easton, 'feed on fears of social isolation that have a basis in reality'.[28] So do soap operas.

For it is crucial to recognize that soap opera allays *real* anxieties, satisfies *real* needs and desires, even while it may distort them.[29] The fantasy of community is not only a real desire (as opposed to the 'false' ones mass culture is always accused of trumping up), it is a salutary one. As feminists, we have a responsibility to devise ways of meeting these needs that are more creative, honest, and interesting than the ones mass culture has come up with. Otherwise, the search for tomorrow threatens to go on, endlessly.

Notes

1 Roland Barthes, *S/Z*, trans. Richard Miller (New York: Hill and Wang, 1974), 76.
2 Dennis Porter, 'Soap Time: Thoughts on a Commodity Art Form', *College English* (Apr. 1977), 783.
3 Madeleine Edmondson and David Rounds, *From Mary Noble to Mary Hartman: The Complete Soap Opera Book* (New York: Stein and Day, 1976), 104–10.
4 Barthes, *S/Z*, 135.
5 John Cawelti, *Adventure, Mystery, and Romance* (Chicago: Univ. of Chicago Press, 1976). 45–6.
6 Laura Mulvey, 'Visual Pleasure and Narrative Cinema', in Karyn Kay and Gerald Peary (eds.), *Women and the Cinema* (New York: E. P. Dutton, 1977), 420.
7 Ibid. 420.
8 Ibid.
9 Edmondson and Rounds, *From Mary Noble to Mary Hartman*, 193.
10 There are still villains in soap operas, but their numbers have declined considerably since radio days – to the point where they are no longer indispensable to the formula. *The Young and the Restless*, for example, does without them.

11 See e.g. Kathryn Weibel, *Mirror Mirror: Images of Women Reflected in Popular Culture* (New York: Anchor Books, 1977), 62. According to Weibel, we quite simply 'deplore' the victimizers and totally identify with the victims.

12 'A soap opera without a bitch is a soap opera that doesn't get watched. The more hateful the bitch the better. Erica of "All My Children" is a classic. If you want to hear some hairy rap, just listen to a bunch of women discussing Erica. "Girl, that Erica needs her tail whipped." "I wish she'd try to steal my man and plant some marijuana in my purse. I'd be mopping up the street with her new hairdo." ' Bebe Moore Campbell, 'Hooked on Soaps', *Essence* (Nov. 1978), 103.

13 'The author, Mary Elizabeth Braddon, belonged to the class of writers called by Charles Reade "obstacles to domestic industry".' Frank Rahill, *The World of Melodrama* (University Park: Pennsylvania Univ. Press, 1967), 204.

14 Elaine Showalter, *A Literature of Their Own* (Princeton: Princeton Univ. Press, 1977), 165.

15 Mary Ellmann, *Thinking About Women* (New York: Harvest Books, 1968), 181.

16 The game, observed by Freud, in which the child plays 'disappearance and return' with a wooden reel tied to a string. 'What he did was to hold the reel by the string and very skilfully throw it over the edge of his curtained cot, so that it disappeared into it, at the same time uttering his expressive "o-o-o-o." [Freud speculates that this represents the German word "*fort*" or "gone".] He then pulled the reel out of the cot again by the string and hailed its reappearing with a joyful "*da*" ["there"].' According to Freud, 'Throwing away the object so that it was "gone" might satisfy an impulse of the child's, which was suppressed in his actual life, to revenge himself on his mother for going away from him. In that case it would have a defiant meaning: "All right, then go away! I don't need you. I'm sending you away myself." ' Sigmund Freud, *Beyond the Pleasure Principle*, trans. James Strachey (New York: W.W. Norton, 1961), 10–11.

17 Speaking of the child's *fort-da* game, Freud notes, 'At the outset he was in a *passive* situation – he was overpowered by experience; but by repeating it, unpleasurable though it was, as a game, he took on an active part. These efforts might be put down to an instinct for mastery that was acting independently of whether the memory was in itself pleasurable or not.' *Beyond the Pleasure Principle*, 10.

18 Porter, 'Soap Time', 783–4.

19 Barthes, *S/Z*, 76.

20 Claire Johnston, 'Women's Cinema as Counter-Cinema', in Bill Nichols (ed.), *Movies and Methods* (Berkeley: Univ. of California Press, 1976), 217.

21 Edmondson and Rounds, *From Mary Noble to Mary Hartman*, 112.

22 Ellmann, *Thinking About Women*, 222–3.

23 In a provocative review of *Scenes from a Marriage*, Marsha Kinder points out the parallels between Bergman's work and soap operas. She speculates that the 'open-ended, slow paced, multi-climaxed structure' of soap operas is 'in tune with patterns of female sexuality' and thus perhaps lends itself more readily than other forms to the portrayal of feminine growth and developing self-awareness (*Film Quarterly* (Winter 1974–5), 51). It would be interesting to consider Kinder's observation in the light of other works utilizing the soap opera format. Many segments of *Upstairs Downstairs*, for instance, were written by extremely creative

and interesting women (Fay Weldon, for one). The only disagreement I have with Kinder is over her contention that 'The primary distinction between *Scenes from a Marriage* and soap opera is the way it affects us emotionally. . . . Instead of leading us to forget about our own lives and to get caught up vicariously in the intrigues of others, it throws us back on our own experience' (p. 53). But soap opera viewers constantly claim that their favourite shows lead them to reflect upon their own problems and relationships. Psychologists, recognizing the tendency of viewers to make comparisons between screen life and real life, have begun to use soap operas in therapy sessions (see Dan Wakefield, *All Her Children* (Garden City, New York: Doubleday & Company, 1976), 140–3). We may not like what soap operas have to teach us about our lives, but that they *do* teach and encourage self-reflection appears indisputable.

24 Porter, 'Soap Time', 788.
25 Michel Foucault, *La Volonté de Savoir* (Paris: Editions Gallimard, 1976), esp. pp. 78–84.
26 Carol Lopate, 'Daytime Television: You'll Never Want to Leave Home', *Radical America* (Jan.-Feb. 1977), 51.
27 Barbara Easton, 'Feminism and the Contemporary Family', *Socialist Review* (May–June 1978), 30.
28 Ibid. 34.
29 A point Hans Magnus Enzensberger makes about mass consumption in general. See *The Consciousness Industry* (New York: Continuum Books, 1974), 110.

2

Sex and the City and Consumer Culture
Remediating postfeminist drama

Jane Arthurs

Originally published in *Feminist Media Studies*, 3:1 (2003): 83–98.

Introduction

A new approach to the representation of women's sexuality in television drama has emerged in the form of Home Box Office's (HBO) hit comedy series *Sex and the City* (1998–). The aim of this article is to show how the success of *Sex and the City* is symptomatic of the forces shaping programmes in the digital, multichannel era of television that allow for innovation in its sexualised mode of address. I also want to suggest how this development might be understood in the light of debates about the politics of postfeminist culture. I will explore how the creation of a successful brand in this crowded market depends on the ability to innovate within a pattern of predictable pleasures to create a recognisable identity for a product that appeals to a commercially attractive audience (John Ellis 2000: 165–9). The novelty of *Sex and the City*, I argue, lies in the migration of a woman-centred and explicit sexual discourse into television drama. Its distinctive appeal arises from its ability to "re-mediate" the familiar forms of the television sitcom and the glossy women's magazine. Re-mediation is used by Jay David Bolter and Richard Grusin as a term to describe the forms in which new media arise, as each medium "responds to, re-deploys, competes with and reforms other media" (1999: 35).

Sex and the City can be compared to previous examples of postfeminist, woman-centred drama produced for prime-time network television in the US. These are dramas that in the wake of second-wave feminism selectively deploy feminist discourses as a response to cultural changes in the lives of their potential audience, an audience that is addressed as white, heterosexual, and relatively youthful and affluent. They emerged out of a hybridisation of genres driven by a desire to maximise audiences by creating drama that appealed to both men and women. The feminisation of crime genres such as cop shows (*Cagney and Lacey*) and legal dramas (*LA Law, Ally McBeal*) allowed for an exploitation of the generic pleasures associated with the masculine, public world of work and the feminised, private world of personal relationships (Julie D'Acci 1987; Bonnie J. Dow 1996; Amanda D. Lotz 2001; Judith Mayne [1988]

1997; Rachel Moseley and Jacinda Read 2002). Their responsiveness to changes in the socio-political context had also allowed for an engagement with liberal feminist issues arising from women's relation to the law and to work. A focus on women as protagonists, whose actions drive the narrative, replaced the marginal and narrow range of roles available previously to women characters in these genres. Although it shares their incorporation of feminist themes and their focus on the liberal, hetero-sexual, white, metropolitan, career woman, *Sex and the City* is very different from these networked dramas. These differences arise, I would argue, from the institutional conditions of its production and distribution. It was made not as prime-time network TV but as subscription cable television. This has a number of consequences for the form that it takes.

One of the consequences of the multiplication of channels has been a diversifica-tion in television's address to audiences. Specialist channels catering to particular social groups or taste cultures have proliferated. It moves the television industry much closer to the magazine industry, which addresses niche markets and where there is very little overlap between men's and women's titles. This has a number of consequences. One is that it draws the audience into a different economic relation to the product, where the tastes of the audience-as-market, as direct purchasers of the channel, are not as obscured by the normalising processes of the mass market. This segmentation allows for a pluralism that recognises previously marginalised cultures, albeit limited by their ability to pay. It also encourages polarisation, especially between male and female audiences (Benjamin Compaine and Douglas Gomery 2000: 524). *Sex and the City* is addressed to affluent, white women as a segment of the market, in which it re-mediates the address developed in the established women's media, namely glossy women's magazines. This reverses the trend towards the hybridisation of masculine and feminine genres that has characterised prime-time drama on network television.

The argument introduced here is developed in the following sections where I look at how the programme remediates the content and address of women's magazines for television and the Internet; how its brand identity is established across the interlocking circuits of the media, celebrity, and fashion to construct an address to the "bourgeois bohemians"; the resultant instability in its aestheticised mode of address as it oscillates between complicity and critique of a consumer lifestyle; and, finally, the consequences this has for its construction of women's sexuality.

Having it all

In the hybrid, women-centred, work-based drama characteristic of postfeminist tele-vision in the 1980s and 1990s, one of the main issues has been the division between the world of work and the private world of the domestic sphere that prevents women "having it all." In *Sex and the City*, the world of work largely disappears from view as a distinct space and set of hierarchical relations, although the women's autonomy from men is underwritten by their economic independence. For three of the four women who make up the main characters in the series, work is collapsed into the private sphere and becomes another form of self-expression, alongside consumption, thereby side-stepping the postfeminist problematic. Carrie's sex life and those of her friends act as research for her weekly newspaper column, which she writes from home. Samantha works in public relations, a job where her physical attractions and personal charm are intrinsic to her success. Charlotte manages an art gallery in a manner that suggests it is more of a hobby. This might be regarded either as a magical resolution of a continuing contradiction in women's lives or a realistic reflection of the opportunities for educated urban women in the contemporary labour market. Only Miranda feels the contradiction between her private life and her career success as a lawyer.[1] Even so, when Miranda accidentally becomes pregnant (in Season 4) and has the baby without getting married, she gets by with the help of her friends, including the child's father.

There is a generic expectation that postfeminist drama will be about single women wanting to get married. Sex and the City was initially marketed as such to feed into those expectations. The video blurb for the first season states "Sexy, hip, smart and sassy, Sex and the City charts the lives and loves of four women and their quest to find the one thing that eludes them all – a real, satisfying and lasting relationship. Is such a thing possible in New York?" (Sex and the City 1999–2001). But unlike other postfeminist narratives, in Sex and the City the responsibility for single women's unhappiness isn't laid at the door of feminist women choosing a career over a man. Of the four women only Charlotte is unequivocal in her desire to get married but is quickly disillusioned when she does. The traditional romance narrative is still there but as a residual sensibility, a slightly old-fashioned version of femininity that doesn't work in practice. Charlotte's belief in romance and saving yourself for your husband is undercut by his impotence on their wedding night and her discovery that he can be aroused only by a porn magazine in the bathroom, thereby completely puncturing the romantic myth (Episode 45 "Hot Child in the City").[2] When Carrie and friends visit a former New Yorker for her baby shower (Episode 10 "The Baby Shower") they aren't shown envying the woman her home in the country, her husband, and her coming baby – rather it accentuates the gulf which separates them from her – and they return to their single lives in New York with a huge sigh of relief.

The women's single state is rather a necessary precondition for their central preoccupation – sexual relationships and how to achieve sexual satisfaction – not previously considered a suitable topic for television drama. The series publicly repudiates the shame of being single and sexually active in defiance of the bourgeois codes that used to be demanded of respectable women. It self-reflexively interrogates media representations of the single woman although the emotional power of these residual stereotypes is acknowledged. For example, when Carrie appears looking haggard and smoking a cigarette on the front of a magazine under the strapline "Single and Fabulous?" it sparks a discussion amongst the four women about why the media want to persuade women to get married (Episode 16 "They Shoot Single People Don't They?"). Despite their intellectual critique, the rest of the episode explores the emotional vulnerabilities of their situation before concluding that it's better to be alone than faking happiness with a man. There is no shame attached to being alone. It ends with Carrie eating by herself in a restaurant, with no book to read as armour, to assert her belief that she really is "Single and Fabulous"! (with no question mark).

This exploration of women's sexuality is enabled by changes in the regulatory regime of television as a consequence of digital convergence. It has moved closer to the freedoms enjoyed by the print media and the Internet as compared to the sensitiv-ity to religious Puritanism historically shown by the television networks.[3] In a context freed from the moral constraints of network television, *Sex and the City* is able to exploit fully the glossy women's magazines' consumerist approach to sexuality, in which women's sexual pleasure and agency are frankly encouraged as part of a con-sumer lifestyle and attitude. In this respect, *Sex and the City* has moved a long way from the kind of family-centred or wholesome peer-group sitcoms that have previ-ously dominated the network schedules, in which embodied desire provided the repressed subtext rather the primary focus of the dialogue and action. Hybridisation of the discourse of women's magazines with the codes of the television sitcom has provided the "licensed space" for an exploration of sexual taboos and decorum (Jane Arthurs 1999; Steve Neale and Frank Krutnick 1990).

This hybridisation has also allowed for the consumer attitude to be lightly satir-ised, a response that is argued to be characteristic of an aestheticised relation to the self. It is this sensibility that allows for the adoption of ironic ways of consuming and a self-reflexive attitude to one's own identity, appearance, and self-presentation. Michael Featherstone (1991) characterises the aestheticised relation to the self as one in which consumers enjoy the swings between the extremes of aesthetic involvement and distanciation, a sensibility he argues is characteristic of the new middle classes of postmodern culture. It is a form of controlled hedonism that oscillates between complicity with the values of consumer culture, and critique. This allows a certain section of the "baby-boomer" generation the simultaneous satisfaction of the sensual pleasures allowed by material success along with the placating of their guilty, liberal conscience. It emerged in the "Yuppie TV" of the work-obsessed 1980s, where both envy and guilt were deliberately evoked in response to the affluent lifestyles of its protagonists. In *LA Law* for example, the guilt was differentiated by gender. For men it was guilt at their material success whereas for women it was guilt at their lost opportunity for marriage and children (Jane Feuer 1995).

The almost exclusive focus on sexual relationships and consumption in *Sex and the City* speaks instead to the wider cultural influence in the 1990s of the "bour-geois bohemians." This class fraction has, David Brooks (2000) argues, replaced the Yuppies as the new dominant class in the US (and other Western economies). The key feature of this new class fraction is their ability to reconcile the contradictions between bourgeois and bohemian values and lifestyles. Sexual permissiveness, that in the bohemian movements of the 1960s was articulated with radical anti-capitalist political values, has been re-articulated to conform, not only with the materialist priorities of consumer culture, but also with the emancipatory politics of the 1970s and 1980s. One effect has been to free white, middle-class women from the sexual constraints required by bourgeois respectability.[4]

A scene from the first season of *Sex and the City* (Episode 6 "Secret Sex") encapsulates this brand identity, that is to say the emotions, attitudes, and lifestyle with which it is associated and the specificity of its address. In an episode that explores the shame that some sexual experiences can provoke, Carrie, the series' central char-acter, gathers a group of her friends together for the launch of a new publicity cam-paign promoting her weekly column called "Sex and the City." They wait on the sidewalk for a bus to pass by carrying the poster for her brand on its side. They are in a mood of excited anticipation, marred only by the regret that Mr Big, the new man in her life, has failed to show up to share this proud moment. The revealing dress she is wearing in the poster is the dress that she had worn on their first date, when, despite her best judgement, they had sex. As the bus approaches, the excitement turns to dismay, and Carrie hides her face in shame. There is the poster with Carrie's body stretched in languorous pose along the full length of the bus, under the strapline "Carrie Bradshaw knows good sex." But as we pan across her body, next to her seductively made-up lips a crudely drawn outline of a large penis is revealed.

This short scene exemplifies the series' dramatic terrain, namely the exploration of women's sexuality in a postmodern consumer culture. It is a culture produced by capital's restless search for new and expanded markets, and characterised by the commodification of the individual's relation to the body, self, and identity, just as we see here in the relation of Carrie to her billboard image. The scene also exemplifies the programme's tone and style which mixes the display of celebrity lifestyles for our emulation, as in women's magazines, with a comic puncturing of these aestheticised images. The idealised image of bourgeois perfection in the image of Carrie on her billboard is momentarily satirised by the obscene graffiti. It is an eruption of the repressed "other" to bourgeois femininity in a deliberate disruption of its codes of sexual decorum. This, plus Big's absence, are both reminders of women's vulnerability to loss of self-esteem when it relies too exclusively on body image and its sexual appeal to men. The presence of Carrie's friends is important though in providing the support and reassurance she needs to regain her composure. Their shared culture of femininity offers an alternative to heterosexual dependence.

Feminist evaluations of *Sex and the City* have conflated it with other examples of postfeminist culture in which comedy and satire have replaced any serious, ethical commitment to challenging the power relations of patriarchy, a challenge that they argue is undermined by complicit critique. The postfeminist irony in texts such as *Bridget Jones* or *Ally McBeal* allows for a constant emphasis on women's appearance and sexual desirability as a source of worth whilst simultaneously subjecting this attitude to ridicule (Germaine Geer 1999; Imelda Whelehan 2000). In this view, the ironic oscillations in our relation to the bourgeois women who people the fictional world of *Sex and the City* are complicit with the aestheticised values of consumer culture and its unequal structuring of the "look." It assumes women in the audience are invited to share this male gaze to the extent that it is internalised in women's narcissistic relation to their own bodies. This objectifies women's bodies and renders them powerless. In a counter-argument, feminine cultures of consumerism and fashion have been considered as a source of pleasure and power that is potentially resistant to male control. Indeed they can offer women an alternative route to self-esteem and autonomy that overcomes the damaging division that second-wave feminism constructs between feminism and femininity (see Joanne Hollows 2000; Celia Lury 1996; Angela McRobbie 1997 for an overview of these debates).

These contradictory evaluations need not be presented as alternatives. Part of the problem for academic feminism is to develop arguments that capture the complex contradictions of postfeminism in popular culture. In her discussion of the emphasis on the spectacle of women's bodies in women's magazines, Hilary Radner (1995) draws attention to the way this is counteracted by a textual commentary that variously endorses or asks us to question the extent to which women's worth resides in her looks. In arguing the limitations to metacritical feminist discourse in capturing women's reading practices in everyday life, Radner highlights the potential of feminine culture to "displace the political onto the minute decisions of a contingent day to day practice in which absolute categories cannot be maintained from moment to moment" (1995: 178). Consumption is thereby redefined as an active process that has unpredictable ideological consequences. In Scott Lash's (1990) view, the ubiquity of images in postmodern consumer culture in itself produces contradictory juxtapositions that undermine any secure position from which to interpret the world. This, he argues, has the potential to produce self-reflexive, nomadic identities in which gender, for instance, is open to re-definition (Lash 1990: 185–98). *Sex and the City* self-consciously explores the instability of feminine identity in a postfeminist, postmodern consumer culture.

Its commodity form precludes a straightforward celebration of the feminist potential of consumer culture, however. This promotes, according to Susan Willis (1991), an alienated and fetishised relationship between people defined by the exchange of commodities. Moreover, the codification of class, race, and gender differences in the stylistic details of commodities normalises and perpetuates notions of inequality and subordination (Willis 1991: 162–3). The professional middle classes have, in her view, been duped by the signs of privilege into confusing the individualised freedom to consume with real political power. Argues Willis, "The production of resistant meanings by individuals will always be assimilated by capitalism for the production of fresh commodities" (1991: 175).

Sex and the City exemplifies these features of the commodity. Its stylistic features contribute to the cultural hegemony of the incorporated resistance of the bourgeois bohemians. Its culture of femininity provides an alternative to heterosexual dependence but its recurring promise of a shameless utopia of fulfilled desire always ends in disappointment for the cycle of consumption to begin again next week.

Remediation

> New technologies of representation proceed by reforming or remediating earlier ones, while earlier technologies are struggling to maintain their legitimacy by remediating newer ones.
>
> (Bolter and Grusin 1999: 61)

Sex and the City is the product of an emerging form of globally dominant television. It is a quality comedy drama series with high production values produced for the subscription cable channel, Home Box Office (HBO). America Online/Time Warner, who merged in 2000, owns HBO. They also bought IPC (International Publishing Corporation), the magazine publisher, in 2001. This economic convergence has produced an international media conglomerate covering the Internet and print media, as well as television. HBO has to sell itself first to its subscribers in the US, on the basis of its appeal to a sufficiently affluent segment of the potential market, before syndicating to other distributors in a global market. Arguably, its relative freedom from government regulation and from the restraints imposed by advertisers in comparison to the networks makes it more responsive to the tastes and values of new social groups (Lury 1993: 40–51).

The high production costs of "quality" drama have provoked fears of its demise when the amounts for production are more thinly spread across a multiplicity of channels. Instead, as the case of HBO demonstrates, it may well migrate to subscription-based services (Ellis 2000: 174). For HBO "quality" drama has been used successfully to enhance both its visibility and its reputation in a context where cable television has had to struggle to gain any cultural status at all. In 2001 *Sex and the City* won the Emmy for Outstanding Comedy series, the first time a cable television show has ever taken top honours for best series in any category (http://www.hbo.com/city/insiders_guide/news). News items and features relating to *Sex and the City* appear regularly in the print media and work to maintain its visibility and status as "must see TV." Its success has been achieved by generic innovation to address a niche market. Rather than offering a mixed schedule or hybridised genres for family viewing, as the networks do, HBO's brand name acts as an umbrella for multiple channels that separate out programmes designed for specific audiences. A whole channel is addressed to women: HBO Signature, "Smart, sophisticated entertainment for women." In a week during July 2001 it was offering a Friday night with "back to back" *Sex and the City*, plus movies themed as "Romance Feature" or "Leading Ladies Feature – a different leading lady every Friday night" (http://hbo.com/schedule).

Print media influence the form of *Sex and the City*. Adapted from a book written by Candace Bushnell ([1996] 1997), a New York journalist, it is structured around the fictionalised writing of a weekly newspaper column. It retains the first-person mode of direct address, using Carrie's voice-over to comment on the action in which a question is posed, journalistic research is undertaken and some conclusions proposed in a personalised, witty and aphoristic style. The questions range from the frivolous to the taboo. They can be serious but not too serious. They don't deal with rape or sexual harassment as in *LA Law* or *Ally McBeal*.

> Can women have sex like a man? . . . Are men commitment phobes? . . . In New York has monogamy become too much to expect? . . . Is motherhood a cult? . . . Can sex toys enhance your sex life? . . . Does size matter?

Each of the ensemble cast provides a different perspective on the week's question. Their stories are told as alternatives for viewers to weigh up, just as articles in women's magazines offer a variety of personal anecdotes to their readers to exemplify a particular issue and how different people have responded in practice. These are loosely tied together by Carrie's final voice over in a provisional conclusion that is often tentative in tone. "Maybe . . . " The bulletin board on the *Sex and the City* website then invites viewers' comments on the episode, asking questions like "What do you think of the new men in Carrie's life? . . . Talk about it with other fans on the Bulletin Board . . . Do you identify with Carrie? . . . Talk about it with fellow fans" (http://www.hbo.com/city/community). Thus multiple perspectives are actively encouraged within a tightly structured, repetitive format in which the characters are bound into a relatively unchanging situation in order to guarantee continuation of the pleasures offered by the brand (Lury 1993: 86–7).

Sex and the City's treatment of sexuality can be understood as a re-mediation of the content and address of women's magazines for television. These women are updated versions of the "Cosmo" woman who is dedicated to self-improvement and economic independence (Ros Ballaster, Margaret Beetham, Elizabeth Frazer, and Sandra Hebron 1991).[5] The function of sexual imagery and talk in *Sex and the City* is quite different from pornographic magazines and cable channels where sexual arousal is assumed as the purpose for consumption. *Sex and the City* dramatises the kind of consumer and sexual advice offered by women's magazines. This is a sphere of feminine expertise in which it has been argued that women are empowered to look – not only at consumer goods but also at their own bodies as sexual subjects (Radner 1995). Sexuality is presented in this context as a source of potential pleasure for which women should make themselves ready, whether through internalising the beauty and fashion advice that will attract the right men, or through following advice on sexual technique. Carrie's billboard slogan draws attention to this pedagogic function; "Carrie Bradshaw *knows* good sex" (emphasis mine). It is an expertise rooted in everyday life and experience. When called upon to give a lecture to a roomful of women on how to get a date, Carrie fails miserably. But she succeeds brilliantly the following week when she takes the women to a bar, where she guides them in how to work the room by reading the sexual signals, giving them the confidence and expertise to act on their desires (Episode 46 "Frenemies").

The series is able to go beyond the catalogue function of magazine fashion spreads, or the list of ten tips on how to improve foreplay. A consumer lifestyle is presented not as a series of commodities to be bought but as an integrated lifestyle to be emulated. The clothes and shoes become expressions of the different moods and personalities of embodied, empathetic characters in an authentic setting. This function is in fact most explicit on the programme's website, which differs in tone and emphasis from the television series and more closely matches the look and address of a woman's magazine. It relies on the relationship fans already have with the programme, guiding viewers in how to convert their knowledge about the series into knowledge they can use in their own lives, as discerning consumers of fashion, as creators of "a look" and a lifestyle. This is represented as a set of active choices that are an expression of individual character and mood. We are invited to conceive of emotional states as a trigger for particular types of consumption and clothing choices, such as the photograph of Carrie that is captioned. "The dress that shows she is finally going to split from Mr. Big" (http://www.hbo.com/city_style). The site anticipates, encourages, and attempts to shape fan behaviour that will convert into consumerism (Miriam Rivett 2000).

Bourgeois bohemians

As a successful brand *Sex and the City* influences the continuing transformations in fashion that characterise consumer culture. News stories about fashion regard it as an important influence. Sarah Jessica Parker (who plays Carrie) is a fashion icon in women's magazines and in newspaper columns; celebrity exposure is being touted as a replacement for the era of catwalk shows and supermodels.[6] The British fashion journalist who tracked down and bought Parker's horse head handbag and then wrote about it in a British national newspaper provided publicity for the TV show, the makers of the bag, and Parker as a celebrity (Victoria Lambert 2001). It also contributed to New York's reputation as city "brand" in the global system of capitalism as a source of new fashion ideas. A report on the New York fashion shows in the *Guardian* was headed "Fashion in the city; cult show underpins style" (Charlie Porter 2001). It comments on the "power of the cult drama" to create a fashion trend, whether for Jimmy Choo stiletto heels, corsages, or purses in the shape of a horse's head. The report is focused on the House of Field who act as stylists for *Sex and the City*. Theirs is a bohemian look, made newly respectable as mainstream fashion, but retaining in the thrift-store elements reference to the anti-materialist values that characterised the hippie bohemianism of the 1960s. It incorporates the psychedelic patterns of that era and an individual eclecticism achieved by mixing retro and new clothing, the avant-garde and the mass-produced.

The horse's head handbag works within this kitsch aesthetic, in which objects are redefined as "cool" through a process of irony. It reminds the *Daily Telegraph* journalist of My Little Pony and her 9-year-old self, and it is cheap to buy in comparison to most designer handbags ($165). The HBO website offers *Sex and the City* merchandise for sale, but they have no pretensions to be designer goods. They are cheap items: T-shirts, mugs, and glasses printed with the *Sex and the City* logo and New York skyline (doubly ironic now). The trash aesthetic of *Sex and the City* anticipates the ironic response that, in the 1980s for example, was developed as a sub-cultural, camp response to *Dynasty* (Feuer 1995: 142). In the decade or so that separates *Dynasty* from the incorporated irony of *Sex and the City's* trash aesthetics, camp irony has moved from the margins to the centre. It exemplifies the way in which an attitude to mass culture originating in a gay response to their cultural marginalisation, has been appropriated by the mainstream media in order to address niche markets in the affluent middle classes. It is the culmination of a trend that accelerated in the 1960s, and is associated with the rise of the consumer society and the generation that grew up with it (Andrew Ross 1989). *Sex and the City* is simply part of a wider cultural trend, one that at its most broad can be described as postmodernism, a commodified aesthetic in which irony is a central component (Naomi Klein 2000).

The style also expresses a bohemian attitude to women's sexuality. But the clothes do not simply replicate the rather demure look for women of the hippie era, when sexual liberation, enabled by the separation between sex and reproduction that the pill made possible, still meant women responding to men's sexual initiatives. The *Sex and the City* version of bohemian fashion is post punk, post Madonna; it incorporates an assertive sexualised imagery for women that consciously plays with the transgressive sexual connotations of leather, bondage, and underwear as outerwear. One garment, "open to below the navel before swooping under the crotch, had an immaculate cut, even if the look was purposefully wanton . . . [Y]ou could easily see Carrie giving the look a try, maybe out at the Hamptons" (Porter 2001). "Wantonness" combined with "a perfect cut" epitomises the reconciliation of bourgeois with bohemian values in the aesthetics and lifestyle that *Sex and the City* expresses and promotes.

The specificity of this taste culture is made clear in the series itself through the way the four main characters' style and codes of sexual behaviour are defined against other social groupings. There are the restrained (and boring) bourgeois women, untainted by bohemian values, in whom sexual expression is kept under strict control. These are exemplified by the women who look increasingly scandalised as Charlotte, the most "preppy" one of the four, at a reunion dinner with her university Fraternity friends, reveals the fact of her husband's impotence and her own frustration. "Don't you ever feel like you want to be fucked really hard"? she enquires as they recoil in disgust (Episode 46 "Frenemies"). Or by Natasha, Big's wife. His boredom with her is defined by her taste in interior design, "Everything's beige." Then there are the people who live outside the city, and whose adherence to traditional gender roles is an indicator of their being either low class or simply old-fashioned. On a trip to Staten Island (the ferry marking the boundary) "real men" offer a tantalising sexual fantasy for Samantha, but when faced with the reality in the cold light of a working day, her liaison with a fireman doesn't seem such a good idea (Episode 31 "Where There's Smoke . . .").

In traditional bourgeois cultures unbridled sexual appetites or loose speech are a mark not only of the lower classes but of the unruly woman, who inverts the power relations of gender and has sex like a man (Arthurs 1999; Mary Russo 1995). Samantha's guilt-free promiscuity is exemplary here, although even she has her limits. She is shocked by a new acquaintance who dives under the restaurant table to "give head" to a man they have just met (Episode 36 "Are We Sluts"). Indecorum is a sign of lack of respectability, which for women has been a sexual as well as class category associated with prostitution. *Sex and the City* works through the problem of establishing the boundaries of respectability in a postfeminist culture where women share many of the same freedoms as men, but in which the residual effects of the double standard are still being felt. It strives to be sexually frank without being "vulgar."

These women are of a generation old enough to have been influenced by feminism (in their thirties and forties) but too old to participate in a newly fashionable queer culture, despite their appropriation of camp as a style. They are resolutely heterosexual, despite occasional short-lived encounters with gays, lesbians, and bisexuals that simply reconfirm it. "I'm a tri-sexual," says Samantha jokingly. "I'll try anything once," and indeed she does, briefly, have one lesbian lover. Carrie's relationship with a 26-year-old bisexual founders when she can't handle the thought that he's been with a man, nor does she feel comfortable with his gender-bending friends. "I was too old to play this game," she tells us in the voice-over (Episode 34 "Boy, Girl, Boy, Girl . . ."). These episodes, like the one where Samantha dates an African American, simply mark where their sexual boundaries are drawn. Thus the women's particular mix of bourgeois bohemianism is normalised.

Their transgression of bourgeois sexual decorum marks the foursome as "unruly," a challenge to patriarchal structures of power, but their adherence to the sleek control of the commodified body makes this compatible with capitalism. Unlike Edina or Patsy, the unruly women in *Absolutely Fabulous* (BBC2 1992–4, BBC1 1995–6), a British comedy that is located in a similar cultural milieu, if the women are made to *look* ridiculous it is a momentary aberration that causes embarrassment (as in the billboard scene). In contrast, the British comedy persistently satirises consumer culture and the feminine world of fashion, PR, and women's magazines, through a farcical exaggeration of fashion styles and a slapstick mode of comedy that undermines the bodily control and discipline that underpins glamour (often as a result of drug-taking or excessive drinking, a bohemian legacy of the 1960s in contemporary consumer society that plays a very minor role in *Sex and the City* in comparison) (see Arthurs 1999; Pat Kirkham and Beverley Skeggs 1998 for further discussion of *Absolutely Fabulous*). The comedy in *Sex and the City* depends instead on verbal wit and ironic distancing, a more intellectual, and, in class terms, a more bourgeois form than slapstick. It also enables the complicit critique that is considered to be characteristic of postmodernism (Feuer 1995; Klein 2000; Lash 1990).

The aestheticised self and sexual relations

The advert for Bailey's Cream, the corporate sponsors of *Sex and the City*, exemplifies how in consumer culture the body as the bearer of sensation replaces the ethical self as an ideal. It presents a sensuous image of swirling, creamy liquid with the slogan "Let your senses guide you." Rachel Bowlby refers to the ideal modern consumer as, "a receptacle and bearer of sensations, poser and posed, with no consistent identity, no moral self" (1993: 23). In this aestheticised culture the question has become, does it look good or feel good rather than, is this a good thing to do? Although *Sex and the City* rejects the traditional patriarchal dichotomy of virgin and whore, insisting in its explorations of the women's multiple sexual experiences their rights to seek sexual satisfaction without shame, this doesn't mean that there are no limits. Aesthetic boundaries replace moral boundaries so that men who can't kiss very well, who smell, who are too short, or whose semen tastes peculiar are rejected on those grounds.

Despite the radical roots of this bohemian attitude, developed in opposition to the rationalist, puritan ethos of nineteenth-century industrial capitalism (in Romanticism and Surrealism as well as Dandyism), it is now fully integrated into consumer marketing and its appeal to our hedonistic impulses and imaginings. Lury explains that:

> [A]n important part of this calculating hedonism is an emotional and cognitive distancing on the part of the individual since it is this distance which introduces the possibility of reflection on consumption and facilitates the adoption of playful and ironic ways of consuming.
>
> (1996: 76)

Yet for women, Lury argues, this relation to an aestheticised, self-reflexive identity in which commodities are used creatively to re-fashion the self is more problematic than for men (1996: 118–55). This is because they occupy an unstable position in relation to the aestheticised self, an instability that is enacted in the oscillations in tone that characterise *Sex and the City* and its exploration of women's sexuality in a consumer culture.

For the women in *Sex and the City*, it often appears as though hedonism and narcissism have displaced the masochist position they occupy in patriarchal structures of desire. The grotesque "other" of sadistic masculinity has been repressed (and displaced into *The Sopranos*, another successful HBO "quality" drama). In this economy of desire the city streets have lost the danger of a sadistic or reproving masculine gaze. Instead of intimating the dark dangers that kept respectable women off the streets, New York is shown to be a place of freedom and safety – the worst that can happen is that their clothes might be splashed by a passing car (as happens to Carrie in the title sequence). These women move freely around the cafes and boutiques, with a confident sense of possession, enjoying the multiple pleasures of consumption in the company of other women and gay men. In this way their dependence on male lovers for emotional and sensual satisfaction is displaced; they always disappoint or disempower, as Mr Big does in the billboard scene by not showing up. A designer stiletto shoe, Carrie's trademark obsession, is different. It's always there to be possessed, offering a fetish substitute for the satisfactions denied by men. The autoeroticism legitimated by the narcissistic structure of the look in consumer culture offers the possibility of doing without men at all. The show's promotion of vibrators as a route to sexual satisfaction has resulted in a huge increase in sales of the "rabbit" model that was featured (Episode 9 "The Turtle and the Hare") (Clarissa Smith 2002).

The programme's representation of the women's dissatisfaction with their male lovers could be regarded as encouraging a rejection of men as a source of emotional and sexual satisfaction in favour of a feminine culture of gossip and shopping. It is the tight-knit relationship of the four women that is the only constant in the series. But they don't live together as in the cosy but adolescent comedy series *Friends*. The recurring message that for grown ups living in Manhattan means living alone constructs the single household as the norm, a trend that has been cited as one of the major stimuli to consumption in modern cities (Lury 1996).

Sex in this context becomes like shopping – a marker of identity, a source of pleasure – knowing how to choose the right goods is crucial. But men in *Sex and the City* are the only objects of desire that create consumer dissatisfaction. The women treat men as branded goods – the packaging has to be right but the difficulty is to find one whose use value lives up to the image. The quest becomes one in which they are looking for the phallus that would bring an end to a seemingly endless chain of desire. "In a city of infinite options there can be no better feeling than that you only have one," is the aphorism Carrie offers at the end of one episode (Episode 7 "The Monogamists"). And yet there is a recognition that the phallus will never live up to its promise of satisfaction and fulfilment. "In a city of great expectations is it time to settle for what you can get?" wonders Carrie (Episode 9 "The Turtle and the Hare"). The women try men out to see if they "fit for size," as Carrie tells a potential husband, but they never do. This is literally the case when promiscuous Samantha unexpectedly falls in love (Episode 12 "Oh Come All Ye Faithful"). When she has sex with her new lover after two weeks of uncharacteristic abstention, she is devastated. His dick is only three inches long! In *Sex and the City* size *does* matter.

Sex and the City incorporates the ambivalence in feminist evaluations of the aestheticised self – showing it to be both a source of confident autonomy and of disempowerment in its unstable oscillations. For instance, Carrie's performance is constructed around her role as a successful and famous journalist researching her newspaper column that bears the same name as the TV show. She is shown as a detached observer of her own and her friends' sexual desires and experiences. She self-reflexively and playfully deliberates on their consequences, not in terms of some overarching ethical position but from an aesthetic point of view of someone who has to write a witty, readable column that will enhance her professional status. Sexual ethics are converted into a controlled display of witty aphorisms and the comedy of embarrassment. The same is true of the show's address to its viewers. As an audience we are positioned as detached observers of this sexual play, not as we would be in pornography for physical arousal and the satisfactions of masturbation, nor as lessons in morality, but to be amused.

When the oscillation swings back to close involvement, the mood is one of unsatisfied yearning not playfulness. Carrie's emotional involvement with the main man in her life produces the feeling that she is out of control – her desire for him can never be fully satisfied. Again this is considered characteristic of a consumer lifestyle in which consumers "experience moderate swings from being in control to being out of control and back again . . . Their lives are balanced between feelings of completeness and incompleteness" (Elizabeth Hirschmann cited in Lury 1996: 77). In this scene the consequences of an aestheticised relation to sexual relations are shown to be debilitating – for women. Carrie craves authenticity, and constantly wants to establish whether her relationship with Big is real or not. In one episode, where she is particularly distressed by her powerlessness in relation to Big, Carrie offers a poignant critique of the masquerade as a strategy of female empowerment.

> I think I'm in love with him, and I'm terrified in case he thinks I'm not perfect . . . you should see what I'm like round him – it's like – I wear little outfits. I'm not like me. Sexy Carrie. Casual Carrie. Sometimes I catch myself actually posing – it's exhausting!
>
> (Episode 11 "The Drought")

Later that evening Big visits her flat for the first time. She is nervous about this as another test of her self-presentation, but is reassured, "I like it just the way it is" he says. On seeing a couple having sex in the flat opposite, offering a distanced but explicit spectacle, Big turns to her and says, "Hell – we can do better than that!" The voice-over from Carrie, "And then he kissed me," places the scene in the realm of a Mills and Boon erotic novel for women – the unobtainable object of the heroine's desire succumbs when he recognises her true worth. Yet it also marks a return to the distancing that characterises the dominant, comic mode of the series. Carrie's worries about her unstable and inauthentic identity are resolved through the aestheticised pleasures of erotic spectacle and generic parody. And there is no end to these oscillations; its serial form doesn't provide the plenitude of narrative closure; instead its repetitions offer the consumer satisfactions of "diversity within sameness that is comfortable and comforting to most people" (Hirschman cited in Lury 1996: 77).

Conclusion

The fragmentation of the television market has allowed a sexually explicit and critical feminist discourse into television comedy, albeit within the parameters of a consumer culture and the limitations this imposes. This is a welcome innovation in women's representation on television in that it assumes and promotes women's right to sexual pleasure and validates women's friendship and culture. At the same time the contradictions of its comedic and serial form expose this culture to interrogation and critique, thereby encouraging intellectual analysis. The analytic approaches used in this article are not confined to an academic elite but are available to a broad segment of educated women, the bourgeois bohemians, who read the quality press alongside women's magazines. An ability to see ourselves in these characters works not simply to confirm our sense of self but to question the costs as well as the benefits of living in a postfeminist consumer culture. It is in the messy contingencies of the everyday that feminism is produced or inhibited in practice, and it is this quality that *Sex and the City* is able to capture.

This establishes a space in popular culture for interrogation of our own complicity in the processes of commodification – women's narcissistic relation to the self, the production of fetishistic and alienated sexual relations – that continue to undermine our self-esteem and contentment. The programme offers evidence of the deleterious effects of economic liberalism in a society where moral and religious values are in decline, with no alternatives to the hedonistic and selfish values of capitalism. Whether this has the power to translate into feminist political action is beyond the scope of this article (but see Klein 2000; Whelahan 2000; Willis 1991 for scepticism in this respect). What remains more hidden from view is the gap between the lifestyle depicted and the experience of the majority of the women in the world, who are often the most disadvantaged by the economic inequalities on which the freedom to pleasurable consumption rests (Klein 2000; McRobbie 1997; Willis 1991). Yet in a post September 11 context, the connotations of *Sex and the City*'s logo of the Manhattan skyline has changed. The guiltless triumph of consumer values no longer seems so secure.

Acknowledgements

I would like to thank Gillian Swanson, Sherryl Wilson, and Helen Kennedy, as well as the anonymous reviewers for this journal, for their helpful comments on earlier versions of this article. Parts of the text are to be included in my book, *Television and Sexuality* (Open University Press, forthcoming).

Notes

1   In a series of interviews with writers of the series that appeared on the website in July 2001 they were asked which characters they identified with most strongly. They all chose Miranda (http://www.hbo.com/cityinsiders_guide; accessed July 26, 2001).

2   The identification of the episodes follows the continuous numbering of the website episode summaries rather than the video compilations, which start again at number one for each season.

3   As technological and economic convergence gathers pace, regulatory frameworks are also converging. The Internet has been an important driver in this respect, resetting the boundaries for the public circulation of sexual material (Bernt Stubbe Ostergaard 1998).

4   The kind of attention given to women's sexual freedom and pleasure in second-wave feminism arises from the very specific social and political history of the

white middle-class women who dominated the movement. It is quite different from the political agenda around sexuality that arises from the historical positioning of black or working-class women as the embodied "other" of the white bourgeoisie (Donna Haraway 1990).

5   The four main characters' signature cocktail is called a "cosmopolitan," signalling this sorority. The show's title echoes that of a book, *Sex and the Single Girl* written by Helen Gurley Brown in 1962 who went on to be the founding editor of *Cosmopolitan* magazine in 1965 (Radner 1995).

6   Radner's (1995: 51–5) discussion of Cybil Shepherd's role in the television comedy *Moonlighting* (1986–7) also highlights the way intertextuality allows for differing inflexions of the same celebrity persona.

References

Arthurs, Jane. 1999. "Revolting Women: The Body in Comic Performance," in Jane Arthurs and Jean Grimshaw (eds.) *Women's Bodies: Discipline and Transgression*, pp. 137–64. London and New York: Cassell.

Ballaster, Ros, Margaret Beetham, Elizabeth Frazer, and Sandra Hebron. 1991. *Women's Worlds: Ideology, Femininity and the Woman's Magazine*. Basingstoke: Macmillan Education.

Bolter, Jay David and Richard Grusin. 1999. *Remediation: Understanding New Media*. Cambridge, MA and London: MIT Press.

Bowlby, Rachel. 1993. *Shopping with Freud*. London and New York: Routledge.

Brooks, David. 2000. *Bobos in Paradise: The New Upper Class and How they Got There*. New York: Simon and Schuster.

Bushnell, Candace. [1996] 1997. *Sex and the City*. London: Abacus.

Compaine, Benjamin and Douglas Gomery. 2000. *Who Owns the Media?: Competition and Concentration in the Mass Media Industry*. Mahwah, NJ and London: Lawrence Erlbaum Associates.

D'Acci, Julie. 1987. "The Case of *Cagney and Lacey*," in Helen Baehr and Gillian Dyer (eds.) *Boxed In: Women and Television*, pp. 203–26. London: Pandora.

Dow, Bonnie J. 1996. *Prime-time Feminism: Television, Media Culture and the Women's Movement Since 1970*. Philadelphia: University of Pennsylvania Press.

Ellis, John. 2000. *Seeing Things: Television in the Age of Uncertainty*. London and New York: I. B. Tauris.

Featherstone, Michael. 1991. *Consumer Culture and Postmodernism*. London: Sage.

Feuer, Jane. 1995. *Seeing Through the Eighties: Television and Reaganism*. Durham, NC: Duke University Press.

Greer, Germaine. 1999. *The Whole Woman*. London: Doubleday.

Haraway, Donna. 1990. "Investment Strategies for the Evolving Portfolio of Primate Females," in Mary Jacobus, Evelyn Fox Keller, and Sally Shuttleworth (eds.) *Body/Politics; Women and the Discourse of Science*, pp. 139–62. London and New York: Routledge.

Hirschmann, Elizabeth. 1992. "The Consciousness of Addiction: Towards a General Theory of Compulsive Consumption," *Journal of Consumer Research* 19 (September): 155–79.

Hollows, Joanne. 2000. *Feminism, Femininity and Popular Culture*. Manchester and New York: Manchester University Press.

Kirkham, Pat and Beverley Skeggs. 1998. "*Absolutely Fabulous*: Absolutely Feminist?," in Christine Geraghty and David Lusted (eds.) *The Television Studies Book*, pp. 287–300. London, New York, Sydney, and Auckland: Arnold.

Klein, Naomi. 2000. *No Logo*. London: Flamingo.

Lambert, Victoria. 2001. "Horseplay with a Handbag," *Daily Telegraph*, July 4: 15.

Lash, Scott. 1990. *Sociology of Postmodernism*. London and New York: Routledge.

Lotz, Amanda D. 2001. "Postfeminist Television Criticism: Rehabilitating Critical Terms and Identifying Postfeminist Attributes," *Feminist Media Studies* 1 (1): 105–21.

Lury, Celia. 1993. *Cultural Rights: Technology, Legality and Personality*. London and New York: Routledge.

Lury, Celia. 1996. *Consumer Culture*. Cambridge: Polity Press.

Mayne, Judith. [1988] 1997. "LA Law and Prime Time Feminism," in Charlotte Brunsdon, Julie D'Acci, and Lynn Spigel (eds.) *Feminist Television Criticism: A Reader*. Oxford and New York: Oxford University Press, pp. 84–97. First published in *Discourse* 10 (2): 30–47.

McRobbie, Angela. 1997. "Bridging the Gap: Feminism, Fashion and Consumption," *Feminist Review* 55 (Spring): 73–89.

Moseley, Rachel and Jacinda Read. 2002. " 'Having It Ally': Popular Television (Post)Feminism," *Feminist Media Studies* 2 (2): 231–49.

Neale, Steve and Frank Krutnick. 1990. *Popular Film and Television Comedy*. London: Routledge.

Ostergaard, Bernt Stubbe. 1998. "Convergence: Legislative Dilemmas," in Dennis McQuail and Karen Suine (eds.) *Media Policy: Convergence, Concentration and Commerce*, pp. 95–106. Euromedia Research Group. London, Thousand Oaks, CA, and New Delhi: Sage.

Porter, Charlie. 2001. "Fashion in the City: Cult Show Underpins Style," *Guardian*, September 10: 5.

Radner, Hilary. 1995. *Shopping Around: Feminine Culture and the Pursuit of Pleasure*. New York: Routledge.

Rivett, Miriam. 2000. "Approaches to Analysing the Web Text: A Consideration of the Web Site as an Emergent Cultural Form," *Convergence* 6 (3): 34–60.

Ross, Andrew, 1989. "The Uses of Camp," in *No Respect: Intellectuals and Popular Culture*, pp. 135–70. New York and London: Routledge.

Russo, Mary. [1994] 1995. *The Female Grotesque: Risk, Excess and Modernity*. New York and London: Routledge.

Sex and the City. 1999–2001 (video recording). Home Box Office. Seasons 1–3.

Sex and the City (website). Home Box Office. On-line. Available: http://www.hbo.com/city (July 2001).

Smith, Clarissa. 2002. "From Oppression to the Jelly Rabbit," paper presented at the Third Wave Feminism Conference, Exeter University, UK, July 23–25.

Whelahan, Imelda. 2000. *Overloaded: Popular Culture and the Future of Feminism*. London: The Women's Press.

Willis, Susan. 1991. *A Primer for Daily Life: Is there More to Life than Shopping?* London and New York: Routledge.

3

Women with a Mission

Lynda La Plante, DCI Jane Tennison and the reconfiguration of TV crime drama

Deborah Jermyn

Originally published in *International Journal of Cultural Studies*, 6:1 (2003): 46–63.

Ever since *Widows* was first transmitted in 1983, writer Lynda La Plante has been at the forefront of British television crime drama. She has earned a reputation as a daring and controversial TV dramatist with a taste for violent and dark subject matter, known for her recurrent interest in traditionally 'male' genres and settings – a diamond heist in *Widows* (ITV 1983, 1985); a serial rape and murder investigation in *Prime Suspect* (ITV 1991);[1] ex-paratroopers readjusting to civilian life in *Civvies* (BBC 1992); a male prison in *The Governor* (ITV 1995, 1996). In 1993 a profile of her in *You* magazine commented, 'Every time she sits down at the word processor . . . what comes out is . . . brutality, blood and guts. The chief characteristic of her work is not optimism but a profound sense of the violence of human existence' (Thomas, 1993: 82). Her interest in 'male' genres, however, has frequently been combined with the presence of central, leading roles for women characters, most notably Detective Chief Inspector Jane Tennison (Helen Mirren), who investigates the murder of six women in *Prime Suspect*'s quest to convict serial killer George Marlow. This has attracted popular plaudits for, and interest in, La Plante's work as a TV writer, opening up the once rather limited repertoire of roles available to women actors in TV crime drama. In 1996 *The Independent* declared her 'The most famous TV dramatist in Britain. She has "above-the-title" stardom . . . responsible for a rash of hard hitting, tough talking, no-holds-barred dramas' (Rampton, 1996: 30). With a pedigree like this behind her, La Plante's work is pivotal to an understanding of the shifts in British TV crime drama over the past two decades.

But despite this engrossing oeuvre, industry accolades including a BAFTA for *Prime Suspect* and international distribution and critical acclaim for *Prime Suspect* (including transmission on the US's respected 'Masterpiece Theatre'), sustained academic acknowledgement and analysis of La Plante's contribution to the genre have been decidedly thin on the ground. Julia Hallam has attributed this to the entrenched 'persistent marginalisation of women writers not only in the TV industry itself but also within the critical institutions of the academy', whereby women writers have been recurrently excluded from the canon of 'quality' television (2000: 141). In a similar vein Glen Creeber's analysis notes with surprise and disappointment how 'despite both its subject matter and international success, *Prime Suspect* has failed to attract the sort of academic attention that one might expect' (2001: 150). In this article I want to redress this neglect further still by arguing that *Prime Suspect* can be seen as a transitional text in the history of TV crime drama for its resituating of both gender and realism in the form. Creeber gives an insightful account of the relationship between gender and genre in the text, but examines it largely through the 'masculine' lenses of film noir and hard-boiled detective fiction, traditional male-centred police TV dramas and Dennis Potter's *The Singing Detective* (1986), arguing convincingly that these are generic precursors that *Prime Suspect* self-consciously echoes. But as a result, even while examining its disruption of them, his analysis sometimes seems to privilege *Prime Suspect*'s indebtedness to male canons – in film, television and litera-ture – rather than, for example, foregrounding La Plante's authorship or the text's place in her oeuvre as paradigmatic foci. Partly, then, I want to open up an analysis that refocuses these 'masculine' lenses and places La Plante and her interventions in the genre at its core, as Hallam (2000) has called for.

In doing so I look again at the representation of Tennison and also the other women – including the victims and Marlow's wife Moyra *and*, crucially, the relation-ships between all of them – and I also look more closely at Marlow in terms of the com-mentary on misogyny that his characterization gives rise to. The text's articulation of gender difference and sexual politics is pursued not just through its *narrative* con-cerns, however, but also through corresponding recurrent *aesthetic* devices. More specifically, as I will show, camerawork is structured around a visual and symbolic gendered dichotomy. Furthermore, there is an explicit concern in the text with who 'looks', and at whom, where the refusal or inability to be able to 'see' the victims becomes a motif that highlights the relative visibility and invisibility of different women and, with it, the gendered power structures contained within the act of looking. The conflicts and contrasts this gives rise to arguably make *Prime Suspect* one of the most troubling yet seminal texts that feminist cultural studies has had to contend with in recent years, making its relative neglect all the more remiss. Yet cultural studies must not risk marginalizing this text or discounting its broader significance by examining it only in the context of feminist concerns, since arguably this would be to perpetuate La Plante's exile from more expansive recognition in the academy. Furthermore, while this essay makes a detailed single-text analysis, a method that traditionally has its heritage in screen studies rather than in cultural studies, this approach is not invoked in order to invite the reader to consider the text in a cultural vacuum. *Prime Suspect* takes up and interrogates motifs familiar from the media's dissemination of 'real-life' sex crime. Its international impact and influence extend to recent generic shifts across TV crime drama, where it set new precedents regarding the parameters of the female investigator's role and the explicit display of the victim's corpse. Beyond the realm of television, it holds a pivotal place in a far wider cultural turn that has seen an explosion of popular interest in forensics. This analysis, then, should be understood both as examining a definitive text in the evolution of the TV crime genre, and as situating that text at the forefront of a much broader cultural shift, the influence of which has been felt across literature, film, television and advertising. It is for these reasons that I return to *Prime Suspect* more than 10 years after it was first broadcast in the UK.

Linked to the above, I want to look at the invocation of realism in the text. With its graphic attention to forensic detail and the foregrounding of the authenticity of the corpse, *Prime Suspect* arguably paved the way in 1991 for the kinds of visual signifiers of realism we now take for granted in the genre. The impact of *Prime Suspect*'s evocation of gender and realism and its contribution to the 'reinvention' of TV crime drama has been internationally resonant; it has become a genre that can now be carried by female leads and routinely figures explicit descriptions and images of forensics that would have been unheard of on prime-time TV in the era before *Prime Suspect*. In the wake of *Prime Suspect*, long-running and hugely successful programmes such as *The X-Files* (Fox, 1993–) (although not altogether a 'crime drama') and *Silent Witness* (BBC, 1996–) now pivot on female investigators and forensic detail – and indeed the exchange between the two.[2] Elsewhere, much of La Plante's later work and crime drama more broadly now regularly integrate female protagonists at the 'gritty' core of the genre – for example, *Trial and Retribution* (ITV, 1997, 1998, 1999, 2000, 2002), *Mind Games* (ITV, 2001) (both La Plante), *Mersey Beat* (BBC, 2001–) in the UK and *CSI: Crime Scene Investigation* (CBS, 2000–), produced in the US. Through an examination of *Prime Suspect*'s seminal narrative and aesthetic systems, then, I hope to show how this text more than any other stands out as a decisive moment in La Plante's ongoing reconfiguration of the boundaries and structures of TV crime drama.

Contextualizing *Prime Suspect*

Clearly, precedents in British TV drama that foregrounded female police officers were already in place before *Prime Suspect*, the much-cited examples being *Juliet Bravo* (BBC, 1980–85) and *The Gentle Touch* (LWT, 1980–84). However, to point to the inclusion of a female detective in these texts as evidence of common territory would be to risk a rather reductive reading. Their titles alone seem to suggest the differences in their approaches; where *Juliet Bravo* and *The Gentle Touch* foreground a feminine angle, nominally at least *Prime Suspect* deflects attention away from the fact that its central protagonist is a woman. This arguably indicates that it sees itself first and foremost as a crime drama, not a female or 'woman's' crime drama. Pioneering US series *Cagney and Lacey* (1982–88) arguably became exactly the latter. Although it was undeniably significant in putting professional women at the forefront of a TV crime drama, exploring social issues and the demands on women juggling family, career and personal lives, its characters, settings, humour and status as a long-running prime-time US series developed into a kind of cosy familiarity quite unlike the characteristic 'grittiness' of *Prime Suspect*. Comparing *Cagney and Lacey* with *Prime Suspect*, Helen Mirren mixes value-judgement with astute observation when she describes how 'it was very much lower-level and developed into a kind of soap opera' (Mirren, in Hayward and Rennert, 1996: 11). Despite the rather dismissive conflation of 'lower-level' TV with soaps, Mirren rightly hints here that aspects of the crime or police procedural elements of the show were somewhat eroded by its domestic angle.

Furthermore, Gillian Dyer has argued, as Creeber notes (2001: 150), that we should be wary of assuming that such female roles in themselves were in any way progressive or that they radically shifted the conventions or 'male police structures' of the genre. More particularly, she points to the specific cultural and social context in which *Juliet Bravo* was made. In the early 1980s the BBC had become sensitive to accusations of excessive violence in crime drama and so was seeking both to 'soften up' the genre and represent the police in a more compassionate light at a time when public cynicism towards them was growing (Dyer, 1987: 11). Far more radically by comparison, *Prime Suspect* has been contextualized as being a response in part to the high-profile and controversial complaint of sexual discrimination brought by Assistant Chief Constable Alison Halford in 1990 (see Purser, 1991: 14). One of Britain's highest-ever ranking female officers, Halford took her case to a Liverpool tribunal when she was allegedly passed over for promotion on nine occasions. Although La Plante has said on the one hand that Halford was not originally an inspiration for Tennison – 'No, no. That was a little bonus if you like' – (La Plante in Purser, 1991: 14), she has also said that she planned for Tennison to 'go up and up the ranks' until 'she would have ended up like Detective Chief Constable Halford, the woman high flier destroyed by male power' (La Plante in Day Lewis, 1998: 23). It is hard, then, not to see echoes of the real-life Halford in Tennison's experiences, and, in the US, *Prime Suspect*'s topicality was made all the more resonant by its appearance in the wake of the sensation wrought by Anita Hill's sexual harassment charges against Clarence Thomas following his nomination to the Supreme Court (Wolcott, 1995: 19–20). Elsewhere, Charlotte Brunsdon has argued that *Prime Suspect*, along with other instances of the genre's rise in the 1980s and 1990s, 'works over and worries at the anxieties and exclusions of contemporary citizenship, of being British and living here, now' (Brunsdon, 1998: 225). *Prime Suspect*, then, seems more overtly motivated than its earlier British counterparts by a desire to engage critically and consciously with the politics of the 'glass ceiling' and the systematic and insidious discrimination that policewomen experience.

'She's not what I expected' – introducing Tennison

Responses to Helen Mirren's first outing as Tennison in 1991 were remarkable, heaping praise on her performance and making Tennison one of British television's most memorable and resonant female characters.[3] This response was all the more striking because Tennison is not a woman who invites immediate empathy by any means. While she seeks to confront those men in the police who are colluding against her, she isn't above dabbling in corruption herself, tampering with records and making a dubious pact with Superintendent Kernan by keeping quiet about Otley's misdemeanours in return for choosing his replacement. While she holds 'feminine' attributes – in the ease with which she befriends the prostitutes and Peter's young son, notes the detail in the clothes and appearance of the victims, dresses in light, tailored clothing (always skirts) and pays careful attention to her make-up – she also displays 'masculine' behavioural traits – punching the air when she scores points, smoking and drinking, wanting to be known as 'guv'nor or boss', apparently relishing the simultaneous prestige and strife wrought by police work. Tennison is up against the presence and spectre of the patriarchal order of the police at every juncture, not just in the daily menace she encounters from Kernan and Otley, but in the gauntlet laid down by Paxman's mythical arrest record and the ever-present threat of Hicock's arrival as her replacement. Yet she seems to offer WPC (Woman Police Constable) Havers little recognition at the end, as one might hope she would for a fellow woman officer, for providing the hunch that breaks the case. Having secured Marlow's confession she stops Havers in the corridor, not to enjoy a little female camaraderie but only in order to enquire 'Any of those lads about?' Despite the text's investigation of institutional-ized and pathological misogyny, and Tennison's apparently inspirational effect on some of her audience (Hayward and Rennert, 1996: 15), this is 'by no means . . . a feminist tract' (Shales, 1991: 38). Rather, it is a text that portrays the compromises and negotiations necessitated by being a woman 'in a man's world' with bleak candour. Inevitably, La Plante was criticized for showing Tennison's private life as recurrently in crisis and thereby denying women the possibility of 'having it all'. As TV commentator Stuart Jefferies put it, 'In a way *Prime Suspect* was kind of reaction-ary. It was saying, well, women can do this kind of stuff but the cost is this: they will not be able to hold their lives together outside of work' (Channel 4, 2001). On a similar note there were concerns that it seemed to feed the paranoia and dread that prevail in our culture regarding women 'of a certain age' outside of conventional heterosexual relationships (Rennert, 1995: 26–8). In Amy Taubin's words, Tennison is 'forced to choose between work and a love-affair that, since she's already middle-aged, may well be her last' (1992: 50). This recurrent and anxious line of criticism says much about how older, independent, assertive and sexually active women pose such a discomforting 'problem' in cultural terms in their challenge to conventional notions of legitimate womanhood – and why *Prime Suspect*'s casting of exactly such a woman at its core was such a remarkable feat.

La Plante also adds another agitating element to the mix by demonstrating that in fact the personal and domestic lives of many of the *male* officers infringe on their professional lives; as the team meets in the pub we overhear Muddyman reassuring an anxious wife or girlfriend who has, we presume, followed him there, that he hasn't been two-timing her (mirroring Marlow's earlier dubious reassurance to Moyra). Meanwhile Birkin (who is later reprimanded for 'fraternising' with prostitutes) mut-ters in the office one evening that he can't stay any later because, 'The wife's mother is staying with us'. In fact, if anyone's private life infringes on their commitment or ability to fulfil the professionalism of the job, it is Shefford, who at one point gets his colleagues at the morgue to sing 'Happy Birthday' down the phone to his son. This scene ultimately points again to the imbalance between the sexes; La Plante is perhaps suggesting that Shefford can do this *because* he is a man, while a woman would rather more likely fear a reprimand for letting parental responsibilities encroach on professional time.

'Everybody seems to like him' – the serial killer as 'everyman'

Creeber (2001) gives considerable attention to both Shefford and Tennison and their positioning within the homosocial world of the police, but an exploration of the wider gender dynamics opened up by *Prime Suspect* also demands that we look closely at the representation of George Marlow, the killer. He is paradoxically perhaps most inter-esting for being so apparently undistinguished, because it is his seeming banality that makes him such a thought-provoking and disturbing 'villain'. The 'refreshing' decision to make Marlow an everyman figure, 'no (outwardly) demonic figure but instead a puppy faced forty-year old' (Shales, 1991: 38), was a crucial casting and characterization move. Through Marlow, La Plante again confronts a history of representation within the crime genre; a serial killer who isn't rendered transparently deviant or unambiguously guilty but is in a long-term relationship, has a steady job where he is well liked and a Mum who (however eccentric) loves him. He is popular, charming, unassuming and gregarious, a 'normal' man in every aspect of his outward appearance, to the extent that even the undercover police watching his house can't help but warm to him. Although he admits to sleeping with prostitutes, in the homosocial world of the text this isn't entirely transgressive after all, since the police themselves indulge in 'off-duty leg-overs' with prostitutes. (As George says confidentially to Shefford in his first interview, 'man-to-man' as it were, 'Well, you know they like to hustle'.)

Indeed *Prime Suspect*'s 'digression' into the private sphere extends not just to Tennison but to Marlow too, when we recurrently see him at home with his common-law wife Moyra. These exchanges work further to humanize Marlow and integrate him into the 'normal' cultural fabric of the social world. The scene where he proposes to Moyra is one that evokes the real warmth and companionship that underlies their relationship. Moyra's affection for him, and his desirability, are evident not only in her loyalty to him but in the quietly observed scene where she watches him in bed, then climbs in and tenderly caresses his back, initiating their love-making. Such a character is far more 'dangerous' than the conventional killer marked by obvious inadequacy, social maladjustment or physical oddity. Indeed, this very point was apparent in the reception of La Plante's first *Trial and Retribution* serial (1997), where a number of reviewers expressed disappointment of some kind with its 'unsatisfying bad guy'. He was described in the *Daily Telegraph*, for example, as:

> a ridiculously weird figure in a long black coat and long stringy hair whose limbs gyrated dervish like as he screamed about Beezlebub . . . in short, a join-the-dots description of a villain. *How much more sinister he would have been had he looked like Mr Ordinary Citizen* – your next door neighbour, or your brother-in-law. . . . Our concern for his fate . . . would have been much greater *had he been one of us*.
>
> (Odone, 1997: 38; emphasis added)

Trial and Retribution's killer was unsatisfying, then, precisely because of his perceived obviousness. In *Prime Suspect* there is no such clarity surrounding Marlow. Instead, like Tennison and everyone who surrounds him, we must ponder for ourselves whether this 'everyman' could indeed, beneath the likeable facade, be a psychopath. He is clearly and 'sinisterly' very much constructed as the 'Mr Ordinary Citizen' evoked in Odone's review above.

Existing work on the conventional depiction of the killer and/or rapist in slasher and rape revenge movies elucidates this point. These genres have been criticized for the dubious pleasure they take in female suffering, appealing to the sadistic side of the 'male spectator'. But the question of identification here is by no means simple. Carol Clover notes that by typically marking the rapist/killer as obviously unbalanced, socially inadequate or physically unattractive, the representation of this character facilitates against identification with him, externalizing him as 'Other' (Clover, 1992).[4] In this light it is arguably far more challenging and potentially politically charged to characterize the rapist/killer as ordinary and likeable. By depicting apparently 'normal' men in these roles and by, in a sense then, 'tricking' the spectator into sympathy or identification with them, a much more problematic and disconcerting audience/text relationship evolves than the 'exteriorization' allowed by more stereotypical representations. There is an implicit suggestion that, like an unmarked police car, men resembling George could be anywhere, moving unseen among us. It is George's very ordinariness that echoes the pervasive and ubiquitous character of misogyny as one that accumulates in the everyday. Indeed, feminist analysis of the reporting of real-life sex crime has similarly critiqued the sensationalist tendency of news to construct sex attackers as aberrant 'monsters' because 'the notion of a sex fiend presents a particular stereotype which hinders the full understanding of the nature and range of sex offences' (Soothill and Walby, 1991: 44). Misogyny lies in the mundane, the easy dismissal of women as 'tarts' and 'slags' that we witness from the male police officers, as much as in the spectacular excess of George's crimes; the difference is one of degree rather than nature.

'Look. Look at her, Moyra!' – female complicity and male sexual violence

Provocatively, too, there is an edgy and discomforting narrative thread suggesting *female* complicity in Marlow's crimes, a motif that has again informed the dissemination of many real life crimes where a woman has featured either as a suspected accomplice, gullible partner or 'stooge' to a prolific male serial killer. Suzanne Moore, writing in the *Guardian* in March 1994 about the Fred and Rose West case,[5] notes how women feature most often in serial killer stories as 'victims and progenitors'. Domineering mothers in particular are often depicted as the root cause of the male psychopath while other women 'figure as tormentors or as unavailable objects', both in some sense then 'to blame' for male sexual violence (Moore, 1994: 5). Both these myths of female accountability neatly describe the psychology we are offered as a means of understanding George Marlow. The representation of Moyra as a harping 'hard-nosed bitch', a wilful if ultimately repentant and misguided accessory who gives him a false alibi, means that she shares a measure of his accountability for the murders. Moyra's silence, her suppression of the fact that he had at one time enacted sexual aggression on her, 'enables' Marlow to kill again. Meanwhile Marlow's apparently unhealthy attachment to his crudely over-made-up mother, the mutual 'flirtation' they enact when he visits her, suggests she too is in some way complicit in his horribly warped perception of women.

Indeed, in its way, the most disturbing scene in *Prime Suspect* comes close to the end when Tennison is interviewing Moyra, who has refused to break her alibi for Marlow. Tennison demands that Moyra admit she had known the victims, Karen Howard and Della Mornay, pulling out Della's police mug-shot. Moyra refuses to look. Tennison pulls out a close-up of Della's corpse, her decomposing face, then another of Karen tied up and bloodied on the floor. We linger, though, not on these pictures but on Moyra's face refusing to look. Tennison grows frustrated and she demands angrily, 'Look. Look! Hands tied behind her back. Look at the marks on her body. Look at her, Moyra!' As Tennison and Moyra's lawyer begin to bicker among themselves, Moyra finally looks. We cut to the photos of the corpses laid out on the desk as Moyra's manicured and bejewelled hand reaches out to touch Della's face and rests on it. The image is a disconcerting one, the juxtaposition of living flesh against the dead and decaying, the carefully groomed against the hideously defiled, an intimate gesture against brutal violence. Moyra speaks at last: 'Get them to leave' she says of the men. There is an odd appeal here, then, to a kind of female solidarity or unity despite the expansive divide between Moyra and the police, excluding the men from the room in a reversal of the gendered exclusion Tennison has suffered so many times herself with her male colleagues. With just Tennison and (WPC) Maureen present, Moyra finally opens up. 'He did it to me once. But I . . . I didn't like it. Tied my hands . . . leather straps'. She breaks off and starts to gag and choke. Yet Tennison watches her without flinching; there is a virtually imperceptible flicker across her face that just might suggest exasperation. She then turns to Maureen and looks at her as if to say, 'This is it!' Maureen too is silent, but the instinctual exchange between them is clear as she gives the faintest of nods and smiles. There is female camaraderie at last then, in this room; the understanding that Moyra had apparently appealed to. But it is one that Moyra is very much excluded from. As Tennison and Maureen let Moyra get on with her retching without comment to share a moment of silent vindication, their exchange of looks rings the most hollow of victories.

It is at once a brilliant and deeply disturbing scene for the ambivalent position it takes on all the women present. Should we feel contempt or understanding for Tennison and Maureen's response? Have the police turned these women into something so horribly unfeeling, so driven only by 'masculine' vindication, that they can revel in their own victory in the face of human collapse? Are they police officers first and women second? Is that the way it should be? And finally, should we pity or loathe Moyra? Isn't she a victim in all this too? In Oldham, the prostitutes told Tennison that Jeannie, the first young prostitute Marlow murdered, 'Never stood a chance. Her foster dad was screwing her at seven. She was out on the streets at fourteen'. In this interview we learn that Moyra was also on the streets as a young woman, appearing on charges of soliciting with Della in Manchester Juvenile Court in 1976. Moyra too, then, is marked as holding an affinity with the dead prostitutes, not visually like Tennison who is recurrently framed against pictures of their corpses, but in the structures of sex, class and powerlessness inscribed in their shared social position.

'I want to see her face' – looking at women, seeing the female corpse

In fact the insistence on looking, or refusal to look, at women – more specifically at Tennison and the spectacle proffered by the female corpses – is marked as a central motif in *Prime Suspect*'s gendered aesthetics and its investigation of male structures of power. La Plante and director Chris Menaul's scrutiny of gender in the genre, then, is not just pursued at the level of narrative. *Prime Suspect* foregrounds the act of looking as one that holds peculiarly potent significance in terms of *recognizing* women, in both senses of the word – that is, in naming and identifying women *and* in acknowledging their position and accomplishments. The disastrous start to the investigation is caused by Shefford's refusal or inability to look at the corpse, leading to the misidentification of Karen's body as being Della's. At the murder scene, as the pathologist Felix examines the body, he asks, 'John do you want a look?', but Shefford shakes his head and lingers by the doorway. Later, as Felix performs the post-mortem, he comments 'Her whole body's badly bruised with extensive bruising to the vagina – want to see?', and again Shefford shakes his head and moves away. It later becomes clear that his reluctance to look at her springs partly from his having been sexually involved with Della, but more broadly this refusal to 'see' Karen is part of a larger narrative motif running throughout the text. It is only when Tennison takes over the case that anyone 'sees' the victim for the first time, not as a collection of injuries and evidence, not as an opportunity to break the station's record for the fastest arrest on a murder enquiry, but as a woman whom the others have failed to rightfully recognize.[6] Later, when Della's body is found dumped on Sunningdale golf course, in the hellish thick of the mud, darkness and rain, Tennison goes to the officer at the scene and says 'I'd like to have a look please'. He is reticent and patronising – 'Are you sure? It's not a pretty sight'. Tennison is forthright – 'I want to see her face'. In a shocking, rotten, terrible image, the earth is rubbed away from the corpse's nose and eye sockets to reveal her face. Tennison recognizes her instantly, nods and stands; 'That's Della Mornay'.

There is a gendered matrix of looking and seeing in operation, then, first, pivoting around who can and can't 'see' both the victims and Tennison and, second, regarding who will meet Tennison's gaze. Looking is inscribed as an empowering act for men who can withhold or grant the gaze, and the recognition it carries, on women. This is a process that does not operate in quite the same way as the objectifying male gaze Laura Mulvey described in classical Hollywood cinema because it is not always constructed as pivoting on sexually motivated voyeurism (Mulvey, 1975). But it is nevertheless a system of looks that is equally embedded in gender and power. Like the victims, Tennison endures a series of encounters where men refuse to look at her, a disavowal of her presence and position that serves as a means of disempowering her. Major Howard, D.S. Eastow at the Sunningdale crime scene, Karen's boyfriend Michael, the policeman in Manchester; all choose in some way not to look at Tennison, typically 'recognizing', gravitating to or addressing the other, less senior, but crucially *male* officer with her.

A similar gendered dichotomy is to be found in the recurrent ways in which the male officers and Tennison are oppositionally framed and shot. The men's solidarity is underlined by the manner in which they are repeatedly grouped together in the canteen and incident room by an expansive, circular, panning or tracking camera movement. In contrast we frequently see Tennison isolated and/or against the images of the victims on one side of the incident room in still, medium close-up. The still camera on a solitary Tennison, then, underlines her difference, contrasting with the recurrent bravura camera movement across a brooding sea of men. Intriguingly, Tennison is ultimately incorporated into the expansive, 'masculine', panning camera at the end, when the men surround her with flowers, champagne and singing in the incident room following Marlow's confession. The camera surveys them in a circular movement as they toast her jubilantly at their centre. As Brunsdon has noted, Tennison's response – 'You bastards. I thought you'd all pissed off home' – underlines her acceptance by the men because she is 'now fully integrated into the language of the lads' (Brunsdon, 1998: 234). Alternatively, Creeber sees the scene as one where her acceptance suggests not the incorporation of Tennison into 'masculine' behavioural traits but the men's recognition, finally, of her femininity; 'The fizzy champagne covers her and all the male officers with white froth and light, the flowers she is given a symbolic triumph of the "natural" and the "feminine" over the "urban", "masculine" and neo-noir world' (Creeber, 2001: 162). But one might also read a hint of menace into these images. Tennison seems almost engulfed by the men when the camera pans around them dizzily, as if trapped in an eerie, overwhelming merry-go-ground. Indeed a psychoanalytic reading of the men would make much of their spraying her here with popping champagne bottles as a symbolically aggressive act connoting sexual dominance over her and phallic power. As later instalments of the serial go on to show, Tennison is still far from affiliated into the male order of the police.

The gendered dichotomy of the camera is evident too in the way Tennison is also recurrently privileged by the still camera when it lingers on her after, or outside of, the dramatic climax of a scene. If *Prime Suspect* owes anything to the conventions of soap opera, it is not so much an interest in the domestic sphere as the visual tradition of staying with a close-up of the protagonist's/Tennison's face for that 'extra beat' beyond the 'end' of a scene. In the hall after her first address to the men and after Birkin ejects her from the room with Major Howard, we do not cut to the next scene immediately or witness the more tangible 'drama' of the men's reactions to her. Instead, as on numerous occasions in the interviews and courtroom for example, we stay with Tennison and are invited to 'read' the subtle, indeterminate shifts on her face. La Plante's ambivalent characterization of Tennison and Mirren's reserved performance style demand that much of how we perceive Tennison emanates from the readings we make of her in these instants. Like Richard Dyer's description of 'the private moment' in classical Hollywood, where a character is allowed a moment of reflective intimacy with the audience that other characters are not privy to (1980: 95), these pauses on Tennison draw one into identificatory processes with her.

Reimagining realism

The centrality of the spectacle of the corpses lies not just in their contribution to the text's gendered dichotomy of looking and its commentary on misogyny, however. They are also crucial in terms of their contribution to the *realism* inscribed in the text, which, like its gender dynamics, is fundamental to the way in which *Prime Suspect* provocatively reconfigured the genre. As the *Sunday Times* review put it, in terms echoed widely elsewhere,[7]

> What separated *Prime Suspect* from a thousand US cop shows however was its realism. The unearthed bodies looked all too much like unearthed bodies . . . the police procedure had almost documentary conviction.
>
> (Anon, 1991)

The use of the terms 'realism' and 'documentary' here are significant. In locating these, the review above points to the authenticity of both the mise-en-scène ('unearthed bodies') and meticulous attention to script and narrative ('police procedure') while also wanting to differentiate it from other generic associates; this is *not* 'a US cop show'. To liken it to a documentary is significant for two reasons here. First, it is a telling descriptive term in that it points to how the programme draws on some of the aesthetic conventions that audiences are likely to associate with the documentary form – for example, the murky lighting, the 'fly-on-the-wall' forays into the forensics labs and, perhaps most strikingly, but frequently overlooked, the muffled, multiple layering and overlapping of sound. But second, this description is also evaluative, it is meant as a *plaudit*; the perceived documentary-like realism of the programme separates it from its peers and transforms it into a particularly accomplished text. Its 'documentary conviction' secures the show an enhanced kudos, bearing out the enduring resilience of the critical tradition that has long seen ' "the documentary" as the art cinema of Britain' (Garnham, 1971: 55). Crucially, this 'realism' is often at its most striking in the representation of the victims; the text's willingness to graphically explore the female corpse, and in its recurrent use of their pictures, of photographic 'evidence', as a signifier of realism. In *Prime Suspect* British television arguably encountered the most consistently explicit series of images of the corpse it had ever known at that time. Clothed and naked, bloodied and bruised, tortured and decomposing, in close-up and in long shot, the corpse is always there, whether haunting the margins of text and screen or, intermittently, centre-stage.

Unsurprisingly, then, perhaps, *Prime Suspect*'s 'unnecessarily explicit visual details of a dead body' along with its 'strong language' prompted 10 complaints to the Broadcasting Standards Council (Broadcasting Standards Council, 1991). Defending themselves in the statement they issued in response, Granada Television observed,

> it was the company's intention to be as *honest and authentic* about the professional and public impact of a case which was distressing and disturbing . . . the production team attempted to make a compromise between the *extreme realism of a similar situation in real-life* and undue sanitization.
>
> (Broadcasting Standards Council, 1991; emphasis added)

Neither complaint, of undue visual or verbal explicitness, was upheld. The BSC Complaints Committee found that the strong language was not inappropriate 'in *the context of a play* giving a realistic account of police investigations' (emphasis added) and although it recognized 'the grimness of the spectacle of the bodies displayed', these images 'did not exceed limits reasonable in a drama of this sort' (Broadcasting Standards Council, 1991).[8] A number of interesting details emerge from the account of these complaints. In its defence Granada Television explains that its aesthetic was led by the desire for 'honesty', 'authenticity' and 'extreme realism'. Granada forges a direct comparison between what it has produced and 'real-life'. The Broadcasting Standards Council's findings are also revealing, indicating how the programme produces kinds of slippage, between 'spectacle' but 'grimness', between 'a realistic account' but also variously a 'drama' and 'play'. This last description, 'a play', seems particularly telling. Britain's penchant for the single play has declined massively over the past two decades but it has always traditionally been seen as the zenith of British television's intelligent, accomplished and meditative programming. John Caughie notes this when he writes that the single play, confers a certain cultural prestige, a 'seriousness', on television as a whole. But in order to function in this way, in order to be 'serious', drama occasionally has to *overstep the limits, to show what has not been shown before.*

(Caughie, 1981: 333; emphasis added)

Like the reference to 'documentary conviction' above, then, the description of *Prime Suspect* as a 'play' in formal terms is a revealing choice of words; it adds dramatic weight and loftiness to the programme's profile and points to the earnestness with which *Prime Suspect* was received. But, furthermore, Caughie's stipulation that the single play has a reputation for 'overstepping limits' also endorses my suggestion that the first *Prime Suspect* pushed the boundaries of the TV crime drama into new territory. It is for these reasons – in its radical aesthetics and sexual politics as well as its striking performances – that *Prime Suspect* managed to distinguish itself from everyday televisuality, rising above 'the flow' in its reception and impact on the genre.

Pushing back genre boundaries

Writing about audience relationships with different forms of film and TV violence and their relative levels of 'realism', David Morrison et al. (1999) have recently formulated the concept of 'the new rules of injury'. It is a premise that seems particularly pertinent here, offering another intriguing way into La Plante's work and its reception by describing a climate that usefully conceptualizes contemporary shifts in the perception of violence and realism in the media. They describe these 'new rules of injury' as 'the changing conventions employed by filmmakers to give more and more "realism" to violent injury: to attempt to show injuries as they would supposedly look in real life, with clinical precision' (Morrison et al., 1999: 8). As this suggests, these 'rules', like genres in fact, are dynamic, constantly being renegotiated by new texts. Morrison et al. continue:

> The sheer cleverness of modern special effects, and the commitment of film makers to ensuring that violence is presented in graphic detail, over-emphasises reality. To construct a violent act on film, using the close focus so often employed in modern films, is to slow it down. . . . In real life, action is never viewed with such concentrated focus . . .

(1999: 21)

Although this description specifically invokes film as its referent, we can transpose the same kind of processes to recent shifts in television's evocation of realism. Morrison's words about the increasing importance and expectation of 'modern special effects', 'graphic detail' and 'close focus' are all relevant to understanding La Plante's oeuvre and its rearticulation of forensic realism in television crime. This theme is very much pursued by her later *Trial and Retribution* serials. These have pushed back the boundaries expanded by *Prime Suspect* further still with even more explicit and detailed forensic imagery, and they have also been striking and contentious for their experimental use of split-screen.[9] La Plante has not just drawn on television's 'new rules of injury' in her crime dramas; she has been a key British proponent in their recent evolution, the impact of whose work has been felt internationally.

This, combined with her ongoing interjection into the genre's inflection of gender, makes greater critical interest in her work a priority for contemporary cultural studies. It seems ironic that Tennison is on a mission to overcome exclusion and win 'recognition' throughout *Prime Suspect* because, while Tennison arguably succeeds (momentarily) in this mission by the end of the first serial, her author's quest for the same outcome seems not yet to have been satisfactorily resolved in the academy. It is La Plante now, then, who must be more broadly recognized, who like Tennison must be properly 'seen' by the institution in which she works; in her case, as arguably the most influential contributor to British crime drama in recent television history.

Notes

1   There were eventually five serials of *Prime Suspect* in total, of which La Plante wrote numbers 1 and 3.

2   Of course, the move towards increasingly explicit depictions of the corpse and forensics since the early 1990s now extends across popular culture wholeheartedly into the rise of crime stories in documentary and reality TV, and indeed beyond TV to literary fiction (for example, novelists Patricia Cornwell and Kathy Reichs) and cinema (for example, *The Silence of the Lambs* (Jonathan Demme, 1991), *Se7en* (David Fincher, 1995), *Copycat* (John Amiel, 1995)). In many of these texts too we can see the concurrent rise of the female investigator in the genre, marking these generic shifts as very often interlinked.

3   Indeed, impressively, *Prime Suspect* took first place in Channel 4's *Top Ten TV: Cops* (tx 29/9/01), another testament to Tennison's remarkable popularity and resonance in the genre. In his commentary, presenter David Soul noted the programme's striking success but also, implicitly, the novelty of this result: 'Yes, our number one TV cop is a woman'.

4   See, for example, Clover's description of 'the threatening rural Other' (1992: 125–7) marked by physical disfigurement and poverty, who is positioned outside the rules of civilization, and how the figure of the 'redneck' has become 'the "someone else" held responsible for all manner of American social ills' (1992: 135).

5   Fred and Rose West were British husband and wife serial killers responsible for the rape, torture and murders of at least a dozen women, and, it is feared, perhaps many others. They were arrested in 1994 when a number of bodies were found buried in their Gloucester home. Fred West committed suicide in custody in January 1995. In November 1995 Rose West was convicted of 10 counts of murder.

6   There are distinct echoes of *The Silence of the Lambs* here, where it is Clarice Starling who 'sees' and articulates the body in the post-mortem scene. Like Tennison in *Prime Suspect* too, Starling is recurrently framed against or played off the image of the victim to suggest parallels between them. Similarly again, Starling also brings 'female' knowledge and camaraderie with the victims' friends to bear, noting in the autopsy that the victim can't be local since 'she's wearing

glitter nail polish' and finally cracking the case through information gleaned from her interview with Frederica Bimmel's friend. See my discussion in Jermyn (2003).

7   For example, Richard Last spoke similarly of its 'admirably hard-edged quasi documentary look' (1991: 15).

8   I am grateful to the Broadcasting Complaints Commission as it is now known for making these records available to me.

9   This is an aesthetic subsequently and more recently adopted by the US crime serial *24* (2001), whose own inventive contribution to 'reimagining realism' in the genre hinges on its use of 'real-time'. Neither split-screen nor real-time are new devices in themselves, of course. But their recent revival in these texts indicates the dynamic nature of genre – which must continually borrow, adapt or pioneer different themes and aesthetics – and the institutional desirability of 'giving an old formula a new angle' (Dyer, 1987: 11).

References

Anon. (1991) Review of *Prime Suspect, The Sunday Times* (14 April).

Broadcasting Standards Council (1991) Finding from BSC Complaints Committee, 28 May.

Brunsdon, Charlotte (1998) 'Structure of Anxiety: Recent British Television Crime Fiction', *Screen* 39(3): 223–43.

Caughie, John (1981) 'Progressive Television and Documentary Drama', in Tony Bennett (ed.) *Popular Film and Television*, pp. 327–52. London: BFI/OUP.

Channel 4 (2001) *Top Ten TV: Cops*, video-recording, tx 29 September.

Clover, Carol (1992) *Men, Women and Chainsaws*. London: BFI.

Creeber, Glen (2001) 'Cigarettes and Alcohol: Investigating Gender, Genre and Gratification in *Prime Suspect*', *Television and New Media* 2(2): 149–66.

D'Acci, Julie (1987) 'The case of *Cagney and Lacey*', in Helen Baehr and Gillian Dyer (eds) *Boxed In: Women and Television*, pp. 203–25. London: Pandora Press.

Day Lewis, Sean (1998) *Talk of Drama: Views of the Television Dramatist Now and Then*. Luton: University of Luton Press.

Dyer, Gillian (1987) 'Women and Television: An Overview', in Helen Baehr and Gillian Dyer (eds) *Boxed In: Women and Television*, pp. 6–16. London: Pandora Press.

Dyer, Richard (1980) 'Resistance Through Charisma: Rita Hayworth and *Gilda*', in E. Ann Kaplan (ed.) *Women in Film Noir*, pp. 91–9. London: BFI (2nd edition 1998).

Garnham, Nicholas (1971) 'TV Documentary and Ideology', *Screen Reader One*, pp. 55–61. Society for Education in Film and Television.

Hallam, Julia (2000) 'Power Plays: Gender, Genre and Lynda La Plante', in Jonathan Bignell and Madeleine Macmurragh-Kavanagh (eds) *British Television Drama: Past, Present and Future*, pp. 140–49. Basingstoke: Palgrave.

Hayward, Anthony and Amy Rennert, eds (1996) *Prime Suspect: The Official Book of the Award-Winning Series*. London: Carlton Books.

Jermyn, Deborah (forthcoming 2003) 'You Can't Keep a Dead Woman Down: The Female Corpse and Textual Disruption in Contemporary Hollywood', in Elizabeth Klaver (ed.) *Representations of the Dead: Images Corporeus from the Early Modern Moment to Cyberspace*. Madison, WI: University of Wisconsin Press.

Last, Richard (1991) 'Murder and Male Prejudice', *Daily Telegraph* (8 April): 15.

Moore, Suzanne (1994) 'Death and the Maidens', the *Guardian* (G2) (11 March): 5.

Morrison, David E. with Brent McGregor, Michael Svennevig and Julie Firmstone (1999) *Defining Violence: The Search for Understanding*. Luton: University of Luton Press.

Mulvey, Laura (1975) 'Visual Pleasure and Narrative Cinema', *Screen* 16(3): 6–18.

Odone, Christina (1997) Review of *Trial and Retribution, Daily Telegraph* (20 October): 38.

Phillips, Geoffrey (1997) 'Sharpening the Mirren Image', *Evening Standard* (16 October): 30.

Purser, Philip (1991) 'Prejudice? It's a Fair Cop', *Daily Telegraph* (10 April): 14.

Rampton, James (1996) 'Prime-time with La Plante', *The Independent* (23 March): 30.

Rennert, Amy, ed. (1995) *Helen Mirren: A Celebration – Prime Suspect*. San Francisco, CA: KQED Books.

Shales, Tom (1991) Review of *Prime Suspect*, reprinted in Anthony Hayward and Amy Rennert (eds) (1996) *Prime Suspect: The Official Book of the Award-Winning Series*, pp. 64–70. London: Carlton Books.

Soothill, Keith and Sylvia Walby (1991) *Sex Crime in the News*. London and New York: Routledge.

Taubin, Amy (1992) 'Misogyny, She Wrote', *The Village Voice* (28 January): 50.

Thomas, David (1993) 'La Plante's Punch', *You* (magazine of *The Mail on Sunday*) (23 May): 82–5.

Wolcott, James (1995) 'An Appreciation', in Amy Rennert (ed.) *Helen Mirren: A Celebration – Prime Suspect*. San Francisco, CA: KQED Books.

4

Divas, Evil Black Bitches, and Bitter Black Women

African-American women in postfeminist and post-civil rights popular culture

Kimberly Springer

Originally published in Diane Negra and Yvonne Tasker (eds), *Interrogating Post-Feminism* (Durham, NC: Duke University Press, 2007), 249–276.

Much of feminist theory recognizes the contributions of women of color, particularly 1980s and 1990s demands for attention to intersectionality as fundamental to social, political, economic, and cultural transformation. To date, studies of postfeminism have studiously noted that many of its icons are white and cited the absence of women of color, but the analysis seems to stop there. Whiteness studies, an area that started with such a bang, appears to have dwindled to a whimper when it comes to thinking about how, say, Miranda, Carrie, Samantha and Charlotte exact racial privilege while they have their sex in the city. The arrival of postfeminist discourse in popular culture, especially, needs to be interrogated for how race is *always* present. Even when they are not on the screen, women of color are present as the counterpart against which white women's ways of being – from Bridget Jones to Ally McBeal to Carrie Bradshaw – are defined and *re*fined. And though there are black women in successful business, intellectual, and cultural industries, there are also, critically, not-so-new manifestations of racism and sexism impacting black women in popular culture.

   This chapter attempts to examine both African-American women's presence and absence in postfeminist manifestations of popular culture. Some critics believe that we must expand campaigns for representational inclusivity to address underlying industrial practices, particularly given the expansion of culture industries from nationally owned entities (e.g. the Big Three Networks, ABC, NBC, and CBS) into the global market (e.g. Viacom, NewsCorp, Vivendi).[1] Undoubtedly the ability of business to capitalize on niche markets continues to evolve beyond US borders. Susan J. Douglas draws our attention to the political stakes of postfeminist culture, noting that: "the seemingly most banal or innocent or peripheral media fare play a central, crucial role in the weekly and monthly engineering of consent around an acceptance of postfeminism as the only possible subjective stand and political position for women to inhabit in the early twenty-first century."[2] Seemingly harmless cultural representations of black women are incorporated into institutional enactments of discrimination, including racist, sexist, classist, and heterosexist social policies. My analysis situates postfeminist and post-civil rights discourses as retrograde and contrary to the interests of women in general, and black women, specifically. The potential political implications of these two discourses for popular culture pick up where misogynistic and racist stereotypes, often now implicit, left off, taking them to a new level of identity construction.

Integrating multiple "post-" positions: postfeminism and post-civil rights

Examinations of postfeminism have defined it as a cultural and political move against feminism and contrary to the goals of the women's movement.[3] It is also emerging that postfeminism includes claims of feminism's demise and accusations that feminism is antisex.[4] Based on content analysis of ninety popular and academic sources, Elaine J. Hall and Marnie Salupo Rodriguez establish the following four claims as central to postfeminism: support for feminism decreased from 1980–1990; antifeminism has increased among young women, women of color, and full-time homemakers; feminism is irrelevant because it has successfully achieved equality for younger women who feel they experience only personal, not institutional, sexism; women who agree with feminist ideals of equality may refuse to claim a feminist identity.[5] They then surveyed public opinion polls to test these claims, finding that, in fact: levels of support increased or remained stable from the late 1980s to early 1990s; women of color and young adults view the women's movement favorably, while homemakers did appear disinclined toward feminism; from 1980–1999, half of their respondents considered the women's movement still relevant; and the "I'm not a feminist but . . ." position was prevalent with the potential to depoliticize feminism.[6]

These findings and emerging definitions indicate, more generally, backlash against the gains and goals of feminism defined broadly as solely rooted in a liberal, pluralist feminist framework of equality. Amber Kinser, in her exploration of Third Wave feminism, observes that today's young women live in a world where, curiously, "feminist *language* is part of the public dialogue, but authentic feminist *struggles* are not accounted for in that dialogue except in terms articulated by the mainstream, which still perpetuates a conservative and sexist status quo."[7] This distinction between language and struggle is crucial because it is this difference that allows postfeminism, perhaps more insidiously than antifeminism, to appropriate feminist language and exploit liberal feminism's key weakness namely a call for equality without including racial analysis. Liberal feminism and postfeminism exclude revolutionary visions of feminism that continue to ask the question: equal to what? Feminists of color long maintained being equal to men of color, who experience disproportionate incarceration compared to white men, unemployment, etc., would mean merely a different kind of oppression. Why would women choose this capitalist fantasy of equality when the reality includes further gender segregation in the burgeoning US service economy, the rapid rise of women of color as incarcerated labor, and the closing of the welfare state? Instead, they argue that feminism needs to fight for radical social transformation, particularly in the U.S. where equality discourse is rooted in a founding national document crafted by slaveholders and begins with the words "all (white) men are created equal."

It is on this basis that I would expose postfeminism's racial agenda. Postfeminism seeks to erase any efforts toward racial inclusion feminism made since the 1980s. It does so through making racial difference, like feminism itself, merely another commodity for consumption. Amber Kinser remarks, "Part of the genius of postfeminism is to co-opt the language of feminism and then attach it to some kind of consumer behavior that feeds young people's hunger for uniqueness . . ."[8] Similarly, postfeminism takes demands for racial inclusion on the feminist agenda and makes race consumable in the form of "ethnic" clothing, mainstreaming the fetishization of a "big, black booty," promoting year-round "bronzed" (brown) skin, and encouraging consumption of fair trade goods without ever questioning the conflation of commerce and democracy. Racialized postfeminism does not move very far from bell hooks' assertion that particular forms of cultural engagement merely amount to "eating the other": a "commodification of otherness" in which "ethnicity becomes spice, seasoning that can liven up the dull dish that is mainstream white culture."[9]

As Imelda Whelehan notes, control became a catchphrase of one 1990s manifestation of postfeminism, power feminism, but this " . . . control always seemed to be about the right to consume and display oneself to best effect, not about empowerment in the worlds of work, politics, or even the home."[10] Women could once again be universalized under the assumption that all women want to "have it all." If, as Diane Negra maintains, "one of the key premises in current antifeminist postfeminist constructions of women's life choices . . . is the need to abandon the overly-ambitious 1980s program of 'having it all' ", does this apply across racial categories?[11] The discourse of having it all has always been a bit lost on black women and anathema to black feminism that aimed, in the 1970s, to dismantle the idea that black women could be Superwomen. The icon of the Black Superwoman or Strongblackwoman[12] is not the racialized equivalent of having it all. Having it all discourse implies that women are lacking something that they need to go out and get: career and family.

Superwoman/Strongblackwoman discourse assumes that a black woman has *too many obligations* but she is expected to *handle her business*. Thus, while postfeminism poses that white women cannot have it all, racialized postfeminism, at least for black women, means continuing to be everything for everyone else *and* maintaining a sense of self. Postfeminism, though, has begun to assimilate black women into the rhetoric of having it all. For instance, Veronica Chambers' book *Having It All? Black Women and Success* accepts the terms of the having it all conceptualization and reflects a postfeminist vision of middle class and aspiring upper class black women's lives. This vision treads a perilous line of a depoliticized *black* postfeminism calling upon black feminist theorists such as bell hooks and incorporating paragons of white beauty such as Audrey Hepburn and Grace Kelly. While I am not implying that black women can only look to black women for inspiration, the reliance on staple icons like Kelly and Hepburn does not advance black feminist, and feminist calls generally, for seeking out role models that do not fit into postfeminism's version of white, upper class, slim, traditionally attractive femininity.

In addition to postfeminism, there is another "post" to be reckoned with in this essay: post-civil rights. As part of a racialized discourse, one must grapple with postfeminism's place in the post-civil rights era. Like critiques that expose the postfeminist fallacy that all of feminism's goals have been achieved, therefore rendering the women's movement unnecessary, post-civil rights language would seem to imply that the goals of the civil rights movement were achieved starting with the Supreme Court desegregation legislation in 1954's *Brown v. Board of Education* to the passage of the 1964 Civil Rights Act and on through the rise of a significant black middle class in the 1980s. However, it is more accurate to conceptualize post-civil rights discourse as a commentary on the drastic rollbacks or, to be consistent with criticisms of post-feminism, backlash against civil rights movement achievements. Patricia Hill Collins outlines the contours of that backlash against efforts to dismantle institutional racism: "In the 1980s, Republican administrations set about dismantling enforcement efforts for equal opportunity, cutting funding for urban programs, incarcerating growing numbers of African-Americans in the burgeoning prison industry, shrinking the social welfare budget through punitive measures, and endorsing historical labor market patterns."[13] The Clinton Administration's dismantling of the welfare system, shifting from Aid to Families with Dependent Children to state-administered welfare-to-work programs, and the second Bush Administration's aggressive stance against affirmative action fall well within the definition of a countermovement to a progressive agenda of racial equality.

The social counterpart to institutional post-civil rights racism was the welfare queen. Poor black women were already vilified as mammies and jezebels in slavery, then later in the 1970s as matriarchs destroying the black community with their female-headed households,[14] and playing the welfare system for undue gain. The 1980s welfare queen image implied that black women not only cheated the system, but they also lived extravagantly from the proceeds. Integrally tied to reproduction, the welfare queen's trump card lay in her alleged disregard for birth control and propensity for having more children than she could afford. In its most perverse trans-formation yet, racist ideology maintained that while white slave masters no longer profited from black women's offspring, black women now claimed public tax dollars for their profligacy. The incongruity of a black woman living the high life in some of the worst public housing in the world was lost on fiscally conservative American taxpayers. Welfare queen iconography remained solidly prevalent until the Clinton Administration ended additional benefits for additional children. While not completely eradicated, the image of the welfare queen morphed into the crack-addicted mother, who became a mainstay of late 1980s and 1990s political rhetoric linking race and gender to the War on Drugs.

Black women, long the subject of racially gendered prejudices from the antebel-lum period through the 1980s, faced the iconography of the mammy, the jezebel, the sapphire, the matriarch, the welfare queen, and the crack-addicted mother in popular culture and social policy. As I have indicated, these stereotypes still exist, but they have also morphed into new ones more appropriate to the postfeminist, post-civil rights era. If we are beyond discriminatory behavior, how do we account for the diva, the black lady, the angry black woman images populating the current cultural landscape?

The remainder of this chapter explores representations of black women in select television programs and films. The range of texts discussed here is by no means comprehensive, but is meant to provide a general theory of black femininity within postfeminist and post-civil rights discourses and illustrate examples of backlash representation.[15] Starting with popular culture more generally, I tackle the usage of the term "diva" as it relates to black women and consider what it has come to signify about "black women with attitude." I also note Patricia Hill Collins' theorizing on the black lady and modern mammy images in popular culture representations. Both in political life and on television, the modern mammy and black lady maintain a striking convergence whether found in the White House or on our television screens. Next, I analyze reality television's often *un*real depictions of black women and responses to these sexist and racist evocations of black womanhood. Lastly, in terms of film, I examine postfeminism and post-civil rights era films about black women and their contradictory messages about black women's race, gender, and class. *Waiting to Exhale* (1995), *Down in the Delta* (1998), and *Diary of a Mad Black Woman* (2005) offer fruitful areas of inquiry for locating postfeminism's racialized agenda.

Deploy the diva!

Much like other stereotypes bestowed upon African-American women, the journey of the appellation "diva" is under-theorized and begs the question: how did the term diva move from denoting a heralded opera singer to its late twentieth century embodiment: a powerful and entertaining, if pushy and bitchy woman? In thinking about how a label once applied to Maria Callas is now applied to Mariah Carey, we need to ask how the diva fits into the postfeminist, post-civil rights agenda.

The association of the diva with singers has continued, but recently changed genres. Hypothetically speaking, it is possible that a film facilitated the term's cross-over from opera to R&B to hip hop. The French film *Diva* (1981) is structured around a twisting plot that was meant as a tribute to the French New Wave. The diva in question is Cynthia Hawkins (Wilhemina Wiggins-Fernandez), a reclusive black American opera singer who refuses to be recorded. A fan records one of her performances setting off a stylized thriller with a number of interested parties all chasing after the same bootleg for various reasons – from adoration to criminal intent. For a generation of college-attending Third Wave feminists, women and men, the film is a cult classic with the diva, even as a recluse, driving the film's action.

If we also consider the career of another soprano we can begin to make the leap from the black opera singer to the black R&B singer. Diana Ross was preceded by a number of talented black women singers who commanded respect in their own ways, but it was Ross who owned the 1960s and 1970s with her music and films. Topping the charts with The Supremes, she was an integral part of creating the distinct Motown sound. Though there were three group members who originally signed with Motown in 1961, in 1964 the Motown record label head, Berry Gordy, designated Ross the permanent lead singer of the group – a move that generated ten number one hit singles making The Supremes the most successful black group of the 1960s. Notably, in 1967 the group was renamed Diana Ross & the Supremes, highlighting Ross' central role and creating tensions in the group that are still commented upon today whenever there is talk of a reunion of The Supremes.

Ross left The Supremes behind and embarked on a solo singing career in 1970. It got off to a rough start until Gordy and Motown's new film production unit showcased Ross as Billie Holiday in the film *Lady Sings the Blues* (1972). This move garnered Ross an Academy Award nomination for Best Actress and she won a Golden Globe award for Best Newcomer. With this new cache and a stunning soundtrack of Billie Holiday cover songs, Ross went on to another Oscar nomination for her glamorous role as a poor project girl turned supermodel in *Mahogany* (1975). It is no wonder that she ended the decade with a critically acclaimed 1979 album appropriately titled *The Boss*.

I highlight Ross as the focus of the transition of the term diva from opera to R&B because in her life (at least the media-generated one), her music, and her films, Ross became the template for contemporary notions of the diva as immensely talented, but selfishly driven and difficult to deal with. It is hard to separate legend from fact, but with her ascension from group singer to lead singer in The Supremes and the larger than life aspects of her film roles, it is near impossible to tell the difference between Diana and the Diva. Then and now, though she is still considered the Boss and a diva, her reported behavior demonstrates the dual nature of divadom. She inappropriately touched the rapper Lil' Kim's already exposed breast at the 1999 MTV Video Music Awards. At London Heathrow Airport Ross vehemently opposed an airport body search she found intrusive by grabbing the security guard's breast. Convicted for drunk driving in 2004, Ross served only a fraction of her time because it was alleged a guard let her have the run of the prison. Ross' later antics only fuelled her reputation as a diva and facilitated the continued (d)evolution of the term.

Just as the diva label is bestowed, women and some gay men claim to be divas as an honorific. A 2002 review of country artist Faith Hill's album *Cry* in *Time Magazine* opined, "By definition, a diva is a rampaging female ego redeemed only in part by a lovely voice. It's hard to imagine why anyone would want to be one, but a new generation of female talent appears to be weirdly enamored of the word and the idea."[16] And, indeed, this was true when adult video music channel VH1 launched its series of *Divas* concerts in 1999. Linking high glamour and a revue format to a charitable cause, VH1 capitalized, if not spearheaded, the latest incarnation of the cult of celebrity by designating new divas for each show. The first concert, *Divas Live*, featured Celine Dion (the romantic diva), Gloria Estefan (the Latina diva), Shania Twain (the pop/country diva), Mariah Carey (the R&B diva), Aretha Franklin (the truly talented diva), and special guest Carol King (singer-songwriter diva).

Each successive *Divas* concert has followed this generational pattern: lesser-talented diva-wannabes supported by genuinely talented, older women who have both style *and* substance. One might argue that truly talented women do not need pop culture entities such as VH1 to certify their abilities, nor do they feel the need to proclaim their greatness. This distinction and that between generations are evident in the number of older female singers who decline the diva label. Motown hit maker and singer Gladys Knight insisted, "Don't call me diva. Diva has become something else now. Now they're throwing the word around. It's supposed to mean some kind of grandeur and that kind of stuff, but some of these people who they call divas have not been here long enough anyway. No, don't call me diva. I'm just here to sing . . . I am not all that. And when I start thinking that it's me, then I get into trouble. It's not about me."[17]

In a post-civil rights and postfeminist context, the diva label would appear to be a dubious homage. Today's divas are unreasonable, unpredictable, and likely unhinged. When a woman is called a diva or accused of exhibiting diva behavior, that woman is usually a woman of color. Jennifer Lopez's extravagant on-set demands; Mariah Carey's highly publicized, if disputed nervous breakdown; singer Mary J. Blige's early reputation as a drink- and drugs-fuelled hellion; Whitney Houston's erratic behavior in private and in an interview with ABC's Diane Sawyer; constant attempts to compare contemporary pop group Destiny's Child (especially the group's early lineup upheavals) with The Supremes, including possibly casting Beyoncé Knowles in the film version of the Broadway tribute to Diana Ross and the Supremes, *Dreamgirls*: these incidents are regularly featured in celebrity news venues as evidence of a woman whose financial success has yielded excess. Clearly, the line of postfeminist reasoning would go, these women do not know how to be humble about their talents and use them in service to others. While a tug-of-war over the empowering or negative connotations of divadom might be fought, it seems the label is ultimately but another form of categorization that classes women according to how well they adhere to race, class, and sexuality norms.

Black ladies and modern mammies

In an In Focus section of *Cinema Journal*, Yvonne Tasker and Diane Negra observe, "Within contemporary popular culture, it is clear that certain kinds of female agency are recognizably and profitably packaged as commodities. Typically, texts of this form are directed at a female audience even while covertly acknowledging male viewers/ voyeurs."[18] They go on to note the ways postfeminism operates on the basis of inclusion and exclusion, all the while assuming gender equality that allows for politically decontextualized racial and ethnic diversity. Much like early feminist generalizations, postfeminism assumes a universal category of women . . . or so it would seem. I maintain, however, that popular culture narrowcasts its representations of women to appeal to audience segmentation. In other words, racial and gender stereotypes are the commodity and the discourse that make difference legible in popular culture.

The image of the angry black woman has always been present on television, particularly in the form of a mouthy harpy. Media critics and African-American historians duly note the image of the nurturing mammy, the loudmouthed Sapphire, and the oversexed Jezebel as staples in television genres from situation comedies to family dramas to comedy sketch programs.[19] Thus reality TV has adapted this stereotype rather than originated it. In the post-civil rights era and with the rise of a black middle class, Collins believes we now have cultural representations and stereotypes of black women stratified by class. If poor and working-class women are defined as bitchy, promiscuous, and overly fertile, these "controlling images . . . become texts of what *not* to be."[20]

Becoming middle class, then, relies on a politics of respectability.[21] Echoing ancestral mandates passed down from the 19th century, black professional women must adhere to the role of the black lady, a role designed to counter accusations of black female licentiousness and one that can accommodate the ascension to middle-class status through work outside the home. Since black women were, and continue to be necessary to the workforce, postfeminist representations make clear that ". . . they cannot achieve the status of lady by withdrawing from the workforce" like white women.[22] An enduring example of the black lady is Clair Huxtable, the upper-middle-class wife, mother, daughter, and lawyer of the most successful post-civil rights black television show, *The Cosby Show* (1984–1992). Though never shown at work like her husband, Heathcliff, Clair's skills as a lawyer usually only emerged in her approach to mediating her children's squabbles.

In an effort to maintain the black lady's status, Collins claims "the image of Mammy, the loyal female servant created under chattel slavery, has been resurrected and modernized as a template for middle-class Black womanhood. Maneuvering through this image of the modern mammy requires a delicate balance between being appropriately subordinate to White and/or male authority yet maintaining a level of ambition and aggressiveness needed for achievement in middle-class occupations."[23]

George Walker Bush's Secretary of State Condoleezza Rice would be the real-life example of the black lady. Disavowing affirmative action, claiming success solely based on merit and determinedly asexual, Rice epitomizes the black professional lady at the height of her success. As the highest-ranking African-American woman ever in a presidential administration, Rice attempts to, paradoxically, depoliticize her presence there as a political actor. Narratives of her Birmingham, Alabama, childhood and current success are consistently separated from the struggle for civil rights. She insists upon a personal and family history of self-reliance, but denies privileges derived from black liberation struggles that accrued to a small, but emerging black middle class long before the Cosbys.

Rice embodies postfeminist and post-civil rights discourses in her adamant adherence to conservative Republic values of individual achievement and empowerment through money. To date, one of the most revealing and extensive articles on her attitudes appeared in the 9 September 2001 *Washington Post Magazine*. In the article Rice is attributed as saying that in her family: "liberation came not through a movement but from generations of ancestors navigating oppression with individual will, wits and, eventually, wallets – long before King or the federal government took up the cause. It is one of her frustrations, she says, that people routinely assume she was beaten down or deprived as a child until the civil rights movement arrived. 'My family is third-generation college-educated,' she says with proud defiance. 'I should've gotten to where I am.' "[24] In Rice's logic, those who are part of America's underclass are undeserving, but her achievements are based solely on merit. Hers is a post-civil rights mentality conditioned by defensiveness against affirmative action and rewarded for maintaining the privileges of the meritocracy.

As a high-ranking woman, Rice's sexuality has also fallen under scrutiny. In the modern mammy role, it is assumed that Rice is asexual and that might be appropriate for a woman of her rank in a presidential administration. Neither the mammy nor the black lady are thought of as sexual or as having sex, but Rice poses a conflicted dilemma for leftists who pride themselves on their anti-racism and anti-sexism. Previously advocating positions that argue against assumptions about black women's sexuality as licentious, supposedly progressive activists and thinkers will not hesitate to make unseemly comments about Rice's sexuality. Just as Anita Hill's single status and sexual harassment claims against Clarence Thomas were pathologized as "erotomania," speculation about Rice ranges from accusations of lesbianism to innuendo that she has an intimate relationship with George W. Bush. In November 2004, British newspaper *The Guardian* made these observations:

> As national security adviser for four years, Ms Rice has been indispensable and constantly available. She has no other life, has never married and a handful of dates with eligible men organised by well-meaning friends have led nowhere romantically.
>
> She spends many of her weekends at Camp David with the president, watching baseball and football and doing jigsaws with the first family. Her only time off appears to be occasional sessions playing the piano with a classical music group in Washington.
>
> At a dinner party with some senior journalists in spring this year, her dedication was revealed in an extraordinary Freudian slip. "As I was telling my husb-" she blurted, before correcting herself. "As I was telling President Bush."
>
> It says a lot about the prim reputation of both that hardly anyone in gossip-ridden Washington interpreted the slip as a sign of a romantic connection.

The Washington newspapers and weblogs may have steered clear of interpreting Rice's slip of the tongue, but notably black liberal news sources ran with it. The website BlackCommentator.com was already deriding Rice as "The Borg Queen" and ran a controversial cartoon in 2003 that implied that Rice, in addition to being a gatekeeper, might have a more intimate relationship with the President.

Most notable of black liberal ire toward Rice was cartoonist Aaron McGruder's series about Rice that ran in November 2004. The strip, which in essence contends that perhaps if Rice (who is single) got some "good old-fashioned lovin' " she would not be "hell-bent" on destroying the world. Possible suitors included Darth Vader as the one man in the universe who Rice might find compatible.

It is noteworthy that black men generated both depictions of Rice; black women academics and activists have been notably silent about her. Their views echo those in email discussion groups and on weblogs that Rice, like Clarence Thomas, is a sell-out to African-Americans. Interestingly, though, it is somehow considered just to raise Rice's sexuality as rationale for her conservative politics. She either simply needs to get laid or, because she is an unmarried successful woman in highly male echelons, she is a lesbian. In this postfeminist, post-civil rights era Rice is a no-win situation: in the eyes of conservatives she is totally devoid of sexuality as a black lady should be; for liberals she is a modern mammy (i.e. a race traitor *à la* Sally Hemmings, an unfortunate spinster, or a lesbian).

Rice poses a dilemma in that her achievements are consistently linked to a conservative agenda for which she appears to be but a prop. Indeed her position in the most powerful government in the world is impressive, particularly growing up in the midst of racist violence. And, yet, when contextualized in the prevalent stereotypes of the day, it is difficult, if nearly impossible, to view Rice as a success of the feminist and civil rights movements. And she would not want that. Instead, she embraces ideologies that claim the end of racism and sexism. While she may not want to be representative of black achievement, Rice enables postfeminist and post-civil rights goals by serving as both the good black lady and the modern mammy.

Collins cites *Law and Order*'s police lieutenant Anita Van Buren and *The District*'s Ella Farmer as examples of television characters that, while respectable, cannot evade the strictures of the modern mammy and the black lady. They may face sexist and racist discrimination, but "they both remain loyal to social institutions of law and order that are run by White men."[25] The same assertion is one possible explanation for the ubiquity of black female judges in television crime dramas. Failing to acurately represent the number of black women in the legal profession or the disproportionate rise in the number of black female inmates, and perhaps fearful of accusations of racism, black lady judges are preferable to 1970s and 1980s representations of black women as prostitutes or drug addicts in television courtrooms.[26]

The editing made me do it! The Evil Black Woman™[27]

"If you've ever seen a reality TV show, chances are you've seen her: a perpetually perturbed tooth-sucking, eye-rolling, finger-wagging harpy, creating confrontations in her wake and perceiving racial slights from the flimsiest provocations. At the very sight of her, her cast mates tremble in fear. And no wonder. She's the Sista With an Attitude."[28]

Reality TV "is a catch-all term, a convenient shorthand for many kinds of television."[29] This genre, borrowing the situationist approach from psychology and applying it to television ("what would happen if . . .?"), includes programs filming people in everyday situations, in unusual situations, in game show competition, on talk shows, and in docusoaps. What all these formats have in common is "the comprehensive monitoring of the unscripted rhythms of daily life" for both advertiser and audience consumption.[30] And just as reality TV is a catch-all, its modes of operation, including casting, are a catch-all for socially constructed identities.

Media critics, reality television aficionados, producers, and especially participants in the genre all acknowledge the stock trade in two-dimensional representation. Reality TV shows are not far removed from unsupervised social psychology experiments that create controlled environments using identity as mere prop.[31] Writing for *The Washington Post*, in an article entitled "The Evil Sista of Reality Television" Teresa Wiltz notes the use of "recognizable stereotypes" as "visual shorthand" in the genre.[32] Writing on "Race and Reality . . . TV," media critic L.S. Kim observes that while there may be more "characters" of color than ever before on television due to the reality genre, editing creates "characters in what can best be described as an 'ensemble cast.' "[33] Omarosa Manigault-Stallworth explains, "Minorities have historically been portrayed negatively on reality TV . . . These types of show [sic] thrive off of portrayals that tap into preconceived stereotypes about minorities (i.e. that we are lazy, dishonest and hostile). Reality TV's 'angry black woman' portrayal strikes again!"[34]

And Manigault-Stallworth should know. In 2004 she became the most infamous black woman in television. For viewers of Donald Trump's reality series *The Apprentice*, Manigault-Stallworth epitomized the Angry Black Woman, the Evil Black Bitch, and every other variation on that particular racist and sexist theme. During her tenure on the show's first season and after she was "fired" as a Trump apprentice,

Manigault-Stallworth, was (and continues to be) vilified as difficult, lazy, obstructive, manipulative, and unnecessarily hostile to her fellow contestants.

Commensurate with Collins' update of stereotypes of black womanhood, in unscripted programming Manigault-Stallworth fell afoul of scripts for black female behavior. Manigault-Stallworth was *The Apprentice*'s antiblack lady. She failed to be the modern mammy. She "played the race card" when she took offense at another cast member telling her "that's calling the kettle black." She was less than nurturing to other women on the show. She appeared to intentionally sabotage the efforts of the other African American, Kwame Jackson, participating in the show, though Jackson came in as runner-up by the end of the competition, Manigault-Stallworth's actions played into divisive perceptions of a black woman trying to hold a black man back. She even beat out Paris Hilton for the title "Most Appalling Reality Show Star of the 2003–2004 Season."[35]

Trump offered contradictory assessments of Manigault-Stallworth. On the show, he berated her, "You were rude. You *are* rude. I've seen it . . . It was very repulsive to me."[36] Yet, in an interview with the infotainment program *Extra TV*, Trump was bewildered, "Omarosa is very smart. She's very beautiful, and she's got an attitude and some of the women have gotten to just hate her. The level of hatred for Omarosa is so unbelievable that I've never seen anything like it."[37] Manigault-Stallworth confounded reality TV's visual codes for women in general and for black women specifically. She's beautiful, but beautiful women are supposed to be dumb. For a man a take-no-prisoners attitude in business would usually be just the thing to succeed in the cut-throat corporate world, but a black woman with attitude has no place in Trump's or any other white-dominated institution. Both her supposed attitude and uncompromising nature cancelled out any black lady or modern mammy roles she might have assumed.

Manigault-Stallworth held her own during an appearance on *Dr. Phil*.[38] Dr. Phil McGraw, a clinical psychologist, met Oprah Winfrey while running a business that focused on providing trial lawyers with psychological expertise for mock trials and jury selection. He soon became a regular fixture on *Oprah*, known for his straight-talking, Texan manner. With his catchphrase "Get real," he launched his own advice talk show in 2002 and took on both Manigault-Stallworth and Donald Trump in May 2005. In the broadcast Manigault-Stallworth admits to both playing to the cameras ("I quickly learned that as a black woman on reality television, if you want to get camera time, then you've got to be quite naughty. I knew that if I was naughty, I could certainly dominate most of the show, and I did. Guilty as charged!") and being manipulated by the editing process ("The Omarosa that America saw is a character. Out of every 300 minutes that they shot, there was only one minute that the American people saw. You don't see the manipulation behind the scenes. You don't see a systematic pattern of how they portray people. I am cast on these shows to be naughty.") Dr. Phil accuses her of complaining and being a victim, but Manigault-Stallworth characterizes her experience as research and critical analysis. She readily accepts partial responsibility for her actions, but only as the performance of a pre-existing role. Her position is a conflicted one that is mired in "the pornography of the performing self."[39] Her objections are to a double standard that paints her and other black women as liars and bitches, but white contestants as smart and shrewd. Yet, her concerns are less tailored toward fair representation and more focused upon how those projections impact her fiscal bottom line.

Audiences and critics are attuned to producers and show participants' motivations, but that does not make them more accepting of the prejudices perpetuated. After a week of racist slights – from the overt to the covert – student press writer Melanie Sims, in a review of reality TV imagines she is being stalked by television producers with hidden cameras intent on catching her out "finger-wagging, neck-popping, eye-rolling, [and] disgruntled."[40] She refuses to play this role saying, "The EBW [Evil Black Woman] is a persona – not a person. For as much as she is respected, she is vilified. She represents only a fraction of the black female consciousness and even less of the black female population as a whole. Reality TV's angry black woman is merely a product of selective studio editing."[41]

But how much can we blame on the editing? Camille McDonald, a contestant in series two of *America's Next Top Model*, claimed that her perceived arrogance, petulance, discord with other contestants, and rudeness was ". . . a media created, or media infused personality due to editing . . ."[42] This disclaimer has become a standard one regardless of identity for reality TV show participants and might be evidence of a widespread postmodern sensibility about constructions of truth and reality. To blame the editing both avoids directly accusing television producers of manipulation, absolves reality TV show participants from accountability for their actions, and keeps them in the good graces of producers who might want to use them in yet another reality TV series.

Yet, in a moment of candor, McDonald admits, "It's a reality show, so I can't sit here and say that we were given characters. Nothing was scripted. Everyone said what they said and did what they did, but it was how it was put together in the editing. You also have to keep in mind that there are other people besides Tyra [Banks, series producer and Supermodel] who have a say in how the contestants are portrayed. The bottom line for them is that if it doesn't make dollars it doesn't make sense." McDonald and other reality TV participants pretend to do the public a favor by cluing them in to what audiences already know: that even a genre claiming to be unscripted and true plays tricks and manipulates sound and image to craft the saleable product. It is an open secret that reality TV participants are also culpable since they, too, are concerned about the bottom line: future fame and fortune in a celebrity-fuelled, famous-for-being-famous culture.

Blaming the editing also allows reality TV participants to explain their consent to misrepresentation. In reality TV logic, a signed consent form assumes that participants are fully informed, thus Manigault-Stallworth and McDonald implicitly agree to negative representations of black women. Jennifer Pozner, executive director of Women in Media & News, writes, "Apologists claim reality TV isn't sexist because no one forces women to appear on these shows."[43] Male rap music video directors and artists use the same rationale to dismiss accusations that they exploit women, making them just another part of the scenery like cars and money. Though audiences are often treated to the hard luck stories of reality TV participants (particularly for the 18–24 demographic there is often an assumed narrative of absent fathers and single mothers incapable of providing for their children), it is more difficult to refute the claim of agency denied for reality TV contestants than it is for women in rap

videos. Whereas there are clear financial benefits in rap video performance, lap dan-
cing, and other related industries that outstrip working in the US service economy,
the incentives for black women and men to play to type are more dubious in reality
television.[44]

Brenton and Cohen contest the idea of consent in reality TV environments
that are often structured, with the help of staff psychologists, around a disorienting
audition process, manipulation of feelings of guilt, appeals to competitive spirit, and a
sense of responsibility to see a given task through to its end. Consent, then, is a deeper
issue than the mere act of a participant signing up for an experience might suggest.
Consent also raises ethical questions for psychologists and legal and intellectual property issues for producers.[45] Manipulating consent, and reality TV participants' sense
of having consented, is integral to the genre's form structure and to the manipulation
of audiences' gender, race, class, and sexual orientation prejudices.

Though audiences have yet to see the Evil Black Woman, or her counterpart
the Angry Black Man, win a reality TV competition, blacks have progressed through
these competitions but at what cost? For contestants across race, Kim defines the
following criteria as integral to winning: a show of gratitude ("A successful or compelling player must be grateful for the text, e.g. by praising and thanking the show (or
God) for the once-in-a-lifetime opportunity to see his/her dream come true."); sympathetic back-story (". . .s/he must have a good pre-existing story, one that follows a
Horatio Alger and/or immigrant tale." *American Idol* winner Ruben Stoddard lived in
a car with his single mother.); and a good work ethic (". . . American viewers must see
these people exerting energy and emotion in order to be worthy of becoming the
winner or hero of a reality television text.").[46] The stock characters that cater to
audiences' prejudices benefit from what Dovey calls reality TV's "regime of truth":
"the foregrounding of individual subjective experience at the expense of more general
truth claims."[47]

Crucially, reality TV participants benefit from this regime of truth only to the
extent that they adhere to dominant ideas about race, class, gender, sexuality, and
physical ability. Thus, Stoddard's sympathetic back-story is authenticated because of
dominant assumptions about black single mothers as incapable of providing for their
children. However, when it comes to racism and sexism, subjective experience is
usually discounted as paranoia and outside the regime of truth. When confident black
women such as McDonald and Manigault-Stallworth, refusing to conform to these
criteria, as well as rejecting historical perceptions of black women as only existing to
make white lives better, do appear in reality TV competitions, not only do they lose,
they also end up maligned. Camille, a student at Howard University (an historically-
black college/university), characterizes her toughness and high self-regard as honor-
ing her parents' sacrifice as immigrants from the Caribbean and refuses to apologize
for her pride: "People have asked me 'why didn't you cry [when you were elimin-
ated]? You're so cold; so distant. You have no emotions.' But I'm like 'cry fi wah?'
If I was to cry my grandmother would be like 'yuh wan mi gi yuh sup'm fi cry
about?' I have the entire West Indies riding on my back. If I make it, they make it."[48]
Her use of dialect in an interview following her *America's Next Top Model* experience
reflects a connection to heritage and values that did not make it into the show. As
she notes, " . . . the show portrayed my confidence as cockiness."[49] Camille, like

other people of color raised similarly, is the product of parents who raised their children to hold their heads high in the midst of racism and to persevere in spite of efforts to hold them back. Reality TV cannot accommodate black women who do not fit the few sanctioned contemporary roles, e.g. the ubiquitous black woman judge, the abusive single mother, the police captain without capacity for significant action.

One must question black feminism's progress in dismantling images of "the black bitch," "the loud black woman," "the sistah with attitude," and a host of other stereotypes if these cues are still considered easily recognizable. Additionally, there is also the notable failure of societal transformation in eradicating these images. A connected question asks whether we can hold black women behaving badly on reality TV accountable for perpetuating an image detrimental to black women. Do we just as readily recognize and remember the names of those black women who represented black women as kind, generous, and likable on reality TV?

Although we cannot assume that any of these women claim feminist politics, we can presume that they do enter into the genre aware of black women's construction in the popular imagination. Like the negative version of the barely talented diva, do reality TV women believe their own hype? Does the reality TV diva take ideas about black women's strength to a perverse extreme, playing to those constructions to succed at the audition stage? In a bid for celebrity or progress in their field, be it modeling, corporate enterprises, acting, sports, or any number of other professions that thrive on effective public relations, some black women in reality TV shows choose to manipulate retrograde prejudices about black womanhood. Some celebrities reject the idea that they are role models and I am not claiming that black participants in reality TV should assume that role. However, no matter how much we adamantly maintain that no one black person should have to be representative of the race, we need to be aware that television disseminates these representations nationally and internationally.

The question very rarely asked, though, is *why* might these black women be angry? The answer lies where postfeminism meets post-civil rights: both discourses erase history and claim equality as today's norm for women and for people of color. Much like 1970s feminism's failure to recognize that black women were already "liberated" in the sense that they have always worked outside the home (if this was the meaning of liberation) since slavery, postfeminism situates black women as always already angry, carrying a chip on their collective shoulders and ready to go off at the least personal slight.

This provides the context for reality TV's Evil Black Woman: reverting to the days before feminism declared the personal as political, postfeminism retrenches women's grievances, especially black women's grievances, as personal – not structural or institutional. How, after all, can racism and sexism be built into the structure of unscripted television? By denying the fabricated nature and ensemble cast character of reality TV, producers can recast their blatant use of racist, sexist, heterosexist and classist iconography as creating a cast that represents one version of a diverse America. In the post-civil rights vision of the world, inclusion means merely having a presence, but not empowerment in terms of self-definition.[50]

Bitter black women

It has been suggested that postfeminism "mask[s] the persistence of a sexual double standard, the persistence of racial stereotyping, and the persistence of efforts to redomesticate women by insisting that their place, first and foremost, remains in the home and subservient to men."[51] Do these conditions apply to all women, however? After all, black women historically have rarely been in *their own homes* as full-time homemakers. Now, more than ever, black women are in the workforce. Chambers notes, "Between 1976 and 2006, the number of black women in the workplace will have increased by 35 percent. This is in comparison with white women, up by 10 percent in the same 30 years. . . ."[52] Though black women are being displaced by other groups of women of color, particularly immigrant populations, they continue to earn advanced degrees at a rate faster than black men and, "in some fields, such as sales and administrative support roles . . . black women are beginning to earn slightly more [than white women]."[53] Given black women's presence and success in the workplace, what does it mean for postfeminism to re-domesticate them with the assistance of racial stereotyping and a sexual double standard?

Postfeminism's racialized narrative takes assumptions about white women's lives and turns them on their heads. Thus the few films that deal with middle-class African-American women call for them to remain in the workplace but in racially prescribed ways. As seen with Manigault-Stallworth, attempting to climb higher than one's racially prescribed station, exhibiting characteristics usually lauded in men, results in a violation of the modern mammy and black lady stereotypes. The post-civil rights narrative in these films relies on the assumption that integration means assimilation and, therefore, a loss of culture. Presumptions in these films are based on problematic notions of racial authenticity. The story usually begins with a black couple who have worked their way up from poverty or the working class. The wife supported her husband through medical/law/dental school or while he developed his business from a small enterprise to a large, successful corporation. The marker of the black man's success in this trope, in line with some 1970s black masculinist discourse, is a white or light-skinned black female secretary who inevitably becomes his lover. In the most callous way possible, the black man reveals to his black wife that he will shortly be moving his secretary/lover into their home and she should pack her things and go.

At this point, the story usually follows the postfeminist script of "retreatism." Analyzing a range of examples of films featuring white female protagonists, Negra concludes, "retreatism has become a recognizable narrative trope. Accordingly, both film and television have incorporated fantasies of hometown return in which a heroine gives up her life in the city to take up again the role of daughter, sister, wife or sweetheart in a hometown setting."[54] Films featuring black women protagonists also portray retreat, but filmmakers attempt to make their departure points and destinations seem racially authentic. The black female heroine goes in one of two directions: the black woman either returns to her family and black community who she has neglected or she turns to a tight network of sister-friends. In the case of *Waiting to Exhale* (1995), the husband of one of the four central protagonists leaves her for his white assistant, and she burns most of his expensive belongings in a fit of rage. She later calmly sells off the rest of his possessions in a yard sale. She turns to her friends for comfort and support, noting that she left her own dreams behind to support her now wealthy husband's ambitions. The 1998 film *Down in the Delta*, directed by Maya Angelou, finds a mother sending her two granddaughters and drug-addicted daughter away from Chicago to live with her brother in Mississippi. It is there that the prodigal daughter learns about ancestral struggles and her heritage – a connection with land and family that restores her self-esteem and facilitates her recovery from addiction. In a slight variation, in *Beauty Shop* (2005) Queen Latifah returns from the white world, specifically a high-end hair salon, to an urban neighborhood where she can own her own salon and hang a picture of the first black female millionaire, Madame C.J. Walker.

Postfeminism's retreatist narrative is seen in effect most clearly in *Diary of a Mad Black Woman* (2005), a compelling film in the postfeminist, post-civil rights era because of its production and narrative. The film is based on one of a series of Tyler Perry gospel stage plays. Other titles include *I Can Do Bad All By Myself* (2000), *Madea's Family Reunion* (2002), *Madea's Class Reunion* (2003), *Meet the Browns* (2004), and *Madea Goes to Jail* (2004). These typically play on the "chitlin" or "urban theatre circuit," a colloquialism for the mainly African-American venues, such as nightclubs and theatres, that host the productions. And the lucrative potential of these plays should not be underestimated: according to Perry, he grossed over $50 million writing and producing plays for urban theatre.[55] *Diary of a Mad Black Woman*'s box office success surprised the industry and critics – the film grossed over $22.7 million and was the number one film its opening weekend.

The mad black woman in question is Helen (Kimberly Elise), a woman who has always lived in the same city where she was raised – Atlanta – but she has moved to an affluent suburb with her husband Charles (Steve Harris). Helen has emotionally and racially left home, though. In the presence of his light-skinned mistress – she will be moving into his home with her infant son whom he has clearly fathered – Charles literally throws his wife out of the house. The mover who rescues Helen will eventually become the love of her life, though she is angry and cast as "one of those bitter black women." Ashamed and disheveled, Helen returns home, to her grandmother Madea.[56] Helen exacts her revenge on her ex-husband by sadistically neglecting and humiliating him after he is paralyzed in an accident and his mistress, who has turned into another stereotype, the Evil Mulatto, has abandoned him. It is only through the religious guidance of the Church, her new lover's spiritual nurturance, and her pistol-packing Granny's wisecracks that Helen once again learns to stand on her own two feet and knows that she can only rely on four men for sure: the Father, the Son, the Holy Ghost, and A Good Black Man.

In *Waiting to Exhale*, *Down in the Delta*, and *Diary of a Mad Black Woman* each heroine has sacrificed her standing as a Strongblackwoman, but the end of the film finds them redeemed. *Down in the Delta* uses drug abuse and urban living to mark a loss of self for its working poor heroine that can only be regained by getting back in touch with her roots. For middle-class women, like those in *Waiting to Exhale* and *Diary of a Mad Black Woman*, the retreat to family or sister-friends is actually a coming back to blackness – the implication being that when a black female protagonist has it all, she becomes a snob and is in danger of no longer being authentically black. Eventually, the middle-class heroine returns to a true sense of herself through an appropriately black small business enterprise (e.g. beauty shop, soul food restaurant), her family and friends' nurturance, a Good Black Man, and *always* a new haircut. Thus, the markers of change for these women are both stylistic changes of appearance and clearly marked as having to do with identity.

How do these films function in the postfeminist era in which they were produced? On the one hand, they can be characterized as black women's films, an updating of the 1930s and 1940s women's film genre: black women suffer but are ultimately triumphant having returned to a place from which they drifted; black family and community are regained. This would seem to be a positive message for black women. Yet, within the context of postfeminist, post-civil rights discourse, what are we do make of black women's position in US society as suggested by the deployment of the diva, the race-inflected fiction of reality TV, and the black "chick flick"?

I propose that, for African-American women, the postfeminist message is that black women need to know their place within the racial and gender hierarchy even if they are permitted, in small numbers to assume places in the middle class. For the films discussed in this chapter, when black women leave work and return to the home, they lose themselves and their connection to being black. Are black mainstream film-makers and authors in a growing area of black chick lit/flicks advocating a feminist position that black middle-class women should remain in the work world because without work they lose their freedom? Or are they saying that black women are incapable of choosing to stay in the (opulent) home because it is considered lazy, indulgent and makes them soft – something black women are not allowed to be if they are to continue to uphold the race? The implication is that educational and career achievement is black women's 21st-century racial uplift work.

Contemporary film and television representations of African-American women offer two racially gendered variations of postfeminist discourse. In relation to white women, still to be defined as the Other, black women continue to be denied access to the pedestal (in this case the option of not working) designated by 19th-century ideals as the sole province of white women. Instead, black women are expected to remain in the workplace performing emotional, if not physical, labor for whites. Black women on reality TV, if they step away from the roles of the modern mammy or the black lady, clearly exceed their place as subservient to whites. Unless it is being mimicked or appropriated by white, mainstream popular culture ("You, go, girl!"), any demonstra-tion of pride or refusal to act like a black lady is characterized as being difficult or having an attitude.

In relationship to black men and black communities, post-civil rights and post-feminist discourses require black women not to have it all, but to continue to do it all. Black women's agreement with feminist principles and continuing resistance to increased numbers of black women being incarcerated, sexual exploitation and a host of other oppressive factors is erased because, in the post-civil rights worldview, they are racial success stories.[57] Middle-class black women are marginally afforded status as women, or ladies more specifically, if they conform to a politics of respectability. If they do not conform, they are relegated to the Evil Black Woman category along with poor and working-class black women.

Postfeminism, post-civil rights, postmodernism – linguistically all these "posts" might seem excessive and merely indulgent jargon. After all, how might constant critique of backlash politics and culture limit visions for social transformation? To always be in the defensive position and reacting, can sometimes leave little room or energy for thinking and acting proactively. As feminist, critical race, and queer critics the prospect that we will find ourselves only able to articulate everything that is wrong with popular culture and unable to give credit to those positive aspects that create a pathway to transformative visions is worrisome.[58] As feminists making incursions into the terrain of postfeminism, recognizing those culture-makers forging ahead because of and in spite of oppression is as important, if not more important, than highlighting those forces counter to ending oppression. Yet when forces determined to maintain the status quo use post formulations to attempt to make us believe we are beyond particular forms of oppression or liberation struggles, the work of critique continues.

To bring current Audre Lorde's metaphor, the master's house has not, in fact, been dismantled, but instead has added additional rooms and annexes in which to harbor oppressive variations of racist, sexist, classist, and heterosexist themes. This move makes interrogating postfeminism and post-civil rights culture very necessary. Critiques of these concepts make visible the political, social and economic changes that shape discriminatory practices and our responses to them. As modes of exploitation change to continue to accommodate oppression, our critiques also need to adapt in language and practice, making "post" political configurations critical sites of analyses.

Notes

1 Herman Gray offers a compelling critique of continued media activism around representation and offers new directions for race and media studies, noting that we no longer live in a world in which media is controlled by local, state, or even national forces. Media activists concerned about racial representation, in his opinion, will need to look for the global implications of media production and distribution and how these impact representation; Herman Gray, *Cultural Moves: African Americans and the Politics of Representation*.

2 Susan J. Douglas, "Manufacturing Postfeminism: Race, Youth Cultures, and the Boundaries Between Feminism and Post-feminism in American Mass Media," panel abstract, International Communications Association Annual Meeting 2003, <http://www.convention.allacademic.com/ica2003/session_info.html>.

3 Amber E. Kinser, "Negotiating Spaces For/Through Third-Wave Feminism," 134–135.

4 Pamela Aronson, "Feminists or 'Postfeminists'?: Young Women's Attitudes toward Feminism and Gender Relations"; Projansky, *Watching Rape*.

5 Elaine J. Hall and Marnie Salupo Rodriguez, "The Myth of Postfeminism," 879.

6 Ibid., 886–899.

7 Kinser, "Negotiating Spaces," 135.

8 Kinser, "Negotiating Spaces," 144.

9 bell hooks, "Eating the Other," in *Black Looks: Race and Representation*.

10 Imelda Whelehan, *Overloaded: Popular Culture and the Future of Feminism*, 4.

11 Diane Negra, "Quality Postfeminism?"
12 Joan Morgan runs the words "strong," "black," and "woman" together to signify the intertwining and seeming inextricability of these words in the lives of black women and expectations of them; Joan Morgan, *When Chickenheads Come Home to Roost: My Life as a HipHop Feminist.*
13 Patricia Hill Collins, *Black Sexual Politics: African Americans, Gender, and the New Racism,* 78–79.
14 Daniel Patrick Moynihan, *The Negro Family: The Case for National Action.*
15 The idea of backlash, of course, assumes there was momentary progress in the representations of black women before the backlash.
16 Josh Tyrangiel, "The New Diva-Disease."
17 Interview, "Gladys Knight Talks About 'At Last' Her First Album in Six Years and Why She's Not a Diva," *Jet,* 5 March 2001.
18 Yvonne Tasker and Diane Negra, "In Focus: Postfeminism and Contemporary Media Studies," 108.
19 Herman Gray, *Watching Race: Television and the Struggle for "Blackness"*; Beretta E. Smith-Shomade, *Shaded Lives: African-American Women and Television.*
20 Collins, 138–140.
21 Evelyn Brooks Higginbotham, *Righteous Discontent: The Women's Movement in the Black Baptist Church, 1880–1920* (Cambridge, MA: Harvard University Press, 1993).
22 Ibid., 139.
23 Ibid., 140.
24 Dale Russakoff, "Lessons of Might and Right: How Segregation and an Indomitable Family Shaped National Security Adviser Condoleezza Rice," 9 September 2001, W23.
25 Collins, *Black Sexual Politics,* 142.
26 Oprah Winfrey, Collins posits, is a successful reflection of the black lady and modern mammy through her nurturance of predominately white female talk show guests and her avocations of personal, individualized transformation. Anita Hill, on the other hand, violates the tenets of black ladyhood and the modern mammy. Though she exhibited all the traits of respectability, once she accused Supreme Court judge nominee Clarence Thomas of sexual harassment, she challenged the social order and was punished for it.
27 J. Danielle Daniels, "Africana's Reality TV Recap," *AOL Black Voices,* 23 January 2003, <http://archive.blackvoices.com/reviews/moviesTV/mTV20040123recap.asp>.
28 Teresa Wiltz, "The Evil Sista of Reality Television."
29 Sam Brenton and Reuben Cohen, *Shooting People: Adventures in Reality TV,* 8.
30 Mark Andrejevic, *Reality TV: The Work of Being Watched,* 8.
31 Brenton and Cohen cogently delineate the devolution from documentary film with social purpose to unsupervised psychology experiments (especially Philip Zimbardo's 1971 Stanford Prison experiment in which ordinary citizens took their roles as guards and prisoners to a psychologically damaging degree) to contemporary psychology professionals' dubious ethical relationship to reality TV productions as series contestants.

32 Wiltz, op. cit.

33 L.S. Kim, "Race and Reality . . . TV."

34 Wiltz, op. cit.

35 "The 2003–2004 Tubey Awards, Part Two," <http://www.televisionwith-outpity.com>.

36 Wiltz, op. cit.

37 Daniels "Africana's Reality TV Recap."

38 "Reality Check," *Dr. Phil*, May 2005, <http://www.drphil.com/slideshow/slide.jhtml?contentId=3148_reality3.xml&start=2>.

39 Brenton and Cohen, *Shooting People*, 53.

40 Melanie Sims, "Angry black woman," Opinion, *Indiana Daily Student News*, 29 January 2004, <http://www.idsnews.com>.

41 Ibid.

42 Adika Butler, "Camille McDonald dispels rumors and sets the record straight," *Where Itz At: The Pulse of the Caribbean People*, <http://www.whereitzatlive.com/the_naked_truth.htm>.

43 Jennifer Pozner, "The Unreal World: why women on reality TV have to be hot, dumb and desperate," *Ms. Magazine*, Fall 2004, <http://www.msmagazine.com/fall2004/unrealworld.asp>.

44 Richard Thomas, "The Power of Women." Applicable to most reality TV shows is *The Apprentice's* tagline: "This isn't a game – it's a week's long job interview." Landing a job with Donald Trump on *The Apprentice*, a recording contract, speaking engagements on college campuses, or hosting *MTV's Spring Break* are all possibilities, but the fickle world of television does not promise a long and lucrative career.

45 Brenton and Cohen, *Shooting People*, 135–144.

46 Kim, "Race and Reality . . . TV.

47 Jon Dovey, *Freakshow: First Person Media and Factual Television*, 25.

48 Butler, op cit.

49 Ibid.

50 Tellingly, of the monographs on reality TV consulted for this chapter, only one indexed "racism" and none of them indexed "race," "whiteness," or any racial grouping. This indicates a failure of the literature, to date, to adequately grapple with race and its role in the genre.

51 Douglas, "Manufacturing Post-feminism."

52 Chambers, 3.

53 Ibid.

54 Negra, "Quality Postfeminism?"

55 Zondra Hughes, "How Tyler Perry Rose from Homelessness to a $5 Million Mansion."

56 Madea, an abbreviation for the endearment "Mother Dear," is Tyler Perry in drag portraying a feisty, gun-waving grandmother.

57 Hall and Rodriguez, "The Myth of Post-feminism."

58 One might, for example, examine more closely and through an academic lens the performance art of Sarah Jones or the production and performance of hiphop impresario Missy Elliott.

References

Andrejevic, Mark, *Reality TV: The Work of Being Watched* (Lanham, MD: Rowman and Littlefield, 2003).

Aronson, Pamela, 'Feminists or Post-feminists? Young Women's Attitudes toward Feminism and Gender Relations', *Gender & Society*, Vol. 17, No. 6 (2003): 903–922.

Brenton, Sam and Cohen, Reuben, *Shooting People: Adventures in Reality TV* (London: Verso, 2003).

Butler, Adika, 'Camille McDonald dispels rumors and sets the record straight', *Where Itz At: The Pulse of the Caribbean People*, http://www.whereitzat.com/the naked truth.htm.

Collins, Patricia Hills, *Black Sexual Politics: African Americans, Gender and the New Racism* (New York: Routledge, 2004).

Douglas, Susan J, 'Manufacturing Post-feminism: Race, Youth Cultures and the Boundaries Between Feminism and Post-feminism in American Mass Media', panel abstract, International Communications Associations Annual Meeting, 2003.

Dovey, Jon, *Freakshow: First Person Media and Factual Television* (London: Pluto, 2000).

Gray, Herman, *Watching Race* (Minneapolis: University of Minnesota Press, 1995).

Gray, Herman, *Cultural Moves: African Americans and the Politics of Representation* (Berkeley, Los Angeles and London: University of California Press, 2005).

Hall, Elaine J. and Rodriguez, Marnie Salupo, 'The Myth of Post-feminism', *Gender & Society*, Vol. 17, No. 6 (2003): 878–902.

Higginbotham, Evelyn Brooks, *Righteous Discontent: The Women's Movement in the Black Baptist Church, 1880–1920* (Cambridge, MA: Harvard University Press, 1993).

hooks, bell, *Black Looks: Race and Representation* (Boston, South End Press, 1992).

Hughes, Zondra, 'How Tyler Perry Rose from Homelessness to a $5 Million mansion', *Ebony*, January 2004.

Kim, L. S. 'Race and Reality . . . TV', *Flow Online Journal*.
http://idg.communication.utexas.edu/flow/index.php?jot=view&id=482

Kinser, Amber E, 'Negotiating Spaces For/Through Third-Wave Feminism', *National Women's Studies Association Journal* Vol. 16, No. 3 (2004): 124–153.

Morgan, Joan, *When Chickenheads Come Home to Roost: My Life as a HipHop Feminist* (New York: Touchstone, 1999).

Moynihan, Daniel Patrick, *The Negro Family: The Case for National Action* (Washington, DC: Office of Policy Planning and Research, U. S. Department of Labor, 1965).

Negra, Diane, 'Quality Postfeminism?: Sex and the Single Girl on HBO', *Genders OnLine Journal* 39 (2004), http://www.genders.org.

Pozner, Jennifer L, 'The Unreal World: Why Women on Reality TV Have to Be Hot, Dumb and Desperate', *Ms. Magazine* (Fall 2004).
http://www.msmagazine.com/fall2004/unrealword.asp.

Projansky, Sarah, *Watching Rape: Film and Television in Post-feminist Culture* (New York: New York University Press, 2001).

Russakoff, Dale, 'Lessons of Might and Right: How Segregation and an Indomitable Family Shaped National Security Adviser Condoleezza Rice', *Washington Post*, September 9, 2001. p.W23.

Smith-Shomade, Beretta, *Shaded Lives* (New Brunswick, NJ: Rutgers University Press, 2002).

Tasker, Yvonne and Negra, Diane, 'In Focus: Post-feminism and Contemporary Media Studies', *Cinema Journal* Vol. 44, No. 2 (2005): 107–110.

Tyrangiel, Josh, 'The New Diva-Disease', *Time*, October 21, 2002.

Whelehan, Imelda, *Overloaded: Popular Culture and the Future of Feminism* (London: The Women's Press Ltd, 2000)

Wiltz, Teresa, 'The Evil Sista of Reality Television', *Washington Post*, February 25, 2004, p.C01.

5

Ellen, Television, and the Politics of Gay and Lesbian Visibility

Bonnie J. Dow

Originally published in *Critical Studies in Media Communication*,
18:2 (June 2001): 123–140.

In their December 1997 year-end issue, the editors of *Entertainment Weekly* named Ellen DeGeneres "Entertainer of the Year," noting that

> at a time when an acknowledgment of homosexuality has entered all aspects of popular culture, when diversity and acceptance are the words of the day but by no means entirely the deeds, and when more and more of the sizeable population of homosexual men and women working in the entertainment industry today are weighing the risks of coming out themselves, DeGeneres allowed herself to become a poster girl – not for lesbianism, but for honesty. . . . DeGeneres risked her professional reputation for personal freedom. And she pulled it off. She did good, important work that continues to shape the public discourse.
>
> (Schwarzbaum, 1997, p. 18)

It is perhaps arguable how widely shared the opinion is that Ellen DeGeneres's poster child status is about honesty rather than lesbianism, but the assertion that DeGeneres's coming-out narrative, in both its "real" and fictionalized forms, has had a profound effect on public discourse, can hardly be questioned (although, as I argue here, the *dimensions* of that effect *are* open to question). DeGeneres's public announcement of her homosexuality made the cover of *Time* magazine (Handy, 1997b), got her an invitation to the White House ("Girls Night Out," 1997), and provoked laudatory comments from Vice-President Al Gore about Hollywood's new openness toward sexual orientation (Price, 1997).

DeGeneres's ascendance as 1997's lesbian media icon was, of course, triggered by the ABC sitcom *Ellen*, which broadcast three episodes, beginning on April 30, 1997, concerning the "coming-out" experiences of its lead character, Ellen Morgan. Prior to the first coming-out episode, DeGeneres, the star of and creative force behind the sitcom, was featured in a media blitz of interviews in three high-profile media forums: *Time* magazine, *20/20*, and *Oprah*, in which she discussed her own struggles with her sexuality, her romantic relationships with women, and the process of creating the *Ellen* episodes. The generally positive response to the coming-out episodes and DeGeneres's sudden media popularity seemed to indicate that previously censored forms of sexuality were gliding rather easily out of the closet and into prime-time.

By the spring of 1998, however, this triumphal narrative had taken another turn. After a season of lackluster ratings, ABC canceled the sitcom. There were accusations from DeGeneres that the network had not been supportive of the show, claims from ABC executives that the program had turned into her personal soapbox, and arguments from television critics and commentators that it had simply ceased to be funny (Cagle, 1998; Gilbert, 1998; Tucker, 1998). Even amid the rancor, there was agreement from both sides that *Ellen* had changed the face of television, and a syndication deal with the *Lifetime* network meant that *Ellen* would live on in re-runs. Indeed, several critics have argued that the success of the NBC sitcom *Will and Grace*, which debuted in the fall of 1998 and focuses on two roommates, a heterosexual woman and a gay man, was made possible by the path that *Ellen* blazed (Hall, 1998; Milvy, 1998; Mink, 1998).[1] Moreover, in February of 1999, the coming-out of a male character on the WB teen soap *Dawson's Creek*, and the revelation that the show's creator, Kevin Williamson, was gay, caused "barely a ripple" in public discourse (Bauder, 1999, p. 7c; see also Connelly, 1999).

Whether or not *Ellen* did, in fact, make it "okay to be gay," is not the primary concern here, although this analysis may make some gestures toward answering that question. Rather, I am concerned with the narrative logic of the coming-out discourses in and around the three *Ellen* episodes in the spring of 1997. As a case study, the *Ellen* coming-out sheds light on the various mechanisms through which the ostensible liberation of the truth of sexuality – from silence, repression, denial – was not a simple case of setting free the truth, but was, rather, the beginning of a discursive construction of that sexuality – of its authenticity, of its form, and of its politics. This construction, from its beginning, was "thoroughly imbued with relations of power" (Foucault, 1978, p. 60) that channeled its rhetorical effect in particular directions and that present implications for our understanding of what gay visibility can and cannot be allowed to mean in commercial media.

Confession, liberation, authenticity

In his explanation of the repressive hypothesis, Foucault argues that, contrary to the belief that the late twentieth century gave rise to ever expanding levels of openness about sexuality, discourse about sex has been proliferating at an excessive rate since the late nineteenth century (1978, pp. 63–65). Confession, originally in the form of penance, but later in a wide variety of forms and within a wide variety of relationships, "was, and still remains, the general standard for governing the production of the true discourse on sex" (Foucault, 1978, p. 63). Importantly, the attraction of confession has, in large part, been linked to a belief in its liberating effect, what Foucault calls "the internal ruse of confession": the assumption that "confessions frees, but power reduces one to silence; truth does not belong to an order of power, but shares an original affinity with freedom" (p. 60).

The implicit notion that "the truth is corroborated by the obstacles and resistance it has had to surmount in order to be formulated," and that "the expression alone, independently of its external consequences, produces intrinsic modifications in the persona who articulates it" is precisely the logic that governs the coming-out discourse in and around *Ellen*. That confession, for the confessor, "exonerates, redeems, and purifies . . . unburdens him [or her] of his [or her] wrongs, liberates him [or her], and promises him [or her] salvation," is a key theme in the language of both Ellen DeGeneres and Ellen Morgan (Foucault, 1978, p. 62).

The April 14, 1997, issue of *Time* magazine featured DeGeneres on its cover in a simple portrait over the words "Yep, She's Gay." The *Time* story was DeGeneres's first act of coming out in the mainstream media, and it is the first instance in the pattern that would emerge. The article describes her coming-out as "the culmination of a long process of struggling with feelings about her own sexuality, her fears about being rejected for it, her wish to lead a more honest and open life in public, her weariness at the effort it took her not to" (Handy, 1997b, p. 78+). DeGeneres is quoted within the article saying, "this has been the most freeing experience because people can't hurt me anymore" (Handy, 1997b, p. 78+). The interview with DeGeneres on ABC's *20/20*, her next major media appearance, began with Diane Sawyer's noting of the "risk" entailed in "deciding to go public with a lifelong secret." DeGeneres herself makes reference to not living her life as a lie anymore, refusing to be ashamed any longer, and the "joy" that coming out gave her.

However, the *Oprah* interview that aired shortly before the coming-out episode was broadcast is perhaps the richest example of the liberation narrative that threaded through DeGeneres's media discourse. Importantly, Oprah Winfrey's facilitation of DeGeneres's revelations on daytime television had additional intertextual power as it was noted during the interview that Winfrey herself had a cameo in the first coming-out episode. She played Ellen Morgan's therapist, who aids Ellen in reaching the realization that she is gay, much as Winfrey herself aids DeGeneres in discussing her sexuality on *Oprah*. Very early in the interview, Winfrey asks DeGeneres, "Now that you have come out, what has been the biggest relief for you?" and DeGeneres replies in the same terms she has elsewhere, describing her confession as a kind of freedom: "To feel completely honest – that's something I've never felt in my life, and I don't know how many people do feel like that. And this is not a gay issue, this is just an issue about truth and about not having anything to hide. No one can hurt me." Within the first *Ellen* episode, as Ellen Morgan is talking with Oprah in character as her therapist, she says something remarkably similar: "I feel like this tremendous weight has been lifted off of me. I mean, for the first time in my life I feel comfortable with myself."

DeGeneres's public confession of her sexuality was saturated with implications of authenticity at different levels. First and most clearly, her revelations were couched in terms of her personal discovery or recovery of authenticity; she was revealing her "true" self to the public. As Joan Scott notes, "What could be truer, after all, than a subject's own account of what he or she has lived through?" (1993, p. 399). Second, these initial revelations occurred in a prominent print news magazine, a prominent television news magazine, both high status non-fiction fora, as well as in a highly rated daytime television talk show well known for its use of intimate confession as a path to personal authenticity (Fiske, 1987, pp. 281–282; Davis, 1999). Despite their status differences, all three of these media contexts share a common methodological and epistemological premise that Scott identifies in historical writing: the "authority of experience" arises from and contributes to its function as a "reflection of the real" (1993, p. 399). Thus, DeGeneres's testimony, coupled with the contexts in which it appears, constructs an authenticity narrative that privileges what Scott calls "the evidence of experience." This epistemological framework,

> whether conceived through a metaphor of visibility or any other way that takes meaning as transparent, reproduces rather than contests given ideological systems – those that assume that the facts of history speak for themselves and those that rest on a naturally established opposition between, say, sexual practice and social conventions, or between homosexuality and heterosexuality.
>
> (1993, p. 400)

Crucially, the authenticity narrative established by DeGeneres's coming-out in non-fiction media appearances carries over to the coming-out episodes of *Ellen*. Not only does the program gain credibility for its representation from the intertextual links with DeGeneres's personal testimony and its interpretation in other venues, but, in many ways, the struggle for the truth and the eventual triumph of authenticity and honesty that DeGeneres described or alluded to in interviews was enacted within the *Ellen* episodes. For example, in the climactic moment in the first coming-out episode, when Ellen first confesses her sexuality to a woman to whom she is attracted, the struggle is clear in the speech pattern itself:

> I can't even say the word. Why can't I say the word? I mean, why can't I just say . . . I mean, what is wrong . . . Why do I have to be so ashamed? I mean why can't I just say the truth, I mean be who I am. I'm thirty-five years old. I'm so afraid to tell people, I mean I just . . . Susan, I'm gay.

Almost immediately, the liberating effects take hold, as Ellen says, "That felt great, that felt so great." In the second episode, as Ellen's mother laments that she misses "the old Ellen," Ellen replies in terms that stress the authenticity that the "new" Ellen has gained: "Which Ellen is that? The Ellen that used to keep her feelings bottled up? The Ellen that used to lie to herself and everybody else? The Ellen that could have spent the rest of her life alone?"

The temporal and thematic convergence of the confessions of Ellen DeGeneres and Ellen Morgan is key to understanding the significance of the repressive hypothesis in the *Ellen* discourse. In both cases, the confession is represented as changing Ellen by allowing her authentic self to emerge, because such a deep truth " 'demands' only to surface . . . and it can finally be articulated only at the price of a kind of liberation" (Foucault, 1978, p. 60). This is an implication articulated repeatedly in coming-out narratives, what Bonnie Zimmerman (1985) calls the " 'tribal' lore," and the "myth of origins" of the lesbian community (p. 262). Zimmerman's study of literary coming-out narratives analyzes the liberatory function of such discourse, in which "speaking, especially naming oneself, 'lesbian,' is an act of empowerment. Power, which traditionally is the essence of politics, is connected with the ability to name, to speak, to come out of silence. . . . Powerlessness, on the other hand, is associated with silence and the 'speechlessness' that the powerful impose on those dispossessed of language" (p. 259). The notion of power at work in this description is one that assumes "a world of discourse divided between accepted discourse and excluded discourse, or between the dominant discourse and the dominated one" (Foucault, 1978, p. 100); it is, in short, the world assumed by the repressive hypothesis, one in which the evidence of experience is transparent and its liberating effect is assured.

For the literary coming-out narratives Zimmerman speaks of, the audience is clear: they are addressed to "a reading community assumed to be (or to have the potential to be) lesbian" (Martin, 1993, p. 278). The politics of such narratives, then, are connected to "self-worth, identity, and a sense of community," and coming out "aims to give lesbian identity a coherence and a legitimacy that can make both individual and social action possible" (Martin, 1993, p. 278). Following Foucault, Biddy Martin (1993) questions the wisdom of rooting political liberation in the "autonomy of the psychological" arguing that the repressive hypothesis works to "mask the actual workings of power" (p. 276). Indeed, this caution is even more necessary when considering the function of the DeGeneres/Morgan coming-out in mass media, a context in which a supportive or identifying audience can hardly be assumed. Lost in the narrative of authenticity and liberation that permeates coming-out stories is, of course, Foucault's claim that to enter the confession ritual may be seemingly to escape from one power relation only to enter another. As La-Fountain (1989) explains, "the whole truth does not rely in the confessor but rather is 'incomplete, blind to itself' and only reaches completion in the one who assimilates and records it." This process "aligns the interpreter with knowledge and truth, and with power. It is to and for power that we are confessing animals" (p. 132).

Television, heteronormativity, and confessional politics

Acknowledged or not, then, the confession ritual demands an audience, for "one does not confess without the presence (or virtual presence) of a partner" (Foucault, 1978, p. 61). Indeed, given DeGeneres's public statements, the presence of the audience was foremost in her mind. Explaining her reservations about coming out in her *20/20* interview, she noted her fear that "if they found out I was gay, maybe they wouldn't applaud, maybe they wouldn't laugh, maybe they wouldn't like me if they knew that I was gay." "They" presumably refers to *Ellen*'s assumed heterosexual audience, as it seems logical to assume that the gay community, to whom DeGeneres was hardly closeted anyway, would hardly condemn her for coming out. Thus, the discourse of the *Ellen* coming-out episodes can most usefully be read as a demonstration that the most powerful implied audience for Ellen's revelations was, in fact, heterosexual. With that in mind, the episodes' discourse must be seen in relation to the logics of control and depoliticization that historically have governed gay representation on television and that governed *Ellen* as well. For *Ellen*, the implied confessional partner, the "authority who requires the confession, prescribes and appreciates it, and intervenes in order to judge, punish, forgive, console, and reconcile," was always heterosexual, both inside the show's narrative and outside, in its viewing audience. Thus, from the first moment, DeGeneres's/Morgan's ostensibly liberating move from silence into speech "unfold[ed] within a power relationship" (Foucault, 1978, p. 61) that, within the *Ellen* discourse, was simultaneously implicitly observed and explicitly denied.

Seen through both DeGeneres's discourse and media treatments of it, the coming-out campaign was clearly geared toward gaining the approval of mainstream, hetero-sexual Americans – the kind of people that ABC wants to watch its sitcoms, for instance. For example, DeGeneres came out to *Time* magazine, rather than, say, *Out*, the most widely read gay newsmagazine, or *Curve*, a popular lesbian publication. In the *Time* article, DeGeneres took pains to insist that she "didn't do it to make a political statement," but merely because "it was a great thing for the show," and that she saw the point of what she was doing as "acceptance of everybody's differences" (Handy, 1997a, p. 86).

Interpreted within this frame, the DeGeneres/Morgan revelations were touted by mainstream media as evidence of progress: in (always presumed to be heterosexual) Americans' tolerance for representation of homosexuality, in network television's willingness to break the sexuality barrier by broadcasting a sitcom with a gay lead character, in Hollywood's embrace of an openly gay actress. The notion that represen-tation of a lesbian on prime time signaled a kind of acceptance of homosexuality was explicitly stated in the *Time* article discussing the show itself. As Bruce Handy (1997b) put it, "Does Ellen Morgan's coming out in what is still our massest medium legitimize homosexuality, or does the sponsorship of a bottom-line business like ABC merely reflect its acceptance by a significant portion of the population? Clearly, the answer is both" (p. 78+). Generally, the reception of the coming-out episodes was framed as a referendum on prejudice against gays and lesbians; as a comment in *People* magazine put it, "Advertisers, networks, producers and fans have to haul out their prejudices and say, 'Does this make a difference in how I feel about this woman?' " (Gliatto, et al., 1997, p. 129+). Frank Rich (1997, p. A29), writing in *The New York Times*, phrased a similar question before the coming-out episode aired: "If [the show] fails, will the character's homosexuality, rather than the series' spotty quality, be held accountable?"

Through the end of the 1997 season, at least, the approval of these various con-stituencies named by commentators seemed clear. The coming-out episode more than doubled *Ellen*'s regular viewing audience, the show was renewed by ABC, and *Ellen* garnered an Emmy for best comedy writing. On the other hand, saying that the success of Ellen's initial coming-out means the end of prejudice against gays and lesbians is like saying that the success of *The Cosby Show* in the 1980s signaled the end of racism (Jackson, 1997). There is, however, a useful parallel to be drawn between *Ellen* and *Cosby*, which is that just as *Cosby* was often interpreted as a sitcom about black people that was largely geared toward the comfort of white people (see, e.g., Gray, 1994), *Ellen* was a sitcom about a lesbian that was largely geared toward the com-fort of heterosexuals.[2] In this sense, it differs little from the history of representations of gays and lesbians on television.

As Foucault has noted about sexuality in general, the history of sexuality in prime-time television is not one of absence and repression, but, rather, one that has followed clear norms for different kinds of silence and speech. Representations of homosexuality have existed since television's earliest days, although, of course, in limited number. A drag queen routine was one of the favorite and most popular items in the repertoire of Milton Berle, one of early television's most popular comedians, and there were powerful gay undertones in the comic relationships of Jack Benny on *The Jack Benny Show* (Doty, 1993). The counterpart in 1950s dramas was to cast homosexual characters, largely, male, as villains. In this context, homosexuality was used primarily to establish an additional level of deviance for such characters. The link of homosexuality with criminality was a dramatic convention that continued for decades, surfacing in series dramas such as *Police Woman, Marcus Welby, Hunter*, and *Midnight Caller* in the 1970s and 1980s (see Fejes & Petrich, 1993; Gross, 1994).

With the growth of the gay rights movement in the 1970s and resultant pressure for more positive representations, television networks began to view homosexuality as an appropriate topic for "socially relevant" programming; that is, programming designed to sensitively treat the "problem" of homosexuality. This motive resulted in television movies such as 1972's *That Certain Summer*, in which a gay man must tell his son about his homosexuality, 1978's *A Question of Love*, in which a lesbian mother fights for custody of her son, 1985's *An Early Frost*, the first TV movie about AIDS, which focuses on a young man who must reveal both his illness and his homosexuality to his family, and 1992's *Doing Time on Maple Drive*, in which a college student comes out to his very traditional (and dysfunctional) family.

These TV movies relied on the general rules for representing homosexuality on television that were also evident in the sympathetic portrayals of gays and lesbians that emerged in series television in the 1970s and 1980s in shows such as *The Mary Tyler Moore Show, Rhoda, Barney Miller, Cheers, Kate and Allie, The Golden Girls*, or *Designing Women*. These rules include the following: First, representations of gays and lesbians were incorporated as "one time" appearances rather than as integral elements or regular characters in a series narrative. (This is why the "one shot" TV movie was such a popular form for dealing with homosexuality.) Second, such characters are never "incidentally" gay; they appeared in episodes or movies in which their sexuality was "the problem" to be solved; third, the problem they represent is depicted largely in terms of its effect on heterosexuals. Homosexual characters are rarely shown in their own communities, homes, or same-sex romantic relationships but are depicted in terms of their place in the lives of heterosexuals. Finally, and perhaps most crucially for a commercial medium like television, representations of gay or lesbian sex, or even desire, are absent (Fejes & Petrich, 1993).

The 1990s witnessed the subversion of some of these rules as recurring gay or lesbian characters were incorporated into both comedy and drama, although, as has historically been true of all marginalized groups, the preponderance of these representations occurred in comedy (Marc, 1989; Taylor, 1989). There were a few exceptions beginning in the 1980s. *Dynasty*, one of the most popular prime-time soaps of the 1980s, contained a storyline about a bisexual male character who had a difficult time deciding between men and women, much to the consternation of his father, the family patriarch. Another 1980s drama, the short-lived medical show *Heartbeat*, has received some critical attention for its depiction of a recurring lesbian character who worked as a nurse in a women's health clinic run by feminist doctors (Hantzis & Lehr, 1994; Moritz, 1994; Torres, 1993). However, the drama only lasted one season, and the lesbian character's sexuality was featured in only two episodes.

Those few prime-time representations of gays or lesbians that have taken the risk of depicting actual gay and lesbian sexual interaction, however brief and avowedly "tasteful," have predictably run afoul of sponsors and conservative interest groups, all of which claim to be representing the interests of the American (presumably heterosexual) public. For example, a 1989 episode of the yuppie drama *thirtysomething* featured a brief scene of two gay men in bed together. The scene prompted advertisers to pull their sponsorship of the show, and, although the episode was still aired, it was removed from the summer rerun schedule (Fejes & Petrich, 1993, p. 413). A 1991 episode of *L.A. Law* featured a brief kiss between two regular characters – one of whom was bisexual and the other of whom was presumably hetero-sexual but was nonetheless intrigued. The Reverend Donald Wildmon's American Family Association brought its wrath to bear on NBC, threatening product boycotts (as it had done with *Heartbeat*), and NBC responded by disclaiming any attempt to create a continuing lesbian storyline (Gross, 1994, p. 151). Indeed, by the end of the season, the intrigued woman was recommitted to her heterosexuality, and the bisexual woman was happily involved with a man – with whom, of course, she was shown having sex. In the early 1990s, *Roseanne* added a regular bisexual female character. The most famous moment in this storyline, however, came when Roseanne herself, in a visit to a lesbian bar, briefly kissed another woman. The episode in which this occurred was preceded by a "viewer discretion" warning from ABC (Roush, 1994).

In 1997–98, the television season following Ellen's coming-out, recurring gay or lesbian characters were featured on *Spin City, Friends, ER, NYPD Blue,* and *Chicago Hope,* just to name a few popular shows. Indeed, when DeGeneres appeared on *Oprah,* a young heterosexual mother in the audience claimed that the abundance of such characters had become overwhelming and that media attention to gay and lesbian sexuality was crowding out traditional family values. As DeGeneres gently pointed out, we are a long way from such a situation. However, the immense attention given to Ellen Morgan's coming-out has been interpreted as indicating a genuine shift in the level of tolerance for gay and lesbian representation. However, this conclusion is not self-evident, as some have claimed, but is rather the product of *Ellen*'s interaction with "the complex and changing discursive processes by which identities are ascribed, resisted, or embraced, and which processes themselves are unremarked and indeed achieve their effect because they are not noticed" (Scott, 1993, p. 408). It is this interaction, of the liberatory coming-out narrative, of television's historical patterns of homosexual representation and of the personalizing of sexuality in the *Ellen* episodes discussed below, that produces the grounds for claiming *Ellen* as emancipatory.

Personalizing sexuality in *Ellen*

Certainly, DeGeneres and *Ellen* brought some visibility to an important issue: the representation of gays and lesbians in mainstream media. Certainly, a lead character that is lesbian is a step beyond what we have seen before. In crucial ways, however, *Ellen* departed little from representational norms. The underlying similarity of the rules of gay and lesbian representation discussed above is that they all contribute to the conclusion that homosexuality is relevant almost exclusively for its impact on personal relationships, and moreover, that the most important personal relationships a gay or lesbian character has are those s/he has with heterosexuals. Stock storylines have included the coming-out narrative (and its effect on spouses, parents, children), the narrative about acceptance of a gay partner, or, increasingly, the ways that family and friends cope with AIDS.

In many cases, such storylines include allusions to larger political or legal issues that affect gays and lesbians, but such issues are alluded to primarily for their utility in prompting interpersonal confrontation, reconciliation, or solidarity. Typically, this kind of plot device results in the moment when the homophobic friend or family member realizes that to hate gays is to hate someone that he or she loves and is instantly transformed as a result. It is the moment when political oppression becomes a personal problem, and the solution to that problem is largely in the hands of heterosexuals. Thus, even when confronting the supposed subversion of hetero-sexuality, heterosexism governs *Ellen*'s representation as well as the production of the "truth" of her sexuality: what it will and will not mean, how it does and does not matter.

There is a moment in the second coming-out episode of *Ellen* that exemplifies this process quite well. In this episode, Ellen comes out to her parents, who are, predictably, shocked and dismayed. Ellen's father has a particularly hard time with her lesbian identity. Although her mother, Lois, is convinced to attend a meeting of PFLAG (Parents and Friends of Lesbians and Gays), she informs Ellen that Ellen's father refused to come. During the meeting, another parent attacks Ellen, saying "Why should your mother accept this [your lesbianism]? It's wrong. It's sick. And you're sick." Ellen's mother jumps to her defense, saying "Don't you talk to my daughter that way. . . . Sure, I'm not happy about this. But I love her and I don't want to lose her." At that moment, Ellen's father arrives unexpectedly and joins in, "You tell 'em, Lois. She's here, she's queer, get used to it!"

The man who attacks Ellen represents the kind of bigotry that she is likely to face as a lesbian. However, the point of this moment is not to draw attention to that fact of lesbian existence; rather, it is to showcase the triumph of Ellen's parents' love for her over their disappointment. Even though Ellen's father recites a slogan popular with queer political activists, it is also clear that he has little idea what it means, as he notes in an aside to Ellen that he read it on a bumper sticker. Moments earlier in this scene, Ellen's mother Lois specifically raised the issue of discrimination, albeit obliquely, by saying that she was concerned for Ellen because "Life is going to be so hard for you now." The immediate reply from the PFLAG counselor was "It's harder to live a lie than it is to live your life openly and honestly," neatly sidestepping the very real issue of discrimination and turning the issue into one of personal integrity.

The treatment of Ellen's homosexuality in the coming-out episodes operates repeatedly to emphasize personal issues over political ones; that is, it presents accept-ance by family and friends as the most crucial issues Ellen faces. The first episode in the series of three treated Ellen's recognition of her attraction to women, her difficul-ties coming out to her friends, and her first encounter with lesbian culture (a trip to a lesbian coffeehouse). The second focused on her coming out to her parents, and the third centered on the conflicts engendered by her sexuality with her best (hetero-sexual) woman friend and with her boss at the bookstore where she is a manager. The majority of the problems treated in these episodes are standard sitcom fare solved in standard sitcom style – fear and ignorance are conquered through love, support, and mutual understanding.

In all of these episodes, the sitcom follows the basic rules of gay and lesbian representation: no sexual interaction, treating Ellen's revelation as a "problem" to be dealt with by her heterosexual friends and family, and minuscule representation of any sort of lesbian community – indeed, it is quite amusing that in the first episode of the 1997 fall season, Ellen's best heterosexual friend bemoans the fact that Ellen is not "clicking" with any of the women she fixes her up with, and she says, "I'm running out of lesbians." Apparently the heterosexuals in her life know more lesbians than Ellen does. In terms of its subversion of television's patterns of representation of homosexuality, the biggest contribution that *Ellen* makes is taking us beyond the "one shot" or "one episode" approach.

When larger issues related to the political status of gays and lesbians are raised in *Ellen*, they are turned into jokes or transformed into personal identity or relationship issues. At a few points in these episodes, the possibility of larger ramifications appears. For example, in the first episode, during a conversation with her therapist, Ellen mentions discrimination against gays and lesbians, but her only specific example is "Do you think I want people calling me names to my face?" Amused by Ellen's attempt to explain discrimination to a black woman, her therapist (played by Oprah Winfrey) sarcastically replies, "To have people commit hate crimes against you just because you're not like them? . . . To have to use separate bathrooms and separate water fountains? Sit in the back of the bus?" Ellen, finally seeing the irony, humorously replies, "Oh, man, we have to use separate water fountains?"

The point of this interaction seems to be to belittle Ellen's fears, or, perhaps, to draw a parallel between prejudice against African Americans and prejudice against gays and lesbians. However, the point that is *not* made in this scene is that the kinds of discrimination that were once legal against African Americans are still legal, in most states, against gays and lesbians. There is no federal civil rights law protecting the rights of gays and lesbians. Unlike African Americans, they have not yet been designated a protected class. In 39 states, it is legal to discriminate against gays and lesbians in employment.

However, *Ellen* assiduously avoids such recognition; indeed, at the end of her interaction with her therapist, Ellen Morgan turns the issue of discrimination back into one of self-acceptance when she says, "You have to admit it's not exactly an accepted thing. I mean, you never see a cake that says 'Good for you – you're gay.' " Continuing the personal turn, the therapist replies, "Okay, then, Ellen, I'll say it: 'Good for *you*, you're gay' " (my emphasis).

This neat turning of the potentially political into the personal becomes a pattern in the coming-out episodes. In the third such episode, Ellen faces the possibility of workplace discrimination, when her boss at the bookstore she manages reacts negatively to the knowledge that she is a lesbian. Importantly, however, his first reaction is not to fire her, which would take the issue into the realm of politics by introducing employment discrimination. Rather, her boss's reaction is manifested in personal terms, as he tells her that he no longer wants her to baby-sit his children, with whom she has a close relationship. When Ellen presses him for an explanation, his response is that he thinks homosexuality is wrong and that he is "just protecting my kids." When Ellen asks him if he sees her as "someone so evil that you've got to keep your children away from me?" he replies that he has to do what he thinks is right. At this point, Ellen quits her job saying that she cannot work with someone who feels this way about her.

Ellen is not fired, a move that would be legal in many states; rather, she makes the decision to quit, turning the issue (again) into one of her own personal integrity. Moreover, it is obvious that she is most disturbed by the break-down of her relationship with her boss and his family rather than by the effect of his homophobia on her workplace environment.

In the coming-out episodes, *Ellen* simply refuses to recognize the existence of organized, systemic, or politically oppressive homophobia, and the political status of gays and lesbians is never raised. When this issue finally surfaces, it is in a fall 1997 episode that appears designed to critique the oppressive nature of gay and lesbian political activism, rather than the political oppression to which such activism responds. In this episode, Ellen's gay friend Peter (a recurring character) invites several of his gay and lesbian friends to a party at Ellen's house, in an effort to introduce her to the gay and lesbian community. Again, politics are played for laughs, as Ellen reacts to meeting a rather militant, politically aware lesbian. The woman hands Ellen a rainbow flag, explaining that "The rainbow is a sign of unity for gays of all sexes, creeds, and colors." Ellen instantly repudiates this political implication, responding that "Well, it's also a sign that it's raining and the sun is still shining."

Later in the party, Ellen offers this same woman some "Señor Crunchy" corn chips, and is refused with the comment that the woman is "boycotting – excuse me – girlcotting. Señor Crunchy's has repeatedly denied benefits to same sex partners." At a loss for words, Ellen replies, "But they're corndelicous." Moments later, Ellen uses the word "straight" and receives an instant lecture: "You really shouldn't use the word straight – it implies that gay people are somehow crooked, or bent." Ellen's cutting response makes it clear that the appropriate reaction to this woman is to dismiss her as humorless and rigid: "Well, what about the word gay? I mean, that's a lot of pressure, to be happy and cheerful all the time. Although I see it didn't touch you at all." The woman does not give up on her relentless pressure to politicize Ellen, proposing "a toast to our new sister Ellen. We hope she will remember, as John Kennedy might have said, had *he* been gay, 'ask not what the gay community can do for you, ask what you can do for the gay community.' "

Incredibly, at the same time that it dismisses the possibility or relevance of the material effects of homophobia, *Ellen* takes pains to establish gay political awareness and activism as oppressive. Indeed, at the end of this episode, the pressure toward political awareness is constructed as a threat to Ellen's newfound authenticity as she discusses the evening with her friend Peter.

Ellen: I don't want people to think that I don't support the community. I do, but I can't keep up – it's overwhelming. I can't keep up with the bumper stickers and the flags and the gay bakeries and the lesbian friendly furniture polish . . . I came out so I could be who I am. I'm not about to change so I can please other people.
Peter: Ellen, the only reason I've been bugging you to get more involved is because I wanted you to know that there's a whole support system out there of people just

like you. The person you are is wonderful . . . And the good news is that you can be any kind of gay person you want to be.

What is most interesting about this is Ellen's claim that she does not wish to change just because she has come out – as if, again, coming out is a purely personal phenomenon that is relevant only in terms of who she decides to date or sleep with and has no impact on her status in the larger world. Her liberation has been so complete that homophobia is no factor at all. Even more interesting, Peter's reply to her complaint is that the primary function of his community is to offer Ellen *personal support* in her quest to be whatever kind of gay person she "wants to be."

The logic of the coming-out episodes, and one which DeGeneres herself explicitly endorses, is that "being gay is okay," and that gays and lesbian need to accept and value themselves and to expect the same from their loved ones. DeGeneres' appearances on talk shows and her interviews in the print media have underscored this message again and again. The episode of *Prime-Time Live* that immediately followed the broadcast of the first coming-out episode was introduced as "a gay daughter and her anxious parents. One family's story," and centered on DeGeneres's relationship with her family, as her mother, father, and brother all discussed their reaction to her coming-out. *Ellen*'s discourse, DeGeneres's discourse, and the media discourse that accompanied them all constructed the DeGeneres/Morgan coming out as a personal phenomenon for whom the appropriate audience was her heterosexual friends, family, and fans.

At times, DeGeneres brought up her hope that her show would have some impact on gay teenagers and adolescents. A 1992 study of gay and lesbians youths, for instance, found that 64% of males and 50% of females said that their self-esteem was affected positively by coming out. Lesbian and gay youths are two to three times more likely to attempt suicide than their heterosexual peers, and gays and lesbians account for 30% of all completed suicides among youths (Singer & Deschamps, 1994, pp. 76–77). If a show like *Ellen* can alter those statistics in a positive way, it deserves praise. Self-acceptance and acceptance by friends and family are important, particularly so in the process of coming-out. However, it is not the entire battle, and to talk about *Ellen* as though it signifies some kind of achievement of equality for gays and lesbians, either in media or in life, is to "confuse autobiographical gestures with [political] liberation" (Martin, 1993, p. 276).

Indeed, proclaiming that "Black is beautiful" hardly ended racial discrimination. As Biddy Martin has argued, the clear implication of Foucault's argument about confession is that "laying claim, then, to one's sexuality and the rights associated with it, insisting on the freedom to speak freely of one's sexuality, risks subjection to regulation and control" (1993, p. 276). *Ellen* demonstrates this most clearly in its adherence to the norms for gay and lesbian representation on television. Equally important, however, is the realization that it is not sexuality that has been repressed in television, but, rather, the *politics* of sexuality. Or, to put it another way, the secret being kept isn't homosexuality; it's homophobia and heterosexism (Crimp, 1993, p. 308). In this sense, *Ellen* only amplifies the silence, demonstrating the powerful mechanisms of power and control at work in mediated discourse about gays and lesbians.

Conclusion

I have emphasized two facets of the *Ellen* coming-out discourse: the reliance on a belief in the liberating effects of confession and a construction of gay identity as primarily, if not exclusively, a personal and relational concern. These two threads in the *Ellen* discourse stem, of course, from the same source: a commitment to the notion that subjectivity is under the control of the individual, that human beings have an authentic sexual and psychological self which can exist outside of social control and cultural pressure, that we are, in fact, only political subjects when we allow ourselves to be such. What it denies, as Jeffrey Weeks (1985) points out, is that

> in a culture in which homosexual desires, male or female, are still execrated and denied, the adoption of gay or lesbian identities inevitably constitutes a *political* choice. These identities are not expressions of secret essences. They are self-creations, but they are creations on grounds not freely chosen but laid out by history.
>
> (p. 209, emphasis in original)

Yet, the romantic narrative of autonomy and liberation that undergirds the rhetoric of *Ellen* allows it to be celebrated by gays and straights alike. For many gays, the fiction of personal authenticity and control provides psychological comfort in a deeply homophobic culture; for sympathetic straights, this narrative facilitates blindness toward the heterosexism and homophobia in which they are complicit and from which they benefit. DeGeneres/Morgan's coming-out was not an escape from power; rather, it was an entry into a different realm of power, one governed by a familiar yet potent narrative that carries its own forms of repression. To see it this way is to "refuse a separation between 'experience' and language and to insist instead on the productive quality of discourse" (Scott, 1993, p. 409).

The narrative produced by discourse in and around *Ellen* is understood here as a discursive construction, not as a transparent rendering of experience. It is discourse that "position[s] subjects and produce[s] their experiences. Experience in this definition then becomes not the origin of our explanation, not the authoritative (because seen or felt) evidence that grounds what is known, but rather that which we seek to explain, that about which knowledge is produced" (Scott, 1993, p. 401). The question, then, is not whether coming-out is liberating or not, but how is it *produced* as liberating and what power dynamics does that production rely upon, produce, and also repress? For example, the liberation narrative in and around *Ellen* allows mainstream media to proclaim increased *visibility* for gays and lesbians as increased *legitimacy* for gays and lesbians, in presumably social and political ways. If acceptance is merely a matter of being heard, of being recognized, of having one's confession acknowledged, so to speak, *Ellen* is progress. This is the claim that both DeGeneres and Morgan make, and it is an easy wish for a heterosexist media culture to grant. If, on the other hand, we are willing to interrogate the "outing fantasy – that the revelation of homosexuality would have a transformative effect on homophobic discourse –," this claim should arouse suspicion, not comfort (Crimp, 1993, p. 308).

Moreover, *Ellen*'s foregrounding of the personal – and its concomitant repression of the political – is classic television strategy in its representation of marginalized groups, and it blinds us to the contradictions inherent in claiming political progress from media representation (see Dow, 1996). Such contradictions are particularly clear in the case of *Ellen* and its relationship to gay and lesbian politics (see Dow, 1998). For instance, President Clinton, who, with much media fanfare, welcomed Ellen DeGeneres and her then-girl-friend Ann Heche to the White House Correspondents' Dinner (and who later invited lesbian poet Adrienne Rich to be the nation's Poet Laureate) is the same President who signed the Defense of Marriage Act and who failed to follow through on lifting the ban against gays and lesbians in the military. Despite the fact that a 1993 *New York Times* poll found that 78 percent of Americans believe that gay and lesbian workers should have equal rights on the job (Jackson, 1997, p. A23), only 11 states have laws forbidding workplace discrimination on the basis of sexual identity. There is no federal civil rights law for gays and lesbians, and a federal statute that would have protected gay and lesbian workers failed in the Senate in 1996 (Price, 1997). More than half of all socially active gays and lesbians have experienced some sort of anti-lesbian and anti-gay violence, and the third most common perpetrators of such violence are police officers (Singer & Deschamps, 1994, pp. 69–70). There are still several states in which one can be imprisoned for same-sex relations. Only 11 states have laws that make sexual orientation irrelevant in custody cases, and, of course, gays and lesbians are denied the right to marry same-sex partners.[3]

The positive visibility given to lesbian identity in *Ellen* is not the same as political progress – or even political *awareness* – and it is a mistake to confuse them. *Ellen*'s interpretation of lesbian identity as an exclusively *personal* issue makes it easier for everyone – especially those viewers in middle America that DeGeneres so desperately wants to reach – to ignore that there is much more at stake here than making TV safe for gays and lesbians. *Entertainment Weekly*'s designation of DeGeneres as a "poster child" that was noted in the opening to this essay is right on target; indeed, one could extend that metaphor to argue that *Ellen* is a fairly clear example of poster child politics, in which the attractiveness of an issue is directly related to who represents it.

Of course we like Ellen. She's pretty and funny, and doesn't take herself too seriously – so we don't have to either. In most episodes, she's just another single woman hanging out with her friends and looking for love – standard fare for a sitcom. She is, in fact, the ultimate user-friendly lesbian for television purposes. Yet, poster child politics are double-edged. On the one hand, they can often bring needed visibility to a deserving issue – witness the turnaround in media and governmental attention to AIDS after the death of Rock Hudson or the activism of Ryan White. However, such politics as practiced in popular culture can serve a masking function as representation is mistaken for social and political change. The success of the *Cosby* show didn't erase racial division in this country – it just meant that middle America liked Cosby. The obvious extension of poster child politics is tokenism, and the success of *Ellen* doesn't mean that discrimination against gays and lesbians – and the formidable, well funded, and influential political organizations that advocate it – is erased either. As Eve Sedgwick (1990) notes, "we have too much cause to know how limited a leverage any individual revelation can exercise over collectively scaled and institutionally embodied oppressions" (p. 78).

Popular culture *can* be political, in the sense that it can empower certain constituencies and can energize political agendas. However, one of popular culture's most salient characteristics is that it is ephemeral – its dependence on the power of personality, hot topics, and quickly shifting tastes makes it a fragile basis for lasting social change. Certainly, DeGeneres herself is aware of pop culture's fickle nature, as indicated by her consistent comments that she has no desire to be pigeonholed as the "lesbian actress" (e.g., Handy, 1997a, p. 86). Moreover, as Sloop and Ono (1997) have noted in their discussion of "outlaw discourse," when "one puts one's focus on individuals rather than on discourses, one makes it more likely that a project will fail because the failure of the individual implies the failure of the discourse" (p. 62). Media construction of the DeGeneres/Morgan coming-out, in which the success of the individual was taken to imply the success of the discourse (presumed to be gay and lesbian liberation), is a precise illustration of this problem.

The personalization of lesbian identity in *Ellen* and its surrounding discourse is what television – and mainstream media practice, to a large extent – do best: making us like characters, not issues. Ellen is a likable lesbian, but her popularity doesn't mean that America suddenly *likes* lesbians nor should it. In the end, what is at stake here are basic issues of civil rights, freedom of choice, and social justice – issues that shouldn't be dependent on liking, anyway. Media avoidance of such political stakes is more than mere omission; it should be recognized as an expression, indeed a production, of power.

Notes

1   In the fall of 2000, *Will & Grace* won three Emmys: for Best Comedy Series, Best Supporting Actor and Best Supporting Actress. A few weeks later, an issue of *Entertainment Weekly* titled "Gay Hollywood 2000: A Special Report" asserted in its lead story that "today, in 2000 A.D. (After DeGeneres), gay characters are so common on television, so unexotic, that their sexual orientation has become all but invisible to most viewers. It is, in a sense, the ultimate sign of acceptance: Gays, like blacks and single moms before them, are now allowed to be every bit as boring (or smart or stupid or ruthless or whatever) as anybody else on TV" (Svetkey, 2000, p. 26). This commentary is a striking example of the hyperbolic claims for progress in gay representation that are attributed to the *Ellen* phenomenon. Svetkey's claims are, at the very least, exaggerated, given that the Gay and Lesbian Alliance Against Defamation's (GLAAD's) figures for the 2000–2001 television season on broadcast and cable put the number of lead, supporting, and recurring gay characters in prime-time series programming at a whopping total of 27. Moreover, the "invisibility" of their sexual orientation also seems questionable, given that the storylines featuring gay characters are often *about* being gay in a way that other programs are not specifically *about* being heterosexual. Finally, while gay characters may be able to be as boring or stupid or ruthless as "anybody else," they are rarely allowed to be as *sexual* as straight characters, something that Svetkey himself seems to imply with his later comment that some see *Will & Grace*'s "straight-laced Will as a cop out, so blandly gay as to seem almost asexual" (p. 28).

2   I do not mean to discount the sizable gay and lesbian audience for *Ellen*. GLAAD
    was heavily involved in publicizing the coming-out episodes, hosting viewing
    parties in major cities, and the gay press certainly paid close attention to the con-
    troversy surrounding the DeGeneres/Morgan coming-out. Moreover, the first
    coming-out episode, in particular, contained a number of "in-jokes" clearly
    designed for a gay and lesbian audience as well as a number of cameo appear-
    ances by such gay and lesbian pop culture figures as k.d. lang, Melissa Etheridge,
    and GLAAD Media Director Chastity Bono. However, the purpose of this analy-
    sis is to analyze the rhetorical/ideological/political function of the coming-out
    phenomenon as constructed in mainstream media culture for its presumed
    heterosexual audience.
3   In the spring of 2000, the state of Vermont passed a comprehensive "civil union"
    bill, making same-sex couples eligible for the many benefits available under
    state law for married couples, although "civil union" is not technically the same
    as marriage. Moreover, although questions about its constitutionality continue,
    supporters of the Defense of Marriage Act signed into law by President Clinton
    in 1996 claim that it permits the federal government and the states to deny
    recognition of all same-sex unions in other states.

References

Bauder, D. (1999, March 17). "Dawson's Creek" gay character gets little notice so far. *The Atlanta Constitution*, p. 7C.

Cagle, J. (1998, May 8). As gay as it gets? *Entertainment Weekly*, 28–32.

Connelly, S. (1999, February 18). Coming out on "Dawson's Creek": Gay story line puts hit teenage series into turbulent waters. *New York Daily News*, p. 43.

Crimp, D. (1993). Right on, girlfriend! In M. Warner (Ed.), *Fear of a queer planet: Queer politics and social theory* (pp. 300–320). Minneapolis: University of Minnesota Press.

Davis, C. J. (1999). B(e)aring it all: Talking about sex and self on television talk shows. In I. Gammel (Ed.), *Confessional politics: Women's sexual self-representations in life writing and popular media*. Carbondale: Southern Illinois University Press.

Dow, B. J. (1996). *Prime-time feminism: Television, media culture, and the women's movement since 1970*. Philadelphia: University of Pennsylvania.

Dow, B. J. (1998). If there's no such thing as reality, has Elvis really left the building? *Critical Studies in Mass Communication*, 15, 471–474.

Doty, A. (1993). *Making things perfectly queer: interpreting mass culture*. Minneapolis: University of Minnesota Press.

Fejes, F., & Petrich, K. (1993). Invisibility, homophobia, and heterosexism: Lesbians, gays, and the media. *Critical Studies in Mass Communication*, 10, 396–422.

Fiske, J. (1987). *Television culture*. London: Routledge.

Foucault, M. (1978). *The history of sexuality, volume I*. New York: Random House.

Gilbert, M. (1998, May 13). "Ellen" was gay, but just not that humorous. *The Boston Globe*, p. Cl.

Girls night out. (1997, May 12). *People Weekly*, 42–43.

Gliatto, T., Tomasoff, C., Griffiths, J., & Zutell, I. (1997, May 5). Outward bound. *People Weekly*, 129–136.

Gray, H. (1994). Television, black Americans, and the American dream. In H. Newcomb (Ed.), *Television: The critical view* (pp. 176–187), New York: Oxford University Press.

Gross, L. (1994). What is wrong with this picture? Lesbian women and gay men on television. In R. Jeffrey Ringer (Ed.), *Queer words, queer images: Communication and the construction of homosexuality* (pp. 143–156). New York: New York University Press.

Hall, S. (1998, December 15). Gay guys don't stir as much ire as "Ellen." *The Indianapolis Star*, p. E07.

Handy, B. (1997a, April 14). "He called me Ellen DeGenerate?" *Time*, 86.

Handy, B. (1997b, April 14). Roll over, Ward Cleaver. *Time*, 78–85.

Hantzis, D., & Lehr, V. (1994). Whose desire? Lesbian (non)sexuality and television's perpetuation of hetero/sexism. In R. Jeffrey Ringer (Ed.), *Queer words, queer images: Communication and the construction of homosexuality* (pp. 107–121). New York: NYU Press.

Jackson, D. Z. (1997, May 2). The aftermath of "Ellen." *The Boston Globe*, p. A23.

Jacobs, A. J. (1995, March 24). Will the real Ellen please stand up? *Entertainment Weekly*, 18+.

LaFountain, M.J. (1989). Foucault and Dr. Ruth. *Critical Studies in Mass Communication, 6*, 123–137.

Marc, D. (1984). *Comic visions: Television comedy and American culture*. Boston: Unwin Hyman.

Martin, B. (1993). Lesbian identity and autobiographical difference[s]. In H. Abelove, M. A. Barale, & D. M. Halperin (Eds.), *The lesbian and gay studies reader* (pp. 274–293). New York: Routledge.

Millman, J. (1995, March 23). Ellen comes subtly out of the closet in "Friends of Mine." *Fargo Forum*, p. A13.

Milvy, E. (1998, September 17). Where "Ellen" blazed trails, 'Will and Grace' follows. *Los Angeles Times*, p. F55.

Mink, E. (1998, August 27). "Ellen" led way, new sitcom "Will" follow. *New York Daily News*, p. 104.

Moritz, M. J. (1994). Old strategies for new texts: How American television is creating and treating lesbian characters. In R. Jeffrey Ringer (Ed.), *Queer words, queer images: Communication and the construction of homosexuality* (pp. 122–142). New York: New York University Press.

Price, D. (1997, October 25). Gore's decade-long commitment to gay rights is no secret. *The Times-Picayune*, p. B7.

Rich, F. (1997, April 10). The Ellen striplease. *The New York Times*, p. A29.

Roush, M. (1994, March 1). "Roseanne" boldly refusing to kiss up. *USA Today*, p. 3D.

Schwarzbaum, L. (1997, December 26/January 2). Ellen DeGeneres: Entertainer of the year. *Entertainment Weekly*, 17–18.

Scott, J. W. (1993). The evidence of experience. In H. Abelove, M. A. Barale, & D. M. Halperin (Eds.), *The lesbian and gay studies reader* (pp. 397–415). New York: Routledge.

Sedgwick, E. K. (1990). *Epistemology of the closet*. Berkeley: University of California.

Singer, B. L., & Deschamps, D. (1994). *Gay and lesbian stats: A pocket guide of facts and figures*. New York: The New Press.

Sloop, J. M., & Ono, K. A. (1997). Outlaw discourse: The critical politics of material judgment. *Philosophy and Rhetoric, 30*, 50–69.

Svetkey, B. (2000, October 6). Is your TV set gay? *Entertainment Weekly*, 24–28.

Taylor, E. (1989). *Prime-time families: Television culture in postwar America*. Berkeley: University of California.

Torres, S. (1993). Television/Feminism: *Heartbeat* and prime-time lesbianism. In H. Abelove, M. A. Barale, & D. M. Halperin (Eds.), *The lesbian and gay studies reader* (pp. 176–185). New York: Routledge.

Tucker, K. (1998, May 8). Four weddings and a . . . *Entertainment Weekly*, 55–56.

Weeks, J. (1985). *Sexuality and its discontents: Meanings, myths, and modern sexualities*. London: Routledge & Kegan Paul.

Zimmerman, B. (1985). The politics of transliteration: Lesbian personal narratives. In E. B. Freedman, B. C. Gelpi, S. J. Johnson, & K. M. Weston (Eds.). *The lesbian issue: Essays from Signs* (pp. 251–270). Chicago: University of Chicago Press.

6

You'd Better Recognize

Oprah the iconic and television talk

Beretta E. Smith-Shomade

Originally published in Beretta E. Smith-Shomade,
Shaded Lives: African-American Women and Television
(New Brunswick, NJ: Rutgers University Press, 2002), 148–216.

[By faith] women received back their dead, raised to life again.
Hebrews 11:35

I believe I will run on . . . See what the end will be. I believe I'll work on . . .
Find out what waits for me . . . Ooh, ooh, ooh, ooh, Oprah."
The Oprah Winfrey Show, 1998–1999

Freedwoman and abolitionist Sojourner Truth ignited an early White Women's Rights group in Akron, Ohio, with her ire: "dey talks 'bout dis ting in de head – what dis dey call it? 'Intellect,' whispered someone near . . . What's dat got to do with women's right or niggers' rights? . . . [S]ay women can't have as much rights as man, cause Christ want a woman. Whar did your Christ come from? . . . From God and a woman. Man had nothing to do with him."[1] A century and a half later another free Black woman, Oprah Winfrey, descended on American consciousness to answer Truth's call for women's and "niggers' rights." Over the history of visual culture Black women's imagery has teetered between disgust and adulation, depravity and excess, objectification and agency. This pendulum has significantly impacted the lives of sentient African-American women, but then came Winfrey. Oprah Winfrey's figure has been positioned as both American and model minority. On her body the binaries created via White American male dominance reconciled, and Americans' quest for spirituality found refuge.

No other name (except perhaps O. J.) commanded comparable national recognition in late-twentieth-century pop culture. *Time* magazine lamented the "full Oprahization" of American politics; *Publishers Weekly* claimed an "Oprah Effect" over book sales; the "Oprah Factor" may have impacted the merger between New World Communications and King World, as well as *Time*'s subsequent buying of the distributor; and Christopher Buckley satirized a fictional conversation between Oprah and Pope John Paul II as "Poprah." Because the name, actuality, and talk show of

Oprah Winfrey resonate with people, the mere enunciation "Oprah" conjures the sublime example of self-help, authority, and release. Depending on the context, the name transforms from subject to verb to adjective. As a multifaceted millionaire and international icon, Oprah Winfrey epitomizes both the objectified and the agency-assuming Black woman as created by the medium of television and exemplified in the preceding chapters.

As I have demonstrated, the latter part of the twentieth century found dramatic and contradictory disturbances within American economic structures, political ideology, and culture. Black firsts continued despite twelve years of Reagan-Bush trickle-down policies. Deregulation forced long-term employee outages. Clinton implemented a progressive yet duplicitous leadership, making way for another George Bush Republican administration. The Internet dominated communication. And of course the beat played on for the fortunate few. The changes and stasis of the -isms (racism, sexism, classism) increased consumer and spectator feelings of alienation, loss, and anger among all groups. Although these cultural shifts were not revolutionary, they took on a heightened significance. Perhaps this significance came from the proximity of the approaching millennium. More likely, however, the aesthetic called postmodernism – that new approach to art, politics, business, education, and entertainment – fostered dread and scorn within and against those whom it pretended to benefit.[2]

Despite, or perhaps in response to, these changes, I argue that Oprah Winfrey's iconic status emerged so pervasively because of two very specific, ongoing, and intermingled phenomena in American society. First, I suggest that Winfrey's figure symbolized and embodied the binaries of American culture, of multiculturalism itself. The confluence of her race and gender always already suggested bipolarity. Yet the duality of her Negroness and Americanness that W.E.B. Du Bois wrote about implicated the identifying characteristics of age, class, and sexuality, bringing to bear the force of "us and Other" configurations.[3] In this multicultural debate the assumption of whiteness established the foundation by which dialogue occurred. Consequently, her presence caused further collisions of race, gender, sexuality, and class with whiteness.

Further, Americans' feelings of instability and angst established by inequity and blame were displaced onto the body of Winfrey. Along with the rhetoric of multiculturalism, historically entrenched binaries – Black/White, rich/poor, privileged/disadvantaged, old/young, us/them, homosexual/heterosexual – elevated the Oprah Winfrey icon as an exemplar of dialogue. In other words, the hypocrisy and complexity of the signifiers – salad bowl/no color lines/melting pot/mosaic – congealed into a configuration of Black womanhood that inevitably alienated the signified – Winfrey – from part of her own identity.

Evelyn Hinz connects multiculturalism to religion. In "What Is Multiculturalism? A 'Cognitive' Introduction," Hinz maintains that although religious overtones pervade the multicultural discourse, they rarely receive acknowledgment or consideration. She likens self-consciousness and self-reflexiveness to Catholic conscience; authenticity, transgression, honesty, and guilt to the site of the confession; and she adds that one should not overlook the "religious resonance of terms like 'purity' and 'impurity' in discussions of ethnicity, and especially when they are accompanied by a moralistic ridicule."[4] Hinz implicitly condemns this religious tone, but I maintain that it is precisely within this vein, this "moralistic ridicule," that Americans express their loss of, search for, and forwarding of the Oprah Winfrey figure.

This brings me to my second assertion. I contend that the decline and virtual absence of spirituality in the lives of Americans have, at least partially, constructed Winfrey as icon. Churches' decline in relevance has caused people to embrace salvation outside the bounds of established religion. Through her race, gender, talk show, and outside projects, Winfrey maintained ties to spirituality in the visual and oral folklore of Black representation. Beyond this, she emerged as a spiritual figure against whom the promise of tomorrow could be recuperated today. Symbolizing "core beliefs" as articulated by Nicholas C. Cooper-Lewter and Henry H. Mitchell in *Soul Theology*, Winfrey's figure achieved and activated an ideal balance for human existence.

According to *Soul Theology*, core beliefs empower individuals to affirm their own racialized, gendered, and ethnic construction while maintaining an other-centeredness and a self-giving focus. Balanced people are dependable without being rigid and are capable of expressing and controlling emotion. This balance results in a positive sense of relationship to God and God's creations, however that relationship is stated or envisioned.[5] In her presence on national and world stages Winfrey served simultaneously as an object of "credible" (implied atheistic) voice while connoting and claiming a balanced, spiritualized subjecthood. Thus, multiculturalism and the binaries that it excavated, coupled with religious absence, conjoined to form and forward the Oprah Winfrey star text. Her iconic status has ignited a complete redefinition of television and its growth. Winfrey has aided this redefinition not as a Black woman per se but as both a highly racialized woman and a de-raced, wealthy, American.

This chapter uses *The Oprah Winfrey Show* as a referential text to examine the genre of the talk show alongside other narratives that circulate about her omniscient presence. I use this strategy to uncover how overlapping discourses impacted representations of African-American women on television in the late twentieth century. Essentially, Winfrey's influence on American society has been examined and expressed through three distinct critical fronts: the scholarly, the production/economic, and the popular. Although they overlap, each possesses unique aspects of the iconic that work in tandem to both exalt and derail her.[6]

The scholarly talk of talk

The television talk show exploded in the 1980s as a distinctively American phenomenon.[7] Prior to this, 1950s talk shows were hosted by entertainers such as Dinah Shore, Merv Griffin, David Frost, Joan Rivers, and Mike Douglas.[8] In 1967 the talk landscape changed when Phil Donahue began broadcasting a television talk program as a phone-in show, similar to talk radio. The innovation of this format was its interactivity with the audience and its mixture of information and service. Donahue, comfortable with hard news topics, conveyed a sympathy toward other, "soft" news. However, viewers found Donahue's empathetic ear wanting. His lack created a space for Oprah Winfrey. Yet it was Donahue's talk show that led academics to begin investigating this new genre.

Television talk, like most daytime television, was theorized as female centered. Advertisers still idealized viewers as female homemakers, and they targeted cleaning women with cleanser, cooking women with food made easy, and mothering women with baby formula. Daytime advertisements were aimed at White women, married, and eighteen to thirty-five years of age.[9] Beyond demographic statistics, the commercials' racial composition reflected this. *The Oprah Winfrey Show* appeared within this very gendered and White weekday.[10]

Gloria-Jean Masciarotte's "C'mon, Girl: Oprah Winfrey and the Discourse of Feminine Talk" situates the talk show as a particularly female and somewhat liberating space. Through the prism of psychoanalysis she examines the Oprah Winfrey talk phenomenon, the history of talk itself, and the often-condemned feminine subject. She believes that the derogatory critical attention paid to the television talk show occurs because of patriarchy's gall at women's unrestrained speech on topics deemed feminine, their "painful experiences, [and] ongoing and ill-defined struggles."[11]

Further, Masciarotte's argument suggests that in the constitution of the subject, a series of *I*s instead of an *I/You* dichotomy forwards its trajectory in talk shows. Therefore, "resolving the issue is not the function of the talk show, [but] displaying the space for stories is."[12] In other words, women's speech and women's concerns become central and validated within the space of television talk. Topics ranging from premenstrual syndrome and breast cancer to plastic surgery and the glass ceiling fill the talk hour. This phenomenon, particularly in the context of a Negra bestowing subjectivity, accorded a quasi empowerment not only to the people (normally women) who were given voice but also to the racialized granter of the speech (Winfrey). In the final analysis Masciarotte maintains that because Winfrey was threatening, seductive, big, and aggressive, she defied and denied objectification and isolation. Hers was an "insistence on resistance, resistance to the dominant, curative, normalizing narrative."[13] This subjugation that Masciarotte claims advances the idea of Winfrey standing as a harbinger and beacon of difference.

Studies such as Wayne Munson's *All Talk: The Talkshow in Media Culture* pose key questions to the talk show genre itself: questioning whether they are more talk or show, conversation or spectacle, both or neither?[14] The familiarity of the format, the host, the audience, the set, and the relatively unscripted dialogue provide a forum in which the exchange of ideas takes place. Talk shows offer lively, useful information along with entertaining tidbits, unusual social practices, painful memories, reflections, and/or discoveries. Whether it is Donahue dressed as a woman on the issue of transvestism or Jenny Jones overwhelmed by her mastectomy, Munson concedes that talk shows "juxtapose rather than integrate multiple, heterogeneous, discontinuous elements. Rather than reconcile, talkshows (barely) contain."[15] But reactivating Masciarotte's point, perhaps containment denies dialogue. Resolution at the end of one hour may be more of a man's thing, a masculine construct that fails to follow women's acculturation or goals. This advocacy of reconciliation and heterogeneity surfaces in other scholars' investigations of the talk show genre as well.

Laurie Haag examines talk show intimacy, whereas Patricia Joyner Priest investigates why people participate. Dana Cloud's "Hegemony or Concordance? The Rhetoric of Tokenism in 'Oprah' Winfrey's Rags-to-Riches Biography" looks at the popularity of the format as dictated by its commercial success, its imitators, and demographic numbers. All engage in a dialectical discourse. Munson suggests that the talk show combines the elements of sensation, advice, and politics into a "promiscuous, hall-of-mirrors inclusiveness."[16] Yet in "Oprah Winfrey: The Construction of Intimacy in the Talk Show Setting," Haag argues that viewers have a certain relationship with Winfrey, parasocial she calls it, which allows them to feel intimately acquainted with her. Winfrey's specific success is attributable to "the evolution of both her personal 'legend' and her accessible communication style."[17]

For example, from *The Oprah Winfrey Show*'s inception participants (audience and guests) have always called and referred to Oprah Winfrey by her first name. This gesture indicated a certain familiarity not accorded or taken up by participants of *Donahue*, at least initially. Winfrey takes her audiences shopping, invites them to her home in pajamas, and rewards them for being "good" people. Haag says, "Only a good friend could tell a friend when she is not as cute as she can be."[18] Understanding and explicating the talk show while also revaluing its place in American culture and within the lives of spectators themselves helps to establish the talk show as a link between the interpersonal and the mass-mediated spectacle.

Munson suggests that this link serves a pragmatic and recuperative function. It reconciles technology and commodification with community, mass culture with the individual and the local, and production with consumption. Seemingly, this assessment reveals similarities among television platforms such as infomercials that feature doctors, psychics, therapists, preachers, and health gurus, as well as among the many reality-based programs that aired in the late 1990s. The televangelist movement falls within this linkage also. Munson maintains that in the combination of industrial and social, "the mythic American past of the participatory town meeting and the interpersonal 'handshake' politics of speech and presence meet the imagined 'present' of technological simulation, reproduction, and commodification."[19] This combination explains why the rhetoric of multiculturalism flourishes when Oprah Winfrey is the subject. Theories of postmodernism, as articulated by Jean-François Lyotard and Fredric Jameson, meld with capitalism. Additionally, they make clear the degree to which talk shows permeate American consciousness through business, education, politics, and consumerism. Yet beyond these concerns, still other substantial issues have pervaded the talk show domain.

I demonstrated in the four previous chapters that race, gender, class, and sexuality resonate within the television framework. In talk shows they predominate and provide much of the subject matter. Scholars such as Herman Gray submit that only within the talk show domain have discussions of race really permeated, despite their lack of depth.[20] Janice Peck disagrees. In her "Talk about Racism: Framing a Popular Discourse of Race on *Oprah Winfrey*," she maintains that because the inevitable goal of discussing racism on talk shows is to change perceptions, real-life problems are "discursively contained."[21] Following Peck's logic, for example, Winfrey's coverage of the 1987 and 1988 disruptions on race in Forsyth County, Georgia, did not alter substantially the demographics and perceptions of its inhabitants toward Blacks wanting to live there.

Similarly, Cloud argues that Winfrey's "tokenist biography" blames the oppressed for their failures. This biography is used to uplift and uphold the meritocratic American dream while justifying the inequities of the actual system.[22] Still further,

Debbie Epstein and Deborah Lynn Steinberg contend in "All Het-Up! Rescuing Heterosexuality on the Oprah Winfrey Show" that Winfrey both problematizes and normalizes the boundaries of heterosexuality. The "common sense," the normalized and institutionalized notions of heterosexual coupling, subverts the complexity of power and patterns of social inequality.[23] Half of the debates about *The Oprah Winfrey Show* address its response to, interpretation of, or inscription of race, gender, class, and sexual orientation. The other half focuses on Oprah Winfrey and the talk show genre through the therapeutic aspects of talk.

Many scholars maintain that the central goal of the talk show is to provide a forum for displaced, and what they deem nonbeneficial, therapy, sabotaging real issues for superfluous coverage and ratings. The catharsis and comfort of confrontation, therefore, often only lead to further problems after airtime. For example, in Mimi White's *Tele-Advising: Therapeutic Discourse in American Television*, White uses psychoanalysis to assess "confessional practices" across differing teletherapy, television formats. White conducts this type of analysis to uncover "an agency for producing new voices and new subjectivities that nonetheless remain in fee to consumer culture, voices that both constitute and evade the forces setting them in motion."[24] Her assessments of the television talk show, and particularly of *The Oprah Winfrey Show*, make valuable and valid assumptions.

Winfrey's program has been filled with experts and needy patients/participants who cling to each other for resolution of problems. The audience is not only induced by but also implicated in this process because most of the issues discussed invoke fundamental malfunctions, curiosities, or joys harbored within human consciousness and families. Besides, these emotive displays elevate the spectator, many of whom feel superior to the talk show participants. But beyond prevailing theories of therapy, commercialization, identity construction, and the genre itself, talk show discourses highlight the binaries of multiculturalism and religious lack as founded by and on Oprah Winfrey.

Validating this assertion, many of the aforementioned theorists mention therapy within religious contexts. For example, Masciarotte likens declarations on talk shows to the religious activity of testifying or witnessing before a group rather than to undergoing therapy. This allows for the constitution of social citizen beyond the private sphere. Winfrey's creation of a particularly woman-centered, spiritual, and industrial space helped her to become therapist and patient, host and audience member. In examining Winfrey's 1992 series on race, Peck suggests that religious and therapeutic discourses blurred when racism was defined as a lack of understanding, "a failure to recognize others as divine creations, a violation of the 'golden rule,' and a resulting spiritual (and hence social) disharmony."[25] According to this logic normally distinct ideological territories now grouped individuals before God, the marketplace, and science in the talk show.

The religious tone permeating the late twentieth century came through politics, a resurgence of religious fundamentalism, televangelism, and the multicultural impulse. Bandied about within educational institutions, this dialogue/debate revolved around storytelling, whose story and who would tell it. On the other hand, the multicultural impulse, according to Ward Churchill, actually amounted to "monolithic pedagogical reliance on a single cultural tradition [which] constitute[d] a rather transparent form of intellectual domination, achievable only within the context of parallel forms of domination."[26]

The figure of Oprah Winfrey was situated somewhere in-between those domains. She acknowledged and completely embraced society's opposition of her being alongside her own life stories, testimonies, and real-life actualities. Fissures, along with her ability to work an audience, positioned her centrality through change, as accessible although completely unreachable and as wholly understood but an unknown quantity. These scholarly debates about Winfrey's figure overlapped with the production texts of her success and her assumption of manly (White) power in product creation.

The production codes

The public economic/production narratives of the real-life, multimillionaire Oprah Winfrey focused on her ongoing monetary deals with King World Productions, her production company, and her new projects. According to *Forbes* magazine, *The Oprah Winfrey Show* earned $115 million in revenue during its first two seasons.[27] Winfrey credits the acquisition of a new agent in 1985 for propelling her from "employee" to mogul: "I had to get rid of that slave mentality. . . . He took the ceiling off my brain."[28] By 2000 Winfrey's name appeared on "The Forbes 400," a list of the four hundred richest Americans, which placed her at number 354, with a net worth of $800 million.[29] By her fifteenth season, Oprah Winfrey had won thirty-four Emmys and had twenty-two million viewers weekly. Shackles, be gone!

Economic narratives increased in proportion to Winfrey's soaring ratings as compared to other talk shows, the program's ability to draw advertisers, and money generated. For example, *Broadcasting* assessed the potential for high ratings at a low cost as a major factor for the rapid increase in talk shows. In 1992 *The Oprah Winfrey Show* led the ratings and earned $705 million in revenue. One analyst remarked that "[t]hese shows really are high profit centers. . . . And you don't have to be Oprah to make money."[30] Not until 1998, in her twelfth year of broadcasting, was *The Oprah Winfrey Show* resoundingly beaten, by *Jerry Springer*, and not permanently.

When Winfrey entered her thirteenth season, in September 1998, King World Productions agreed to pay her $150 million dollars per year to continue the show through the 2002 season.[31] By 1998 she accounted for 40 percent of King World's annual revenue or about $200 million dollars.[32] This same year Winfrey entered into an equal partnership with Geraldine Laybourne, Marcy Carsey, Tom Werner, and Caryn Mandabach to create a new cable station for women called Oxygen.[33] One of the largest cablers, TCI, committed to adding Oxygen to its basic service of seven million subscriber homes. Oxygen's premier in early 2000, along with the launch of her Web site, www.oprah.com, and *O, the Oprah Magazine* (the most successful magazine launch ever) all added to Winfrey's media omniscience.

Since 1986 Winfrey has produced several television works under the proviso of her Harpo Productions (*Oprah* spelled backwards and, coincidentally, the name of her character's husband in *The Color Purple*). They include *Women of Brewster Place* (March 1989), *Brewster Place* (May–June 1990), *Scared Silent* (September 1992), and *There Are No Children Here* (November 1993). The first two programs showcased Black women in dramatic fiction. The next two examined traumas that Winfrey herself endured in hopes that the exhibition thereof would end similar traumas. Her first feature film in collaboration with Touchstone Pictures, *Beloved* (1998), was produced also under the Harpo banner.

For "Oprah Winfrey Presents" Winfrey has delivered *Before Women Had Wings* (1997), *The Wedding* (February 1998), *David and Lisa* (November 1998), *Tuesdays with Morrie* (December 1999), and *Amy and Isabelle* (March 2001). *The Wedding* dramatized the 1996 book of the same title by Dorothy West. *David and Lisa* remade a 1962 classic of the same name. *Tuesdays with Morrie* won three Emmy awards, including one for Outstanding Made-for-Television Movie. All except *Beloved* and those projects under the "Oprah Winfrey Presents" logo appeared with the endorsement of nonprofit organizations. I will look more closely at the production and critical narratives surrounding the making of Toni Morrison's *Beloved* later in this chapter.

In September 1996 Winfrey launched the monthly "Oprah's Book Club" feature on her talk show. Its success gave an "atomic-powered boost" to sales of books selected and the authors themselves.[34] For example, the first book featured, Jacquelyn Mitchard's *The Deep End of the Ocean,* soared from an initial printing of one hundred thousand to eight hundred thousand after its announcement as a book club selection.[35] This ability to translate profits – to just speak it and have it be – gave Winfrey the status of a higher being. In fact, Vicki Abt called her a god, saying, "She has probably the highest Q [popular identification] rating of anyone on television. There may be better interviewers and smarter people elsewhere on TV, but no one markets charisma like Oprah does."[36]

While couched within the context of media moguls or media changes, *Variety, Broadcasting and Cable, Forbes,* and *Fortune* closely monitored the finances of this woman and of Harpo Productions. Similar to the coverage of professional Black athletes, Harpo Productions and Winfrey were discussed in terms of net worth and contracts. The racialized chutzpah of money and blackness propelled media propaganda about her. In other words, Winfrey's propensity to draw large sums of money both fascinated and appalled. Disgust came not so much in the amount of money per se (although that had a significant part) but more through ongoing arguments for racial reparations sought by some Black American citizens and a Caucasian sense that equality has been achieved. These types of production/economic narratives fed and merged with the scholarly to forward popular discourses.

The popular

Popular texts surrounding the Oprah Winfrey phenomenon have covered the star-generated projects, gossip, and fandom not addressed in the previous two arenas. From the beginning, articles appeared in magazines ranging from *Good Housekeeping, People,* and *Ebony* to *Ms., Nation, Time,* and *Essence.* Over twelve books have been written about Winfrey, specifically, and the talk show more generally. Many, quite tabloid-like, narrativize her life, increasing her fame. Several of these texts provide limited or no documentation and assume validation through pictures from *The Oprah Winfrey Show,* her character Sophia in *The Color Purple* (Spielberg, 1985), or Winfrey accepting one of several Emmy awards.

Her "rags to riches" story aired on the talk show through discussions of weight;

her longtime suitor/fiancé, Stedman Graham; health; and wealth. Home, hairstylists, and favorite dishes were also popular narrative fodder. The personal and intimate details of her life came to existence through the realm of the popular. Even on the Internet she has received cultural and Web space in the form of tributes by fans, star biographies, promotions by stations airing the talk show, and through the *TV Guide* international schedule.[37] Her own site, www.oprah.com, promoted her talk show format, viewer participation, and new projects. John Fiske suggests that many of the sites related to fandom are cultural forums denigrated by the dominant value system. Thus through these fan formations the talk show became further associated with the cultural taste of disempowered people, the people Christians assert will be saved.[38]

For her role as Sophia in *The Color Purple* Winfrey received Oscar and Golden Globe nominations, as well as being named Woman of Achievement by the National Organization for Women in June 1986. Her role of Bigger Thomas's mother in *Native Son* (Jerrold Freeman, 1986) failed to receive the same accolades but kept her in the forefront of American cinematic consciousness. These acutely racialized, gendered, and age-specific roles did not tarnish her star status. In fact, a 1988 survey asked college students to give descriptors most frequently associated with television talk show hosts. For Oprah Winfrey they characterized her by her appearance and her concern.[39]

Although Winfrey distinctly personifies the accoutrements of success, her name and figure escape many of the stereotypical constructions of others who look like her, the damning relations of those as wealthy as her, and the pigeonholing of those as famous. This may be because of the sense of crisis that accompanies the construction of what Richard Dyer calls star texts. How stars speak to, embody, or condense crisis may reaffirm the "reality of people as individuals or subjects over against ideology and history, or else in terms of exposing precisely the uncertainly and anxiety concerning the definition of what a person is."[40] This need for crisis (and dialogue thereof) forwarded Winfrey's narratives.

In multiple unauthorized biographies Winfrey's rise from abject poverty to the *Forbes* fortune list predominated. Also popular was her own self-distancing from "blackness." She was quoted amply as not being into "that stuff" (dashiki-wearing, "power to the people" mantras) when in college, preferring to foster "excellence" as the key to combating racism, framed as if the two sit in opposition. Nods toward bootstrapping (à la Clarence Thomas and Anita Hill) loomed just below the surface. Yet Dana Cloud's analysis of these popular discourses found that tokenism promoted by Winfrey's stories elided the real-life barriers to success and wealth confronted by the majority of African-Americans.

Cloud suggests that this tokenism participates in the "hegemony of liberal capitalism in so far as it acknowledges black voices, but redefines oppression as personal suffering and success as individual accomplishment."[41] This idea harkens to Coco Fusco's expression of difference (see chapter 1) and to bell hooks's assessment of poverty and Black communities' historic response (see chapter 4). Similar to many now successful marginalized members, Winfrey's figure helped to lessen the significance of economic, racial, and cultural disparities. Moreover, within and through *The Oprah Winfrey Show* and her image, the dual selves of Oprah Winfrey confronted America's ability to just get along.

The Oprah Winfrey Show and the woman behind it

Americans' love affair with this Black woman began with her talk show and her role in *The Color Purple*. Winfrey began her rise to iconic status when *The Oprah Winfrey Show* initially aired as *AM Chicago* in 1983. In the first six months the ratings for her show beat then reigning Phil Donahue in the same time slot. The King World Distribution Company saw the program and her appearance in *The Color Purple*. They approached the twenty-six-year-old Winfrey about syndicating her program nationally. In Winfrey, King World saw someone to compete against the virtually solo *Donahue*. Taking up the gauntlet, *The Oprah Winfrey Show* began broadcasting nationally in September 1986.[42] On initial syndication *The Oprah Winfrey Show* carried 120 stations. By the end of its first season the talk show held the number one rating position for daytime talk.

As *Donahue* provided the format for the daytime talk show's interactive style, Winfrey's program served as the progenitor to talk content as currently articulated. Winfrey supplied a warm, loving, and inviting space for viewers (women) and the in-studio audience to come and discuss their problems, concerns, secrets, and successes before millions. Aimed at a specific demographic, the show addressed and captured that audience in an unprecedented fashion. Coming to national attention on civil rights/affirmative action gains and battling (albeit subtly) Reagan/Bush attempts to reverse them, the show became the narrativization of one Black woman's life. This point proved to be imperative to her rise.

In succinct Americanesque storytelling Winfrey, the woman, grew up poor, struggled, overcame, and succeeded. Not trying to minimize or make light of her circumstances and successes, this brief account sums up her story. For marginalized folks dreaming of America, success must follow this type of narrativized trajectory. If the pitfalls had not occurred, similar situations would have been created. Indeed, it is the mandatory condition of the American dream. Like music video artists, talk show hosts submit to careful construction. Perhaps this construction aligns more closely with the actual lives of the hosts, but they are fashioned in a way that will make the host similar to the consumer, leaving room for and endorsing achievement. Although access to the American dream remained restrictive, scenarios such as Winfrey's were not unheard of for Black women growing up in this country in the late 1950s. Winfrey's tribulations began with her own conception.

Born to unmarried, teenaged parents, she suffered the shame of illegitimacy but benefited from the embracing of family. Although the phenomenon of children conceived by unmarried parents was fairly common in the United States, the progeny of that coupling often sustained open condemnation. For Afro-Americans W.E.B. Du Bois claims that a "red stain of bastardy" meant not only the loss of ancient African chastity but also held racialized implications of "the hereditary weight of a mass of corruption from white adulterers, threatening almost the obliteration of the Negro home."[43] This imagery played itself out in the public persona of Winfrey and other Black women. It underlies Halle Berry's and Mariah Carey's biracial status, Salt-N-Pepa's out-of-wedlock children, and Tawana Brawley's and the now defunct *Emerge* writer Lori Robinson's rape. It surfaced also within the context of Winfrey's show and other similar details of her life's tale. The importance of discussing these personal narratives was that they, particularly, became a part of Winfrey's talk show and iconic persona.

Most critiques extended from these personal tragic accounts. Criticisms of her talk show ranged from personal infusion to openly soliciting confessions without professional knowledge to handle them. But the judgment most pertinent to my argument was one that charged Winfrey with denying her blackness to ensure commercial success. Many African-Americans believed that Winfrey hugged more Whites than Blacks and befriended them more readily. For example, in a 1989 segment her guests included parents whose children had been fatally shot accidentally. Accidental shootings and gun control (which in and of itself bore a racialized component) were the topics. Winfrey, in tears, sat between a colored (Latina) woman and a White couple mediating and negotiating the ideological position of gun control and the personal feelings of loss.[44] In her brown body Winfrey effectively stood in for nonrepresented Black women who have lost their children through gunfire. But within a White articulation/framework of the problem, she decolorized it to assume salvation status. In other words, by embodying both the notion of mother and motherless with multiracialness, she positioned herself as someone for all people.

Like her audience, most of Winfrey's staff were White women. Winfrey justified and likened this racial composition to the viewership of her program. The demarcation between Winfrey's colored body and her White audience proved her ability to cross racial lines not only thematically but also through the use of her own body.

The girth of this body, her weight, probably represented Winfrey's predominate discussion segment, promotion ploy, and personal challenge in the show's first ten years. When *The Oprah Winfrey Show* began, Winfrey, at five feet seven inches, weighed 190 pounds. She lamented in the popular press, "I'm overweight. People tell me not to lose weight, I might lose my personality. I tell them, 'Honey it ain't in my thighs.' "[45] Often using her battle with weight gain as a springboard, she claimed that the turning point in her approach to weight came under the looking glass of a public event, the acceptance of the 1992 Emmy for best daytime talk show. Upset and depressed at her winning because of the necessity to go onstage, she wondered if someone was looking at the enormity of her butt. At the time she wore a size 24.[46]

Winfrey's weight and epiphanic experiences surrounding it commanded screen time and space, even beyond the talk show. As I pointed out in chapter 2, television condemns and devalues fat. Its enormity denies productivity and seems to allow women to take up too much space. Jeremy Butler argues, however, that Delta Burke's Suzanne in *Designing Women* became feminist in direct response to her weight gain. He remarks that Suzanne "shed the masquerade of femininity that women must preserve if they wish to remain visible *and powerful* in patriarchal culture."[47] Roseanne Barr, in person and in performance, reveled in the girth of her body, and Kathleen Rowe noted a power in Barr's self-described feminine fat and unruly laughter. But these women, in their anomalous bodies, retained the normality, the "possessive investment," of whiteness.[48]

With no such defense or cover Winfrey allowed America's obsession with thinness and youth to define her approach to weight. Ironically, although her weight fluctuations incited laughter in comedy, they helped to retain her power and popularity with everyday women. With a personal trainer and chef, Winfrey stabilized her weight by 1995. Both the trainer and the cook produced best-selling books based on their work with Winfrey. Indeed, the topics on *The Oprah Winfrey Show* and her own discourses played an important role in the construction of Winfrey as icon but also in rethinking Black womanhood and multiculturalism.

Oprah, the multicultural icon

Labeling Oprah Winfrey an icon of American success and credible voice requires definition and grounding. According to C. S. Peirce and Peter Wollen, icons are formed through linguistic sign systems that imply that language and meaning do not necessarily have direct correlation.[49] To Wollen the iconic is, "a sign which represents its object mainly by its similarity to it; the relationship between signifier and signified is not arbitrary but is one of resemblance or likeness."[50] As I mentioned earlier, Dana Cloud maintains that Winfrey's iconic positioning arose only through the rhetoric of tokenism. Cloud asserts that "liberal individualism requires the 'rags-to-riches' story as 'proof' that the dream of the individual achievement against all odds is real. This dream, in turn, justifies continuing inattention to structural factors, like race, gender, and class, that pose barriers to the dream for some Americans."[51] Yet in her Colored, big/small gendered body, Winfrey took on all the binaries and contradictions of the American dream for racialized, gendered, lower-classed, and sexualized Others. She epitomized the "give me your tired, your poor, your huddled masses" mantra of America. She became the Dream incarnate.

Beyond this, the rhetoric of multiculturalism turned increasingly from understanding, teaching, and accommodating difference to appreciation. Food, music, clothes, and arts became the essence of multiculturalism with the same hierarchical and privileging structures firmly in place. The social conservative movement astutely made multiculturalism synonymous with quotas, reverse discrimination, language, and anti-Americanness. Winfrey, however, eluded these distinctions by embracing and denying stigmas.

Even in a topic as superfluous as the "MTV Dance Party" Winfrey both defined and contained the -isms.[52] In the segment she defied stereotypes of Blacks' natural rhythm. She has none, nor can she sing. She possessed knowledge of contemporary cultural product but struggled with nouveau lyrics and beats. Her clothes reflected current trends but were not always suited to her frame. These types of minor, maybe superficial, contradictions signified larger ones that Winfrey strategically internalized, manipulated, and then exemplified as uniquely her own.

Certainly other iconic figures have emerged in American culture. Almost always appearing through the arts (music, literature, film, television) they include such figures as Marilyn Monroe, Elvis Presley, and, more recently, Madonna and O. J. Simpson. Perhaps the ability to say the icon's first name and have instant recognition across race, gender, generation, and class gives rise to their iconic stature. Yet only Madonna rivaled the space Winfrey occupied in the late twentieth century and in the psyche of national culture. Both singer and actress, through her own self-promotion and transgressive actions, Madonna inverted (or at least challenged) America's notions of sex, gender, and power. Madonna publicized her appropriation of the unspoken and taboo areas of America's moralist rhetoric and capitalized on it through the scandalization and titillation of the consumer.

Some have argued, however, that Madonna's insistence on solidarity with marginal groups and on moving between worlds was duplicitous. Dan Rubey suggests that she "presents herself as a female icon of white power functioning without sign or against white men. In this context, the assertion, 'It makes no difference if you're black or white, if you're a boy or a girl' seems cynical rather than naive."[53] bell hooks believes that her "power to the pussy" credo worked only to solidify Madonna's positioning on the backs of the marginalized. But Madonna, as producer of cultural ambiguity and openness, which was her profit center, marketed Madonna the performer. The sexual icon she constructed may indeed, then, accord power to the pussy.[54]

Yet despite Madonna's influence, her iconic status markedly differed from Winfrey's and in some ways was eclipsed by Winfrey's presence in American culture. In the 1990s Madonna's popularity declined. Lamenting that decline, Andrew Ferguson suggested that her "real crime" had been longevity. He maintained that "[t]he revolution craves novelty; it is rooted in the short attention span. And because its craving never slackens, it must create new icons and dismantle old ones with amazing speed."[55] But I suggest that the difference between Madonna et al. and Winfrey surfaced through Winfrey's ability to attack and control variant consumer visual venues.

Although all of the iconic figures mentioned were performers, including Winfrey, most lacked the ability to transcend their initial contact with the American spectator. Only Winfrey far exceeded her initial impact with television talk. She possessed a different persona. She acts, owns a production company (and restaurant, magazine, cable channel, and Web site), donates substantial amounts of money and time to various causes, and holds a college degree. These spaces not only mark her difference but also her scope and ability to reach ever more diverse sectors of the United States and the world. Even within this book, deciding whether to reference her by last name or the "Oprah" moniker sparked debate and reflection, a testament to the pervasiveness of her figure. Like religion, Winfrey assumed an omniscient presence, to be everywhere at once and to be all things to many. This religious resonance pervaded all her media forums and helped shape America's response to her.

The impact of Christianity

Alongside the free-love movement, the rise in religious fundamentalism grew steadily from the 1970s. Codified in social conservatism, it attacked multiple fronts simultaneously – politics, education, and media. Much of its rhetoric, particularly of the far right, positioned race, sexuality, and changing gender roles at the center of what's wrong with America. Dan Quayle's bemoaning of the "poverty of values" was only part of a larger move to restore the country to its previous hierarchical, conservative, and Eurocentric order. Prayer in schools, abortion, and gay rights were some of its core issues. By 1994 a study found that 90 percent of Americans considered themselves religious with 93 percent of those claiming Christianity.

Religious media became one of the most prevalent means to further the Moral

Majority's agenda, reach backsliders, and make new converts. The National Religious Broadcasters organization claimed over thirteen hundred radio stations and television channels by 2000. With historic ties to religion and spirituality already, African-Americans, and especially Black women, faced a unique dilemma to this growing tide.

Against this backdrop a debate of Christianity's viability for African diasporic people began to rage in academic communities. One film of the period, Haile Gerima's *Sankofa* (1992), challenged the role of Christianity in the United States and its relationship to Africans in America, particularly. In this fiction about a Black American successful model in Ghana for a photo shoot, Gerima transports this woman metaphorically to pre-emancipation, where she confronts her blackness, the past, and its relationship to her future – all through the bonds of slavery. Christian doctrine served as a fundamental theme of this film to justify and maintain slavery. One biracial character (his mother a slave, his father an overseer) kills his mother in the name of God. Ultimately, the film questioned whether Christianity should hold a place for African-Americans wanting to remove the figurative shackles from their minds and souls.

Yet many African-American scholars fought the perennial charge that Christianity, as a compensatory and otherworldly religion, distracted Negroes from their tenuous American predicaments, as it encouraged them to accept their lot as the will of God, to "take this world but give me Jesus." Albert Raboteau writes that the Black men and women he remembers growing up with spoke with righteous anger and prophetic certainty about the destruction awaiting this nation unless it repented from the evil of racism. In that same vein he urges that "[a]ny form of Christianity that condones slavery or racial discrimination is to that extent false and will be punished [–] Ain't everybody talking 'bout heaven, gonna go to heaven."[56] Regardless of one's position, the idea of Christianity's fundamental necessity to the nation and the lives of the people elevated figures like Oprah Winfrey.

American evangelists such as Oral Roberts, Robert Schuller, Jerry Falwell, Jimmy Swaggart, Pat Robertson, and Creflo Dollar took their pulpits to the altar of television. Organizations such as Concerned Women for America, the Family Resource Council, and the Christian Coalition formed and mobilized to impress the word of Jesus on a drifting world and to castigate those outside of their "divine" interpretation. All of these so-called prophets prepared the American audience for a figure such as Winfrey – not in a one-leads-the-other way but as phenomena that mutually fed and forwarded each other. Through her sense and use of familiar Christian practices – testimony, catharsis, touch, resurrection, and salvation (her own spiritual, televisual style) – Winfrey gave voice to the unspeakable for intellectuals and atheists and confirmation for believers.

Confession and testimony

A part of Winfrey's style emerged through the use of confession and testimony. Confession makes up part of the Catholic principles of sacrament and penance. As articulated, God's grace and forgiveness come through the confession of sin to an ordained priest, who then directs, blesses, and forgives on God's behalf.[57] The confession always begins, "Forgive me Father for I have sinned," followed by admission of the sins of action, thought, and heart. This type of confessional practice appeared often in the talk show, particularly in the early *Oprah Winfrey Show* programs, and has been taken up by copycat programs spawned hence.

In 1985, for example, one of the most discussed confessional episodes occurred when an incest guest confessed that she had been raped by her own father. With that admission Winfrey broke into tears and called for a commercial break. On the show's return Winfrey revealed that at nine years old, she too had been raped by an older cousin. This confession, this on-air disclosure, drew 878 telephone calls to the show.[58] People accosted Winfrey on the street to thank her for bringing to light a secret they shared and endured. Early talk show confessions like this fueled the deluge of programs that succeeded hers in the late 1980s and 1990s.

With the introduction of talk shows hosted by the likes of Geraldo Rivera, Jenny Jones, Sally Jesse Rafael, Ricki Lake, Montel Williams, Morton Downey Jr., and Jerry Springer assorted sexual, relationship, self-centered, and work practices poured from the mouths and screens of the American public. In these programs no small amount of African-American women and men aired as defrauders of the welfare system, cheaters on their spouses, carriers of alternative men's children, and exhibitionists, all targeted at White women's consumption. One climactic case came from a murder resulting from a confession on *Jenny Jones*.[59] By the end of 1994 Winfrey publicly announced her disgust of the talk forum and vowed to rid hers of the "sleaze" factor. This change was visualized largely through another religious practice, testimony.

Winfrey's subsequent guests subscribed to the Protestant/Black Christian practice of testifying rather than to the confessional practices of Catholicism. The corollary to confession, testimony receives validation and actualization within the preponderance of television talk shows through celebratory pieces of success, ordinary heroes, miraculous deflections of death, and celebrity transformations. Yet for Black women on *Ricki, Jenny Jones,* and *Jerry Springer* their testimonies remained in the framework of stories that objectified their sexual and bodily travails.

Winfrey accelerated her commitment to affirming stories when she introduced "Change Your Life TV," the theme for her 1998–1999 season. The host turned singer in the show's opening credits. In the music video-like scenario, Winfrey stands/dances at a microphone surrounded by an ethnically diverse, young, pop choir. She says, "What I believe is that we all are looking for something deeper, greater."[60] This new program thrust, as the words at the beginning of the chapter indicate, was on making audiences' lives better through the uniting of spirit, mind, and body. In some ways Winfrey offered a nod to "new age" religion, with weekly appearances by the author of *Men Are from Mars, Women Are from Venus*, John Gray; Dr. Philip McGraw; and author Iyanla Vanzant, a Yoruba priestess whose 1993 *Acts of Faith* had more than seven hundred thousand copies in print. Winfrey's official Web site confirmed that, indeed, Winfrey recognized and assumed a certain spiritual testament and responsibility. Between changing people's lives and Oprah's Angels, this icon looked to make a difference.[61] This new direction, this new Oprah, overtly positioned Winfrey as a religious figure.

Fire in the bones: catharsis, Holy Spirit, and the laying on of hands

I have mentioned that criticism of Winfrey in Colored communities sometimes suggested that she favored her White guests and audience members over her Negro ones. Beyond language and quantity of Colored guests, this charge had some grounding in the quantity of touch she bestowed on guests. The religious denotation of the laying of hands on a person involves the transference of the Holy Spirit or Holy Ghost from one person to another in order to heal, cure, liberate (from curse), or relieve.

The general secretary of the National Council of Churches, Joan Brown Campbell, explained that the laying on of hands is an ancient form of ministry filled with spiritual richness. It symbolizes the outpouring of God's spirit through those present to one who is facing a time of crisis.[62] One audience member remarked that Winfrey touches people and that everybody needs touch in their lives. Touching seems to provide a space and means for catharsis to occur. Winfrey's touches, literally and visually, connected her to both the specific audience member and the at-home spectator. For people who lacked touch in their day-to-day lives this televised figure achieved a certain tactility.

This assessment may exude a Hallmark feel, yet many have used the power of touch to both embrace and condemn African-American women. Negra touches were invited into the homes of White Americans whose babies needed nursing and whose children needed raising. In Black homes the same rules have applied. Touch has received validation to harvest food, cultivate the lives of children in segregated schools, and rock abandoned crack babies in hospitals. Conversely, however, tactility endured condemnation when these same women possessed too much melanin, were designated as whores (at least in public), or retained too much education, drive, or attitude. Winfrey's tactility harbors a perceived healing quality normally reserved for White religious persons, the visualized White Jesus himself, whereas the racial component of her being was relegated to the nurturing and historic comforts of mammy.

Resurrection

Winfrey's biblical associations did not confine themselves to her talk show persona. They pervaded all of the discourses and visual manifestations that created her figure. In *The Color Purple* (1985), for example, the potential volatility of its White director, Steven Spielberg, visioning a Black woman's story and the issues presented brought to the forefront many of America's foibles, even though the story is set in the past. According to media of the time, Winfrey enjoyed her television talk show because of her success at it. But with acting, she felt that "you lose your personality in favor of the character you're playing but you use it to provide energy for your character."[63]

Alice Walker's *The Color Purple* (1982) chronicles the lives of several women and their relationships to a family of men, male culture, and themselves. But unlike the book, the film revolves solely around issues of power, particularly men's power over women, home, and sexuality. For example, in the book Celie and Shug engage in an intimate, passionate, and long-lasting lesbian relationship that the film barely acknowledges. Further, Walker incorporates a strong, anti-Christian, pro-God sentiment within the text. The film, however, revises the anti-Christian plot. These religious and sexual subversions, particularly as they impact Shug's behavior and sexuality, illuminate the lack of sexual power simultaneously accorded and denied to African-American women. They show also the impact this constant denial has on Black women and men's relationships in visual culture.[64] The denial of sexual freedom along with moral condemnation was critical to the disempowerment of African-American women and the elevation of a Christian ethos.

With this revisionist tactic in mind Winfrey played a central character in the construction of the film and, within it, offered the possibility of resurrection. One poignant scene opens with a shot of a white dinner plate with Sophia's (Winfrey) face reflected in it. At first the reflection and plate are indistinguishable. When the shot widens to frame her full figure, the spectator sees that Sophia appears either asleep or subdued, rocking gently in her chair without speaking. This scene is the family's Thanksgiving meal celebration. Squeak (Rae Dawn Chong) asks Sophia how she feels. She replies, "Confused." Harpo (Willard E. Pugh) questions, "Aren't you glad to be home?" She responds, "Maybe." While the scene's dramatic tension actually concerns Celie's (Whoopi Goldberg) breaking away from Mister (Danny Glover), Sophia's presence confers a Christian ethos.

Celie calls Mister "dead horse shit," causing Squeak to laugh. The camera cuts to Sophia as she begins to stare meekly at Celie. Harpo commands Squeak to shut up, saying, "You know it's bad luck for a woman to laugh at a man." This declaration brings forth laughter from Sophia, a slow, loud, continuous, and solitary chortle. Her laughter silences everyone. Mr.'s daddy (Adolph Caesar) turns slowly toward her and remarks, "My God. The dead has arisen." With that, Sophia recounts the misery of her jail time: "I know what it like Miss Celie. Wanna go somewhere and cain't. I know what it like wanna sing, have it beat out ya. I want to thank you Miss Celie, for everything you done for me. . . . When I see'd you, I know there is a God . . . and one day I'se goin get to come home."

The possibility of resurrection has been key to African-Americans' ability to survive in the United States. Resurrection became a central mantra during Reconstruction. Reminiscent of Scarlett's declaration before God in *Gone with the Wind* (1939), Sophia's resurrection and her laughter made profound and progressive statements about Black women and their ability to survive and insert themselves into patriarchy, despite Spielberg's reconceptualization of the text. Thereby, Winfrey as Sophia and as a spiritual icon symbolized the possibility of resurrection.

Jacqueline Bobo examined Black women's responses to this film and literary text in *Black Women as Cultural Readers*.[65] Following the scene in which Sophia packs up her children in order to leave Harpo, the women in Bobo's study came to an interesting verdict about fictionalized representation and real-life situations:

Phyllis: You folks be talking about she [Celie] should have gone with her [Sophia], but you have to remember, girlfriend's mouth got her in jail for a while.

Whitney: That's true. Well, you gotta do what you gotta do. It's all about integrity.

Phyllis: First, it's about survival. Then it's about integrity.[66]

Therein lies the dilemma: whether to suffer in silence either through racialized, gendered, generational, or sexualized tropes and to, at some level, be saved, or to speak your mind and endure the consequences, which may be fatal. Inevitably, Sophia was punished for speaking her mind in this narrative, and the other Black women endured some form of oppression. Yet it was Sophia's specific oppression that represents issues of sight and, more poignantly, sound.

In the role of Sophia Winfrey occupied that anonymous space of the inner eye that I discussed in chapter 2. Sophia became a literal servant, but, more significant, within this designated sphere she failed to receive recognition (as in the scene with Miss Millie in the store and car). Although new to the visual realm, Winfrey used the words written by Alice Walker and the art of performance to secure her own resurrection from dire circumstances connected to her own biography. As borne out in subsequent visual texts, Winfrey's personal tragedies paralleled and equaled Sophia's, forcing the tangential connection linking the character in the film, the host of the talk show, and the actual lived narrative of Oprah Winfrey. These connections suggested that if Oprah could rise after all her trials, certainly the members of her audience could too.

Salvation

According to Cooper-Lewter and Mitchell, everyone possesses a belief system that enunciates certain value judgments. Whether expressed or kept within, "an assumption inescapably involving some sort of faith determines all conscious choices and influences all unthinking response."[67] In the biblical text of Mark the demon-possessed, the leper, the paralytic, the dying child, the hemorrhaging woman, and the blind man all, in the face of apparent hopelessness, received divine blessings and mercy through God's freeing them from their pains and problems.[68] In this century these same types of individuals, broken through the loss of children, abandoned by friends, and alienated from society's norms, found themselves on and spectators of the talk show. The producers strove for a certain salvation-like peace at the end of each installment of *The Oprah Winfrey Show*, at least visually. For example, on the 1992 coming-out day segment for abusive parents, tears flowed, confessions and apologies were offered, and testimonials were given. In this milieu Winfrey represented a saving grace, a conciliator. She brought warring parties together, initiated and directed the touch of flesh, and asked appropriate questions to elicit salvific responses.[69]

Outside the confines of the talk show Winfrey represented salvation through her philanthropy. In September 1994 she announced her "Families for a Better Life" program, which literally attempted to rescue people from the life of poverty inhabited by members and residents of Chicago's inner city (that is, the areas where poor Blacks and Latinos live). Although Winfrey gave a considerable amount of money to initiate the program, it ceased operations after helping only five families.[70] In 1997 she challenged viewers to volunteer to help build 202 houses with Habitat for Humanity, one house in every city where a station carried *The Oprah Winfrey Show*. Donating monies to educational institutions and nonprofit children's organizations, Winfrey sought to make a difference, in cash. Interestingly, even when her efforts failed, as they did with Families for a Better Life, the failure inconsequentially impacted the perception of Winfrey's salvation ability. Winfrey was seen as a giver, but beyond financial philanthropy. She appeared to give of herself. In essence, then, salvation came to those who believed and followed her example. *The Oprah Winfrey Show*'s shift in focus from "Get with the Program" to "Change Your Life TV" confirmed it.

Beyond her prominence as a spiritual icon Winfrey pursued her dreams of stardom. In 1989 Winfrey's Harpo Productions produced Gloria Naylor's *Women of Brewster Place*. This four-hour, two-part television special showcased Naylor's novel with Winfrey as coexecutive producer. Winfrey starred as the central character, Mattie Michael, in a cast of African-American actresses who found themselves in a poor tenement on a street blocked by a brick wall. The program opens and closes with Mattie framed in the middle of a hole created by the women finally fed up with the horror of their lives.

Despite the visual flaws in Winfrey's aging process,[71] the project made a significant statement. The financial and popular wherewithal to bring a story about Black women to television spoke to the political and economic American culture of the late 1980s and the commercialization of Black women's stories. By then Black women seemed bankable. The main proponent of that profit was Winfrey herself.

Her most ambitious film project, however, has been the production of Toni Morrison's *Beloved*. Published in 1987, the book traces an escaped slave woman's encounters with her past, her present, and her future. For eleven years Winfrey struggled to produce a film version. She ultimately succeeded in 1998, bankrolling a coveted director who would allow her to assume the lead role of Sethe.

The film sets forth powerful iconography and performances to try to capture this painful and dense historical moment. However, audiences failed to value its efforts. Despite an enormous marketing blitz by Disney Communications and Winfrey herself,[72] the film ran only eight weeks. It generated just over $22 million, but it had cost $80 million to make.[73]

Critics faulted the surrealist nature, the "irrelevant protracted sequences, which sidestep the tragedy and pathos which should be its core,"[74] and, in some circles, Winfrey. Frank Rich complained that "the audience feared more sermon than drama from the increasingly more preachy Oprah."[75] I agree with some of this criticism, but the reality of the reasons for the film's failure goes deeper.

Despite Winfrey's popularity, this project positioned her squarely in her blackness. Beyond its economic agenda, slavery in the United States dehumanized one group of people (Black) for the sole benefit of another (White). Being 150-plus years past slavery's abolishment has failed to lessen its impact and has further shaped its legacy. Who can humanely reconcile Black women's bloody, beaten, and raped bodies and perceived animalistic tendencies (particularly those who still have Black and brown women in their kitchens and nurseries)? It seemed not many. Winfrey's recuperation of blackness at the expense of the multicultural impulse helped tank the film from the start.

Oprah as fictionalized narrative referent

Beyond the discourses that circulated in the everyday lives of Winfrey's talk show viewers and her own acting forays, Hollywood utilized her omniscient name recognition for profit. In the blending of fact and fiction television comedy featured Winfrey, the actress, within their texts as "Oprah, the talk show host." The layers produced by this intertexuality harkened to both the historic nature of television and the post-modern aesthetic. But as I have shown, Winfrey moved beyond intertext to intratext. Winfrey's status coupled with her credibility made her opinions, her roles, and her personal life pervasive and intimately open to the spectator. In sitcoms and feature films Winfrey grounded self-referentiality and reality. She performed herself, was played upon, and used as a real-life construct in the world of fiction.

For example, in an episode of *The Fresh Prince of Bel-Air* the Banks family appear on *The Oprah Winfrey Show*. Winfrey plays "Oprah," – the talk show host, when the family comes as guests on a segment of political candidates. The episode, "A Night at the Oprah," illustrated once again why Winfrey became ingrained so firmly in the minds of the American public. She offers to buy Hilary a dress just like hers (in Hilary's size), features two families (one Black, one White), and draws out the secrets of her guests (Hilary living with Treavor, her fiancé). Even citizens who claimed not to watch television possessed an "Oprah" referential understanding.

An early *In Living Color* episode parodied Winfrey, *The Oprah Winfrey Show*, and her obsession with weight. The scene opens with Kim Wayans as Winfrey, dressed very elegantly in a blue silk dress, moving through the crowd. Announcing the day's subject, "men unable to commit," she comforts a young woman by pulling the girl onto her lap and rocking her. Returning to the audience, she opens a candy bar. She then begins to lament over her relationship with Stedman, to eat uncontrollably, and to rotisserie three whole chickens simultaneously, consoling herself by exclaiming, "Homeboy still throwing down in the bedroom."

Wayans as Winfrey gorges, cries, and rants about Stedman's spending her money and living in her condo. Visually, her body gradually expands, literally, as she yells, "Food is my lover; food is my friend." Presumably, the sheer weight of her enlarged body lifts her into the air outside of the frame until finally the body explodes, raining all types of food disgustingly to the ground. In this skit Wayans played the "Oprah legend" against the metanarratives that surrounded her. Food and fat, her relation-ship with Stedman Graham, her interaction with audiences, and her hybrid speech collided and exploded before the viewers' eyes.

These metanarratives not only formed a part of her star discourse but also, particularly in this case, lauded the Negro wit that helped frame and proclaim the Winfrey impact on the lives of African-Americans. In this instance Wayans's parody of Winfrey's performance confronted and extended the fiction in service to humor and grace. In mainstream television programming Winfrey was equally prevalent. For example, she served as Ellen's therapist in Degeneres's much-heralded coming-out episode, putting Winfrey on the cutting edge of cultural sexuality despite academic assessment otherwise.[76]

In cinema the beginning of *The Nutty Professor* (1996) played into the Winfrey mythos by dominating the fictional characters' dinner conversation. The Klump fam-ily (Eddie Murphy) are an obese, African-American, middle-class family, seemingly comfortable with their weight. The only concern comes from the eldest brilliant son, Sherman. When Sherman removes the skin from his chicken, the dinner conversation turns to America's obsession with weight. Father Klump exclaims, "You know where that come from? Watchin that damn TV. Every time you turn it on they got somebody on there talkin about lose weight. Get healthy. Get in shape. Got everybody lookin all anorexic talkin bout that's healthy. I know what healthy is."

As Father Klump rants, he piles his plate with greens, chicken, peas, and potatoes, followed by a dousing of gravy. Ironically, the fat content of this meal exemplifies one of the most pernicious causes of heart disease, obesity, and high blood pressure in Black communities. Nevertheless, the musing continues, and Winfrey becomes the subject of critical examination:

Father Klump:	And tell you somethin else. I don't know why everybody tryin to lose weight in the first place. Ain't everybody suppose to be the same size. We supposed to be all different. Big. Small. Medium. Midgets. You supposed to have all that . . . Like that Oprah Winfrey. She gone lose her weight. Whatn't nothin wrong wit her. She was fine. Oprah was a fox. She lost all that weight, her head look all big, skin hangin all off her . . . Oprah and Luther need to keep their ass one way cause I'm confused.
Mother Klump:	Yes, I hope nothing's wrong with Oprah. She doesn't look real.
Grandmother Klump:	Ain't nothin wrong with Oprah. I seen Oprah on *Hard Copy* last week. Was the picture of health. Got her a tall, young; strong gentleman named Stedman, so handsome . . .

These constant references to Winfrey's real and constructed selves fuse fiction and reality.

Next, on Oprah

The figure of Oprah Winfrey exemplified the psychosis of American society in the latter part of the twentieth century. For Black and White, dirt-poor and disgustingly rich, fat and thin, beautiful and unattractive, fiercely independent and completely dependent on male companionship, producer and consumer, this woman (and the man in her power) embodied and exploited accepted binaries. Although this ideological and polysemic displacement benefited the consumers of her texts (mostly White women in the case of the talk show), it virtually denied Winfrey's agency as a Black woman.

The surplus of her body, her presence, her talk, and her life marked out the territory of her iconic figure as individualistic, exemplary, and isolated. Winfrey personified a method for the coexistence of difference. She strove to present a moral and spiritual beacon for a country moving away from spiritual underpinnings as a sign of progress and intellectualism. The splitting of binaries across her body enabled her figure to move beyond the -isms. She achieved subjecthood while satisfying consumer demand. But the producer, Winfrey herself, paid a price. She was absent in her presence. Standing on the ground of "excellence," her achievements were stripped from her colorized and gendered form and, in turn, were partially denied to women who look like her.

Winfrey bridged a gap that had been simply ignored for quite a long time. She encouraged victims of dubious circumstances to appear before a compassionate and similarly (but not identically) composed audience to hear them. The discussions on institutional problems (racism, sexism), relationship problems (marriage, adultery, dysfunction), and unspoken problems (rape, incest, molestation) touched nerves that ate at American consciousness. Although Phil Donahue's program covered similar categories, Donahue lacked the ability to move beyond the surface. Successful talk show hosts not only sympathize with but empathize with their audience and guests. Yeast production, for example, was not a topic of familiarity for Donahue.

Winfrey, like Jesus, placed herself in the framework of her guests and audience (often quite literally in the case of rape and weight issues), which endeared and promoted her as the voice for and the ear of the spiritual unseen and unspoken. However, as she continued to do this, to perpetually disclose information, her figure reinscribed sexist and racist constructions of Black womanhood. This propensity may eventually lead to her downfall. The beginning of this decline can be seen in spectators' responses to *Beloved* and in comments by Tom Shales, who says, "Of course Winfrey is wonderful and living-saintly and all things bright and beautiful. We all know that. But her evangelistic tendencies are beginning to spin out of control."[77]

Talk shows that emerged subsequent to *The Oprah Winfrey Show* featured Black women and lower-class Whites ad nauseam, often conflating the two. From young Negro girls impregnated by their sisters' husbands to those afraid of commitment (as in the *In Living Color* skit), African-American women represented the base and mythologized sexual vamps that permeated welfare debates, sexual harassment cases, and energized musical bodies. Talk show hosts Ricki Lake, Jenny Jones, and Jerry Springer exploited these women and their stories to get dramatic boosts in their ratings.[78] Lake would question incredulously, "You were pregnant, and he was only coming to sleep with you?" Her audience would respond, "Go Ricki! Go Ricki!" Even expressions such as these, extracted from Black talk, fed and fueled this kind of exploitation.

In these talk shows Black faces and bodies performed for predominately White audiences in a White, serialized context. Although most of the counselors, therapists, and audiences were White, the overwhelming proportion of guests on these shows were Black and Latina, poor, young, and unemployed. Jill Nelson describes these shows: "Young women of all colors are victims; or stupid, sex-addicted, dependent baby-makers, with an occasional castrating bitch thrown in. . . . It was initially interesting to see that a significant number of these couples are interracial, but the subtext quickly became clear: Penis-waving black men prey not only on black women who deserve/are used to it, but on White Women."[79] In her talk show and as her real star persona, Winfrey spoke in an inappropriate, private speech. Using terms of endearment, she comforted the broader American mainstream yet made them uncomfortable. Phrases such as "child," "girlfriend," "honey, please," beyond their tangential relationship to the South, erected notions of mythic internal relationships between African-Americans themselves that incorporated Whites.

The splitting of the American psyche played itself out across Winfrey's body. Few Americans remained unaware of Winfrey's success story. The discourses surrounding her personal, professional, and production life were documented on the television and through popular publishing. Her life story began in poverty, strife, abuse, and neglect then bloomed into Cinderella's night at the ball and an ongoing dance with the prince. Only in this case Winfrey served as both the Colored Cinderella and Prince Charming. She helped create the vision and guided its progress. After the ball Cinderella and the prince stormed visual fronts and conquered a good portion of them. Quintessentially American, the dream became accessible through Oprah Winfrey along with the contentious identity issues that buttressed that dream. Consequently, the dichotomies that divided her body never departed but dangled the potential to unite across difference.

Notes

1 Sojourner Truth, *Narrative of Sojourner Truth* (Boston: printed for the author, 1850).
2 The ideas of Jean-François Lyotard's postmodernism are well described in Steven Best and Douglas Kellner, *Postmodern Theory: Critical Interrogations* (New York: Guilford, 1991), 165.
3 See W.E.B. Du Bois, *Souls of Black Folk* (Chicago: A.C. McClurg & Co, 1903), 215.
4 Evelyn J. Hinz, "What Is Multiculturalism? A 'Cognitive' Introduction," *Mosaic* 29, no. 3 (September 1996): xiii.
5 Nicholas C. Cooper-Lewter and Henry H. Mitchell, *Soul Theology: The Heart of American Black Culture* (San Francisco: Harper and Row, 1986), 5–6.
6 Unlike others of her stature, Winfrey achieved ideological proportions similar to the concepts of the American dream, nation, capitalism, and democracy.
7 I am not suggesting that the United States held a monopoly on television talk. However, the talk show's contemporary articulation made it a uniquely American genre.
8 See Wayne Munson, *All Talk: The Talkshow in Media Culture* (Philadelphia: Temple University Press, 1993), 61.
9 Sara Welles, "Taming the TV Talk Show," *Television Quarterly* 28, no. 3 (summer 1996): 41–48.
10 Winfrey was not the first African-American woman to have a television talk show. Della Reese had a combination talk-variety show called *Della* (1969–1970).
11 Gloria-Jean Masciarotte, "C'mon, Girl: Oprah Winfrey and the Discourse of Feminine Talk," *Genders* 11 (Fall 1991): 82.
12 Ibid., 88.
13 Ibid., 103.
14 Munson, *All Talk*, 15.
15 Ibid., 10.
16 Ibid., 5.
17 Laurie L. Haag, "Oprah Winfrey: The Construction of Intimacy in the Talk Show Setting," *Journal of Popular Culture* 26, no. 4 (Spring 1993): 115.
18 Ibid., 120.
19 Munson, *All Talk*, 6–7.
20 Herman Gray, *Watching Race* (Minneapolis: University of Minnesota Press, 1995), 174.

21   Janice Peck, "Talk about Racism: Framing a Popular Discourse of Race on Oprah Winfrey," *Cultural Critique* 27 (Spring 1994): 120.

22   Dana L. Cloud, "Hegemony or Concordance? The Rhetoric of Tokenism in 'Oprah' Winfrey's Rags-to-Riches Biography," *Critical Studies in Mass Communication* 13, no. 2 (1996): 115–137.

23   Debbie Epstein and Deborah Lynn Steinberg, "All Het-Upl Rescuing Heterosexuality on the *Oprah Winfrey Show*," *Feminist Review* 54 (Autumn 1996): 88–111.

24   Mimi White, *Tele-Advising: Therapeutic Discourse in American Television* (Chapel Hill: University of North Carolina Press, 1992), 186 n. 9.

25   Peck, "Talk about Racism," 104.

26   Ward Churchill, "White Studies: The Intellectual Imperialism of U.S. Higher Education," in *Beyond Comfort Zones in Multiculturalism: Confronting the Politics of Privilege*, ed. Sandra Jackson and José Solís (Westport, Conn.: Bergin and Garvey, 1995), 18.

27   Robert La Franco and Josh McHugh, "Piranha Is Good," *Forbes*, October 16, 1995, 66–67.

28   Ibid.

29   See <http://www.forbes.com/finance/lists> (accessed February 15, 2001).

30   Steve McClellan, "Look Who's Talking: Potential for High Ratings at Relatively Low Cost Attracts New Talk Shows," *Broadcasting*, December 14, 1992, 22–23.

31   "King World Agrees to Pay $150 Million in 'Oprah' Deal," *Wall Street Journal*, September 25, 1998, B7. Her contract was then renegotiated and extended to 2004.

32   Of the $200 million, King World banks roughly 35 percent for distribution fees. Cynthia Littleton, "Oprah to Talk through '02," *Variety*, September 28–October 4, 1998, 69.

33   Richard Katz and Cynthia Littleton, "Oxygen Moves Forward with Oprah," *Variety*, November 30–December 6, 1998, 25.

34   Littleton, "Oprah to Talk," 69.

35   Stephen Braun, "The Oprah Seal of Approval," *Los Angeles Times*, March 9, 1997, Calendar sec., 81.

36   Ibid.

37   Winfrey's Web presence is ubiquitous. A Google search for "Oprah Winfrey" brings up more than 105,000 pages. See, among others, a tribute to her by a fan <http://www.geocities.com/Hollywood/Lot/2891/oprah.html> (accessed November 19, 2001); and Mr. Showbiz's biographies on entertainers et al. like Oprah <http://www.mrshowbiz.go.com/celebrities/people/oprahwinfrey/index.html> (accessed October 2000); to find *The Oprah Winfrey Show* on international television schedules, see <http://www.eurotv.com/rtv5.htm> (accessed November 19, 2001).

38   See John Fiske, "The Cultural Economy of Fandom," in *The Adoring Audience: Fan Culture and Popular Media*, ed. Lisa A. Lewis (London: Routledge, 1992), 30.

39   James R. Walker, "More Than Meets the Ear: A Factor Analysis of Student Impressions of Television Talk Show Hosts," paper presented at the 74th

Annual Meeting of the Speech Communication Association, New Orleans, November 3–6, 1988, *ERIC*, ED 299630.

40   Richard Dyer, *Stars* (London: British Film Institute, 1979), 183.

41   Cloud, "Hegemony or Concordance?" 119.

42   An alternative version of King World and Winfrey's meeting suggests that her agent approached King World about distributing the program.

43   Du Bois, *Souls of Black Folk*, 14.

44   "Gun Control," *The Oprah Winfrey Show*, syndicated program, June 27, 1989.

45   Quoted in Thomas Morgan, "Oprah Winfrey: Troubled Youth to TV Host and Nominee," *New York Times*, March 4, 1986, 26.

46   As late as 1997, even in her slimmed-down, healthy version, Winfrey returned to her outreach mainstay, weight. In the March 5, 1997, *Oprah Winfrey Show* she retraced the moment she decided to change her lifestyle. She aired a portion of the skit done by the *In Living Color* cast satirizing her persona and the discussion of her weight around the dinner table in *The Nutty Professor* as different lows and highs of her weight roller coaster.

47   Jeremy G. Butler, "Redesigning Discourse," *Journal of Film and Video* 45, No. 1 (Spring 1993): 15.

48   This phrase comes from George Lipsitz, *The Possessive Investment in Whiteness: How White People Benefit from Identity Politics* (Philadelphia: Temple University Press, 1998).

49   Terry Eagleton, *Literary Theory: An Introduction* (Minneapolis: University of Minnesota Press, 1983), 101.

50   Peter Wollen, *Signs and Meaning in the Cinema* (Bloomington: Indiana University Press, 1972), 122.

51   Cloud, "Hegemony or Concordance?" 119.

52   "MTV Dance Party," *The Oprah Winfrey Show*, syndicated, August 7, 1991.

53   Dan Rubey, "Voguing at the Carnival" *South Atlantic Quarterly* 90, No. 4 (Spring 1997): 901–902.

54   Madonna's pussy is apparently so powerful that full texts are dedicated to its examination. See, e.g., Lisa Frank and Paul Smith, eds., *Madonnarama: Essays on Sex and Popular Culture* (Pittsburgh: Cleis, 1993); and Matthew Rettenmund, *Encyclopedia Madonnica* (New York: St. Martin's, 1995).

55   Andrew Ferguson, "Bad Girls Don't Cry," *National Review*, May 30, 1994, 72.

56   Albert J. Raboteau, "Fire in the Bones: African-American Christianity and Autobiographical Reflection," *America*, May 21, 1994, 4.

57   "The Sacrament of Penance," *New Advent*
     <http://www.newadvent.org/cathen/11618c.htm> (accessed July 22, 2001).

58   Morgan, "Oprah Winfrey," 26.

59   In 1995 Jonathan Schmitz murdered his best friend, Scott Amedure, three days after the two appeared on the *Jenny Jones* show. On the episode Amedure confessed that he had romantic feelings for Schmitz. Schmitz was convicted twice (the first time it was overturned) in 1999. Subsequently, the Amedure family won a $25 million lawsuit against *Jenny Jones* and its parent Warner Bros. in a Missouri court.

60 Quoted in Bob Longino, "Channel Surfer Oprah Exhorting Fans to 'Change Your Life,' " *Atlanta Journal and Constitution*, September 10, 1998, D6.

61 For proof of Winfrey's spiritual determination see her official Web site at <http://www.oprah.com>.

62 See "Christian Leaders Consult with Clinton," *Christian Century*, December 6, 1995, 1169.

63 "Oprah Winfrey," *Current Biography Yearbook* (New York: H. H. Wilson, 1987), 611. The writer compiled the biography from several sources, including the *Chicago Tribune, Ebony, New York Daily News, Miami Herald, Newsweek, Washington Post*, and Robert Waldon's book *Oprah!*

64 I thank Michelle Fang from my U.C.L.A. course, "Representations of Women of Color in Contemporary Visual Culture," Spring 1997, for alerting me to this discrepancy.

65 One key issue Black women noticed about Winfrey's Sophia was the color of her skin. As extensively discussed in two previous chapters, the melanin quotient always plays a role in the way Colored people perceive themselves and certainly in the way that they are visualized.

66 Jacqueline Bobo, *Black Women as Cultural Readers* (New York: Columbia University Press, 1995), 110.

67 Cooper-Lewter, *Soul Theology*, 1.

68 James Ayer, "Mark 3:20–35: Between Text and Sermon," *Interpretation: A Journal of Bible and Theology* 51, no. 2 (April 1997).

69 "Coming Out Day for Abusive Parents," *The Oprah Winfrey Show*, syndicated program, January 13, 1992.

70 Louise Kiernan, "Oprah's Poverty Program Stalls: Despite High Hopes, Only 5 Families Graduate in 2 Years," *Chicago Tribune*, August 27, 1996, N1.

71 In the opening Winfrey portrays a girl in her late teens or early twenties. The spectator may mark some incongruity as a result of the disparity between Winfrey's actual thirty-five-year-old body and the age of the character. Also, by the time the program ends, she appears to be seventy-five instead of the fifty that she should have been.

72 The film was the subject of twenty-four television news magazine pieces and eleven magazine covers. Frank Rich, "The Oprah Gap," *New York Times*, December 12, 1998, A21.

73 The first week *Beloved* garnered $8 million and placed number five in terms of box office receipts. By the end of the second week ticket sales had dropped 50 percent. Because films exploring African-American themes are marketed almost exclusively domestically, the film was a financial failure. "*Beloved* It's Not," *Economist*, November 21, 1998, 3–4.

74 Raphael Shargel, "Epic Mice," review of *Beloved, New Leader*, November 30, 1998, 18–19.

75 Rich, "Oprah Gap," A21.

76 For this academic view, see Epstein and Steinberg. "All Het Up!"

77 Tom Shales, "Oprah's Preachiness Becoming a Turn-Off," *Atlanta Journal and Constitution*, November 5, 1998, D6.

78 *Ricki Lake* began in 1993. The show targets a young audience but concentrates on the eighteen-to-thirty-four-year-old demographic.
79 Jill Nelson, "Talk Is Cheap," *Nation*, June 5, 1995, 800.

References

Ayer, James, "Mark 3:20–35: Between Text and Sermon," *Interpretation: A Journal of Bible and Theology* 51, No. 2 (April 1997).

Best, Steven and Kellner, Douglas, *Postmodern Theory: Critical Interrogations* (New York: Guilford, 1991).

Bobo, Jacqueline, *Black Women as Cultural Readers* (New York: Columbia University Press, 1995).

Braun, Stephen, "The Oprah Seal of Approval," *Los Angeles Times*, March 9, 1997.

Butler, Jeremy G. "Redesigning Discourse: Feminism, the Sitcom and Designing Women," *Journal of Film and Video* 45, No. 1 (Spring 1993): 13–26.

Churchill, Ward, "White Studies: The Intellectual Imperialism of U.S. Higher Education," in *Beyond Comfort Zones in Multiculturalism: Confronting the Politics of Privilege*, ed. Sandra Jackson and José Solis (Westport, Conn.: Bergin and Garvey, 1995): 17–36.

Cloud, Dana L, "Hegemony or Concordance? The Rhetoric of Tokenism in 'Oprah' Winfrey's Rags-to-Riches Biography," *Critical Studies in Mass Communication* 13, No. 2 (1996): 115–137.

Cooper-Lewter, Nicholas and Mitchell, Henry H, *Soul Theology: The Heart of American Black Culture* (San Francisco: Harper and Row, 1986).

Du Bois, W. E. B, *Souls of Black Folk* (Chicago: A.C. McClurg & Co., 1903).

Dyer, Richard, *Stars* (London: British Film Institute, 1979).

Eagleton, Terry, *Literary Theory: An Introduction* (Minneapolis: University of Minnesota Press, 1983).

Epstein, Debbie and Steinberg, Deborah Lynn, "All Het-Up! Rescuing Heterosexuality on the *Oprah Winfrey Show*," *Feminist Review* 54 (Autumn 1996): 88–115.

Ferguson, Andrew, "Bad Girls Don't Cry," *National Review*, May 30, 1994.

Fiske, John, "The Cultural Economy of Fandom," in *The Adoring Audience: Fan Culture and Popular Media*, ed. Lisa A. Lewis (London: Routledge, 1992): 30–49.

Frank, Lisa and Smith, Paul, eds., *Madonnarama: Essays on Sex and Popular Culture* (Pittsburgh: Cleis, 1993).

Gray, Herman, *Watching Race: Television and the Struggle for the Sign of Blackness* (Minneapolis: University of Minnesota Press, 1995).

Hagg, Laurie L, "Oprah Winfrey: The Construction of Intimacy in the Talk Show Setting," *Journal of Popular Culture* 26, No. 4 (Spring 1993).

Hinz, Evelyn J, "What is Multiculturalism? A 'Cognitive' Introduction," *Mosaic* 29, No. 3 (September 1996).

Katz, Richard and Littleton, Cynthia, "Oxygen Moves Forward with Oprah," *Variety*, November 30–December 6, 1998.

Kiernan, Louise, "Oprah's Poverty Program Stalls," *Chicago Tribune*, August 27, 1996.

La Franco, Robert and McHugh, Josh, "Piranha is Good," *Forbes*, October 16, 1995.

Lipsitz, George, *The Possessive Investment in Whiteness: How White People Benefit from Identity Politics* (Philadelphia: Temple University Press, 1998).

Littleton, Cynthia, "Oprah to Talk Through '02," *Variety*, September 28–October 4, 1998.

Longino, Bob, "Channel Surfer Oprah Exhorting Fans to 'Change Your Life'," *Atlanta Journal and Constitution*, September 10, 1998.

Masciarotte, Gloria-Jean, "C'mon, Girl: Oprah Winfrey and the Discourse of Feminine Talk," *Genders* 11 (Fall 1991): 81–100.

McClellan, Steve, "Look Who's Talking: Potential for High Ratings at Relatively Low Cost Attracts New Talk Shows," *Broadcasting*, December 14, 1992.

Morgan, Thomas, "Oprah Winfrey: Troubled Youth to TV Host and Nominee," *New York Times*, March 4, 1986.

Munson, Wayne, *All Talk: The Talkshow in Media Culture* (Philadephia: Temple University Press, 1993).

Nelson, Jill, "Talk is Cheap," *Nation*, June 5, 1995.

Peck, Janice, "Talk About Racism: Framing a Popular Discourse of Race on Oprah Winfrey," *Cultural Critique 27* (Spring 1994): 89–126.

Raboteau, Albert J., "Fire in the Bones: African-American Christianity and Autobiographical Reflection," *America*, May 21, 1994.

Rettenmund, Matthew, *Encyclopedia Madonnica* (New York: St. Martin's, 1995).

Rich, Frank, "The Oprah Gap," *New York Times*, December 12, 1998.

Rubey, Dan, "Voguing at the Carnival: Desire and Pleasure on MTV," *South Atlantic Quarterly* 90, No. 4 (Spring 1997): 871–906.

Shargel, Raphael, "Epic Mice," *New Leader*, November 30, 1998.

Shales, Tom, "Oprah's Preachiness Becoming a Turn-Off," *Atlanta Journal and Constitution*, November 5, 1998.

Truth, Sojourner. *Narrative of Sojourner Truth* (Boston: printed for the author, 1850).

Walker, James R, "More Than Meets the Ear: A Factor Analysis of Student Impressions of Television Talk Show Hosts," paper presented at the 74th Annual Meeting of the Speech Communication Association, New Orleans, November 3–6, 1988.

Welles Sara, "Taming the TV Talk Show," *Television Quarterly* 28, No.3 (Summer 1996): 41–48.

White, Mimi, *Tele-Advising: Therapeutic Discourse in American Television* (Chapel Hill: University of North Carolina Press, 1992).

Wollen, Peter, *Signs and Meaning in the Cinema* (Bloomington: Indiana University Press, 1972).

7

"Take Responsibility for Yourself"
Judge Judy and the neoliberal citizen

Laurie Ouellette

Originally published in Susan Murray and Laurie Ouellette (eds), *Reality TV: Remaking Television Culture* (New York: New York University Press, 2004), 231–250.

A woman drags her ex-boyfriend to court over an overdue adult movie rental and unpaid loan. A woman is heartbroken when her best friend betrays her and ruins her credit. A smooth-talking ex-boyfriend claims money from his ex was a gift. Welcome to *Judge Judy*, queen of the courtroom program, where judges resolve "real-life" disputes between friends, neighbors, family members, roommates, and lovers on national television. For critics who equate television's role in democracy with serious news and public affairs, altercations over broken engagements, minor fender benders, carpet stains, unpaid personal loans, and the fate of jointly purchased household appliances may seem like crass entertainment or trival distractions. But such dismissals overlook the "governmental" nature of courtroom programs like *Judge Judy*, which gained cultural presence – and a reputation for "zero tolerance when it comes to nonsense" – alongside the neoliberal policies and discourses of the 1990s.[1]

Judge Judy took the small claims-based court format from the fringes of commercial syndication to an authoritative place on daytime schedules when it debuted in 1996, the same year the U.S. Telecommunications Act was passed.[2] While the legislation has been critiqued for its deregulatory ethos as well as its affinity with the broader neoliberal forces behind welfare reform and the privatization of public institutions from the penal system to the post office, the cultural dimensions of these parallels remain less examined.[3] There is a tendency within policy studies to take the cultural impact of neoliberalism as self-evident – to presume that the laissez-faire principles codified by the Act will erode democracy in predictable ways that typically involve the decline of journalism, documentaries, and other "substantial" information formats found unprofitable by the culture industries. While such concerns have some validity, the metaphor of subversion needs to be jettisoned, for it reifies untenable cultural hierarchies, and neglects neoliberalism's productive imprint on contemporary television culture and the "idealized" citizen subjectivities that it circulates.

Reality programming is one site where neoliberal approaches to citizenship have in fact materialized on television. From makeover programs (such as *What Not to*

Wear and *Trading Spaces*) that enlist friends, neighbors, and experts in their quest to teach people how to make "better" decorating and fashion choices, to gamedocs (like *Survivor* and *Big Brother*) that construct community relations in terms of individual competition and self-enterprising, neoliberal constructions of "good citizenship" cut across much popular reality television. The courtroom program is a particularly clear example of this broader trend because it draws from the symbolic authority of the state to promote both the outsourcing of its governmental functions and the subjective requirements of the transition to a neoliberal society. *Judge Judy* and programs like it do not subvert elusive democratic ideals, then, as much as they *construct* templates for citizenship that complement the privatization of public life, the collapse of the welfare state, and most important, the discourse of individual choice and personal responsibility.

This chapter situates *Judge Judy* as a neoliberal technology of everyday citizenship, and shows how it attempts to shape and guide the conduct and choices of lower-income women in particular. As we shall see, *Judge Judy* draws from and diffuses neoliberal currents by fusing an image of democracy (signified in the opening credits by a gently flapping U.S. flag, stately public courthouse, and gavel-wielding judge) with a privatized approach to conflict management and an intensified government of the self. *Judge Judy* and programs like it supplant institutions of the state (for instance, social work, law and order, and welfare offices), and using real people caught in the drama of ordinary life as raw material, train TV viewers to function without state assistance or supervision as self-disciplining self-sufficient, responsible, and risk-averting individuals. In this way, the courtroom subgenre of reality TV exemplifies what James Hay has called a cultural apparatus for "neoliberal forms of governance."[4]

Neoliberalism and television culture

To understand *Judge Judy*'s neoliberal alignments, a brief detour through the concept of neoliberalism is in order. My understanding of neoliberalism begins with political economy and the activism it inspires. From this vantage point, neoliberalism is generally understood as a troubling worldview that promotes the "free" market as the best way to organize every dimension of social life. According to activists Elizabeth Martinez and Arnoldo Garcia, this worldview has generated five trends that have accelerated globally since the 1980s: the "rule" of the market; spending cuts on public services; deregulation (including the deregulation of broadcasting); the privatization of state-owned institutions, "usually in the name of efficiency"; and "eliminating the concept of the public good or community and replacing it with individual responsibility."[5] For critics like Robert McChesney, the upshot of neoliberalism and the reforms it has spawned is that a "handful of private interests are permitted to control as much as possible of social life in order to maximize their personal profit."[6]

While I share these concerns, I have found Foucauldian approaches particularly useful for analyzing the subjective dimensions of neoliberalism that circulate on reality TV. Drawing from Michel Foucault, Nikolas Rose theorizes neoliberalism less as a simple opposition between the market (bad) and welfare state (good) than as a "changing network" of complex power relations. If neoliberal regimes have implemented an "array of measures" aimed at downsizing the welfare state and dismantling the "insitutions within which welfare government had isolated and managed their social problems," they still rely on "strategies of government."[7] This manifests as various forms of "cultural training" that govern indirectly in the name of "lifestyle maximization," "free choice," and personal responsibility, says Rose. This diffused approach to the "regulation of conduct" escapes association with a clear or top-down agenda, and is instead presented as the individual's "own desire" to achieve optimum happiness and success. As Rose points out, the "enterprising" individual crafted by this discourse has much in common with the choice-making "customer" valorized by neoliberal economics. Both presume "free will," which means that those individuals who fail to thrive under neoliberal conditions can be readily cast as the "author of their own misfortunes."[8]

Rose makes several additional observations that can help to illuminate neoliberalism's cultural manifestations. First, he contends that the ideal of citizens working together to fulfill mutual and "national obligations" has given way to the "ideal of citizens seeking to fulfill and protect themselves within a variety of micro-moral domains." Second, he observes that the requirements of "good" citizenship have come to include adopting a "prudent" relationship to fate, which includes avoiding "calculable dangers and avertable risks." Finally, Rose cites the media as a cultural technology operating outside "public powers" that works to govern the "capacities, competencies and wills of subjects," and in so doing, translate the goals of "authorities" into the "choices and commitments of individuals."[9]

James Hay has extended this argument to television studies specifically. Because a "neoliberal form of governance assumes that social subjects are not and should not be subject to direct forms of state control, it therefore relies on mechanisms for governing at a distance," through the guiding and shaping of "self-disciplining subjects," Hay explains. Television plays an important role in this governmental process, he contends, one that is not limited to sanctioned forms of news and public affairs. In fact, popular reality TV may be better suited to the indirect, diffuse mode of cultural governmentality that Hay describes. The court program is an acute and therefore symptomatic example of popular reality TV's role in mediating, as Hay puts it, "a kind of state control that values self-sufficiency and a kind of personal freedom that requires self-discipline."[10]

While Hay theorizes television's part in bringing neoliberal techniques of "governmentality" into the home, feminist scholars have shown the extent to which neoliberal policies intersect with an acceleration of self-help discourse aimed at women. From advice books on intimate relationships to self-esteem-building initiatives for welfare mothers, this discourse has been critiqued for presuming to "solve social problems from crime and poverty to gender inequality by waging a social revolution, not against capitalism, racism and inequality, but against the order of the self and the way we govern the self."[11] As Barbara Cruikshank has pointed out, the solution to women's problems is construed as having the right attitude, making smart decisions, and taking responsibility for one's life in the name of personal "empowerment."[12] In this sense, self-help is a cultural manifestation of neoliberalism, a technology of citizenship that encourages women to "evaluate and act" on themselves so that the social workers, medical establishment, and police "do not have to."[13]

Judge Judy fuses television, neoliberalism, and self-help discourse in a governmental address to women living out what feminist philosopher Nancy Fraser has called the "postsocialist" condition.[14] The program presents the privatized space of the TV courtroom as the most "efficient" way to resolve microdisputes steeped in the unacknowledged politics of gender, class, and race, but it also classifies those individuals who "waste the court's time" as risky deviants and self-made victims who create their own misfortunes by making the "wrong" choices and failing to manage their lives properly. The imagined TV viewer is the implied beneficiary of this litany of mistakes, for one's classification as "normal" hinges on both recognizing the pathos of "others" and internalizing the rules of self-government spelled out on the program. The courtroom program has, for precisely this reason, been institutionally positioned as a moral and educational corrective to "permissive" entertainment, suggesting that the discourse of the "public interest" in broadcasting has not been squashed but rather reconfigured by neoliberal reforms. Indeed, it could be that television is increasingly pivotal to neoliberal approaches to government and the citizen subjectivities on which they depend.

"The cases are real, the rulings are final"

Judge Judy is not the first television program to resolve everyday microconflicts in simulated courtroom settings. The genre can be traced to 1950s programs like *People in Conflict* and *The Verdict Is Yours*. In the 1980s, retired California Superior Court judge Joseph Wapner presided over *The People's Court*, while *Divorce Court* used actors to dramatize "real" legal proceedings.[15] *Judge Judy* did, however, rework and revitalize the format, and the program's "no-nonsense" approach to family and small claims disputes generated notoriety and imitators (examples include *Judge Joe Brown*, *Judge Mathis*, *Judge Hatchet*, *Curtis Court*, a revitalized *People's Court*, and *Moral Court*). Well into the new millennium, courtroom programs abound on television, competing with talk shows, game shows, and soap operas for a predominantly female audience.

On *Judge Judy*, real-life litigants are offered travel costs and court fees to present their cases on national television. The price is to drop out of the public judicial process and submit to the private ruling of Judith (Judy) Sheindlin. A former New York family court judge, Sheindlin was recruited for the "tough-love" philosophy she first spelled out in an influential *60 Minutes* profile, and later expanded on in her best-selling book *Don't Pee on My Leg and Tell Me It's Raining*, which faulted the overcrowded court system as a lenient bureaucracy that reflects "how far we have strayed from personal responsibility and old-fashioned discipline."[16] Spotting ratings potential, Larry Lyttle, president of Big Ticket Television, a Viacom company, invited Sheindlin to preside over "real cases with real consequences in a courtroom on television." Called a "swift decision maker with no tolerance for excuses" by the program's publicity, Sheindlin claims to bring to her TV show the same message she advocated in the courts: "Take responsibility for yourself, your actions and the children you've brought into the world."[17] In interviews, she situates *Judge Judy* as a public service that can solve societal problems by instilling the right attitudes and choices in individuals:

It's a much larger audience. Whatever message I spew – "Take responsibility for your life. If you're a victim, it's your fault. Stop being a victim. Get a grip! You're the one who's supposed to make a direction in your life." All those messages I tried in Family Court to instill in people – primarily women. [The TV show] sounded like something that would not only be fun, but worthwhile as well.[18]

Like other TV judges, Sheindlin now hears noncriminal disputes that rarely exceed several hundred dollars or the equivalent in personal property. While these conflicts often speak to broader social tensions and inequalities, the program's governmental logic frames the cases as "petty squabbles" brought about by the deficiencies of individuals. Sheindlin's courtroom is filled with feuding relations and typically devoid of people who wish to sue businesses, bosses, or least of all, big corporations. This focus makes perfect sense, for the program's impetus as a technology of citizenship is to scrutinize ordinary people who require state mediation of everyday affairs, a process that hinges more on the moral radar Sheindlin claims to have developed in the public court system than on time-consuming democratic processes (she has been known to snap, "I don't have time for beginnings" and "I don't read documents"). While TV viewers are situated outside Sheindlin's disciplinary address to litigants derided as losers, cheaters, liars, and "gumbos," their status as "good" citizens presumes the desire to adhere to the neoliberal templates for living she espouses.

While the opening credits promise "real people" involved in "real cases," a male narrator differentiates the program from the public court system with the reminder: "This is Judy's courtroom," where the "decisions are final." Onscreen, Sheindlin plays judge, prosecutor, professional expert, and punctilious moral authority, handling an average of two cases per thirty-minute episode and dispensing justice at "lightning speed," according to the program's publicity. Participants must abide by the program's rules, which include speaking only when spoken to, accepting the authority of the judge ("Just pay attention, I run the show," she tells litigants), and taking humiliating remarks and reprimands without rebuttal or comment ("Are you all nuts?" and "I'm smarter than you" are typical examples). More important than the details of any particular case is Sheindlin's swift assessment of the choices and behaviors of the people involved in them. Just as, according to Foucault, the delinquent is characterized not so much by their "acts" as by their life biography, Sheindlin questions litigants about their employment history, marital and parental status, income, drug habits, sexual practices, incarceration record, and past or present "dependency" on public welfare.[19] Such information transcends the evaluation of evidence as the principal means whereby Sheindlin determines who is at fault in the citizenship lesson that accompanies every ruling. Sheindlin is also known to belittle the accents of non-English speakers, accuse litigants of lying and abusing the "system," and order individuals to spit out gum, stand up straight, and "control" bodily functions to her liking. In one episode, a male litigant who denied her accusations of pot smoking was ordered to take a live drug test. *Judge Judy* thus both duplicates and extends the surveillance of the poor and working class carried out by welfare offices, unemployment centers, and other social services.[20]

Judge Judy is part of the current wave of reality TV in that "real" people (not actors) involved in "authentic" disagreements are used as a selling point to differentiate the show from fictional entertainment. While scripts are not used, reality is, as John Fiske reminds us, "encoded" at every level.[21] The program scours small claims dockets for potentially "interesting" cases; would-be litigants must complete a questionnaire, and only those "actual" disputes that can be situated within the program's logic are presented on television. Offscreen narration, graphic titles, video replays, and teasers further frame the meaning of the cases by labeling the litigants, characterizing their purportedly real motivations to viewers and highlighting scenes from the program that reiterate Sheindlin's governmental authority. Due to increased competition for conflicts among the growing cadre of courtroom programs, viewers are now invited to bypass the courts altogether and submit their everyday disputes directly to *Judge Judy*. On-air solicitations like "Are You in a Family Dispute? Call Judy" promise an efficient, private alternative to public mediation of conflicts – and yet, individuals who accept the invitations are ultimately held responsible for their "mistakes" on cases like "The Making of a Family Tragedy."

Judge Judy's focus on everyday domestic conflicts has led some critics to denounce the courtroom program as a new twist on the sensational "low brow" daytime talk show.[22] Yet Sheindlin insists that her program is a somber alternative to the participatory, carnivalesque atmosphere of the genre it now rivals in the ratings. Indeed, the court setting and overtly disciplinary address of the *Judge Judy* program "code" it in distinct ways that are easily distinguishable to TV viewers. Sheindlin's strict demeanor and authoritative place on the bench are accentuated by camerawork that magnifies her power by filming her from below. The silence of the studio audience, the drab, institutional-like setting of the simulated courtroom, and the presence of a uniformed bailiff also separate the court program from talk shows, a format that feminist scholars have characterized as a tentative space for oppressed groups (women, people of color, and the working classes) to discuss the politics of everyday life. Jane Shattuc, for example, sees talk shows as an offshoot of the social movements of the 1960s to the extent that they draw from (but also commercially exploit) identity politics, consciousness-raising techniques, and an awareness that the "personal is political."[23] For Sonia Livingstone and Peter Lunt, talk shows offer a counterpoint to the white, male, bourgeois-dominated sphere of "serious" news and public affairs; talk shows provide a popular forum that enables women in particular to participate, however haltingly, in democratic processes.[24] Of course, talk shows also operate with their own disciplinary dynamics, as Janice Peck has shown. Relying on psychosocial experts (such as health workers, therapists, or self-help gurus), talk shows present a "televised talking cure" that "manages conflict and crisis" by folding women's personal stories into a "confessional" discourse and "therapeutic" narratives, she contends.[25]

As Mimi White has observed in her analysis of *Divorce Court*, court programs reconfigure the confessional/therapeutic orientation of the talk show in subtle, but important ways: "To the extent that the couple no longer confesses with ease, the injunction to confess must be enforced through the agencies of the . . . legal establishment."[26] On *Judge Judy*, the authority represented by the simulated courtroom setting is often enlisted to "force" such confessions. Sheindlin claims that her past experience as a frustrated state official has enabled her to "see through the bull" ("She can always tell if you're lying. All she has to do is make eye contact," reported *USA Today*). Litigants who refuse to "confess" to suspected actions have been subjected to live background checks, but more often than not Sheindlin simply discounts "false" confessions and replaces the version of events offered by the litigant with an expert interpretation gleaned through biographical information as much as "evidence."

Court programs also magnify the disciplinary logic present on the talk show by disallowing audience participation, controlling the flow of personal revelations, and fusing the therapeutic ethos of the "clinic" with the surveillance of the welfare office and the authoritative signifiers of law and order. This distinction, as much as the absence of the carnivalesque, is what has allowed courtroom programs to be institutionally positioned as a cultural corrective to "tabloid" television. *Judge Judy* is the "antithesis of Jerry Springer," insists Sheindlin. "Jerry Springer encourages people to show off their filthiest laundry, to misbehave. I scrupulously avoid doing that. I cut them off."[27]

The television industry has also been quick to assert that courtroom television "educates" as well as entertains – a claim to public service that is rarely made of most popular reality formats. Big Ticket's Larry Lyttle maintains that courtroom programs function as a positive moral force because unlike on talk shows, where "conflicts are aired and tossed around," a court show like *Judge Judy* "ends with a decision that someone was right and someone was wrong."[28] WCHS-TV in Charleston, West Virginia, similarly praises the program's "unique ability to act as a true moral compass for people seeking guidance, insight and resolution."[29] Characterizing the courtroom genre as a technology of citizenship that can temper the "effects" of fictional television, one TV judge explained in an interview that

> America's been looking at soap operas for going on 50 some years, and they legitimize the most back-stabbing, low-down, slimeball behavior. That's gotten to be acceptable behavior. . . . We find ourselves confronted with a lot of soap-opera behavior in our courtrooms. And we resolve them and say, no, we know you may have seen this, but it's not right.[30]

Privatizing justice, stigmatizing "dependency"

Judge Judy's claim to facilitate "justice at lightning speed" boldly implies that commercial television can resolve problems faster and more efficiently than the public sector. In this sense, the program affirms neoliberal, rationales for "outsourcing" state-owned institutions and services. *Judge Judy* also complements neoliberal policies by conveying the impression that democracy (exemplified by the justice system) is overrun by individuals embroiled in petty conflicts and troubles of their own making. If the program feeds off of real-life microdisputes, Sheindlin chastises litigants for failing to govern their "selves" and their personal affairs. In addition to lecturing guests about their personal history, she often accuses participants of "wasting the court's time," conveying the idea that "normal" citizens do not depend on the supervision of the judiciary or any public institution for that matter. People who rely on professional judges (including TV judges) to mediate everyday problems are cast as inadequate individuals who lack the capacity or, worse, desire to function as self-reliant and personally responsible citizens.

On *Judge Judy*, citizenship lessons are often directed at people who reject marriage, the nuclear family, and traditional values; unmarried couples who live together are of particular concern. While Sheindlin (who is divorced) does not condemn such behavior as moral disconduct, she does present rules and procedures for navigating modern relationships, which include getting personal loans in writing, not "living together for more than one year without a wedding band," and not "purchasing homes, cars, boats or animals with romantic partners outside of wedlock."[31] On *Judge Judy*, individuals are told that they must impose these rules on themselves – both for their own protection and because, as Sheindlin explains, there is "no court of people living together. It's up to you to be smart. Plan for the eventualities before you set up housekeeping." When former lovers dispute an unpaid car loan, Sheindlin takes the disagreement as an opportunity to explain the dos and don'ts of cohabitation without marriage. Sheindlin finds the couple incompatible and "irresponsible," and rules that it was an "error of judgment" for them to share an apartment together. This judgment is tied to a broader failure of appropriate citizenship when Sheindlin lectures the pair for then "asking the courts" to resolve a domestic property dispute. "You're not married – there is a different set of rules for people who choose to live together without marriage," she asserts, reiterating that people who stray from state-sanctioned conventions have a particular duty to monitor their own affairs.

If the idealized citizen-subject constructed by *Judge Judy* complements the choice-making neoliberal customer discussed by Rose, that individual is also a self-supporting worker. People who receive any form of public assistance are cast as deviants in particular need of citizenship lessons. The advice they receive evokes Nancy Fraser and Linda Gordon's observation that welfare has become cloaked in a stigmatizing discourse of "dependency" that presumes gender, class, and racial parity. As Fraser and Gordon point out, women (including single mothers) are now held accountable to the white, middle-class, male work ethic, even as they lack the advantages and resources to perform as traditionally male breadwinners. While this marks a shift away from the patronizing assumption that all women are helpless and therefore "naturally" dependent on men or, in their absence, the state, it conceals the structural inequalities that lower-income women in particular continue to face.[32] On *Judge Judy*, all women are presumed to be capable of supporting themselves and their children financially; accepting welfare is construed not as a reflection of gender or economic inequality but as a character flaw. Women are routinely asked to disclose their past or present reliance on government "handouts," and those who admit to receiving benefits are subsequently marked as irresponsible and lazy individuals who "choose" not to work for a living. Welfare recipients are also constructed as morally unsound citizens who cheat taxpayers, as was the case in an episode where Sheindlin demanded to know whether an unmarried woman with three children by the same father had "avoided" marriage merely to qualify for welfare benefits. In another episode, an unemployed twenty-something mother being sued by her baby's would-be adoptive parents was scolded for relying on public assistance to raise the child she had decided not to give up for adoption. While adoption law doesn't allow adoptive parents to reclaim monetary "gifts" to birth mothers, Sheindlin stressed the woman's "moral" obligation to repay them. Presuming that the mother had chosen poverty, Sheindlin also sternly advised her to get a job and "not have more babies she can't take care of."

Judge Judy's disdain for so-called welfare dependency extends to charity and other forms of assistance. If individuals are told to take care of themselves and their families, empathy and social responsibility for others are discouraged. "No good deed goes unpunished," Sheindlin advised a family friend who took in a homeless woman who had spent some time in jail. At the societal and community level, the public good is cast in neoliberal terms, as a system of individual responsibilities and rewards.

According to Rose, neoliberal citizens are conceived of as private individuals who must ensure their own well-being through risk management strategies and prudent "acts of choice."[33] *Judge Judy* instills this template for citizenship by discouraging personal contact with deviant and allegedly risky individuals, and by instructing women to make "smart" choices to avoid "victimization." The program functions as a "panoptic" device to the extent that it classifies and surveils individuals deemed unsavory and dangerous.[34] This same point has also been made of reality-based crime shows like *Cops* and *America's Most Wanted*.[35] Sheindlin contends that criminals are largely unreformable, and *Judge Judy* extends this philosophy to people who are not official criminals but are nonetheless judged to possess amoral tendencies, psychological imbalances, drug addictions, and other character flaws. The more pressing message, however, is that all citizens must take personal responsibility for protecting themselves from con artists, "manipulators," abusers, and other risky individuals. In this sense, one of the program's most important governmental roles is to instruct TV viewers how to detect and avoid the risks that certain individuals are shown to represent.

Since the litigants on *Judge Judy* are introduced by name and occupation – this information also appears in onscreen titles – viewers know that individuals cast as risky are often working-class men who drive trucks, wait on tables, enter data, do construction, or perform low-paying forms of customer service. If female welfare recipients are cast as irresponsible nonworkers, men lacking middle-class occupations and salaries are routinely scorned for "choosing" a life of poverty, as was the case when Sheindlin lectured a middle-aged male Wal-Mart cashier for failing to obtain more lucrative employment. In the adoption episode mentioned above, a similar evaluation of male employment was tied to a failure of citizenship. The infant's father, who had worked on and off as a gas station attendant but was currently unemployed, was characterized as a personal failure and societal menace, not just because he refused to admit "personal moral responsibility" to repay the money to the adoptive parents but because he "refused" to enterprise himself in accordance with the middle-class work ethic.

Cases involving men who manipulate women out of money, gifts, rent, or property are a staple on *Judge Judy*, and in these cases, male unemployment and insolvency are closely tied to the detection and avoidance of romantic risk. In a case where a woman met a man on the Internet, loaned him money, and was dumped, Sheindlin fused a harsh judgment of the boyfriend's opportunism and dishonesty in his romantic relationship to an undeveloped work ethic. Demanding to know when he last "held a full-time job," she swiftly identified the man as a freeloader and "con artist," implying that men without economic means are especially dangerous and therefore not to be trusted when it comes to intimate relationships. Female litigants can also be categorized as identifiable romantic risks, as was the case in "Opportunity Knocks," where Sheindlin accused an attractive young woman in court to resolve whether money from her ex-boyfriend was a gift or loan of "using" the man financially with "no intention of marrying him." In most cases, though, it is lower-income men who play this role in a gender reversal of the gold digger stereotype that complements the program's focus on solving the problem of female victimization through better self-management.

Women are typically cast as "self-created" victims in terms that articulate neoliberal currents to female self-help culture. Rejecting what she terms the "disease of victimization" or tendency to blame society for one's hardships, Sheindlin claims, in her books and on her TV program, that all women can achieve happiness and success with a little knowledge along with the right attitude. On *Judge Judy*, women's problems are blamed on their own failure to make good decisions, whether that means pulling one's self up from a life of poverty, "preparing" wisely for financial independence, or avoiding entanglements with unstable, manipulative, or abusive individuals. In her book *Beauty Fades, Dumb Is Forever*, Sheindlin elaborates on the value of personal responsibility, contending that

> victims are self-made. They aren't born. They aren't created by circumstances. There are many, many poor, disadvantaged people who had terrible parents and suffered great hardships who do just fine. Some even rise to the level of greatness. You are responsible for nurturing your roots, for blooming. No one can take that away from you. If you decide to be a victim, the destruction of your life will be by your own hand.[36]

In some cases, female "victims" are lectured for allowing themselves to be mistreated by other women. In "The Kool-Aid Debacle," where a young waitress sued her female ex-roommate over Kool-Aid stains on the carpet and a couch that got smelly, Sheindlin scolded the plaintiff for getting herself into such a situation: "You make a mistake when you let someone into your house who is a slob," she explained. Other times, women are deemed responsible for making their own misfortunes. In a case involving former lovers at odds over an unpaid loan, the program's neoliberal dismissal of female victimization is spelled out. The woman claims that her ex-boyfriend helped cover her hospital bill when she miscarried their baby. The man asserts that she promised to pay him back. As is typical, Sheindlin focuses less on the details of the loan than on the moral and behavioral lessons she discerns from the case. She lectures the young woman (but not the man) for not using birth control, and attributes her "situation" to her own unwise and irresponsible conduct. Refusing to accept this ruling, the young woman insists that the ex-boyfriend should help pay for the cost of the miscarriage since she was uninsured and it "was his baby too." Defying Sheindlin's orders to speak only when addressed, she demands to know what *she* as a woman would do in such circumstances, Rejecting the female litigant's appeal to a sense of female solidarity on the question – and ignoring the broader issue of health care access raised by the episode – Sheindlin tells the litigant that she wouldn't be in her shoes because she's "smarter than that."

Women who claim to have been abused by men appear frequently on *Judge Judy*, where they too are lectured for creating their circumstances. Domestic abuse is never the basis of a legal case, but is typically revealed in the course of Sheindlin's interrogation of the participants involved. In a case involving cousins fighting over a family collection of knick-knacks, Sheindlin determines that the man is a deranged and unstable individual, while the woman he bullied and harassed is an "adult" who has "chosen to let someone do this to her." When Sheindlin learns that an ex-boyfriend in court over a minor car accident has battered his former teenage girlfriend, she maintains that the girl made unwise "choices," sternly advising, "Never let a man put his hands on you." In a case involving former lovers disputing overdue phone and gas bills, the woman reveals that in refusing to pay household expenses, her former boyfriend was addicted to heroin and had spent time in jail for assaulting a minor. She also implies that he physically abused her. Typifying the program's neoliberal solution to the problem of domestic violence as well as the complexities of gender and class, Sheindlin faults the woman for failing to accept responsibility for her own conduct. Taking the troubled relationship as the raw material for a citizenship lesson aimed at women, Sheindlin determines that "being with him doesn't speak well of your judgment." As "young as you are, you allowed someone with a criminal history and no job to live with you . . . and you want the courts to fix that?"

Judge Judy seeks to instill in women a desire to avoid the "disease" of victimization along with the overreliance on state assistance and intervention it is said to have spawned. This message carries traces of liberal feminist discourse to the extent that it promotes female independence and agency. Presuming that barriers to social and gender equality have long been dismantled, the program places the onus to achieve these goals on individuals. Sheindlin, who considers herself a positive female role model, contends that all "women have the power to make decisions, to call it as they see it, to take no gruff."[37] She claims that all women, however positioned by an unequal capitalist society, can reap the benefits of happiness and success so long as they exercise good judgment and cultivate self-esteem. Economic security and "feeling good about yourself" are thus closely bound in Sheindlin's blueprint for successful female citizenship. The responsibility for cultivating self-esteem is placed not on society but on individual women, whose job it is to train themselves and their daughters "to have a profession, have a career . . . so they will never be dependent on anybody."[38] On *Judge Judy*, female litigants are advised to avoid "depending" on boyfriends and husbands for financial assistance in particular. This message has less to do with dismantling dominant ideologies and institutions than it does with ensuring that women "take care of themselves" so that the state doesn't have to. *Judge Judy* conveys the idea that women can no longer "claim" a victim status rooted in bifurcated and hierarchical gender roles; nor, however, can they expect public solutions to the inequalities that structure women's lives.

Sheindlin presents "independence" as a responsibility that all women must strive to achieve, but she also promotes the hegemony of the nuclear family, reconstituted as a two-wage-earning unit. Family troubles underscore many of the cases heard on *Judge Judy*, where mothers suing daughters, children suing their parents, and parents suing each other are the norm. This steady stream of feuding relations paints a portrait of a troubled institution that clearly isn't working, yet Sheindlin uses her authority to promote the sacred importance of family bonds. The contradiction exists in perpetual tension, as illuminated by the treatment of family in two key episodes. In the first, a male cashier is suing his unemployed ex-fiancée for bills paid when they lived together; she is countersuing for "mental distress." After Sheindlin interrogates the woman about why she wasn't working at the time, the woman replies that she quit her job to "build a home together." She also tells Sheindlin that her fiancé stalked her and threatened to come after her with a gun when they broke up. Although this scenario contains the material to cast the male as a deviant individual, Sheindlin rejects the woman's story as an "excuse" smacking of victimization. Comparing her own success as a married working woman who didn't "quit her job to pick out furniture and dishes" to the failure of the "alleged victim of harassment," she orders the woman to pay the back rent. In this episode, the female litigant's embrace of traditional family values is denounced because it includes the desire for "dependency" on a male bread-winner, thereby violating the neoliberal mantra of self-sufficiency that *Judge Judy* espouses. In a dispute involving an estranged mother and daughter, though, the nuclear family is valorized against a woman's quest for independence. The mother, who divorced her husband when she came out as a lesbian, is implicitly cast as selfish and irresponsible for abandoning the heterosexual family unit to pursue her own personal fulfillment. While Sheindlin doesn't condemn the woman's homosexuality, she harshly criticizes her performance and "choices" as a mother, and recommends family counseling to repair the damage. As these examples attest, *Judge Judy*'s advice to women does not seek to expand women's choices, it merely guides them in particu-lar directions. Operating as a technology of citizenship, the program steers women toward neoliberal reforms that are presented as their own responsibilities and in their own "best interests." In this sense, *Judge Judy* seeks to transform what Rose calls the "goals of authorities" into the "choices and commitments of individuals."[39]

Judge Judy and the normative citizen

Judge Judy constitutes the normative citizen – the TV viewer at home – in opposition to both risky deviants and "self-made" victims. By scrutinizing the dos and don'ts of everyday life as it is presumed to be lived by "troubled" populations, it promotes neoliberal policies for conducting one's self in private. It scapegoats the uneducated and unprivileged as "others" who manufacture their hardships, and thus, require nothing more than personal responsibility and self-discipline in the wake of shrinking public services. Those who reject this logic are deemed abnormal and often unre-formable: "I'm not going to get through to her. I have a sense that she's a lost cause at fourteen," Sheindlin once said of a female litigant.[40] TV viewers are encouraged to distance themselves from the "deficient" individuals who seep into Sheindlin's court-room, therefore avoiding any recognition of the societal basis of women's problems and concerns. While Sheindlin's harshest derision is aimed at the socially "unrespect-able," her governmental advice is intended for all women – particularly middle-class viewers – for according to the program's neoliberal logic, their happiness and success hinge on it.

It is untenable to presume that viewers respond to *Judge Judy* in seamless or uniform ways. The program can be read as an authoritarian spectacle that unravels what Foucault has called the "ideology of bourgeois justice." The running parody of *Judge Judy* on *Saturday Night Live*, where Sheindlin is portrayed as an exaggerated version of her insulting, authoritarian television persona, suggests that *Judge Judy* may partly dislodge an image of the courts as inherently objective and fair.[41] Women on the wrong end of unequal class and gender relations may also see in *Judge Judy* a glaring example of class prejudice and professional gumption. Yet these possibilities do not prevent the program from exemplifying a neoliberal form of governing that in various dimensions and forms, cuts across the newest wave of reality TV.

We can see variations of the neoliberal currents examined here in makeover programs, gamedocs, and other reality formats that "govern at a distance" by instilling the importance of self-discipline, the rewards of self-enterprise, and the personal consequences of making the "wrong" choices. *Judge Judy* represents one of the clearest examples of this trend because it articulates neoliberal templates for citizenship to the privatization of public life while self-consciously bringing what Foucault called "the minute disciplines" and "panopticisms of the everyday" into the home.[42] The citizen subjectivities constructed on *Judge Judy* complement a model of government that disdains state authority and intervention, but demands a heightened form of personal responsibility and self-discipline from individuals. Reality TV as exemplified by the courtroom program is not outside democracy, then, but is an active agent in its neoliberal transformation.

Notes

1 The popular press has emphasized the "no tolerance" ethos of the programs, contributing to the cultural context in which they are received. See, in particular, Melanie McFarland, "Tough Judges Show There's Justice in Watching Television," *Seattle Times*, 30 November 1998, http://archives.seattletimes.

2 See ibid.

3 For a critical analysis of the Telecommunications Act of 1996, see Patricia Aufderheide, *Communications Policy and the Public Interest* (New York: Guilford, 1999); and Robert McChesney, *Rich Media, Poor Democracy: Communication Politics in Dubious Times* (New York: New Press, 2000).

4 James Hay, "Unaided Virtues: The (Neo)-Liberalization of the Domestic Sphere," *Television and New Media* 1, no. 1 (2000): 56.

5 Elizabeth Martinez and Arnoldo Garcia, "What Is Neoliberalism?" *Corpwatch*, 1 January 1997, www.corpwatch.org.

6 Robert McChesney, introduction to *Profit over People: Neoliberalism and Global Order*, by Noam Chomsky (New York: Seven Stories Press, 1999), 7, 11.

7 Nikolas Rose, "Governing 'Advanced' Liberal Democracies," in *Foucault and Political Reason: Liberalism, Neoliberalism, and Rationalities of Government*, ed. Andrew Barry, Thomas Osborne, and Nikolas Rose (Chicago: University of Chicago Press, 1996), 55, 58–59. For a Foucauldian approach to "governmentality," see also Graham Bruchell, Colin Gordon, and Peter Miller, eds., *The Foucault Effect: Studies in Governmentality* (Chicago: University of Chicago Press, 1991). I have also found Toby Miller's analysis of citizenship and subjectivity helpful for thinking through neoliberal modes of government. See his *The Well-Tempered Self: Citizenship, Culture, and the Postmodern Subject* (Baltimore, Md.: Johns Hopkins University Press, 1993).

8   Rose, "Governing 'Advanced' Liberal Democracies," 57–59.
9   Ibid., 57, 58.
10 Hay, "Unaided Virtues," 54.
11 Barbara Cruikshank, "Revolutions Within: Self-Government and Self-Esteem," in *Foucault and Political Reason: Liberalism, Neoliberalism, and Rationalities of Government*, ed. Andrew Barry, Thomas Osborne, and Nikolas Rose (Chicago: University of Chicago Press, 1996), 231.
12 In addition to Cruikshank, "Revolutions Within," see Heidi Marie Rimke, "Governing Citizens through Self-Help Literature," *Cultural Studies*, 14, no. 1 (2000): 61–78.
13 Cruikshank, "Revolutions Within," 234.
14 Nancy Fraser, *Justice Interruptus: Critical Reflections on the "Postsocialist" Condition* (New York: Routledge, 1997).
15 Judge Wapner was brought back to resolve disputes between pet owners on the Animal Channel's *Animal Court*.
16 Luaine Lee, "Judge Judy Has Always Believed in the Motto 'Just Do It,' " *Nando Media*, 28 November 1998, www.nandotimes.com; and Judy Sheindlin, *Don't Pee on My Leg and Tell Me It's Raining* (New York: HarperPerennial, 1997), 3.
17 Cited on www.judgejudy.com.
18 Cited in Lee, "Judge Judy."
19 Michel Foucault, "Complete and Austere Institutions," in *The Foucault Reader*, ed. Paul Rabinow (New York: Pantheon, 1984), 219–20. See also Michel Foucault, *Discipline and Punish* (New York: Random House, 1995).
20 See Frances Fox Piven, *Regulating the Poor: The Functions of Public Welfare* (New York: Random House, 1971); and John Gillion, *Overseers of the Poor* (Chicago: University of Chicago Press, 2001).
21 John Fiske, *Television Culture* (New York: Routledge, 1987).
22 Michael M. Epstein, for example, argues that courtroom programs are an extension of the talk show to the extent that they use law and order to legitimate a sensationalist focus on personal conflict. Epstein also points out that the judge figure is construed as an "ultimate" moral authority less concerned with legal procedures than with the evaluation of personal behaviors. Presuming the "low" status of the genre and concentrating on its misrepresentation of the actual law, however, his critique overlooks the governmental nature and implications of this focus on everyday conduct and behavior. See Michael M. Epstein, "Judging Judy, Mablean, and Mills: How Courtroom Programs Use Law to Parade Private Lives to Mass Audiences," *Television Quarterly* (2001), http://www.emmyonline.org/tvq/ articles/32–1–1.asp.
23 Jane Shattuc, *The Talking Cure: TV Talk Shows and Women* (New York: Routledge, 1997).
24 Sonia Livingstone and Peter Lunt, *Talk on Television: Audience Participation and Public Debate* (London: Routledge, 1994).
25 Janice Peck, "The Mediated Talking Cure: Therapeutic Framing of Autobiography in TV Talk Shows," in *Gender, Race, and Class in Media*, ed. Gail Dines and Jean Humez (Thousand Oaks, Calif.: Sage, 2002), 538, 545.

26 Mimi White, *Tele-Advising: Therapeutic Discourse in American Television* (Chapel Hill: University of North Carolina Press, 1992), 69.

27 Cited in Barbara Lippert, "Punchin' Judy," *New York Magazine*, 15 June 2001, www.newyorkmetro.com.

28 Cited in *Judge Judy* publicity, www.wchstv.com/synd_prog/judy.

29 Cited in www.wchstv.com/synd_prog/judy.

30 Cited in McFarland, "Tough Judges Show There's Justice."

31 Judy Sheindlin, *Keep It Simple Stupid* (New York: Cliff Street Books, 2000), 2.

32 Nancy Fraser and Linda Gordon, "A Genealogy of 'Dependency': Tracing a Keyword of the U.S. Welfare State," in Fraser, *Justice Interruptus.*

33 Rose, "Governing 'Advanced' Liberal Democracies," 58.

34 Michel Foucault defines panopticism as surveillance or "systems of marking and classifying" (*Power/Knowledge: Selected Interviews*, ed. Colin Gordon [New York: Pantheon, 1977], 71).

35 See Elayne Rapping's essay in this volume, "Aliens, Nomads, Mad Dogs and Road Warriors: The Changing Face of Criminal Violence on TV," in Susan Murray and Laurie Ouellette (eds.) *Reality TV: Remaking Television Culture* (New York: New York University Press, 2004), 214–230; and Anna Williams, "Domestic Violence and the Aetiology of Crime in America's Most Wanted," *Camera Obscura* 31 (1995): 65–117.

36 Judy Sheindlin, *Beauty Fades, Dumb Is Forever* (New York: Cliff Street Books, 1999), 112–13.

37 Ibid., 105.

38 Sheindlin, cited in Lee, "Judge Judy."

39 Rose, "Governing 'Advanced' Liberal Democracies," 58.

40 The clip was replayed during an interview with Sheindlin on *Larry King Live*, CNN, 12 September 2000.

41 Michel Foucault, "On Popular Justice," in Gordon, *Power/Knowledge*, 27.

42 Michel Foucault, "Panopticism," in *The Foucault Reader*, ed. Paul Rabinow (New York: Pantheon, 1984), 212.

8

Feeling Like a Domestic Goddess
Postfeminism and cooking

Joanne Hollows

Originally published in *European Journal of Cultural Studies*, 6:2 (2003): 179–202.

Nigella Lawson has become one of the UK's bestselling cookery writers. A food writer for British *Vogue*, Nigella has published four bestselling cookery books, *How to Eat* (1999), *How to Be a Domestic Goddess* (2000), *Nigella Bites* (2001) and *Forever Summer* (2002), the latter two based on the Channel 4 prime time cookery shows of the same names. She has also been a columnist for the UK newspaper the *Observer* (where she was frequently interpreted as representing a 'feminist' voice), writes a beauty column for *The Times* and, perhaps not insignificantly for what follows, has been a former member of the editorial board of *Critical Quarterly*. She has also gained an iconic status in the UK, becoming known simply by her first name like the UK's Delia (Smith) and the US's Martha (Stewart). Press commentary about Nigella has extended far beyond her food writing to reflect on her heritage (she is the daughter of former Conservative MP Nigel Lawson), the tragedies in her life (she lost her mother, sister and, most recently, her husband to cancer) and her love life (a well-publicized relationship with millionaire art collector Charles Saatchi). However, most commentary betrays a fascination with her 'beauty' (in a British survey, she was voted the third most beautiful woman in the world) and with the 'Nigella lifestyle' and what it represents.[1]

The publication of *How to Be a Domestic Goddess* (hereafter referred to as *Domestic Goddess*) in the UK served to highlight the distance between feminism and cooking, at least within 'the popular'. The book provoked a huge debate in the press about the relationship between feminism, femininity and baking, with Nigella being variously positioned as the prefeminist housewife, as an antifeminist Stepford wife, as the saviour of downshifting middle-class career women and as both the negative and positive product of postfeminism. In the process, while many columnists couldn't get past odes to Nigella's beauty, many others equated baking with false consciousness and suggested that there was but a short step from baking to domestic enslavement (Tyrer, 2000) and a prefeminist world of back street abortions (Moore, 2000).

The coverage devoted to the book would seem to support Julia Hallam's argument that 'feminism as a (contradictory and unfixed) subject position is widely circulating as a interpretive strategy amongst . . . journalists' (cited in Read, 2000: 119). From reading some of these accounts about the significance of a collection of recipes, it is easy to get the impression that while feminism might be 'contradictory and unfixed', the feminist's cake-making 'other' – the housewife – is 'fixed' in a non-contradictory 1950s of both the popular and feminist imagination (although see, for example, Clarke, 1997; Meyerowitz, 1994). While columnist for the *Guardian* Charlotte Raven claims that for wannabe domestic goddesses 'the housewife represents stability and security' (2000: 5), the critiques levelled at Nigella frequently suggest that the house-wife might represent this for feminism. If, as Charlotte Brunsdon argues, 'the oppos-ition feminist/housewife was polemically and historically formative for second-wave feminism' (2000: 216), then it also seemed to be alive and well in the British press in 2000.

In feminist cultural studies, there has been a concern with the new postfeminist identities that have emerged 'between feminism and femininity' (see Brunsdon, 1997; McRobbie, 1994; Moseley and Read, 2002). However, such work has largely been concerned with youthful and/or non-domestic femininities (although exceptions exist such as Rowe, 1997). What remains less clear is what emerges between the feminist and the housewife. It is in this context that I examine Nigella's cookery writing and television shows to identify what kind of postfeminist identity can emerge in a domestic context. In doing so, I avoid the more pejorative and celebratory con-ceptualizations of postfeminism, preferring the more historically informed idea of postfeminism. Such an approach is offered by Brunsdon, who argues that the term postfeminism 'is quite useful if used in an historically specific sense to mark changes in popularly available understanding of femininity and a woman's place that are generally recognized as occurring in the 1980s' (1997: 101). From this perspective, Nigella's conception of cooking is historically *post*-1970s feminism; while her con-struction of the cook does not conform to 1970s feminism, it nonetheless is a product of a historical period informed by feminism.

However, in what follows, Nigella's construction of the cook is not simply dis-cussed in terms of gender, but also in terms of class. If the press coverage about Nigella has shown a preoccupation with the relationship between the author and feminism, it has also demonstrated a preoccupation with her privileged background and the lifestyle she represents. The reception of her TV show *Nigella Bites* frequently characterized it as primarily about lifestyle and it was situated in terms of wider debates about the proliferation of lifestyle programmes on TV (see Bell, 2000, 2002; Moseley, 2000, 2001). While I have little desire to dispute the image of Nigella as a cover girl for the new middle class, an examination of her work begins to problematize some of the assumptions that underpin sociological theories of the new middle classes. These theories frequently show little explicit concern with gender, while implicitly gendering the new middle classes as masculine (see Featherstone, 1991a; for a critique, see Hollows, 2002). While Nigella does not specifically address a female reader, she nonetheless addresses specific conflicts and problems that are experienced by those inhabiting middle-class feminine identities. As I go on to discuss below, these centre around the problem of time scarcity in the face of the competing demands of paid labour, domestic labour and 'leisure-work' (Bell, 2002) that is crucial to new middle-class identity.

Finally, the article argues that the sheer extent of the debate about Nigella as a 'domestic goddess' and the other figures of middle-class femininity that were produced and reproduced in the debate demonstrates the multiple femininities that are in circulation and in competition in current times. The article draws on the work of Elspeth Probyn to examine how, in debates about the significance of Nigella, the issue of choice – and making the 'right' choice – is presented as both a freedom and a problem that represents rather more than a change of wardrobe, as implied in some of the work on more youthful femininities.

The postfeminist cook

For those unfamiliar with Nigella's output, it is perhaps necessary to give a sense of her style – a style recognizable enough to now be parodied on British television.[2] The television shows *Nigella Bites* (2000), *Nigella Bites II* (2001) and *Forever Summer* (2002) draw on some of the elements established in Jamie Oliver's show *The Naked Chef* (see Moseley, 2001), in which the cooking takes place in the context of everyday life in her home and during which we see her feed herself, her children and her friends. It is interspersed with images of the Nigella lifestyle: dropping off and picking up the kids, shopping for food, photo shoots for her books, writing on the computer, playing with the children, socializing with friends. Furthermore (and again comparisons with *The Naked Chef* are useful here), a narrative about Nigella's life is constructed across the series as she moves from the role of wife and mother in *Nigella Bites*, to widowed single parent in *Nigella Bites II*, to a more carefree and newly-in-love partner in a reconstituted family in *Forever Summer*.[3]

Her cooking style is carefully distanced from the prim and proper efficiency of the (female) home economist and from the decontextualized precision of the (male) professional chef. Instead, Nigella makes a virtue of messiness (she throws egg shells into the sink and gets chilli seeds all over the floor), acknowledges her own laziness ('it's not *just* because I'm lazy') and demonstrates her own incompetence as a sign of both the foolproof nature and the pleasure of her cooking (she loves her mezzaluna 'because I'm incredibly clumsy and it makes me feel like one of those super confident people', *Nigella Bites*, 1, 'Fast Food'). For Nigella, it is all about 'cooking in context' (Lawson, 1999: 7). Her address to camera is frequently arch and flirtatious and peppered with quips: 'trust me, I'm not a doctor', she says as she puts on rubber gloves to chop chillis, and 'now I'm going to disrobe, de-rubber', as she takes them off (*Nigella Bites*, 1, 'Fast Food'). Likewise, as she picks up kitchen tongs to turn steak on the griddle, she quips 'I like a little tong action' (*Nigella Bites*, 3, 'Family'). Her television shows and books are also laced with a range of popular and high cultural references that position her as a cultural omnivore: on TV she refers to her conical sieve as 'my Jean-Paul Gaultier'; in *Domestic Goddess* she compares tine marks on shortbread to 'the scrappy lines that drive Gregory Peck mad in *Spellbound*' (Lawson, 2000: 11); and in *How to Eat* she compares making mayonnaise to reading Henry James (Lawson, 1999: 13). However, this omnivorousness also extends to her culinary tastes: *Nigella Bites* contains a section on 'trashy' food, with fried chicken in 'Roseanne-like quantities' and 'Elvis Presley's Peanut-Butter and Banana Sandwiches' (Lawson, 2001: 136–40). Such omnivorousness 'enables the middle-class to re-fashion and retool itself through the use and association with tastes that were once associated with the working-class' (Skeggs, forthcoming). In this way, Nigella's taste for the trashy serves less to dissolve the relationship between class and taste and more to reaffirm the distinction of the new middle class (see also Warde et al., 2000).

However, the sense of fun displayed in both television shows and books also relates to what one might characterize as the Nigella cooking philosophy that cooking should be pleasurable and should start from the desire to eat. As she tells us at the opening of the first episode ('Fast Food') of *Nigella Bites*: 'The idea here for me is food that I love eating but doesn't give me a nervous breakdown to cook. . . . What I'm after is minimum effort for maximum pleasure in both the cooking and the eating.' Throughout her television series, she constantly highlights the sensuous pleasures of the cooking process: a lemon pasta sauce smells 'so fragrant, so comforting' and is described as 'harmonious, calm, voluptuous and creamy'; the smell of coriander is 'like a drug, it's so strong' (*Nigella Bites*, 1, 'Fast Food'); squeezing out gelatine leaves becomes play: 'There's something curiously satisfying about all that squelching – oh, how lovely is this? Yaaah – creature from the deep' (*Nigella Bites*, 2, 'Entertaining'). Nigella not only advises her audience about how to free cooking of stress ('it's the sort of food you can make when you're so stressed out that just the idea of cooking makes you want to shriek'), but also to use cooking to combat stress ('squish it around in here and really kind of bash it round and this will get rid of the day's stresses. Better to do that *before* the guests come!'). Yet Nigella's approach isn't simply about fast food that fits with the demands of modern life, it's also about 'comfort cooking' as an escape from the demands of modern life. A lemon risotto is presented as not only comforting to eat, but also 'immensely comforting to make: in times of strain, mindless repetitive activity – in this case, 20 minutes of stirring – can really help' (Lawson, 2001: 43). Likewise, the more time-consuming pleasures of baking are presented as 'feeling good, wafting along in the warm sweet-smelling air, unwinding, no longer being entirely an office creature' (Lawson, 2000: vii).

As the discussion above suggests, this sense of cooking as pleasure goes in tandem with the idea of eating as pleasure. Throughout the television shows, we see Nigella literally biting into a whole array of food, and the show customarily ends with her picking from the fridge or attacking a freshly cut piece of cake (usually at night). While Delia Smith, the UK's top television cook, informs the viewer of the nature of wheat so they can get a better understanding of bread-making, Nigella denies knowing much about where salmon comes from: 'I'm a city girl, I'm not expected to know these things. My skill lies in eating' (*Nigella Bites*, 1, 'Fast Food'). While Delia has declared that she will never eat the dishes she cooks on TV, Nigella 'has nothing to declare but my greed' (Lawson, 1999: viii). While many of the professional male television chefs tell the viewer how excellent a dish is, Nigella demonstrates the pleasure the food induces as the camera lingers on her face as she eats and groans with satisfaction. Eating, like cooking, also offers access to the druglike qualities of food: 'Happiness Soup' has such 'a sunny, mood-enhancing yellowness' that it can 'banish the blues' (Lawson, 2002: 28).

The significance of this emphasis on the pleasure of cooking and eating is the extent to which it differs from the accounts of the meanings women bring to cooking and eating in feminist sociology. This work has tended to situate cooking and food within debates about the sexual division of labour. These studies demonstrate that women are positioned as providers of food for others, but maintain a difficult relationship with eating itself: women frequently use food to offer pleasure to family members, yet have difficulty experiencing food as pleasurable themselves, particularly in a domestic context (Charles and Kerr, 1988; Martens, 1997). For example, the title of Anne Murcott's article 'It's a Pleasure to Cook for Him', taken from a comment by one of her respondents, illustrates the extent to which the women she studied saw cooking, and the choice of *what* to cook and eat, as something done 'in the service of some other(s)' (1995: 94). As a result, women rarely cooked just for themselves. Similar findings are reported by Charles and Kerr, who show how this is exacerbated by women's fear of gaining weight. Women 'deny themselves pleasure whereas one of their aims in preparing food for others is to give pleasure; women fundamentally cook to please men in particular' (Charles and Kerr, 1988: 153). However, a few women in their study did seek to 'treat' themselves when they were home alone (1988: 70) and Shaun Moores has pointed to the similarity between this and the 'guilty pleasures' enjoyed by the woman who indulges her televisual tastes when no one else is around (1993: 53).[4] For Charles and Kerr, the pleasure gained from cooking 'for him' is the pleasure of demonstrating 'care' for others and, in Marjorie DeVault's work, it is this relationship between cooking and caring (for others) that cements the relationship between cooking and femininity: caring work is the 'undefined, unacknowledged activity central to women's identity' (1991: 4).

What I want to suggest is that the representation of cooking in Nigella's work starts from the importance of satisfying and caring for the self rather than others and in this way offers an alternative mode of representing the pleasures of domestic femininity. I have already demonstrated how cooking as pleasure is represented in her shows and writing, but by linking the pleasures of cooking and eating, Lawson represents not only a feminine self that eats, but one that is very aware of what it wants to eat rather than deferring to the preferences of others:[5] 'I don't deny that food, its preparation, is about sharing, about connectedness', she writes (and, indeed, much of her writing testifies to this), 'But that's not all that it's about. There seems to me to be something robustly affirmative about taking trouble to feed yourself; enjoying life on purpose rather than by default' (Lawson, 1999: 134). By bracketing cooking, however fleetingly, from the demands of 'cooking *for*', she suggests that we can learn how to see cooking as 'a pleasure in itself' (1999: 135). Furthermore, by relating both cooking and eating to contexts, Nigella connects both with recognizable situations in everyday life. Chocolate fudge cake 'serves 10. Or 1 with a broken heart' (Lawson, 2001: 47) and comfort food 'soothes' when we 'get tired, stressed, sad or lonely' (2001: 31). Even low-fat food is linked with pleasure rather than deprivation; it's what we eat when we want to feel *as if* our body is a temple, not about 'deprivation or restraint, but rather the holy glow of self-indulgently virtuous pleasure' (2001: 223).

This emphasis on the pleasure of cooking and eating and the need for restraint appears to fit with the 'calculated hedonism' that has been seen to characterize the consumption practices of the new middle classes, in which 'discipline and hedonism are no longer seen as incompatible' (Featherstone, 1991b: 171). Here, the ability to shift from eating chocolate fudge cake to vegetable miso broth is linked to a 'calculated decontrol', characterized by 'an ability to move in and out of the condition of self-control thereby to experience a greater range of sensations' (Warde, 1997: 92–3). For Bourdieu (1984), the ability to both pursue hedonistic pleasure as an aesthetic experience and maintain a disciplined and controlled relationship with the body distinguishes the new middle classes from both the restraint of the old middle classes and the lack of discipline and aesthetic distance that is seen to characterize working-class taste. In Featherstone's work, calculated hedonism involves a shift from the pleasures of hedonism to the denial of pleasure as the body is disciplined in the gym or on a diet. However, as Nigella's 'temple food' demonstrates, discipline may also be linked with pleasures of asceticism rather than deprivation, and Lupton (1996) suggests that these pleasures may be gendered insofar as they relate more closely to the way many women experience their relationship with both food and the body. Lury has suggested that calculated de-control is a disposition best associated with a masculine middle class, as women often experience an 'enforced de-control' in which they feel little sense of the mastery and control over 'the self' that (some) men possess (1996: 242). What Lawson offers in its place is a sense of feeling *as if* we were in control, *as if* the body was a temple. If women frequently lack control over 'the self' because they have also been excluded from constructions of 'the individual', this form of 'imagining' at least offers a means of exploring what it would feel like to be in control (see Cronin, 2000).

However, while acknowledging the pleasures of cooking and eating, Nigella cannot ignore the anxieties produced by cooking. Work by DeVault, among others, suggests that while men do cook, they do not 'feel the force of the morally charged ideal of deferential service that appears in so many women's reports' (1991: 149). Cooking as caring is one of the key ways in which femininity is performed, in which 'a woman conducts herself as recognizably womanly' (1991: 118). Failure to perform in such a way is seen as a failure to be 'properly feminine', as demonstrated by the press coverage of the Greenham Common women which focused on 'rancid' and 'burnt' food and their 'dirty' pots and pans (Creswell, cited in Morley, 2000: 70). Therefore, while Nigella advocates that the cook should take pleasure from their own eating and should largely avoid cooking practices that cause displeasure, she also acknowledges that cooking does not occur in a vacuum.

For these reasons, Nigella's cookery attempts to negotiate the demands of both pleasing the self and pleasing and caring for others, addressing the anxieties associated with cooking that frequently arise from a fear of being judged as 'improperly' feminine. This is dealt with in two key ways. First, the 'sisterly' conversational tone adopted by Nigella is an attempt to assuage anxiety: 'I have wanted to make you feel that I'm there with you, in the kitchen, as you cook' (Lawson, 1999: x). Potential failures are anticipated and the reader is assured that mistakes are not only 'normal', but also need not be read as failures. For example, *Domestic Goddess* contains a photograph of an 'Easy Almond Cake' that has been patched up after it stuck to the tin: 'these things happen to us all and I wanted to show it wasn't the end of the world. . . . Life isn't lived in a lab' (Lawson, 2000: 6).[6] This reference to a scientific approach to cookery located in the public sphere relates to the second way in which Lawson seeks to negotiate anxiety by stressing the values of a feminine domestic culinary tradition. On a basic level, this is an attempt to inspire confidence, but more crucially it is a way of acknowledging the pressures and pleasures of the feminine while refusing the need to be judged according to multiple culinary standards. The standards refused are those of the postwar dinner party which made the cook feel as if she had 'to slave, to strive, to seat, to *perform*' and those of restaurant chefs who have 'to innovate, to elaborate, to impress the paying customer' (Lawson, 1999: 330; emphasis in original). In this way, while she acknowledges that 'feeding work' may not be unproblematic, she also claims that home cooking is 'the antithesis of restaurant cooking' (*Nigella Bites II*, 6, 'Legacy'), refusing the demands to combine the 'caring self' and the 'performing self' and be judged by extra-domestic standards.

What is noticeable in Nigella's writing and television shows is that cooking and caring have been divorced from the 'for him', yet remain closely associated with motherhood. Her children feature frequently in her television shows, where they eat some of her creations, sometimes join in the cooking and participate in constructing the Nigella lifestyle of the middle-class working mother. Cooking as a means of performing motherhood by both feeding children and socializing them into culinary competence is also integral to her books. Despite the fact that much of her output demonstrates the 'Nigella lifestyle', in her writing, her husband John Diamond is rarely mentioned and his fleeting appearances in the television shows portray him as father, dinner party co-host and occasional cook rather than eater. Given the amount of press coverage given to Diamond's cancer (which made it difficult to eat) and subsequent death, many of Nigella's audience would have been aware that there was no 'him' to cook for.[7] For these reasons, the roles of 'mother' and 'wife' become largely divorced. As a result, 'the caring self' produced within Nigella's work embodies the same contradictions as 'the caring self' produced by feminist criticism on cooking as domestic labour. As Daniel Miller argues, 'It is noticeable that for all the critique of normative marriage implied by DeVault, there is very little attempt by her to challenge a mother's love' (1998: 98). In this way, Nigella's postfeminist cooking reproduces some of the tensions found in feminist critiques of cooking.

In many ways, Nigella's cookery writing, with its emphasis on extracting pleasure where possible from the cooking process, sits easily within the frameworks established for understanding the aesthetic dispositions of the new middle classes. Cooking practices are presented as 'aestheticized leisure activities' (Lupton, 1996: 126) and as part of a wider lifestyle based around 'a morality of pleasure as duty' which 'makes it a failure, a threat to self-esteem, not to "have fun" ' (Bourdieu, 1984: 367). This can be understood within the context of what Featherstone calls the 'aestheticization of everyday life' (1991a), which is capitalized upon by the new middle classes as they invest in the art of lifestyle. For Featherstone, 'the new heroes of consumer culture make lifestyle a life project . . . the modern individual in consumer culture is made conscious that he speaks not only with his clothes, but with his home, furnishings, car and other activities' (1991a: 86), including, presumably, cooking and eating. These 'new heroes' appear as masculine in Featherstone's account (Lury, 1996: 148), begging the question of what happens to this conception of the new middle classes when gender is made a structuring form of differentiation rather than remaining implicit (see Hollows, 2002).

On the one hand, there would appear to be nothing particularly 'new' about middle-class (and non-middle-class) women's responsibility for using the domestic sphere as a site for aesthetic display in which class tastes are both constructed and reproduced (see, for example, Attfield, 1995; Sparke, 1995). Furthermore, taking a 'heroic' disposition towards everyday life is problematic for women as they have traditionally been associated with a conception of 'everyday life' as 'mundane' and 'non-heroic' (Felski, 2000).

On the other hand, the home as a site for the practice of a 'morality' of pleasure and play is problematized for women, for whom it has been traditionally seen as a site for labour and the performance of a morality of 'respectability' through which women are judged as to whether they are 'appropriately' feminine (see Skeggs, 1997). The following section explores further how the position of the domestic goddess may respond to middle-class women's experience of the home as both a site of domestic labour and 'leisure-work'. Furthermore, this problematizes the extent to which women among the new middle classes share an ethic of 'calculating hedonism' in the same ways as middle-class men. Lupton notes how this has

> spatial and temporal dimensions: the workplace, the working day and the working week are characterized by production and aesthetic self-discipline, while the evening, the weekend, the holiday and festival days, the home and public spaces such as shopping malls, pubs, bars, and restaurants are the times and spaces within which consumption and hedonistic indulgence take place.
>
> (1996: 151)

If the home is both a site of labour and leisure, it is neither temporally nor spatially divorced from sites of production and discipline. It is these issues that are developed in the next section, which examines how a relationship between time and domesticity is negotiated in Nigella's construction of a postfeminist cook.

Between Sophia Loren and Debbie Reynolds: nostalgia, time and fantasy

Much of the press coverage that surrounded the publication of *Domestic Goddess* suggested that the book was a manifesto for Stepford wives, part of a 'recidivist trend' in which 'housework was the new sex' (Gordon, 2000, Part 2: 7) and had 'an unreconstructed housewife agenda' (Burnside, 2000: 16). Charlotte Raven in the *Guardian* claimed that Nigella had produced 'a heritage park impression of house-wifery' and was baffled by 'Nigella's apparent conviction that the only problem with domestic servitude was the time it took to perfect. Her nostalgia for the side-effects of female oppression – that atmospheric fug in the kitchen – would be offensive if it wasn't so curious' (2000: 5). Likewise, Moore in the *Mail on Sunday* argued that the book's nostalgia 'for a simpler time when men earned the dough and women stayed home kneading it' was a product of 'anxiety about changing gender relations' (2000: 31). While the book did find a more positive reception among some journalists, in comments like the ones above the journalist takes on the identity 'feminist' in opposition to the position of 'the housewife'. Instead, I want to suggest that an identification with the position of the 'domestic goddess' negotiates the opposition between the feminist and the housewife by being offered as a position that is only available in fantasy – in Nigella's words, 'not *being* a domestic goddess exactly, but *feeling* like one' (Lawson, 2000: vii; emphases in original).

Before proceeding to examine more closely what is at stake in the desire to *feel* like a domestic goddess, it is worth addressing this issue of nostalgia. While a nostalgia for an imagined 'golden age' is frequently apparent in popular commentary that bemoans the decline of the 'family meal' (Murcott, 1997) and the replacement of a living tradition of 'authentic home-cooking' with an 'inauthentic' system of industrial mass production of food (Laudan, 1999), nostalgia is also evident in more academic work on women and cooking. While one dominant trend in feminist scholarship identified earlier is to situate cooking and feeding work within debates about domestic labour, another trend has been to celebrate feminine kitchen cultures. However, this celebration is situated within a narrative of cultural and culinary decline which rests on a nostalgia for a simpler time before commerce interfered too much with cooking – a kind of feminist version of what Laudan (1999) has called 'culinary Luddism'.

For example, the French sociologist Luce Giard, while seeking to validate the practice of 'doing cooking' and its role in women's culture, also employs a narrative of cultural decline that employs some of the tropes of mass culture theory. The skilled and inventive female cook of yore, she argues, is being transformed into an '*unskilled spectator* who watches the machine function in her place' (1998: 212; emphasis in original). Although Giard warns of the dangers of 'archaistic nostalgia' (1998: 213), her culturalist analysis nonetheless rests on a distinction between an 'authentic' popular culture, reproduced in a living tradition of women's culture, and an 'inauthentic' mass-produced and industrialized culture that is produced *for* women rather than by them. Another example offered in Mary Drake McFeeley's (2001) history of American women's kitchen cultures is fuelled by what Bourdieu has called a 'populist nostalgia' (1984: 58), in which a Missouri farming community of the 1920s represents 'the world we have lost'. For McFeeley, the 1950s represent a nadir in women's culinary history, a time when the creative and productive housewife in a living kitchen culture was replaced by a deskilled housewife-consumer, marooned in a kitchen where she prepared homogeneous and standardized dishes 'handed down, not from Great-grandmother, but from General Foods' (2001: 99). While McFeeley's liberal feminism means that she ends on a rather more optimistic note than Giard when she claims that 'we do not need to lose our kitchens to keep our freedom' (2001: 169), both critics share a feminist 'culinary Luddism' in their nostalgia for the time before capitalist rationalization destroyed a living tradition of feminine culinary culture. For these critics, the modern is presented as 'an alien, external force bearing down on an organic community of the disempowered' and, in the process, they tend to ignore the multiple ways 'the modern becomes real at the most intimate and mundane levels of experience and interaction' (Felski, 2000: 66).

While press commentary that drew on feminist discourses to criticize *Domestic Goddess* equated a nostalgic view of the kitchen, and women's place in it, with prefeminism, both McFeeley and Giard seek to celebrate and validate a prefeminist feminine practice located in a world 'outside' capitalist industrialization. What I want to suggest is that *Domestic Goddess* negotiates a space between these oppositions. In the preface, Nigella claims that 'baking stands as a useful metaphor for the familial warmth of the kitchen we fondly imagine used to exist, and as a way of reclaiming our lost Eden' (2000: vii). While the negative criticism of the book in the British press frequently swooped on the phrase 'lost Eden' as indicative of a prefeminist 1950s, instead it could also be read as a mythical place, somewhere we 'imagine' existed, rather than a literal past, positive or negative. In the process, Nigella refuses the fantasies of the past upon which feminism itself depends, creating in their place an alternative fantastic space that acknowledges that it *is* a fantasy.

Likewise, the position of the domestic goddess presented by Nigella is not simply a prefeminist figure of femininity, a throwback to a 'real' past, but instead offers a point of feminine identification that responds to the contradictions of the present. The position of the domestic goddess is presented as an imagined and unfixed position, 'a fond, if ironic, dream: the unexpressed "I" that is a cross between Sophia Loren and Debbie Reynolds in pink cashmere cardigan and fetching gingham pinny' (2000: vii). In this way, criticisms of the 'unreality' of the domestic goddess miss the point that 'textual constructions of possible modes of femininity . . . do not function as role models but are symbolic realizations of feminine subject positions with which viewers can identify in fantasy' (Ang, 1990: 83). The clarification that Nigella makes in the preface is significant here: she is not offering guidance on how to *be*, but how to *feel* like a domestic goddess. In *Watching Dallas*, Ien Ang argues that fantasy offers the opportunity to experience feminine identities 'without having to experience their actual consequences' (1985: 134). While feeling like a domestic goddess does translate into practice, it is a practice (like S&M) that is engaged in at a fantasy level: 'The good thing is that we don't have to get ourselves up in Little Lady drag and we don't have to renounce the world and enter into a life of domestic drudgery' (Lawson, 2000: vii).

Ang's work is useful here because it points to the ways in which fantasy enables us to experiment with identities that 'the structural constraints of everyday life' (1990: 84) might prohibit, while also reminding us that such fantasies are necessary: 'no one subject position can ever cover satisfactorily all the problems and desires an individual encounters' (1990: 85). In what follows, I suggest that the key 'structural constraint' that the fantasy of the domestic goddess addresses is time scarcity. If Campbell sees the new domesticity as 'perversely time-consuming' (2001: 4), then I want to examine what is at stake in this perversity.

Time scarcity is seen to be acutely felt by women as they engage in paid work while the domestic division of labour proves relatively resistant to change. Not only does this result in a need for 'multitasking', but women may also find it more difficult than men to organize their time effectively because there is always the risk of interruption from competing domestic responsibilities and the demands of others (Southerton et al., 2001: 9). While this may not seem class-specific, it may well be experienced as such: because the 'work' of consumption and leisure is crucial to new middle-class identities, this is seen to produce a pressure on 'free time'. As a result, the increased use of paid domestic labour by the middle class in the UK can be seen as a means of creating time to concentrate on the more 'pleasant' and 'creative' elements of domestic life which make a more significant contribution to maintaining distinctive and distinguished lifestyles (Bell, 2002; Gregson and Lowe, 1995). An alternative response can be seen in the desire to escape the demands of both work and play to create 'more time' through down-shifting (Southerton et al., 2001). However, both these responses can be seen in relation to an increased sense of 'harriedness'. This creates a pressure to create what Gary Alan Fine, in a different context, describes as 'temporal autonomy' through the creation of 'temporal niches', an attempt to control time 'in the face of uncontrollable and unpredictable durations and tempos' (1996: 55).

For this reason, it is perhaps not surprising that the first episode of *Nigella Bites* was entitled 'Fast Food', with an emphasis on 'minimum effort for maximum pleasure'. But, as Lawson points out in *How to Eat*, producing something to eat on a daily basis is not straightforward when 'we have less time for cooking as we have more interest in food' (1999: 178). Furthermore, she claims that the entry of more women into paid employment means that the problem of producing a meal (for either men or women) is now faced at the end of a day working outside the home, a problem that doesn't just involve the cooking process, but also the other elements, such as shopping, that go into what DeVault calls 'feeding work'. Inviting friends for a midweek dinner, Nigella claims in her TV series, seems like 'a great idea – and then, as the day dawns, you really begin to panic about how you're going to do the shopping, the cooking, the lot. I have an answer 'cos we've all been there' (*Nigella Bites*, 1, 'Fast Food'). Everyday cooking is therefore presented as something that must negotiate the contradictory demands of care and convenience (Warde, 1997). While the need to negotiate the opposition between care and convenience is not new, this contemporary sense of being harried may not simply be about a shortage of time but, more generally, a changing experience of time itself as the need to organize and manage time becomes more important, as 'scheduling strategies', once features of an industrialized public sphere, have become part of everyday life (Warde, 1999: 524). In this context, the fragmented images of activities that comprise the Nigella lifestyle, which are interspersed between cooking sequences, can begin to look like a visual illustration of the need to order 'work appointments, physical exercise, journeying to the shops, transporting children, using leisure facilities and visiting friends [which] require complex and anxiety provoking organization' (1999: 523).

Within such a context, Nigella's call to cake-baking can appear at first as rather ridiculous. However, some studies suggest that the contemporary middle classes' experience of time may also involve scheduling 'quality time' which is outside of both paid labour and the less pleasant aspects of unpaid domestic labour (tasks which can be carried out by paid domestic labour; see Gregson and Lowe, 1995: 159). Cooking in quality time can, therefore, be contrasted with, and in some senses bracketed off from, everyday cooking and, in *Domestic Goddess*, these are equated with different modes of femininity. As Lawson argues, modern cookery has produced a

> mood . . . of skin-of-the-teeth efficiency, all briskness and little pleasure. Sometimes that's the best we can manage, but at other times we don't want to feel like a post-modern, post-feminist, overstretched woman but, rather, a domestic goddess trailing nutmeggy fumes of baking pie in our languorous wake.
>
> (2000: vii)

If, as Hilary Radner argues, the pleasure of spending money on make-up is 'precisely because it is excessive, without any "real" purpose' (1989: 311), then, when time is a scarce commodity for the new middle classes, it is the excessive expenditure of time on baking a loaf or making bagels that offers one a source of pleasure. This also explains why cooking like a domestic goddess, for Nigella, takes place in time opposed to the rhythms of the (masculine) professional workplace where 'chefs and their minions have to conjure up the finished dish within minutes' (1999: 178).

Richard Dyer has explored how some forms of popular entertainment contain five different types of 'utopian possibilities' which offer the sense of what 'utopia would feel like rather than how it would be organized' (1985: 222; see also Geraghty, 1991). These respond to 'particular inadequacies in society' (1985: 227) as they are experienced at particular historical moments. For example, Dyer argues, entertainment may offer the sense of what material abundance would feel like as a response to the experience of material scarcity. I would suggest that Nigella's work offers the sense of what temporal abundance might feel like as a response to the feeling of harriedness and time scarcity. However, in the figure of the domestic goddess, two further 'utopian solutions' discussed by Dyer overlap with the promise of temporal abundance: first, she offers the sense of an 'energy' that arises when work and play are 'synonymous', which responds to feelings of exhaustion; and, second, feelings of 'intensity', 'the affectivity of living in response to the "dreariness" and "instrumentality" of the daily round' (1985: 228). While Nigella's work acknowledges and offers sympathetic advice on dealing with these structural constraints, in the figure of the domestic goddess three possible utopian possibilities coalesce to offer her readers the experience of what life would feel like outside them.[8]

If the meaning of cooking is 'in the process' rather than the end product (Lawson, 2001: 99), then these meanings are not necessarily gender-specific. Indeed, studies suggest that men who enjoy cooking are more likely to take responsibility for preparing labour-intensive 'special occasion' meals than for everyday family meals (see, for example, Charles and Kerr, 1988; Kemmer, 1999; Lupton, 1996). User comments and reviews on amazon.com and amazon.co.uk (an online book supplier) also suggest that it is not only women who use her books and that the position of the 'domestic goddess' is undoubtedly also open to men. Nonetheless, the figure of the domestic goddess is not only literally a gendered figure, it is also used to validate feminine practices and 'traditions' to produce a homology between cooking, eating, reading and femininity based around ideas of comfort. While Nigella is careful not to invoke a nostalgia for a 'real' rose-tinted past, she nonetheless uses the relationship between food and (real and imagined) memories to suggest the emotional components of both cooking and eating as a source of social and psychological sustenance. The memories and histories drawn on here are less a nostalgia for a previous epoch of domestic culture and more micronarratives of matrilineal relations in which both lived or imagined experiences are intertwined with emotions that are a source of comfort in the present. As Lupton argues:

> Preparing a meal may evoke memories of past events at which that meal has been prepared and eaten, conjuring up the emotions felt at that time, or the experience may look forward to the sharing of the meal with another, anticipating an emotional outcome.
>
> (1996: 32)

It is in both the cooking and the eating of roast chicken that Nigella draws on her mother's practices and childhood memories to produce food that 'to me, smells of home, of family, of food that carries some important extra-culinary weight' (1999: 8). But these do not need to be recreations of the past, but a means of connecting with the past and producing new memories of comfort through practice. For example, in a discussion of whitebait which Nigella recalls as '*the* restaurant starter' in her childhood, the memories are neither of eating nor home-cooking. As she recollects, 'I didn't eat it then, but my father and sister, Thomasina, always ordered it, and it is partly in her memory, and with the wish that she was still here to eat it, that I present it to you now' (2001: 158).

However, memory and tradition are not offered as a basis for simply recreating the past in the present. As Felski argues, 'even as they bear witness to the otherness of the past, traditions are always dynamic, unstable and impure' (2000: 70). On the one hand, Nigella calls for a need to respect the 'legacy' she inherits from female relations and authors who act as culinary maternal figures. However, on the other hand, she refuses the passivity that comes from reproducing both feminine and familial traditions. There is an acknowledgement here that not all the emotions surrounding food and cooking are positive: for example, 'Christmas can induce panic and depression' (1999: 55) when tradition can become 'a source of pressure rather than pleasure' (2000: 247). Instead, Nigella advocates a more reflexive and active relationship to tradition: 'you can decide which rituals and ceremonies you want to adopt to give shape to your life and which you want to lose because they just constrain you. . . . I've consciously enjoyed setting my own pattern here' (2000: 247). In this way, the domestic goddess is freed from the 'real' force of tradition and the modes of feminine labour, self-sacrifice and obligation associated with it: tradition is presented as a choice.

However, this does not lead to an invalidation of feminine histories and maternal influences. Lawson also takes the opportunity to not only recreate recipes from her forebears, but also to reflect on the practice of compiling recipes as an everyday feminine tradition. Family cookbooks are compared to photograph albums, and the episode of *Nigella Bites* dealing with dishes from her childhood is intercut with old photographs of family members (*Nigella Bites II*, 6, 'Legacy'). For example, 'Granny Lawson's Lunch Dish' is not presented in terms of memories of cooking and eating, but in terms of memories embedded in the material culture of cooking. The source of the dish is her grandmother's 'old battered cookery notebooks', which operate as 'domestic diaries, half-filled with recipes torn out of papers, the rest a handwritten mixture of tips passed on by friends or accounts of lunches served to them. Cooking isn't just about ingredients, weights and measures: it's social history, personal history' (Lawson, 2001: 162). For Janet Theophano, such books are not only the products of those elements of the private sphere where women have been able to wield authority, they also act as a form of property that women can bequeath to other women (2002: 86). Furthermore, 'The traces women left behind in cookbooks anchored their contemporary relationships to the pages of their books and also connected the living with the dead' (2002: 115). The encouragement to maintain this practice is built into *Nigella Bites* where pages are left for notes (although more cynically this could be seen as a form of padding in what is a relatively slight collection). The aim, Nigella suggests, is to create a space for responses to her recipes so that there is a form of 'conversation' rather than a 'monologue'. In the process, her books become not only part of a more 'official' history of cookbooks, but also records of multiple microhistories that are written as the books are used.

In this way, the figure of the domestic goddess not only offers a point of identification in fantasy, but she is also positioned within a fantasy scenario in which maternal relations between women offer a source of comfort. While this might suggest a psychoanalytic reading, drawing on Chodorow's (1978) work on the relationships between mothers and daughters, this is at odds with the specific construction of the domestic goddess as a historicized figure of middle-class femininity. A more useful way of understanding the ways in which fantasy operates in the relations between women that are established within *Domestic Goddess* is offered by Cora Kaplan, who draws on the observation made by Laplanche and Pontalis that 'Fantasy is not the object of desire, but its setting' (Kaplan, 1986: 150). Kaplan examines the ways in which fantasy does not simply work to confirm subjectivities, but allows the exploration of what multiple subjectivities might feel like by allowing us to move between them. In this way, the fantasy scenarios constructed between domestic goddesses allow the reader the pleasure of moving between the positions of the mother and the mothered and the uses of this fantasy need not be gender-specific.

This discussion has aimed to highlight the ways in which the figure of the domestic goddess offers a form of identification inscribed in a textual fantasy which can translate into practice. The figure of the domestic goddess allows women to deal with 'specific forms of psychical and emotional satisfaction and dissatisfaction, and specific ways of dealing with conflicts and dilemmas' (Ang, 1990: 83). In particular, it offers a retreat from the complexities of time management and scarcity and from juggling roles, in the process offering the potential for feelings of comfort and security that, while not located in an idealized 'real' past, are nonetheless connected with 'real' and imagined feminine figures and scenarios that maintain a sense of tradition. As with the pleasures of investing in make-up, an investment in taking time to enjoy the pleasures of cooking appears to do little to disturb the traditional contours of femininity. Yet, in a postfeminist landscape in which it is often manifest that contemporary femininity is multiple and complex, the desire to temporarily inhabit a figure of femininity which appears stable, which is of another time (literal or mythical) in which things seem simpler and less contradictory than the present, can also appear to offer a sense of escape from the pressures of managing and ordering both everyday life and feminine selves.

'I choose my choice': postfeminism, middle-class femininity and domesticity

In an episode from *Sex and the City* (55, 'Time and Punishment'), Charlotte tells her three single friends that she is thinking of giving up her job in a gallery to create enough time for the other interests she wants to pursue: having a baby, taking an Indian cookery class, learning pottery and doing volunteer work in a paediatric AIDS ward. The single girls look distraught and pour scorn on the idea of becoming 'one of those women we hate' who quit their jobs once they get married. Perturbed by their response, Charlotte phones Miranda, the character most closely identified with the figure of the 'career woman', early the following morning to ask her to stop being judgemental and to get behind her choice: 'The Women's Movement is supposed to be about choice and if I choose to quit my job, that's my choice. . . . It's my life and it's my choice. . . . I am behind my choice. . . . I choose my choice. I choose my choice.' The episode provides a useful dramatization of the ways in which femininity for the new middle classes can be inhabited as a choice in which not only are certain modes of femininity embraced but, in the process, others are also refused. It also demonstrates that these choices are far from straightforward. And, at the end of the episode, we see career woman Miranda playing hookie from her job in a law firm, sitting on the sofa watching a cookery show on TV, enjoying a bit of her domesticated 'other'. Carrie's voiceover tell us: 'And, for the first time in her life, Miranda learned the joys of cooking and of not working. Of course, she'd have to back down eventually, just to prove Charlotte wrong.'

Charlotte's comments provide a valuable illustration of how rhetorics of feminism, contemporary femininity and middle classness are articulated around ideas of choice (although, at the same time, Charlotte's increasingly hysterical assertions of 'I choose my choice' allow the show to also undercut these ideas, suggesting that the compulsion to make a choice constitutes a lack of choice). Commenting on the work of Marilyn Strathern, Skeggs observes how 'the middle class continually have to make choices, of viewpoints, of resources, of what to attach to themselves' (forthcoming). The idea that there are 'no rules, only choices' that has been associated with the new middle classes (see, for example, Featherstone, 1991a) also coincides with what some feminist critics have seen as a brand of 'popular individualistic feminism' that emerged in the 1980s, which served to cement a relationship between feminism and middle-class privilege (Skeggs, 1997: 153). For Probyn, writing about US television shows of the same period, class and gender are articulated in 'a new age of "choiceoisie" ' which is part of a wider postfeminist landscape (1990: 152).

The commentary surrounding the publication of *Domestic Goddess*, like the discussions between Carrie and her friends, was also couched in terms of choice. Some commentators demonized Nigella in the name of 'feminism'; as Gillian Glover asked, 'didn't Marilyn French, Erica Jong and Germaine Greer free us from our need to please the genie of the Fairy Liquid bottle?' (2000: 9). Such comments frequently assumed a straightforward choice between feminism and domestic femininity in which feminism could be the only 'rational' response; 'Could it be that the real reason women hate baking is because cake-baking epitomizes our status as domestic slaves? Most men secretly love the idea of a Stepford Wife, programmed to eager servitude, be it sex or baking' (Tyrer, 2000: 47). Burnside sneered that, 'For women who have given up career jobs to make packed lunches and sew Tweenie costumes', *Domestic Goddess* was 'affirming stuff' (2000: 16). However, she also acknowledged that this was not simply about a choice between the identities of feminist and domestic goddess, but about the inability of most women to choose between or effortlessly combine family and work, as they lacked Nigella's privileged background. Likewise, Raven suggested that Nigella peddles a fantasy that women don't need to choose and can 'have it all': 'the fear of choosing one thing at the expense of the other is soothed by the subtextual message that ambition does not preclude the domestic idyll they all yearn for' (2000: 5).

These readings of *Domestic Goddess* are obviously at odds with the one I have made above. My point in rehearsing them here is less to criticize them and more to demonstrate the extent to which they, like Nigella and like the women in *Sex and the City*, also constitute a wider landscape in which middle-class femininities are seen as a product of choices between femininities, 'in which feminism itself is bound up with the discourse of choice' (Probyn, 1993: 284). Choices are offered between feminism and domesticity, between workplace and family, between paid work and domestic labour, between 'work-work' and 'leisure-work'. These 'discourses of choice construct positions for women – they place us in relation to other discourses and in relation to our everyday lives' (1993: 282). While, as Skeggs (forthcoming) rightly points out, this 'begs the question of what about those who have no choice?', it also suggests that the 'no rules, only choices' mentality that is supposed to be characteristic of the new middle classes is rather more fraught for women when 'having it all' is constituted within the popular as yet a further, compromised and problematic choice.

On the one hand, these representations of choice not only serve to denaturalize modes of femininity (including 'feminist femininities'), but also gesture to the ways in which femininities are crosscut by class. On the other hand, however, they do far more than this. Probyn's analysis of choice is useful because it highlights the ways in which representations of choice are not simply about the opportunity to change our lives, but may more modestly simply allow us to 'feel differently'. For Probyn, it is necessary to analyse 'the affective implications of the images of choice as they circulate within the material structure of our lives' (1993: 283). It is here that 'feeling like a domestic goddess' may offer rather more than a compensation for living in the present. The representation of a mode of femininity that is based around cooking and eating as pleasure, rather than servitude and denial, may begin to offer a way of experiencing cooking and eating differently. It also provides an alternative means of representing women's relationship with food to that offered by (some very good) feminist criticism. Furthermore, for this author at least, while there are times when I want to feel 'like a feminist', there are other times when I really do want to feel 'like a domestic goddess' (and, seemingly, I am not alone in this; see Campbell, 2001: 5). While I have no wish to offer my own fantasies as a prescription for anything, 'this rearrangement of the feel of the material' (Probyn, 1993: 283) enables one way of experiencing what it would feel like to live between the dichotomies upon which feminist authority frequently depends.

Alison Light has argued that fantasy allows us to explore 'desires which may be in excess of the socially possible or acceptable' (1984: 7). This suggests that, while the social and cultural constraints which the fantasy of being a domestic goddess addresses are important, so are judgements of taste about 'acceptable' and 'unacceptable' femininities. As Sara Thornton argues, 'Distinctions are never just assertions of equal difference; they usually entail some claim to authority and presume the inferiority of *others*' (1995: 10; emphasis in original). Within the popular, versions of feminism do have an impact on constructions of cultural distinctions between femininities and, like the more 'official' feminisms of second-wave feminism, they sometimes suggest that it is our duty to make a choice. The morally charged judgements against Charlotte's decision to make pots and have a baby, like the vilification of Nigella in some portions of the British press, suggest that the 'choice' between femininities is not straightforward, but bound up within a series of moral 'rules' – feminist and otherwise.

Notes

1   Indeed, of the kind people who discussed this with me, many commented on what I was going to do about her 'beauty' and the implications of this in terms of her representation of anxiety and her own eating, on the one hand, and her relationship to a sizeable heterosexual male fan base on the other. These remain issues to address, but are beyond the scope of this article.

2   See, for example, the trailer for Channel 4's *Does Doug Know?*, in which Daisy Donovan flirts mercilessly with the camera in the style of Nigella, and BBC1's *Alistair McGowan's Big Impression*, where a hassled Nigella 'prepares' Mars bars as a pudding for her children ('I prefer to open them with my teeth').

3   I am grateful to one of the readers of this article for these comments. It should also be noted that there is far less emphasis on Nigella as working mother and far more emphasis on a leisured lifestyle in *Forever Summer*.

4   And indeed Nigella introduces us to her own very solitary pleasure in fried pig's ear which no one else will eat (*Nigella Bites*, 4, 'Home Alone').

5   It is interesting to note that in Garry Marshall's *Runaway Bride* (1999), Maggie Carpenter (Julia Roberts) only deems herself ready to marry once she stops eating her eggs in whatever style her current man favours and does a tasting session to discover her own preferences.

6   This reference to the lab can be seen as a way in which Nigella's approach to cooking is not only distinguished from a tradition of domestic science, on the one hand, and industrial food production, on the other, but also from the hyperscientific approach to cookery associated with figures such as the chef and contributor to the *Guardian* Heston Blumenthal.

7   While this changes in *Forever Summer*, when Charles Saatchi is introduced, the emphasis in this series, as befits the new couple, is largely on eating with friends rather than everyday domestic cookery.

8   The importance of fantasy is also employed in her later work, when the reader is invited to act *as if* it could be 'forever summer'. As Lawson explains:

> Summer, then, is an idea, a memory, a hopeful projection. Sometimes when it's grey outside and cold within, we need to conjure up the sun, some light, a lazy feeling of having all the wide-skied time in the world to sit back and eat warmly with friends. (2002: vii)

Furthermore, cooking is something that can be done both 'in lieu of travelling' and as a means of evoking a memory of past travels, a means of acting *as if* we were temporarily in another country (2002: 76). In the television series, Nigella compares the pleasure she takes from the displays in a British Italian deli to those she has experienced in European markets. In this way, Nigella again employs a means of using cooking to play with time and to create a sense of leisured time that is associated with holidays. This is accentuated in the television series where much of the cooking is taken out into the garden or relocated to the kitchen of a seaside holiday home. In this way, summer cooking becomes associated with both a time and a space that are presented as a holiday from the demands of everyday domestic cookery.

References

Ang, I. (1985) *Watching Dallas: Soap Opera and the Melodramatic Imagination*. London: Methuen.

Ang, I. (1990) 'Melodramatic Identifications: Television and Women's Fantasy', in M.E. Brown (ed.) *Television and Women's Culture: The Politics of the Popular*, pp. 75–88. London: Sage.

Attfield, J. (1995) 'Inside Pram Town: A Case Study of Harlow House Interiors, 1951–61', in J. Attfield and P. Kirkham (eds) *A View from the Interior: Women and Design*, pp. 215–38. London: Women's Press.

Bell, D. (2000) 'Performing Tastes: Celebrity Chefs and Culinary Cultural Capital', paper presented at the Crossroads in Cultural Studies conference, Birmingham University, July.

Bell, D. (2002) 'From Writing at the Kitchen Table to TV Dinners: Food Media, Lifestylization and European Eating', paper presented at the Eat, Drink and Be Merry? Cultural Meanings of Food in the 21st Century conference, Amsterdam, June. [http://www.cf.hum.uva.nl/research/asca/Themedia-reader.htm]

Bourdieu, P. (1984) *Distinction: A Social Critique of the Judgement of Taste*. London: Routledge.

Brunsdon, C. (1997) *Screen Tastes: Soap Opera to Satellite Dishes*. London: Routledge.

Brunsdon, C. (2000) *The Feminist, the Housewife and the Soap Opera*. Oxford: Oxford University Press.

Burnside, A. (2000) 'Lessons from a Goddess', *The Sunday Herald* (3 Sept.): 16.

Campbell, D. (2001) 'Housewives Choice?', *Trouble and Strife* 42: 2–12.

Charles, N. and M. Kerr (1988) *Women, Food and Families: Power, Status, Love, Anger*. Manchester: Manchester University Press.

Chodorow, N. (1978) *The Reproduction of Mothering: Psychoanalysis and the Sociology of Gender*. Berkeley: University of California Press.

Clarke, A.J. (1997) 'Tupperware: Suburbia, Sociality and Mass Consumption', in R. Silverstone (ed.) *Visions of Suburbia*, pp. 132–60. London: Routledge.

Cronin, A. (2000) 'Consumerism and "Compulsory Individuality": Women, Will and Potential', in S. Ahmed, J. Kilby, C. Lury, M. McNeil and B. Skeggs (eds) *Transformations: Thinking through Feminism*, pp. 273–87. London: Routledge.

DeVault, M. (1991) *Feeding the Family: The Social Organization of Caring as Gendered Work*. Chicago, IL: University of Chicago Press.

Dyer, R. (1985) 'Entertainment and Utopia', in B. Nichols (ed.) *Movies and Methods*, Vol. 2, pp. 200–32. Berkeley: University of California Press.

Featherstone, M. (1991a) *Consumer Culture and Postmodernism*. London: Sage.

Featherstone, M. (1991b) 'The Body in Consumer Culture', in M. Featherstone, M. Hepworth and B. Turner (eds) *The Body: Social Process and Cultural Theory*, pp. 170–96. London: Sage.

Felski, R. (2000) *Doing Time: Feminist Theory and Postmodern Culture*. New York: New York University Press.

Fine, G.A. (1996) *Kitchens: The Culture of Restaurant Work*. Berkeley: University of California Press.

Geraghty, C. (1991) *Women and Soap Opera: A Study of Prime-time Soap Operas*. Cambridge: Polity Press.

Giard, L. (1998) 'Doing Cooking', in M. de Certeau, L. Giard and P. Mayol *The Practice of Everyday Life*, Vol. 2: *Living and Cooking*, pp. 149–247. Minneapolis: University of Minnesota Press.

Glover, G. (2000) 'New Sex and Old Dusters', *The Scotsman* (20 Sept): 9.

Gordon, J. (2000) 'Men Belong in the Kitchen Too', *The Times* (4 Oct.), Part 2: 7.

Gregson, N. and M. Lowe (1995) ' "Too Much Work": Class, Gender and the Reconstitution of Middle Class Domestic Labour', in T. Butler and M. Savage (eds) *Social Change and the Middle Class*, pp. 148–65. London: UCL Press.

Hollows, J. (2002) 'The Bachelor Dinner: Masculinity, Class and Cooking in *Playboy*, 1953–61', *Continuum* 16(2): 143–55.

Kaplan, C. (1986) '*The Thorn Birds*: Fiction, Fantasy, Femininity', in V. Burgin, J. Donald and C. Kaplan (eds) *Formations of Fantasy*, pp. 142–66. London: Methuen.

Kemmer, D. (1999) 'Food Preparation and the Division of Domestic Labour among Newly Married and Cohabiting Couples', *British Food Journal* 101(8): 570–9.

Laudan, R. (1999) 'A World of Inauthentic Cuisine', paper presented at the Cultural and Historical Aspects of Food: Yesterday, Today, Tomorrow conference, Oregon State University, 9–11 April.

Lawson, N. (1999) *How to Eat: The Pleasures and Principles of Good Food*. London: Chatto & Windus.

Lawson, N. (2000) *How to Be a Domestic Goddess: Baking and the Art of Comfort Cooking*. London: Chatto & Windus.

Lawson, N. (2001) *Nigella Bites*. London: Chatto & Windus.

Lawson, N. (2002) *Forever Summer*, London: Chatto & Windus.

Light, A. (1984) 'Returning to Manderley: Romantic Fiction, Female Sexuality and Class', *Feminist Review* 16: 7–25.

Lupton, D. (1996) *Food, the Body and the Self*. London: Sage.

Lury, C. (1996) *Consumer Culture*. Cambridge: Polity Press.

McFeeley, M.D. (2001) *Can She Bake a Cherry Pie? American Women and the Kitchen in the Twentieth Century*. Amherst: University of Massachusetts Press.

McRobbie, A. (1994) *Postmodernism and Popular Culture*. London: Routledge.

Martens, L. (1997) 'Gender and the Eating Out Experience', *British Food Journal* 99(1): 20–6.

Meyerowitz, J. (ed.) (1994) *Not June Cleaver: Women and Gender in Postwar America, 1945–60*. Philadelphia, PA: Temple University Press.

Miller, D. (1998) *A Theory of Shopping*. Cambridge: Polity Press.

Moore, S. (2000) 'Did We Fight for the Right to Bake?', *Mail on Sunday* (22 Oct.): 31.

Moores, S. (1993) *Interpreting Audiences: The Ethnography of Media Consumption*. London: Sage.

Morley, D. (2000) *Home Territories: Media, Mobility and Identity*. London: Routledge.

Moseley, R. (2000) 'Makeover Takeover on British Television', *Screen* 41(3): 299–314.

Moseley, R. (2001) ' "Real Lads *Do* Cook – But Some Things Are Still Hard to Talk About": The Gendering of 8–9', *European Journal of Cultural Studies* 4(1): 32–9.

Moseley, R. and J. Read (2002) 'Having it *Ally*: Popular Television (Post)Feminism', *Feminist Media Studies* 2(2): 231–49.

Murcott, A. (1995) ' "It's a Pleasure to Cook for Him": Food, Mealtimes and Gender in Some South Wales Households', in S. Jackson and S. Moores (eds) *The Politics of Domestic Consumption*, pp. 89–99. Hemel Hempstead: Harvester Wheatsheaf.

Murcott, A. (1997) 'Family Meals: A Thing of the Past?', in P. Caplan (ed.) *Food, Health and Identity*, pp. 32–49. London: Routledge.

Probyn, E. (1990) 'New Traditionalism and Post-feminism: TV Does the Home', *Screen* 31(2): 147–59.

Probyn, E. (1993) 'Choosing Choice: Winking Images of Sexuality in Popular Culture', in S. Fisher and K. Davis (eds) *Negotiating at the Margins: Gendered Discourses of Resistance*, pp. 278–94. New Brunswick, NJ: Rutgers University Press.

Radner, H. (1989) ' "This Time's for Me": Making Up and Feminine Practice', *Cultural Studies* 3(3): 301–22.

Raven, C. (2000) 'A Half-baked Fantasy: On Why Nigella Lawson Has Become an Icon', *Guardian* G2 (3 Oct.): 5.

Read, J. (2000) *The New Avengers: Feminism, Femininity and the Rape-Revenge Cycle*. Manchester: Manchester University Press.

Rowe, K. (1997) '*Roseanne*: Unruly Woman as Domestic Goddess', in C. Brunsdon, J. D'Acci and L. Spigel (eds) *Feminist Television Criticism*, pp. 74–83. Oxford: Oxford University Press.

Skeggs, B. (1997) *Formations of Class and Gender*. London: Sage.

Skeggs, B. (forthcoming) *Class, Self and Culture*. London: Routledge.

Southerton, D., E. Shove and A. Warde (2001) ' "Harried and Hurried": Time Shortage and the Co-ordination of Everyday Life', CRIC Discussion Paper 47. Manchester: Centre for Research on Innovation and Competition.

Sparke, P. (1995) *As Long as it's Pink: The Sexual Politics of Taste*. London: Pandora.

Theophano, J. (2002) *Eat My Words: Reading Women's Lives through the Cookbooks They Wrote*. New York: Palgrave.

Thornton, S. (1995) *Club Cultures: Music, Media and Subcultural Capital*. Cambridge: Polity Press.

Tyrer, N. (2000) 'Who Wants to Be a Domestic Goddess Anyway?', *Daily Mail* (19 Oct.): 47.

Warde, A. (1997) *Consumption, Food and Taste: Culinary Antinomies and Commodity Culture*. London: Sage.

Warde, A. (1999) 'Convenience Food: Space and Timing', *British Food Journal* 101(7): 518–27.

Warde, A., M. Tomlinson and A. McMeekin (2000) 'Expanding Tastes? Cultural Omnivorousness and Social Change in the UK', CRIC Discussion Paper 37. Manchester: Centre for Research on Innovation and Competition.

9

Feminism Without Men
Feminist media studies in a post-feminist age

Karen Boyle

Originally published in James Curran and Michael Gurevitch (eds),
Mass media and Society, 4th edn (London: Arnold, 2005).

Post-ing feminism

The terms "feminism" and "post-feminism" are widely used both in the media and in media studies, yet their meaning is difficult to pin down. As Amanda Lotz writes:

> Confusion and contradiction mark understandings of feminism in US popular culture at the turn of the 21st century. Surveying the terrain of both feminist theory and popular discussions of feminism, we seem to have entered an alternate language universe where words can simultaneously connote a meaning and its opposite.
>
> (Lotz, 2001: 105)

This article considers how this confusion and contradiction impact upon feminist media studies, focusing on the ways in which "post-feminism" features in these debates. The final section works through these issues in relation to *Buffy the Vampire Slayer* and feminist criticism of the show.

At the outset, a definition of terms must be provided, although this is no easy task. Indeed, a quick perusal of any book dealing with feminist theory provides an array of feminism*s*: liberal feminism, socialist feminism, radical or revolutionary feminism, lesbian feminism, black feminism, postmodern feminism, first, second or third wave feminisms to name just a few. Clearly, these feminisms are defined less by commonality than by difference – of membership, generation, allegiance with other political movements, modes of organisation and relationship to the academy – but they do share a common recognition of gendered inequality and a determination to change that reality. Or, as bell hooks (2000: 1) puts it: "feminism is a movement to end sexism, sexist exploitation, and oppression." So, until sexism, sexist exploitation and oppression have been consigned to the dustbin of history, there will be a need for feminism.

In this context, what can "post-feminism" offer?

If defining feminism is complicated, then defining post-feminism is even more so, requiring a definition both of the feminism to be "post-ed" and of the "post-ing" itself. The feminism most often at stake here is second-wave feminism, which, in both the UK and US, can be dated to the development of the women's liberation movement in the late-1960s. Many contemporary writers – whether they define themselves as post-feminist or not – characterise the WLM as a consensus-based political movement, noting the movement's rejection of conventional modes of femininity and its assumption of a universalised feminist sisterhood (e.g. Brooks, 1997; Hollows, 2000). There is a certain amount of truth in this characterisation. There was (and still is) a tension between feminism and femininity that alienated many women, and the 1960s-70s movement was rightly criticised – particularly by women-of-colour, lesbians and working-class women – for ignoring structural differences between women in the often naïve conception of "sisterhood" (e.g. Carby, 1982; hooks, 1982). However, it is not true that the second wave completely failed to recognise difference (Richardson, 1996). In the British context, for example, debates at the National Women's Liberation Movement conferences held between 1971–78 repeatedly foregrounded women's different positions of privilege in relation to regional, class and sexual identities. Difference, here, was not simply an issue for theory (though it *was* an issue for theory), but related to the organisation and priorities of the movement itself. At the regional and local level, groups organised around single issues (including reproductive rights, wages for housework and violence against women) or sought to bring women together on the basis of commonality *and* difference, in relation, for example, to racial, ethnic or national identities, class, sexuality or experience of motherhood.[1]

However, what is perhaps most worrying about the (re-)construction of the second wave as a period of consensus is the way this functions to take the movement out of feminism or to equate movement with the "post" era (see Brooks, 1997). Feminism's practices have never remained static but have developed and responded to change, both in the contemporary period and in feminism's first-wave (see Littlewood, 2004: 149–50). Acknowledging difference, then, is not to "post" feminism, but to *do* feminism. As hooks (2000: 58) argues:

> There has been no contemporary movement for social justice where individual participants engaged in the dialectical exchange that occurred among feminist thinkers about race which led to the re-thinking of much feminist theory and practice. The fact that participants in the feminist movement could face critique and challenge while still remaining wholeheartedly committed to a vision of justice, of liberation, is a testament to the movement's strength and power. It shows us that no matter how misguided feminist thinkers have been in the past, the will to change, the will to create the context for struggle and liberation, remains stronger than the need to hold on to wrong beliefs and assumptions.

The understanding of feminism upon which post-feminism relies is, therefore, flawed. To be clear, this is not to argue that there is one authentic feminism that post-feminism has simply mis-understood. Rather, it is to point to the very multiplicity of feminisms – within as well as outside of the second wave – and the inherent difficulty of attempting to fix feminism in order to "post" it.

The meaning of the "post" in post-feminism also requires consideration. Broadly speaking, there are three overlapping ways in which the term is used – to imply a periodisation, a rejection or a development of second-wave feminism – and I will briefly consider each of these, reflecting on the way these meanings are constructed in popular representations and by feminist media critics. It should also be noted, how-ever, that I am – of necessity – glossing over important national and disciplinary differences in the usage of the term (Lotz, 2001: 112). Partly, this is a practical decision – mapping the terrain is already complicated enough and my aim is to give a broad overview of debates rather than a strictly comprehensive account – but it is also an acknowledgement that the ways in which discourses about (post-)feminism circulate, within media studies and within the media, are not bound by national or disciplinary boundaries even as they may exhibit national or disciplinary peculiarities.

Periodising feminism

In implying a periodisation, post-feminism speaks of a time *after* feminism.

As Sarah Projansky (2001: 70) notes, the death of (second-wave) feminism has been regularly proclaimed in the media since the early 1980s. The reasons given for its passing are two-fold: either feminism's successes have rendered the movement obsolete because women now have equality; or, feminism's failures have rendered the movement obsolete in demonstrating the absurdity of feminist demands and the intractability of material differences based on gender. However, to go back a step, the very existence of feminism's second wave depends upon a first wave (usually associ-ated with the struggle for suffrage). To the extent that it ignores this legacy and reduces all feminisms to one feminist moment (in the late 1960s-1970s), post-feminism is profoundly ahistorical (Brunsdon, 1997: 102).

Moreover, proclaiming the "death" of feminism in this way depends upon an assumption that feminism's movement is a linear one. This is difficult to sustain, not least because so much feminist work has to be continually rediscovered by new gener-ations (Spender, 1982). As a result, constructing a feminist lineage is fraught with difficulty. For example, Ann Brooks' (1997) attempt to fix writers and ideas within a chronology culminating in post-feminism leads her to describe Ann Kaplan's work of the early 1980s as "pre-postfeminist" and Teresa de Lauretis' work of the same period as "early postfeminist". Both of these designations imply that there is a moment, in time as well as in theory, before which it is not possible to talk of post-feminism and after which it is not possible to talk about feminism without qualifica-tion (hence, "pre-postfeminism" rather than simply "feminism"). Leslie Heywood and Jennifer Drake (1997: 4), attempt to fix their moment even more precisely, defin-ing feminists born between 1963–74 as third wavers. Clearly, the history of feminist theory and practice is important. However, it is difficult to see how this kind of fixing of pre-feminist, feminist, post-feminist *moments* is useful on a theoretical, political or even on a personal, level. After all, how many of us experience feminism in this way?

To give a personal example: my birthdate places me within Heywood and Drake's third wave and my teenage years were clearly shaped by the gains of the second wave, but I only encountered feminist activism and theory as a young adult in the academy. This academic encounter – which privileged the texts and theories of the second wave – led to my involvement with feminist organisations working to challenge male violence and support women survivors, an on-going involvement that feeds into my academic writing and thinking about feminism and the media. How I "do" feminism (and how I do feminist media criticism) therefore continues to shift as I encounter new ideas, practices and challenges and as – through my academic work – I encounter old ideas, practices and challenges that are, nevertheless, new to me. I am continually learning about feminism's present and its history, and that conjunction shapes the kind of feminism I "do". But it also makes the need to fix and precisely define that feminism impossible and rather redundant. On a broader scale, the intellectual effort to fix and define feminism(s) is often counter-productive in that it makes feminism and feminists (not sexism, sexist exploitation and oppression) the subject of our criticism.

One result of this within feminist media studies is that we have numerous studies that explore the "feminism" of women-centred media texts, but very little work that examines the daily playing out of gender relations in non-feminist or male-centred shows. "Post-feminism" has been a key concept in much of this scholarship since the early 1990s (Lotz, 2001). Charlotte Brunsdon (1997: 81–102), for example, uses the term in an essay on *Working Girl* (Nichols, 1987) and *Pretty Woman* (Marshall, 1990) to signal how these films are formed by, yet disavow, feminism. She argues that the female protagonists have a specific relation to femininity, being neither trapped in femininity (pre-feminist), nor rejecting of it (feminist), but, rather, using it to their own advantage in the workplace and the bedroom. Whilst the heroines' uses of femininity often look decidedly pre-feminist, their desires and aspirations – for career advancement, equality in interpersonal relationships, financial independence and sexual satisfaction – are expressed in a vocabulary that is historically specific in its debt to feminism. It is precisely this combination of traditional femininity with the gains of second-wave feminism that many cultural critics – both within and outside of the academy – have labelled post-feminist.

For these critics, post-feminism is not a movement or theory, but a way of acknowledging the complex relationship to feminism exhibited in mainstream cultural texts and, indeed, the term is sometimes used as though it is synonymous with popular feminism. It is the apparent tension between feminism and femininity that is central here and, as a result, a majority of this work is concerned with women and girls. So, for example, we have numerous studies addressing the (post-)feminist attributes of Madonna (Schwichtenberg, 1993), *Sex and the City* (Arthurs, 2003; Kim, 2001; Henry, 2004), *Ally McBeal* (Moseley and Read, 2002; Kim, 2001) and *Buffy the Vampire Slayer* (Owen, 1999; Daugherty, 2002; Vint, 2002), to name just a few of the most popular topics. Of course, it is not incidental that these texts/performers have also become central to popular debates about feminism, from the much-discussed *Time* cover (June 29, 1998) that used Ally McBeal to symbolise the death of feminism, to debates in the quality press about whether Madonna/Carrie/Ally/Buffy et al. can be defined as "feminist". As Moseley and Read (2002) convincingly argue, it is important for feminist cultural critics to engage with and interrogate these popular (post-)feminisms. However, my concern is that we allow the popular debate to set the parameters of our own study. Thus, the emphasis of much of this work is on women (critics) judging women (performers, characters) on behalf of a third group of women (viewers, fans, consumers) who look to the media for suitable role models.

In discussing the suitability of these characters as role models for (other) women, it is important to note that physical appearance and dress are recurring concerns. Whilst there are important questions to be asked about the media's construction of feminine beauty, there is a danger that this obsessive focus on women's appearance as the marker of their worth – albeit, this time as feminist role models – replicates the construction of women as objects of the (male) gaze in the mainstream media. The emphasis on appearance and clothing also contributes to the construction of feminism as an out-dated fashion or performance, associated with repression and replaced by this season's post-feminism with its lipgloss, designer shoes and push-up bras. In other words, much of this criticism emphasises the (re-)construction of the self rather than providing a framework for action.

In a paper reflecting on the field of feminist television scholarship, Brunsdon (2004) makes a broadly similar argument, noting that much recent work in the field has taken the form of what she dubs the "ur-feminist article". This ubiquitous article begins by noting how a text (or character) aimed at women or focusing on women characters has been denounced or claimed by feminists and goes on to explore whether the text/character fits the author's definition of feminism. Thus, the very project of much feminist television criticism involves an articulation of dis-identity, as though it is only possible for the critic to identify herself (or her object of study) as feminist by saying what kind of a feminist she/ it is not. Moreover, to the extent that feminist television criticism has developed around this ur-article, it has focused primarily on character, appearance and story with the result that other aspects of the television text – seriality, flow, aesthetics, sound and so on – have been rather marginalised. Feminism, not television, has become the critical focus.

Rejecting feminism

While the term post-feminism has a certain validity in describing the simultaneous debt to and disavowal of feminism in contemporary media discourse, it is less useful as a description of feminist theory and activism as it consigns that theory and activism to the past and erases its future. For, if post-feminism represents the evolution of the second wave then it also implies the end of the sequence: how can there be a third, fourth or fifth wave post (i.e. after) feminism? It is in this sense that post-feminism has been associated with a rejection of, or backlash against, feminism.

Post-feminism and the backlash are not new phenomena. Indeed, Susan Faludi (1992: 70) notes that the term post-feminism first surfaced in the US press in the 1920s and was used to construct an opposition between younger women and their feminist elders at the very point that feminist gains began to re-shape the public sphere. In the contemporary context, Faludi links the re-invention of post-feminism to the political conservatism of the 1980s and the attempt to solicit women's consent for anti-women policies by presenting feminism, rather than sexism and oppression, as the source of women's discontent. For Faludi, then, post-feminism is virtually synonymous with the backlash, both in the moments of their emergence and in their ideological projects of pitting generations of women against one another.

The construction of post-feminism as generational requires comment. Admittedly, the language, organisation, style and even some of the key demands of the 1970s' women's movement seem alien to many daughters of the second wave. However, this does not mean that a decisive and antagonistic split is necessary. Indeed, those identifying themselves as third-wave feminists often have a clear sense of how their own politics and activism continue and develop the struggles of an earlier, but still active, generation.[2]

In contrast, the label "post-feminist" – certainly as it is applied in the media – is more often used to indicate a decisive break with and rejection of the more radical politics of second-wave feminism. Nowhere was this more apparent than in the early-1990s when books by Camile Paglia (1993), Naomi Wolf (1994), Katie Roiphe (1994) and Christina Hoff Sommers (1994) very publicly asserted that it was feminism (and not the backlash) that was failing women, and young women in particular. These writers – variously labelled as post-feminists, anti-feminists, power-feminists and new feminists – have little in common, except, perhaps, a general concern with rejecting what they argue is the "victimising" tendency of radical feminism and with exploring women's autonomy and sexual desire. Their arguments are, in many ways, attractive. It is, after all, much less depressing to think about what gives us pleasure than to focus on situations where women are relatively powerless, and easier to change the self than to change society. Indeed, the individual is the main focus of these books and while these authors typically criticise feminism's second wave for ignoring differences between women, the fierce individualism of these texts allows for little constructive consideration of difference. The extensive media coverage these authors received on both sides of the Atlantic replicated this individualism, turning the authors' physical appearances and personal lives into the subject of analysis. This Projansky (2001: 71) describes as an anti-feminist feminist post-feminism: a feminism that insists upon the death of other feminisms in proclaiming its own birth.

The post-feminism born out of this conjuncture is a feminism that is focused on the aspirations and possibilities for individual women (typically, white, affluent, American women) but rejecting of second-wave feminism's demands for structural change. In particular, this post-feminism seems designed to let men (and patriarchy) off the hook, either by celebrating men's feminism or by turning individual men into objects of fun and derision whilst affirming the ideal of masculinity. This phenomenon is not, of course, consigned to theoretical texts and, indeed, a number of feminist media critics and commentators have explored its manifestation in popular culture. For example, in their analyses of rape representations in US film and television, both Projansky (2001) and Moorti (2002) demonstrate that it is on-screen men who most frequently give voice to feminist arguments and teach women about feminism, often in the face of other women's opposition. It might seem counter-intuitive to argue that this is an anti-feminist move, however, when men are cast as "better" feminists than women, women (and feminists) are once more positioned as redundant.

The redundancy of women was, of course, taken a stage further in many texts emerging during the 1980s where women were, quite literally, absent. It was this absence that led Tania Modleski (1991) to describe the post-feminist age as "feminism without women", a description that has two meanings, pointing both to a feminist anti-essentialism (of which, more later), and to the triumph of a male feminist perspective that excludes women. It is important to emphasise that Modleski's "feminism without women" is a popular feminism, that is, it is (post-)feminism *as represented* in media texts (factual and fictional), rather than a development within theory – and, indeed, it is in this guise that post-feminism has most often featured in media criticism.

However, while Modleski saw women being obliterated in the cultural landscape of the 1980s, any review of feminist media studies must conclude that it is men who are missing in action. Feminist media studies' focus on women is not, however, a post-feminist innovation. For example, Brunsdon (1995) identifies four main categories of *feminist* television scholarship: the real world of women working in television; content analyses of the presence of women on the screen; textual studies of programmes for and about women; and studies focusing on female audiences. More specifically, in the introduction to *Feminist Television Criticism*, Brunsdon, D'Acci and Spigel (1997:1) suggest that feminist television criticism is defined by an engagement, "with the problems of feminism and femininity – what these terms mean, how they relate to each other, what they constitute and exclude". Yet, despite its women-centeredness, much of this work sets about deconstructing the very category "woman", with the result that it becomes very self-reflexive, individualistic and difficult to relate to a feminist politic. Indeed, in the early 21st century, we seem to have reached a point where the legacy of feminism in relation to both television content and television scholarship is being repeatedly, indeed almost exclusively, measured by the performances of individual women and girls (Madonna, Carrie, Ally, Buffy et al.). The critical focus on individual women allows the challenge of feminism to disappear as it is positioned as a lifestyle choice (being feminist) rather than a movement (doing feminism). If feminism is equated with women's agency, choice and subjectivity, then questions about gender, about structural inequalities, discrimination, oppression and violence are allowed to slip from view.

Finally, it is instructive to consider the gleeful men-bashing indulged in by female-centred 1990s texts such as *Bridget Jones' Diary* (Fielding, 1997) or *Sex and the City* (1998–2004) which are also routinely dubbed "post-feminist" by critics. In a *Guardian* column reflecting on *Sex and the City*'s first series, Charlotte Raven (1999) describes the show's male characters as:

> commitment-phobes, smug marrieds, posers, nerds, swingers, clingers, workaholics, slackers, culture bores, philistines, predators, romantics, porn freaks, computer geeks, emotional illiterates, needy jerks, fastidious queens, slobs, liars, confessors, fashion victims, dorks, virgins, perverts, twentysomething bimbos, thirtysomething creeps, fortysomething saddos and – most contemptible of all – losers with tiny dicks.

– hardly a prestigious roll-call. It is not surprising, therefore, that many of the column inches devoted to *Sex and the City* were reports on the battle of the sexes. Yet, whilst this battle might look considerably different to that conducted by the feminist men of Projansky and Moorti's rape narratives, there are important parallels: both pre-empt feminist critiques of male power and privilege by showing men to be either willing to give up that power (feminist) or incapable of wielding power (pathetic). In both instances power is dispersed to the point where it becomes impossible to analyse the structural inequalities that have concerned feminists. To return to Raven:

> [Feminists'] man-hating wasn't a bar-room grudge but a response to a political situation. It wasn't about individuals – most feminists got on fine with individual men, even as we also denounced masculinity as an idea. These days, the situation is reversed. The modern man-hater hates specific men but worships the idea of masculinity.

Nevertheless, it would be too simplistic to state that authors like Roiphe or programmes like *Sex and the City* are simply anti-feminist, for both the texts themselves and the extensive public debate they generate also provide feminism's most public face. As Projansky (2001: 70) argues in her discussion of yet-another magazine editorial proclaiming the "death" of feminism, such texts ensure that feminism lives on in the public imaginary even if only to instigate the question about its demise. Or, as Faludi (1992) argues, the intensity of the backlash is very real evidence of the clear and present danger to the status quo that feminism represents.

Developing feminism

In this section, I want to consider how the term "post-feminism" is used to describe a regeneration and development of feminist theory within the context of broader developments in post-modernism and post-structuralism. "Feminism without women" in this context refers to an anti-essentialist challenge to the very category "woman" (and "man", though this is rarely made explicit) and the abandonment of grand narratives and universalising theories. For anti-essentialists, it should not matter whether we do our feminism without women or without men: the point is that gender-categories per se are mutable. But it is important to ask whose interests are best served by such a deconstruction?

For Brooks (1997: 4), whose *Postfeminisms: Feminism, Cultural Theory and Cultural Forms* provides a valuable summary of these debates, the term "post-feminism" denotes a "conceptual shift within feminism from debates about equality to debates about difference". A fundamental problem with this formulation is, of course, the way in which it reduces the history and diversity of feminisms to one strand of the 1960s–70s movement (liberal, or equity feminism), suggesting that feminism depended upon a consensus (however fragile) among women and an ignorance of the differences that shape our experiences under patriarchy. For Brooks, the recognition of difference so fundamentally challenged feminism as to warrant the invention of this new label, though many of the critics she cites (including bell hooks) resist the post-feminist label and, instead, see their work as contributing to the development of *feminist* theory and practice. It is also worth noting that this version of post-feminism is largely an academic one – that is, it is based in theory rather than practice – and has had particular currency in writing about the media and culture. This is, in part, due to the emphasis on discourses rather than on over-arching structures. Yet it is also a reflection of the fact that it is far easier to de-stabilise gender in the representational field than in our daily lives where our gender-presentation continues to have very concrete material effects. It is telling, in this respect, that Brooks devotes much of her chapter on post-feminism and popular culture to a consideration of Madonna, a performer whose continual re-invention of herself works to de-stabilise categories of gender and sexual identity. However, at this juncture, it is important to ask how Madonna's performances relate to the lived experiences of other women (see Schwichtenberg, 1993). Lisa Henderson (1993: 123), for example, notes that whilst cultural critics might celebrate the destabilisation of fixed gender and sexual identities in Madonna's performances, the political struggles of feminists and queer activists depend upon fixing these identities, both for our own protection and because these identities remain the basis of material inequalities in the social world:

> It is difficult, finally, to acknowledge the divided self and engage the pleasure of masquerade while at the same time fighting a strikingly antagonistic legal and social system for your health, your safety, your job, your place to live, or the right to raise your children. Indeed, this is the other contradiction of lesbian and gay resistance: to be constructionists in theory, though essentialists as we mobilize politically, demanding that the state comply because this, after all, is *who we are*, not who we are today or who we have become in recent history.

Part of the difficulty with much contemporary (post-)feminist writing on the media is that the link between the representational and material spheres has been severed as studies of representational practices have become divorced from a broader feminist political project and history. Moreover, the de-stabilising of the category "woman" has – in practice – led to a very narrow focus on individual women as the objects of study. As a result, much of this writing ends up replicating the focus on the white, middle-class self that was the basis of the critique of the second wave, the difference being that post-feminists do not claim any universal status for this self. In focusing on the individual it becomes, by definition, almost impossible to say anything meaningful about difference: what can an analysis of Madonna, Carrie, Ally or Buffy tell us about differences between women? More damagingly, the failure to connect these analyses to a broader feminist praxis makes the analyses – no matter how interesting and well argued – seem rather pointless. As Modleski (1991: 15) puts it:

> The once exhilarating proposition that there is no 'essential' female nature has been elaborated to the point where it is now often used to scare 'women' away from making any generalizations about or political claims on behalf of a group called 'women'.

Making the personal political should not mean that the personal is the *only* site of political contestation and change. In short, if analysing Madonna can only tell us about Madonna then, frankly, why should we bother?

My intent in providing this brief survey of these complex debates is not to try to fix the meaning of post-feminism once and for all – indeed, this seems to be a rather pointless, if not impossible, task – but to highlight the way in which these "post-ings" repeatedly focus on women, feminism and femininity as the problem, as the objects of investigation and critique. As a result, much recent feminist media studies presents a feminism at war with itself and the political relevance of feminism is in danger of being lost. Moreover, whilst all this deconstructing of the female gender has been going on, men and masculinity have, once again, been allowed to slip under the radar: hence my reformulation of Modleski's title. As a political theory and practice, feminism without men is surely as limited as feminism without women.

Buffy binaries and *Buffy's* boys

So far, my argument has been fairly abstract. The remainder of this article seeks to rectify this by providing a case study centred on *Buffy the Vampire Slayer*. My intention is not to argue that *Buffy* (or Buffy) is or is not feminist, rather, I want to consider the ways in which the show's "feminism" has been framed in existing criticism and how this framing has allowed other issues of importance to feminism (and to *Buffy*) to escape critical scrutiny.

In an oft-quoted account, *Buffy* creator Joss Whedon describes the show as,

> my response to all the horror movies I had ever seen where some girl walks into a dark room and gets killed. So I decided to make a movie where a blonde girl walks into a dark room and kicks butt instead.
>
> (Whedon quoted by Early, 2001)[3]

Whedon's creation tale is the starting point for numerous articles (both popular and academic) dealing with the show's feminism and, indeed, Whedon's willingness to use the f-word in discussing the show's ideology and appeal has meant that *Buffy*'s relationship to feminism has been consistently foregrounded both on-screen and in responses to the show.

The blonde girl in question is, of course, Buffy Summers (Sarah Michelle Gellar), a former cheerleader who is also the vampire slayer. The first two seasons repeatedly return to the apparent incongruity of conjoining "Buffy" with "vampire slayer" and play on and with characters' and viewers' expectations of the blonde girl, expectations that clearly change as show and character develop. Nevertheless, in the early seasons, a large part of the show's humour and drama comes from the apparent conflict between the demands and gains of feminism and femininity and it is this conflict – and the various ways in which it is played out within the show and in secondary texts – that has been the major concern of those interested in its relationship to feminism. Patricia Pender (2002: 35), for example, notes that much of the debate revolves around opposing value judgements about the feminist credentials of the central character and the show: "Put simply, is *Buffy* good or bad?" As a physically strong, assertive and sexually desiring heroine Buffy is claimed as a (good) feminist. As a young woman concerned with her appearance, clothing and desirability to the opposite sex, she is a bad feminist, but – depending on the position of the author – she might still be a good post-feminist. For many critics, the combination of feminism and femininity places *Buffy* firmly in the "post" era.

Asking the question "is *Buffy* good or bad" for feminism seriously limits the

scope of feminist enquiry to how we define feminism and construct a feminist identity. Moreover, to return to Lotz, with confusion and contradiction marking popular
definitions of feminism, it should hardly be surprising that the same characteristics
are variously read as feminist, anti-feminist or post-feminist, and celebrated or condemned on these grounds by different critics. To give an example, Buffy's appearance
is a central concern in many early responses to the show. Buffy – as played by Gellar –
is blonde, petite, nubile, perfectly made-up and, above all, fashionable. Her favoured
daywear in the early seasons is a short skirt, spaghetti-strap top and high heels: clothing designed to expose and shape her body according to conventional standards of
feminine beauty. For some critics, this conjunction of feminism and femininity is to be
celebrated in extending feminism's appeal to a new generation of women and girls; for
others, it compromises the show's feminist premise by constructing Buffy/Gellar as a
sexualised object.[4]

I am less interested here in which group of critics are "right" than in the fact that
Buffy/ Gellar are so often the focus of critical consideration. The reason often given to
justify this is their importance as role models for young girls who use media figures to
help them construct their own sense of identity and agency (e.g. Vint, 2002). Yet, this
depends upon a very limited notion of identification and fails to account for the
possibilities and pleasures of cross-sex identification and same- and cross-sex desire.
Indeed, while Whedon talks about selling feminism to boys as a major concern,[5] boy
fans have been the subject of little (if any) feminist scholarship. As Anthony Easthope
(1986: 1) pointedly argued nearly 20 years ago, the effect of this critical interest in
women is to allow masculinity to pass itself off as natural and universal, placing it
beyond critique.

Morever, much of the good Buffy/ bad Buffy debate fails to consider the show *as
television*. In other words, this criticism (particularly in its more populist versions) is a
harking back to the "images of women" approach that characterised feminist critiques of the media in the late 1960s and early 1970s and paid little attention to
medium specificity (Walters, 1995). For example, whilst the concern regarding sex-
object-Buffy may well be justified at a meta-textual level (Vint, 2002), the television
show rarely constructs Buffy/Gellar as the object of a sexualised male gaze. It is
undoubtedly true that her daywear – in the early seasons in particular – is flesh-
shaping and exposing, however, the camera rarely lingers on or fetishises her body.
Further, when it comes to night-time slayage, Buffy rarely wears such obviously
sexualised attire: indeed, when she does – as in Season 2's opening episode "When
She Was Bad" – it is a sign that all is not well. More typically, in fight scenes Buffy
is shown in long shot, her face and form obscured by shadow and dark lighting as
well as by her loose clothing and long hair.[6] Combined with the specular and narrative privileging of the woman's point-of-view in the show, this makes it difficult
to argue that *Buffy* privileges a male gaze in any straightforward way (Daughtery,
2002).

As Pender also notes (2004), the need to resolve Buffy/*Buffy*'s feminist credentials seems to serve for some critics as a justification of their own engagement, pre-
venting an acknowledgement of the show's complexities and contradictions. I am
reminded here of Modleski's warning that feminist media criticism risks becoming
increasingly narcissistic, "based on an unspoken syllogism that goes something like

this: 'I like *Dallas*; I am a feminist; *Dallas* must have progressive potential" (1991: 45). One of the implications of this in *Buffy*-studies has been a marked reluctance among feminists to consider the show's less liberatory aspects – such as its treatment of race and class – as though this would somehow tarnish the object of study (Pender, 2004). Alternatively, a post-feminist approach might seek to embrace these contradictions as part of the post-feminist fabric of the show. In either case, the effect is the same: the marginalization of difference and an emphasis on the individual.

To the extent that we allow the popular television text – and the growing body of critical work on such texts – to define our "feminism", we marginalize many of the most important challenges feminism *as a movement* posed and continues to pose. From my own perspective, as a feminist working mainly on gendered violence, it is pertinent to note that whilst (post-)feminist action heroines have been the subject of recurring critique within feminist media studies (e.g. Inness, 1998; Helford, 2000; Early and Kennedy, 2003; Tasker, 2004), there has been relatively little academic work that considers media representations of male violence from a perspective informed by feminism. In this respect, the critical silence on male violence in *Buffy* – particularly from those critics interested in the show's relationship to feminism – can be read as evidence of the way that the post-feminist frame works to banish the spectre of the radical ("victim") feminist and her analysis of patriarchy. Yet, radical feminism is more than a spectral form in the show itself, which – although inconsistent on this point – often seems to offer a surprisingly radical analysis of the systematic nature of male violence. My intent here is not to demonstrate that *Buffy* conforms to my version of feminism (as in Brunsdon's ur-article), rather, I want to point to some of the themes that are too often neglected within feminist media studies in this "post-feminist" age.

Buffy's primary focus may be to "take back the night" for the living, but it is notable that the undead and demonic are – with few exceptions – male.[7] This, in itself, is hardly exceptional – content analyses of prime-time television consistently find that the majority of both perpetrators and victims of on-screen violence are white males (Gunter and Harrison, 1998; Center for Communication and Social Policy, 1997, 1998a, 1998b) – but the very routine nature of male violence should surely make it more, not less, worthy of feminist comment and analysis (Boyle, 2004). Yet, the first book-length feminist studies of television violence were not published until the early 2000s (Cuklanz, 2000; Projansky, 2001; Moorti, 2002) and it is notable that these studies all focus on a very specific form of violence, namely, rape. Certainly, *Buffy*'s treatment of sexual violence is worthy of feminist attention. However, so too are unexceptional, routinised examples of male violence which may, indeed, be invisible as violence given the cultural value attached to aggression as an expression of normative masculinity. Where *Buffy* is relatively unusual (and potentially radical), is in the way in which this link between heterosexual-masculinity and violence is critically and provocatively kept in view. This is perhaps most explicit in the figure of Caleb (Nathan Fillion), the final season's misogynist villain, but comments about the aggressive and morally questionable behaviour of men, as a group, are made throughout. Interestingly, it is often left to recurring male figures to comment on the limits of masculinity. When the hapless Xander (Nicholas Brendon), is possessed by a hyena in "The Pack" (1.06), for example, Buffy's Watcher, Giles (Anthony

Stewart Head), resists labelling his sexually aggressive, condescending behaviour as demonic:

Giles: Xander's taken to teasing the less fortunate? [. . .] And there's been a notable change in both clothing and demeanour? [. . .] And otherwise all his spare time is spent lounging about with imbeciles?
Buffy: It's bad isn't it?
Giles: It's devastating, he's turned into a 16-year-old boy. Course, you'll have to kill him.
Buffy: Giles, I'm serious.
Giles: So am I, except for the part about killing him. Testosterone is a great equalizer, it turns all men into morons. He will, however, get over it. [. . .] Buffy, boys can be cruel. They tease. They prey on the weak. It's a natural teen behaviour pattern.

Although Giles' essentialist account is quickly proved wrong, he is not wrong in pointing out that a level of aggression, competition and misogyny is an accepted part of normative constructions of masculinity within the Buffyverse (and beyond). This recognition of what men as a group stand to gain from violence (both in terms of their status with other men, and in terms of material and sexual power), whilst central to feminist critiques, is in direct contrast to accounts of male violence in other mainstream media contexts where the focus is typically on drawing a clear distinction between violent men (monsters, beasts, perverts, fiends) and "normal" men (Benedict, 1992; Boyle, 2004). In contrast, *Buffy* continually draws parallels between its monsters and its men, making masculinity both visible and problematic.

Admittedly, this might not seem immediately obvious from the above example where "evil" Xander, possessed by a hyena, is, quite obviously, *not* Xander. More generally, in the early episodes there does appear to be a relatively clear-cut distinction between man (the conscious, socially situated agent) and monster (the inhuman, asocial beast) that is underlined by the mise-en-scène: the monsters look monstrous, inhabit dark spaces on the margins of Sunnydale and are often in full or partial shadow. Yet, such an *absolute* distinction is difficult to sustain. The vampire, the werewolf and the possessed teen are liminal figures: humans who become monsters and retain the human's visage (at least some of the time) and memories. One of the more interesting complexities of the Angel/Angelus character,[8] for example, is that it is the demonic Angelus who has the most in common with Liam, the drunken, sexually aggressive and immoral man the vampire once was. As Angel comments in "Doppelgangland" (3.16), the traces of the vampire are in the human. Equally, those who are introduced as demons frequently express human emotions and complexities. As major characters move from one position to another any ideas of "absolute" evil become increasingly complicated and this, too, is visually rendered through changes in costume, make-up, lighting and so on. Whilst it could be argued that this de-stabilisation of identity is quintessentially post-feminist, to follow this argument is once more to re-direct the focus of our enquiry from a quintessentially feminist issue (gendered violence), to feminism itself.

Finally, *Buffy*'s centuries-old demons are also associated with the past and, specifically, with a pre-feminist past that they bring with them into the show's present. In this sense, while Buffy (the character and the show) might be beneficiaries of feminism, it is clear from the outset that Sunnydale is not a post-patriarchy. In other words, an analysis of the Buffyverse (like an analysis of our own world), demonstrates the difficulty of fixing pre-feminist, feminist, and post-feminist *moments* and the necessity of considering movement, organisation and behaviour at both the individual and societal level.

In conclusion, as feminist media critics we need to continually keep in focus the ways in which our analyses of cultural texts contribute to broader struggles both within and outside of the academy. We need to think about our methods, about our objects of study and, perhaps most importantly, about the *purpose* of our study. For example, examining representations of men's violence against women has long been seen as part of the broader feminist struggle to challenge and de-naturalise that violence – as the preceding discussion of *Buffy* begins to suggest. As Benedict (1993) argues, changes in representation don't only follow on from changes in reality, they can also lead the way. This is why struggles over language and meaning matter and why analysing, challenging and changing how we – and others – speak about or otherwise represent men's violence (or other forms of gendered realities and inequalities) is an important part of feminism's transformative project. This does not mean that feminists cannot also study music videos, or shoe shopping, or romance novels, but it helps to remind us that in all our work we need to retain a sense of the broader picture. In this respect, we cannot afford to lose sight of how debates about feminism (and feminists) are used within the media. It is hardly surprising that disputes over the feminist identities of figures like Madonna, Carrie, Ally or Buffy have received such widespread media attention for, as I have argued in this article, such a focus allows the more difficult challenges posed by feminism – challenges to male privilege and power, to the lived tensions of all of our daily lives – to slip from view. To let these debates define our "feminism" in the early 21st century would be a truly regressive move.

Notes

1   To get to grips with the diversity of debate it helps to get beyond academic sources and examine documents produced within the movement – newsletters, conference materials, oral histories, and so on. These documents can be accessed in a variety of feminist archives, including (in the UK) the Glasgow Women's Library (see http://www.womens-library.org.uk/), the Women's Library (see http://www.thewomenslibrary.ac.uk/) and the Feminist Library (see http:// www.feministlibrary.org.uk/).

2   See, for example, essays collected in Heywood and Drake (1997), Mirza (1997) and in Gillis, Howie and Munford (2004).

3   Buffy made her first appearance in a 1992 film, written by Whedon and directed by Fran Rubel Kuzui.

4   For more on this, see Owens (1999), Fudge (1999), Vint (2002) and Pender (2002).

5   Whedon comments: "If I can make teenage boys comfortable with a girl who

takes charge of the situation, without their knowing that's what's happening, it's better than sitting down and selling them on feminism" (cited in Esmonde, 2003).

6   The need to disguise the stunt doubles used in the fight sequences provides a practical reason for this.

7   Whedon himself describes *Buffy* as a chance for horror's prototypical blonde girl to "take back the night" (in Esmonde, 2003), an allusion to on-going feminist campaigns. *Not once* in 144 episodes does Buffy battle a lone female or an all-female gang in her patrols. This is not to suggest that *Buffy*'s female characters never act violently with evil or morally questionable intent, but morally reprehensible violence does *not* bring female characters together in the way that it routinely unites male gangs.

8   Angel (played by David Boreanaz) is Buffy's first love. A vampire cursed with a soul, Angel loses that soul (reverting to Angelus) after he and Buffy have sex.

References

ARTHURS, J., 2003: '*Sex and the City* and Consumer Culture: Remediating Postfeminist Drama', *Feminist Media Studies*, Vol. 3, No. 1.

BENEDICT, H., 1992: *Virgin or Vamp: How the Press Covers Sex Crimes*, New York & Oxford: Oxford University Press.

BENEDICT, H., 1993: 'The Language of Rape' in Buchwald, E., Fletcher, P.R. and Roth, M. (eds), *Transforming a Rape Culture*, Minneapolis: Milkweed.

BOYLE, K. 2004: *Media and Violence: Gendering the Debates*, London: Sage.

BROOKS, A., 1997: *Postfeminisms: Feminism, Cultural Theory and Cultural Forms*, London: Routledge.

BRUNSDON, C., 1995: 'The Role of Soap Opera in the Development of Feminist Television Criticism' in, Brunsdon, C. (ed), 1997: *Screen Tastes: Soap Opera to Satellite Dishes*, London: Routledge.

BRUNSDON, C., 2004: 'Feminism, Post-Feminism, Martha and Nigella' Paper presented at: Interrogating Post-Feminism: Gender and the Politics of Popular Culture, University of East Anglia, 2–3 April 2004.

BRUNSDON, C., D'ACCI, J. and SPIGEL, L., 1997: 'Introduction' in Brunsdon, C., D'Acci, J. and Spigel, L. (eds), *Feminist Television Criticism: A Reader*, Oxford: Oxford University Press.

CARBY, H.V., 1982: 'White Woman Listen! Black Feminism and the Boundaries of Sister-hood' in Centre for Contemporary Cultural Studies (ed), *The Empire Strikes Back: Race and Racism in 70s Britain*, London: Hutchinson.

CENTER FOR COMMUNICATION AND SOCIAL POLICY (ed) 1997: *National Television Violence Study: Volume 1*, Thousand Oaks: Sage.

CENTER FOR COMMUNICATION AND SOCIAL POLICY (ed) 1998a: *National Television Violence Study: Volume 2*, Thousand Oaks: Sage.

CENTER FOR COMMUNICATION AND SOCIAL POLICY (ed) 1998b: *National Television Violence Study: Volume 3*, Thousand Oaks: Sage.

CUKLANZ, L.M., 2000: *Rape on Prime Time: Television, Masculinity and Sexual Violence*, Philadelphia: University of Pennsylvania Press.

DAUGHERTY, A. M., 2002: 'Just a Girl: Buffy as Icon' in Kaveney, R. (ed) *Reading the*

Vampire Slayer: An Unofficial Critical Companion to Buffy *and* Angel, London: Tauris Parke.

EARLY, F., 2001: 'Staking Her Claim: *Buffy the Vampire Slayer* as Transgressive Woman Warrior', *Journal of Popular Culture*, Vol. 35, No. 3.

EARLY, F., and KENNEDY, K. (eds) (2003) *Athena's Daughters: Television's New Women Warriors*, Syracuse, NY: Syracuse University Press.

EASTHOPE, A., 1986: *What A Man's Gotta Do: The Masculine Myth in Popular Culture*, London: Paladin.

ESMONDE, J., 2003: 'Ghoul Power: Buffy Sticks it to the System', *New Socialist*, No. 40. Available at: http://www.newsocialist.org/magazine/40.html (Accessed August 2004.)

FALUDI, S., 1992: *Backlash: The Undeclared War Against Women*, London: Chatto & Windus.

FIELDING, H., 1997: *Bridget Jones' Diary: A Novel*, London: Picador.

FUDGE, R., 1999: 'The Buffy Effect: Or, a Tale of Cleavage and Marketing', *Bitch*, No. 10. Available at: http://www.bitchmagazine.com/ (Accessed September 2004.)

GILLIS, S., HOWIE, G., and MUNFORD, R. (eds) 2004: *Third Wave Feminism: A Critical Exploration*, London: Palgrave MacMillan.

GUNTER, B. and HARRISON, J., 1998: *Violence on Television: An Analysis of Amount, Nature, Location, and Origin of Violence in British Programmes*, London: Routledge.

HELFORD, E.R. (ed) 2000: *Fantasy Girls: Gender in the New Universe of Science Fiction and Fantasy Television*, Lanham: Rowman & Littlefield.

HENDERSON, L., 1993: 'Justify Our Love: Madonna and the Politics of Queer Sex' in Schwichtenberg, C. (ed) *The Madonna Connection: Representational Politics, Subcultural Identities and Cultural Theory*, Boulder: Westview Press.

HENRY, A., 2004: 'Orgasms and Empowerment: *Sex and the City* and the Third Wave Feminism' in Arkass, K. and McCabe, J. (ed), *Reading Sex and the City*, London: I.B. Tauris.

HEYWOOD, L. and DRAKE, J. (1997) 'Introduction' in Heywood, L. and Drake, J. (eds) *Third Wave Agenda: Being Feminist, Doing Feminism*, Minneapolis: University of Minnesota Press.

HOLLOWS, J., 2000: *Feminism, Femininity and Popular Culture*, Manchester: Manchester University Press.

HOOKS, B., 1982: *Ain't I a Woman?: Black Women and Feminism*, London: Pluto.

HOOKS, B., 2000: *Feminism is for Everybody: Passionate Politics*, London: Pluto.

INNESS, S.A., 1998: *Tough Girls: Women Warriors and Wonder Women in Popular Culture*, Philadelphia: University of Pennsylvania Press.

KIM, L.S., 2001: ' "Sex and the Single Girl" in Postfeminism', *Television & New Media*, Vol. 2, No. 4.

LITTLEWOOD, B., 2004: *Feminist Perspectives on Sociology*, Harlow: Pearson.

LOTZ, A.D., 2001: 'Postfeminist Television Criticism: Rehabilitating Critical Terms and Identifying Postfeminist Attributes', *Feminist Media Studies*, Vol. 1, No. 1.

MIRZA, H. S., 1997: *Black British Feminism: A Reader*, London: Routledge.

MODLESKI, T., 1991: *Feminism Without Women: Culture and Criticism in a "Postfeminist" Age*, London: Routledge.

MOORTI, S., 2002: *Color of Rape: Gender and Race in Television's Public Spheres*, Albany: State University of New York Press.

MOSELEY, R. and READ, J., 2002: ' "Having it *Ally*": Popular Television (Post-)Feminism', *Feminist Media Studies*, Vol. 2, No. 2.

OWEN, S.A., 1999: '*Buffy the Vampire Slayer:* Vampires, Postmodernity and Postfeminism,' *Journal of Popular Film and Television*, Vol. 27, No. 2.

PAGLIA, C., 1993: *Sex, Art and American Culture*, London: Pénguin.

PENDER, P., 2002: ' "I'm Buffy and You're . . . History": The Postmodern Politics of *Buffy*' in Wilcox, R. V. and Lavery, D. (eds), *Fighting the Forces: What's at Stake in* Buffy the Vampire Slayer, London: Rowman & Littlefield.

PENDER, P. 2004: 'Whose Revolution Has Been Televised?: *Buffy*'s Transnational Sisterhood of Slayers'. Paper presented at: Slayage Conference on *Buffy the Vampire Slayer*, Nashville, June 2004. Available at: http://www.slayage.tv/SCBtVS Archive/index.htm (Accessed August 2004.)

PROJANSKY, S., 2001: *Watching Rape: Film and Television in Postfeminist Culture*, New York & London: New York University Press.

RAVEN, C., 1999: 'All Men Are Bastards: Discuss . . .' *The Guardian*, 9 February.

RICHARDSON, D., 1996: ' "Misguided, Dangerous and Wrong": On the Maligning of Radical Feminism' in Bell, D. and Klein, R. (eds) *Radically Speaking: Feminism Reclaimed*, London: Zed.

ROIPHE, K., 1994: *The Morning After*, London: Hamish Hamilton.

SCHWICHTENBERG, C., (ed) 1993: *The Madonna Connection: Representational Politics, Subcultural Identities and Cultural Theory*, Boulder: Westview Press.

SOMMERS, C.H., 1994: *Who Stole Feminism? How Women Have Betrayed Women*, New York: Simon & Schuster.

SPENDER, D., 1982: *Women of Ideas and What Men Have Done to Them: From Aphra Behn to Adrienne Rich*, London: Routledge & Kegan Paul.

TASKER, Y., 2004: 'Family/Romance: Reading the Post-Feminist Action Heroine'. Paper presented at: Media Research Conference, University of Tampere, January 2004. Available at: http://www.uta.fi/laitokset/tiedotus/Mediatutkimuspaivat/PAPERIT/MTP04Yvonne Taske r.pdf (Accessed September 2004.)

VINT, S., 2002: 'Killing us Softly? A Feminist Search for the "Real" Buffy' *Slayage: The On-line International Journal of Buffy Studies* 5 http://www.slayage.tv (Accessed August 2004.)

WALTERS, S.D., 1995: 'From Images of Women to Woman as Image' in Walters, S.D., *Material Girls: Making Sense of Feminist Cultural Theory*, Berkeley & London: University of California Press.

WOLF, N., 1994: *Fire With Fire: The New Female Power and How to Use It*, New York: Fawcett Columbine.

10

Girls Rule!

Gender, feminism, and Nickelodeon

Sarah Banet-Weiser

Originally published in *Critical Studies in Media Communication*,
21:2 (2004): 119–139.

In June 2000, the Museums of Television and Radio in both New York and Los Angeles presented a three-month retrospective that honored the children's cable network Nickelodeon. The retrospective, "A Kid's Got To Do What A Kid's Got To Do: Celebrating 20 Years of Nickelodeon" featured screenings of past and current programming, hands-on workshops, an interactive gallery exhibit, and seminars for families. One of the seminars, titled "Girl Power! Creating Positive Role Models for Girls," lauded Nickelodeon's efforts over the past 20 years to challenge traditional gender stereotypes on children's television by featuring girls as primary lead characters. A "girl power" seminar had a particular cultural resonance in 2000: the connection between these two concepts – "girl" and "power" – once thought to be completely absent from the world of children's popular culture, had become normalized within the discourses of consumer culture. In the contemporary cultural climate, in other words, the empowerment of girls is now something that is more or less taken for granted by both children and parents, and has certainly been incorporated into commodity culture.

Indeed, the rhetoric of girl power has found currency in almost every realm of contemporary children's popular culture. In the mid-1990s, The Spice Girls, a manufactured, pop-music girl-group, adopted "Girl Power!" as their motto. And, at the same time, the alternative internet community the Riot Grrrls incorporated girl power ideology in their efforts to construct a new kind of feminist politics (see, for example, Baumgardner & Richards, 1999; Currie, 1999; Douglas, 1999; Driscoll, 2002; Kearney, 1998; Shugart, Waggoner, & Hallstein, 2001). T-shirts emblazoned with "Girls Kick Ass!" and "Girls Rule!" became hot new items for both high-school and elementary school girls, and Nike's "Play Like a Girl" advertising campaign skillfully used the concept of "commodity feminism" to sell athletic gear (Goldman, 1992; Sturken & Cartwright, 2001). In the sporting world, the success of the 1999 Women's Soccer World Cup tournament, the public focus on tennis superstars Venus and Serena Williams, and the creation of the Women's National Basketball Association brought new attention and prestige to powerful female athletes. In the world of popular psychology and everyday culture, books such as Mary Pipher's (1995) *Reviving Ophelia: Saving the Selves of Adolescent Girls* and Rosalind Wiseman's (2002) *Queen Bees and Wanna-Bes: Helping Your Daughter Survive Cliques, Gossip, Boyfriends, and Other Realities of Adolescence*, recognized problems unique to young girls growing up in the 1990s and immediately became bestsellers.

In the world of children's television, programs about self-confident, assertive, and intelligent girls such as Nickelodeon's 1991 hit, *Clarissa Explains It All*, and more recent animated programs such as *As Told By Ginger, Rocket Power*, and *The Wild Thornberries* initiated a new trend in programming that actively rejected the conventional industry wisdom that children's shows with girl leads could not be successful (see, for example, Seiter, 1995). Aside from these types of entertainment programs, Nickelodeon also addresses gender issues on its non-fiction news program, *Nick News*, with episodes devoted to body image, bullying, and girls' sports, among others. This essay focuses on the cultural context that produces girl power practices and commodities, and specifically situates the cable television network Nickelodeon as a key producer of girl power culture. Is contemporary media – and Nickelodeon in particular – simply capitalizing on a current trend, or does girl power ideology signify a new direction for feminist politics? I argue here that girl power is not just a fad, although it is that; it is not just about empowerment, although it is that as well. Girl power powerfully demonstrates the contradictions or tensions that structure Third Wave feminist politics, especially for young girls. It is not my aim to "resolve" these tensions or to expose Third Wave feminism or girl power as a commercial hoax. It is my goal, rather, to theorize how the often contradictory media representations of girl power function as a kind of feminist politics. Because of the importance of media representation to all kinds of politics, it is also important to situate media powerhouses within this kind of context. Nickelodeon, for example, does not simply exploit the commercial market of girl power; the network is also a significant *producer* of girl power culture – especially since Nickelodeon is one of the most influential producers of children's programming and media in the U.S., and it attracts a large audience of pre-adolescent and adolescent girls.

It is this tension between Nickelodeon's embrace of the girl power consumer market and its role as a producer of girl power ideology that I will explore here. But what does it mean to say that a huge corporate entity such as Nickelodeon enables girls to be *producers* of their own culture? Certainly, it can be argued, as Mary Celeste Kearney does, that alternative cultural productions along the margins of mainstream popular culture – 'zines, for example, or Riot Grrrl websites – illustrate how girls can produce girl power culture (Kearney, 1998). But Nickelodeon programs are hardly "alternative," and are squarely a part of mainstream, commercial culture. To get at how Nickelodeon demonstrates the tensions within girl power culture, I analyze three of the network's programs: *Clarissa Explains It All*, which first aired in 1991; *As Told By Ginger (ATBG)*, a contemporary popular animated series, and *Nick News*, the weekly news program for children that is hosted and produced by Linda Ellerbee. I chose to examine *Clarissa* because the program is widely noted as a "break-through" show in girl power programming – it was among the first children's series to feature a strong, independent girl lead character, and through this program Nickelodeon became well-known in the industry as a champion for girls. I then look at *ATBG* as a way to account for the trajectory of girl power ideology in the decade since Clarissa first aired, taking specific note at the program's use of irony and self-reflexivity as a more current rhetorical strategy of girl power. Finally, I examine *Nick News* for its representation of girl power themes, as well as its role as a producer of girl power culture through both the themes of the episodes and the figure of the host, Ellerbee, herself. Although *Nick News* differs from the other programs in that it is non-fiction, the themes on the news program – body image, popularity, parental authority – are similar to the themes in the entertainment programs, and thus it makes sense to look at all three as rich examples of mass-mediated girl power. The content of these particular Nickelodeon programs illustrates some of the contradictions within the relationship between media visibility, commercialism, and the production of girl culture – the same kinds of contradictions that also structure Third Wave feminism.

Girl power and generational differences: feminism for whom?

Girl power programming on Nickelodeon is part of a general trajectory in the contemporary mass media that can, in part, be attributed to Third Wave feminism.[1] Third Wave feminism (or sometimes "Girlie feminism") embraces commercial media visibility and enthusiastically celebrates the power that comes with it. In this way, Third Wave feminism situates issues of gender within commercial and popular culture, and insistently positions Third Wave feminist politics as not only fundamentally different from Second Wave feminist politics,[2] but because of the embrace of media visibility and the commercial world, as also more representative for a new generation of women. Indeed, one of the most impassioned discourses involving feminism lately has not been generated by differing particular political platforms, or a specific egregious act of discrimination against women, but from the arguments, contradictions, and general disavowals between Second and Third Wave feminism. The lack of generational cohesion here between the two movements makes it difficult to figure out one's position within feminism; as Susan Douglas (1994) has argued, the different stances on the consumer world between generations leads to a broader ambivalence about feminism: "Once this sense of generational collectivity *as a market* evaporates, so does the sense of political collectivity" (p. 292, my emphasis). That is, differences between Third Wave and Second Wave feminists are often represented as a generational rather than political problem. And yet, as Lisa Hogeland (2001) points out, generation is not a significant explanation for differences. The alternative, recognizing problems within feminism, means confronting the "unevenness" of the movement itself and "fundamental differences in our visions of feminism's tasks and accomplishments" (p. 107). One of these differences concerns media visibility. Whereas many Third Wave feminists seem to regard consumer culture as a place of empowerment and as a means of differentiating themselves from Second Wave feminists, Second Wave feminism has tended, on the whole, to be critical of the misogyny of popular consumer culture.

The embrace of consumer culture is the site for tension within girl power programming on Nickelodeon as well. Once feminism (as represented through girl power), becomes part of the mainstream it has traditionally challenged, can we still talk about it as political? Can feminism be represented and enacted within popular culture, or is popular culture by design hostile to feminism? Are we simply living in, as Naomi Klein (2000) claims in her book *No Logo*, a "Representation Nation," where visibility in the media takes precedence over "real" politics? Jennifer Baumgardner and Amy Richards (2000), authors of the Third Wave feminist tract *Manifesta: Young Women, Feminism, and the Future*, argue to the contrary, and claim that this kind of media visibility is absolutely crucial to politics. On Nickelodeon, not only are there strong female characters on the programs, there is a general tone of empowerment and activism that shapes the network's self-image.

In fact, we have arrived at a point where much of (liberal) feminism is part of mainstream media culture; that this is not a problem could be taken as a measure of what Second Wave feminism has accomplished (Dow, 1996). Baumgardner and Richards (2000) argue that young women who make up the Third Wave are "born with feminism simply in the water," a kind of "political fluoride" that protects against the "decay" of earlier sexism and gender discrimination (p. 83). The struggle for positive representations in the media is certainly not over, but we also do not experience the same media that we did even ten years ago, when, as Douglas (1999) contends, the most pervasive media story remained "structured around boys taking action, girls waiting for the boys, and girls rescued by the boys" (p. 293). There has been a clear historical trajectory of incorporating feminist ideologies into mainstream popular culture, ranging, as Bonnie Dow (1996) points out, from the 1970s television show *One Day at a Time* to shows in the 1980s and 1990s such as *Murphy Brown* and *Designing Women*. And yet, as Dow argues, while the liberal feminist politics of equal opportunity and equal pay for equal work have been somewhat normalized (although the material reality of these politics is not always or even often achieved), it is also the case that the process of mainstreaming an oppositional politics often functions as a hegemonic strategy to dilute those very politics. In other words, the normalization of feminism has prevented it from existing as a discrete politics; it rather emerges as a kind of slogan or a generalized "brand."

As a contemporary social and political movement, then, feminism itself has been rescripted (but not disavowed) so as to allow its smooth incorporation into the world of commerce and corporate culture – what Robert Goldman (1992) calls "commodity feminism." Current feminist politics involve a complex dynamic that is not only directly concerned with general gender issues, but also with issues of cultural territory: as part of a general self-identification, Second Wave feminism is at times overly romanticized in terms of its commitment to social protest politics, and there seems to be a kind of reluctance on the part of Second Wave feminists to rethink and redefine politics according to the stated needs and desires of Third Wave feminism (Susan Brownmiller, in a now infamous *Time* magazine interview about Third Wave feminists claimed, "they're just not movement people"; Bellafante, 1998, p. 60). This territorialism that surrounds some of the current politics of feminism seems to be about salvaging the name of feminism (and, presumably, the politics that ground and historicize the name). Baumgardner and Richards (2000), Barbara Findlen (1995), and Naomi Wolf (1994), for example, participate in this kind of salvation project, the project of not necessarily appropriating a historical concept of feminism, but widening its borders to include more contemporary manifestations of the politics. While in theory this makes sense, and certainly these authors at times do justice to the legacies of feminisms, Baumgardner and Richards (2000) also insist that "underneath all of these names and agendas is the same old feminism" (p. 80). However, it is precisely *not* the same old feminism that structures the politics of Third Wave feminism. The insistence that it is stems from a range of sentiments, from nostalgic yearnings for real social protest movements to respectful acknowledgements of political practices that open up economic and social opportunities to a sheer base desire to belong to something. Without discounting these sentiments, it is also the case that lingering in this generational territory battle between Second Wave and Third Wave feminism has paralyzed the debate, and prevented the further development and refinement of a feminist praxis and material feminist politics. As Hogeland (2001) points out, "Generational thinking is always unspeakably generalizing: one reason we react so vehemently to accounts of 'our' generation is that changes in feminist ideas, and the social, political, and institutional impact of feminism itself have been so uneven" (p. 110).

In fact, the idea that we all share a feminist politics, that we all want the same thing, is highly problematic. Not only does this make the same mistake as many Second Wave feminists who insisted on a universal feminist standpoint, but it also functions as a kind of refusal to identify what the "thing" is that we all apparently want (see particularly Hartsock, 1998). The politics of feminism are quite obviously different for different generations, and Third Wave feminists are produced in a very different cultural and political context to Second Wave feminists. This, then, is what situates the specific politics of girl power as a politics of contradiction and tension: the dynamics between the ideological claims of this cultural phenomenon – girls are powerful, strong, independent – and the commercial merchandising of these claims demonstrate a profound ambivalence about these feminist politics in general.

Nickelodeon produces its own kind of commodity feminism through its original programming. The television shows on Nickelodeon engage the audience member as an important consumer group, but the other components of girl power – media visibility and cultural production – are also part of the programming. The girl power programming on Nickelodeon, as well as the network's outspoken commitment to girls as lead characters, forces us to interrogate the connections and contradictions between children's television and empowerment. In fact, "empowerment" became the buzzword of the 1990s – not in marginalized political communities, but squarely within mainstream commercial culture. While this kind of empowerment obviously references economic power and the recognition of adolescent (and pre-adolescent) girls as an important market segment, it also seems to address a politico-social power represented in terms of feminist subjectivity. Indeed, Nickelodeon has built its entire self-image around this concept of empowerment. Addressing children as empowered beings, as kids with rights, is a very different message from earlier television programming, which tended to address children as either unsophisticated or in need of protection (Hendershot, 1999; Jenkins, 1998; Kinder, 1999; Seiter, 1995; Spigel, 1992). And, within the context of girl power, the relationship between empowerment and children's television is especially charged because of television's history as a medium that favors boy characters and boy-based programs. Thus, while part of an emphasis on the empowerment of youth signals a larger cultural shift in definitions of childhood itself, it is also reflective of shifting feminist politics, where access to female empowerment is increasingly found within commercial culture, rather than outside the hegemonic mainstream.

Obviously, to invoke the term "power" in direct connection with girls is an ideologically complex move, and has several different facets. The most economically significant way in which power connects to girls is the increasing recognition of young girls and adolescents as an important consumer group – a group that has more and more money to spend each year on girl power products (McNeal, 1992; Quart, 2003).[3] Another important way in which power is connected with girls in the media context of Nickelodeon is through the particular gender representations on the network's original programming. As Ellen Seiter (1995) points out, it was not really until the 1980s that children's television began creating shows that featured girls as lead characters. Although the heroines of such 1980s programs as *My Little Pony* and *Strawberry Shortcake* were not necessarily powerful, intelligent characters, they were at least female, which challenged the earlier invisibility of girls on children's television. Historically, a "cross-over" audience has seemed to work only in favor of boys (in other words, according to conventional wisdom, boys *and* girls would watch boys on television, but boys would not watch girls on television). In the past decade, however, the representation of girls on television has been influenced by the more general mainstreaming of feminist rhetoric, and Nickelodeon has led the way in terms of children's television.

In 1991, Nickelodeon launched its hit "tween" program, *Clarissa Explains It All*, featuring a young girl as its lead character. The network's commitment to strong girl characters (a commitment that has demonstrated itself in more and more programming that features girls as lead characters) is an important part of its public persona: the aforementioned Museum of Television and Radio's retrospective on Nickelodeon featured the network's commitment to girls as a main focus. Curator David Bushman commented:

> I think Nickelodeon has empowered kids in a lot of ways . . . but I think they've specifically empowered young girls, and that's a really important thing that Nickelodeon deserves a lot of credit for. This whole idea that you could not make girl-centric shows because boys wouldn't watch them, they disproved that theory.
> (Heffley, 1999, p. 45)

Indeed, some industry professionals mark the debut of *Clarissa Explains It All* as a crucial turning point for Nickelodeon, the moment in which the network established itself as an organization dedicated to taking risks to more accurately represent and appeal to a child audience. In this sense, Nickelodeon is an important *producer* of girl power politics, as it explicitly connects commercial representation and the sheer visibility of girls on television with a larger recognition of girls as important empowered subjects in the social world.

Of course, the claim that representation and greater visibility of girls in the media result in a particular kind of empowerment assumes several things. First, to assume that media visibility leads to empowerment is to consider adolescent television audiences as active agents who position themselves in a variety of relationships with the ideological structures and messages of the media. While this may be true, it is also certainly true that these very same ideological structures and messages of the media privilege a commercial context that connects social power with consumption activity. Second, the acknowledgement that adolescent girls comprise an active, empowered audience does not necessarily free them from the commercial power of the mass media. To the contrary, as we witness with the increasing visibility of gay and lesbian representations on television, this kind of recognition insists on the ever-more important connection with the commercial power of the mass media (see, for example, Canclini, 2001; Dow, 2001; Gross, 2001; Miller, 1998). The cultural dynamics that produced girl power within the constant flux of media representations of gender in the 1990s not only produced a hip new slogan, but were also part of a more general shift toward mainstreaming feminism into popular and dominant culture (Dow, 1996). Undoubtedly, this kind of media visibility carries with it a kind of power, in a cultural context where visibility is so often conflated with power and influence.

Another aspect of empowerment behind the girl power movement is a more institutional one and involves the accounting of girls as producers of their own culture (rather than simply consumers). It also entails the transformation of the media industry itself, where more and more executives and producers are female. While, as Joy Van Fuqua (2003) argues, the relationship between women in positions of power at networks and the proliferation of strong female characters is certainly not guaranteed, it is also worth noting that, for example, the former president of Nickelodeon, Geraldine Laybourne, led the way in the children's television market in terms of creating programming with powerful girl lead characters. *Nick News* is not only hosted but also produced by Linda Ellerbee, a known feminist and children's activist. This institutional side of girl power production coexists with a proliferation of less mainstream forms of girl power culture, such as 'zines including *Bust* and *Hues* and "do it yourself" (DIY) forms of cultural production (Kearney, 1998).

These elements of empowerment – as a consumer group, as media visibility, and as cultural producers – are all part of girl power. The dynamics between these variations within the theme of empowerment are complicated, and represent significant tensions and even ambivalence within feminisms. Media visibility is an important component of empowerment, but it is far from unproblematic, as scholars such as Stuart Hall (1997), Herman Gray (1997), Larry Gross (2001), and Bonnie Dow (2001) have pointed out. As Gross (2001), writing about the increasing media visibility of gays and lesbians, succinctly put it: "as we're learning, visibility, like truth, is rarely pure and never simple" (p.253). The power behind girl power is also complex, and is often contradictory. One of the key tensions regarding girl power exists not between the mainstream media and feminism, but rather within feminism itself, and the assumed generational differences between Second and Third Wave feminists.

Nickelodeon and girl power programming

Catherine Driscoll (2002), in her recent study of adolescent girl culture, points out that

> the opposition between pleasure in consumption figured as conformity and pleasure against the grain of such conformity does not provide a useful model for considering girl culture, where resistance is often just another form of conformity and conformity may be compatible with other resistance. (p. 12)

In other words, concepts such as conformity and resistance are assumed to be oppositional, but in fact are mutually constituitive categories. The ideological themes of girl power that are represented in Nickelodeon programs such as *Clarissa Explains it All* and *As Told by Ginger*, where the girls are strong, independent, and often unruly are situated in relation to normative definitions of girls as obedient and docile – even as these "resistant" themes are marketed as a particular kind of product. So, for example, during the commercial break for an episode of *As Told by Ginger*, an animated program that features a group of intelligent and often ironic middle-school girls, one could often see an ad for a girl power doll: girls playing with Barbie, or something similar, dressed up in sporty clothes carrying a skateboard (or one for the new Mattel Flavas dolls, hip-hop dolls of various ethnicities positioned on a cardboard wall covered in grafitti). Indeed, this kind of juxtaposition so often shown on the media, between a kind of political agency and a commitment to consumerism, is one of the reasons that it is so difficult to theorize what exactly girl power is, as well as whether or not it is a feminist discourse and practice. That is to say, the typical categories that are used to talk about agency do not really apply to this contemporary context, since girl culture is ambiguous from the ground up (see, for example, Driscoll, 2002).

Discussing the exaggerated negative reaction to the Spice Girls and the subsequent dismissal of the group by critics as inauthentic and manufactured, Driscoll (2002) asks: "Can feminism be a mass-produced, globally distributed product, and can merchandised relations to girls be authentic?" (p. 272). Driscoll understands girl culture to be primarily characterized by "unresolvable tensions" between agency and conformity. She argues, "To actually embrace the community alternative girl culture imagines requires a degree of complicity with systems with which they claim to be incompatible, and they produce legitimated models of agency within the systems they say exclude them" (p. 278). This complicity with the system is precisely where Nickelodeon steps in; the discourse of girl power created a new niche in television programming and led to the creation of girl-centered and girl-powered shows. Nickelodeon programs can be seen as potentially innovative efforts to address gender representation in children's television. However, the presentation and rescripting of gender identity for girls on Nickelodeon are not as seamless as the network's subtext of girl power would lead one to believe. Nickelodeon demonstrates Driscoll's point about the unresolvable tensions between agency and conformity: the network overtly situates gender identity (or positive gender portrayal) as an important element of programming, and was the first children's network to air a program that featured a girl character in a leading role, with their 1991 live-action show, *Clarissa Explains It All*. At the same time, the network's definition of empowerment is part of a larger system of consumer citizenship, where the recognition of an audience as a potentially lucrative one confers power on that same audience.

Clarissa Explains It All

With the debut of *Clarissa*, Nickelodeon became known for risk-taking in programming, and was specifically recognized as a champion for girls in television. The success of *Clarissa* has undoubtedly been a motivation for not only Nickelodeon to continue to produce shows about girls – it has followed *Clarissa* with other successful programs: *The Secret World of Alex Mack* (1994), *The Mystery Files of Shelby Woo* (1996), *The Wild Thornberries* (1998), *The Amanda Show* (1999), and *As Told By Ginger* (2000), among others – but also for other networks to create programming that challenges "the boys-won't-watch-girls" myth. According to the Nickelodeon press release about the show, the main character, Clarissa Darling (played by Melissa Joan Hart) "is an imaginative and very contemporary teenager who makes no bones about detailing her likes, dislikes, and fantasies. Breaking many conventions of the sitcom and using special video effects to highlight Clarissa's thoughts and plans, the series examines life through her eyes" (Nickelodeon press release, 2000). The idea of portraying life through the eyes of a young girl is innovative in and of itself, especially given the historical context of 1991. Nickelodeon very purposefully marketed *Clarissa* as a break-out kind of show, and the success of the program illustrated the effective marketing: boys seemed to watch the program along with girls, and the show clearly seemed to tap into the burgeoning cultural climate of girl power. The early 1990s were already emerging as a new era for pre-adolescent and adolescent boys and girls in terms of their spending power and consumption habits, and the character of Clarissa seemed to fit perfectly in this context. Indeed, Clarissa is not the stereotypical feminine heroine who relies on a man (or a boy, in this case) to save her from the various scrapes of contemporary teenage life. Although boys are featured regularly on the show – Clarissa has a younger brother, Ferguson, who often provides the annoying foil for Clarissa's thought processes, and her best friend, Sam, is a boy her own age with whom she has a platonic relationship – the program truly does revolve around the antics of Clarissa.

As the lead character, Clarissa is portrayed as an unusually mature teenager who narrates her life to the audience as one that is full of surprises, haphazard coincidences, and typical teen dilemmas. Her parents, Janet and Marshall Darling, are caricatured as ex-hippies, and their (media-defined) sense of social responsibility shapes each episode (for example, Clarissa's mother, Janet, is a health nut, and her father, Marshall, is an environmentally aware architect). Each episode opens with a monologue by Clarissa, where she voices some clever remark about the theme of that day's show. Often these opening remarks are sarcastic and self-reflexive; for example, in the episode "The Misguidance Counselor" (June 14 1992), Clarissa begins the show with a sardonic statement: "Okay, time for another normal start of another normal day in the ever-normal Darling household." This episode goes on to spoof normal families, with the central narrative organized around an obviously ridiculous plan of the school's guidance counselor for Clarissa to "fit in." The program in general is very intertextual in that other television shows and films are often referenced and used as part of the plot: for example, at one point in this specific episode, the show parodies early family television shows such as *Ozzie and Harriet* by depicting a black and white television set featuring the show *Oh! Those Darlings*, complete with a head shot of Clarissa in nostalgic 1950s garb, and a credit line "Clarissa Darling as Big Sis" underneath. Another episode also demonstrates this kind of ironic self-construction, where the opening line of "A Little Romance" (August 14, 1993) has Clarissa saying: "I think that it was either William Shakespeare or Sting who said, 'love is blind; love is madness; love is reason without reason.' Personally, I agree. Love is nuts!"

John Hartley (1999) identifies *Clarissa* as an interesting example of a particular kind of potential civic behavior. Locating the politics of citizenship within a variety of cultural artifacts and technologies within the "mediasphere," he argues that within media and commercial culture, we have moved through a series of different levels of citizenship, ranging from civic to cultural citizenship. The present moment is characterized by yet another form of citizenship, called DIY or "Do It Yourself" citizenship (p. 179). DIY has its roots in British punk rock and has been recognized as a particular kind of alternative cultural production (especially in terms of girl power ideology) such as 'zines and riot grrl websites (Kearney 1998; McRobbie, 1991). Interestingly, Hartley identifies the very mainstream *Clarissa Explains It All* as illustrative of DIY citizenship because the character of Clarissa is smart, in control of her environment, and she disrupts conventional modes of representation by talking directly to the camera. As Hartley argues, the character of Clarissa marks an important departure from conventional representations of young girls on television because she is the "undisputed centre of her show ... a mainstream, fully-formed, 'adult' character, articulate, interesting, full of initiative, clever and congenial" (p. 184).

Hartley continues by arguing that Clarissa is a particular kind of citizen (albeit a problematic kind of citizen), in a world of children's media that often excludes children as citizens, both ideologically and in practice. He identifies *Clarissa Explains It All* as a program that specifically attends to issues of citizenship for girls and, in that way, the show disrupts cultural mythologies of gender for young girls: the victim, the unintelligent, the dependent. Clarissa is quite plainly the opposite of all of these personality characteristics, but not only that, the show itself is often organized as a kind of *critique* of the constructed nature of cultural mythologies – of girls, of boys, of romance, of popularity. In this way, the character of Clarissa represents the kind of contradictions present in the broader politics of girl power: she is the typical powerless adolescent girl in the sense of her position in a larger culture that privileges both adults and males, but she is nonetheless a powerful figure within commercial culture. Hartley describes DIY citizenship as bringing about a kind of "semiotic self-determination" where representation of agency *becomes* agency in a particular televisual society; in this way, Clarissa represents a kind of girl power feminism that makes sense in this particular historical moment, and under these particular conditions.

Through its intertextuality, its unconventional methods such as narrating directly to the camera, and its casting as lead a kind of wacky teenage girl, the show represents some of the important themes of girl power ideology. For example, in the episode "Can't Buy Me Love" (September 8, 1992), Clarissa opens the show with these remarks: "What's in and what's out: two harmless little questions that make otherwise rational people break out in hives." The recognition here of both the importance of fitting in socially, and the superficiality of that desire to fit in, mirrors the larger tensions of girl power ideology. The episode continues when Clarissa's brother Ferguson is befriended by the local rich kid, predictably named J. Elliot Fundsworth III, and is asked to pledge to join an exclusive yacht club, the Young Americans' Junior Yacht Club. Within this relationship, Ferguson is transformed from the solidly middle-class boy that he is to a pretentious snob, interested only in elite membership at the club. J. Elliot Fundsworth III, not surprisingly, is a fraud who befriends

Ferguson only to gain access to Clarissa, on whom he has a crush. Although Ferguson is constantly at odds with Clarissa in the show, it is Clarissa who saves him from the clutches of the elitist, arrogant boy.

The episode is peppered with subtle (and some not so subtle) messages about class politics; although they are certainly not radical in that the episode focuses only on the very wealthy, there is nonetheless a pro-social message intended. More interesting, however, is the role that Clarissa herself plays as the savior of her brother, and the one who rejects the love interest of the selfish rich boy. She is the lead character in the program, and each episode centrally revolves around not only her experiences as a young adolescent girl, but also around the contradictions between political action and individual subjectivity that are inherent in current definitions of girl power culture. The last episode of the program, "The Last Episode," which aired October 1, 1994, depicted these contradictions on several different levels. The episode revolved around Clarissa's decision to go to college in Cincinnati to study journalism. Although her decision about college had ostensibly been made, when Clarissa wrote an article for a local newspaper about teen angst and malls (could there be a more illustrative girl power topic?), she was offered an internship at the *New York Daily Post*. She then was faced with choosing between college and career, a plot theme that carried on the show's explicit connection of gender identity with a kind of agency or citizenship.

Clarissa can be seen as an important Third Wave feminist icon. Her empowerment as a particular kind of citizen is assumed to be more generally connected to an increase in empowerment in the media and in the larger social world (in fact, "The Last Episode" is reminiscent of another media power player when Clarissa plays Murphy, of *Murphy Brown* fame, in a spoof called "Murphy Darling"). And, like Third Wave feminism itself, the agency of the character of Clarissa is reflective of a contradictory version of citizenship; the empowerment that it articulates for young girls does not include a model for how to *access* that citizenship except through representation. Indeed, girl power is defined by the tensions between representing girl power citizenship through the media and accessing that citizenship in a way that has larger implications for gender ideologies and practice.

As Told By Ginger

As Told By Ginger (ATBG) is a Nickelodeon original animated production, currently airing twice a week. The show features a main cast of five 12–13-year-old girls, and generally revolves around the issues that surround this group in their school, Lucky Middle School. Although the program does feature three younger boys (all of whom are siblings of the main characters), the episodes are primarily concerned with issues that pertain to the girl characters. The program has enjoyed some critical acclaim: it has been nominated twice for an Emmy award (Animated Series in Less Than an Hour category), but lost to *The Simpsons* and *Futurama*. Like those other animated programs, *ATBG* also presents social commentary within each episode; the girl power issues that garner a kind of social power, such as popularity, cliques, the culture of "cool," are presented in this program within a context of critique. *ATBG* is at times self-reflexive, using parody and irony to critique social norms and standards about gender and class. The main theme of the show revolves around some of the very same issues that *Nick News* covers in real life; Ginger Foutley, the lead character, is accepted into both the popular, cool clique at school, as well as by her long-time friends who are also represented as intelligent nerds.

In fact, one fan describes Ginger is described in the following manner:

> Ginger Foutley is a regular kid – although maybe a bit more reflective than most – who's still trying to figure out who she is. The social structure of Lucky Junior High grosses her out, but she's also kind of obsessed with it. If she were part of the cool clique, she swears she would do things differently. Yet her bluff is called when Courtney, a princess of cool, decides Ginger can hang. With one foot in each crowd, Ginger constantly flip-flops between her loyalty to her old friends and her desire to be cool with a capital C . . . Welcome to junior high!
>
> (*As Told By Ginger*, 2003a)

The profound tensions that define Ginger's character are mirrored by the contradictions that surround girl power culture specifically and Third Wave feminism more generally. In particular, the tensions between wanting to "be cool with a capital C" in a commercially driven culture and the dedication to genuine female friendship are a marker of girl power. While this is certainly not a new theme in children's programming (the subject of the cool crowd seems to be a staple of programming targeted to the tween segment of the market), the refusal to resolve the issue makes *ATBG* unique.

In other words, most other children's programs that deal with issues of popularity seem to claim the moral high ground and come out for "genuine" friendship at the expense of the obviously more superficial popular social group. Yet *ATBG* plays with the tension more, even with characters other than Ginger. For example, Courtney Gripling, "the princess of cool," is cast in a Professor Higgins sort of role, a popular girl who wants to re-make Ginger:

> Totally self-absorbed and opportunistic, Courtney takes her position as Most Popular Girl very seriously. She prides herself on the diplomatic control and manipulation of her classmates. She's intrigued and baffled, however, by Ginger's backbone and real friendships. So she sets out to pluck the "unknown" from the dregs of everyday life and make her a "Popular Girl."
>
> (*As Told By Ginger*, 2003a)

In this role, Courtney is at times more successful than others, but there is a general refusal to cast the characters universally as either superficial or genuine. Again, this kind of ambiguity, formulated within the dynamics of consumerism (the foundation upon which the concept of cool hangs) and a discourse of the genuine, is symptomatic of Third Wave feminism and girl power culture, a politics which at times rather defensively insists that these two discourses and practices are not mutually exclusive.

This tension is not simply a side theme of *ATBG*; rather, it forms the substance of almost every episode. The tension is often represented through a strategy of parody and self-reflexivity: there is a general subtext that mocks the distinctions between social groups and characterizes the groups as trivial, even while the show constantly focuses on social groups, thus legitimating them for the tween audience. For example, in one episode, "Family Therapy" (May 25 2002), the contradictions between the superficial cool group and the genuine real group are brought into bold relief through the figure of Ginger's friend Macie Lightfoot. Macie, definitely not a member of the cool group, is riddled with neuroses and is an incredibly insecure, self-conscious character. In this particular episode, the program's theme revolves around the fact that Macie and one of the cool girls, Mipsy, both have birthdays on the same day. While Mipsy's birthday is announced at a school assembly and the cool girls immediately begin to plan a party (complete with a sushi chef flown in from Japan), Macie waits for what she anticipates will be a surprise party given by her parents. Unfortunately, her parents, both child psychologists, forget her birthday, and need to be reminded about the date by Ginger. In an effort to compensate for their forgetfulness, they shower Macie with attention. However, they are so unconnected to their daughter that they don't realize that she is turning 13, and treat her instead as if she was a five-year-old – they throw her a party with a petting zoo, they give her a swingset for a present and, for her party, she dresses in a dress more appropriate for a very young child.

The social commentary of the program – the child psychologists forgetting their own child's birthday, the hyperbolic character of Mipsy's birthday party, the embrace of the juvenile attention by Macie – characterizes this program within the same popular cultural realm as *The Simpsons* or other programs like it that offer ironic critique as part of the entertainment. *ATBG* is different from *Clarissa* – for one thing, it is produced at a very different historical moment to *Clarissa Explains It All*, and the increased normalization of feminist rhetoric since 1991 (when *Clarissa* was first aired) has an obvious presence on the program. The issue of cliques, although always part of the landscape in adolescent culture, occupies a new position of salience in the early 21st century, where attention to girls has not only led to an increase in commercial products for this audience, but also increased public attention to the issues that characterize girl culture.

Nick News

Cliques, popularity, intelligence and empowerment are some of the girl power themes in Nickelodeon's original entertainment programming. These themes, however, not only provide interesting entertainment content, but are also represented in the nonfiction programming on the network's award-winning children's news program, *Nick News*. *Nick News* is a half-hour weekly news program, shown every Sunday evening. Each regular edition *Nick News* covers three or four topics, and there is also a special edition *Nick News*, which devotes an entire show to one theme or special topic. *Nick News* is clearly different from *Clarissa* or *ATBG* because it is non-fiction; as a news program, it arguably provides a kind of "public sphere" for its youth audience. As David Buckingham (2000a) has argued, "for all its shortcomings, news journalism remains the primary means of access to the public sphere of political debate and activity" (p. 186). The show is hosted by Linda Ellerbee, a public figure who is not only well known as a feminist, but also as an important children's advocate.

According to Buckingham, the key to *Nick News*'s success is the willingness of the program to be more adventurous with information and to "rethink politics" for children and thus address the youth audience as a slightly different kind of citizen. *Nick News* at times achieves the goal of establishing the relevance of traditional politics, but it is also an example of the kind of tension present in girl power programming, a tension between a more official political rhetoric and the rhetoric of consumer politics. At times, *Nick News* does address children as "political actors," as Buckingham asserts. That is to say, children's voices, desires, and opinions are treated with respect and without condescension, and the program offers specific instruction on how to act politically – by writing to one's congressperson, by refusing the social rules of an elitist clique, or simply by educating the child audience in what free speech means. So, for example, in one episode of *Nick News* (October 6, 2002), the first story involved cross-burning, after a recent case in the southern U.S. This was a significant program in that it articulated the complexities surrounding issues of free speech, and Ellerbee asked the children in the studio whether, for example, the KKK has a right to free speech, pushing the children to answer why and why not.

After this story, the show cut to a commercial break. At the return of *Nick News*, Ellerbee immediately began the program by discussing how one's dreams can come true – but as a rock star. The program then went on to detail the story of "O-Town," a manufactured boy-band that came into existence as a result of the reality television show, *The Making of the Band*. The odd juxtaposition of these two stories exemplifies the specific tension found in girl power programming between a more typically political form of address and a more commercial address that emphasizes consumer choice. In fact, in a special episode of *Nick News*, "The Fight To Fit In" (December 2 2002), Ellerbee specifically references the contradictions I am identifying more generally in girl power ideology: "Grown ups will tell you how easy it is to be a kid. Kids know better. There is, at your age – at any age really – a natural struggle between the desire to be part of a group and the desire to be an individual."

Nick News more expressly addresses girl power in several different ways: there are some special editions, such as "The Fight To Fit In," or "The Body Trap" (November 25, 2002), that focus on issues thought to be relevant to girl culture such as body image, girls' personal identity, as well as on issues of inclusion in a male-dominated world. (Indeed, many of the girl power issues covered on *Nick News* explicitly reference the social world as largely male dominated, surely a recognition of the mainstreaming of feminist thought into children's consumer culture.) In "The Body Trap," *Nick News* devoted an entire issue to problems related to body image and contained a scathing critique of the popular culture industry's privileging of thin girls as ideals. Featuring not only celebrity Rosie O'Donnell as an "expert," but also graphic visual footage of a young girl suffering from anorexia, "The Body Trap" is an important counter-argument to the hundreds of images of impossibly thin models within popular culture that so powerfully become the norm for young girls. The episode featured a group of children and adolescents, both boys and girls, telling their personal stories about wanting to be thin, feeling stigmatized, and so on. Although this kind of personalized, individual story-telling is important in terms of recognizing the problem, it also functions to distract audiences from larger social issues that are a result of "The Body Trap," such as gender discrimination, racism in the media, and so on.

Even in the regular *Nick News* schedule, girls are often featured as important story subjects (there are, of course, many stories that appeal to a cross-over audience of both boys and girls). For example, issues such as the fledgling National Women's Football League was covered in one episode, where the story made an explicit argument about the unequal playing field for girls and boys sports, and argued that girls "are as tough as boys" (October 20, 2002). Other episodes of *Nick News* dealt with the issue of cruelty and gossip among girl cliques. For example, in an episode of *Nick News* aired on November 3, 2002, Ellerbee begins by saying: "Sugar and Spice and everything Nice, that's what little girls are made of . . . NOT!" In fact, Ellerbee continues, girls can be just as mean as boys, and even meaner. The episode then depicts several young girls recounting their stories of cruelty at school, featuring author Rosalind Wiseman (of the aforementioned *Queen Bees and WannaBes*) on the voice-over stating that the "girl who has the most social power gets to do what she wants to the girl who doesn't." The episode also discusses the contradictions between societal expectations of girls – primarily that they be silent and passive rather than aggressive and active – and that this expectation has led to a unique kind of cruelty that relies not on overt aggression but rather a more subtle, and arguably more insidious, type of malice such as gossip and secrets. Directly connecting girl cruelty to popular culture, *Nick News* argues that girls learn "that to move up they have to pull somebody else down" through glossy magazines, music videos and other forms of popular culture that privilege a kind of brutal competition among girls. The segment ends with a discussion of Wiseman's "empower program," *Owning Up*, where she encourages girls to stand up for themselves if another girl is being cruel. As *As Told By Ginger* suggests in an entertainment format, some of the more pressing issues of the early 21st century, at least when it comes to children, have to do with the dominant practices of femininity, self-esteem, and popularity in the social and cultural world. These topics have provided a broader cultural context for *Nick News* to address similar sorts of issues.

Finally, another way in which *Nick News* is an example of girl power programming comes not in the form of representation, but in a more extratextual way, through the host Linda Ellerbee herself. Ellerbee is a well-known journalist who has been outspoken on the problems of sexism and ageism in the field of journalism. Her production company, Lucky Duck Productions, not only produces *Nick News*, but also programs for Lifetime Television and WE (Women's Entertainment Network). Her work in journalism has garnered numerous awards, including several Emmys and the duPont Columbia award (*Nick News* itself has won three Peabody awards). Ellerbee is also a public speaker; she is a breast cancer survivor and speaks nationally about her experience. She is well known for her respect for both women and children, and is the author of an adolescent reading series, "Get Real," about a young girl reporter.

Henry Jenkins (1998) positions Ellerbee as an important figure in the world of children's media regarding the treatment of children as political and social agents, rather than impressionable beings that need protection from the media. He argues that Ellerbee

creates television programs that encourage children's awareness of real-world problems, such as the Los Angeles riots, and enable children to find their own critical voice to speak back against the adult world. She trusts children to confront realities from which other adults might shield them, offering them the facts needed to form their own opinions and the air time to discuss issues. (p. 32)

As the producer of *Nick News*, Ellerbee is also a producer of children's culture – and in this specific case, a producer of girl power culture. Although *Nick News* is clearly not a DIY form of cultural production, or an alternative girl power 'zine, it nonetheless manages to function as an important producer of girl power ideology (Kearney, 1998).

Nick News is shaped in part by these different dimensions of girl power. The program's focus on girl power issues, in a children's news program that targets a youth audience, is an important form of media activism. *Nick News* claims to specifically empower children through the distribution of information. As Nickelodeon describes the show, "Every week *Nick News* keeps you in the know about the issues that are important to you, from personality profiles to interviews to polls and special guests . . . It's the news the way YOU want it, with help from kids everywhere!" (Nickelodeon website, 2003). However, not only is it difficult to determine precisely what issues are important to all kids, but *Nick News* has the same problem as most news programs: how to connect the issues on the program with the politics of a child's material life. As Buckingham (2000b) argues, "young people need to be provided with opportunities to engage in political activity, rather than simply observing it from a distance – in other words, that they are entitled to be political actors in their own right" (p. 187). *Nick News* is a program that, like citizenship itself, is fraught with tension about the various meanings of empowerment, and what it means to be a political actor. The girl power episodes on *Nick News* create even more of a contradiction: on the one hand, the programs do encourage an awareness of the various issues surrounding contemporary gender politics. On the other hand, these very same gender politics are the products not necessarily of political action, but of media visibility and the commercial realm. The issue of body image, for example, is an important feminist concern, and *Nick News* acknowledges this, but also approaches it from within the commercial realm of the media – a site that helps to produce dominant norms of femininity in the first place.

Girl power: citizenship or consumerism?

Nickelodeon's efforts to include girls as lead characters may be understood as a lucrative market strategy to capitalize on the cultural fad of girl power, but programs such as *Clarissa Explains It All*, *As Told By Ginger*, and *Nick News* nonetheless provide a different cultural script for both girl and boy audience members, a script that challenges conventional narratives and images about what girls are and who they should be. Susan Douglas (1999), writing about the Spice Girls, argues that

when adolescent girls flock to a group, they are telling us plenty about how they experience the transition to womanhood in a society in which boys are still very much on top. Girls today are being urged, simultaneously, to be independent, assertive, and achievement oriented, yet also demure, attractive, soft-spoken, fifteen pounds underweight, and deferential to men. (pp. 47–48)

Nickelodeon programming, including the shows discussed in this essay, incorporates these kinds of tensions as part of their narrative logic, and in so doing provides a context in which both girls and boys can question dominant narratives of gender.

Bonnie Dow (1996), when discussing prime time television shows of the 1980s and 1990s that were assumed to contain a feminist message, argues that while the gender ideology on shows such as *Murphy Brown* and *Designing Women* may not create policy change or affect material politics, they nonetheless represent a kind of feminism. In other words, that these shows are being aired in the mainstream media (a place that historically has demonized feminism) does not mean they are anti-feminist:

> To use the word "feminist" to describe them is not a mistake: within the limits of commercial television, they offer a version of feminist ideology. However, that ideology is one suited to television's needs, not to the needs of a feminist politics committed to the future of all women regardless of race, class, sexuality, or life situation. (p. 214).

Indeed, I see girl power shows on Nickelodeon as also representing a kind of feminism, one that is fundamentally about tension and contradiction. Girl power television is more closely aligned with Third Wave feminism than any kind of post-feminist ideology that disavows feminism. On the contrary, girl power programs such as *Clarissa* and *As Told By Ginger* are visibly situated within a Third Wave ethos, where empowerment and agency define girls more than helplessness and dependency. However, this empowerment is represented as an individual choice, and at times resembles other commercial choices we all make. In other words, Nickelodeon is an important producer of a kind of feminism, but commercial and media visibility is an important part of what *legitimates* that feminism. This does not mean that girl power television is *not* feminism; but it does mean that a significant component of Third Wave and girl power feminism is about media visibility. The mixing of political addresses within the programming and advertising on Nickelodeon – both feminine and feminist, both social and individual – reflects the kind of dynamic Third Wave feminists adopt as part of their subjectivity. Thus, the network itself speaks to its child audience in a mix of conflicting feminist voices.

The images young girls and adolescents watch on Nickelodeon – images of Clarissa Darling, or Ginger Foutley, or the real girls on *Nick News* – are empowering, at least within a specific context. They are diverse, and they represent a range of options and models, and in many ways these images are a refreshing and politically authorizing change from traditional images of femininity. While obviously the commercial shaping of girl power cannot be denied, girl power, like other forms of feminism, is about a particular kind of recognition. This is not simply a recognition that so-called "women's issues" such as sexual harassment, equal work for equal pay, and legal policies on rape and abuse are important issues that need to be addressed in the public sphere. It is also a recognition of women as contributing members of society now meriting a kind of visibility. And increasingly, the kind of visibility that carries with it an important dimension of power is media or cultural visibility.

In this sense, the easy dismissal of girl power as a media-created new commercial avenue that has no connection with any kind of real politics is both inaccurate and misleading about the nature of reality in the 21st century. The charge by Second Wave feminists regarding the apparent lack of real politics in Third Wave feminism may very well indicate, in part, the latter's preoccupation with personal issues and individualism. But this sentiment not only romanticizes the feminist movements of the 1960s and 1970s as concerned only with the social and material spheres; it also caricatures feminist politics of the 1990s as narcissistic and vacuous. As Susan Douglas (1994) has pointed out, the representation of women and girls in the media has historically encouraged a kind of love/hate relationship, where seemingly contradictory messages about being strong and weak, beautiful and business-like, assertive yet demure, have been offered to female (and male) audiences as a model for subjectivity. The media address of Third Wave feminism and girl power ideology is no different: it is also tension and contradiction, about the individual pleasures of consumption and the social responsibilities of solidarity. Although obviously the political landscape has changed since the 1960s, and it seems evident in many contemporary examples that individual concerns have taken precedence over larger community or social issues, it is too easy to dismiss girl power as only or simply media fluff. The collectivist drive that defined the feminist movement during the Second Wave emerged not only because the feminists of that era were particularly politically minded, but also because the civil rights movement, the gay rights movement and the anti-war movements (as well as other political upheavals during this time) provided a rich context for collective protest. For contemporary women, the focus on individualism and the increasing significance of commercial culture provides a context for a very different kind of feminism to materialize. One project for feminists, then, is to attempt to understand the discourse of Third Wave feminism on its own terms, and not always through comparison to an imagined and nostalgic golden age of feminism of the 1970s.

Notes

1 Third Wave feminism is generally characterized as a movement centering on female self-empowerment that emerged in the 1990s. Third Wave feminism often uses both mainstream and marginalized popular and commercial cultures as mechanisms to celebrate female sexuality and access empowerment. The cultural expression of Third Wave feminism is often playful and ironic, exemplified in television such as *Buffy the Vampire Slayer*, activist groups like Riot Grrrl and 'zines such as *Hue* and *Bitch*. Third Wave activists, most often in their 20s and 30s, are focused on a broad range of feminist issues, ranging from abortion rights to individual self-esteem.

2 Second Wave feminism generally refers to the women's movements of the 1960s and 1970s. Second Wave activists were focused on fighting for gender equality in the workplace, abortion rights, economic parity, violence against women, and other issues. The Second Wave of feminism was defined by the collectivist drive

that motivated the movement, and focused not only on the equality of women with men, but also on the liberation of women from patriarchy. Some of the important legislative measures that occurred as a result of the efforts of Second Wave feminists are, to name a few, the Equal Pay Act 1963, Title VII, the Civil Rights Act 1964, and the Equal Rights Amendment.

3   Boys also influence the purchasing power of their parents. Children in general have been increasingly recognized as a very important market because of not only their own power as a group, but also the extended power that comes from their influence on their parents' commercial decisions.

References

As Told By Ginger website. Retrieved March 1 2003, from Character section, http://www.cooltoons.com/ginger

Aucoin, D. (1999, March 21). At 20, Nickelodeon is top-rated – and it's the channel that changed kids TV. *The Boston Globe* p. N4.

Baumgardner, J., & Richards, A. (1999). *Manifesta: Young women, feminism, and the future*. New York: Farrar, Straus and Giroux.

Bellafante, G. (1998, June 29). It's all about me! *Time*, p. 57.

Buckingham, D. (2000a). *The making of citizens: Young people, news and politics*. London: Routledge.

Buckingham, D. (2000b). *After the death of childhood: Growing up in the age of electronic media*. London: Polity Press.

Canclini, N. G. (2001). *Consumers and citizens: Globalization and multicultural conflicts*. Translated and with an Introduction by George Yudice. Minneapolis: University of Minnesota Press.

Currie, D. (1999). *Girl talk: Adolescent magazines and their readers*. Toronto: University of Toronto Press.

Douglas, S. (1994). *Where the girls are: Growing up female with the mass media*. New York: Times Books/Random House.

Douglas, S. (1999). Girls 'n spice: All things nice? In Daniel M. Shea (Ed.), *Mass politics: The politics of popular culture* (45–49). New York: St. Martin's Press.

Dow, B. (1996). *Prime-time feminism: Television, media culture, and the women's movement since 1970*. Philadelphia: University of Pennsylvania Press.

Dow, B. (2001). *Ellen*, television, and the politics of gay and lesbian visibility. In *Critical Studies in Media Communication, 18* 123–140.

Driscoll, C. (2002). *Girls: Feminine adolescence in popular culture and cultural history*. New York: Columbia University Press.

Findlen, B. (Ed). (1995). *Listen up: Voices from the next feminist generation*. New York: Seal Press.

Goldman, R. (1992). *Reading ads socially*. New York: Routledge.

Gray, H. (1997). *Watching race: Television and the struggle for the sign of blackness*. Minneapolis: University of Minnesota Press.

Gross, L. (2001). *Up from invisibility: Lesbians, gay men, and the media in America*. New York: Columbia University Press.

Hall, S. (1997). *Representation: Cultural representations and signifying practices*. London: Sage Books.

Hartley, J. (1999). *Uses of television*. London: Routledge.

Hartsock, N. (1998). *The feminist standpoint revisited and other essays*. Colorado: Westview Press.

Heffley, L. (1999, June 3). Family arts zone: Then along came lively shows for kids, in the nick of time. *Los Angeles Times*, p. 45.

Hendershot, H. (1999). *Saturday morning censors: Television regulation before the V-chip*. Durham: Duke University Press.

Hogeland, L. M. (2001). Against generational thinking, or, some things that "Third Wave" feminism isn't. *Women's Studies in Communication, 24* 107–121.

Jenkins, H. (1998). *The children's culture reader*. New York: New York University Press.

Kearney, M. C. (1998). Producing girls: Rethinking the study of female youth culture. In S. A. Inness (Ed.), *Delinquents and debutantes: Twentieth century American girls' cultures* (pp. 285–310). New York: New York University Press.

Kinder, M. (Ed.). (1999). *Kids' media culture*. Durham, NC: Duke University Press.

Klein, N. (2000) *No logo*. New York: Picador.

McNeal, J. U. (1992). *Kids as customers: A handbook of marketing to children*. New York: Lexington Books.

McRobbie, A. (1991). *Feminism and youth culture: From Jackie to Just Seventeen*. Boston: Unwin, Hyman.

Miller, T. (1998). *Technologies of truth: Cultural citizenship and the popular media*. Minneapolis: University of Minnesota Press.

Nickelodeon press release (2000, September). In press packet for "A Kid's Got to Do What a Kid's Got to Do: Celebrating 20 Years of Nickelodeon." New York: Museums of Television and Radio, June 1, 2000.

Nickelodeon website. Retrieved May 13 2000, from http://nick.com/all_nick/tv_supersites/display_show.jhtml/?show_id = new

Pipher, M. (1995). *Reviving Ophelia: Saving the selves of adolescent girls*. New York: Ballantine Books.

Quart, A. (2003). *Branded: The buying and selling of teenagers*. Cambridge: Perseus Publishing.

Seiter, E. (1995). *Sold separately: Parents and children in consumer culture*. New Jersey: Rutgers University Press.

Shugart, H. A., Waggoner, C. E., & O'Brien Hallstein, D. L. (2001). Mediating Third Wave feminism: Appropriation as postmodern media practice. *Critical Studies in Media Communication, (18)* 194–209.

Spigel, L. (1992). *Make room for TV: Television and the family ideal in postwar America*. Chicago and London: The University of Chicago Press.

Sturken, M., & Cartwright, L. (2001). *Practices of looking: An introduction to visual culture*. London: Oxford University Press.

Van Fuqua, J. (2003). "What are those little girls made of?": *The Powerpuff Girls* and consumer culture. In C. A. Stabile & M. Harrison (Eds.), *Prime time animation: Television animation and American culture* (pp. 205–219). New York: Routledge.

Wiseman, R. (2002). *Queen bees and wannaBes: Helping your daughter survive cliques, gossip, boyfriends and other realities of adolescence*. New York: Crown Publications.

Wolf, N. (1994). *Fire with fire: The new female power and how to use it*. New York: Fawcett Books.

11

The (In)visible Lesbian
Anxieties of representation in *The L Word*

Susan J. Wolfe and Lee Ann Roripaugh

Originally published in Kim Akass and Janet McCabe (eds), *Reading The L Word: Outing Contemporary Television* (London: I. B. Tauris, 2006), 43–54.

As Eve Sedgwick observes in '*The L Word: Novelty* in Normalcy', Showtime's series creates a lesbian ecology – '[a] visible world in which lesbians exist, go on existing, exist in forms beyond the solitary and the couple, sustain and develop relations among themselves of difference and commonality' (2004: B10). However, Sedgwick also points out that to meet this 'obvious and modest representational need' the show must also enact a Faustian bargain because television is a genre which ultimately caters to the desires and expectations of mainstream audiences. As noted in *The Advocate* by Showtime President Bob Greenblatt, '*The L Word* has not only proven itself to be a signature show for Showtime but also one that has captured the imagination of a large mainstream audience with its bold, sexy storylines and talented cast' (Anon 2005).

Not surprisingly, *The L Word* has elicited highly ambivalent and hotly debated responses among its lesbian viewers, revealing intense anxieties regarding lesbian identity and representation, as evidenced by the wildly disparate reviews published after the show's debut in early 2004. The show's detractors, for example, criticised the show as shamelessly pandering to the male, heterosexual gaze. Winnie McCroy, in her review of *The L Word* in *New York Blade*, 'L is for Invisible', stated:

> If lesbians have to choose between remaining invisible to the mainstream, or being represented by Showtime's clipped and plucked lesbians, I choose invisibility. After all, real lesbians will still remain invisible, at least until our lives become more than a marketing tool or cottage industry or pud fodder for Joe Sixpack.
>
> (2004)

Similarly, Malinda Lo, in 'It's All About the Hair: Butch Identity and Drag on *The L Word*', laments the lack of 'hair diversity' on the show:

> [If] we are committed to fighting discrimination and stereotypes about women in general – not only lesbians – it is not enough to have a show full of slender,

beautiful, femmy women who just happen to be lesbians. We really need to have a few butch haircuts too.

(April 2004)

Conversely, proponents of the show praised it as 'ghetto-busting' and focused on its deconstruction of 'negative' lesbian stereotypes. Stacey D'Erasmo, in her review from the *New York Times*, 'Lesbians on Television: It's Not Easy Being Seen', hailed the show as:

> a breakthrough in the annals of television's fantasy life. Being an L myself, a member of a group that has had a spotty presence on the small screen, I can testify with authority to the despair of bouncing along a life of risk, mystery and heartbreak only to turn on the TV and see two women in bad pantsuits gingerly touching one another on the forearm. *The L Word* tosses those pantsuits to the wind, and good riddance to them. A mini-series of one's own is progress, undeniably.

(2004)

Along similar lines, Jacqueline Cutler noted in '*The L Word* Breaks Lesbian Ground' that, 'Indeed, clichés are avoided. There are no plaid flannel shirts or fat, hairy women in sight' (2004). And in a *LesbiaNation* article appearing on the verge of the second season première, '*The L Word*: Paragon Paradox', Shona Black, fending off criticism of the show, exhaustedly queried, 'Have we not reached a point where we can admit and celebrate the fact that women can be just as shallow as men, that lesbians appreciate some eye-candy just as much as the next guy?' (2005).

While these reviews demonstrate conflicting responses to the show, they also reveal a consistent sense of anxiety about lesbian representation: assimilationist visibility vs. marginalised invisibility, identitarian 'authenticity' vs. Revlon revolution 'passing', second-wave vs. third-wave feminism, lesbianism vs. post-lesbianism, and policing of commodified mainstream image making vs. the policing of negative stereotypes. Interestingly, these anxieties have also surfaced repeatedly in the past decade's scholarly discourse on lesbian identity and representation. In her book *The Lesbian Menace*, for example, Sherrie Inness (1997) critiques the phenomenon of the 'frilly lesbian' in popular women's magazines – a representation which she argues is calculated to reassure a heterosexual viewing audience that lesbians are, indeed, just like them. Inness writes:

> Viewers are given a fantasy image of lesbians, which is as unrealistic as the image that all lesbians are ugly. Also, using models who look stereotypically heterosexual pretending to be lesbians provides titillation without threat as there is an implicit understanding that these are not 'real' lesbians.

(65–6)

Along similar lines, in an analysis of cinematic conventions governing lesbian representation in eighties cinema, Judith Halberstam complains that, 'the butch character is played as a shadow of her former self' (1998: 217), going on to state that:

The shades of butch are still readable (Patrice Donnelly as a jock, Mary Stuart Masterson as a rough-and-tumble southern dyke), but their embodiments are definitely feminized. Wherever a novel has been turned into a film (*Fried Green Tomatoes, Desert Hearts*), the characters in the novels who were coded as butch have been noticeably softened into femmey butches or soft butches.

Halberstam goes on to assert that 'the butch is a *type* of lesbian as well as a lesbian stereotype.' This erasure of the butch from 1980s lesbian cinema, Halberstam argues, seriously undermines lesbian visibility within these films – rendering lesbian erotic relationships as ambiguously submerged, or virtually indistinguishable from platonic friendship and thus invisible, as in the case of *Fried Green Tomatoes* (220–1).

Conversely, post-lesbian scholarly perspectives reveal anxieties about identity and representation that centre primarily around a perceived need to uncouple lesbian and feminist identities, as well as a desire to dismantle, usurp, and transgress against prior generations' identitarian formations of lesbian identity. (And perhaps tellingly, it is these former incarnations of lesbian-feminist identities which have been frequently caricatured and perpetuated as 'negative' stereotypes by mainstream media.) In *Not My Mother's Sister: Generational Conflict and Third-Wave Feminism*, Astrid Henry writes:

> as in straight third-wave writing, young dykes tend to portray the previous generation of feminists as frumpy and unsexy. The word 'frumpy', like 'dowdy', suggests a look that is not only unsexy but out of fashion. Fashion plays a central role in staging this generational divide, both in terms of literal fashion – that is, style of dress – and in terms of the desire to be 'in fashion' in a larger sense.
>
> (2004: 124)

Charlotte Ashton notes the same trends in 'Getting Hold of the Phallus: "Post-Lesbian" Power Negotiations', stating that, 'With big hair, short skirts, lipstick and lycra, post-lesbians are holding up a mirror to the mainstream and reclaiming the components of "passing" as totems of transgression. Or, put another way, as overheard at a chic London dyke club: "This is the Revlon revolution, Sister!" ' (1996: 163). Going on to argue that the Revlon revolution comes at a cost, however, Ashton claims that:

> The reason for post-lesbianism's current popularity with the mainstream media lies in the fact that it doesn't *look* or *act* any differently from other forms of accepted femininity. For as long as men can look at post-lesbians and see sexy women they want to fuck, and who indeed might even fuck them back, they will not consider that they have been forced to concede any ground.
>
> (172)

Rather than resisting commodification as a form of exploitation and invisibility, though, post-lesbianism embraces its subversive potential. In 'Lesbian Bodies in the Age of (Post)mechanical Reproduction', Cathy Griggers writes that we are:

> bearing witness to the military becoming lesbian, the mother becoming lesbian,

straight women becoming lesbian, fashion and Hollywood and the sex industry becoming lesbian, middle-class women, corporate America, and technoculture becoming lesbian, and so on. That is, the lesbian body of signs, like all minority bodies, is always becoming majority, in a multiplicity of ways. But at the same time, in a multitude of domains across the general cultural field, majority bodies are busy *becoming lesbian*.

(1993: 184)

Clearly, *The L Word* emerges as a site of contestation for precisely these types of anxieties regarding lesbian identity and representation. Perhaps more interestingly, however, it could be argued that the show itself *enacts and critiques* these anxieties of representation during moments when the show turns the lens in on itself through the use of meta-narrative, or the insertion of what Candace Moore (2005) refers to in an *AfterEllen.com* piece as a *meta-eye*. These moments of meta-narrative serve to complicate and implicate acts of representation, acts of performance, and acts of consuming/ viewing, thereby creating a self-reflexive commentary on the anxieties of lesbian identity and representation that is, ultimately, quite nuanced and rich.

From the outset, viewing and voyeurism play a significant role throughout the first two seasons of *The L Word* and, indeed, the show seemingly attempts to distinguish between negative vs. positive modes of representation and viewing through periodically framing the episodes with opening credit vignettes with distant narrative connections to the episodes themselves. These opening credit vignettes often depict abject circumstances, such as the exploitation of young women via lesbian porn-ography, lesbian self-denial and self-hatred, and homophobic discrimination or violence, among others. On occasion, the vignettes also seem to function as overtly constructed and explicitly fictionalised representations of lesbian identity, including scenes from movies, dreams/fantasies or fiction.

The enclosure of the episodes within these framing vignettes does several interesting things: on the one hand, the framing vignettes create the illusion of a lesbian third space. Within the protective folds of these framing vignettes, the episodes themselves – particularly in juxtaposition to the overt (and frequently negative) constructedness of the vignettes – are privileged as positive and 'authentic' lesbian representations. Furthermore, the vignettes immediately place the audience member in a voyeuristic relationship to the episodes via the implication that they are being allowed a titillating glimpse into a fictional 'inner sanctum,' so to speak.

By the same token, the very constructedness of the opening vignettes cannot help but signal the presence of meta-narrative devices within the show – serving as a constant reminder that what the viewer sees might *seem* like the 'real deal' but is, in fact, a deliberately constructed fiction as well. This perspective prevents the potentially salacious voyeur from becoming too comfortable about peering into this fictional 'inner sanctum'. Viewers who hope to lapse into a complacent and pleasurable voyeurism will instead find themselves repeatedly bumping up against the boundary of the television screen and reminded that what they are viewing is a representation which serves as a sort of screen or shield to the real. In this sense, the screen almost serves as a symbolic fencing device, separating viewers from characters in much the same way that voyeurs are separated from the fictional lesbians they attempt to spy upon, forced to view them through windows and lenses. The use of the opening vignettes, like the examination of the role of the voyeurs in the episodes, establishes from the outset that the act of viewing is a complex activity that is never innocent, passive, or neutral.

Meta-narrative, or the introduction of the *meta-eye*, is even more explicitly introduced in the pilot episode of *The L Word*, when the character of Jenny Schecter – at this stage a heterosexual, engaged woman – glimpses two women having sex in her next-door neighbour's pool. Fascinated, Jenny crouches down in order to remain unobserved herself, and then spies on the women through the slats of her fence. The audience is thus immediately implicated in a voyeuristic observation of lesbian sex, rendering the act of viewing as both titillating and inappropriately transgressive. Furthermore, the camera not only cinematographically forces the viewer to spy on the lovers through Jenny's point of view, but to also spy on Jenny spying on the lesbian lovers. What is particularly fascinating about this scene is that the fence through which jenny spies does, in fact, form a visual fencing device, and what she, as an outsider, sees through the slats of the fence (along with the viewer, through Jenny's point of view) is only a partial, obscured, and incomplete image.

Similarly, the scene eventually evolves into one of *mistaken identity* when Jenny later describes the women in the pool to her fiancé, Tim Haspel, and asks if his next-door neighbours are gay. Assuming that Jenny is referring to long-term partners Bette Porter and Tina Kennard, Tim, at first incredulous, is then turned on by the idea, and encourages Jenny to continue her narration. He seems particularly aroused by Jenny's interest in what she describes as the blonde woman's 'really beautiful breasts'. The women in the pool that Jenny describes, however, are not Bette and Tina (as Jenny and Tim imagine), but rather Bette and Tina's friend, Shane McCutcheon, enjoying an afternoon fling in Bette and Tina's pool with an anonymous woman. In this sense, lesbian identity is foregrounded as slippery and difficult to pin down or essentialise, and what the viewers *think* they have seen may not in fact be what they've actually seen.

Furthermore, this act of viewing has profoundly disturbing and unexpected effects on both Jenny and Tim. For Jenny, what she has witnessed functions as a lesbian primal scene of sorts – opening the door to latent desires which first initiate a full-blown homosexual panic but later culminate in her affair with Marina Ferrer. Tim, on the other hand, learns that he gravely mistakes his own (imagined) sexual desires when he casually appropriates Jenny's interest in the lesbians to fuel his own fantasy fodder. Later in the season, when Tim accidentally walks in on Jenny having sex with Marina ('Lies, Lies, Lies', 1:4), he (predictably) doesn't find the scene remotely sexy, but rather feels upset, betrayed, excluded and emasculated. Thus, as viewers, we witness fantasy and reality colliding in ways that do not necessarily mesh with one another, while simultaneously being reminded that what we are witnessing on the small screen is also a representation, or form of fantasy.

Another rich instance of meta-narrative which similarly questions lesbian identity and representation occurs during a strip club outing when the friends arrange to take the pregnant and grieving Tina out for a lap dance in order to distract her from her painful break-up with Bette ('Lap Dance', 2:3). Upon their arrival at the strip club Tina, who is dubious about the evening's agenda, says that she thinks it's hideous, but

Alice Pieszecki gives her a little pep talk. 'Well, they're all different, you know,' Alice says. 'Some have real boobies. You just keep looking. You'll find something you like.' Her comment seems to adumbrate two key strands of representation which are explored in this particular meta-narrative. On the one hand, the visual juxtaposition of the strippers on stage with the cast members is immediately striking. Once again, the artificial constructedness of the dancers – their bodies, costumes and rhetorical gestures of seduction – is acutely highlighted in contrast to the bodies, costumes and casual posturing of the show's cast members in such a way as to privilege the show's characters as 'natural', positive and authentic representations of lesbian identity. Furthermore, the entry of the characters into the male-dominated space of the strip club – with all of the concomitant rights and entitlements symbolically contained therein (i.e. symbolic power of the gaze, symbolic power of choice and symbolic control of capital) – seems to playfully enact a post-lesbian appropriation of the phallus. Playfulness is key here, as if there's no need to take the phallus *too* seriously, and while the characters enjoy the show and distribute tips to the dancers, they nonetheless continue to talk and carry on among themselves. In other words, their narratives are foregrounded and continue to unfold against the backdrop of the dancers. This is in stark contrast to the male clientele of the club, who all appear to be grimly riveted to their seats and tractor-beamed onto the stage – held in thrall to the dancers and rendered semi-paralytic by their own gazing. The presence of these submissively cow-like male viewers at the strip club once again seems to unflatteringly implicate an 'outsider' or purely voyeuristic gaze – brushing it off as both laughably reductive and impotent.

At the same time, anxieties of lesbian representation do not go uninterrogated here. Before they go out to the strip club, for example, the women have dinner at a Chinese restaurant, where Tina foregrounds salient issues about representation, lesbian visual pleasure, political correctness, and power when she states, 'I don't think women, especially lesbians, should exploit other women.' Shane likewise interrogates assumptions regarding agency and sexual abjection when she counters, 'Well, the strippers I know do it because they love it.' Also as before, the highly constructed performances of the fictional dancers on stage inevitably serve as a reminder that the characters we are viewing on the screen are likewise actresses who are similarly performing roles for an audience. In another interesting layer of meta-narrative, when Tina is finally cajoled into accepting a lap dance, her friends immediately observe that the woman she has chosen resembles Bette. Tina's wistful expression during the seductive lap dance seems to suggest she is pretending or imagining that the dancer is, in fact, Bette. Later on at home, Tina attempts to masturbate, but the imaginary representation fails her and she ends up weeping instead. Like Tina, we learn that the dancer is an inadequate substitute for Bette, who is more than just her body. Viewing has stimulated a desire which cannot be satisfied by a visual fantasy, and once again, the failure of a representation to stand in for the real is thematically underscored.

Perhaps the most overt instance of meta-narrative, however, occurs in the second-season storyline involving the character of Mark Wayland – a would-be amateur film-maker who, after becoming Shane and Jenny's roommate, embarks upon a film project titled *A Compendium of Lesbianism*. This project involves videotaped interviews with Jenny, Shane, and their friends, as well as tape taken from 'strategically and respectfully placed' hidden cameras planted throughout the house without their knowledge. On the one hand, Mark's instrusive presence in the house as a narrative embodiment of the male gaze can be read, in part, as a response to first-season criticism that the show pandered too much to the imagined needs of this gaze. The hidden cameras seem to serve as a reminder that perhaps the viewer and not the 'panderer' bear responsibility for the acts of gazing. Interestingly, though, while the non-consensual nature of Mark's film is characterised as violating, his obsessive viewing and interaction with the women nonetheless has a transformative effect, in that his film starts to become less prurient and more 'anthropological'. Early in the storyline ('Lynch Pin', 2:4), Mark explains his desire to pin down lesbian authenticity in his documentary – a discussion that perhaps explores criticisms of inauthenticity raised by viewers during the first season of *The L Word*. He says he can't quite figure out the 'lesbian thing' but, with access to 'real' lesbians, he's determined to 'put his finger on it anyway'. Here, Mark's ludicrous assertion seems to foreground the impossibility of representing a non-existent, essentialised lesbian identity. When he questions Jenny's long hair and remarks that she doesn't exude that 'thing', Jenny – in a gesture that also seems to be a calculated response to first-season critics – gets a short haircut.

In episode nine ('Late, Later, Latent'), Mark emerges as misguidedly earnest when he pitches his film to his repulsive sidekick Gomey (Sam Easton) and their sleazy financial backer. *A Compendium of Lesbianism*, Mark enthusiastically gushes, is replete with insights into lesbian life: 'The women talk all the time, it's not all just about sex, it's about a way of life, they have a culture of their own, it's revelatory, it's anthropological.' In response to Mark's description of his film's aims (aims which would seem to echo the representational aims of *The L Word* itself), the financial backer becomes incensed, screaming, 'Red-blooded men don't give a fuck about this anthropological bullshit.' Rather, 'They want hot lesbian sex and they want it now.' Gomey suggests that Mark is turning into a homosexual and indeed, by this point, Mark has a decidedly queer crush on Shane – a crush that reverses the stereotypical fetishising of hyper-feminine lesbians in favour of a model that seems to have overtones of male homoerotic desire and therefore speaks to the potential of trans-semiotic queering.

While Mark emerges as a not entirely unsympathetic character, his intrusive and non-consensual viewing has serious consequences for which he is ultimately held accountable. Given that network executives insisted on writing in a straight male character for straight male audience members to relate to, it is probably no coincidence that the scripts render this character, a creative intrusion, as a vehicle by which to examine and critique the theme of male intrusion. In particular, in 'Land Ahoy' (2:10), when Jenny discovers that Mark has been taping the house without permission, she confiscates his video camera and lures Mark to her room. Having scrawled 'Is This What U Want' in black magic marker on her naked body in a disturbing sexual parody, Jenny then turns the tables on Mark and issues one of the show's strongest feminist speeches. Training his video camera on him, she demands that he ask his younger sisters about the very first time they were intruded on by a man or a boy. Asked by Mark why she assumes his sisters have been intruded upon, Jenny replies, 'Because there isn't a single girl or woman in this world that hasn't been intruded upon, and sometimes it's relatively benign, and sometimes it's so fucking painful. But you have no idea what this feels like.' Later on, when Mark tries to make amends to Jenny, insisting that she and Shane have made him a better man, Jenny takes a radical feminist view, arguing that women, and by extension the show itself, are not responsible for educating men: 'It's not a fucking woman's job to be consumed and invaded and spat out so that some fucking man can evolve' ('Loud and Proud', 2:11). Furthermore, Mark then dramatically removes his clothes to demonstrate his vulnerability, asking Jenny if that's what *she* wants. Jenny's explanation points out that making any female body available to the male gaze poses a danger which he, as a man, has never experienced. At the same time, on the level of meta-narrative, the statement also reflects the inherent difficulty of representing lesbians (or any women) on the screen because female characters are always open to exploitative readings:

> What I want is for you to write 'Fuck Me' on your chest. Write it. Do it. And then I want you to walk out that door and I want you to walk down the street. And anybody that wants to fuck you, say, 'Sure, sure, no problem.' And when they do, you have to say, 'Thank you very, very much.' And make sure that you have a smile on your face. And then, you stupid fucking coward, you're gonna know what it feels like to be a woman.

Given the relative lack of viable lesbian protagonists in mainstream media, *The L Word* has good reason to be anxious over its portrayal of lesbians; as the first show of its kind, the show bears inordinate responsibilities and impossible representational burdens, particularly when it must perform competitively to ensure its continued existence. As Stacey D'Erasmo ruefully confesses in 'Lesbians on Television: It's Not Easy Being Seen':

> A peculiar consequence of so rarely seeing your kind on television, in movies, in plays, what have you, is that you can become, almost unwittingly, attached to a certain kind of wildness: the wildness of feeling not only unrepresented but somehow unrepresentable in ordinary terms. You get so good at ranging around unseen (and finding less obvious characters to identify with, from Tony Soprano to Seven of Nine) that it can feel a little limiting to be decanted into a group of perfectly nice women leading pleasant, more or less realistic lives. You can think, ungratefully: Is that all there is?
>
> (2004)

Perhaps inasmuch as certain burdens of representation are impossible to meet within the scope of a single television show, arguments about whether or not *The L Word* attains any sort of representative 'normalcy' with regard to lesbian identity are moot. However, through the moments of self-reflexive meta-narrative under discussion here and present in numerous other examples, *The L Word* ultimately makes a sophisticated attempt to acknowledge, speak to, and address these anxieties of representation in ways that are ultimately both savvy and subversive.

Part 2

AUDIENCES, RECEPTION CONTEXTS, AND SPECTATORSHIP

This section explores the practices of viewing television and television's relationship to women's pleasure and social subjectivity. Over the past four decades feminist critics have contributed to and often shaped debates about the public's relationship with and reception of television. As is generally true of the work on spectatorship and audiences, feminist scholarship in this area has been interdisciplinary in nature – mixing models from literary and film theory with those drawn from sociology and anthropology. From literary and film theory, television scholars inherited an interest in the ways texts encourage women to identify with a 'subject position' or what is often also called a 'spectator position', 'reading position', 'implied reader', and the like. From sociology and anthropology, critics inherited a focus on the empirical audience. For example, how do viewers use television programmes like *Buffy* to form fan communities? How are reality shows like *Who Wants to Be a Millionaire?* or *Survivor* used as the stuff of everyday conversation at school or work, or since the 1990s, in Internet chat rooms? Or how do diasporic populations use television programs to recall a sense of home and to re-imagine national or ethnic ties while living in a host country? How are programs like *Sex and the City* received in places where western feminism and postfeminism are out of sync with many women's lived experiences and aspirations? How are Japanese serials received in Korea? Or how do telenovelas appeal to Mexican American girls? Rather than being text based or context based by design, much of the work in this area is often both at once. The hybrid quality of the research can be seen in many articles featured in this section. The articles engage and at times mix together relatively diverse research methods (from narrative analysis of 'modes of address' to historical recovery to more audience-centered and ethnographic approaches). They also span the diverse set of national contexts in which this research is conducted.

The section begins with two relatively early essays on audiences and spectators. Annette Kuhn's much-cited 1984 article 'Women's Genres' offers an overview of the different theoretical paradigms and disciplinary origins from which much of the work on female spectators has been generated. Focusing on the early work on soap opera and women's 'weepies' in the cinema, Kuhn suggests that while these 'gyno-centric' genres may appear to appeal to women in common ways, the research generated by television scholars on soaps is generally different from the work in film studies. Kuhn argues that while film scholars of the 1970s and early 1980s tended to use textual analysis to understand how films implicate spectators in various modes of identification and subjectivity, television scholars had gravitated toward the analysis of the social and reception context in which women watch television. Kuhn goes on to argue that attention to both – a subject/spectator implied by a text and a social audience – is important to any sophisticated understanding of the popularity of these genres with women, and that therefore we must look both to text and context in our analyses. Since the publication of Kuhn's essay, many scholars (including those published here) did just that.

Similarly concerned with texts, contexts, and interpretation, Ien Ang's essay 'Melodramatic Identifications' reprises some of the findings of her influential study of *Dallas* fans conducted in the early 1980s in the Netherlands. In this study, Ang used ideas of fantasy (then more commonly associated with studies of film melodrama) to help her empirical investigation of viewers' letters about *Dallas*. In the article reprinted here, Ang speculates on the attractions that *Dallas* characters like Sue-Ellen held for women and she also considers the appeal of the tougher Christine Cagney (from *Cagney and Lacey*). She suggests that women's strong affection for and identification with these characters testifies to the complexity of the task of 'being a woman', while she also points out that not all, and not *only*, women like melodrama. She speculates that identification is less stereotypically gender-divided than much early feminist film and television criticism assumed, an argument she expands in work later than that reproduced here.[1]

The following four essays expand ethnographic and qualitative audience research in connection with narrative and/or ideological analysis to consider how an increasingly global and transnational media/consumer culture relates to women's experiences in different national contexts. Based on her book *Screening Culture, Viewing Politics* (1999), Purnima Mankekar's 'National Texts and Gendered Lives' is an ethnographic study of television viewers in New Delhi. Using insights from Stuart Hall, feminist film and television theory, and anthropology, Mankekar explores viewers' interpretations of the gendered and nationalist meanings in primetime television serials on Doordarshan, the state-run Indian channel. She argues that the serials (a cross between Hindi cinema and soap opera) promote an ideal of Indian Womanhood that imagines women as the protectors of the nation, but that viewer responses to the serials vary according to gender, class, age and other life circumstances. Through participant observation and interviews with television viewers in their homes, Mankekar finds that women's and men's everyday viewing practices are affected by the larger gender system. For example, women tend to cook or clean while watching TV, but men tend to relax and pay full attention to the set. In addition, she claims, male and female viewers often identify with women characters and plots about Indian womanhood in very different ways. Moreover, she argues that viewers' intense involvement in the shows does not necessarily translate into passive acceptance of the programmes' nationalist framework. Instead, she claims, 'Intensive emotional involvement occurs simultaneously with a critical awareness that sometimes enables viewers to "see through" the narrative to the state's agenda. "Resistance" and "compliance" are not mutually exclusive categories.' In this respect, the essay provides a rich example of how ethnographic method can help to nuance our understanding of television's ideological effects and viewers' use of television within the gender systems that help to organize the everyday 'commonsense' discourses and practices of the nation.

Elizabeth MacLachlan and Geok-lian Chua's 'Defining Asian Femininity: Chinese Viewers of Japanese TV Dramas in Singapore', continues this section's interest in television's relation to nationalism and sexuality, in this case with an emphasis on transnationalism. Using a focus group composed of twenty Singaporean women of Chinese ethnicity, the authors explore how the women (some single women in their twenties, some older and married) respond to a Japanese '(post)-trendy' serial shown on Singaporean television. MacLachlan and Chua find that the married women tend to reject the sexual liberalism in the (post-trendy) drama. These women see the sexual content as part of Japan's loss of traditional Asian values in favour of modernity and the loose mores associated with the West. But younger women identify with the more liberal sexual content in the programme (including pre-marital sex and adultery), seeing this as a welcome aspect of globalization, even while they still believe in traditional values of womanhood associated with marriage and childrearing. Based on this case study of transnational consumption, MacLachlan and Chua argue that we need to consider popular culture in the context of Joseph Straubhaar's concept of 'cultural proximity' (or shared identities, gestures, fashions, lifestyles, etc.). Developing this concept, they further draw on the work of Koichi Iwabuchi to argue that some Asian populations (such as their young interviewees) share a sense of 'real time' resonance with other non-western modernities, even as they simultaneously recognize differences.[2]

Transnational media consumption also serves as the focus for Ksenija Vidmar-Horvat's 'The Globalization of Gender: *Ally McBeal* in Post-socialist Slovenia'. In this essay (Chapter 16) Vidmar-Horavat considers the global popularity of a US programme, widely seen as a representative example of western postfeminism. Why is the programme so widely popular among women in post-socialist Slovenia, and how does it resonate (or not) with women's lived experiences? In particular, how does a US postfeminist heroine resonate in a part of the world where women have often resisted western feminism and postfeminism by proxy? To answer the question, Vidmar-Horvat provides her college-age students with a questionnaire, the answers to which suggest that despite historical resistance to western feminism, and despite the fact that students understood Ally to be a neurotic poster girl for western postfeminism, they often mobilized her character in their own life aspirations for women's justice and progress. For example, numerous students embraced Ally as a 'progressive chapter in the emancipation of women' and some saw her as a relevant role model for women's liberation and a counter to traditional views of women's roles. The author concludes that despite its often contradictory and contested meanings, 'In the post-socialist cultures, post-feminism may be seen as granting, in its female form of consumption, a compensation for state-controlled bars to commodity culture and female pleasure in socialism.' Thus, despite *Ally McBeal*'s hegemonic western ways of understanding women, worldwide audiences may adapt its postfeminist sensibilities to local histories and gender inequities, and use it to re-imagine their own futures.

The next essay continues with the transnational success of television among female publics, this time by looking at television within the context of beauty ideals and 'make-over' fantasies so common to television since its inception. Taking this as her focus, Yeidy Rivera's 'The Performance and Reception of Televisual "Ugliness" in *Yo soy Betty la fea*' discusses the transnational success of the Colombian telenovela (which first aired in 2001 and was subsequently adapted to dramatic form in the US as *Ugly*

Betty). Rivero first lays out the narrative dynamics of *Betty*, which revolves around Beatriz, a young, clumsy, working-class yet brilliant woman employed as a secretary at a high fashion company (packed with beautiful models). Rivero asks how Latina, Latin American, and Spanish Caribbean women understood beauty ideals promoted in *Betty* and why audiences were so engaged by this programme. Analyzing the way *Betty* enforced Eurocentric notions of beauty (and undermined black, brown, and mulatta bodies), she then attempts to understand how audiences interpret the text. Using a focus group of mostly middle- and upper-class women, Rivero considers how white Eurocentric notions of beauty dominate the Latin American imagination and how race and class serve to further affect the beauty system. She finds that women in her study often accepted the beauty ideals and notions of ugliness which were connected to blackness and lower-class taste in *Betty*. Nevertheless, some women also spoke critically of *Betty*'s race and class bias and saw the beauty system as a media construction that made women feel they had to conform to Eurocentic ideals. In the end, as Rivero suggests, the programme itself performs the 'ugly duckling' happy ending in a sequel in which Beatriz and the other 'ugly' women in the show adapt western ideals of beauty – a makeover which is connected to Beatriz's rise in class and her marriage to her boss.

The final essay in this volume represents a strain of feminist scholarship concerned specifically with the historical audience for television. In 'Sob Stories, Merriment, and Surprises: The 1950s Audience Participation Show on Network Television and Women's Daytime Reception', Marsha Cassidy develops feminist work on the 1950s suburban housewife and her relation to the new medium of television. Rather than seeing television as a medium that simply enforced women's isolation in the home, Cassidy argues that daytime television was replete with audience participation shows that worked as a prototype for the cyber-communities of today. Shows like *Strike It Rich* and *It Could Be You* allowed television viewers to call or mail in, while they also offered women opportunities to become studio audiences (or participate vicariously with the female studio audiences on screen). Adapting film historian Miriam Hansen's work on the female audiences for early cinema and their use of cinema as a subaltern public sphere, Cassidy claims that the audience participation show granted women at home a bridge between private and public life, thus offering a decidedly ambivalent mode of female subjectivity. These programmes, Cassidy suggests, created a metaphysic of female electronic presence even while women were physically home alone.[3] In this regard, she concludes that the programmes balanced the period's tensions between television's home-centredness and its allure as a fantasy space for imagined community and public amusement.

Although we have chosen the articles in this section for their diversity of approach, national origin, and subject matter, they by no means fully represent the enormous amount of audience-centred approaches to television. We did not have space, for example, to include the proliferating work on Internet fandoms; the engagement with girls as audiences and producers; and the considerable amount of attention to diasporic television viewing in many parts of the globe. Nevertheless, as with this book more generally, we hope to spark interest in further reading and to inspire inquiry into this considerably productive area of research.

Notes

1 See Ien Ang and Joke Hermes, 'Gender and/in media consumption', in James Curran and Michael Gurevitch (eds) *Mass Media and Society* (Sevenoaks: Edward Arnold, 1991), 307–28.
2 Joseph D. Straubhaar, 'Distinguishing the global, regional and national levels of world television', in Annabelle Sreberny-Mohammadi, Dwayne Winseck, Jim McKenna, and Oliver Boyd-Barrett (eds) *Media in Global Context: A Reader* (New York: Edward Arnold, 1997); Koichi Iwabuchi, *Recentering Globalization: Popular Culture and Japanese Transnationalism* (Durham, NC: Duke University Press, 2002); Koichi Iwabuchi, 'Becoming culturally proximate: the a/scent of Japanese Edo dramas in Taiwan', in Brian Moeran (ed.) *Asian Media Productions* (Honolulu: University of Hawaii Press, 2001), 121–57.
3 Miriam Hansen, *Babel in Babylon: Spectatorship and American Silent Film* (Cambridge, MA: Harvard University Press, 1989).

12

Women's Genres
Melodrama, soap opera, and theory

Annette Kuhn

Originally published in *Screen*, 25:1 (1984): 18–28.

Television soap opera and film melodrama, popular narrative forms aimed at female audiences, are currently attracting a good deal of critical and theoretical attention. Not surprisingly, most of the work on these 'gynocentric' genres is informed by various strands of feminist thought on visual representation. Less obviously, perhaps, such work has also prompted a series of questions which relate to representation and cultural production in a more wide-ranging and thoroughgoing manner than a specifically feminist interest might suggest. Not only are film melodrama (and more particularly its subtype the 'woman's picture') and soap opera directed at female audiences, they are also actually enjoyed by millions of women. What is it that sets these genres apart from representations which possess a less gender-specific mass appeal?

One of the defining generic features of the woman's picture as a textual system is its construction of narratives motivated by female desire and processes of spectator identification governed by female point of view. Soap opera constructs woman-centred narratives and identifications, too, but it differs textually from its cinematic counterpart in certain other respects: not only do soaps never end, but their beginnings are soon lost sight of. And whereas in the woman's picture the narrative process is characteristically governed by the enigma-retardation-resolution structure which marks the classic narrative, soap opera narratives propose

> competing and intertwining plot lines introduced as the serial progresses. Each plot . . . develops at a different pace, thus preventing any clear resolution of conflict. The completion of one story generally leads into others, and ongoing plots often incorporate parts of semi-resolved conflicts.[1]

Recent work on soap opera and melodrama has drawn on existing theories, methods, and perspectives in the study of film and television, including the structural analysis of narratives, textual semiotics and psychoanalysis, audience research, and the political economy of cultural institutions. At the same time, though, some of this work has exposed the limitations of existing approaches, and in consequence been

forced if not actually to abandon them, at least to challenge their characteristic problematics. Indeed, it may be contended that the most significant developments in film
and TV theory in general are currently taking place precisely within such areas of
feminist concern as critical work on soap opera and melodrama.

In examining some of this work, I shall begin by looking at three areas in which
particularly pertinent questions are being directed at theories of representation and
cultural production. These are, first, the problem of gendered spectatorship; secondly, questions concerning the universalism as against the historical specificity of
conceptualizations of gendered spectatorship; and thirdly, the relationship between
film and television texts and their social, historical, and institutional contexts. Each of
these concerns articulates in particular ways with what seems to be the central issue
here – the question of the audience, or audiences, for certain types of cinematic and
televisual representation.

Film theory's appropriation to its own project of Freudian and post-Freudian psychoanalysis places the question of the relationship between text and spectator firmly
on the agenda. Given the preoccupation of psycho-analysis with sexuality and gender,
a move from conceptualizing the spectator as a homogeneous and androgynous effect
of textual operations[2] to regarding her or him as a gendered subject constituted in
representation seems in retrospect inevitable. At the same time, the interests of feminist film theory and film theory in general converge at this point in a shared concern
with sexual difference. Psychoanalytic accounts of the formation of gendered subjectivity raise the question, if only indirectly, of representation and feminine subjectivity.
This in turn permits the spectator to be considered as a gendered subject position,
masculine or feminine: and theoretical work on soap opera and the woman's picture
may take this as a starting-point for its inquiry into spectator–text relations. Do
these 'gynocentric' forms address, or construct, a female or a feminine spectator?
If so, how?

On the question of film melodrama, Laura Mulvey, commenting on King Vidor's
Duel in the Sun,[3] argues that when, as in this film, a woman is at the centre of the
narrative, the question of female desire structures the hermeneutic: 'what does *she*
want?' This, says Mulvey, does not guarantee the constitution of the spectator as
feminine so much as it implies a contradictory, and in the final instance impossible,
'phantasy of masculinisation' for the female spectator. This is in line with the author's
earlier suggestion that cinema spectatorship involves masculine identification for
spectators of either gender.[4] If cinema does thus construct a masculine subject, there
can be no unproblematic feminine subject position for any spectator. Pam Cook, on
the other hand, writing about a group of melodramas produced during the 1940s at
the Gainsborough Studios, evinces greater optimism about the possibility of a feminine subject of classic cinema. She does acknowledge, though, that in a patriarchal
society female desire and female point of view are highly contradictory, even if they
have the potential to subvert culturally dominant modes of spectator–text relation.
The characteristic 'excess' of the woman's melodrama, for example, is explained by
Cook in terms of the genre's tendency to '[pose] problems for itself which it can
scarcely contain'.[5]

Writers on TV soap opera tend to take views on gender and spectatorship rather different from those advanced by film theorists. Tania Modleski, for example, argues with regard to soaps that their characteristic narrative patterns, their foregrounding of 'female' skills in dealing with personal and domestic crises, and the capacity of their programme formats and scheduling to key into the rhythms of women's work in the home, all address a female spectator. Furthermore, she goes as far as to argue that the textual processes of soaps are in some respects similar to those of certain 'feminine' texts which speak to a decentred subject, and so are 'not altogether at odds with . . . feminist aesthetics'.[6] Modleski's view is that soaps not only address female spectators, but in so doing construct feminine subject positions which transcend patriarchal modes of subjectivity.

Different though their respective approaches and conclusions might be, however, Mulvey, Cook, and Modleski are all interested in the problem of gendered spectatorship. The fact, too, that this common concern is informed by a shared interest in assessing the progressive or transformative potential of soaps and melodramas is significant in light of the broad appeal of both genres to the mass audiences of women at which they are aimed.

But what precisely does it mean to say that certain representations are aimed at a female audience? However well theorized they may be, existing conceptualizations of gendered spectatorship are unable to deal with this question. This is because spectator and audience are distinct concepts which cannot – as they frequently are – be reduced to one another. Although I shall be considering some of its consequences more fully below (pp. 228–30), it is important to note a further problem for film and television theory, posed in this case by the distinction between spectator and audience. Critical work on the woman's picture and on soap opera has necessarily, and most productively, emphasized the question of gendered spectatorship. In doing this, film theory in particular has taken on board a conceptualization of the spectator derived from psychoanalytic accounts of the formation of human subjectivity.

Such accounts, however, have been widely criticized for their universalism. Beyond, perhaps, associating certain variants of the Oedipus complex with family forms characteristic of a patriarchal society and offering a theory of the constructions of gender, psychoanalysis seems to offer little scope for theorizing subjectivity in its cultural or historical specificity. Although in relation to the specific issues of spectatorship and representation there may, as I shall argue, be a way around this apparent impasse, virtually all film and TV theory – its feminist variants included – is marked by the dualism of universalism and specificity.

Nowhere is this more evident than in the gulf between textual analysis and contextual inquiry. Each is done according to different rules and procedures, distinct methods of investigation and theoretical perspectives. In bringing to the fore the question of spectator–text relations, theories deriving from psychoanalysis may claim – to the extent that the spectatorial apparatus is held to be conterminous with the cinematic or televisual institution – to address the relationship between text and context. But as soon as any attempt is made to combine textual analysis with analysis of the concrete social, historical, and institutional conditions of production and reception of texts, it becomes clear that the context of the spectator/subject of psychoanalytic theory is rather different from the context of production and reception constructed by conjunctural analyses of cultural institutions.

The disparity between these two 'contexts' structures Pam Cook's article on the Gainsborough melodrama, which sets out to combine an analysis of the characteristic textual operations and modes of address of a genre with an examination of the historical conditions of a particular expression of it. Gainsborough melodrama, says Cook, emerges from a complex of determinants, including certain features of the British film industry of the 1940s, the nature of the female cinema audience in the post-World War II period, and the textual characteristics of the woman's picture itself.[7] While Cook is correct in pointing to the various levels of determination at work in this sentence, her lengthy preliminary discussion of spectator–text relations and the woman's picture rather outbalances her subsequent investigation of the social and industrial contexts of the Gainsborough melodrama. The fact, too, that analysis of the woman's picture in terms of its interpellation of a female/feminine spectator is simply placed alongside a conjunctural analysis tends to vitiate any attempt to reconcile the two approaches, and so to deal with the broader issue of universalism as against historical specificity. But although the initial problem remains, Cook's article constitutes an important intervention in the debate because, in tackling the text–context split head-on, it necessarily exposes a key weakness of current film theory.

In work on television soap opera as opposed to film melodrama, the dualism of text and context manifests itself rather differently, if only because – unlike film theory – theoretical work on television has tended to emphasize the determining character of the contextual level, particularly the structure and organization of television institutions. Since this has often been at the expense of attention to the operation of TV texts, television theory may perhaps be regarded as innovative in the extent to which it attempts to deal specifically with texts as well as contexts. Some feminist critical work has in fact already begun to address the question of TV as text, though always with characteristic emphasis on the issue of gendered spectatorship. This emphasis constitutes a common concern of work on both TV soaps and the woman's picture, but a point of contact between text and context in either medium emerges only when the concept of social audience is considered in distinction from that of spectator.

Each term – spectator and social audience – presupposes a different set of relations to representations and to the contexts in which they are received. Looking at spectators and at audiences demands different methodologies and theoretical frameworks, distinct discourses which construct distinct subjectivities and social relations. The *spectator*, for example, is a subject constituted in signification, interpellated by the film or TV text. This does not necessarily mean that the spectator is merely an effect of the text, however, because modes of subjectivity which also operate outside spectator–text relations in film or TV are activated in the relationship between spectators and texts.

This model of the spectator/subject is useful in correcting more deterministic communication models which might, say, pose the spectator not as actively constructing meaning but simply as a receiver and decoder of preconstituted 'messages'. In emphasizing spectatorship as a set of psychic relations and focusing on the relationship between spectator and text, however, such a model does disregard the broader social implications of filmgoing or televiewing. It is the social act of going to the cinema, for instance, that makes the individual cinemagoer part of an audience. Viewing television may involve social relations rather different from filmgoing, but in its own ways TV does depend on individual viewers being part of an audience, even if its members are never in one place at the same time. A group of people seated in a single auditorium looking at a film, or scattered across thousands of homes watching the same television programme, is a *social audience*. The concept of social audience, as against that of spectator, emphasizes the status of cinema and television as social and economic institutions.

Constructed by discursive practices both of cinema and TV and of social science, the social audience is a group of people who buy tickets at the box office, or who switch on their TV sets; people who can be surveyed, counted, and categorized according to age, sex, and socio-economic status.[8] The cost of a cinema ticket or TV licence fee, or a readiness to tolerate commercial breaks, earns audiences the right to look at films and TV programmes, and so to be spectators. Social audiences become spectators in the moment they engage in the processes and pleasures of meaning-making attendant on watching a film or TV programme. The anticipated pleasure of spectatorship is perhaps a necessary condition of existence of audiences. In taking part in the social act of consuming representations, a group of spectators becomes a social audience.

The consumer of representations as audience member and spectator is involved in a particular kind of psychic and social relationship: at this point, a conceptualization of the cinematic or televisual apparatus as a regime of pleasure intersects with sociological and economic understandings of film and TV as institutions. Because each term describes a distinct set of relationships, though, it is important not to conflate social audience with spectators. At the same time, since each is necessary to the other, it is equally important to remain aware of the points of continuity between the two sets of relations.

These conceptualizations of spectator and social audience have particular implications when it comes to a consideration of popular 'gynocentric' forms such as soap opera and melodrama. Most obviously, perhaps, these centre on the issue of gender, which prompts again the question: what does 'aimed at a female audience' mean? What exactly is being signalled in this reference to a gendered audience? Are women to be understood as a subgroup of the social audience, distinguishable through discourses which construct a priori gender categories? Or does the reference to a female audience allude rather to gendered spectatorship, to sexual difference constructed in relations between spectators and texts? Most likely, it condenses the two meanings; but an examination of the distinction between them may nevertheless be illuminating in relation to the broader theoretical issues of texts, contexts, social audiences, and spectators.

The notion of a female social audience, certainly as it is constructed in the discursive practices through which it is investigated, presupposes a group of individuals already formed as female. For the sociologist interested in such matters as gender and lifestyles, certain people bring a pre-existent femaleness to their viewing of film and TV. For the business executive interested in selling commodities, TV programmes and films are marketed to individuals already constructed as female. Both, however, are interested in the same kind of woman. On one level, then, soap operas and women's melodrama address themselves to a social audience of women. But they may at the same time be regarded as speaking to a female, or a feminine, spectator. If soaps and melodramas inscribe femininity in their address, women – as well as being already formed *for* such representations – are in a sense also formed *by* them.

In making this point, however, I intend no reduction of femaleness to femininity: on the contrary, I would hold to a distinction between femaleness as social gender and femininity as subject position. For example, it is possible for a female spectator to be addressed, as it were, 'in the masculine', and the converse is presumably also true. Nevertheless, in a culturally pervasive operation of ideology, femininity is routinely identified with femaleness and masculinity with maleness. Thus, for example, an address 'in the feminine' may be regarded in ideological terms as privileging, if not necessitating, a socially constructed female gender identity.

The constitutive character of both the woman's picture and the soap opera has in fact been noted by a number of feminist commentators. Tania Modleski, for instance, suggests that the characteristic narrative structures and textual operations of soap operas both address the viewer as an 'ideal mother' – ever-understanding, ever-tolerant of the weaknesses and foibles of others – and also posit states of expectation and passivity as pleasurable:

> the narrative, by placing ever more complex obstacles between desire and fulfilment, makes anticipation of an end an end in itself.[9]

In our culture, tolerance and passivity are regarded as feminine attributes, and consequently as qualities proper in women but not in men.

Charlotte Brunsdon extends Modleski's line of argument to the extratextual level: in constructing its viewers as competent within the ideological and moral frameworks of marriage and family life, soap opera, she implies, addresses both a feminine spectator and female audience.[10] Pointing to the centrality of intuition and emotion in the construction of the woman's point of view, Pam Cook regards the construction of a feminine spectator as a highly problematic and contradictory process: so that in the film melodrama's construction of female point of view, the validity of femininity as a subject position is necessarily laid open to question.[11]

This divergence on the question of gendered spectatorship within feminist theory is significant. Does it perhaps indicate fundamental differences between film and television in the spectator–text relations privileged by each? Do soaps and melodramas really construct different relations of gendered spectatorship, with melodrama constructing contradictory identifications in ways that soap opera does not? Or do these different positions on spectatorship rather signal an unevenness of theoretical development – or, to put it less teleologically, reflect the different intellectual histories and epistemological groundings of film theory and television theory?

Any differences in the spectator–text relations proposed respectively by soap opera and by film melodrama must be contingent to some extent on more general disparities in address between television and cinema. Thus film spectatorship, it may be argued, involves the pleasures evoked by looking in a more pristine way than does watching television. Whereas in classic cinema the concentration and involvement proposed by structures of the look, identification, and point of view tend to be paramount, television spectatorship is more likely to be characterized by distraction and diversion.[12] This would suggest that each medium constructs sexual difference through spectatorship in rather different ways: cinema through the look and spectacle, and television – perhaps less evidently – through a capacity to insert its flow, its characteristic modes of address, and the textual operations of different kinds of programmes into the rhythms and routines of domestic activities and sexual divisions of labour in the household at various times of day.

It would be a mistake, however, simply to equate current thinking on spectator-text relations in each medium. This is not only because theoretical work on spectator-ship as it is defined here is newer and perhaps not so developed for television as it has been for cinema, but also because conceptualizations of spectatorship in film theory and TV theory emerge from quite distinct perspectives. When feminist writers on soap opera and on film melodrama discuss spectatorship, therefore, they are usually talking about different things. This has partly to do with the different intellectual histories and methodological groundings of theoretical work on film and on television. Whereas most TV theory has until fairly recently existed under the sociological rubric of media studies, film theory has on the whole been based in the criticism-orientated tradition of literary studies. In consequence, while the one tends to privilege contexts over texts, the other usually privileges texts over contexts.

However, some recent critical work on soap opera, notably work produced within a cultural studies context, does attempt a *rapprochement* of text and context. Charlotte Brunsdon, writing about the British soap opera *Crossroads*, draws a distinction between subject positions proposed by texts and a 'social subject' who may or may not take up these positions.[13] In considering the interplay of 'social reader and social text', Brunsdon attempts to come to terms with problems posed by the universalism of the psychoanalytic model of the spectator/subject as against the descriptiveness and limited analytical scope of studies of specific instances and conjunctures. In taking up the instance of soap opera, then, one of Brunsdon's broader objectives is to resolve the dualism of text and context.

'Successful' spectatorship of a soap like *Crossroads*, it is argued, demands a certain cultural capital: familiarity with the plots and characters of a particular serial as well as with soap opera as a genre. It also demands wider cultural competence, especially in the codes of conduct of personal and family life. For Brunsdon, then, the spectator addressed by soap opera is constructed within culture rather than by representation. This, however, would indicate that such a spectator, a 'social subject', might – rather than being a subject in process of gender positioning – belong after all to a social audience already divided by gender.

The 'social subject' of this cultural model produces meaning by decoding messages or communications, an activity which is always socially situated.[14] Thus although such a model may move some way towards reconciling text and context, the balance of Brunsdon's argument remains weighted in favour of context: spectator–text relations are apparently regarded virtually as an effect of socio-cultural contexts. Is there a way in which spectator/subjects of film and television texts can be thought of in a historically specific manner, or indeed a way for the social audience to be rescued from social/historical determinism?

Although none of the feminist criticism of soap opera and melodrama reviewed here has come up with any solution to these problems, it all attempts, in some degree and with greater or lesser success, to engage with them. Brunsdon's essay possibly comes closest to an answer, paradoxically because its very failure to resolve the dualism which ordains that spectators are constructed by texts while audiences have their place in contexts begins to hint at a way around the problem. Although the hybrid 'social subject' may turn out to be more a social audience member than a spectator, this concept does suggest that a move into theories of discourse could prove to be productive.

Both spectators and social audience may accordingly be regarded as discursive constructs. Representations, contexts, audiences, and spectators would then be seen as a series of interconnected social discourses, certain discourses possessing greater constitutive authority at specific moments than others. Such a model permits relative autonomy for the operations of texts, readings, and contexts, and also allows for contradictions, oppositional readings, and varying degrees of discursive authority. Since the state of a discursive formation is not constant, it can be apprehended only by means of inquiry into specific instances or conjunctures. In attempting to deal with the text–context split and to address the relationship between spectators and social audiences, therefore, theories of representation may have to come to terms with discursive formations of the social, cultural, and textual.

One of the impulses generating feminist critical and theoretical work on soap opera and the woman's picture is a desire to examine genres which are popular, and popular in particular with women. The assumption is usually that such popularity has to do mainly with the social audience: TV soaps attract large numbers of viewers, many of them women, and in its heyday the woman's picture also drew in a mass female audience. But when the nature of this appeal is sought in the texts themselves or in relations between spectators and texts, the argument becomes rather more complex. In what specific ways do soaps and melodramas address or construct female/feminine spectators?

To some extent, they offer the spectator a position of mastery: this is certainly true as regards the hermeneutic of the melodrama's classic narrative, though perhaps less obviously so in relation to the soap's infinite process of narrativity. At the same time, they also place the spectator in a masochistic position of either – in the case of the woman's picture – identifying with a female character's renunciation or, as in soap opera, forever anticipating an endlessly held-off resolution. Culturally speaking, this combination of mastery and masochism in the reading competence constructed by soaps and melodramas suggests an interplay of masculine and feminine subject positions. Culturally dominant codes inscribe the masculine, while the feminine bespeaks a 'return of the repressed' in the form of codes which may well transgress culturally dominant subject positions, though only at the expense of proposing a position of subjection for the spectator.

At the same time, it is sometimes argued on behalf of both soap opera and film melodrama that in a society whose representations of itself are governed by the masculine, these genres at least raise the possibility of female desire and female point of view. Pam Cook advances such a view in relation to the woman's picture, for example.[15] But how is the oppositional potential of this to be assessed? Tania Modleski suggests that soap opera is 'in the vanguard not just of TV art but of all popular narrative art'.[16] But such a statement begs the question: under what circumstances can popular narrative art itself be regarded as transgressive? Because texts do not operate in isolation from contexts, any answer to these questions must take into account the ways in which popular narratives are read, the conditions under which they are produced and consumed, and the ends to which they are appropriated. As most feminist writing on soap opera and the woman's melodrama implies, there is ample space in the articulation of these various instances for contradiction and for struggles over meaning.

The popularity of television soap opera and film melodrama with women raises the question of how it is that sizeable audiences of women relate to these representations and the institutional practices of which they form part. It provokes, too, a consideration of the continuity between women's interpellation as spectators and their status as a social audience. In turn, the distinction between social audience and spectator/subject, and attempts to explore the relationship between the two, are part of a broader theoretical endeavour: to deal in tandem with texts and contexts. The distinction between social audience and spectator must also inform debates and practices around cultural production, in which questions of context and reception are always paramount. For anyone interested in feminist cultural politics, such considerations will necessarily inform any assessment of the place and the political usefulness of popular genres aimed at, and consumed by, mass audiences of women.

Notes

1 Muriel G. Cantor and Suzanne Pingree, *The Soap Opera* (Beverly Hills: Sage, 1983), 22. Here 'soap opera' refers to daytime (US) or early evening (UK) serials . . . not prime-time serials like *Dallas* and *Dynasty*.

2 See Jean-Louis Baudry, 'Ideological Effects of the Basic Cinematographic Apparatus', *Film Quarterly*, 28/2 (1974–5), 39–47; Christian Metz, 'The Imaginary Signifier', *Screen*, 16/2 (1975), 14–76.

3 Laura Mulvey, 'Afterthoughts on "Visual Pleasure and Narrative Cinema" ', *Framework*, 15/16/17 (1981), 12–15.

4 Laura Mulvey, 'Visual Pleasure and Narrative Cinema', *Screen*, 16/3 (1975), 6–18.

5 Pam Cook, 'Melodrama and the Woman's Picture', in Sue Aspinall and Robert Murphy (eds.), *Gainsborough Melodrama* (London: BFI, 1983), 17.

6 Tania Modleski, *Loving with a Vengeance: Mass Produced Fantasies for Women* (Hamden, Conn.: Archon Books, 1982), 105. See also Tania Modleski, 'The Search for Tomorrow in Today's Soap Operas', *Film Quarterly*, 33/1 (1979), 12–21 (Chapter 2 in this volume).

7 Cook, 'Melodrama and the Woman's Picture'.

8 Methods and findings of social science research on the social audience for American daytime soap operas are discussed in Cantor and Pingree, *The Soap Opera*, ch. 7.

9 Modleski, *Loving with a Vengeance*, 88.

10 Charlotte Brunsdon, '*Crossroads*: Notes on Soap Opera', *Screen*, 22/4 (1981), 32–7.
11 Cook, 'Melodrama and the Woman's Picture', 19.
12 John Ellis, *Visible Fictions* (London: Routledge & Kegan Paul, 1982).
13 Brunsdon, '*Crossroads*: Notes on Soap Opera', 32.
14 A similar model is also adopted by Dorothy Hobson in Crossroads: *The Drama of a Soap Opera* (London: Methuen, 1982).
15 Cook, 'Melodrama and the Woman's Picture'. E. Ann Kaplan takes a contrary position in 'Theories of Melodrama: A Feminist Perspective', *Women and Performance: A Journal of Feminist Theory*, 1/1 (1983), 40–8.
16 Modleski, *Loving with a Vengeance*, 87.

13

Melodramatic Identifications
Television fiction and women's fantasy

Ien Ang

Originally published in Mary Ellen Brown (ed.), *Television and Women's Culture: The Politics of the Popular* (London: Sage, 1990), 75–88.

Contemporary popular television fiction offers an array of strong and independent female heroines, who seem to defy – not without conflicts and contradictions, to be sure – stereotypical definitions of femininity. Heroines such as Maddie Hayes (*Moonlighting*) and Christine Cagney (*Cagney and Lacey*) do not fit into the traditional ways in which female characters have generally been represented in prime-time television fiction: passive and powerless on the one hand, and sexual objects for men on the other.

Christine Cagney, especially, and her partner Mary-Beth Lacey, are the kind of heroines who have mobilized approval from feminists.[1] *Cagney and Lacey* can be called a 'socialist realist' series, in which the personal and professional dilemmas of modern working women are dealt with in a serious and 'realistic' way. Cagney explicitly resists sexual objectification by her male colleagues, forcefully challenges the male hierarchy at work, and entertains an adult, respectful, and caring friendship with her 'buddy' Lacey.

Maddie Hayes is a little more difficult to evaluate in straightforward feminist terms. However, while she often has to cope with the all-but-abusive, but ever-so-magnetic machismo of her recalcitrant partner David Addison, *Moonlighting*, as a typical example of postmodernist television, self-consciously addresses, enacts, and acknowledges metonymically the pleasures and pains of the ongoing 'battle between the sexes' in the context of the series' characteristic penchant for hilarious absurdism and teasing parody.[2] In that battle, Maddie is neither passive nor always the loser: she fights and gains respect (and love) in the process.

Many women enjoy watching series such as *Cagney and Lacey* and *Moonlighting*, and it is likely that at least part of their pleasure is related to the 'positive' representations of women that both series offer. But this does not mean that other, more traditional television fictions are less pleasurable for large numbers of women. On the contrary, as is well known, soap operas have traditionally been *the* female television genre, while prime-time soaps such as *Dallas* and *Dynasty* have always had a significantly larger female audience than a male one.

Personally, I have often been moved by Sue Ellen of *Dallas* as much as I am at times by Christine Cagney. And yet, Sue Ellen is a radically different heroine from Cagney: she displays no (will for) independence whatsoever, she derives her identity almost entirely from being the wife of the unscrupulous and power-obsessed J.R. Ewing, whom she detests because he is never faithful, but whom she does not have the strength to leave.[3] As a consequence, Sue Ellen's life is dominated by constant frustration and suffering – apparently a very negative representation of 'woman' indeed. Despite this, the Sue Ellen character seems to be a source of identification and pleasure for many women viewers of *Dallas*: they seem not so much to love to hate J.R. but to suffer with Sue Ellen.

An indication of this can be derived from the results of a small-scale research that I conducted a few years ago.[4] Through an advertisement in a Dutch weekly magazine, I asked people to send me their views about *Dallas*. From the letters, it was clear that Sue Ellen stood out as a character whom many women viewers were emotionally involved with. One of the respondents wrote:

> I can sit very happy and fascinated watching someone like Sue Ellen. That woman can really get round us, with her problems and troubles. She is really human. I could be someone like her too. In a manner of speaking.

Another wrote:

> Sue Ellen is definitely my favourite. She has a psychologically believable character. As she is, I am myself to a lesser degree ('knocking one's head against a wall once too often') and I want to be (attractive).

It is interesting to note that another *Dallas* character whose structural position in the narrative is similar to Sue Ellen's has not elicited such committed responses at all. Pamela Ewing (married to J.R.'s brother, Bobby) is described rather blandly as 'a nice girl', or is seen as 'too sweet'. In fact, the difference of appeal between the two characters becomes even more pronounced in the light of the findings of a representative Dutch survey conducted in 1982 (around the time that the popularity of *Dallas* was at its height). While 21.7 per cent of female viewers between 15 and 39 years mentioned Sue Ellen as their favourite *Dallas* character (as against only 5.9 per cent of the men), only 5.1 per cent named Pamela as their favourite (and 4.2 per cent of the men).[5]

Clearly Sue Ellen has a special significance for a large number of women viewers. Two things stand out in the quotes above. Not only do these viewers assert that the appeal of Sue Ellen is related to a form of realism (in the sense of psychological believability and recognizability); more importantly, this realism is connected with a somewhat tragic reading of Sue Ellen's life, emphasizing her problems and troubles. In other words, the position from which Sue Ellen fans seem to give meaning to, and derive pleasure from, their favourite *Dallas* character seems to be a rather melancholic and sentimental structure of feeling which stresses the down-side of life rather than its happy highlights; frustration, desperation, and anger rather than euphoria and cheerfulness.

To interpret this seemingly rather despondent form of female pleasure, I shall examine the position which the Sue Ellen character occupies in the *Dallas* narrative, and unravel the meaning of that position in the context of the specific fictional genre to which *Dallas* belongs: the melodramatic soap opera. The tragic structure of feeling embodied by Sue Ellen as a fictional figure must be understood in the context of the genre characteristics of the *Dallas* drama: just as Christine Cagney is a social-realist heroine and Maddie Hayes a postmodern one, so is Sue Ellen a melodramatic heroine. In other words, articulated and materialized in Sue Ellen's identity is what in 1976 American critic Peter Brooks called a melodramatic imagination.

Of course, fictional characters may be polysemic just as they can take on a plurality of meanings depending on the ways in which diverse viewers read them. Thus, Sue Ellen's melodramatic persona can be interpreted and evaluated in several ways. Whilst her fans tend to empathize with her and live through her problems and troubles vicariously, others stress her bitchiness and take a stance against her. In the words of one *Dallas* viewer:

> Sue Ellen has had bad luck with J.R., but she makes up for it by being a flirt. I don't like her much. And she's too sharp-tongued.

Others have called her a frustrated lady. One of my respondents was especially harsh in her critique:

> Take Sue Ellen. She acts as though she's very brave and can put up a fight, but she daren't make the step of divorce. What I mean is that in spite of her good intentions she lets people walk over her, because (as J.R. wants) for the outside world they have to form a perfect family.

According to Herta Herzog, who interviewed German viewers about *Dallas* in 1987, older viewers tend to see in Sue Ellen the woman ruined by her husband, while younger ones tend to see her as a somewhat unstable person who is her own problem.[6] However, despite the variation in emphasis in the different readings of Sue Ellen, a basic agreement seems to exist that her situation is an extremely contentious and frustrating one, and her personality is rather tormented. This is the core of the melodramatic heroine. But while many viewers are put off by this type of character, some are fascinated, a response evoked not only by the dramatic content of the role, but by the melodramatic style of the actress, Linda Gray. As one fan discloses,

> Sue Ellen (is) just *fantastic*, tremendous how that woman acts, the movements of her mouth, hands, etc. That woman really enters into her role, looking for love, snobbish, in short a real woman.

As a contrast, the same viewer describes Pamela as a Barbie doll with no feelings!

It is not my intention to offer an exhaustive analysis of the Sue Ellen character as melodramatic heroine. Nor do I want to make a sociological examination of which segment of the audience is attracted to characters like her. Rather, I use her as a point of departure to explore women's pleasure in popular fiction in general, and melodramatic fiction in particular. Women who use Sue Ellen as a source of identification while watching *Dallas* do that by taking up, in fantasy, a subject position which inhabits the melodramatic imagination.[7] The pleasure of such imaginary identification can be seen as a form of excess in some women's mode of experiencing everyday life in our culture: the act of surrendering to the melodramatic imagination may signify a recognition of the complexity and conflict fundamental to living in the modern world.

Soap opera and the melodramatic imagination

I now move to summing up some of the structural soap opera characteristics of *Dallas* which contribute to its melodramatic content.[8] It should first be noted, however, that because *Dallas* is a prime-time programme, some of its features are different from those of the traditional daytime soaps. Most importantly, because the programme must attract a heterogeneous audience it will include a wider range of themes, scenes, and plots. For example, male characters, as well as themes, scenes, and plots which traditionally are mainly appreciated by male audiences, such as the wheelings and dealings of the oil business, and the cowboy/Western elements of the show, occupy a much more prominent place in the fictional world of *Dallas* than in regular daytime soap. Nevertheless, the general formal characteristics of *Dallas* do remain true to the soap opera genre, and are very important for the construction of melodramatic meanings and feelings in the text.[9]

First of all, as in all melodrama, personal life is the core problematic of the narrative. Personal life must be understood here as constituted by its everyday realization through personal relationships. In soap operas, the evolution of personal relationships is marked out through the representation of significant family rituals and events such as births; romances, engagements, marriages, divorces, deaths, and so on. It is the experience of these rituals and events (and all the attendant complications and disputes) on which soap opera narratives centre. This does not imply that non-personal issues are not addressed. However the way in which they are treated and take on meaning is always from the standpoint of personal life:

> the action of soap opera is not restricted to the familial, or quasi-familial institutions, but everything is told from the point of view of the personal.[10]

Thus, while J.R.'s business intrigues form a focal narrative concern in *Dallas*, they are always shown with an eye to their consequences for the well-being of the Ewing family members, not least his wife Sue Ellen.

A second major melodramatic feature of soap opera is its excessive plot structure. If family life is the main focus of the *Dallas* narrative, the life of the Ewings is presented as one replete with extraordinary conflicts and catastrophes. To the critical outsider this may appear as a purely sensationalist tendency to cliché and exaggeration – a common objection levelled at melodrama since the late nineteenth century. It is important to note, however, that *within* the fictional world of the soap opera all those extreme story-lines such as kidnappings, bribery, extramarital affairs, obscure illnesses, and so on, which succeed each other at such a breathtaking pace, are not treated in a sensational manner, but are taken entirely seriously.[11] The parameters of melodrama require that such clichés be regarded and assessed not for their literal, referential value – that is, their realism – but as meaningful in so far as they solicit a highly charged, emotional impact. Their role is metaphorical, and their appeal stems from the enlarged emotional impact they evoke: it is the feelings being mobilized here that matter. An excess of events and intensity of emotions are inextricably interwined in the melodramatic imagination.

Sue Ellen's recurrent alcoholism is a case in point. Even though she has stayed away from alcohol for a long time loyal viewers are reminded of this dark side of her past every time she is shown refusing a drink. Do we detect a slight moment of hesitation there? Alcoholism is a very effective narrative motif that, in a condensed way, enables the devoted viewer to empathize with her feelings of desperation. She is married to a man she loathes but who has her almost completely in his power. In other words, Sue Ellen's propensity for alcoholism functions as a metaphor for her enduring state of crisis.

Such a state of crisis is not at all exceptional or uncommon in the context of the soap opera genre. On the contrary, crisis can be said to be endemic to it. As a result, Sue Ellen's predicament, as it is constructed, is basically unsolvable unless she leaves the *Dallas* community and disappears from the serial altogether. Here, a third structural characteristic of the soap opera makes its impact: its lack of narrative progress. *Dallas*, like all soap operas, is a never-ending story: contrary to classic narratives, which are typically structured according to the logic of order/disorder/restoration of order, soap opera narratives never reach completion. They represent process without progression and as such do not offer the prospect of a conclusion of final denouement, in which all problems are solved. Thus, soap operas are fundamentally anti-utopian: an ending, happy or unhappy, is unimaginable. This does not mean, of course, that there are no moments of climax in soap operas. But, as Tania Modleski has observed, 'the "mini-climaxes" of soap opera function to introduce difficulties and to complicate rather than simplify the characters' lives'.[12] Here, a basic melodramatic idea is conveyed: the sense that life is marked by eternal contradiction, by unsolvable emotional and moral conflicts, by the ultimate impossibility, as it were, of reconciling desire and reality. As Laura Mulvey has put it,

> The melodrama recognises this gap by raising problems, known and recognisable, and offering a personal escape similar to that of a day-dream: a chance to work through inescapable frustrations by positing an alternative ideal never seen as more than a momentary illusion.[13]

The life of the Sue Ellen character in *Dallas* exemplifies and dramatizes this melodramatic scenario. She even expresses an awareness of its painfully contradictory nature. In one dialogue with Pamela, for example, she states:

> The difference [between you and me] is that you're a strong woman, Pam. I used to think I was, but I know differently now. I need Southfork. On my own, I don't amount to much. As much as I hate J.R., I really need to be Mrs J.R. Ewing. And I need him to be the father of John Ross [her son]. So I guess I just have to lead a married life without a husband.

In general then, it could be said that the soap operatic structure of *Dallas* opens up a narrative space in which melodramatic characters can come to life symbolically – characters who ultimately are constructed as victims of forces that lie beyond their control. A heroine like Sue Ellen will never be able to make her own history: no matter how hard she tries, eventually the force of circumstances will be too overwhelming. She lives in the prison of an eternally conflictual present. No wonder that she reacts with frustration, bitterness, resignation, and cynical ruthlessness on the rebound. As she neatly summarizes her own life philosophy:

> If J.R. seeks sex and affection somewhere else, so why shouldn't I? All Ewing men are the same. And for you to survive you have two choices. You can either get out, or you can play by their rules!

In fact, this frame of mind has led her to give up all attempts to find true happiness for herself: although she has her occasional moments of joy (a new lover, for example), they are futile in the face of her biggest self-imposed passion: to use all the power she has to undermine J.R.'s projects, to ruin his life just as he has ruined hers. She even refuses him a divorce to keep him from marrying another woman (by which he expects to win an extremely advantageous business deal). It is such small victories which make her feel strong at times. But they are ultimately self-destructive and will never allow her to break out of her cage.

Against this background, identifying with Sue Ellen implies a recognition of the fact that Sue Ellen's crisis is a permanent one: there seems to be no real way out. She may experience happy moments, but as viewers we know that those moments are bound to be merely temporary and inevitably followed by new problems and difficulties. At stake, then, must be a rather curious form of pleasure for these viewers. Whereas in other narratives pleasure comes from the assurance and confirmation of a happy end – as with the romantic union of a man and a woman in the formulaic 'they live happily ever after', involvement with a character like Sue Ellen is conditioned by the prior knowledge that no such happy ending will ever occur. Instead, pleasure must come from living through and negotiating with the crisis itself. To put it more precisely, many female Sue Ellen fans tend to identify with a subject position characterized by a sense of entrapment: a sense in which survival is, in the words of television critic Horace Newcomb, 'complicated by ambiguity and blurred with pain even in its most sought-after moments'.[14]

If this is true (and I have already given some indications that this is indeed the case) how do we interpret this kind of identification, this form of pleasure in popular fiction?

Pleasure, fantasy, and the negotiation of femininity

One could assert that melodramatic heroines like Sue Ellen should be evaluated negatively because they attest to an outlook on life that stresses resignation and despair. Isn't the melodramatic imagination a particularly damaging way of making sense of life because it affirms tendencies of individualistic fatalism and pessimism? And isn't such an impact especially harmful for women as it reinforces and legitimizes masochistic feelings of powerlessness? Wouldn't it be much better for women and girls to choose identification figures that represent strong, powerful, and independent women who are able and determined to change and improve their lives, such as Christine Cagney?

Such concerns are, of course, often heard in feminist accounts of popular fiction, but it is important to note here that they are often based upon a theoretical approach – what could be called a role/image approach, or more conventionally, 'images of women' approach – which analyses images of women in the media and in fiction by setting them against real women. Fictional female heroines are then seen as images of women functioning as role models for female audiences.[15] From such a perspective, it is only logical to claim that one should strive to offer positive role models by supplying positive images of women. And from this perspective, feminist common sense would undoubtedly ascribe the Sue Ellen character to the realm of negative images, reflecting a traditional, stereotyped, or trivialized model of womanhood.

However, this approach contains both theoretical and political problems. Most importantly here, because it implies a rationalistic view of the relationship between image and viewer (whereby it is assumed that the image is seen by the viewer as a more or less adequate model of reality), it can only account for the popularity of soap operas among women as something irrational. In other words, what the role/image approach tends to overlook is the large *emotional involvement* which is invested in identification with characters of popular fiction.

To counteract this attitude, we first of all need to acknowledge that these characters are products of *fiction*, and that fiction is not a mere set of images to be read referentially, but an ensemble of textual devices for engaging the viewer at the level of fantasy.[16] As a result, female fictional characters such as Sue Ellen Ewing or Christine Cagney cannot be conceptualized as realistic images of women, but as textual constructions of possible *modes of femininity*: as embodying versions of gendered subjectivity endowed with specific forms of psychical and emotional satisfaction and dissatisfaction, and specific ways of dealing with conflicts and dilemmas. In relation to this, they do not function as role models but are symbolic realizations of feminine subject positions with which viewers can identify *in fantasy*.

Fantasy is central here. In line with psychoanalytic theory, fantasy should not be seen as mere illusion, an unreality, but as a reality in itself, a fundamental aspect of human existence: a necessary and unerasable dimension of psychical reality. Fantasy is an imagined scene in which the fantasizing subject is the protagonist, and in which alternative scenarios for the subject's real life are evoked. Fantasizing obviously affords the subject pleasure, which, according to the psychoanalysts, has to do with the fulfilment of a conscious or unconscious wish. Here I would suggest more generally that the pleasure of fantasy lies in its offering the subject an opportunity to take up positions which she could not do in real life: through fantasy she can move beyond the structural constraints of everyday life and explore other situations, other identities, other lives. It is totally unimportant here whether these are realistic or not. As Lesley Stern has remarked, 'gratification is to be achieved not through acting out the fantasies, but through the activity of fantasising itself'.[17]

Fantasies, and the act of fantasizing, are usually a private practice in which we can engage at any time and the content of which we generally keep to ourselves. Fictions, on the other hand, are collective and public fantasies; they are textual elaborations, in narrative form, of fantastic scenarios which, being mass-produced, are offered ready-made to audiences. We are not the originators of the public fantasies offered to us in fiction. This explains, of course, why we are not attracted to all the fictions available to us: most of them are irrelevant. Despite this, the pleasure of consuming fictions that do attract us may still relate to that of fantasy: that is, it still involves the imaginary occupation of other subject positions which are outside the scope of our everyday social and cultural identities.

Implicit in the theoretical perspective I have outlined so far is a post-structuralist theory on subjectivity.[18] Central to this is the idea that subjectivity is not the essence or the source from which the individual acts and thinks and feels; on the contrary, subjectivity should be seen as a product of the society and culture in which we live: it is through the meaning systems or discourses circulating in society and culture that subjectivity is constituted and individual identities are formed. Each individual is the site of a multiplicity of subject positions proposed to her by the discourses with which she is confronted; her identity is the precarious and contradictory result of the specific set of subject positions she inhabits at any moment in history.

Just as the fictional character is not a unitary image of womanhood, then, so is the individual viewer not a person whose identity is something static and coherent. If a woman is a social subject whose identity is at least partially marked out by her being a person of a certain sex, it is by no means certain that she will always inhabit the same mode of feminine subjectivity. On the contrary, many different and sometimes contradictory sets of femininities or feminine subject positions (ways of being a woman) are in principle available to her, although it is likely that she will be drawn to adopt some of those more than others. Certain modes of femininity are culturally more legitimate than others; and every woman knows subject positions she is best able to handle. This does not mean, however, that her identity as a woman is something determined in the process of socialization. On the contrary, the adoption of a feminine subjectivity is never definitive but always partial and shaky: in other words, being a woman implies a never-ending *process* of becoming a feminine subject: no one subject position can ever cover satisfactorily all the problems and desires an individual woman encounters.

All too often women (and men too, of course, but their relationship to constructions of masculinity is not at issue here) have to negotiate in all sorts of situations in their lives – at home, at work, in relationships, in larger social settings. In this women are constantly confronted with the cultural task of finding out what it means to be a woman, of marking out the boundaries between the feminine and the unfeminine. This task is not a simple one, especially in the case of modern societies where cultural rules and roles are no longer imposed authoritatively, but allow individualistic notions such as autonomy, personal choice, will, responsibility, and rationality. In this context, a framework of living has been created in which every individual woman is faced with the task of actively reinventing and redefining her femininity as required. The emergence of the modern feminist movement has intensified this situation: now women have become much more conscious about their position in society, and consequently are encouraged to take control over their own lives by rejecting the traditional dictum that anatomy is destiny. Being a woman, in other words, can now mean the adoption of many different identities, composed of a whole range of subject positions, not predetermined by immovable definitions of femininity. It would stretch beyond the purpose of this article to explore and explain in more detail how women construct and reconstruct their feminine identities in everyday life. What is important to conclude at this point then is that being a woman involves *work*, work of constant self-(re)construction. (The ever-growing array of different women's magazines is a case in point: in all of them the central problematic is 'how to be a true woman', while the meanings of 'true' are subject to constant negotiation.) At the same time, however, the energy women must put in this fundamental work of self-(re)construction is suppressed: women are expected to find the right identity effortlessly. (Women's magazines always assume an enthusiastic, 'you-can-do-it!' mode of address: work is represented as pleasure.)

It is in this constellation that fantasy and fiction can play a distinctive role. They offer a private and unconstrained space in which socially impossible or unacceptable subject positions, or those which are in some way too dangerous or too risky to be acted out in real life, can be adopted. In real life, the choice for this or that subject position is never without consequences. Contrary to what women's magazines tell us, it is often *not* easy to know what it means to be a 'true' woman. For example, the social display of forms of traditional femininity – dependence, passivity, submissiveness – can have quite detrimental and self-destructive consequences for women when strength, independence, or decisiveness are called for. In fantasy and fiction, however, there is no punishment for whatever identity one takes up, no matter how headstrong or destructive: there will be no retribution, no defeat will ensue. Fantasy and fiction then, are the safe spaces of excess in the interstices of ordered social life where one has to keep oneself strategically under control.

From this perspective identification with melodramatic heroines can be viewed in a new way. The position ascribed to Sue Ellen by those identifying with her is one of masochism and powerlessness: a self-destructive mode of femininity which, in social and political terms, could only be rejected as regressive and unproductive. But rather than condemn this identification, it is possible to observe the gratification such imaginary subject positions provide for the women concerned. What can be so pleasurable in imagining a fantastic scenario in which one is a self-destructive and frustrated bitch?

In the context of the discussion above, I can suggest two meanings of melodramatic identifications. On the one hand, sentimental and melancholic feelings of masochism and powerlessness, which are the core of the melodramatic imagination, are an implicit recognition, in their surrender to some power outside the subject, of the fact that one can never have everything under control all the time, and that consequently identity is not a question of free and conscious choice but always acquires its shape under circumstances not of one's own making. Identification with these feelings is connected with a basic, if not articulated, awareness of the weighty pressure of reality on one's subjectivity, one's wishes, one's desires. On the other hand, identification with a melodramatic character like Sue Ellen also validates those feelings by offering women some room to indulge in them, to let go as it were, in a moment of intense, self-centred abandon – a moment of giving up to the force of circumstances, just-like Sue Ellen has done, so that the work of self-(re)construction is no longer needed. I would argue that such moments, however fleeting, can be experienced as moments of peace, of truth, of redemption, a moment in which the complexity of the task of being a woman is fully realized and accepted. In short, whilst indulgence in a melodramatic identity in real life will generally only signify pathetic weakness and may have paralysing effects, fantasy and fiction constitute a secure space in which one can be excessively melodramatic without suffering the consequences. No wonder melodrama is often accompanied with tears.

Final remarks

This interpretation of the appeal of melodramatic characters among women must, of course, be contextualized and refined in several ways. First of all, by trying to explain what it means for women to identify with a melodramatic fictional character, I have by no means intended to justify or endorse it. I have tried to make it understandable, in the face of the ridicule and rejection that crying over melodramatic fiction (as if it were irrational) continues to receive. However, my analysis does not extend to any further impact upon the subjects concerned. Whether the release of melodramatic feelings through fantasy or fiction has an empowering or paralysing effect upon the subject is an open question and can probably not be answered without analysing the context of the fantasizing.

Secondly, we should not overlook the fact that not all women are attracted to melodrama, and that some men can be moved by melodrama too. If anything, this fact suggests that femininity and masculinity are not positions inhabited inevitably by biological women and men, but that identity is transitory, the temporary result of dynamic identifications. Further research and analysis could give us more insight into the conditions, social, cultural, psychological, under which a surrender to the melo-dramatic imagination exerts its greatest appeal. Melodrama has been consistently popular among women in the modern period, but this does not have to be explained exclusively in terms of constants. The fundamental chasm between desire and reality, which forms the deepest 'truth' of the melodramatic imagination, may be an eternal aspect of female experience, but how that chasm is bridged symbolically and in prac-tice is historically variable. In fact, there is a fundamentally melodramatic edge to feminism too. After all, are not the suffering and frustration so eminently materialized in melodramatic heroines the basis for the anger conveyed in feminism? And does not feminism stand for the overwhelming desire to transcend reality – which is bound to be a struggle, full of frustrations and moments of despair? While the melodramatic heroine is someone who is forced to give up, leaving a yawning gap between desire and reality, the feminist is someone who refuses to give up, no matter how hard the struggle to close that gap might be.

Christine Cagney, too, shares more with Sue Ellen than we might expect. Of course, the manifest dramatic content of *Cagney and Lacey* is more in line with femi-nist ideals and concerns, and as such the Cagney and Lacey characters can provide an outlet for identification with fantasies of liberation for women viewers.[19] Despite the fact that Christine Cagney is an independent career woman who knows where she stands, she too must at times face the unsolvable dilemmas inherent in the lives of modern women: how to combine love and work; how to compete with the boys; how to deal with growing older . . . Often enough, she encounters frustration and displays a kind of cynical bitchiness not unlike Sue Ellen's. I would argue that some of the most moving moments of *Cagney and Lacey* are those in which Cagney gives in to the sense of powerlessness so characteristic of the melodramatic heroine.

Notes

1 See J. D'Acci, 'The Case of *Cagney and Lacey*', in H. Baehr and G. Dyer (eds.), *Boxed-In: Women and Television* (London: Pandora Press, 1987); also D. Clark, '*Cagney and Lacey*: Feminist Strategies of Detection', in M. E. Brown (ed.), *Television and Women's Culture: The Politics of the Popular* (London: Sage, 1990), 116–33.
2 See S. R. Olson, 'Meta-Television: Popular Postmodernism', *Cultural Studies in Mass Communication*, 4 (1987), 284–300.
3 At one point, Sue Ellen decided to become a businesswoman – and with great success. However, even this major structural change in her life was motivated by a wish to mess up J.R.'s schemes and plans. She started her business (Valentine Lingerie) as a shrewd tactic to get rid of J.R.'s mistress.
4 See I. Ang, *Watching* Dallas: *Soap Opera and the Melodramatic Imagination*, trans. D. Couling (London and New York: Methuen, 1985).
5 These figures come from a survey of the Department of Viewing and Listening Research, NOS, Hilversum, May 1982.
6 See M. H. Herzog, 'Decoding *Dallas*: Comparing German and American Viewers', in A. A. Berger (ed.), *Television in Society* (New Brunswick, NJ: Transaction Books, 1987).
7 It should be noted, however, that watching a television programme does not necessarily involve identification with only one character. On the contrary, numerous subject positions can be taken up by viewers while reading a television text. Consequently, a *Dallas* viewer may alternate between positions of identification and positions of distance, and thus inhabit several, sometimes contradictory imaginary structures at the same time.
8 See R. C. Allen, *Speaking of Soap Operas* (Chapel Hill: Univ. of North Carolina Press, 1985).
9 See Ang, *Watching* Dallas: J. Feuer, 'Enterprises: An Overview', in J. Feuer, P. Kerr, and T. Vahimagi (eds.), *MTM: 'Quality Television'* (London: BFI, 1984); also for melodrama in general see P. Brooks, *The Melodramatic Imagination: Balzac, Henry James, Melodrama and the Mode of Excess* (New Haven: Yale Univ. Press, 1976); C. Gledhill (ed.), *Home is Where the Heart is* (London: BFI, 1987).
10 C. Brunsdon, '*Crossroads*: Notes on Soap Opera', *Screen*, 22/4 (1981), 34.
11 The moment a soap opera becomes self-conscious about its own excess, which is sometimes the case with *Dynasty*, and no longer takes its own story seriously, it presents itself as a parody of the genre, as it were, accentuating its status as discourse through stylization and formalism (such as slow-motion techniques). Sections of the *Dynasty* audience that read the show as a form of camp, for instance, are responding to this aspect of the *Dynasty* text.

12   T. Modleski, 'The Rhythms of Reception: Daytime Television and Women's Work', in E. A. Kaplan (ed.), *Regarding Television* (Los Angeles: American Film Institute, 1983), 107.

13   L. Mulvey, 'Notes on Sirk and Melodrama', *Movie*, 25 (1978), 30.

14   H. Newcomb, *TV: The Most Popular Art* (New York: Anchor Books, 1974), 178.

15   T. Moi, *Sexual/Textual Politics: Feminist Literary Theory* (London: Methuen, 1986); L. F. Rakow, 'Feminist Approaches to Popular Culture: Giving Patriarchy its Due', *Communication*, 9 (1986), 19–41.

16   V. Walkerdine, 'Some Day my Prince will Come: Young Girls and the Preparation for Adolescent Sexuality', in A. McRobbie and M. Nava (eds.), *Gender and Generation* (London: Macmillan, 1983), 168. See also E. Cowie, 'Fantasia', *m/f* 9 (1984), 71–105; C. Kaplan, '*The Thornbirds*: Fiction, Fantasy, Femininity', in V. Burgin, J. Donald, and C. Kaplan (eds.), *Formations of Fantasy* (London and New York: Methuen, 1986).

17   L. Stern, 'The Body as Evidence', *Screen*, 23/5 (1982), 56.

18   See C. Weedon, *Feminist Practice and Poststructuralist Theory* (Oxford: Basil Blackwell, 1987).

19   G. Dyer, 'Women and Television: An Overview', in H. Baehr and G. Dyer (eds.), *Boxed-In: Women and Television* (London: Pandora Press, 1987), 10.

14

National Texts and Gendered Lives
An ethnography of television viewers in a North Indian City

Purnima Mankekar

Originally published in *American Ethnologist*, 20:3 (1993): 543–563.

Recent trends in anthropology reflect an increasing acknowledgment of the signifi-cance of mass media to processes of identity formation (see, for instance, Appadurai and Breckenridge 1988; Ivy 1988; Russell 1991; Traube 1989). In this essay I analyze the ways in which men and women in New Delhi actively engage with and interpret Indian television, and I explore the place of their interpretations in their constitution as national and gendered subjects. Given the tendency of some scholars to depict audiences of mass media as passive consumers and, in the case of women who live in the "Third World," as helpless victims of a totalizing patriarchal "system," my approach to popular culture and subjectivity represents important theoretical and political gains.

Studies attempting to link television with the construction of identity have tended to focus on the effects of popular texts upon the lives of those who interact with them. For instance, Modleski (1979, 1983) stresses the centrality of the pleasures of television's texts to the construction of femininity. Similarly, Colin MacCabe has emphasized the various ways in which the "terrain of the political is being redefined" by television in the establishment of "enormous machineries of desire" (MacCabe 1986, cited in Caughie 1986: 165). Such studies have far-reaching implications for those of us concerned with the relations of power that suffuse everyday life and the constitution of subjectivities. For when mass media such as television are treated as part of a whole range of cultural products, as texts to be "read" according to interpre-tive strategies, we see that literary conventions and forms have greater sociocultural significance than we might first suspect: analyses of mass media thus enable us to see how we are fashioned by our interactions with what we read, watch, and listen to.[1]

However, in the analysis that follows I extend these propositions by *ethnographic-ally* examining viewers' variable and active interpretations of televisual texts. I hence highlight the fact that meaning is unstable and is frequently contested by viewers, historical subjects, living in particular discursive formations, rather than positioned by any single text.[2] I go beyond approaches that focus exclusively on the implications of specific viewing conditions (for example, Brunsdon 1984; Modleski 1979, 1983), on the construction of subject positions by televisual and cinematic texts (as in Lakshmi 1988; Mulvey 1989; Thomas 1985; Vasudevan 1989),[3] or on the relationship between texts and the sociopolitical conjunctures in which they are embedded (Krishnan and Dighe 1990; Punwani 1988; Taylor 1989). The questions I raise in this essay emerge from my understanding of the gaps in primarily textual or sociological analyses. What is the place of television in the construction of viewers as national and gendered subjects? How do audiences, themselves historically and spatially located, simultaneously "submit" to and "resist" the texts produced by a hegemonic state apparatus such as Indian television?[4] By examining viewers' *active* interaction with television's texts, we can envision popular culture as a site of struggle and not simply of domination, as an "arena of consent and resistance . . . partly where hegemony arises, and where it is secured" (Hall 1981: 239).[5]

My analysis of television enables me to situate viewers in particular sociohistorical contexts, to demonstrate that subject positions vary according to the conjunctures in which viewers are interpellated,[6] and to show how class, community, gender, age, and household position mediate people's interactions with televisual texts.[7] Thus, while previous research on Indian television has dwelt on the political and cultural effects of *texts* (see, for instance, Krishnan 1990; Singhal and Rogers 1989), I have focused on the ways in which *viewers* interpret specific themes and images. Because I am interested in tracing connections between responses to television and the continuous constitution of national and gendered subjectivities, I situate viewers' interpretations in the context of life-narratives that those viewers constructed in conversations with me. I am concerned with relationships between the narratives of television and those that viewers weave of themselves, between popular culture and the viewers' perceptions of themselves as Indian men and women.

In what follows I analyze the manner in which men and women living in New Delhi interpret serials on Indian television, in particular those reflecting and reconstructing discourses of gender and nationhood. This constellation of discourses is of crucial significance because the Indian state has attempted to use television to construct a pan-Indian culture (Krishnan 1990: Women's Studies supplement [WS] 103). In particular, I examine the consequences of the state's projects of national integration and development for the *re*constitution of notions of "Indian Womanhood" predominant in popular discourse.[8] "Indian Womanhood" is an indigenous symbolic construct that predates the contemporary nation-state. Although it became a major site of contention in colonial and nationalist discourses, in which women were often represented as icons or "carriers" of tradition (Mani 1987) and nation (Chakravarti 1989; Sangari and Vaid 1989), notions of Indian Womanhood, modified in the postcolonial context, continue to have profound significance for the construction of identity.

The historical and political context

In this section I outline the contexts in which television's discourses were produced and received by the people I worked with. I do so by delineating the historical and political specificity of television as a medium of mass communication and by analyzing the implications of the state's programming policies for the production of culture in postcolonial India. The notion of ethnographic context, usually conceived in terms of a "thick description" of "local communities," is hence expanded to include the broader political-economic conjuncture.[9] Next, I sociologically locate the core of Indian television's target audience, the expanding middle class, and attempt to describe the immediate context in which the viewers I worked with interpreted their favorite serials: the city and neighborhoods in which they lived, their class positions, and the household politics that framed their understandings.

Television neither simply "reflects" nor "reinforces" discourses: it is, in and of itself, a "cultural form" (Williams 1974) and must be analyzed as part of a larger discursive field.[10] Outlining the history of television in India enables us to better understand the politics of representation underlying constructions of gender and nationhood in a postcolonial context. Indian television (officially and popularly known as Doordarshan) is state-owned and state-controlled. It was first introduced in September 1959 as an experimental service for schools and rural audiences ("rural" meaning villages in the immediate vicinity of New Delhi). The only station was the Delhi Kendra (Center), which broadcast programs for a couple of hours a day on one channel. The Ministry of Information and Broadcasting (under whose aegis television continues to function) next began expanding the reach of television: centers were set up in Bombay (1972), Srinagar (1973), Amritsar (1973), Calcutta (1975), Madras (1975), and Lucknow (1975). Concurrently, transmission times were lengthened, and the telecasting of entertainment programs increased. But for the most part television was, and continues to be, primarily geared to what the Indian nation-state clearly sees as a major objective of mass media: the project of nation building (Joshi 1989). Thus, the major themes in most television today include communal harmony and national integration (as in serials such as *Tamas* and *Sanjha Choola*), national development (exemplified by the countless public information spots promoting family planning or public health education), the reconstruction of anticolonial movements (as with serials like *Kahan Gaye Woh Log*), and the need to improve the status of women (illustrated in serials like *Yugantar*).

The Asian Games of 1982, when teams from different nations assembled in New Delhi for sports events, functioned as a major public relations exercise for the Indian state, both within and outside the country. They marked a turning point in the history of Indian television. As Pendakur has pointed out, the state wanted to capitalize on the pomp and pageantry of the Games; to enable wide reception, it relaxed import restrictions not just on television sets for individuals but, more important, on television technology kits for manufacturers (Pendakur 1989a: 182). Television sets appeared in countless homes across the country, and the skylines of Indian cities were soon filled with the scraggly silhouettes of antennas.

The setting up of low-power transmitters in various parts of the country to relay programs beamed from metropolitan centers by satellite dramatically increased both the reach of television and the hours of transmission. Today, over 75 percent of the population is "covered" by television.[11] Further, whereas audiences in the early years could watch television for two hours in the evening, audiences in many parts of the country can now watch from 7:30 to 9:00 a.m., 2:00 to 3:00 p.m., and 5:30 to

11:00 p.m. on weekdays and from 9:00 a.m. to noon on Sundays on Channel 1, and from 7:30 to 10:00 p.m. on Channel 2.

Until the advent of commercial sponsorship in 1980, most programs were produced by employees of government-owned television centers. Media critics, producers, and indeed television officials often contended that the introduction of private production and sponsorship promoted artistic "freedom" and generated the financial resources required for the production of entertainment serials. At the same time, public discourse on television repeatedly emphasized that a poor country like India could not afford the luxury of "pure" entertainment, that what it needed, instead, were programs such as soap operas harnessed to the (modernist) project of national development (see, for example, Government of India 1985). In keeping with the Indian government's anti-West, pro-Third World stance, the source of Indian soaps was said to be not the United States but Mexico, where *telenovelas* supposedly entertain as well as educate people about the benefits of family planning, modern education, and the rights of women as citizens.[12] From this paradigm of "social change through entertainment" was born the new, hybridized form of the *Indian* television serial.

Today, despite the fact that many serials are privately produced, state-appointed selection and screening committees play a powerful role in the formulation of television's discourses.[13] Discourses about nation building and national integration are directly incorporated into and, in fact, underlie the structuring of transmissions. Prime-time segments (from 8:40 to 11:00 every evening and from 9:00 to noon on Sunday mornings) are all part of what is known as the "National Programme." The National Programme is beamed by satellite to small towns, district headquarters, and villages with electricity. About three-fourths of its programs are in Hindi; the remainder are in English. Variations exist only where regional protests have been vociferous: for example, in Tamil Nadu there is no Hindi news, and because attempts to dub Hindi serials in Tamil have failed, a relatively large number of locally produced serials are shown during prime time. Very few entertainment programs (a maximum of two or three per week) are imported. Some local programs produced in metropolitan centers are in regional languages. But all programs seen during prime time – when people are home from work – and an overwhelming majority of the serials are part of the National Programme. The National Programme is a major component of the effort to construct a pan-Indian "national culture," and at present, when relations between the national and the state governments are particularly turbulent, it is part of the center's attempt to exert hegemonic control over the regional governments.[14]

In this essay I focus on teleserials shown during prime time – that is, as part of the National Programme – from July 1990 through March 1991. A cross between American soap operas and popular Hindi films, they speak the "metalanguage" of the popular Hindi film (evident, for instance, in the types of sets, dialogue, costumes, and music used [Krishnan 1990: WS 104]), while they resemble soaps in terms of audience engagement and narrative structure: multiple plots, the deferment of narrative closure, and the build-up of suspense are important aspects of their narrative tone and texture. Further, like the audiences of American soaps, those of Indian serials deeply identify with characters on the screen; unlike their more distant (although still passionate) attachment to film heroes and heroines, viewers' regular and relatively

extended interactions with television characters foster familiar, even intimate, relationships.[15] However, because most serials are telecast in the evenings rather than the
afternoons, they are targeted not exclusively at women or at people who stay at home
but at families. The family, then, is the basic viewing unit, a fact evident from the
design of advertisements and confirmed by my observations and by what I inferred
from conversations with television officials and the directors of serials.[16]

Serials have ranged in genre from the mythological (*Ramayana* and *Mahabharata*)
and the epic (*The Sword of Tipu Sultan*) to the comic (*Yeh Jo Hai Zindagi*). Many
serials, such as *Hum Log* and *Buniyaad*, resemble the Hindi film genre known as
"the social" in their use of melodrama and social realism (cf. Chakravarty 1989;
Vasudevan 1989), and in their focus on the destinies of families, neighborhoods, and
communities as well as those of individuals.[17] Most serials on Indian television have
explicit "social messages," with themes related to family planning, national integration, and the status of women woven into the narratives. And at any given moment,
more than half of the eight to ten serials shown per week during prime time deal
explicitly or implicitly with nationalist themes. Although the social messages woven
into the narratives have varied according to political contingencies (such as particular
national crises or the needs of a ruling party), an astonishing number continue to deal
centrally with women's issues. More important, even where gender is not an overt
theme, it features prominently as a critical subtext. In nationalist serials the nationalist
metanarrative is reinforced by its appropriation of discourses on gender. In *Param
Veer Chakra* and *The Sword of Tipu Sultan*, for example, the male protagonists' relationships with women are *constantly* posed against their devotion to their country, and
the female characters' attitudes and behavior complement or serve as a foil to the
men's heroic patriotism.

From 1990 to 1992 I conducted numerous interviews with viewers living in two
neighborhoods in New Delhi: Vikas Nagar and Basti.[18] Working with urban women in
multiethnic neighborhoods enabled me to see how reactions to nationalist discourses
were mediated by the ways people negotiate and construct their identities in such
contexts.[19] Moreover, New Delhi was a particularly appropriate setting for the study
of nationalism: the presence of the state is more overwhelming there than in any other
Indian city I have known. The state is a major employer in New Delhi. The city's
landscape is dotted with government buildings, government housing colonies, minis-
terial bungalows, and other reminders of the nation-state. And, like Washington, DC,
New Delhi does not belong to a regional state; it therefore has no regional roots of
its own and its population is composed largely of migrants. People from Old Delhi
characterize themselves as laid-back, courteous, and cultured in comparison with the
allegedly brash, rude, aggressive residents of New Delhi. Old Delhi, they say, has
"tradition"; New Delhi is a place where everything is in disarray. New Delhi's identity
ultimately issues from its role as the capital of the postcolonial nation-state. For all
these reasons, it has the ambience of a quintessentially "national" city.

Nationalism has been characterized as a middle-class phenomenon (Chatterjee
1989), and the relationship between "middle-classness" and nationalism is a fundamental one.[20] Personal observations and conversations with Doordarshan officials
and media critics have led me to believe that the middle and lower middle classes form
the core of the target audience for Indian television (as opposed to, say, popular Hindi

films, which are aimed at all classes).[21] The past two decades have witnessed a dramatic expansion of the Indian middle classes: they now constitute over 20 percent of the population. This demographic change has created an enormous market for consumer goods. The new middle classes that once invested in bicycles, transistor radios, scooters, and refrigerators now want to buy color television sets (Pendakur 1989a: 186). Indeed, owning a color television is itself a mark of being middle class.

As mentioned above, the relaxation of restrictions on the import of television technology around the time of the Asian Games of 1982 promoted an enormous rise in the production and purchase of television sets. This change in policy reflected a major shift in the allocation of financial and technical resources, from community-owned television sets in rural areas to those owned by urban middle-class and lower-middle-class households (Pendakur 1989a). Programming priorities changed accordingly, from the dissemination of development information to entertainment (although, as noted, sustained efforts are still made to weave social messages into serials). The expansion of television thus indicated the power of the growing middle classes (Krishnan 1990; Pendakur 1989b), a power also evidenced by the launching of color television in 1982, the introduction of advertisements and commercial sponsorship (whereby private companies finance the production of entertainment programs), and the subsequent establishment of a second channel.[22] Television's discourses are designed to draw these upwardly mobile classes – "captured" simultaneously as a market for consumer goods advertised by the sponsors of programs and as an audience for nationalistic serials – into the project of constructing a national culture.[23]

The interpretations provided by the lower middle and upwardly mobile working classes are also significant because of those groups' interstitial, comparatively fluid location. The people I worked with felt they were struggling to cross the threshold of "middle-classness." They were acutely aware of their vulnerable position, and the various ways in which that awareness surfaced in their self-presentation made it clear to me that financial insecurity was a major part of their discursive consciousness.[24]

Vikas Nagar is a lower-middle-class government "colony" that houses junior clerks and stenographers occupying the lowest rungs of the state bureaucracy. Each flat in Vikas Nagar consists of an 8' by 10' room, which functions as a living room by day and a bedroom by night, and an even tinier kitchen. Residents share common latrines and bathrooms. Basti was a village until the city of New Delhi engulfed it from all sides. Like many other "urban villages" forced to coexist with middle-class neighborhoods, Basti has "developed" unevenly. Pressure on land and housing has resulted in the sale of about one-fourth of the plots to middle-class people who have gone on to build new, relatively fancy homes with modern plumbing and other trappings of upward mobility. All the people I worked with lived in older, ramshackle houses. Much poorer than their middle-class neighbors, they all sublet tiny rooms within larger units. Yet most of them were somewhat upwardly mobile: while many of the older generation were employed as household help in adjacent upper-middle-class neighborhoods, most of the younger men and women worked on assembly lines in factories or as clerks in private corporations. Unlike upper-middle-class viewing groups, in which servants watch television with the rest of the household, these lower-middle-class and upwardly mobile working-class viewing groups, just a generation away from poverty, were fairly homogeneous in terms of class composition.

I see the household (loosely defined to include not just the extended family but, in many cases, neighbors and their children) as a politically, hence emotionally, charged context in which people watch television. Although I noticed few conflicts over which show should be watched (as mentioned above, most of the serials were telecast on one channel as part of the National Programme), age and gender influenced people's preferences. Women particularly enjoyed the serials, and even though all the men I met also watched the serials with great relish (and usually made no bones about it), they told me that they made it a point to watch the news. Indeed, watching the news was considered an adult, usually male, activity. Most schoolchildren I met would try to watch as many television programs as the demands of homework and the reprimands of parents would permit. Parents often tried to censor the films their children, particularly their young daughters, watched: they made sure the youngsters were asleep before the weekly late-night film, usually an imported one with relatively explicit "love scenes," came on.[25]

In general, gender, household position, and age were the crucial factors influencing viewers' styles of interaction with what they watched. Power relations within families were sometimes reflected in how people arranged themselves around the television set: the older generation (usually men but sometimes older women as well) would be seated on the few chairs; the children would squat on the floor. Very seldom did I see women, especially daughters-in-law, sitting with the rest of the family: not only was it considered inappropriate for them to sit with the men (particularly in North Indian families), but more important, they were the ones responsible for the housework.[26] The men of the household were usually the most avid viewers because they could afford not to be distracted by household tasks, which kept the women busy in the evenings when dinner was being prepared and served or on Sunday mornings when the house had to be cleaned, clothes washed, and water buckets filled. While the men and children kept up a running commentary on the show, the women were usually silent, instead discussing it among themselves the next day.

One woman told me that she made up for all the evening hours she was unable to sit in front of the television set by insisting on watching the Sunday morning shows undisturbed. Another woman, much to the irritation of the rest of her family, kept her television set at its loudest so she could listen to the soundtrack over the din of her housework. These women were relatively successful in their attempts to gain some control of their time. But not all the women I worked with were in a position to be openly assertive: very often, the younger women (daughters-in-law, in particular) would keep up with their favorite shows by listening to the soundtrack and by getting fleeting glimpses from the kitchen as they cooked or from the veranda as they washed clothes. But despite the fact that most of the women half-watched, half-listened while cooking, serving food, doing dishes, or sweeping the floor, they were nonetheless able to engage intimately with what they "viewed."

Most women I worked with did not have the luxury of sitting "glued to the television set"; the following analyses are therefore predicated on the premise that notions of "viewing" have to encompass more than the visual act of watching television. Further, the cultural and political significance of viewing has to be seen in terms of its restructuring of social relations within the family. As Morley has pointed out, viewing has to be conceptualized simultaneously as a "ritual whose function is to structure domestic life and to provide a symbolic mode of participation in the national community" and as an "active mode of consumption" (Morley 1991: 5). The processes of engagement that I describe were, therefore, necessarily inflected by the fields of power in which people watched television, for they watched not only in the setting of the household – that is, in the immediate context of the politics of the family[27] – but also in settings embedded in the larger sociopolitical conjunctures of community and nation.

What role did the viewers' intense engagement with television play in their constitution as national and gendered subjects? I spent a fair amount of time trying to get a sense of how they related what they watched to their own lives, and of how they identified with characters as their favorite narratives unfolded before their eyes. I will now address the viewers' interpretations of representations of "Indian Womanhood," the slippery presence of "oppositional" readings, and the significance of interpretive processes to the conceptualization of popular culture.

Notions of Indian womanhood

Discussions with viewers helped me obtain a glimpse of their engagement with the ideologies of nationalism and gender inscribed in *everyday* discourses on "appropriate behavior" for Indian women: on women's place in the family, their relationship with men, and, most powerfully, their duties to the nation.[28] Creating a sort of double bind, the convergence of discourses of cultural nationalism and gender sometimes fostered particularly oppressive subject positions for women. It raised the expectations women had of themselves and, equally important, those their men had of them. This double bind was most obvious when their "womanhood" was seen to both contribute to and detract from their role as patriotic citizens.

Selapan and his wife, Padmini, came from Tamil Nadu. Selapan worked as a junior clerk with an army intelligence organization. Tall and broad-shouldered, he sported a bushy, somewhat theatrical, military moustache. He loved to talk and was one of the warmest, most articulate people I met. Like many South Indians raised in the North, Selapan spoke very *filmi* Hindustani (a somewhat melodramatic Hindustani imbibed from Hindi films).[29] He often distressed me by passing rude comments about his wife in her presence. Yet I knew that he spent days and nights nursing her when she was sick (which was quite often). Padmini was tall and skinny. She was usually silent when her husband held forth, but when she and I were alone together, she unhesitatingly contradicted and sometimes belittled him. Selapan's favorite serial was *Param Veer Chakra*: he felt it showed "real stories" of men who died for their country. Hence, he said, viewers could see what "real patriotism" (*sacchi deshbhakti*) and sacrifice were all about.[30] He continued: "Young people who see this program can know that instead of frittering their energies, they can do things that will prove they are worthy of the wombs of their mothers."

One morning soon after an episode of *Param Veer Chakra* had ended, I asked Selapan what he thought of the heroine's courage in persuading her reluctant husband to go to the battlefront on the morning after their wedding night. Selapan had been impressed by her. "But," he went on to say, "Indian women are not all like that. If all women were like that, no one would be able to look disrespectfully at India [*koi bhi aankh utha kar dekh nahi payega].*" His statements reveal an elision, an imperceptible slide from "mother" to "motherland": women are "subjectified" as mothers and held responsible for inspiring their children to safeguard India's honor; at the same time, India is feminized as the mother and made the object of protectionist discourse.

How did these notions affect Selapan's behavior toward his wife? I found that he seemed to apply similarly exacting standards to her. In one episode of *Param Veer Chakra* the mother of the hero, Abdul Hamid, persuades his father to get him married by saying, "Put a ring through the bull's nose. That will prevent him from roaming around." I had been deeply offended by this metaphor and, while the episode was still on, asked both Selapan and Padmini (Padmini was sitting quietly after serving us tea) what they thought of it. Selapan replied that he agreed with Hamid's mother: "Women these days cling to their husbands' feet and don't allow them to go anywhere. My wife even stops me from going by bus these days, let alone allows me to go to war."[31]

I silently turned to Padmini, willing her to reply. She did not contradict her husband directly. Instead she pointed out that Hamid's wife, despite all her fears, had run after him to bid him farewell. "When he was so keen to go, what could she do? She had to submit to his wishes," she replied, her voice heavy with resignation. But both Abdul Hamid's mother and Selapan saw women (more specifically, wives) as sources of constraint: while she had implied that they helped rein in the restlessness of young men, Selapan seemed to feel that men had to curb their "courageous" impulses because of women's cowardly fears for their safety. In both cases, women were conceived as obstacles to masculine heroism.

Selapan felt that *Param Veer Chakra* might have a beneficial effect on women because after watching it, they might also become "brave" (*bahadur*) and encourage their husbands to fight and sacrifice for the country. "Don't you think there are already women who are brave, women who themselves do brave things?" I persisted. He replied that there were, only they were very rare. He gave an example of a soldier's wife in South Arcot whose husband had died in Operation Bluestar (the Indian government's 1984 raid on the Golden Temple in Punjab). When the government organized a function to honor him and presented her with a check, she returned it, saying that the glory her husband had earned defending his country was compensation enough for her. And what was more, he continued, she had insisted on wearing her *mangalsutra* (the necklace worn by some Hindu women that signifies their married, as opposed to single or widowed, status). According to Selapan, she had said, "My husband is not dead, he is a martyr [*shaheed*]." Selapan was so moved by this sentiment that he repeated the sentence at least three times. Then, after keeping quiet for a few seconds, he shook his head and said in a low voice, "Indian women are great."

I asked him if he blamed women for worrying about their husbands and sons going to war. When he replied that he would be proud to admit his son into the army, I turned to his wife and asked her what *she* thought of that. She smiled ruefully, put her son's head against her chest (he was sitting between his parents on the bed), and started to stroke his hair. For a minute she was silent. Then after pausing awhile, she turned to me and said: "He is my only child. How can I put him in the army?"

Selapan burst out laughing. "See!" he exclaimed genially. "See how cowardly [*buzdil*] she is! If all mothers start getting scared like this, who will protect the country?"

I felt horrible that I had exposed Padmini to her husband's derision. It was all right for men, whose position in society was relatively secure, to be "brave," I protested, but how could he blame women, who were so socially vulnerable, for being worried? Referring particularly to the plight of women whose husbands die in war, I asked if their fear was unfounded given the low status of widows in Indian society. In any case, I continued, was militant nationalism the only context in which women could be courageous? Ignoring my second question, he replied that while it was true that widows had a hard time in India, if one conducted herself "properly" (*sahi tarah*), even criminals (*goondas*) would fold their hands and call her "sister" (*behenji*). Obviously the onus was on the widow to prove that she deserved respect!

I then asked him what he thought of television's depiction of Indian women in general. His answer, an anecdote, was only apparently off-track. He said that one day, while going somewhere by bus, he had seen a girl wearing a "very short" skirt. She was being teased by some men. "Now, how can you blame boys for teasing her?" he asked, continuing:

> Being modern is all right, but there are some rules [*niyam*] in this culture. This is not the way Indian women should dress. . . . Look at what happens with foreign women. They divorce five, six times. What is the meaning of marriage then? What happens to the children, to the family, then? If there is no family, where is society? Indian women have different rules.

He insisted that the most important "duty" (*kartavya*) of an Indian woman to her country was to protect her family and "see that it never falls apart."

"But what happens if the man is bad, if he ill-treats her?" I asked. "Should she still stay with him?"

"Everything is in the wife's hands," he replied. "If she wants, she can save him, she can put him on the right path [*sahi raaste par*]. It is her responsibility to do so."

In Selapan's view, clearly, women's place in the nation is analogous to their place in the family: it is their duty to protect and to sacrifice for the family. As with the family, so with the nation. But in this scheme women do more than play a supporting role: it falls to them to protect the integrity of family and nation and to do so by inspiring and, if necessary, inciting their men to fight for the motherland. And women alone have the strength (the *shakti*) to do so.[32] Indeed, this is why only heroic sons can be "worthy of the wombs" of their mother/motherland.

This response has to be seen in light of the "mythicizing" of motherhood in nationalist ideologies. Its continuing potency is evident in the prevalence in popular discourse of the notion of *Bharat Mata* (Mother India), which, being rooted in the Hindu concept of the Mother-Goddess, has created a space for notions of women's energy as active and heroic (Bagchi 1990: WS 69). Politicized by Hindu nationalists like Bankim Chandra, who thus forged one of the most powerful icons of the nationalist struggle, this concept has been appropriated by mainstream nationalist ideology.[33]

The conception of Indian Womanhood in terms of heroic motherhood is evident both in Selapan's discourse and in that of *Param Veer Chakra*, which dwells on the motif of women inspiring their sons to fight for the motherland. Nationalists during colonial rule spoke of how the mother(land) was ravished by the British, but Selapan and many other viewers I talked with appeared to have picked up a major theme of *Param Veer Chakra*, that of the mother(land) threatened by hostile neighbors. The purported heroism of the ideal Indian Woman (the *bhartiya naari*) is thus measured by her capacity to incite or inspire her children to fight for their country, and not simply by her ability to bear patriotic sons.

Discussions about popular female characters also revealed a fascinating convergence between discourses of gender and those of nationalism. In July 1989 I witnessed a public controversy over the depiction of two mythological heroines on television, Sita of the *Ramayana* and Draupadi of the *Mahabharata*. Everyone, from vegetable vendors and cab drivers to upper-class intellectuals who usually dismissed television serials, was discussing it. A leading newsmagazine ran a poll to ask which of the two better represented "the modern Indian Woman." Many comparisons and contrasts were drawn between Sita, who symbolizes devotion and patience, and Draupadi, noted for her intelligence and fiery strength. Historically, both Sita and Draupadi have served as symbols of Indian Womanhood (ideal types of the *bhartiya naari*). For instance, nationalist ideologues have appropriated both Draupadi's rage and Sita's resilience to encourage orthodox Hindu women to join anticolonial movements (Mankekar 1990). In 1989 the question on many people's lips was: which of the two is more pertinent to *contemporary* Indian Womanhood?

And so it came as no surprise when conversations about Sita and Draupadi led to discussions on Indian Womanhood. Many viewers, both men and women, had strong opinions on which of the two better represented Indian Womanhood. My conversations with women of different ages were particularly interesting because they illustrated how notions of Indian Womanhood were being *re*constituted (rather than radically transformed) across generations. Uma Chandran lived in Vikas Nagar. Her father was a retired clerk, and her mother, Jayanthi, worked as a stenographer in a government department. Uma had just got a job as a secretary in a private corporation, where she felt out of place because most of the other employees came from much wealthier families. This sense of alienation did nothing to strengthen her fragile self-confidence. While my conversations with all others were in Hindi, she and I spoke English heavily laced with Hindi.

One Sunday morning a couple of weeks after the *Mahabharata* had come to an end, Uma and I were sitting on her veranda. We had been shooed out of the inner room by her father, who wanted to watch the news. Uma talked of how, as a young woman from a poor family, she felt isolated by her wealthier colleagues. She felt she wasn't assertive enough. We soon began talking about the depiction of Sita in the television version of the *Ramayana*. Uma had just started comparing Sita with Draupadi when her mother joined our conversation. This excerpt from the exchange between Uma and Jayanthi illustrates the change and continuity inherent in their notions of volition, suffering, and strength, and it clearly shows the intimate relationship between ideologies of cultural nationalism and those of gender:[34]

Uma: I liked Draupadi better than Sita. Sita was a complete wash-out. . . .

Jayanthi: Why is that? I liked Sita more. I liked her more because she did not have as much glamour. She was simple. You could see devotion [*bhakti*] more clearly in Sita. At every step.

Uma: But why did she submit at every step [*kyon dab jaati hai*]?

Jayanthi: But this was not so in the case of Draupadi. . . . They did not show her with *pativrata dharma* [roughly translates, in this context, as "duties of a wife"].[35] In this *zamana* [era] there is no *pativrata dharma*. There can't be as much as there was in Sita's time. There shouldn't be less. But people don't see the reality of that *shakti* [strength].

Uma, doubtfully: I don't know. Where will this *shakti* take us Indian women today? [She turns to me.] Aren't American women where they are today because they are more independent than we are?

According to Jayanthi, Sita was much stronger than Draupadi. Her strength, her *shakti*, came from her capacity to suffer for her *pativrata dharma*, that is, her duty toward her husband. But Uma disagreed. She felt that modern times required a *shakti* more akin to Draupadi's rage. And Indian women, she seemed to say, were essentially different from American women, who were more independent. Indeed, another young woman with whom I spoke went so far as to claim that Draupadi seemed "less Indian" than Sita: when I tried to probe her meaning, I discovered that she felt Draupadi was "Westernized" because the heroine questioned and challenged her elders on the propriety of their actions. Explicit contrasts between essentialized "Indian women" and "foreign women" thus reflect the ways in which cultural nationalism, through notions of what constitutes "Indian culture," circumscribes discourses on gender. Ideal Indian Womanhood is constructed in terms of values deemed fundamentally womanly, essentially Indian: modesty, patience, and, above all, a strong sense of duty toward the family, the community, and the nation.

The convergence between cultural nationalism and discourses of gender became clearer when, several months later, Uma compared Indian women with "foreign" or "Western" women. Uma and I usually watched *Phir Wahi Talaash* together. In this serial the heroine is forced into an arranged marriage. After a couple of years of trying to make a go of it, she asks her husband for a divorce so that she can reunite with her lover. Once, just as that episode was drawing to a close, Uma responded with bewilderment and some outrage:

Uma: It's not possible to get a divorce that easily in India. In India a divorce means that it's a very free-wheeling lady, all kinds of things. I don't think there are many women who do that Okay, the number has increased, but Indian women are still not so keen on divorce.

Purnima: Why is that?

Uma: I think it's because of our culture. Because marriage means it's for keeps; it's not as if you can get a divorce that easily. The thought doesn't come into our minds.

Purnima: You think this is more true of Indian marriages and Indian women?

Uma: Very much so, very much so.

Uma firmly believed that the heroine was at fault because she had not tried hard enough to save her marriage:

Uma: I still feel she didn't try to make the marriage a success. In between, she is so curt with him. I didn't like that. Why doesn't she make an effort to make a go of the marriage? She's got married, now she should try that the marriage stays safe [*sic*]. It seems to me that she was very casual about it all. That's not how it happens.

Purnima: What do you mean?

Uma: Well, you know, it's very unbecoming for an Indian woman.

It was plain that she strongly disapproved of the heroine's actions because she deemed them inappropriate for Indian women and felt that they had no place in what she called "our culture." Uma, like some other young women with whom I spoke, seemed to be caught between two sets of beliefs about women's independence. She felt that it was "unbecoming" for Indian women to divorce their husbands – women's independence should never be allowed to break up an unhappy marriage. Yet in an earlier conversation she had argued that as a young woman she was better off emulating the "independence" of "American women" and that Draupadi's fiery strength was appropriate to contemporary times. Like Selapan, Uma invoked idealized notions of Indian Womanhood in comparing Indian and Western women.

Thus, although heroic motherhood figures as a primary theme in *Param Veer Chakra* and in Selapan's discourse, it represents only one of several constructions of Indian Womanhood in postcolonial India. Indeed, it is important that we acknowledge the *proliferation* of discourses on Indian Womanhood, some more essentialist than others, all of them reflecting what Foucault (1980: 119) has termed the productive aspects of power. This "incitement to discourse" (Foucault 1978: 18) is reflected in television's preoccupation with "women-dominated serials" – that is, those in which the protagonists are women. The Doordarshan Software Committee, set up by the government to formulate guidelines for television programming, has emphasized the significance of the portrayal of women. Its report, significantly titled *An Indian Personality for Television*, proposes that "women be shown in terms of the complex roles they play . . . as workers and significant contributors to family survival and the national economy" (Government of India 1985: 1, 144–5). However, as seen in the responses of Uma and Selapan, attempts to depict positive and progressive images of women are circumscribed by metanarratives of nation and family. In many serials, for instance, women's anger is portrayed as legitimate only when channeled to the nationalist task of social reform (as in the serial *Rajni*). Marriage is portrayed as the most desirable state for women (as in *Sambandh*; cf. Punwani 1988: 226). Not surprisingly, women are usually portrayed in the context of the family (as in *Hum Log* and *Param Veer Chakra*); those who work outside the home by choice are represented as callous home-wreckers (as in *Khandaan*; cf. Punwani 1988). In serials and in popular discourse in general, Indian Womanhood is now beginning to be conceived in terms of patriotic citizenship, productive labor, and selfless social activism; in short, the ideal Indian Woman is one whose energies are harnessed to the task of promoting national progress in various and multiple ways.

Viewers as critics

As noted above, viewers' interpretations are profoundly influenced by the broader social discourses in which they are interpellated; they are shaped by events in the viewers' lives and by the relationships in which those viewers define themselves. Thus, there is a two-way relationship between viewers' lives and the narratives in serials: what people watch is mediated by and at the same time helps illuminate developments in their lives. I was astonished by how frequently viewers linked their favorite serials with their lives: it seemed to be the easiest way for many of them to discuss not just what they watched but, more significant, their own experiences. Indeed, in many of our conversations the boundaries between texts and lives often blurred so that I found it hard to discern whether we were talking about a television character or about the viewer.

Aparna Dasgupta was a middle-aged Bengali woman. She had never been to school, and said that she had learned a lot from observing people. I know she thought that I, for all my "foreign" education, was extremely naive about "what really goes on in families." In spite – or perhaps because – of being a silent witness to her husband's and son's brutalization of her young daughter-in-law, Aparna insisted on advising me about how to "shield" myself from the alleged "cleverness" of *my* mother-in-law. (My protestations that I didn't really need her advice served only to make her more protective of me.) Aparna felt that television was powerful because one could learn from it (*shiksha milti hai*). When she was growing up, she said, women were not allowed to go to the cinema. Even though she had been living in Delhi for the past 25 years, she never got to watch films until she started to see them on television. In many ways, she told me, television was her window on the rest of the world. However, she insisted, not everyone could learn from watching television: one had to have a particular *bhaav* (loosely, "feeling" or "emotion"; neither of these words quite captures the meaning of *bhaav*) in one's heart. One morning a couple of days after the last episode of her favorite serial, the *Mahabharata*, had been aired, I asked her what she thought of it. She replied: "When you read the Gita, you should read it with a certain *bhaav* in your heart. It's the same thing when you watch something on television."

But what was this *bhaav*? I pressed her. Did it reside in the heart, only to surface when one watched something touching? Or was it a state induced by what one watched, that is, by the experience of seeing something emotional unfold on the screen? If that were the case, wouldn't everyone learn something, the same thing perhaps, from a particular serial? But *bhaav*, Aparna replied, was not quite so simple. She explained it with reference to her experience of Hindi films:

> The first time I watched a Hindi film nothing much happened. But then I saw a second, then a third, then a fourth. Then one day as I watched, *bhaav* came to me [*bhaav aa gaya*] . . . By then I too had a family. I was watching this film called *Bhabhi*. It was all about how this young woman suffers after she gets married. It was all about how you suffer in the world. How much the *bhabhi* [brother's wife] suffers! I just couldn't stop crying. I thought, suppose I have to face what she is going through, what will happen?

This encounter taught Aparna how to watch films and television serials. According to her, one had to surrender to the mood of what was being watched; to learn from it, one had to be immersed in that state of being. And one had to be at a point in life where what was watched made sense personally, at a level beyond mere empathy. This mode of watching, indeed of interacting, became clearer when Aparna recounted what had happened to her daughter Sushmita when she saw a *Mahabharata* scene in which the female protagonist, Draupadi, is publicly disrobed in her in-laws' court:

> My daughter, when she saw [what happened], cried and cried. She cried all morning. Imagine what happened to Draupadi! And in public, in front of her in-laws! A feeling came to my daughter [*bhaav aa gaya*]: What will happen to me when I get married and go to my in-laws' home? Isn't this what happens?

According to Aparna, we learn about life from the emotions (*bhaav*) television's discourses arouse in us. However, interpretation operates within a larger set of discursive practices.[36] As Aparna patiently explained to me, one has to *acquire* the ability to learn from what is watched, and this ability comes from, among other things, frequent exposure. In addition, one must be at a particular point in one's trajectory, in one's development as a person; hence, the film *Bhabhi* would not have aroused *bhaav* in her had she watched it before she was married. She also insisted that not just anyone could learn: only those who, in her words, had an ability to "enter the soul" of what they watched could do so.

However, it is important to emphasize that *bhaav* do not emerge in a vacuum, a result of a text's "impact" on an isolated viewer; we have to foreground the sociocultural hases of these experiences. Aparna was socially "habituated" to read the Gita and to watch the *Mahabharata* with a particular *bhaav* in her heart. Her unmarried daughter's tears at Draupadi's disrobing arose from fear about her own future, a fear reinforced when she saw how other daughters-in-law (including the one in her family) were treated. These *bhaav*, these feelings and emotions, were products of the *social* relations in which they were embedded. In other words, emotions do not emerge from an "inner essence" distinct from the social world; emotions are "social practices organized by stories that we both enact and tell," and "persons are constructed in a particular cultural milieu" of experiences, meanings, relationships, and images, all of which are socially mediated (Rosaldo 1984: 143, 138). I have shown that some experiences, "stories," and representations involve interactions between viewers, located in particular sociocultural contexts, and the texts of mass media such as television: far from being innate, many emotions are themselves produced by the social practices that television's narratives mediate and, indeed, sometimes create.

But are we to think that everyone who watches serials will automatically assume the subject positions created by the discourses of television? I found that even as they deeply identified with characters on television, even as they experienced profound *bhaav*, many viewers were simultaneously able to stand back and criticize what they watched. Neither they nor I saw any contradiction between these two apparently divergent modes of viewing. Viewers loved to critique the acting ability of the cast or the competenece of the director. Similarly, they would often comment that, for example, a particular set was "stagey" or the "photographer" had done a "boring job" (in this case I think the person was saying something about camera angles).[37]

Many viewers had definite opinions about what television "ought to" depict – that is, about appropriate or inappropriate subject matter. Surjeet Kaur worked as an unskilled assembly-line employee in a garment factory. An accomplished storyteller, she would narrate the sagas of serials (and of her life) in intricate detail and with great flourish. She had a stormy relationship with her husband, a junior clerk in the Education Ministry, and often said that watching television was one of the few ways in which she could calm herself. But, she complained, some serials encouraged people's "superstitions." She felt that there was no place for "this sort of thing" (*aisi batein*) in serials because "superstition" (*andh vishwas*) was "wrong" (*galt*). She thought television producers were sometimes very careless about how they constructed stories: "You know how they make serials – they pull from here, cut from there, try to patch a story together somehow."

Her thoughts on the appropriate subject matter for television were based on a theory of the relationship between reception and class, a belief that television could lead "certain types" of people astray. For she went on to say:

People shouldn't believe everything they see on TV, but they often do. . . . Because people are uneducated they believe everything they hear. People should not be guided [she used the English word][38] in this way. Imagine if village women or women who live in *jhuggi-jhopdis* [huts in the shantytown some 20 yards from her house] see all this! They will believe every word. . . . Someone has to guide [Eng.] them, to explain to them that this is not how things really are.

Herself illiterate and precariously lower middle class, Surjeet Kaur was conscious of what she clearly perceived as the privileges of her class position, which, she felt, gave *her* a critical awareness that poorer people lacked. Her discourse on the effects of television constructed viewers who lived in slums as the "other," the gullible, ignorant masses who had to be "guided."[39]

Further, Surjeet Kaur, like many other women I spoke to, had definite ideas about style and plot, especially the resolution of narrative tensions and conflicts. What she disliked most were the conclusions of many serials.[40] She insisted that they concluded too abruptly, that nothing seemed to be resolved (*koi faisla hi nahi hota*), that one never got a sense of "what really happened" in the end. She speculated that perhaps most of the time they ended before "the original story" (that is, the script) had concluded.

More important, most people I talked with were acutely conscious that the serials they watched had been selected, censored, and shaped by the state.[41] They often commented that when secessionist movements threatened the integrity of the nation-state, there would be a spate of serials dealing with Punjab and Kashmir. One young woman complained that although she enjoyed the stories, she was getting tired of the same old themes. Some people saw even more direct connections between the plots of serials and the political motivations of the ruling party. When I asked one viewer if he enjoyed watching serials, he replied that he had enjoyed them until a few months ago but that ever since V. P. Singh, then prime minister of India, had come to power, the programs had deteriorated. "All they show now," he complained, "is villagers and their problems." The prime minister was then making statements about a need to "bridge the gap" between cities and "the real India," that is, "village India." This viewer, along with countless others who pointed out the same thing, was quite astute in grasping why audiences were suddenly being subjected to a number of hastily produced serials set in villages.

Television watching, I sense, is gradually becoming an opportunity for people to sit around and complain about the power (and, very often, the stupidity: "they must be very stupid [*bewaqoof*] to think we're this gullible!") of the government. However, we need to be extremely cautious about concluding that this critical awareness signifies that people are somehow "outside" the reach of the state or that they simply "resist" dominant discourses received through television. Viewers' responses to what they watch cannot be encompassed by categories such as "resistance" and "submission." Oppositional readings, as I hope to demonstrate, are a great deal more complex and slippery.

For instance, the viewers I interviewed would often "submit" to one of the multiple discourses constituting a serial but would appropriate another to criticize the government. One of my conversations with Surjeet Kaur began with her recapitulation of an emotional episode of *The Sword of Tipu Sultan*, a controversial depiction of an eighteenth-century Muslim king. The main theme of that episode, according to not just Surjeet Kaur but also the others present, was the loyalty and kindness of Haider Ali, a central character. Surjeet Kaur used the episode to contrast Haider Ali with present-day politicians who betrayed their supporters. She launched into a detailed description of the joy experienced by Haider and his friend Ramchander when they reunited after several years, and she pointed out that when he became king, Haider remembered his promise to help Ramchander. She exclaimed: "Haider never betrayed his childhood friendship [*bachpan ki dosti*]; he bridged the huge divide between himself and Ramchander." Surjeet Kaur summarized the story thus: "This story is about a king and his friend, about a poor friend and a king [*yeh kahani hai ek dost aur ek raja, ek garib dost aur ek raja ke bare mein*]." She continued:

> Isn't that the way it should be? Not as it is in our country now. That's not how it is now. Whether it's a *raja* [king] or a P.M. [Eng.], they're only interested in keeping their seat [Eng.], their treasury. The people can starve to death, but they don't care. Who cares about the people? When it's time for the election, [politicians] come with their hands folded and say, we'll do this for you, we'll do that for you. What will you [they; that is, politicians] do [*Kya karoge tum*]? You only come to us when you need us. Otherwise who asks about us? Now look, we have to pay Rs. 5 a kilo for onions. Imagine [*Bataiye*]! How are people like us to manage? It's true that the government has increased pay scales. But it doesn't make any difference. I would rather they kept prices down.[42]

Padmini and I once watched an episode of her husband's favorite serial, *Param Veer Chakra*, while he was away visiting an ailing relative. This was one of the few times I saw Padmini actually sitting down to watch television. She had clearly been looking forward to it: she had finished all her work for the morning and was waiting, bathed and ready, when I arrived at her house one chilly Sunday. The episode was particularly melodramatic: by the time it ended I was having a hard time holding back my tears; Padmini was weeping.[43] But was she crying because she was moved by its display of patriotic fervor? I am quite sure she was not. For as soon as the show finished, she turned to me and said, "These men go off. But it's the women who have to suffer because [the men] have gone to fight." It was obvious that she saw the show entirely from the perspective of the wife who had been left behind, and as far as she was concerned, militant nationalism did not seem to be worth the tragedy of war. This response is particularly significant in light of her silence when her husband waxed eloquent on the glories of patriotic Indian Womanhood.

Thus, intense emotional involvement occurs *simultaneously* with a critical awareness that sometimes enables viewers to "see through" the narrative to the state's agenda. "Resistance" and "compliance" are not mutually exclusive categories, and the role of television in the constitution of viewers' subjectivities cannot be conceived in terms of just one or the other. With many viewers, one level of engagement slides into the other all the time. The complexity of resistance has been well demonstrated by Abu-Lughod (1990), who talks of how Bedouin women both resist and support existing systems of power (ibid: 47), and by Radway (1984), who describes how women's resistance is embodied in the act of reading romance novels even as it is sometimes undercut by the content of what they read. This reconception of resistance and compliance helps us see popular culture as a site of *struggle* between dominant discourses and forces of resistance. Popular culture contains "points of resistance" as well as "moments of supersession"; it forms a "battlefield where no once-for-all victories are obtained but where there are always strategic positions to be won and lost" (Hall 1981: 233). Thus, while many of the viewers I met seemed extremely aware of the power of the state, let us not forget Aparna's explication of the role of *bhaav*: it informed viewers, in a frighteningly fundamental way, about their place in the world. They learned about their position as gendered subjects, and as Indians, from *bhaav* as it mediated their interpretations of television's discourses.

Conclusion

My objectives in this essay have been twofold: to analyze the place of television in the constitution of national and gendered subjects and, thus, to arrive at an understanding of how popular texts can be conceptualized. I have tried to argue that nationalism and gender are inherently linked. Discourses on gender seem to crystallize most clearly in discussions centered on the qualities of particular types of women, *Indian* women. Similarly, as evident in the responses of viewers to serials like *Param Veer Chakra*, nationalism is intrinsically both gendered and engendering, creating specific subject positions for men and for women. But, as we have seen, viewers variously interpret, appropriate, resist, and negotiate these subject positions. Discourses of nationhood regulate those of gender and vice versa: I have tried to draw attention both to the multiplicity of interpretations and to the parameters within which those interpretations are made.

Hence, although television plays an unmistakably critical role in the constitution of discursive practices, its cultural and political significance cannot be understood simply in terms of a clear-cut division between the hegemonic text and the passive viewer. By foregrounding viewers' interpretations, we can conceive of popular culture as a site for resistance as well as domination. And by studying the different ways in which viewers actively engage with what they watch, we can break away from theories of popular culture that foreclose the process of interpretation in the production of meaning (for example, Horkheimer and Adorno's (1969) "mass culture" hypothesis, or analyses in which the subject's position is dictated by the text).

I wish to highlight the fact that the viewer is positioned not simply by the text but also by a whole range of other discourses, with those of gender and nationalism being dominant in Indian television. Viewers are reconstituted as subjects not just by the form and content of serials but by the manner in which these texts resonate with the viewers' experiences of dominant social discourses. Viewers' deep emotional engagement with television, the *bhaav* that a text arouses in them, spurs them to introspection about themselves and their lives. For better or for worse, they learn through *bhaav* about their place in the world. Uma's apparently confused views on women's independence, Selapan's ambivalence about women's ability to be "patriotic citizens," and Surjeet Kaur's "submission" to and appropriation of *The Sword of Tipu Sultan* to criticize the contemporary Indian state indicate that television often offers people contradictory subject positions. Foregrounding viewers' active, intimate engagement with television's texts enables us to explore the place of spectatorship in the construction of selves, specifically in the constitution of gender and national identities.

Further, I wish to highlight the importance of delineating the specific contexts in which viewers engage with the texts of television. Morley has described "the average sitting room" as a

> site of some very important political conflicts – it is, among other things, one of the principal sites of the politics of gender and age. . . . The sitting room is exactly where we need to start from if we finally want to understand the constitutive dynamic of abstractions such as "the community" or "the nation."
>
> (Morley 1991: 12)

I argue that we must examine the viewing subject's position in particular networks of power within the family as well as in the broader political conjuncture.

Focusing on specific contexts also helps us comprehend television's role in the construction of gender identity, especially that of women. To assume that *all* women are positioned and "manipulated" by the patriarchal discourses of television is to fall into the trap of universal notions of oppression, as well as to underrate women's abilities to "resist, challenge and subvert" relations of inequality (Mohanty 1984: 345). The depiction of women viewers as active subjects is especially important in light of the tendency to depict "Third World" women as passive victims. Hence, instead of perceiving television's role in the construction of gender identities as unvarying, we need to analyze the construction of gendered subjectivities in *particular* political and social contexts. It is therefore important that we also consider the location of men in specific asymmetrical power networks, and that we examine men's interactions with women in varying relations of domination and interdependence.

Notes

1 For example, feminists have pointed to the significance of representations of romantic love in cultural constructions of gender (Johnson 1986: 59).

2 My positioning of viewers as subjects is based on the premise that "ideologies do not operate through single ideas; they operate in discursive chains, in clusters, in semantic fields, in discursive formations" (Hall 1985: 104; see also Althusser 1971).

3 Feuer (1983) and Modleski (1983) have described some of the factors that distinguish the television experience from that of film: the technological features of the medium itself (for example, the way images are produced and presented); the different texts (commentaries, commercials); the significance of the ties between programs and their commercial sponsors; and the impact of the sites of reception (whether the cinema hall or the living room). Also important are questions of enunciation: Whose voices are being represented in the texts? Who do the texts address? And how are the discourses of television, embedded in specific capitalist relations of production, ideologically charged?

4 Notable exceptions to the preoccupation with textual and sociological analyses are offered by Bobo (1988), Gillespie (1989), Morley (1980), Radway (1984), and Seiter, Borchers, Kreutzner, and Warth (1989).

5 According to the framework used in this essay, popular culture includes folk traditions that may have metropolitan or elite roots, as well as elements of mass culture incorporated into the everyday lives of ordinary people. The concept of "mass culture" formulated by theorists like Horkheimer and Adorno (1969) is modified by the use of Gramsci's notion of hegemony.

6 Drawing on Lacan (1977), Althusser describes "interpellation" in terms of the relationship between ideology and subjectivity: "ideology 'acts' or 'functions' in such a way that it 'recruits' subjects among the individuals . . . or 'transforms' the individuals into subjects (it transforms them all) by that very precise operation which I have called interpellation or hailing. . . . The existence of ideology and the hailing or interpellation of individuals as subjects are one and the same thing" (Althusser 1971: 163). Hall explains interpellation further as the point of recognition between subjects and ideological or signifying chains (Hall 1985: 102).

7 In demonstrating television's place in the discursive construction of subjectivities, I draw on Trinh Minh-ha's (1989: 22) notion of plural, nonunitary subjects. I conceive of subjects as *in medias res*, constantly being formed, never coming wholly to fruition. I thus reject the notion of a unitary consciousness, arguing that each person can be a contradictory subject, "traversed" by a variety of discursive practices (Alarcon 1990: 357, 365).

8 Notions of Indian Womanhood have as much currency and are as central to discourses of cultural nationalism in India as the ideology of the "American Dream" in the United States.

9 See Appadurai (1986) for an excellent critique of the preoccupation with "local" and "face-to-face" communities.

10 Hence, overstressing the dichotomy between television producers and viewers can be extremely problematic.

11 In many parts of the country, "coverage" does not necessarily enable regular viewership. Additional critical factors are ownership of or access to television sets, a reasonably regular supply of electricity, and other infrastructural facilities.

12 In an interview on January 23, 1992, the secretary to the Ministry of Information and Broadcasting, S. S. Gill, confirmed that Indian teleserials were inspired by telenovelas.

13 Selection Committee members Akshay Kumar Jain and Razia Ismail provided this information during interviews in November 1990.

14 I would like to thank one of my anonymous reviewers for emphasizing this point.

15 According to Punwani (1988: 224) the serial *Hum Log* aroused such "intense viewer identification" that producers received regular mail advising them on how the story should develop.

16 This conception of audiences acquires particular significance in light of the fact that audiences do not exist *a priori* but are constructed by discursive and marketing practices. For excellent discussions of this aspect of audience formation, see Ang (1990) and Radway (1988).

17 See Mukherjee (1985) on the unresolved tension between "indigenous" concepts of personhood and notions of the individual in modern Indian fiction.

18 I use pseudonyms to protect the identities of the people I worked with.

19 As an Indian student of anthropology in the United States, I have frequently been startled by how often the typical anthropological discourse on South Asia, craving authenticity, has obsessively attempted to represent "village India" as "the true India" and has stubbornly resisted acknowledging the presence of dynamic, cosmopolitan cultural formations in postcolonial India (scholarship such as that of Appadurai and Breckenridge [1988] is an exception). Hence, my insistence on focusing on urban women is, at least in part, a result of my awareness of the silences in the anthropology of South Asia.

20 The larger project of which this essay is a part details the links between "middle-classness," gender, and notions of national citizenship (Mankekar 1993a).

21 In January 1992 I interviewed both S. S. Gill, the official responsible for the production of the first teleserial (*Hum Log*), and R. Srinivasan, the marketing correspondent of the *Times of India*, a major national daily.

22 Pendakur points out that the state and the middle classes, along with advertising agencies and the growing consumer industries, are highly influential in shaping television policy (Pendakur 1989a: 186). The state competes with producers of television serials (many of whom hail from the Bombay Hindi film industry), private corporations, and advertising agencies for the power to influence cultural production.

23 This point was corroborated by television critic Iqbal Masud in an interview on December 15, 1990.

24 Among my upper-caste interviewees, anxiety about their vulnerable class position reached a peak when the government attempted to introduce the Mandal Commission Bill, which proposed to provide lower and "backward" castes special quotas in educational institutions and state jobs. This bill prompted widespread rioting and street violence all over North India, including New Delhi. My upper-caste but precariously lower-middle-class informants were enraged

at the government because they felt their only hope for upward mobility was being snatched; lower-caste people with whom I spoke were, not surprisingly, unequivocally in favor of the legislation. At stake for all concerned was upward mobility.

25 Many parents, however, confessed that such attempts were futile because the children usually slept (or rather pretended to sleep) in the room where the television set was.

26 Because I was generally treated as a visiting "daughter of the house" by most of these families (and, undoubtedly, because of my class position), I would often be made to sit on a chair or, as they became more informal with me, on the floor with the older daughters.

27 I would like to thank Edgar Winans (personal communication, 1991) for emphasizing the significance of this fact.

28 I am indebted to critiques of Anglo-American feminist theory by feminists such as Alarcon (1990) and Lorde (1984), who have shown us the pitfalls of conceptualizing gender as a category *sui generis*.

29 Hence, his speech was rife with words such as *shaheed* (martyr), *buzdil* (cowardly), and *haqiqat* (reality).

30 Once, when I asked him how the theme of the brave wife had been handled in the "last story," Selapan took exception to my choice of words. "It's not a story. It is reality [*haqiqat*]. It is history," he insisted. He was mollified only when I hastened to explain that I did not mean the episode was fictitious but that I was referring to the dramatization of the hero's dilemmas. In an article entitled "Notions of the Real and Indian Television Serials" (Mankekar 1993b), I attempt to analyze discourses about realism that are deployed by the producers and viewers of television serials.

31 Selapan was referring to the public unrest fomented by the anti-Mandal Commission movement. The presence of phrases like "these days," "this era," and "modern times" reflects a certain image of the "traditional" constructed in contradistinction to modernity. This nostalgic reconstitution of tradition is fed by Doordarshan's depiction of "the glorious Indian past" in serials like the *Ramayana*, the *Mahabharata*, and *Chanakya*. The implications of these serials for Hindu nationalism are discussed in Mankekar (1993a).

32 See Wadley (1980) for discussions of the concept of women's *shakti*.

33 The religious origins of notions such as *Bharat Mata* (Mother India) point to the Hindu hegemony of "mainstream" nationalist discourse. This reveals the slippage between Hindu nationalism and Indian nationalism from the outset and is worth a separate investigation.

34 By no means do I intend to assert a "generational cleavage" of any sort: in fact, as I show, Uma herself seemed to be caught between different discourses on Indian Womanhood. This example simply foregrounds the fact that notions of Indian Womanhood are not static, and it highlights the role played by television in their gradual transformation.

35 See Chakravarti (1986) for an excellent analysis of the hegemonic construction of *pativrata dharma*.

36 The *rasasutra* refers to the "aesthetic organization" of a state of being or emotion

(*bhaav*) found in classical Sanskrit literature (Gerow 1974: 216), and it singles out the following emotions for aesthetic exegesis: love, mirth, grief, energy, terror, disgust, anger, wonder, and peace. Works of art "transmute" each of these into a corresponding mood (*rasa*) – for instance, grief inspires the mood of compassion – and *rasas* "render the personal and the incommunicable generalizable and communicable" (Ramanujan 1974: 118). Effective realization of a *rasa* depends not only on whether a particular performance or other work of art is "suited" to its construction, but also on the capacity of the viewer or reader to apprehend and therefore affirm the prevailing *rasa* (Gerow 1974: 221). Hence *rasa* refers at once to an aesthetic tradition and to a philosophical state of being. Perhaps the *rasa-sutra* provided a vocabulary, if not a conceptual apparatus, for viewers like Aparna, who often spoke of the street plays and musical performances she had watched in her village during her childhood.

However, attempting to identify "indigenous traditions" of spectatorship is tricky because it can sometimes lead one to overemphasize continuity and to underestimate change and borrowing: this danger is particularly acute in the case of popular culture, which necessarily operates in an increasingly transnational world. Therefore, we must pay particular attention to the sociopolitical contexts in which interpretive processes occur. For example, what happens when cultural production is shaped by the modernist discourses of the state? And how are particular themes and images interpreted by viewers who live in a postcolonial, cosmopolitan setting? We must also emphasize the fact that aesthetic categories are neither static nor totalizing and that there is no single "Indian" tradition of aesthetics; instead, many different traditions exist, often in conflict with one another. I explore the relevance of *rasa* theory to analyses of television watching in urban India in "Notions of the Real and Indian Television Serials" (Mankekar 1993b).

37 Pendakur reports that he had a similar experience when he did fieldwork in a small town: when he spoke to lower-middle-class children they demonstrated an astonishing knowledge of production techniques, such as freeze shots and instant replay (Pendakur 1989a: 178).

38 As those familiar with Indian metropolitan centers would know, it is not unusual for even illiterate city dwellers to use English words like "guided."

39 Although a detailed exploration of class consciousness and subjectivity is outside the scope of this essay, Surjeet Kaur's thoughts on how her reception of television differed from that of women living in slums showed clearly how people sometimes construct their identities in relation to prototypical others.

40 Surjeet Kaur's opinion is interesting in light of Modleski's (1983) attempt to link the lack of narrative closure on American soaps with the subject positions of women in suburban US culture.

41 Their suspicion of the state came as no surprise to me: when I was growing up in India, strangers in trains, buses, and other public spaces frequently treated me to long, often vitriolic, discourses on the government's inefficiency, corruption, and so on.

42 Although this particular example tells us nothing about gender ideologies *per se*, it does show how viewers appropriate television's discourses to criticize their own

world. It also reflects the creation of certain notions of citizenship that allow viewers to feel they have the right to expect accountability from their elected leaders.

43 For an excellent analysis of melodrama and the construction of gendered subject positions, see Vasudevan (1989).

References

Abu-Lughod, Lila 1990. The Romance of Resistance: Tracing Transformations of Power through Bedouin Women. *American Ethnologist* 17: 41–55.

Alarcon, Norma 1990. The Theoretical Subject(s) of This Bridge Called My Back and Anglo-American Feminism. In *Making Face, Making Soul*. G. Anzaldua, ed., pp. 356–69. San Francisco, CA: Aunt Lute.

Althusser, Louis 1971. Ideology and Ideological State Apparatuses (Notes towards an Investigation). In *Lenin and Philosophy and Other Essays*, pp. 121–73. New York: Monthly Review Press.

Ang, Ien 1990. *Desperately Seeking the Audience*, London: Routledge.

Appadurai, Arjun 1986. Theory in Anthropology: Center and Periphery. *Comparative Studies in Society and History* 28: 356–61.

Appadurai, Arjun and Carol A. Breckenridge 1988. Why Public Culture? *Public Culture Bulletin* 1(1): 5–9.

Bagchi, Jasodhara 1990. Representing Nationalism: Ideology of Motherhood in Colonial Bengal. *Economic and Political Weekly* 25 (42–3): WS 65–71.

Bobo, Jacqueline 1988. The Color Purple: Black Women as Cultural Readers. In *Female Spectators*. D. Pribram, ed., pp. 90–109. New York: Verso.

Brunsdon, Charlotte 1984. Crossroads: Notes on Soap Opera. *Screen* 22 (3): 32–7.

Caughie, John 1986. Popular Culture: Notes and Revisions. In *High Culture/Low Theory*. C. MacCabe, ed., pp. 156–71. Manchester, England: Manchester University Press.

Chakravarti, Uma 1986. Pativrata. *Seminar* 318: 17–21.

—— 1989. Whatever Happened to the Vedic Dasi? Orientalism, Nationalism and a Script for the Past. In *Recasting Women: Essays in Colonial History*. K. Sangari and S. Vaid, eds., pp. 27–87. New Delhi: Kali for Women.

Chakravarty, Sumita S. 1989. National Identity and the Realist Aesthetic: Indian Cinema of the Fifties. *Quarterly Review of Film and Video* 11 (3): 31–48.

Chatterjee, Partha 1989. The Nationalist Resolution of the Women's Question. In *Recasting Women: Essays in Colonial History*. K. Sangari and S. Vaid, eds., pp. 233–53. New Delhi: Kali for Women.

Feuer, Jane 1983. The Concept of Live Television: Ontology as Ideology. In *Regarding Television: Critical Approaches – An Anthology*. E. A. Kaplan, ed., pp. 12–22. Frederick, MD: University Publications of America.

Foucault, Michel 1978. *The History of Sexuality. Vol. 1: An Introduction*. New York: Vintage Books.

—— 1980. Truth and Power. In *Power/Knowledge*, pp. 109–33. New York: Pantheon Books.

Gerow, Edwin 1974. The Rasa Theory of Abinavagupta and Its Application. In *The Literatures of India: An Introduction*. E. C. Dimock, Jr., et al., eds., pp. 212–27. Chicago, IL: University of Chicago Press.

Gillespie, Marie 1989. Technology and Tradition: Audio-Visual Culture among South Asian Families in West London. *Cultural Studies* 2 (2): 226–39.

Government of India 1985. *An Indian Personality for Television: Report of the Working Group on Software for Doordarshan.* 2 vols. New Delhi: Publications Division, Ministry of Information and Broadcasting.

Hall, Stuart 1981. Notes on Deconstructing "The Popular." In *People's History and Socialist Theory.* R. Samuel, ed., pp. 227–40. London: Routledge and Kegan Paul.

—— 1985. Signification, Representation, Ideology: Althusser and the Post-Structuralist Debates. *Critical Studies in Mass Communication* 2 (2): 91–114.

Horkheimer, Max and Theodore W. Adorno 1969 [1944]. The Culture Industry: Enlightenment as Mass Deception. In *Dialectic of Enlightenment.* J. Cumming, trans., pp. 120–67. New York: Continuum.

Ivy, Marilyn 1988. Tradition and Difference in the Japanese Mass Media. *Public Culture* 1(1): 21–30.

Johnson, Richard 1986. What Is Cultural Studies Anyway? *Social Text* 6 (1): 38–80.

Joshi, P. C. 1989. *Culture, Communication and Social Change.* New Delhi: Vikas.

Krishnan, Prabha 1990. In the Idiom of Loss: Ideology of Motherhood in Television Serials. *Economic and Political Weekly* 25 (42–3): WS 103–16.

Krishnan, Prabha and Anita Dighe 1990. *Affirmation and Denial: Construction of Femininity on Indian Television.* New Delhi: Sage.

Lacan, Jacques 1977 [1966]. *Écrits: A Selection.* A. Sheridan, trans. New York: International.

Lakshmi, C. S. 1988. Feminism and the Cinema of Realism. In *Women in Indian Society.* R. Ghadially, ed., pp. 217–24. New Delhi: Sage.

Lorde, Audre 1984. *Sister Outsider.* Freedom, CA: Crossing Press.

MacCabe, Colin 1986. Defining Popular Culture. In *High Culture/Low Theory.* C. MacCabe, ed., pp. 1–10. Manchester, England: Manchester University Press.

Mani, Lata 1987. Contentious Traditions: The Debate on Sati in Colonial India. *Cultural Critique* 7: 119–56.

Mankekar, Purnima 1990. "Our Men Are Heroes, Our Women Are Chaste": A Nationalist Reading of the "Disrobing" of Draupadi. Paper presented at the panel "The Body and the Categorization of People", American Ethnological Society Annual Meeting, Atlanta, April 26–29.

—— 1993a. Television and the Reconstitution of Indian Womanhood. Ph.D. dissertation, Department of Anthropology, University of Washington.

—— 1993b. Notions of the Real and Indian Television Serials. MS, files of the author. Minh-ha, Trinh 1989. *Woman, Native, Other: Writing Postcoloniality and Feminism.* Bloomington: Indiana University Press.

Modleski, Tania 1979. The Search for Tomorrow in Today's Soap Operas. *Film Quarterly* 32(1): 266–78.

—— 1983. The Rhythms of Reception: Daytime Television and Women's Work. In *Regarding Television: Critical Approaches – An Anthology.* E. A. Kaplan, ed., pp. 67–75. Frederick, MD: University Publication of America.

Mohanty, Chandra Talpade 1984. Under Western Eyes: Feminist Scholarship and Colonial Discourses. *Boundary* 213 (1): 333–58.

Morley, David 1980. *The "Nationwide" Audience.* London: British Film Institute.

—— 1991. Where the Global Meets the Local: Notes from the Sitting Room. *Screen* 32: 1–15.

Mukherjee, Meenakshi 1985. *Realism and Reality: The Novel and Society in India.* Delhi: Oxford University Press.

Mulvey, Laura 1980. *Visual and Other Pleasures.* Bloomington: Indiana University Press.

Pendakur, Manjunath 1989a. Indian Television Comes of Age: Liberalization and the Rise of Consumer Culture. *Communication* 11: 177–97.

—— 1989b. New Cultural Technologies and the Fading Glitter of Indian Cinema. *Quarterly Review of Film and Video* 11 (3): 69–78.

Punwani, Jyoti 1988. The Portrayal of Women on Indian Television. In *Women in Indian Society*. R. Ghadially, ed., pp. 224–32. New Delhi: Sage.

Radway, Janice 1984. *Reading the Romance: Women, Patriarchy, and Popular Literature* Chapel Hill, NC: University of North Carolina Press.

—— 1988. Reception Study: Ethnography and the Problems of Dispersed Audiences and Nomadic Subjects. *Cultural Studies* 2 (3): 359–76.

Ramanujan, A. K. 1974. Indian Poetics: An Overview. In *The Literatures of India: An Introduction*. E. C. Dimock, Jr., et al., eds., pp. 115–18. Chicago, IL: University of Chicago Press.

Rosaldo, Michelle Z. 1984. Towards an Anthropology of Self and Feeling. In *Culture Theory: Essays on Mind, Self, and Emotion*. R. Shweder and R. LeVine, eds., pp. 137–57. Cambridge: Cambridge University Press.

Russell, John 1991. Race and Reflexivity: The Black Other in Contemporary Japanese Mass Culture. *Cultural Anthropology* 6: 3–25.

Sangari, Kumkum and Sudesh Vaid, eds. 1989. Recasting Women: An Introduction. In *Recasting Women: Essays in Colonial History*. K. Sangari and S. Vaid, eds., pp. 1–26. New Delhi: Kali for Women.

Seiter, Ellen, Hans Borchers, Gabriele Kreutzner, and Eva-Maria Warth, eds. 1989. *Remote Control: Television, Audiences, and Cultural Power*. London: Routledge.

Singhal, Arvind and Everett M. Rogers 1989. *India's Information Revolution*. New Delhi: Sage.

Taylor, Ella 1989. *Prime-Time Families: Television Culture in Postwar America*. Berkeley: University of California Press.

Thomas, Rosie 1985. Indian Cinema: Pleasures and Popularity. *Screen* 26: 123–35.

Traube, Elizabeth G. 1989. Secrets of Success in Postmodern Society. *Cultural Anthropology* 4: 273–300.

Vasudevan, Ravi 1989. The Melodramatic Mode and the Commercial Hindi Cinema. *Screen* 30: 29–50.

Wadley, Susan S., ed. 1980. *The Powers of Tamil Women*. Syracuse, NY: Syracuse University Press.

Williams, Raymond 1974. *Television: Technology and Cultural Form*. New York: Schocken Books.

15

Defining Asian Femininity
Chinese viewers of Japanese TV dramas in Singapore

Elizabeth MacLachlan and Geok-lian Chua

Originally published in Koichi Iwabuchi (ed.), *Feeling Asian Modernities: Transnational Consumption of Japanese TV Dramas* (Hong Kong: Hong Kong University Press, 2004), 155–175.

The tendency of popular culture forms to spread to areas within geocultural – rather than simply regional – markets is commonly attributed to what Straubhaar calls "cultural proximity." Cultural proximity is the notion that cultural similarities, including "shared identity, gestures and non-verbal communication; what is considered funny or serious or even sacred; clothing styles; living patterns; climate influences and other relationships with the environment" are key elements in determining preference patterns of certain imported cultural forms over others (Straubhaar 1997, p. 291). With regard to the popularity of Japanese dramas in Asia, this notion is recalled in terms such as "shared sensibilities" (Iwao 1994, p. 74), "the East Asian psyche" (Honda 1994, p. 76), "cultural commonalities," and "common sensibility" (Igarashi 1997, p. 11).

Yet as Iwabuchi (2001, 2002) argues, the concept of cultural proximity does not necessarily explain the pleasures that viewers derive from popular culture forms of different origins. In the case of Japanese dramas in Taiwan, he points out that while Taiwanese viewers claim to watch Japanese programs for their cultural proximity, their comments reveal that what may be equally pleasurable about Japanese dramas is the presentation of ideas and attitudes that do not appear in local productions. Furthermore, viewers may reject programs from their own society because they refer to elements of their own cultural value system that they choose to reject. Ultimately he argues that what may be most significant about cultural proximity is not the sum of shared cultural features, but rather the "dynamic process" of "feeling 'real time' resonance in other non-western modernities while simultaneously recognizing difference" (2001, p. 73).

Central to Iwabuchi's argument is the notion that cultural proximity is based not on ontological cultural similarities between producer and audience, but rather an awareness of this similarity and its association as something pleasurable. Cultural proximity, as he puts it,

... is not something "out there," but needs to be subjectively identified and experienced by the audience. Thus cultural proximity is articulated when audiences identify cultural similarities in a specific programme and context ... (p. 58)

In reworking cultural proximity this way, Iwabuchi thus rescues the concept from cultural determinism and opens up avenues to theorize it not merely as a psychological process, but also as a political one as well. Following his lead, we will explore the notion that cultural proximity is not only selective, but also strategic in its articulation, a notion already hinted at in Iwabuchi's reminder to "pay attention to how certain cultural similarities are reworked to become attractive in a particular text" (ibid). Under what circumstances might it become advantageous to identify similarities *as* similarities, and how and among whom does this occur?

In this chapter, we look at the transnational consumption of Japanese dramas by Chinese Singaporean women, and how articulations of cultural proximity position viewers as women both within the text and against broader government discourses on femininity. We take as our starting point Ang's (1997) simple, but important observation that for a woman,

... many different and sometimes contradictory sets of femininities or feminine subject positions (ways of being a woman) are in principle available to her, although it is likely that she will be drawn to adopt some of those more than others. Certain modes of femininity are culturally more legitimate than others; and every woman knows subject positions she is best able to handle,

(Ang 1997, p. 163)

As we will show, Singaporean government discourses promote highly conservative and patriarchal ideals of femininity in contrast to the more liberal and sexually explicit portrayal of femininity in Japanese dramas. How women relate to Japanese dramas within this larger context of government policies and rhetoric, and where specifically they find points of identification is the subject of this chapter.

In this project, we interviewed twenty Singaporean women of Chinese ethnicity about their responses to an episode of a Japanese drama series that had recently aired in Singapore. These interviews were divided into four focus groups containing four to five individuals each. Half of the groups consisted of single women in their twenties (average age of 23) who are fans of the genre and had followed this particular drama when it ran on Singaporean television. The other half were made up of married mothers in their thirties and forties (average age of 42) who prefer local Chinese and Hong Kong dramas over Japanese ones. The focus groups began with a brief overview of the plot followed by a screening of the one-hour episode and a discussion of their impressions. The drama was shown in Japanese with Chinese subtitles and the interviews were conducted in English and Mandarin, the two main languages of Singapore.

Over Time and Japanese dramas in Singapore

The episode selected for screening was the tenth installment of *Over Time*, a program produced by Fuji Television and originally aired in Japan in January 1999. This

13-hour program was first broadcast in Singapore in March–June 2000 on Monday nights from 10:30 PM to 11:30 PM. It was re-broadcast less than six months later in November 2001 on Saturday mornings from 10:00 AM to 11:30 AM.[1] In both cases, the drama was dubbed into Mandarin.

Audience ratings for first-run Japanese dramas tend to hover between 4 and 5% of the nation's Chinese population, or about 160,000, to 200,000 viewers. These ratings are higher than that for American dramas which average 3.2% audience share, but fall well below the hugely popular local Chinese language dramas (averaging 20.3%) and Hong Kong dramas (averaging 18.6%).[2] Breaking it down into age groups, ratings for Japanese dramas are highest among those in the 15 to 24 age bracket, second highest for those in the 9 to 14 age bracket, and lowest for those in the 35 to 44 age bracket. In terms of ethnicity, viewers are overwhelmingly Chinese.[3] Judging by *Over Time*'s slightly above average rating of 3.4% on its second airing (ratings for the initial broadcast are unavailable; ratings for Japanese drama rebroadcasts averages 3.3%) this drama can be considered to be fairly typical of Japanese dramas in Singapore.

The local press have actually identified two distinct waves of Japanese drama popularity in Singapore.[4] The first occurred in the early 1980s when the government, in a campaign to get more Chinese Singaporeans to speak Mandarin, instituted a "Language Improvement Learning Programme Unit" to dub all Chinese dialect programs on television into Mandarin.[5] As part of this effort, Japanese dramas were brought in and dubbed into Mandarin. These programs enjoyed a brief period of popularity peaking in the mid 1980s when an average of eight new dramas were being shown each year on the government-run, free-to-air television station, but by the late 1980s interest subsided and Japanese dramas were dropped from Singaporean television entirely.

The second wave is part of a larger trend of Japanese drama popularity in Asia (see Iwabuchi 2002). It began in the early 1990s with the introduction of "(post-)trendy dramas" that targeted viewers in their teens and twenties, and were first broadcast in Singapore on free-to-air stations and then later on several cable channels. The popularity of these dramas has also been boosted by the easy availability of pirated copies on VCDs (video compact discs) that can be played on computers and are extremely cheap, a twelve-hour box-set costing as little as US$5. Today, an average of 28 new dramas a year are broadcast on Singaporean television with many more titles being circulated through pirate VCDs and cable reruns.

The plot and setting of *Over Time* is also typical of contemporary Japanese (post-)trendy dramas shown in Singapore. There are eight main characters (four male and four female), all in their 20s and 30s and living and working in present day Tokyo. The cast is led by Sorimachi Takashi and Esumi Makiko, two popular "idols" in Japan, and the background theme song is performed by the popular band, The Brilliant Green. Like most contemporary dramas, it is 12 episodes long.

The episode screened was number 10, the climax in a 12-part series. It was chosen because of the explicit manner in which it deals with issues of feminine sexuality through the trope of a love triangle between a heroine and her two lovers, namely

Natsuki (29), a beautiful office worker who is anxious about approaching 30 and is eager to find Mr. Right and settle into married life.

Kuga (35), a successful doctor and married father of one

Soichiro (25), a free-spirited freelance photographer who shares a house with Natsuki and two other female characters

In the previous episode, Kuga announced to Natsuki that he had decided to accept a research position in New York and would be leaving Japan shortly. He apologized to her for not consulting her on his decision and for giving her the wrong impression that he would marry her. In the beginning of this episode, one of Natsuki's roommates convinces her to go to the airport and see Kuga off. When Natsuki first sees Kuga she refuses to speak to him, but just before he passes through the gates, she shouts out to him, wishing him luck in his new life.

Upon returning, Natsuki is very upset. That night, she enters the bedroom of Soichiro seeking solace and the two end up making love. The following morning, Natsuki tells the two other roommates what happened and they convince her that she and Soichiro are not right for each other. She then approaches Soichiro, asking him to forget the incident in the interest of their friendship. Although he is secretly in love with her, he agrees.

Female characters like Natsuki are representative of those featured in (post-) trendy dramas. In this episode, Kuga's departure has left her emotionally vulnerable and her subsequent sexual relationship with Soichiro is seen as a moment of weakness. Yet despite her transgressions, Natsuki is neither berated for her behavior, nor made to bear sanctions of any kind. Instead, she is given the opportunity to reconsider her perceptions of love, sex, and marriage, and ultimately is presented with a chance to face Soichiro again and re-establish their status as friends. She is, in short, given the liberty to choose between two men. This treatment of female sexuality differs markedly from that outlined in official discourses of the Singaporean government.

Government policies and Singaporean femininity

To locate the image of a "proper" Singaporean woman, one needs look no further than the government policies and rhetoric surrounding marriage and childbirth. The bedrock of these is a social engineering policy to simultaneously encourage women of higher education to have more children while providing disincentives for those of lower education from having more than two. At the time of introduction in 1983, this package of incentives included tax breaks, medical insurance privileges, and guaranteed slots in top-ranking schools for the children of university graduate women, while disincentives for lesser educated working class women included higher charges at public hospital maternity wards after the second child and an offer of S$10,000 (US$5,725) to any working class woman who would undergo tubal ligation after a second child (Heng and Devan 1991, p. 200). While these plans met with controversy (with critics pointing out the uncomfortable coincidence that "graduate" women were overwhelmingly of the Chinese ethnic majority while working class women were of the Malay and Indian ethnic minorities), the policies remain intact today with remarkably little change.

Government policies on marriage are less controversial, but no less subtle in their aims. The Public Education Committee on Family, a government body which promotes family life, recently identified single women in their 30s as a source of concern because of their negative views on marriage.[6] In seeking to promote early unions and discourage divorce, the government has legislated a series of monetary inducements, including income tax exemptions for married couples, eligibility restrictions for singles over the age of 35 to purchase low cost government housing (there is no age requirement for married couples), and the withholding of welfare and working mother benefits such as maternity leave and tax deductions for the hiring of domestic help to mothers of "illegitimate" children. To assist those who would like to get married and cannot find spouses on their own, the government also runs its own matchmaking services, including recently, one run in conjunction with the National Library Board which links couples based on the books they like to read.

These policies are reinforced through criteria of media censorship that identifies certain aspects of non-reproductive (and over-reproductive) female sexuality as obscene, including images of uncovered female breasts, visual depictions of heterosexual intercourse, and virtually any reference to homosexual acts. Given the facts that (1) the high cost of censoring material is borne by the importer of media products (about US$170 per 12 part drama series according to one retailer), (2) costs increase with each deletion that is required, (3) each registered company is allowed only three submissions to the censorship board each week, and (4) programs which have been rated "G" by international ratings agencies are automatically exempt from this process, it makes economic sense for importers to promote "clean" material to their customers.

Underpinning these policies is the notion of a set of Asian Values that exists in opposition to Western Liberalism. This rhetoric, according to Chua (1997), was given new life in the early 1990s when a re-initiation of an Asian values national ideology was launched by the ruling People's Action Party government. In the lead up to this policy shift, Prime Minister Goh Chok Tong outlined his position in a speech before Parliament:

> Traditional Asian ideas of morality, duty, and society, which have sustained and guided us in the past, are giving way to a more Westernized, individualistic, and self-centered outlook on life. Not all foreign ideas and values are harmful. We cannot shut out the outside world, and turn inwards on ourselves. As Singapore develops, we must adapt our customs and traditions to suit new circumstances. However, the speed and extent of the changes to Singapore society is worrying. We cannot tell what dangers lie ahead, as we rapidly grow more Westernized.[7]

In the White Paper that followed, a list of new trends identified as being most harmful to Singapore included "alternate lifestyles, casual sexual relationships, and single parenthood" (1991, p. 3). Chua characterizes the strategy of political rhetoric as the juxtaposition of all the virtues of Asian society with

> . . . all the perceived ills of contemporary Western capitalist nations. Among these alleged social ills are relatively high rates of divorce, crime and unemployment,

and a high level of social welfarism which allegedly undermines the work ethic while generating expanded demands, based on claims of citizenship rights and entitlements, on the largess of the state . . .

(1997, p. 31)

In this official formulation, Japan comes out strongly on the side of Asia as it is "eulogized" for its ability to modernize without losing its traditions (Chua 2000, p. 148) and embraced as "the first Asian nation state which has attained culturally empowered Asian confidence" (Wee 1997, p. 42). Images of women in Japanese dramas such as *Over Time*, however, would seem to bear more similarities to stereotypes of sexually promiscuous Western women rather than traditional and chaste Asian women. How Chinese Singaporean female views of *Over Time* apprehend these contradictions is the subject of the following section.

Married mothers

Japanese dramas appeal predominantly to young people in Singapore. This is also what married women in the focus groups emphasized throughout their interviews. Japanese dramas center on themes which these women believe have no relevance to their lives, the "lovey dovey" stuff of "people who take it easy" rather than the more practical concerns of their daily lives such as earning money to feed the family, overseeing their children's education, and taking care of their husbands and aging parents. These women overwhelmingly prefer to watch Singaporean and Hong Kong dramas which they feel feature more high-paced action and down-to-earth characters, in contrast to Japanese dramas where story lines "tend to drag" and where "all the girls look alike." These Hong Kong dramas are also broadcast in the early evening, a time better suited for their viewing schedules than Japanese dramas, which are broadcast late at night or on Saturday mornings. Of the few who do occasionally watch Japanese dramas, they watch them on Saturday mornings with their children.

The married women's lack of interest in Japanese dramas was clearly evidenced by their disengagement with the program during the focus group screening. Throughout the program, women would poke fun at the text, feigning concern for the characters ("oh no, why did she say that!"), giggling over lines they felt were over-dramatized, and providing humorous commentary on the action. They distanced themselves further by taking the perspective of the program producers in answering questions about the plot.

Interviewer: Why is there a fuss about sex and getting married to the man you went to bed with?
Angelia: The objective is there!
Interviewer: What do you mean?
Angelia: The main point is there.
Interviewer: Whose main point?
Angelia: The people who wrote this! They probably thought, "Okay, for this episode we are going to show this."
Florence: She is asking you why.

Angelia: Why? Ask the producer. Maybe for the next episode they want to explore money problems.

Joyce: Maybe their viewership is mostly made up of young people so they need to capture and maintain that market. (focus group 1)

This unwillingness to engage with the dramas clearly derives from the women's subject position as both wives and mothers. The fact that Natsuki, the lead female character, is involved in an adulterous relationship with a married man Kuga not only prevents these women from empathizing with the protagonist's dilemma, but also serves as an unpleasant reminder of how vulnerable any marriage is to such outside threats. When asked to describe the main characters of the episode, viewers in focus group 2 refer to Natsuki as a "destroyer of other people's families," Kuga as a "worthless husband," and Soichiro as a "bum."

Throughout the discussions, women continuously refer to the one character that is not featured in the episode, the wife of the adulterous doctor. The absence of this character in the episode does not prevent the women from making an association between the wronged wife and themselves, as demonstrated in one telling moment when the conversation shifts from a discussion of the plot to an emotional retelling of the experience of a friend who found out her husband had a mistress.

Dorine: (talking about Natsuki) If you think that he might be married, then you should avoid this thing. Unless you are very sure that you love him and you want to destroy his family. I feel that a man, if he can divorce you for another woman, is not worthy of your love. One day, he may do the same thing to you.

Katherine: I thought this thing happened to your friend.

Dorine: Yes. (She describes how her friend caught her husband with another woman.) He said he did it only once. Let me ask you. If a man did it once, would there be a second time? Can any one of you guarantee that there will not be a second time? I feel that if a man does that to you, you have no need of him at all. (focus group 2)

The root of the problem in Japanese dramas, according to these women, is in the differences between Japanese and Chinese cultures. The Japanese lack "traditional values" and "are more open towards sex" (Katherine, focus group 2), in contrast to "our tradition from China [where] there should be no premarital sexual behavior" (Josephine, focus group 1). These differences are cause by a modernity in which the Japanese

> . . . want to be first in everything. Their technology is first, and this may affect them. They want to be advanced in everything . . . And unconsciously, it may influence their thinking, their attitude towards sex, their values.
>
> (Angelia, focus group 1)

Significantly, this modernity in Japan is seen as a phenomenon of Westernization.

Angelia: This actually comes from the West, is spread slowly from the West to the East.

Josephine: America started it first. Asia followed them because our customs and traditions are from China. This is really conservative, very traditional. And now the present generation is affected by the culture of the West. (focus group 1)

In some cases, it is even indistinguishable from Western practices.

Joyce: I have a wish. I wish these Japanese dramas would not encourage our youths to accept those one-night love relationships so easily, sleep with each other and that's it. This is very unacceptable.

Angelia: Actually, you can't say that. For those youngsters, they feel that "wow, this is what we call 'cool.' I am going to be like that too!"

Katherine: I wonder if this show would encourage those one-night stand kind of relationships.

Joyce: Yeah right. Because American youngsters are sometimes, you know, they have sex at such an early age! (focus group 2)

In light of these perceived differences in social values between Chinese culture on the one hand, and Japanese and Western cultures on the other, women in this group express concern over the possible negative effects Japanese dramas such as *Over Time* might have on their children. These effects include tempting youths to move out on their own and neglect their parents, encouraging young adults to postpone marriage and not have enough children, and creating an atmosphere of tolerance with regard to one-night stands and teenage sex. Their lack of engagement with Japanese dramas, in other words, results not only from the fact that as married mothers they do not personally relate to shows for and about single youths, but also from the fact that they fear single youths will be unduly influenced by these programs and, as a consequence, reject the values of traditional sexual morality.

Single women

The younger group of single women, all in their 20s, have markedly different readings and levels of engagement with the program. As fans of the genre, they pick up easily on the pace and logic of the story structure and approach the viewing process with seriousness and even intensity. All of them had seen the drama before, and some own a pirated copy on VCD.

These viewers all identify with the main character, Natsuki. This identification takes place at several levels. First, and most obvious, is the closeness in age and social situation of the viewers and characters. Both the viewers and the characters in the dramas are generally in their 20s, single, and working for a living. As such, single viewers believe that Natsuki is "like any of us here. Anyone walking in the street." While acknowledging that the lifestyles of the characters are a bit more luxurious than they could afford in their own lives ("How many of us can really rent our own apartments in Singapore?"), these viewers sympathize with her dilemmas, particularly her worries about approaching 30 without any good marriage prospects, and her confusion when her married lover leaves her.

Unlike their married counterparts, single women do not see Natsuki as a home wrecker, but as a victim of circumstance, someone who happened to fall in love with someone who happened to be married. Likewise, they do not condemn Kuga for the failure of his own marriage and see him as someone who could eventually offer Natsuki "the kind of commitment to stay together, to have the kind of relationship that could last" (Grace, focus group 3).

In discussing the moment in the episode when Natsuki initiates sex with Soichiro on the night Kuga leaves, viewers in this group do not condemn her for wantonness or weakness of character, but rather empathize with her confusion:

> At that point in time, actually, she herself is not very sure whether she really likes this guy. It was a really bad night and it's [sic] like so confused. Everything was just [sic], she just totally lost her confidence.
>
> (Kaslin, focus group 3)

> Such things can happen anywhere in this world. It's just that it is filmed in Japan and the characters are Japanese. But when you are talking about love, sex, and marriage, it happens anywhere in the world where someone, out of a situation, has sex with someone else on a fateful night and then thinks about it and, you know, wonders, "Why did I do it?"
>
> (Lorraine, focus group 4)

> When it comes to affairs of the heart, indecision is inevitable in everyone. I can safely say that. Unless you are one of those very independent people, unless you are the kind that knows what you want, that you are very sure who your partner is going to be, then I think that indecisiveness would be very natural. This is how I see Natsuki's position.
>
> (Joyce, focus group 4)

For these single female viewers, the notion of romance is central to their enjoyment of Japanese dramas. These programs allow viewers to give themselves up in emotional abandonment to feelings of love without regard for consequences or practical concerns.

> I remember this guy who said a century ago that modern man would worship the goddess of getting on. And I think this is still very real today. Everybody's just worried about getting on with life and nobody is really preoccupied with love. That's why when we watch all these shows, we tend to get attracted by it because we know that it is this kind of vicarious experience. You know, I have never experienced it in real life, so I want to experience it in a "reel life" kind of thing.
>
> (Grace, focus group 4)

> I really enjoy watching Japanese shows because I always find that – wow! – they really love each other! They go crazy for each other, they would die for each other.

But in real life I do not really see it this way. And I think one of the reasons why they really attract me is because I do not see it in my life. I want to have that experience somewhere, and this is why I get addicted to this type of show. I don't see friends around me who are going through this as well, so I watch it in a show, in a romantic fairy tale show that doesn't happen to me.

(Loraine, focus group 4)

Integral to this notion of romance is the quality of "innocence," in which expressions of love are made subtly and without pretense. Japanese dramas, according to single viewers, excel in depictions of such scenes of romance because of the qualities inherent in the Japanese language itself, which favors indirect and vague styles of communication, in contrast to those found in romances in American and Singaporean contexts.[8]

Joyce: In an American setting or even a Singaporean setting, everyone would just whisper sweet nothings. And, you know, stuff like that, very direct messages of love. But in Japanese culture, the way they speak, they don't speak very directly. They just have this unique way of expressing themselves.
Janice: It is quite innocent.
Joyce: Yes, very innocent. And when they go out, they sit in the park and they just talk. They try to find out how each other feels. Whereas in other cultures, they say "Oh, I am feeling this way," or "I am feeling that way." They are very direct. They just express how they feel. It is just different I think, very romantic. That's why such romanticism cannot be found in the local scene. (focus group 4)

Viewers contrast this notion of Japanese romance with experiences in their own lives where pragmatism operates as the prevailing social norm. When asked how the drama would change if Singaporean characters were substituted in for Japanese ones, single viewers claim that the stories would appear "100% fake," noting that Singaporeans are simply too practical to indulge in the vagaries of uncertain love.

Joyce: Let's say a Singaporean lady, I think she would have gone to bed with that man, and the two of them would just treat it as if nothing had ever happened.
Janice: Yes.
Joyce: They will just treat it as if nothing had ever happened the next day. They won't kick up a big fuss like trying to think "what did we do?" I mean, they would just chuck it aside and move on with life.
Janice: I think Singaporeans are very pragmatic. . . . We are not as romantic as they are and I don't think we have time for romance either. So I don't think there will be that kind of romantic indecisiveness kind of thing. I think we are very pragmatic, and if she slept with him, then okay, you know, but that's over, just move on, no point in mulling over the whole issue. (focus group 4)

The notion of a Japanese-style romance as innocent is further developed through its differentiation from marriage. Viewers see Natsuki's decision to marry Kuga, the doctor, over Soichiro, the photographer, as a choice of "stability over love." While many prefer the character of Soichiro, most feel that choice of Kuga makes sense in the drama as he is more stable and able to provide Natsuki with a more secure foundation. Again, this idea is articulated through its contrast with Western dramas.

> For American [dramas] it's more skewed towards marrying the person you love. Because to them, marriage is not only once. It's like first marriage, second marriage, third marriage, that kind of thing . . . To an Asian, the decision making process actually goes through very different sets of criteria because it's like for an Asian, once I make this decision, all of us would first assume that it must last throughout the whole life. It's an irreversible thing.
>
> (Kaslin, focus group 3)

Viewers thus see Natsuki's choice as a rational and responsible one – "if you are talking about a stable relationship, a marriage commitment, Kuga is the man" (Grace, focus group 4); "she is making a choice of responsibility and not really of love" (Lorraine, focus group 4); "there are a lot of people who marry the person they are not necessarily in love with" (Kaslin, focus group 3) – and in doing so place Natsuki firmly in the realm of "Asian" reality as opposed to an American fairy tale of romance and happily-ever-after.

In discussing sex, love, and marriage in contemporary Singaporean society, single women agree with their married counterparts that foreign television programs have played a central role in promoting the more liberal attitudes that prevail among the younger generation. Yet while married women paint a bleak picture of the relationships between Japanese television dramas and the moral decline of contemporary Singaporean youths, single women see these changes as a positive response to globalization rather than a negative sign of losing Asian morality.

> I think that the change is being led by globalization. We are beginning to develop as well, and there are many influences and exchanges of values with the West. The world is basically very intertwined now, there is a lot of exchange of values and ideas, and Asia as a whole is opening up. I think people are beginning to question their own values, to adopt other people's values and systems as well. So I think that's where the change comes from.
>
> (Janice, focus group 4)

With regard to sex, single women see relaxed attitudes towards premarital or "casual" sex not as an outright rejection of traditional values, but rather as a consequence of youthful curiosity and naïve emotions in which "teens may be falling in love with love, and not falling in love with their partners" (Angelia, focus group 3). They see the "casual attitudes" and "general acceptance towards premarital sex" in Western societies not as a lack of morality, but rather as a difference of moral judgment. And when comparing themselves with other Asian countries, a few even acknowledge the possibility that it may be that Singapore that is the exception in its highly conservative attitudes towards sex.

Seriously, if you look at Hong Kong or Taiwan, they are actually very open about [sex]. I guess it is their media exposure. In Singapore we are in a very controlled environment. So a lot of people in our generation still feel very conservative towards – not taking this casual attitude towards – sex. If you watch cable, or if you look at some of the Taiwanese, Hong Kongers, Japanese, and Koreans, they are actually very open. It's only the Singaporeans who are different.

(Kaslin, focus group 3)

Change in the attitudes of the younger generation towards sex, love, and marriage, according to single viewers, is not a matter of blind acceptance of Western values, but rather the thoughtful process of adapting individual values to new conditions. Single viewers talked about the challenge of "trying to find a balance" between Western and Asian ideals (Yew Mae, focus group 3); letting your own beliefs and values "guard your choices and the decisions you make" (Janice, focus group 4); and "accepting the [behavior of others] which doesn't necessarily mean having to agree with what they are doing" (Lorraine, focus group 4).

Yet despite the acceptance, even endorsement, of more open attitudes towards sex and marriage in Singapore, every one of the single informants declared that if put in the same place as the heroine, she would have responded differently. In particular, single viewers said they would have responded differently from Natsuki in (1) having sex with her best friend Soichiro when she was not sure about her feelings for him, and (2) continuing a relationship with Kuga even after she found out he was married.

In terms of Natsuki sleeping with her best friend, Soichiro, the women felt in varying degrees that it was wrong to treat sex so lightly. Comments ranged from "No casual sex!" (Angelia, focus group 3), and "I wouldn't go into another relationship with Soichiro so fast and have premarital sex with him" (Yew Mae, focus group 3), to the less conclusive "I think I might have kissed him but wouldn't have slept with him" (Janice, focus group 4) and "it goes against what I would rationally do, but then human nature is weak" (Grace, focus group 4).

As for the relationship with Kuga, single viewers agreed that it was wrong to carry on the relationship once it became apparent that he was married. While acknowledging the difficulty of leaving a man with whom they had already fallen in love, especially when "he was only dragging [his marriage] on because of his daughter" (Joyce, focus group 4), they were unanimous in their resolve never to knowingly commit adultery themselves.

Cultural proximity and Singaporean femininities

Singaporean government discourses promoting marriage and childbirth divide women by conferring status to those who have conformed to state-set ideals (i.e. married mothers) and identifying as potentially problematic those who have not (i.e. single adults). Responses to Japanese dramas by women from both these groups reflect the different subjectivities produced through these government discourses. Married women overwhelmingly reject Japanese dramas as too Western in their open attitudes toward casual, pre- and extramarital sex, and express concern over the potential for dramas like these to corrupt the youths of Singapore today. They contrast these dramas to the more culturally proximate Chinese productions from Hong Kong, Taiwan, and Singapore, which teach traditional and pro-family values such as "filial piety," "sexual restraint," and "marital fidelity" and consequently secure their social status as married mothers.

Single viewers see Japanese dramas in terms of the resonance these programs have with their own personal experiences, and it is largely the fact that these dramas are Asian and *not* Western that makes them so enticing. At one level, this articulation of cultural proximity vis-à-vis a shared Asian culture is purely pragmatic: by identifying these dramas as Asian, single women protect themselves from criticism that these programs are conveyors of Western liberalism. At another level, the identification of particular features of Japanese dramas as Asian points to profoundly different perspectives of how live in Singapore should be experienced. In comparison to married women, single viewers see lifestyles portrayed in Japanese dramas as an Asian alternative to the lives they experience in Singapore as women who have yet to meet their social obligations to the state. Japanese dramas, through their focus on the romantic and sexual intrigues of young adults provide a forum for Singaporean women to live vicariously in an "Asian" society without "Asian values" of patriarchy and social expectations of pragmatism that are strongly emphasized in Singaporean discourses. Japanese dramas, in other words, give pleasure not simply because they allow women to experience the feelings of giving into sexual temptation without suffering any social consequences, but also because they give recognition to the difficulty and self-sacrifice that *not* giving into temptation requires in real life! By thus laying bare the challenges of sexual abstinence – the difficulty of resisting temptation and pressure, the ease in which one can accidentally fall for the wrong man – Japanese dramas acknowledge the commitment to remain "traditional" in a globalizing and Westernizing world is not an easy one. In contrast to married viewers who see liberal sexual practices as a lack of "proper" moral education and discipline, single female viewers see sexual abstinence as a matter of extreme self-discipline and individual commitment. These differences are most clearly articulated in the attitudes towards the Japanese dramas themselves. Where married viewers voice concern over the negative messages in the drama and the need for government authorities to intervene in programming through the monitoring of content, the single viewers value the vicarious pleasures engaging in sexual and romantic relationships precisely because they maintain they would not do such things in real life.

If the pleasures derived from watching Japanese dramas by single viewers imply a rejection, then it is not a rejection of "Asian values" concerning feminine chastity, but of the heavy-handed manner in which they are implemented. Political appeals to "Asian traditions," implying that, among other things, female chastity is a natural element of Asian society, deny the possibility that refraining from sex might require discipline, determination, and a suppression of biological urges. Government economic policies regulating marriage and childbirth further devalue the self-control needed for sexual abstinence outside marriage by implying that the exchange of money for "good behavior" is an equal and legitimate one. By embracing Japanese dramas as Asian, single female viewers remind themselves and others that feminine sexuality is a complicated and intensely private matter, and not simply a problem that can be solved through an education of proper and morally accepted behavior befitting an "Asian" woman, or bartered for with monetary inducements and disincentives.

Notes

1 Broadcasts of Japanese dramas are typically shown in one-hour slots during their first run and 90-minute slots during reruns.
2 These statistics provided by Philip Jones at Taylor Nelson Sofres and reflect average ratings for dramas shown in 2001–2.
3 This is not surprising given the fact that three-quarters of the island's population identifies itself as Chinese. Official statistics published in the 2000 report of the Singapore Department of Statistics break down the ethnic groupings in Singapore into the following: 76.8% Chinese, 13.9% Malay, 7.9% Indian, and 1.4% other.
4 "Complete Guide to Japanese Television Dramas," *I-weekly*, No. 114, 8–15 January, 2000; "God, Give Me More Japanese Television Dramas!" *Lianhe Zaobao*, 20 August 2000; "Ha de ke shi zhen de ri ben?" (Is this craze over an authentic Japan?), *Lianhe Zaobao*, No. 10, August 2000; "You jian dong feng cui" (The Eastern trend is in again), *Lianhe Zaobao*, 30 December 2000.
5 "TV Dubbing Team Aims to Promote Use of Mandarin," *The Straits Times*, 20 July 1982.
6 Results of a 2001 survey of over 1000 Singaporeans reveal that single women in their 30s are "least likely to think that marrying and having children is better than staying single." Other attitudes identified as problematic are increased tolerance toward homosexuality, divorce, and cohabitation. "Single Women? And in Your 30s? Oh Dear!" Wong Sher Maine and Sim Chi Yin, *The Straits Times*, 27 September 2002.
7 *White Chapter on Shared Values*. Presented to Parliament by Command of the President of the Republic of Singapore, 2 January 1991.
8 Todd Gitlin's description of the English language provides an interesting contrast to viewers' impressions of Japanese. "American English in particular is pungent, informal, absorptive, evolving, precise when called upon to be precise, transferable between written and verbal forms, lacking in sharp distinctions between 'high' and 'low' forms, and all in all, well adapted for slogans, headlines, comic strips, song lyrics, jingles, slang dubbing, and other standard features of popular culture. English is in a word, the most torrential language" (2001, p. 186).

References

Ang, Ien. "Melodramatic Identifications: Television Fiction and Women's Fantasy." In *Feminist Television Criticism: A Reader*, edited by C. Brunsdon, J. D'Acci, and L. Spigel. Oxford: Clarendon Press, 1997.
Chua, Beng-Huat. "Where Got Japanese Influence in Singapore!" In *Japan in Singapore: Cultural Occurrences and Cultural Flows*, edited by E. Ben-Ari and J. Clammer. Surrey: Curzon, 2000.
—— "Between Economy and Race: the Asianization of Singapore." In *Space, Culture and*

Power: New Identities in Globalizing Cities, edited by A. Oncu and P. Weyland. London: Zed Books, 1997.

Gitlin, Todd. *Media Unlimited: How the Torrent of Images and Sounds Overwhelms Our Lives.* New York: Henry Holt and Company, 2001.

Heng, Geraldine and Devan, Janandas. "State Fatherhood: The Politics of Nationalism, Sexuality, and Race in Singapore." In *Nationalisms and Sexualities*, edited by A. Parker, M. Russo, D. Sommer, and P. Yaeger. New York: Routledge, 1991.

Honda, Shiro. "East Asia's Middle Class Tunes in to Today's Japan." *Japan Echo* 21, 4 (1994): 74–9.

Igarashi, Akio. "From Americanization to 'Japanization' in East Asia!?" *The Journal of Pacific Asia* 4(1997): 3–20.

Iwabuchi, Koichi. *Recentering Globalization: Popular Culture and Japanese Transnationalism.* Durham: Duke University Press, 2002.

—— "Becoming 'Culturally Proximate': The A/Scent of Japanese Idol Dramas in Taiwan." In *Asian Media Productions*, edited by B. Moeran. Surrey: Curzon, 2001.

Iwao, Sumiko. "Popular Culture Goes Regional." *Japan Echo* 21, 4(1994): 4.

Straubhaar, Joseph D. "Distinguishing the Global, Regional and National Levels of World Television." In *Media in Global Context: A Reader*, edited by A. Sreberny-Mohammadi, D. Winseck, J. McKenna and O. Boyd-Barnett. New York: Edward Arnold, 1997.

Wee, C. J. W.-L. "Buying Japan: Singapore, Japan, and an 'East Asian' Modernity," *The Journal of Pacific Asia* 4(1997): 21–46.

White Paper on Shared Values. Presented to Parliament by Command of The President of the Republic of Singapore, 2 January 1991. Singapore: Singapore National Printers.

16

The Globalization of Gender
Ally McBeal in post-socialist Slovenia

Ksenija Vidmar-Horvat

Originally published in the *European Journal of Cultural Studies*,
8:2 (2005): 239–255.

This article examines the American TV series *Ally McBeal* and its reception in post-socialist Slovenia. During the past few years, the series has generated substantial interest among critics. Much of the interest has been rooted in the programme's innovative approach to TV drama and its unique representational techniques, which even led some to compare David Kelly's commercial product to David Lynch's *Twin Peaks* and Dennis Potter's *The Singing Detective*, a masterpiece of television work (Nochimson, 2000: 26–7). Simultaneously, the positioning of the young, attractive and professionally successful lawyer as the lead character has inspired critical inspection of the series' representations of the contemporary 'new woman'. Because the series' target audience has been defined as the '18–34 female market', one key concern regards how the programme's politics of representation relates to and articulates the social experiences of this generation of women. Because the generation has been described also as having 'grown up taking for granted the feminist victories won by their mothers and thus for whom feminism exists at the level of popular common sense rather than at the level of theoretical abstraction' (Moseley and Read, 2002: 238), inadvertently, the construction of women's 'post-feminist' identity triggers questions regarding the programme's relation to the feminist agenda (Dow, 2002; Dubrofsky, 2002; Kim, 2001; Moseley and Read, 2002). In this article, this second line of enquiry will be chosen as a starting point for an examination of Ally McBeal as a post-feminist female television character. Also, it will look at possible shifts in the meaning of post-feminism when the series' audiences are young college women in post-socialist Slovenia.

As a post-feminist character, no doubt Ally offers a fruitful terrain for inspecting television's relationship with feminism and, more broadly, the popular politics of remembering feminism. However, the global success of the series also puts into question the ideologically exclusive equation between the series' politics of representation and the implied western female spectator (Cooper, 2001) involved in a cultural war over the feminist past. A different, non-western-oriented analysis might indeed give rise to a different set of meanings than the prevailing literature suggests. In view of recent ethnographic media scholarship, it can be argued that the success of the programme cannot be explained properly without considering local social and political histories of gender, which define structures of identification for the audiences and help to create their worlds of pleasure (Ang, 1996). As will be argued within the limited scope of this article, the global popularity of the series and its post-feminist character can be illustrated by the fact that it provides a global cultural site which allows local audiences, and women's audiences in particular, to imagine and re-imagine *their own* social biographies. As these biographies in many ways depart from western feminist politics and history, they both deploy and contest the meaning of post-feminism in its current, commercial televisual discursive form.

My own interest in the meaning of global media idols such as Ally McBeal arose from the classroom experience. In the 2000/2001 sociology of culture class, we spent some time discussing the cultural impact of global media products and female icons in particular. By then, I had become an avid viewer of *Ally McBeal* and formed my own 'way of seeing', which was based primarily on questioning the ideological effect of the lead character and her alleged 'progressiveness' in terms of gender and sexual politics. However, the debate with the students in which I presented Ally as a case revealed that they had developed different views of the programme. Intrigued by the difference, I asked them to spend some more time on the issue by answering a short question-naire: 49 first- and second-year undergraduate sociology students (40 female and nine male) responded. The responses obtained cast an interesting light on the dynamic interplay of cultural products and local audiences as they form the imagined, global media community. Both pedagogically and analytically, watching *Ally McBeal* in post-socialist Slovenia calls for reconsideration of the construction of meaning of global ideals of femininity and their involvement in local social histories of gender and sexual conflicts.

The comic female and historical constructions of femininity

Critics emphasize that as a televisual character, Ally McBeal addresses an emergent market niche of professional, middle- and upper-middle-class (white) women,

> who actually like working, who have discovered a job can be both absorbing and worthwhile, who feel their own salary is something to be treasured and who, although defining themselves through their jobs, are not excluding men from their lives.
>
> (Slaughter, quoted in Gough-Yates, 2003: 89)

Consequently, they see her arrival as a positive turn in the politics of representation of women in commercial media: 'One can't expect total satisfaction, yet issues may get presented, and more sympathetically, than elsewhere – for example, in mainstream cinema' (Rapping, quoted in Margolis, 2000). Joan Gershen Marek observes along similar lines that since 'women now account for about one half of the new lawyers in the United States', the mere fact that Ally is represented as a professional woman who is not 'defined by [her] relationship to a man', suggests a novel approach to portraying professional women, which can be 'a positive thing for both sexes' (Marek, 1999).

As a commercial medium, television relies on rationalization of its success by taking into account its target audiences (Ang, 1991). Consequently, TV programmes cannot ignore audiences and their lifeworld experiences. Yet, to assume a simple reflective mode of the series, mirroring the worlds of a social group or generation of women, as this body of work does, risks missing the complex work of television as a fictional medium. As Ella Taylor (1989: 3) writes, 'Television comments upon and orders, rather than reflects, experience, highlighting public concerns and cultural shifts'. By the same token, it can be argued that the contemporary, post-feminist 'new woman' has addressed the 'fortunate minority of women' as much as it has constructed the 'symbolic of femininity' (Gough-Yates, 2003: 38); that is, it has provided a visual – narrative field of selection, exclusion and repression of other, alternative forms of femininity. In other words, female characters on television play a role in both representing and constructing the norms and ideals of contemporary femininity. The latter is not arrived at arbitrarily but in relation to the governing power maps of sexual and gender relations.

The double process of reflection–construction of femininity was at work prior to Ally McBeal's arrival. Ally's predecessors, a 'long line of strong heroines' (as the promotional booklet to the three-volume video series calls them), attest to television's simultaneous ability to speak to real women while channelling their desires towards socially accepted gendered positions. Two of them, Lucy Ricardo of *I Love Lucy* and Mary Richards of *The Mary Tyler Moore Show*, which have been considered by the industry to be crucial to the character's genealogy, are the most popular and paradigmatic cases to observe. Based on her ambition to become a star, Lucy's plots could be seen as reflections of postwar women's audiences condemned to 'domestic containment'. 'Weekly, for six years, [Lucy] accepted domesticity, only to try to escape again the next week' (Mellencamp, 1986: 88). However, as Patricia Mellencamp (1986: 90) writes, granting a woman the place of the performative winner could not secure her escape from the 'confinement and the tolerance of kindly father[s]'. Finding herself in the new work environment, the comic female of the 1970s represented the single woman as a 'content individual who did not need a heterosexual partner to define her identity' (Lotz, 2001: 107); but she had to trade her newly-gained independence for being positioned back in the patriarchal scenario of domestic entrapment – this time in the symbolic form of the family at work.

In contrast to Mary Richards, who was 'situated as both daughter and mother in the show's 'family' of co-workers' (Lotz, 2001: 107), in *Ally McBeal* a woman's substitution of family for career is replaced by searching for a symbiosis between career and personal life. Personal and professional lives become integrated and inseparable:

> She can be an excellent lawyer in court – not quite as outrageous as her boss Cage, infinitely superior to her boss Fish – but her legal arguments almost invariably serve as a lens on her private life or on romance, her personal cause even when the romance in question doesn't concern her.
>
> (Appelo, 1999: 11)

Most importantly, as she progresses in the male world, Ally does not try to imitate the masculine mode of practising law but insists on feminine qualities, combining sensitivity with sexuality, care with availability. 'Ally is a living fictional proof that, in our day, a female character can wear a miniskirt and still play on the boys' field' (Appelo, 1999: 4). In the series, femininity becomes an identity to be valued, not repressed.

It is the series' rehabilitation of femininity which presents an upfront difficulty for most of the feminist critique. *Ally McBeal* openly celebrates femininity but proposes it in a sexual rather than political form. L.S. Kim (2001) has argued that post-feminist sexual liberation has been an act of masquerade based on self-objectification. Self-objectification, she writes, 'does not necessarily achieve subjectivity, and it can be a false freedom' (2001: 324). Kim's view can be supported further by looking at Ally's sexuality, which is expressed in the regressive form of a growing female adolescent rather than that of a mature woman. Her bodily transformations – from the shrunken pose in the chair to the inflated breasts or lips – visually revisit the time of adolescence which, as we know from the character's family biography (concerning especially her parents' divorce), is operative in Ally's inability to form a lasting intimate relationship (Margolis, 2000). In contrast, in Lucy's time, the body of the adolescent fairytale character was transfigured to comment on postwar women's flight from domesticity (Vidmar, 1995). The 1950s cultural representation of the adolescent girl articulated women's resistance to social confinements of domesticity and motherhood, whereas the 1990s comic female resists abandoning adolescence. She remains a young girl in the symbolic, corporate world of the tolerant fathers.

Last but not least, the restoration of femininity unfolds within a male-dominated cultural field. For example, Moseley and Read find evidence of the series' rehabilitation of femininity in representation of Ally's subjectivity by allowing the viewer access to her emotions. It is interesting that they refer to what Lydia Curti has called 'famous window scenery'. The visual expression of her inner thoughts and feelings is given to us 'as she stands at her office window, looking out over the city – a position to which the series returns her repeatedly' (Moseley and Read, 2002: 243). The window is a classic Hollywood reference, a culturally specific generic code, which stands as a 'fundamental icon of melodrama, with its obvious reference to prison, closure, victimization' (Curti, 1992: 147). It prefigures the woman's social place as a spectator '*outside* the "real" arena of social relations and power, with all the connotations of passivity, waiting, and watching normally attached to the function of spectatorship' (Doane, 1987: 78; emphasis in original). While 1990s television rehabilitates the comic woman's inner, intimate worlds by making them visible, it also subjects them to the masculine visual codes of power and control.

Taken together, all three sites of construction of femininity are a justifiable object of critique. Above all, they put into question the narrative of progress in the politics of representation of women in mass media in the past few decades.

Post-feminist reinvention of feminism

From the perspective of the scholars who have examined the programme's construction of post-feminist femininity, the series becomes most problematic at the point where it constructs a narrative of femininity in the (feminist) past. Moseley and Read find an explanation for the programme's appeal in the fact that it attempts to reconcile 'feminist desires' with 'feminine desires' (Moseley and Read, 2002: 238). The reconciliation suggests, however, that the two were essentially exclusive in the past and that it is only within post-feminist discourse that the act of merging can be complete. The proposition legitimates the post-feminist politics of identity. In so doing, it also fabricates a certain memory of feminism.

The process of fabrication is evident in the construction of Ally's 'glorified single status'. In his review of the urban comedy genre, Michael Tueth has described its universe as having been 'about the risk and the discomfort of alternatives. It is not a rush toward a monolithic, mainstream ideal, but a tumbling convergence of various channels of information and values' (Tueth, 2000: 107). Ally's character resonates this new, postmodern politics of identity by occupying simultaneously different, often exclusive subject positions:

> Women should be married. Society drills it into us. Smart people should have careers. Society drills it into us that women should have children and mothers should stay at home. And society condemns the working mother that doesn't stay at home. What chance do you really have when society keeps drilling us? We can change it, Renée. Society is made up of more women than men and if women really wanted to change society, they could do.
>
> I plan to change it. I just want to get married first.
>
> (*Ally McBeal*, 'Silver Bells')

Marketed as 'McBealisms', the statements such as the ones above form the multivocal and polysemantic universe which, as aforementioned, has attracted so much critical acclaim for the show. Moreover, Ally entertains the idea of the lack of closure on identity, understanding – not unlike women's readers of popular romances (Radway, 1986) – that the pleasure of fulfilment is in anticipating, not reaching the end. As Ally reveals at the end of the first episode:

> The real truth is that I probably don't wanna be too happy or content, because then what? . . . I actually like the quest, the search. That's the fun – the more lost you are, the more you have to look forward to . . . What do you know? I'm having a great time and I don't even know it.
>
> (*Ally McBeal*, 'Pilot')

As the series progresses, however, the open-ended structure of a woman's fantasy turns out to be a claustrophobic scenario. Singlehood does not liberate Ally, but makes her a prisoner of past choices, formulated in the post-feminist fashion as the question, as Kim has put it, 'What's a girl to do?' (Kim, 2001: 319).

'So, here I am – the victim of my own choices,' Ally states in the opening episode. The choice to which she is referring concerns the decision to study law at Harvard after she had just broken up with her sweetheart Billy, who enrolled at Princeton. Although the opening scene of the first episode reveals that Ally has passed the exam which Billy has not, and therefore posits women as intellectually superior, it is none-theless played out against a backdrop of a woman's drama or, better still, of the drama of womanhood in patriarchy: of the irreconcilable marriage between romance and career in a woman's life. Throughout the series, the comic side of the character soothes this conflict. It also inscribes an ironic distance which, in contrast to Lucy's gesture of self-ridicule, is oriented toward the extra-diegetic space of the feminist spectator.

Ally's choice implies a feminist gesture, although with a new meaning. Rachel Dubrofsky has argued that, as a television character, Ally performs a reactionary, post-feminist gesture of aestheticization of the political; that is, in Rayna Rapp's words, 'the reduction of feminist *social* goals to individual "lifestyles" ' (quoted in Dubrofsky, 2002: 278; emphasis in original). Moreover, Dubrofsky laments:

> [N]ot only is the show not political, it actually encourages political stasis and reinforces and reinscribes the present political structures – the very same ones that cause Ally so many problems . . . by diverting our attention away from these back to the personal.
>
> (2002: 279)

The 'lifestyle feminism' is evident when, for example, Ally states: 'The definition of the nuclear family is constantly evolving. The time is coming. It has to start some-where. And it would have to start with me' – making feminist politics looking like a commodity that can be purchased and abandoned at will.

As a post-feminist comic character, Ally never reflects upon the feminist history which has secured her social privileges as a white, middle-class, educated woman, but she does engage in dialogue with feminism when her personal happiness is at stake. As Dow (2002: 263) writes, an implied assumption of the series' discourse is that 'it is feminism that has landed women like Ally in their predicament – educated and professionally successful, yet loveless and childless'. Dow goes on to argue that 'feminism has never promised women happiness – only justice' (2002: 263). Yet the rehistorization of feminist politics is crucial to the process of consolidation of post-feminist ideology. By merging women's social gains with the personal agenda of (sexual) liberation, post-feminist memory obliterates the interconnectedness and codependency of both, yet paradoxically falls into its own trap when blaming feminist restructuring of the sexual relations and politics of gender for not finding personal fulfilment.

The series' post-feminist politics of representation present a problem of inter-pretation. As Moseley and Read have suggested, it can be seen as a successful drama-tization of the coming together of 'traditional feminist values with a historically and materially different experience of being young and female' (Moseley and Read, 2002: 240) in the age of post-feminism. It can also be observed as it reconstructs the popular memory of feminism as a means to force hegemonic interpretive lenses on women's audiences and their social experiences. In either case, this body of critical work suggests that an important part of the meaning of the series resides in the troubling relationship between femininity, feminism and post-feminism.

Post-feminism and transitional fantasies

The problematic treatment of feminism by the series and its sexual and gender polit-ics is a legitimate cause of concern for the critical western viewer who has lived through both phases: second-wave feminism and its aftermath. In the global context this culturally specific, albeit subtle televisual battle over the legacy of feminism, acquires a different meaning. In post-socialist transition societies, which have all wit-nessed women's resistance to western feminism, certainly this can be argued to be the case. Jacqueline Andall (2003: 6) explains the rejection of feminist politics on the grounds of the 'difficulties that Eastern Europeans have experienced in articulating their difference to Western feminism'. The resistance may also have to do with a memory, this time of the socialist, rather than the feminist, past.

The image of Ally McBeal was first used in my sociology of culture class to introduce a debate about the relationship between media images of independent and autonomous women, women's actual social experiences and global consumerism. It was only after I had heard consenting voices towards Ally's picture, suggesting that she presents a positive novelty compared to the politics and practices of representa-tion in Slovene past and present media, that I became intrigued. In the questionnaire which followed this classroom experience, I therefore decided to ask the students openly about the social portrait of Ally McBeal; whom they thought she represented; how her image compared to cultural representations of women in Slovenia; and, under the title 'Ally and Feminism', what in their opinion were the local social effects of global female icons like her.

The students described Ally in such contradictory terms as 'romantic, confused, with a wild imagination', 'confused, searching for her man, which she cannot find because of her over-idealized expectations'. Further, she was seen as 'weird, hyster-ical, sometimes pathetic, sometimes likeable', but also as 'self-confident, daring, feminized but human, vulnerable, caught up in fantasies (like all of us)'. Some emphasized the character's strength of being professionally 'successful, self-confident and independent', while others pointed out her emotional instabilities and weaknesses and, interestingly in one response, overdependency on men and their paying attention to her. It was this latter aspect that in one student's mind made Ally an improper role model to be adopted by Slovene audiences. A female student supported the first one's view that she could be a role model, 'considering her economic independence and professional success, but harder when taking into account her emotional intelligence'. As another contradicted, it was a nice change for the lead role to be 'given to a woman who is financially independent and, although anorexic, beautiful and smart'.

Notwithstanding conflicting views of the meaning of the character's emotional (in)stability, Ally was described almost unanimously as the embodiment of the new social group (or class) of career women. Although some were suspicious of Ally as a caricature, there seemed to be a shared consensus that she represented the social advancement of women in the West (especially the United States) and imprinted a progressive chapter in the social history of women's emancipation in general. 'The series tries to show a typical representation of the western generation of women', a student wrote. Another agreed: '[Ally] is representative of a growing number of emancipated women who in the West are becoming more and more independent.'

Interestingly, however, it was only in one response that a student observed a paradox, that this new western figure 'still nurtures idealized visions of the traditional woman, especially in relation to the family'.

When asked about the social effects of the 'new woman' in Slovenia, multiple investments in the character were laid out. 'This is one of the few series (foreign, there are no Slovene ones) that show the emancipation of women', a female student wrote. Another saw in Ally's figure an incentive for women to 'dare to do more for themselves'. Two other girls wrote that Ally carried the promise of having 'a positive effect on stereotypes about women who are supposed to be housewives and take care of the family. Women would at least contemplate their fate', and that Ally would 'help to improve the social position of women in Slovenia'. These responses clearly articulate a belief in the liberating effect of the character, even when the series' politics of representation was perceived in an antagonistic sense as a threat:

> [Ally] increasingly corresponds to the figure of a career woman who does not care or have time for her family; more important to her are professional success, career . . . Slovene women have resented these influences so far, but the growing emancipation of women is putting pressure on the value of a career.

In this student's view, Ally-like characters 'would create growing tensions between the sexes, which could cause the crisis of the family as the basic social unit'.

A recurring theme was the character's challenge to the 'traditional', 'conservative' and 'stereotypical' cultural depictions of womanhood. The traditional clearly signified the local culture, while the progressive was identified with the West. 'Traditional is not the only proper way' as far as representing women is concerned, a student responded to the question of whether they would like to see more characters like Ally on Slovene television: 'Media representations are different here, linked more to traditional understanding of women's roles.' The same female student also pointed out that she believed that in Slovenia, the role of mother is valued over a career. Another pointed to stereotypical depictions of women as housewives and taking care of the family. The implied understanding was that the series destabilized this politics of representation with progressive messages. The students were aware of media practices of idealization, which they associated with the economic logic of American commercial television and/or American culture in general ('Americans have a tendency to complicate and overreact'). Yet because 'Slovenia is still traditional in terms of representing women in the public sphere', programmes such as *Ally McBeal* were seen as having positive impacts on Slovene television production as well as on popular consciousness in a broader sense. Characters such as Ally would eventually evolve on Slovene television, a 'logical consequence of Americanization'; 'Slovenia is moving with the times (dictated by the US) and it is right to present the different, more equal and independent position of women in society'.

The 'traditional' in the equation signalled the transitional encounters with the socialist past. 'Slovenia has not grown out of socialism entirely', a student commented. The vision of repressed femininity that has spilled over from the socialist past came up a number of times (students spoke of a sense of stiffness, the rigidity and pessimism of the culture), one which I have encountered in the classroom ever since. This is puzzling, especially when taking into consideration the specific political and historical context of Slovene society and its socialist past. Slovenia (and Yugoslavia) invented its own version of socialism, marked by periods of economic and political liberalism and greater openness to the West (Ramet, 1999). As the most western of the former Yugoslav states, Slovenia in particular was involved in the daily exchange of labour and commodities with neighbouring Italy and Austria. Moreover, after Tito's break with Stalin's Informbureau in 1948, the country became less rigid in its distancing from anything remotely western. On the contrary, 'American culture was a strong force in setting the norms of various aspects of everyday life, including things such as bodily beauty, desirable objects (cars, houses, clothes, furniture), or romantic affairs' (Crnković, 2003: 159). My own research on the Slovene leading women's magazine of the postwar period reveals a similar, early trend to introduce consumerism and lifestyle cultures to female audiences, while replacing the working mother imagery with modern and independent urban ideals of femininity (Vidmar, 2002; Vidmar and Antic, forthcoming). Hence, for women living in socialist Slovenia, insertion of individuality and femininity has not been an entirely novel experience.

As viewers, we have different unconscious stakes in either identifying with or refuting characters such as Ally; this goes for ascribing historical meanings to them also. Growing up within socialism, which invented its own version of gender equality through the 'woman's question', one would expect at least some evidence of its residual form to compete for ideological space with the global media's depictions of the post-feminist mode of women's liberation. However, in her study of TV re-runs, Lynn Spigel observed a tendency to construe a sharp discontinuity between the present and the past concerning women's progress, when in her class she asked students to compare sitcom female stars, such as Lucy from the 1950s television show. She also observed that this tendency was enforced by their distillation of simplified notions of the women in the past from the reruns. This should not be read merely as a sign of illiteracy in the field of critical media and television studies, Spigel points out, for professional readings are as selective as popular ones. However, they can be seen as a way of negotiating the place in the present to make it 'more tolerable' (Spigel, 1995: 21). As Steven Knapp (1989: 142) writes, 'the focus of authority is always in the present; we use, for promoting and reinforcing ethical and political dispositions, only those elements of the past that correspond to our sense of what presently compels us'.

According to Spigel, this historical, cartoonish depiction of women can be seen as a way of celebrating the audiences' own 'enlightenment in the present' (Spigel, 1995: 20). In transitional Slovene culture, the notion of repressed, socialist femininity has been used in different ideological service to negotiate women's gendered positions in post-socialist times. This is certainly evident in the conservative project to 'redomesti-cate' women, seen in the former eastern bloc countries as well as in former Yugoslav states. The appeals for the repatriarchalization of society and acceleration of right-wing androgyny have been borne on the depiction of socialism as an anomaly, a 'totalitarian vestige' which forced women to occupy unnatural roles outside the family and domesticity (Jogan, 2000: 22). This politically mastered view has ruled over public discourse and mass media during the past decade and has acquired in the process a 'commonsense' quality. Identifying with Ally in this sense may be seen as a defence strategy to confront the post-socialist ideology of women's proper social place in the family. However, two other elements can be highlighted that may relate to Ally's popularity with the students. Both have to do with the 'production of expectations' (Jogan, 2000) in respect to gender and power relations in transition societies.

In the case of Slovenia, when in 1991 the country began its 'transition' to market economy and democracy, a promise that women would increase their political visibility and economic independence was articulated. Soon, the promise proved problematic. The mid-1990s witnessed an actual decline in women's political participation (the number of women in parliament dropped from 12 in 1992 to seven in 1996, climbing back to 12 in 2000) while the politics of sexual segregation in formal and informal work, as well as the income gap, have continued to sustain gender inequality in the economic and social life of the country's post-socialist state. The editor of a popular women's magazine commented on the missed opportunity: 'Because, as it appears, women should not be pushed to the front, the problems, which concern a good half of the population, will continue to be handled by the male minority' (Lupša, 2001: 3). Moreover, as already mentioned, the conservative forces embarked on misogynistic discourses, disguised as moral calls for redomestication and repatriarching of women. Paradoxically, as Slovene sociologists have noted, processes of democratization were operative within this because they were borne on assumptions about the self-propelling of social and political rights, fought by and for women in socialism. Without giving any serious thought to perseverance of sexual and gender inequality in private life from the socialist past, as one Slovene sociologist put it, transition did not accelerate the erosion of androgyny; it temporarily blocked it (Jalušić, 1999; Jogan, 2000).

It appears that this development has had a gender-specific impact on the younger generation as well. According to recent research, titled 'The Social Vulnerability of the Young' (Ule et al., 2000), young adolescent girls have lost out the most in the transition period in Slovenia. Although gender difference in education in Slovenia is declining, and in certain cases women actually excel in terms of formal education (in 1998, out of 8612 graduates, 5043 or 58.5 percent were female graduates), the research shows statistically that young girls increasingly show a lower degree of self-respect and self-worth. Contrary to previous studies showing the assertiveness of young girls, a recent tendency seems to be their withdrawal into inner worlds. The study concludes that instead of solving problems, young girls are facing them with insecurity and anxieties. As the authors summarise, young women have been the hidden losers of the transition society (Rener, 2000).

'It is almost impossible to expect more characters like Ally on Slovene television,' a student wrote, 'because despite democracy, the woman is still subordinate, even though she is a lawyer or a politician.' With regard to readers of women's magazines, Joke Hermes (1995: 51) has argued that 'fantasies of ideal selves that may or may not correspond to real life, or to one another . . . give readers the feeling [that] they will be able to cope'. By the same token, images of autonomous and professionally successful women on television can be seen to provide terrain for audiences to cope with their own expectations. 'Ally encourages women to begin to think that they deserve to be equal to men.' She proves to us that 'we are not alone in this', she makes women realize 'that they should stand up for themselves'. A female student highlighted Ally's status as an educated woman: 'Ally is an educated, emancipated woman, who sees the

world in her own way.' Education for women can be seen as one of the more important social achievements of Yugoslav socialism. Yet, as the above-mentioned study
reveals, the promise to accelerate social advantage via education has been stalled for
women by the transition. Encountering the post-feminist character as a representative
of the educated and emancipated woman therefore provides an outlet for the hope
and belief in what Giddens has called the 'reflexive project of the self' (Giddens,
1991). Considering the 'wealth of the images' coming from the West (Miller, 1992),
mass media icons play a role in this project, but their deployments relate to the local
worlds. As one student put it, watching global media, the Slovene women would get
'their "ally" whom they could, for different reasons, identify with'.

In conclusion, considering the disappointments and society's abridgement of
young women's 'production of expectation', the image of an independent and
professionally accomplished woman, no matter how neurotic or troublesome her
post-feminist masquerade of femininity, begins to complicate any notion of the self-
evident, transparent correlation between global media idols and their local audiences.
It certainly debunks the myth of women's audiences as 'natural collectivity with a
constant identity' (Ang and Hermes, 1996: 118). In contrast to their western sisters
watching TV re-runs, the primary concern of Slovene college women's audiences is
not to strike a pose of a liberated female agency, of a 'coming age of a different law', to
use Foucault's (1990: 7) words. In light of conservative attempts to pull women back
into family and domesticity, theirs may rather be to secure it. How and why this
position departs from the critical feminist reading of Ally in this respect is not a
superficial question, but a critical one – both pedagogically and theoretically.

Global culture and local meanings

Post-feminism as a term has acquired a wide range of meanings which are often
mutually exclusive and contradictory in respect to whether they are deployed in theoretical, political or media discourses (Gough-Yates, 2003; Jones, 2003; Lotz, 2001;
van Zoonen, 1994). Whereas some have used the term 'post-feminism' to delineate a
new theoretical terrain of possibilities to contest the modernist, patriarchal and
imperialist frameworks still operating behind western feminist epistemology, others
have seen it more in terms of a reactionary body of political discourses and cultural,
mass-mediated practices of recasting women in a traditionalist, family-oriented fashion, depoliticizing feminist struggles. The two narratives reconstructed in this article
suggest that post-feminism should be used less as a taxonomic category of ordering
political and ideological realms concentrated around popular and official definitions
of the woman in the West, but more as a global meeting point of cultural discourse
and popular forms of women's self-reflexivity. In the West, post-feminism may constitute a potent ideological vehicle while its visual rhetoric in mass media allows the new
generation of women to insert their separate identity and disassociate themselves from
their mothers' political dreams (Jones, 2003: 318). In the post-socialist cultures, post-
feminism may be seen as granting, in its female form of consumption, a compensation
for state-controlled bars to commodity culture and female pleasure in socialism
(Einhorn, 1993). For a younger generation, it offers a way of inserting a generational
divide as well as projecting a future. In its combined, global effect, post-feminism at

once proposes new hegemonic ways of looking at women and provides grounds for women's audiences worldwide to challenge, through proposed Western imagery, their own local gendered histories.

The challenge in Slovenia relates to the social experience of the 'transition' and restructuring of gender relations. For young viewers, especially women in Slovenia, *Ally McBeal* is but one of many global cultural sites on which to imagine their *own* world, to come to terms with their *own* social histories. These histories are enmeshed in narratives of the past as well as social fantasies of the future. Erika Harris (2002: 192) writes that the pressures of globalization contribute to 'fragmentation of cultures': 'These cultures are a result of memories, local ways of thinking, customs and norms that grew out of the necessities of local struggles, or out of reinterpreted histories and retold stories.' Many of the local struggles, entangled in new global mass-mediated fantasies, concern expectations about the effects that the shift to the market economy and democracy will have on social relations and structures of gender. This 'production of expectation' is entwined within contradictory notions of social history and progress. With respect to the former, paradoxically, it is precisely the projection of patriarchal imagery of the domesticated female – the very one that socialist discourse and politics tried to dismiss as the ideological property of the capitalist system – which for the young viewers symbolizes the remnants of the socialist social history of gender. Regarding the latter, in contrast to their mothers who lived under the spell of socialist ideology, which told them that once women had entered the production force their liberation was achieved, the transition generation perceives socialism as a regime that oppressed women. For them, real liberation comes from the West. Avoiding the legacy of the 'token woman', however, they also 'try to avoid "feminist conflicts" and try to build their public promotion above all as good professionals and experts' (Jalušić, 1999: 125). This is in fact a meeting point between feminism and socialism. By a strange stroke of fate, western feminism and socialism come to play a shared role of the Other.

Engaging in the fictional life of *Ally McBeal* provides different fantasy materials for different audiences. As any fantasy contains omissions, this one lacks historical facts concerning past and present women's struggles both in the West and the former socialist states. This gives us no reason to dismiss popular receptions of global culture. As Slavoj Žižek writes:

> Few things are worthy of more contempt, few views are more ideological . . . than those of the Western academic leftist with a job who arrogantly dismisses (or, worse, paternalistically 'understands') the Eastern European from a communist state who yearns for Western liberal democracy and some commodities.
>
> (2003: 10)

Read from the perspective of young Slovene female audiences consuming the image of Ally McBeal, this view provides solid ground for historical sensitivity when engaging in political debates about the promises and pitfalls of global culture. But this should not prevent us from engaging ourselves in critical readings of global cultural texts. As I was completing this article, national TVS was showing the seventh episode of *The Mary Tyler Moore Show*. Not only is contemporary television becoming globally available, but also television history. Thus, studying global genres may provide a good starting point for both cultural criticism and classroom pedagogy to begin to intercept global popular fantasies with cultural memory.

Acknowledgements

I wish to thank Gordana Crnković for her encouragement to complete this article. I also express my gratitude to anonymous reviewers, and especially Joke Hermes for constructive criticism and useful comments.

References

Andall, J. (2003) 'Introduction: The Space Between – Gender Politics and Immigration Politics in Europe', in J. Andall (ed.) *Gender and Ethnicity in Contemporary Europe*, pp. 1–20. Oxford: Berg.

Ang, I. (1991) *Desperately Seeking the Audience*. London: Routledge.

Ang, I. (ed.) (1996) *Living Room Wars. Rethinking Media Audiences for a Postmodern World*. London: Routledge.

Ang, I. and J. Hermes (1996) 'Gender and/in Media Consumption', in I. Ang (ed.) *Living Room Wars. Rethinking Media Audiences for a Postmodern World*, pp. 109–29. London: Routledge.

Appelo, T. (1999) *Ally McBeal: The Official Mini Guide*. Los Angeles, CA: Twentieth Century Fox Home Entertainment.

Cooper, B. (2001) 'Unapologetic Women, "Comic Men" and Feminine Spectatorship in David E. Kelly's *Ally McBeal*', *Critical Studies in Mass Communication* 18(4): 416–35.

Crnković, G.P. (2003) ' "Have a Nice Day": From the Balkan War to the American Dream and the Things that Shape the Way We See Each Other', in S.P. Ramet and G.P. Crnković (eds) *Kazaaam! Splat! Ploof! The American Impact on European Popular Culture Since 1945*, pp. 158–72. Lanham, MD: Rowman and Littlefield.

Curti, L. (1992) 'What Is Real and What Is Not: Female Fabulations in Cultural Analysis', in L. Grossberg, C. Nelson and P. Treichler (eds) *Cultural Studies*, pp. 134–53. New York: Routledge.

Doane, M.A. (1987) 'The Moving Image: Pathos and the Maternal', in *The Desire to Desire: Women's Film of the 1940s*, pp. 70–95. Bloomington: Indiana University Press.

Dow, B.J. (2002) '*Ally McBeal*, Lifestyle Feminism, and the Politics of Personal Happiness', *Communication Review* 5: 259–64.

Dubrofsky, R. (2002) 'Ally McBeal as Post-feminist Icon: The Aestheticizing and Fetishizing of the Independent Working Woman', *Communication Review* 5: 265–84.

Einhorn, B. (1993) *Cinderella Goes to Market. Citizenship, Gender and Women's Movements in East Central Europe*. London: Verso.

Foucault, M. (1990) *The History of Sexuality*, Vol. 1. New York: Vintage.

Giddens, A. (1991) *Modernity and Self-identity. Self and Society in the Late Modern Age*. Stanford, CA: Stanford University Press.

Gough-Yates, A. (2003) *Understanding Women's Magazines. Publishing, Markets and Readerships*. London: Routledge.

Harris, E. (2002) *Nationalism and Democratisation. Politics of Slovakia and Slovenia*. Burlington: Ashgate.

Hermes, J. (1995) *Reading Women's Magazines*. Cambridge: Polity Press.

Jalušić, V. (1999) 'Women in Post-socialist Slovenia: Socially Adapted, Politically Marginalized', in S.P. Ramet (ed.) *Gender Politics in the Western Balkans*, pp. 109–29. University Park: Pennsylvania State University Press.

Jogan, M. (2000) 'Postsocializem in androcentrizem', *Družboslovne razprave* 16(34–5): 9–30.

Jones, A. (ed.) (2003) 'Feminism, Incorporated: Reading "Post-feminism" in an Anti-feminist Age', in *The Feminism and Visual Culture Reader*, pp. 314–29. London: Routledge.

Kim, L.S. (2001) ' "Sex and the Single Girl" in Postfeminism', *Television and New Media* 2(4): 319–34.

Knapp, S. (1989) 'Collective Memory and the Actual Past', *Representations* 26: 123–49.

Lotz, A. (2001) 'Postfeminist Television Criticism: Rehabilitating Critical Terms and Identifying Postfeminist Attributes', *Feminist Media Studies* 1(1): 105–21.

Lupša, M. (2001) 'A Country of Women?', *Jana* (16 Oct.): 3.

Marek, J.G. (1999) '*The Practice* and *Ally McBeal*: A New Image for Women Lawyers on Television?', *Journal of American Culture* 22(1) (electronic version, Academic Search Premier).

Margolis, H. (2000) 'This Is Not a Show about Lawyers', *Australian Screen Education* 20–1 (electronic version, Academic Search Premier).

Mellencamp, P. (1986) 'Situation Comedy, Feminism and Freud. Discourses of Gracie and Lucy', in T. Modleski (ed.) *Studies in Entertainment*, pp. 80–95. Bloomington: Indiana University Press.

Miller, D. (1992) 'The Young and the Restless in Trinidad: A Case of the Local and the Global in Mass Consumption', in R. Silverstone and E. Hirsch (eds) *Consuming Technologies: Media and Information in Domestic Spaces*, pp. 163–82. London: Routledge.

Moseley, R. and J. Read (2002) ' "Having it *Ally*": Popular Television (Post)Feminism', *Feminist Media Studies* 2(2): 231–49.

Nochimson, M. (2000) '*Ally McBeal*: Brightness Falls from the Air', *Film Quarterly* 53(3): 25–32.

Radway, J.A. (1986) *Reading the Romance. Women, Patriarchy and Popular Literature*. Chapel Hill: University of North Carolina Press.

Ramet, S.P. (ed.) (1999) 'Introduction', in *Gender Politics in the Western Balkans*, pp. 3–10. University Park: Pennsylvania State University Press.

Rener, T. (2000) 'Adolescentke' ['Adolescents'], *Družboslovne razprave* 16(34–5): 207–17.

Spigel, L. (1995) 'From the Dark Ages to the Golden Age: Women's Memories and Television Reruns', *Screen* 36(1): 16–33.

Taylor, E. (1989) *Prime Time Families*. Berkeley: University of California Press.

Tueth, S.J.M. (2000) 'TV's Urban Situation Comedies of the 1990s', *Journal of Popular Film and Television* 28(3): 99–107.

Ule, M., T. Rener, M. Mencin Čeplak and B. Tivadar (2000) *The Social Vulnerability of the Young*. Maribor, Ljubljana: Aristej/Office for Youth.

Van Zoonen, L. (1994) *Feminist Media Studies*. London: Sage.

Vidmar, K.H. (1995) 'The Importance of Being *Mad*: The 1950s Comic Imagination and Discourses on Youth', paper presented at the Sixth Annual Berkeley Symposium, 11–12 March, Berkeley, California.

Vidmar, K.H. (2002) '*Naša žena* and the Image of Mother: Contradictions and Oppositions, 1991–2000', in M. Hrženjak (ed.) *Making Her Up: Women's Magazines in Slovenia*, pp. 34–55. Ljubljana: Peace Institute.

Vidmar, K.H. and M. Antić (forthcoming) *The Construction of Woman's Identity in Socialism: The Case of Slovenia*.

Žižek, S. (2003) 'Kje je prava nevarnost' ['Where Is the Real Danger?'], *Delo* 22(3): 10–12.

17

The Performance and Reception of Televisual "Ugliness" in *Yo soy Betty la fea*

Yeidy M. Rivero

Originally published in *Feminist Media Studies*, 3:1 (2003): 65–82.

In 2001 a televisual cultural artifact from Colombia occupied the center of a transnational cultural dialogue, partially destabilizing the "narrations of violence" that characterize local, national, and global constructions of the embattled South American nation.[1] The *telenovela Yo soy Betty la fea* [*Betty*], produced by Colombia's RCN television and written by Fernando Gaitán, became a mega hit and captured audiences in various Latin American and Spanish Caribbean nations. According to a *Variety* magazine report, *Betty* was broadcast in fifteen Western countries and had 80 million viewers in Latin America (Mary Sutter 2001). In the US *Betty*, which aired on Telemundo's network, captivated audiences in major cities such as New York and Miami and briefly challenged Univision's dominance in the US Spanish language television market (Michael Freeman 2002; Mimi Whitefield 2000).

In both the US and in Latin America, audiences created Internet chat rooms in English and Spanish where *foristas* [women who participate in the forums] discussed the *telenovela*'s narrative, character development, possible endings, and even embraced the *Yo soy Betty la fea* jargon. After witnessing *Betty*'s success, Univision bought the rights to *Betty*'s reruns in the US and co-produced a sequel with RCN titled *EcoModa*. Finally, for the first time in the history of US English language commercial television, a Latin American televisual concept might cross over to the US mainstream market. NBC acquired *Betty*'s rights and planned to transform the *telenovela* genre into a culturally and commercially familiar US situation comedy (Mary Sutter and Josef Adalian 2001).[2]

Betty is a product of globalization wherein the flow of audiovisual images transcends the local realm of signification, creating, as Nestor García Canclini argues, de-contextualized cultural and political histories (2001: 160).[3] However, *Betty*'s transnational success should be examined both in terms of globalized commercial television exchanges and more importantly, in terms of the *telenovela*'s thematic construction. In contrast to other televisual cultural products, *Betty*'s main theme revolved around discourses of female "beauty" and "ugliness," depicting a principal character who might be considered the "ugliest" of all *telenovela* heroines. *Betty*'s narrative re-articulated colonial, gendered, class, racial, and Eurocentric dominant discourses of female aesthetics, thus, creating a trans-cultural space for debates about socially constructed ideologies of "ugliness" and "womanhood."

In view of its transnational success, one is prompted to ask, how did Latina, Latin American, and Spanish Caribbean women understand ideologies of female physical "beauty" and "ugliness" in *Betty*? Were audiences mesmerized by the principal character (Beatriz) and her best friends *el cuartel de las feas* [the bunch of "ugly" women], because they identified with their marginality? This essay seeks to answer these questions by analyzing the ways in which Colombian, Colombian-American, Mexican, Mexican-American, and Puerto Rican women perceived *Betty*'s construction of "beauty" and "ugliness." By establishing points of connection between *Betty* and some of its diverse audiences, this essay argues that *Betty* created a space for gender/cultural identification and provided a source of contestation regarding ideologies of female "beauty."

In this essay I am not suggesting that as a cultural product, *Betty* was inherently emancipatory, or that the participants only produced counter-hegemonic readings. As Douglas Kellner (1995: 39) observes regarding media cultures and audiences, "a system of power and privilege conditions our pleasures so that we seek certain socially sanctioned pleasures and avoid others." In the case of *Betty* and the research participants, perceptions of "beauty" and "ugliness" operated between dominant, negotiating, and in some cases, oppositional meanings (Stuart Hall 1980). However, what was particularly evident in the participants' responses was the fact that regardless of the dominant discourses of gendered, racial, and class-based "beauty" presented in *Betty*, the text offered a space for mediation on the origins of female aesthetic categorizations and the ways in which the participants saw themselves as "women."

To contextualize *Betty* and the audience study, I first examine the construction of female "beauty" and "ugliness" in the Latin American and US contexts. Then, I discuss the method used for the research, the selection of participants, and my personal attachment to the subject of study. A textual analysis of *Betty* follows, paying special attention to "ugliness" and *el cuartel de las feas* [the bunch of "ugly" women]. Finally, I examine audiences' readings of *Betty*'s narrative. This section will focus on the participants' responses regarding the narrative's construction of female "beauty"/"ugliness" and the origins of these aesthetic classifications. I conclude the essay by positioning *Betty*'s success as a product of the *telenovela*'s thematic construction and as a possible result of audiences' desire for diverse themes and representations of "womanhood" in the *telenovela* genre.

The Latin American/Latina "beautiful" and "ugly" body

While *Betty* is situated in contemporary Colombia, the participants in this study (and indeed a large portion of *Betty*'s audience in general) come from various ethnic backgrounds that hint at the complex nature of local/global politics of representations and interpretations. Ideologies of female "beauty"/"ugliness" are social constructions which relate to historical, social, economic, and racial processes in specific cultural spaces. However, even though there are multiple differences regarding what is considered "attractive" or "non-attractive" in particular regions such as Latin

America, the Spanish Caribbean, and the US, one can map distinctive discursive formations regarding the female "beautiful"/"ugly" body. Furthermore, since *Betty* depicts both "white" and "black" women/principal characters, I will focus on the racialization of "white," "black," and *mulata* women through the *mestizaje* discourse.

Colombia, similar to other nations in Latin America and the Spanish Caribbean, developed ideologies of cultural and racial *mestizaje* in their nation-building processes, molding the nation with rudiments of the colonial past (Peter Wade 1997, 2000). While the ideology of cultural and racial *mestizaje* posits a racially equal and culturally hybrid national space, hierarchies exist which define the nation's citizens based on the axes of "race" and class. Central to the *mestizaje* ideology is the racist process of *blanqueamiento* [whitening] in which racial mixing with "white" (European) people means becoming "whiter" and "improving the race" for the "black" and indigenous populations. Still, this racial mixing is also constrained by class. While there may be some mixing among upper classes, it is a much more common practice among lower classes, who might see it as an avenue to material gain and improved status (T. Edmund Gordon 1998; France Winndance Twine 1998). Although it would be a false generalization to say that all the people at the bottom of the economic ladder in Colombia and other Latin American regions are "black," "mulatto," or indigenous people, research has demonstrated that "race" is nonetheless a key factor in social, economic, and political mobility (Wade 1985, 1997). These intertwined racial, cultural, and social ideological discourses circumscribe the social constructions of female aesthetics.

In various Latin American and Spanish Caribbean nations the Eurocentric-patriarchal gaze delimits the ways in which "beauty" is represented, situating "white-ness" (with both "race" and class connotations) as the epitome of purity and elegance for the female body (Frances Aparicio 1998; Ella Shohat and Robert Stam 1994). Conversely, "black" and *mulata* women have been socially constructed as hyper-sexual/sensual bodies, creating a distinction in terms of racialized gendered sexuality and perpetuating the stereotypes embedded in Western ideologies of civilization and primitivism.

Michael Hanchard notes that elites in Latin America imitated the Western model of modernity by situating blacks and indigenous peoples as the "antithesis of the modern nation" (1994: 173). Thus the discourse of modernity becomes intertwined with "race" ("whiteness"), Western/Christianized ideologies of sexual constraint, and civilization in which "blackness" and "black" bodies serve as repository symbols of primitivism and hyper-sexuality. For example, this process is evident in Colombia's coastal region. Characterized by its African heritage, discourses of primitivism foster a racially sexualized "cultural topography" of the nation (Wade 2000: 242). Subsequently, "black" women are generally stereotyped as sexually unrestrained and women with "weak morals" (Wade 1985: 19–23). Similarly, in Puerto Rico and Cuba, the Eurocentric/patriarchal gaze historically constructed "black" and *mulata* as primitive sexual objects at the disposal of the "civilized" upper-class "white" males (Aparicio 1998; Vera M. Kutzinski 1993).

In addition, the racialized "beautiful"/"ugly" rubric in Latin America intersects with ideologies of class. Not only is the "beautiful" female body informed by "white-ness" and sexual constraint, but it is also permeated by the *habitus* of the upper middle-class social fields (Pierre Bourdieu 1984). Upper-class/bourgeois codes of conduct and appearance – related to one's manner of walk, dress, and style, as well as to notions of "proper" manners, elegance, and "correct" use of the language – inform some of the socially constructed elements of female "beauty." This does not mean that a poor *campesina* [peasant] would not be considered "beautiful." However, beyond physical appearance, the *campesina* would have to incorporate the cultural practices of the upper middle class. Thus, one might say that the dichotomy between "beautiful" and "ugly" female bodies in Latin American is broadly informed by intertwined Eurocentric, patriarchal, racial, Western/Christianized ideologies of primitivism/civilization and class.

Eurocentrism, primitivism, and sexualized ideologies of the racial "Other" also permeate the construction of the Latina body in the US context. Nonetheless, US racial discourses and the location of Latinos/as in the national imaginary transform the racial/class representations of "Latinas" present in the Latin American cultural context. Hegemonic racial discourses in the US are framed in "black"/"white" ancestry-related terms. This binary construction erases the multiplicity of "races" that are part of the generic term "Hispanics" and situates the "Latina" body as generally "brown," ethnically undifferentiated, and "working class" (Angharad N. Valdivia 1998).

The socially constructed *brownness* also rearticulates Eurocentric and primitivist sexual ideologies. As bell hooks asserts, "in mass culture, imperialist nostalgia takes the form of reenacting and reritualizing in different ways the imperialistic, colonizing journey as narrative fantasy of power and desire, of seduction by the Other" (1992: 25). Although one might say that the "Latina body" (similar to the African American body), its media representations, and the actual "Latina" performers present an alternative to the ("white") "beauty" normativity that characterizes US constructions, the "Other" female body carries elements of the colonial gaze. Obviously, "Latinas" might find pleasure in these representations and might create counter-hegemonic readings. Nevertheless, as Susan Bordo (1993: 25) argues, US cultural representations of racial "Otherness" are "framed as exotica" and do not transgress the homogenized Anglo-Saxon constructions of "beauty."

In sum, "race," class, and Eurocentric ideologies of "beauty" inform the ways in which female aesthetics have been socially constructed in both Latin America and in the US. Furthermore, other cultural practices and norms such as youth, "body fitness," and plastic surgery permeate representations of the "beautiful" female body (Bordo 1993; Wendy Chapkis 1986; Kathy Davis 1995; Elizabeth Haiken 1997). All the aforementioned elements directly and indirectly inform *Betty*'s construction of female "beauty"/"ugliness" and the participants' responses to the *telenovela*'s aesthetics' categorizations.

The "authentic insider" and the limits of focus groups

The intricacies of examining "Other" cultures have occupied the center of various academic debates, particularly in the area of cultural anthropology and more recently television's audience studies. From the interactions and power dynamics between researcher and participants to the narrations of the dialogic encounter, scholars have contested the "translation of stories," the narrative strategies, and the "political sub-jectivities of researchers" (Ien Ang 1996; Barbara Kauffman 1992; Purnima Mankekar 1999; Ellen Seiter 1999; Barbara Tedlock 1991). In addition, anthropologists in par-ticular, have tried to eradicate the distinctions between "native" and "non-native" scholars which impose a burden on the "authentic insider" and homogenize people from a particular nation or culture (Kirin Narayan 1998: 163–6). With this ongoing dialogue in mind, I will explain my own position in relation to the object of study and the participants, taking into account the power differences and the limitations of the method used for this study.

My selection of the *telenovela Yo soy Betty la fea* as an object of study was primarily influenced by my own "addiction" to the show, the opportunity to work with other Latin American scholars who were also enchanted by *Betty*, and my curiosity about why other women were fascinated with the *telenovela*.[4] I and another member of the research team selected group interviewing (focus groups) as one of the method-ological research tools primarily to establish a space wherein participants could share their opinions about *Betty*'s narrative. Although weekly focus groups combined with interviews would have provided a better understanding of the participants' readings and further space for dialogues, time and money constraints limited the possibilities for expanding the research methods. The participants did not receive any remuner-ation for their involvement in the project. They chose to be part of the research because they were interested in other women's perceptions of *Betty* and wanted to share their opinions about their "most favorite show."

One of my main concerns regarding the focus groups was that some participants may have thought that they were being "tested." In an attempt to alleviate this poten-tial problem, I informed all of the participants at the beginning of each focus group that I was also a *Betty* fan and that I was quite interested in their opinions. Openness and informality permeated the dialogue since most of the participants within each focus group knew each other.[5]

The focus groups were conducted in San Antonio, Texas, on May 2 and 9, 2001, and in Río Piedras, Puerto Rico, on June 19 and 20, 2001.[6] The focus groups included Colombians (nine), a Colombian-American, Mexicans (two), Mexican-Americans (two), and Puerto Ricans (ten). Each participant's age determined her placement in a specific group (18–30 and 40 +). The Colombian 40 + group was comprised of women who had been living in the US for fifteen to forty-two years. The 18+ San Antonio group consisted of Mexicans (two), Colombians (two), Mexican-Americans (two), and one Colombian-American. The Mexican and Colombian women had been living in the US for less than two years. All of the Puerto Rican participants were born and raised on the island.

To create a comfortable arena for discussions, the groups consisted of middle-class and upper middle-class women only. Their educational level ranged from community college to graduate school and their "race" roughly emblemized the racial spectrum of Latin American and Latino communities: "white," *mestizas*, and "blacks."[7] Since I did not want to impose a specific racial or ethnic categorization on any of the participants, I provided a sheet for each woman to record her ethnicity, age, education, and "race."

One important element regarding the participants and myself relates to similar class location, language, gender, and cultural connections which created a comfortable level of communication. This does not mean that as a born and raised "white"/ "brown," middle-class, educated Puerto Rican (my "race" is "translated" differently in the US), I have endured the racism that one of my "black" Puerto Rican participants discussed in the conversations or the oppression of growing up as a *mestiza* Mexican-American in economically, socially, and racially segregated San Antonio, Texas. On the other hand, I have not attained the economic solvency that many of the Colombian 40+ participants have obtained (conclusions drawn from the new Mercedes-Benz, expensive clothing, and jewelry). Still, the fact that I am the one writing this essay illustrates the power differences and my privileged position in relation to the participants.

The following section presents a textual analysis of *Betty*'s narrative, paying special attention to Beatriz (the principal character), *el cuartel de las feas*, and the performance of "beauty," "ugliness," and gender in the text.

Beatriz and *el cuartel de las feas*: too tall, too fat, too black, too sexual . . . in sum, too lower class

Yo soy Betty la fea narrated the story of an "ugly," clumsy, working-class, yet brilliant and hard-working woman who was employed as a secretary at EcoModa, a high-fashion company. Following the *telenovela* genre, which generally recreates the complexities of an almost impossible love between a woman and a man from different social classes, Beatriz fell in love with Armando, the president of the company (Ana López 1995; Omar Rincón 2000). After a series of misunderstandings and suffering, Beatriz and Armando married and one assumes (or more likely questions) that they lived happily ever after.[8] Yet, *Betty* was more than an impossible love between a poor woman and a rich man. As previously mentioned, its narrative revolved around discourses of the female's "physical" appearance.

Betty's construction of "the beautiful" and "the ugly" did not interconnect representations of a particular ethnic or racial group to moral/philosophical questions of human goodness or evilness. The narrative's aesthetic divisions centered around class and, as previously observed, reflected Eurocentric racial and patriarchal discourses of what is generally considered "beautiful" or "ugly" in Colombia and other Latin American cultures. By replicating what Naomi Wolf (1991) categorizes as the "beauty myth," upper-class "white" males/characters constructed aesthetic categories situating "whiteness," upper-class taste, and slim and young bodies as the chief qualifications for women's "beauty." As a result, "dominant discourses of the body enable[d] privileged groups . . . to transcend their own material bodies and take on a god's eye view as disembodied subjects" (Davis 1995: 51). In *Betty*, men functioned as aesthetic judges, and while both "beautiful" and "ugly" men and women reappropriated discourses of "beauty" to judge themselves and others, the ones who suffered harsh aesthetic discrimination and humiliation were Beatriz and *el cuartel de las feas* – the working-class women.

El cuartel de las feas was a categorization created by Hugo Lombardi, EcoModa's flamboyant queen and star designer. Even though Hugo's homosexuality and class would have positioned him outside EcoModa's "beautiful," upper-class, and heterosexual space, his gender, and more important, his "symbolic capital," allowed him to create alliances with both "beautiful" upper-class women and heterosexual males (Bourdieu 1984).

Besides the troupe of high-fashion models who were symbolically or actually present at EcoModa, there were two "beautiful" women who appeared regularly: Marcela and Patricia. Marcela, one of EcoModa's co-owners, was an educated and sophisticated woman who worked as an art designer for the company. Patricia was Marcela's childhood friend who worked at EcoModa as a secretary. Although Patricia's profession, financial status, and sexual behavior (she exchanged her body for financial and professional favors) would have positioned her as part of *el cuartel de las feas*, her family name, prestige, and previous class location (upper class) situated her as a member of the "beautiful" people.

El cuartel de las feas was comprised of seven women who worked at EcoModa. Like Beatriz (the principal character), Sandra, Mariana, Aura María, Berta, and Sofía were secretaries, while Inés worked as a tailor. The narrative presented each of these women as "ugly" based on a series of characteristics that were part of their bodies or their personalities. Although there were gradations of "ugliness" based on Hugo's and the upper-class characters' classifications of the women's bodies and behavior, the underlying assumption was that at EcoModa only working-class women were unattractive.

Beatriz epitomized "ugliness" according to social and cultural constructions of "beauty." She had facial hair (a thin mustache), was clumsy, wore passé clothing and thick-framed glasses, wore braces, and had a peculiar laugh which many characters considered annoying. Although Beatriz was a brilliant woman who obtained a master's degree in finance, she was also shy and insecure. Beatriz was aware that her "ugliness" and marginality created both a socially real and an internalized barrier that prevented her from advancing in her profession and finding (heterosexual) love. However, at EcoModa, Beatriz had the moral support of her friends (*el cuartel de las feas*) who respected her loyalty, honesty, and intelligence.

The other women who formed *el cuartel* (Sandra, Mariana, Berta, Sofía, Aura María, and Inés), although not considered as "ugly" as Beatriz, were nonetheless "unattractive." For example, Sandra was a tall, conservative woman in her late twenties who dressed in an old-fashioned way and was frequently compared to a giraffe. Other characters constantly made fun of her tallness and rigid personality, identifying her as the group's spinster. Mariana was a "black" woman in her mid-twenties, whose "race" automatically situated her as part of *el cuartel*. Her "blackness" carried a stereotype associated with "black" and "mulatto" citizens in parts of Latin America and the Spanish Caribbean. Although Mariana was not constructed as "hyper-sexual," her "blackness" was linked to the "occult." Mariana was a "good witch" who believed in the oracles of the tarot and used her expertise to help her friends "resolve" their personal struggles.

At EcoModa the epitome of hyper-sexuality was Aura María, a "white" woman in her mid-twenties who flirted with every man she encountered. Aura María dressed "provocatively" and tried to use her body, sensuality, and sexuality to attract men. Like Patricia ("beautiful"), Aura María sometimes used sex to improve her economic condition. However, both Patricia and Aura María were mere objects for powerful male sexual pleasures. Even though Aura María would be considered "beautiful" according to dominant standards, her constructed "hyper-sexuality," body, and class subsumed her "whiteness," locating her as a sensual/sexual objectified "black"/ *mulata*.

The rest of *el cuartel* were "older," thus their "ugliness" (class) was interconnected to age. Berta, a woman in her mid- to late thirties was represented as "fat." She was happily married to *el gordo* [the fat man] and had children. As a "fat" woman, Berta could not control her appetite, consequently she devoured everything that appeared in front of her. In addition, Berta entertained herself and her friends with gossip. Sofia was the divorced woman. Her husband had an affair with a younger woman who occasionally worked at EcoModa as a model. According to the narrative Sofia's "ugliness" resided in her shortness. Inés was a woman in her sixties. Constructed as a mother figure, Inés constantly advised her friends regarding personal or professional problems.

Despite the fact that *el cuartel*'s label functioned to ostracize and ridicule Beatriz and her friends, these women appropriated and reconfigured its original meaning, creating a space for class and gender identification. In other words, their "common context of struggle" reaffirmed their friendship, gender, and class solidarity (Chandra Talpade Mohanty 1991). With the exception of Beatriz, *el cuartel* was unconcerned about other people's opinions of their bodies and were generally depicted as being content with themselves. Furthermore, these women constantly transgressed their dominated position at EcoModa. They gossiped about their supervisors, spied on them, came to work late, and took breaks collectively without asking for permission to gather and talk. Although there were limits to their disobedience, they nonetheless resisted their oppression by subverting EcoModa's (capitalistic) work ethics.

In *Betty*'s narrative the working-class female body became a metaphor for ideologies of "beauty" that encompassed class, gender, "race," and age. Yet, one could argue that *Betty*'s aesthetic divisions were staged representations on three main levels: (1) performance of "beauty," (2) performance of gender, and (3) performance of "ugliness." These three levels normalized gender distinctions regarding physical "beauty" and male power, while limiting the narrative discussions of the ideological discourses that inform gendered "beauty"/"ugliness" in Latin American cultures.

First, according to the narrative, the female body was not inherited as "beautiful," rather, it was performatively constructed and represented as "beautiful." In *Betty*, "beauty" could be acquired by accommodating Western/"white" middle-class patriarchal norms of femininity. Through bodily transformations (for example, electrolysis) and adornments (hairstyle, clothing, contact lenses, and make-up), Beatriz and *el cuartel de las feas* (and, therefore, any woman) could become socially and sexually desirable for the male gaze. This performance of "beauty" required more than simply having the economic resources to buy products or transform the body. To become/be "beautiful" women had to learn and incorporate the "tastes" and practices of the upper classes (Bourdieu 1984). According to the narrative, working-class women could obtain this knowledge through the (patronizing) tutelage of "trained specialists" at EcoModa (the fashion industry – upper class).

The performance of "beauty" not only reproduced social norms of femininity, but it also articulated gender divisions. Judith Butler observes that "gender is an act which has been rehearsed, much as a script survives the particular actors who make use of it, but which requires individual actors in order to be actualized and reproduced as reality once again" (1990: 277). In *Betty*'s second level of performance male/female characters acted their roles of "women" and "men," reproducing societal-power differences between these socially and culturally constructed categories. These performances of gender contained the ideologies of *machismo* that generally permeate Latin American cultures.

In Latin American cultures where the feminine identity is informed by ideologies of women as mothers/wives/sacred virgins, women are victimized as they concomitantly internalize and assume the identity of victims (Sonia Montecino 1995: 75). In *Betty*'s narrative, men were generally constructed as possessing innately beautiful bodies and power. More important, all women characters were continuously oppressed and verbally, physically, and sexually abused by men. For example, Beatriz's father (Don Hermes), had complete control over Beatriz and Julia (the mother) and neither of these characters ever contradicted the orders of the father. The characters assumed the role of passive women as daughter and wife, respectively. In the workplace, all of the EcoModa male characters who possessed power screamed at and harassed their female employees while none of the female characters ever challenged their subjugated position. *Betty*'s narrative normalized Latin American gender constructions and the power inequalities between "women" and "men."

"Ugliness" was a third level of performance in *Betty*'s narrative. "Ugliness" was a staged representation, an impersonation in which a series of "characters" depicted what might be considered unattractive in Colombia and some Latin American cultures. However, none of the actresses who played the "ugly" characters were visually unpleasant. Through *Betty*'s narrative and meta-narrative (magazine interviews, television talk shows, web pages, and *Betty*'s "behind the scenes" television specials), audiences were able to confirm the performance of "ugliness." Thus, the underlying assumption, common knowledge, and general expectation of many of the *telenovela* audiences was that through cosmetic/staged transformations Beatriz and *el cuartel de las feas* could and would become "beautiful." *Betty*'s meta-narrative, the *telenovela* genre, and the market/audience pressures limited the textual/narrative possibilities of examining dominant ideologies of "beauty" and women's subjugation.

Since the main context of struggle in *Betty* was class, multiple locations of domination such as "race," sexual orientation, or women's objectification and the patriarchal structures that inform these power dynamics were never examined in the narrative. Certainly, *Betty* presented "sisterhood" as a way of coping with male oppression. Within this "sisterhood" space, there were instances in which women from middle and upper classes created some type of solidarity. However, in these inter-class connections the upper middle-class women claimed the position of "defending" the voiceless working-class women. This "sisterhood" homogenized the category of "womanhood" without revising power differences within the gendered group. In some ways, middle/upper-class women became channels for the working-class route to Western "modernization" and "civilization."

Betty's construction of "beauty" did not consider Eurocentric/racial ideologies which locate "black" and "mulatto" female bodies as unable to comply with social discourses of the ideal "white" "beauty." Nor did it problematize cultural and social constructions of youth, body fitness, and plastic surgery as dominant norms/practices of "beauty." In sum, *Betty* never challenged the gendered power systems that characterize Western cultures.

At the end of the *telenovela* Beatriz and *el cuartel* were able to transform themselves. In the rather simplistic rhetoric of working-class empowerment (i.e., anybody can "make it"), Beatriz's hard work and intelligence allowed her to become the company's president. However, this success in the workplace came with a price; she had to alter her physical appearance. Naomi Wolf argues that "the closer women come to power, the more physical self-consciousness and sacrifice are asked of them" (1991: 28). Beatriz could not be an "ugly" professional woman. More degrading was that a woman/character associated with Colombia's "beauty" pageant (another cultural site where the female body becomes a "performance") was "in charge" of Beatriz's cosmetic and morally painful metamorphosis. Furthermore, in the last episodes, Beatriz politely required her employees (*el cuartel*) to change their physical appearance and dress in a more "professional" manner. Finally, Beatriz married Armando, a man who had humiliated and sexually abused her throughout the entire narrative. *Betty* presented women as objects with limited agency regarding their bodies, appearance, and power. Beatriz and her friends colluded with the "beauty" system. They became what EcoModa/Western capitalistic/patriarchal societies wanted them to be – copycats of "beautiful" women and mere objects for/properties of males.

Despite the fact that *Betty* presented dominant ideologies regarding female "beauty" and "womanhood," the participants problematized the narrative by analyzing the gendered ideologies that delimit these socially constructed categories in Latin American, Spanish Caribbean, Latino, and Western cultures.

What does it mean to be "ugly"?

When asking participants what made a woman "ugly" or "beautiful" in *Betty*'s narrative and who was responsible for the aesthetic categorizations, the participants located three primary, sometimes autonomous and sometimes interconnected sources: gender relations and power; class and "race"; and society/media constructions of women as idealized "beauty" objects. All of the participants agreed that even though there were "ugly" men/characters in *Betty*, the narrative never examined these characters' "ugliness." According to the participants, this construction responds to gender differences regarding men and women's "beauty" and Latin American/Latino cultural norms which establish that men do not have to be "beautiful." Many of the participants declared that in these transnational communities, women have internalized the socially constructed proverb: *el hombre es como el oso, mientras más feo más hermoso* [man is like a bear, the uglier he is, the prettier he becomes]. Although it is extremely difficult to translate this phrase, the general meaning is that men's physical appearances do not matter since as men they are "beautiful" (i.e., powerful).

With the exception of two women, the participants declared that they did not want to see Beatriz and Armando romantically involved or married. Some participants wanted Beatriz to experience her "new life" as a professional and independent woman while others wanted her to marry *el francés* [the French man/ Michelle], a character who romantically pursued Beatriz during the final episodes.

The participants wanted a transformation of the traditional *telenovela* ending where the principal characters finally resolve their moral, class, and existential conflicts. However, they understood that a different ending was almost impossible since "all *telenovelas* end the same way," and some of them already knew *Betty*'s ending.

All of the participants also recognized the objectification and oppression of women in *Betty*. The Colombian 40 + participants and the San Antonio 18 + group were offended by the abuse endured by all female characters and similarly Puerto Rican women wanted to incarcerate Beatriz's father and Armando under the charge of domestic violence. All of them expected that at least one of the female characters would transform her subjugated position at the end of the *telenovela*. As I previously noted, that transformation never occurred. Yet, when we discussed Beatriz's physical transformation, the women admitted that they wanted her to become "beautiful." They observed that Ana María Orozco, the actress who played Beatriz, and the other actresses who performed *el cuartel*'s characters were not "ugly." Thus the participants distinguished between "beauty"/"ugliness" in performance versus "reality."[9] Nonetheless, what was relevant about these discussions is that they created an arena for analyzing the origins of gendered "beauty." The following sections examine the participants' responses regarding female aesthetics and the sources of these ideological discourses.

Female "beauty" and "ugliness" as male constructions

For some participants, aesthetic categorizations in *Betty* were a product of patriarchal ideological discourses and the power inequalities between men and women. One woman noted that:

> "Beauty" or "ugliness" is based on men's images of women. Women's "beauty" comes from their own confidence and who provides confidence to women? Men. Women, especially Latina women, depend on men's perceptions of themselves.
>
> (San Antonio, 40 +, participant #3)

For this participant, women's self-esteem relies primarily on physical attributes, heterosexual attraction, and the ways in which men judge women's "beauty"/bodies. "Beauty" and "ugliness" are then unstable categories which are constantly defined or redefined by men to create ideal standards that are impossible to obtain because they change according to a particular man's perceptions. For this participant, women have no agency since they are trapped in a hierarchical gender and power structure wherein they have no control of their bodies or minds. However, she specifically makes a distinction between women as a general gender categorization and Latina women. It seems that this participant sees the Latina woman as a subject who has internalized the ideologies of male superiority that are part of the Latin America/Latino cultural imaginary.

Following the issue of gender construction and "beauty," another participant observed that:

> In *Betty*, men classified women based on their appearance. Men can get away

with a lot more because that is the way they are classified. A man can be not attractive at all but if he dresses nice and if he has money, any woman would like him because he has money and he has class. If you see an "ugly" woman who has money, what are the chances that you will see that woman with a very handsome man?

(San Antonio, 18+, participant #11)

Similar to the previous participant, this woman situates men as powerful subjects who create aesthetic categorizations. However, she includes other elements such as class and social stereotypes of women and men. Women who were enamoured with financial mobility was a recurring element in *Betty*'s narrative. As previously observed, both Patricia ("beautiful") and Aura María ("ugly") used their sexuality/sensuality to try to improve their socio-economic position. However, for this participant all women are attracted to wealth and social status and would have relationships with any man based on these conditions. On the other hand, since men are only attracted to women's physical appearance, "ugly" women from any socio-economic class will have limited or no opportunities of finding sexual/romantic relationships. In this heteronormal representation, women do not have any power to select their sexual partners. In some ways, the participant's gender depictions rearticulate popular culture and social constructions of women as greedy, as dependent on men, and as mere objects who are desired and judged based on their appearance (Bordo 1993; Chapkis 1986; Wolf 1991).

"Beauty" is a product of class and sometimes "race"

For other participants, "beauty" and "ugliness" in *Betty* were social constructions related to class. In general, these participants reproduced *Betty*'s ideological discourses, since, as I previously discussed, the text represented "beauty" as a commodity that only people with financial resources could obtain. As one participant expressed:

El cuartel represents the working-class woman. They are part of that group because of their lack of economic resources. They are not "ugly." They represent the common woman. Thus, considering that "beauty" is a social construction, the ones who have the economic resources have the power to be "beautiful."

(Puerto Rican, 40 +, participant #16)

Some of the participants who located class as the main source of "beauty" also claimed that to "be beautiful" involved more than having the economic resources to buy clothing and products. "Beauty" was related to "taste" and knowing "how to dress." Therefore, "beauty" becomes one of the symbols and practices of the dominant class. One participant explained:

The "ugly" women are the poor ones. Marcela has money and social status, she knows how to present herself. The "ugly" women are the secretaries. Look at the "black" woman [Mariana]. She is striking, very attractive but she is "ugly" because she comes from the working class.

(San Antonio, 18+, participant #12)

For this participant Marcela's upper-class status is the main element of her constructed "beauty." However, she situates Mariana as one of the most physically beautiful women, which can be viewed as an oppositional reading of the traditional "white" female "beauty." When I asked this participant if elements other than class influenced the construction of "ugliness" in *Betty*'s narrative, neither she nor the other women explored the racial ideologies that construct the dominant discourse of "beauty." Still, it should be noted that none of the other participants in San Antonio's 18 + or 40 + or in Puerto Rico's 40 + focus groups selected the "black" woman as beautiful.

The issue of "race" and "blackness" was reintroduced by the 18 + focus group conducted in Puerto Rico. When describing *el cuartel de las feas*, one participant noted that Mariana was part of that group because of her "race."

Mariana is "ugly" because she is "black" and poor. "Black" women are always rejected . . . There is a lot of racism in our society. For example, I work in a store and my boss is nicer to people who are "white" and dressed elegantly.

(Puerto Rico, 18 +, participant #20)

This participant articulates the multi-axial system of oppression related to "race," gender, and class. Mariana's marginality comes from the color of her skin which contains a realm of significations in Latin American/Western societies. More than being poor, Mariana is "black," a racial signifier that locates her in a more subjugated position than other women in *el cuartel* since, as the participant observed, "black women are always rejected." This participant goes beyond *Betty*'s narrative by locating the racist practices that are part of Puerto Rican and other Latin American societies. It should be noted that this participant identified herself as "black." Although racial categorization does not translate to racial consciousness, in this case the participant's daily experiences as a "black" woman who sees the rejection of "black" people in her workplace might have influenced her oppositional/counter-hegemonic reading.

"Beauty" is a media construction

Another group of participants located female "beauty" as a product of society/media standards. Television, magazines, and media in general construct idealized female bodies that do not correspond to their "real life counterparts." According to these participants, Beatriz, *el cuartel de las feas*, and all women feel social and psychological pressures to comply with the media's idealized parameters of female "beauty." For these participants, *Betty*'s narrative was a reflection of what society/media dictates as "beautiful."

An interesting exchange occurred during the San Antonio 18 + focus group. The following dialogue exemplifies the complex relations between socially constructed female "beauty" and the burden that these participants feel to "be beautiful."

We make ourselves suffer you know, buying magazines, looking at models. Maybe one is not so "ugly" but not as "beautiful" as the models . . . thus one gets obsessed thinking that one is "ugly" but if you look around you will see that most women are like you. *Betty* is a reflection of society. Society dictates who is young and attractive.

(participant #7)

I think that what she says is true since "beauty" standards are too high. For example, in the *telenovela* none of the women are "ugly." All of *el cuartel de las feas* are really "beautiful."

(participant #8)

Exactly their "beauty" does not correspond to EcoModa's beauty standards. That is the problem.

(participant #12)

These participants problematize society's/media's construction of idealized "beauty." Through their own experiences as women and *Betty*'s narrative the participants interconnect some of the Western/mediated ideological discourses of female idealized "beauty" and the ways in which the "beauty" system pressures women to conform to these mythic standards.

Conclusion

Several studies in Latin America have enhanced our understanding of *telenovela* consumption in the household; gender, power, and class relations; and the ways in which women's daily chores determine their interactions with particular media products (Rosa María Alfaro 1988; Mercedes Charles 1995; Jesús Martín Barbero and Sonia Muñoz 1992). These studies provide important information on audiences' readings of texts, situating audiences as active decoders of televisual narratives. However, contrary to previous *telenovelas* produced in Latin America, *Betty*'s theme and transnational success provided a unique opportunity to explore the ways in which women from various ethnic, racial, and age backgrounds understood ideologies of gendered "beauty."

The dichotomy of "beautiful"/"ugly" female bodies in the context of Latin American/Western cultures represented the main point of commonality between participants and *Betty*'s theme. The participants' readings were interconnected to their own gendered position in society, the marginality of the common female body, the social pressures to be "beautiful," and the gender/power differences in Latin American/Latino communities. These women provided multiple answers regarding the origins of female aesthetic classifications and some of the ideological discourses that permeate these socially constructed categories.

If one considers the ways in which gendered "beauty" and "ugliness" were constructed in *Betty*, then the participants' responses created both dominant and negotiated meanings. Certainly, the participant who selected Mariana (the "black" woman) as "beautiful" and the woman who located "race"/"whiteness," and racism as the ideological discourses of "beauty," produced counter-hegemonic readings. As I previously observed, "race" (like other cultural and social norms and practices that inform the "beauty" system) was never directly discussed in the narrative as one of the main qualifications of "beauty." In addition, all of the participants understood aesthetic divisions as social constructions and explored the struggles that women endure to become or "feel" "beautiful." In spite of that, they wanted to witness a transformation of Beatriz and *el cuartel's* physical appearances.

Maybe, as Susan Bordo (1993) argues, women are trapped in the "beauty" system and cannot surpass their domination. Or perhaps, as Dorothy Smith (1990) suggests, women are active agents in their process of body transformations (Smith cited in Davis 1995: 60–2). Thus, the participants understood Beatriz's and *el cuartel's* physical "renovations" as a re-articulation of their subjectivity. Considering that the participants were upper middle class, maybe they wanted Beatriz and *el cuartel* to appropriate the cultural practices of their class while concomitantly redefining "beauty" as a more flexible categorization. After all, that was the main message behind *Betty*. In other words, a "beautiful" woman can be "old," "fat," "tall," "black," and working-class as long she incorporates, re-presents, and performs the cultural practices of the upper middle-class social field. If that was the case, then the depiction of an intelligent and "ugly" protagonist and the possibilities of reconstructing a "common" female body as "beautiful" may have accounted for the *telenovela's* success among the participants and other audiences. Still, are we ready to transform the performance of televisual "beauty"/"ugliness"? Audiences may have been ready for that, however, Univision was not. *EcoModa (Betty's* sequel) focused on the marriage of Beatriz and Armando and the "beautiful," intelligent, yet insecure Beatriz who feared losing "her man."[10]

I wonder what types of performances of televisual "beauty"/"ugliness" will be represented in the NBC version of *Betty*. It is too soon to tell and I am not sure if the sitcom will be ever produced. Nonetheless, and as we already know, the pressures of being "beautiful" transcend a *telenovela* story . . . this is a real-life issue which will not be neatly resolved *vis-à-vis* the *telenovela* or situation comedy genre.

Acknowledgements

I would like to thank Raquel Morris, Izabara Hernández, and Magali García Ramis for helping me locate participants in Texas and Puerto Rico. Thanks to Barbara Klinger for her helpful comments. Special thanks to Clemencia Rodríguez for her mentorship and support.

Notes

1 For an examination on the ways in which Colombia has been constructed in the media, see Clemencia Rodríguez (2000).
2 It should be noted that national differences inform the *telenovela* genre's conventions. For example, the Colombian *telenovela* includes comedy as part of the narrative and is generally characterized as depicting human interactions in a more "realistic" and complex way than its Mexican and Venezuelan counterparts. For

more information about the *telenovela* genre and its national differences, see Ana López (1995) and Omar Rincón (2000).

3 Although some of *Betty*'s characters made indirect references to Colombia's political, social, and economic struggles, the narrative never explored the nation's social and political turmoil. Most of these references were constructed in a nostalgic sense in lines such as, "the way Colombia used to be," or "even though we have many problems, we can enjoy life."

4 This research is part of a larger project organized by Clemencia Rodríguez. The audience research was divided into focus groups and personal interviews. I was in charge of the focus groups in San Antonio, Texas and in Río Piedras, Puerto Rico.

5 The selection process was quite different in each geographical location. Thanks to a Colombian friend in San Antonio, I was able to find Colombians for the two age-differentiated focus groups. All of the Colombian 40 + women were part of a Colombian cultural organization while the younger generation of Colombians were friends. On the other hand, one of my students helped me find Mexicans and Mexican-Americans for the 18 + San Antonio group. The selection of participants in Puerto Rico was easier thanks to contacts at the University of Puerto Rico's (UPR) Communication School. The 40 + group was selected before I traveled to the island and all of the participants have known each other for years. The 18 + Puerto Ricans were part of one of the summer courses of UPR's Education school.

6 The questions were divided into three thematic categories: *telenovela* genre, representations of "beauty" and "ugliness," and gender constructions and love relations. Each meeting lasted one hour, was tape recorded, and later transcribed. All the group interviews took place before the end of *Betty*. With the exception of the San Antonio 18 + group which was bilingual (Spanish and English) the other focus groups were conducted in Spanish. I translated the participants' responses in Spanish into English.

7 "Race" in Latin America and the Spanish Caribbean is comprised of a multiplicity of racial categorizations related to physical appearance, and, in some instances, class. Thus, besides the categories "white" and "black," I included the term *mestiza*.

8 Nora Mazziotti (1996) and Robert Allen (1995) argue that the *telenovela* genre revolves around the characters' search and discovery of their identities. The "happy ending" is also part of the genre and this convention is usually depicted with a wedding between the principal characters (Mazziotti 1996: 13–16).

9 It should be noted that none of the Colombian participants made references to Colombia's social turmoil. Only the Puerto Rican participants mentioned Colombia's current political-social problems. For them, *Betty* presented a depiction distinct from the "Colombia" they see in the news.

10 *EcoModa* was a commercial disappointment. Univision aired *EcoModa* on Sundays, changed its time-slot three times, and packaged the product as a one-hour "comedy" à la *Ally McBeal*. After twenty-six episodes *EcoModa* was canceled on June 2, 2002.

References

Alfaro, Rosa María. 1988. "Los usos socials populares de las telenovelas en el mundo urbano." *Estudios sobre las culturas contemporaneas* 2 (4/5): 223–59.

Allen, Robert. 1995. *To Be Continued . . . Soap Operas Around the World*. Chapel Hill: University of North Carolina Press.

Ang, Ien. 1996. *Living Room Wars*. London: Routledge.

Aparicio, Frances. 1998. *Listening to Salsa: Gender, Latin Popular Music, and Puerto Rican Cultures*. London: Wesleyan University Press.

Bordo, Susan. 1993. *Unbearable Weight: Feminism, Western Culture, and the Body*. Berkeley: University of California Press.

Bourdieu, Pierre. [1974] 1984. *Distinctions: A Social Critique of the Judgment of Taste*. Trans. Richard Nice. London: Routledge.

Butler, Judith. 1990. "Performative Acts and Gender Constitution: An Essay in Phenomenology and Feminist Theory," in Sue Elle Case (ed.) *Performing Feminism: Feminist Critical Theory and Theatre*, pp. 270–82. Baltimore, MD: The Johns Hopkins University Press.

Chapkis, Wendy. 1986. *Beauty Secrets*. London: The Women's Press.

Charles, Mercedes. 1995. "Women and Men in the Latin American Media." *Communication Research Trends* 15 (3): 3–10.

Davis, Kathy. 1995. *The Dilemma of Cosmetic Surgery*. London: Routledge.

Freeman, Michael. 2000. "Telemundo gains new ground." *Electronic Media*, December 11: 8.

García Canclini, Nestor. 2001. *La globalización imaginada*. Buenos Aires: Paidós.

Gordon, Edmund T. 1998. *Disparate Diasporas: Identity and Politics in an African Nicaraguan Community*. Austin: University of Texas Press.

Haiken, Elizabeth. 1997. *Venus Envy: A History of Cosmetic Surgery*. Baltimore, MD: The Johns Hopkins University Press.

Hall, Stuart. 1980. "Encoding/decoding," in Stuart Hall, Daniel Hobson, Andrea Lowe, and Paul Willis (eds.) *Culture, Media, Language*, pp. 128–38. London: Hutchinson.

Hanchard, Michael. 1994. "Black Cinderella?: Race and the Public Sphere in Brazil." *Public Culture* 7: 165–85.

hooks, bell. 1992. *Black Looks: Race and Representation*. Boston, MA: South End Press.

Kauffman, Barbara. 1992. "Feminist Facts: Interview Strategies and Political Subjects in Ethnographies." *Communication Theory* 2: 187–206.

Kellner, Douglas. 1995. *Media Cultures: Cultural Studies, Identity and Politics Between the Modern and the Postmodern*. London: Routledge.

Kutzinski, Vera M. 1993. *Sugar's Secrets: Race and the Erotics of Cuban Nationalism*. Charlottesville: University Press of Virginia.

López, Ana. 1995. "Our Welcomed Guests: Telenovela in Latin America," in Robert Allen (ed.) *To be Continued . . . Soap Operas Around the World*, pp. 256–84. London: Routledge.

Mankekar, Purnima. 1999. *Screening Culture, Viewing Politics*. London: Duke University Press.

Martin Barbero, Jesús and Sonia Muñoz (eds.). 1992. *Televisión y melodrama: género y lecturas de la telenovela on Colombia*. Bogotá: Tercer Mundo.

Mazziotti, Nora. 1996. *La industria de la telenovela: la producción de ficción en América Latina*. Buenos Aires: Paidós.

Mohanty, Chandra Talpade. 1991. "Cartographies of Struggle," in Chandra Talpade Mohanty, Ana Russo, and Lourdes Torres (eds.) *Third World Women and the Politics of Feminism*, pp. 1–47. Bloomington: Indiana University Press.

Montecino, Sonia. 1995. "Identidades de género en América Latina: mestizajes, sacrificios y simultaneidades," in Luz Gabriela Arango, Magdalena Leon, and Mara Viveros (eds.)

Género e identidad: ensayos sobre lo femenino y masculino, pp. 265–99. Bogotá: Tercer Mundo.

Narayan, Kirin. 1998. "How Native Is a 'Native' Anthropologist," in Thapan Meenakshi (ed.) *Anthropological Journeys: Reflections of Fieldwork*, pp. 163–87. Hyderabad, India: Orient Longman.

Rincón, Omar. 2000. "Alabadas sean las ellas de pantalla." *Gaceta* 47:14–19.

Rodríguez, Clemencia. 2000. "Tan lejos de dios y tan cerca del New York Times: los medios y el conflicto internacional," unpublished paper.

Seiter, Ellen. 1999. *Television and New Media Audiences*. Oxford: Clarendon Press.

Shohat, Ella and Robert Stam. 1994. *Unthinking Eurocentrism*. London: Routledge.

Smith, Dorothy. 1990. *Texts, Facts and Femininity: Exploring the Relations of Ruling*. New York: Routledge.

Sutter, Mary. 2001. " 'Ugly Betty' turns tables on telenovela formula." *Variety*, January 22–28: 54.

Sutter, Mary and Josef Adalian. 2001. "NBC betting on 'Betty'." Variety.com, September 19. Lexis-Nexis Academic Universe. On-line. Available: http://www.lexisnexis.com (October 3, 2001).

Tedlock, Barbara. 1991. "From Participant Observation to the Observation of Participation: The Emergence of Narrative Ethnography." *Journal of Anthropological Research* 47: 69–94.

Twine, France Winddance. 1998. *Racism in a Racial Democracy: The Maintenance of White Supremacy in Brazil*. New Brunswick, NJ: Rutgers University Press.

Valdivia, Angharad N. 1998. "Stereotype or Transgression? Rosie Pérez in Hollywood Films." *Sociological Quarterly* 39 (3): 393–408.

Wade, Peter. 1985. "Race and Class: The Case of South American Blacks." *Ethnic and Racial Studies* 8 (2): 233–49.

Wade, Peter. 1997. *Race and Ethnicity in Latin America*. Chicago: Pluto Press.

Wade, Peter. 2000. *Music, Race, and Nation: Música Tropical in Colombia*. Chicago: The Chicago University Press.

Whitefield, Mimi. 2000. "New Formulas Keep Spanish-language Soap Operas Rolling in the Dough." *The Miami Herald*, November 20: 57–8.

Wolf, Naomi. 1991. *The Beauty Myth*. New York: Anchor Books.

18

Sob Stories, Merriment, and Surprises
The 1950s audience participation show on network television and women's daytime reception

Marsha F. Cassidy

Originally published in *The Velvet Light Trap*. 42 (Fall 1998): 48–61.

The women who watched daytime television during the 1950s have not been lost to history. Their images flicker to life on the black-and-white kinescopes that chronicle the decade's audience participation shows. These images, and the narrative structures of the genre in which they appear, open up a new territory of investigation into daytime television reception and television's place in women's public and private leisure during the post-war era.

A profusion of audience participation programs filled daytime scheduling throughout the 1950s, a trend underexamined in earlier television histories.[1] This essay documents the vitality of the network genre across the decade[2] and argues that its mode of narration held in synchronous parallel two disparate spaces consigned to feminine television reception, each space bearing its own version of television's part in feminine relaxation and diversion – the television studio theater and the home. The television studio theater, centered in New York and Hollywood, emerged during the 1950s as a popular new entertainment space that drew crowds of women to daily live broadcasts. In this space, daytime television was linked to visions of feminine leisure, travel, and fun, sequestered from household obligations. Within domestic space, however, daytime television viewing was caught up in discourse that warned women against the perils of television addiction, advising the homemaker to keep working as she watched. The audience participation show raised contradictions about television's place in women's daytime leisure by narratively linking these reception sites. The genre's projection of festive studio diversion into the home, coupled with the promise of active at-home play, collided with homemaking ideals that forbade women from watching television during the day except in a state of distraction.

A close scrutiny of women's relation to television pleasure in these parallel spaces, exemplified in the programs *Strike It Rich* and *It Could Be You*, suggests that the textual strategies of the audience participation genre held these dual spaces and their bipolar expectations for feminine television reception in an uneasy tension. Exploiting early television's capacity for liveness and immediacy to establish what William Boddy calls "a metaphysic of presence" (80), the audience participation show conjoined these contradictory spaces to build a national community of daytime women viewers that was both virtual and mobile. In this conflation, the audience participation show did not simply cast its ideal viewer as a ceaselessly preoccupied home worker who occasionally glanced at her console but called into being a more ambivalent subject, an interactive participant who might indulge in attentive daytime viewing as a release from the household grind. Unlike the closed texts of other daytime genres, which restricted the viewer to the distractions of the domestic zone, the audience participation show hailed a female subject who could freely traverse the home's threshold – either materially or electronically – to engross herself in the amusements made possible by the decade's new medium. The audience participation show sanctioned both the *flâneuse* seen mobilized in the studio theater and her domestic counterpart loafing in front of the television set at home (see Friedberg 2–3).

By devising an interactive mode that invited a home viewer's undivided attention, the audience participation show allayed advertisers' growing fears that daytime commercial messages were being broadcast into empty rooms. The dual discursive spaces occupied by the genre served to legitimate and promote television's prescripts for consumption. Like the turn-of-the-century department store, the television studio theater authorized women's public visibility in the pursuit of commercialized goals, while the daily transmission of a vibrant community of women into domestic space, paired with the possibility for homebound interaction and sorority, justified paying close attention to commercials, a mandatory preface to shopping.

Studying the audience participation show proves to be historically valuable because its very mode of narration suggests that the television industry's ideal daytime viewer was not limited to the distracted housewife so often described by network executives of the era (Allen 124–25; Boddy 20–21; Spigel 77–89). The audience participation show, driven by the industry's commercial imperatives, addressed a more ambiguously constructed spectator, a woman who was concomitantly urged to absorb herself in television as a new form of acceptable feminine recreation and leisure, enjoyed both in the public realm of the television studio and in the privacy of her home.

The audience participation show on daytime television

During the 1950s, the term "audience participation show" was a standard phrase in broadcasting's informal taxonomy; it delineated a prolific category of radio and television programs that integrated ordinary people into the broadcast performance. A 1956 television production manual explained that the key components of the audience participation show were "an MC, various assistants which may include musicians," and people chosen from "the studio audience, from the home viewers, or from both" (Stasheff and Bretz 130).

Consistent with the decade's own sweeping and porous classification (Stasheff and Bretz 131; Lindemann), this study considers the audience participation show not to be a narrowly defined genre but a broader narrational mode whose strategies overarched a range of popular program types, including the quiz show, the stunt show, the human interest show, the "give-away," and even those talk/variety shows that integrated an aggregate studio audience into the performance.

Malleable as it was, the audience participation program played a crucial role in the early development of daytime programming for women. In 1957, NBC research concluded that the audience participation show, in its various incarnations, was one of two forms of programming most successfully attracting female viewers during the day, soap opera being the other (Lindemann). Yet audience participation shows out-numbered soap operas throughout the postwar decade. During the first half of the 1950s, soap operas accounted for only 100 quarter hours of daytime programming, while audience participation shows (including human interest versions) totaled 232. Even during the second half of the decade, the discrepancy continued; soap opera quarter hours grew to 314, but audience participation offerings accumulated 520 quarter hours (Sterling and Kittross 652).

These plentiful programs on daytime television employed varying degrees of audience participation. At the minimal end of the continuum was the en masse visual and aural participation of the studio audience, *The Garry Moore Show* and *Arthur Godfrey Time* serving as two prime examples. More commonly, however, individual members of the studio audience and individual viewers at home were carefully inserted into program narratives. Studio audience guests were either invited up on stage, as they were on *Truth or Consequences* and *Queen for a Day*, for example, or singled out for participation within the audience space, as occurred daily on *Art Linkletter's House Party* and *It Could Be You*. Less centrally, home viewers entered the performance, too, by letter (*Stand Up and Be Counted, The Garry Moore Show, Strike It Rich*) or by telephone (*Strike It Rich* and *Truth or Consequences*).

Orchestrating the dual realms of the home viewer and the studio audience was a "male personality" (Lindemann). *Time* magazine called these pivotal hosts the "charm boys." While in 1954 the "unquestioned king" was Arthur Godfrey, *Time*'s list also named Robert Q. Lewis, Garry Moore, Bob Crosby, Art Linkletter, and Tommy Bartlett (*Welcome Travelers*). Other engaging emcees also populated the dec-ade's airwaves on weekdays: Bob Barker, Bill Leyden, Bert Parks, Bud Collyer, Harry Babbitt, Bill Cullen, Bob Russell, and Warren Hull, among the most famous. In the words of *Time* magazine, from morning to sunset, television "turns loose an avalanche of masculine charm that would overwhelm any audience less hardy than U.S. house-wives" ("Charm"). Mediated by masculine charm, the audience participation genre assumed many profitable guises during the 1950s. Variations proliferated as the format delivered impressive daytime ratings at a moderate cost and reliably attracted lucrative advertising.

Audience participation shows spelled success in daytime ratings. In 1956, for example, *Strike It Rich* on CBS pulled an average rating of 7.25, overpowering the ambitious *Home* show on NBC, which could only muster a 3 (Lichty). In April of the same year, *Arthur Godfrey Time* and *The Big Payoff* performed even better than *Strike It Rich*, ranking among the top ten "multiweekly" ratings grabbers, close com-petitors to four soap operas on the same list ("Katz").[3] And it was only after new leadership at NBC in 1957 programmed *Truth or Consequences, The Price Is Right*, and *Queen for a Day* in vanguard positions that NBC took the lead in daytime numbers ("NBC-TV's" 27; Castleman and Podrazik 111). In the 11 A.M. to 1 P.M. slot in

January of 1957, *Truth or Consequences* and *The Price Is Right* helped procure a 7.2 average rating for the network (up 29 percent from the year before), while *Queen for a Day*'s performance increased NBC's average afternoon rating to 10.2, up 44 percent from the previous year. Delivering 4,222,000 homes for NBC every day, *Queen for a Day* attracted more viewers than twenty of ABC's primetime offerings ("NBC-TV's" 46, 27).

High ratings sold the alternating and multiple sponsorships that were fast becoming the trend in 1950s television advertising (Boddy 159). In August 1956, *It Could Be You* held yearly contracts with eight alternating sponsors, including a solid 26-quarter-hour sponsorship for Mondays purchased by American Home. *Queen for a Day* dominated NBC's selling bonanza, boasting fifteen committed sponsors, among them television's advertising giant, Procter & Gamble, which purchased 65 quarter hours (Barris).

Audience participation shows not only garnered competitive ratings that attracted loyal sponsors, they did so at a cost-effective price. A cross-genre comparison of daytime production numbers in the mid-1950s demonstrates the moderate cost of the audience participation show in relation to the slightly less expensive soap opera and the much more costly *Home* and *Matinee Theater*. Based on estimated weekly costs for one half hour of daily programming five days a week, *Matinee Theater* was budgeted at $50,000 (MacDonald 112) and *Home* between $25,000 and $50,000, depending upon the number of remote broadcasts scheduled ("For the Girls" 92; "TV Hits the Road" 88). In contrast, *Search for Tomorrow* was produced for $19,600 (MacDonald 112), while *Queen for a Day* spent $25,000 ("In Review: *Queen*") and *It Could Be You*, $35,000 ("In Review: *It Could*"). As these figures confirm, the audience participation show, like the soap opera, offered networks a programming format that kept costs down and viewership up, a winning combination.

Guided by this persuasive arithmetic, the flow of daytime television during the 1950s was deluged with daily visions of a participating audience. To indicate more fully the extent of the genre's ubiquity, I have included a chart which describes some of the decade's most popular offerings (Fig. 1). As evidenced in the chart, every day for ten years a steady stream of programs both invited women to enter television's performance space and pictured women who were already there – marrying (*Bride and Groom*); competing for a makeover (*Glamour Girl; The Big Payoff*); telling if a husband was an optimist or a pessimist (*House Party*); parking a steamroller (*Truth or Consequences*); weeping over life's misfortunes (*Queen for a Day, Strike It Rich*); being surprised (*It Could Be You*); or merely giggling, applauding, putting away their hankies, and heading for the exits ("Program" 96).

Despite novel permutations, these programs all fundamentally relied upon the ongoing apposition of two social realms: a newly codified public space for feminine leisure located in the television theater and the privatized domestic workspace to which 1950s women were increasingly confined. By holding these two spheres in perpetual juxtaposition, the audience participation show affirmed both a woman's access to publicly visible leisure during the day – a leisure integrally connected to at-home participation and diversion – and her contradictory obligation to stay home and keep her nose to the grindstone, her television set a mere backdrop to disciplined labor. To better illustrate how the audience participation show mediated these incongruities, I turn first to the space of the television theater, which sprang to life in the 1950s.

A new public space for women: the television studio theater

As the 1950s began, audience participation programs, already a mainstay on radio, struggled to define themselves in television terms (e.g., "On the Happy"; Settle and Glenn 259). Like their radio antecedents, these new programs required a physical space in which audiences could assemble, yet the cumbersome technology of early television posed challenging production problems if the audience was to be visible on camera.

Translating the aurality of audience participation on radio to the "proper language of television" (Herridge) demanded an inventive redesign of existing facilities and directorial experimentation. Responding to the need for theaters that could house television equipment, the broadcast networks began to lease and convert a string of major theatrical spaces up and down Broadway beginning in 1949, some seating over a thousand patrons (Cotler 19). By 1955, NBC had remodeled the International Theatre, the Century Theatre, the Center Theatre, and the Colonial to meet television's technical demands without sacrificing the benefits of a live audience (Liebman). The impressive color-ready Ziegfeld Theatre was converted a year later ("NBC's $5M" 25). Innovative stage remodeling – like equipment aprons, camera runways (Settel and Glenn 145), and platforms that jutted deeply into audience space – enabled cameramen to frame studio patrons in versatile long-shots, pans, trucking shots, close-ups, and zooms. Other ingenious constructions concealed control boths under stages in order to keep lines of sight open ("NBC's $5M" 25) or nestled cameras strategically among audience seats to allow hosts to direct their gaze at both the camera and the studio guests (O'Meara Fig. 13). At the Ziegfeld, innovator Sol Cornberg even devised an aerial camera track located along the balcony ("NBC's $5M" 25). In new construction, CBS's $8 million "Television City" in Los Angeles was blueprinted in 1952 to provide two large audience studios that could each seat 350 visitors ("CBS TV"), while NBC completed a vast new three-million-dollar studio called Brooklyn Two in 1956 ("NBC's $5M" 25).

As rapidly as studio facilities were revamped, versions of popular daytime radio programs that featured a participating audience were shifted to the television screen: *The Garry Moore Show* (talk/variety, based on Moore's radio version, *Club Matinee*) in October 1950; *Strike It Rich* (considered radio's preeminent sob show) in May 1951; *Arthur Godfrey Time* and *Art Linkletter's House Party* (which mixed "talk" and audience participation) in 1952; and *The Bob Crosby Show* in 1953.

Televisual proficiency varied widely among these earliest radio transplants (see MacDonald 48). *Arthur Godfrey Time*, which in 1952 began simulcasting a segment of the radio show on television every weekday morning ("Arthur" 62), minimized camera positions that highlighted the audience. The show's tiny radio facility permitted only occasional shots of women seated on folding chairs in front of Godfrey's raised platform. During an episode from 1953, for example, when Godfrey mentions a CBS promotional shopping bag distributed to his guests (filled, of course, with sponsors' products), the camera cuts briefly to a shot of the seated women, their bags propped awkwardly beside them on the floor. In this rudimentary rendition, the television camera merely documented a studio audience watching the performance of a radio show.

In contrast, *Art Linkletter's House Party* (1952–1969), which joined daytime television nine months later, solved the transition to television in an exemplary way. *House Party's* spacious theater was cleverly designed to detail on camera Linkletter's frequent interchanges with the studio audience in a way that would not disrupt his rapport with home viewers. In a program production manual from 1955, the show's studio layout was cited for its ideal serviceability to the demands of the audience participation format. The caption under a photograph of the show in progress, which pictured a camera aimed at Linkletter from the audience space and another camera directed into the audience from the stage, called the design "[a]n ideal studio arrangement for audience participation show. Setup enables efficient entrance of MC to audience area. Preset lights are turned on the audience and cameras merely wheel around to pick up the action" (O'Meara Fig. 13). This studio arrangement permitted Linkletter's trademark opening, a long shot that panned a cheerful audience chatting and laughing together, as well as his many humorous sallies into the audience space, microphone in hand (Munson 52).

By mid decade, following the lead of *House Party*, a wide range of audience participation programs, including *Strike It Rich, Queen for a Day, Stand Up and Be Counted*, and *It Could Be You*, had freed up the creative potential of the camera to secure the participating audience within the text. Part of a newly conventionalized televisual style, a whole repertoire of innovative shots and cuts dramatized the actions and reactions that gave life to performances.

As the television industry surmounted the challenges of the medium's technical and aesthetic demands and maintained an assortment of well-appointed studios, viewers across the country responded by flocking to production centers to attend live broadcasts. In 1954, an article in the *New York Times Magazine* reported that average attendance in New York television studios alone was over 1.5 million visitors per year; together CBS and NBC received fifteen hundred ticket requests per day during "off-season," while requests increased 25 percent during the summer months, when out-of-towners planned vacations to New York City. The essay's reporter, Gorden Cotler, declared that "television broadcasts rank among New York's chief amusements" (19). By 1957, attending a live broadcast in Los Angeles had also captured the public's imagination. *Sunset: The Magazine of Western Living* headlined, "If you are in Los Angeles . . . want to see a TV broadcast?" and outlined in detail how to obtain tickets to shows at CBS, NBC, and ABC, advising, "apply for tickets at least four weeks in advance" to "avoid disappointment" ("Want to See"). Almost overnight, the television theater had evolved into a novel public space for entertainment and leisure. For the first time, people could gather together both to view a staged performance and to participate visibly in a performance designed to entertain others.

During television's first decade, studio audiences for all telecasts were skewed feminine, but daytime broadcasts in particular were viewed as a public amusement linked predominantly to women's leisure. "Rarely is an audience composed of less than 60 percent women," reported Cotler in 1954, "and the figure is sometimes close to 100 per cent" (19). The studios of the daytime audience participation shows were

ART LINKLETTER'S HOUSE PARTY (9/1/52 to 9/5/69, CBS)
Host: Art Linkletter Producer: John Guedel
A "variety" show that featured comic interviews with schoolchildren and members of the studio audience. When asked where his cast was, Linkletter replied, "In the audience." An intrepid ad-libber, Linkletter was noted for his forays into audience space, microphone in hand, asking people to tell things like "their narrowest escape, their luckiest break, their dearest wish..." (La Cossitt 26, 69, 70; Munson 52–54; McNeil 58).

BEAT THE CLOCK (3/23/50 to 9/28/58, CBS; 10/13/58 to 1/30/61, ABC)
Host: Bud Collyer Producers: Mark Goodson and Bill Todman
Couples hurried to perform stunts for prizes before time ran out (McNeil 82).

THE BIG PAYOFF (12/31/51 to 3/27/53, NBC; 3/30/53 to 10/23/59, CBS)
Host: Bert Parks Producer: Walt Framer
A man or boy explained why the woman in his life deserved a reward, most often a mink coat. In 1951 the show gave away $300,000 worth of furs, modeled by Bess Meyerson ("Winning"; McNeil 94–95).

BRIDE AND GROOM (1/25/51 to 2/5/53, CBS; 12/7/53 to 8/27/54, NBC)
Host: John Nelson Producers: John Nelson, John Reddy, and John Masterson
Daily live weddings from New York were preceded by interviews with the couple. Awarded gifts included honeymoon trips, vacuum cleaners, stoves, and silverware ("For Richer"; McNeil 118).

THE GARRY MOORE SHOW (10/50 to 6/58, CBS)
Host: Garry Moore Producer: Herb Sanford
Music, skits, and "gab" were woven together daily. Moore encouraged audience feedback. During his work in Baltimore radio as "Thomas Garrison Morfit," he held a listener contest to come up with a better stage name; a woman won $100 for suggesting "Garry Moore." During his television career, he regularly asked viewers to tell him what they did not like about the show. One day, just "for laughs," he encouraged his viewers to each send a nickel to Mrs. Margaret Deibel, a housewife visiting the broadcast from Mount Pleasant, Michigan. At week's end, she had collected $7,000 ("Craziest"; McNeil 314 15).

GLAMOUR GIRL (7/6/53 to 1/8/54, NBC)
Host: Harry Babbitt Producer: Jack McCoy
Four women from the audience explained why they should be awarded a glamorous Cinderella make-over. Winners returned the next day to show off their new look (McNeil 329). Filmed in Hollywood.

IT COULD BE YOU (6/4/56 to 12/29/61, NBC)
Host: Bill Leyden Creator: Ralph Edwards
"The show of surprises" that told funny or touching stories about members of the studio audience or viewers at home and awarded prizes. Each episode ended with the "reunion climax," when three members from the studio audience were invited up on stage. Silhouetted behind a screen was a long-lost friend or relative of one of the contestants who gave clues about her identity (McNeil 413–14).

ON YOUR ACCOUNT (6/8/53 to 7/2/54, NBC; 7/5/54 to 3/31/56, CBS)
Hosts: Eddie Albert, Win Elliot, Dennis James
Contestants told hard-luck stories to a panel and won money by answering quiz questions correctly (McNeil 618).

THE PRICE IS RIGHT (11/26/56 to 9/6/63, NBC)
Host: Bill Cullen
Producers: Mark Goodson and Bill Todman
Four contestants chosen from the audience tried to guess the correct price of a variety of items, from clothing to a roomful of furniture. The studio audience, while never seen, was frequently heard hooting, shouting advice, sighing in disappointment, and clapping (McNeil 671–72).

QUEEN FOR A DAY (1/3/56 to 9/2/60, NBC; 9/28/60 to 10/2/64, ABC)
Host: Jack Bailey Producer: Harry Mynatt
    Five contestants, all women, were selected each day from the studio audience to. tell what they wanted if they were chosen queen for a day:' The studio audience, who were assembled around tables at the Moulin Rouge, selected winners by applauding. The winner, who not only received her wish but also a deluge of prizes, sat on a throne, wearing a crown and an ermine-trimmed cape (Blake; "Program"; "Queen"; "Troubles"; McNeil 680).

STAND UP AND BE COUNTED (5/28/56 to 9/6/57, CBS)
Host: Bob Russell
    Contestants were home viewers selected by letter. As they sat with Bob Russell behind the wooden railing of a "front porch," they explained a personal dilemma to a live studio audience. Later, members of the studio audience came forward to stand at the railing and offer advice to the contestants while home viewers sent their opinions by mail. Guests returned the following day to announce their decisions and collect their prizes (Munson 54–55; McNeil 784).

STRIKE IT RICH (5/7/51 to 1/3/58, CBS)
Host: Warren Hull Producer: Walt Framer
    Contestants in need from the studio or home audience answered quiz questions to win up to $500. During the "helping hand" segment, celebrities played the game for deserving home-bound contestants. A telephone was set up on stage as a "Heart Line"; home viewers could call the show and make private donations to guests whose stories touched them. The show was widely censured for capitalizing on human misery, and in 1954 NewYork City tried to require the program to obtain a charity license, a move rejected by the state legislature. Although the scandal forced the cancellation of the primetime version, the daytime version continued for four more years ("Framer"; "Giveaway"; "Then the House Burned"; "Winning"; McNeil 796).

TIC TAC DOUGH (7/30/56 to 10/30/59, NBC)
Hosts: Jack Barry, Gene Rayburn, Bill Wendell
    Contestants were selected from the studio audience and played tic-tac-toe on a game board for money. When the quiz show scandals rocked broadcasting, the nighttime version was pulled from the airwaves, but the daytime version remained untouched (Castleman and Podrazik 133; Blum 265; McNeil 839).

TRUTH OR CONSEQUENCES (1/14/52 to 5/16/52 and 12/31/56 to 9/24/65, NBC)
Host: Bob Barker Creator: Ralph Edwards
    Contestants who failed to answer a question before the buzzer sounded were forced to perform a stunt. Not only did the show select contestants from the studio audience, but Barker also called home contestants, selecting them randomly from submitted postcards (McNeil 867).

WELCOME TRAVELERS (9/8/52 to 7/2/54, NBC; 7/5/54 to 10/28/55, CBS)
Host: Tommy Bartlett Creator: Tommy Bartlett
    Set in Chicago, the program interviewed travelers passing through the city, asking them to tell their personal stories for prizes (McNeil 901).

WHO DO YOU TRUST? (DO YOU TRUST YOUR WIFE?) (9/30/57 to 3/62, ABC)
Host: Johnny Carson Producer: Don Fedderson
    Couples from the audience were interviewed and had the chance to answer questions for prizes (Castleman and Podrazik 120; McNeil 911).

WINNER TAKE ALL (2/12/51 to 4/20/51, CBS; 2/25/52 to 10/5/52, NBC)
Hosts: Barry Gray, Bill Cullen Producer: Gil Fates Creators: Mark Goodson and Bill Todman
    Two contestants chosen from the studio audience answered questions about skits performed on stage (McNeil 918).

Figure 1 Audience Participation Programs 1950–1959

visibly inhabited by women enjoying themselves. On a 1957 episode of *Truth or Consequences*, for example, after a studio audience rules through boisterous applause that women are better drivers than men, Bob Barker jokes, "We've proved one thing beyond a reasonable doubt ... there are more women here than men!" (8 January

1957). Indeed, while a few men could be seen scattered throughout the audiences of daytime programs, the overwhelming majority was female.

For these women, attendance at a television broadcast constituted a special occasion, a holiday excursion split off from the routine of everyday drudgery. Program hosts took care to identify women in the audience either as local suburban or ex-urban housewives who were taking the day off with friends to enjoy a festive treat or as out-of-towners who had traveled to the studio theater as part of a fun-filled vacation. This aura of holiday excitement was heightened in part by the possibility of being seen on live television. One studio visitor, Lynn Swalbe, reported that she and her mother got "all dressed up to the nines, with hats, gloves, and suits, because they knew they'd be on TV" when they attended a *Queen for a Day* broadcast in 1954 (Ganas). Photographs and kinescopes from the decade record the lavish display of dressed-up 1950s femininity that decorated television studios. Crinoline skirts, pinched waistlines, tailored dresses, gloves, purses, and a sea of hats fill the audience space, camera-ready. Visual details like these, combined with shots of women laughing, smiling, talking together, and applauding, served to designate the daytime audience participation program as convivial feminine gatherings set apart from everyday life.

Miriam Hansen has argued that early cinema "opened up a space – a social space as well as a perceptual, experiential horizon – in women's lives, whatever their marital status, age, or background" (117). Like early nickelodeons, the live television broadcast was a "cheap amusement" that drew women together from all walks of life (Peiss). Only this time, the tickets were free. As one network guest relations supervisor said in 1954, "A television studio is one of the few places you can see live talent nowadays without laying out a lot of dough" (qtd. in Cotler 19).

While the audience's generational diversity was readily apparent when cameras panned across faces of all ages, other social differences were discernible through individual interviews. Needy audience members were most evident on the "misery shows," where it was not uncommon to meet women who were too poor to own a washing machine, who were holding down a job while raising seven children alone, or who needed a dining room table big enough for all family members to eat together. At other times, participants identified themselves as wives of army officers or bankers. Occasionally, minority women also appeared on camera. A native American contestant, part Cherokee, was honored for her charity work on one episode of *It Could Be You*, for example (21 May 1957). Loretta Williams, a "full-blooded Pima Indian," competed as a contestant on *Queen for a Day* in March 1956, while a Mexican American contestant, a widow with three young children, was voted queen for a day on February 24, 1956.[4]

The diverse social collectivity of women gathered in the television theater also demonstrated a geographic admixture. Unlike the neighborhood nickelodeons of an earlier generation, the network television theaters were anchored in urban space, divorced from local communities. Television broadcasts originated from the entertainment capitals of America, and participants from around the country made pilgrimages to these media meccas. The audience participation programs prided themselves on the geographically heterogeneous crowds that assembled daily. Each participant was asked to declare her town of origin. Although the composition of audiences shifted from day to day – at times two thirds local residents (Cotler 19) and at other times 75 percent out-of-towners (Bracker 17) – producers in New York and Hollywood routinely preferred featuring "people from far-off places" (Cotler 21), a production strategy that further joined television pleasures to far-flung travel. This new form of commercialized leisure, which attracted feminine celebrants from diverse classes, ages, backgrounds, and localities, built a studio space that seemed freely accessible to any woman.

Like other commercial spaces, however, the television theater was both regulated and disciplined. Competition for tickets was often fierce. Even in 1953, well before the quiz craze swept across America, television quiz shows maintained waiting lists thousands of names long; the fortunate few who held tickets often stood two hours in line to acquire prime seating (Bracker 17). When *Queen for a Day* traveled to New York's eleven-hundred-seat Ziegfeld Theater in 1960, three hundred hopefuls were turned away from each performance ("Program" 96). In another act of regulation, network page-boys monitored audience compositions daily by weeding out any "rabid fans" who attempted to attend their favorite shows too often. Called "steady customers," "regulars," or "eighty-sixes," these fans – usually women over thirty-five "with time on their hands" – were often barred from the studio (Bracker 17; Cotler 19).

Audience participation shows followed an even more rigorous regulatory procedure in the selection of guests who participated individually. By 1953, many studio guests selected for individual participation on quiz shows were required to wait twenty-four hours while their backgrounds were carefully screened; half of all participants were selected ahead of time by mail and were pre-interviewed by telephone (Bracker 17). After New York City's commissioner of welfare took *Strike It Rich* to court in 1954 to force the show to seek a charity license, the program tightened its selection procedures even further: guests who competed for money were chosen by invitation only, and the background of each applicant was thoroughly investigated ("Give-away"). In 1955, a television manual warned producers in no uncertain terms about the dangers of amateur participation:

> As time allows, interrogate all audience guests as thoroughly as possible before they come to the microphone . . . Consider appearance, speaking ability, presence, sense of humor, personality, knowledge and poise . . . One word of caution in this strange business of selecting unknown personalities for sudden exposure to millions. Remember that the very nature of the opportunity afforded by the program invites chronic exhibitionists with low IQs, irresponsible fame-seekers, indiscriminate "wits," and even cranks and mental cases.
>
> (O'Meara 195)

Although disciplined by strictures like these, the television studio evolved into a novel recreational space for women during the 1950s – a subaltern site for feminine conviviality, where women from different classes, ages, backgrounds, and geographic places gathered together in an atmosphere of sisterhood and sociability. Its geographic diversity aside, the television studio that housed this celebratory feminine community resembled the "alternative public space" Miriam Hansen suggests neighborhood nickelodeons provided for women during cinema's early days (92), where mothers "could disappear in the darkness . . . for a few hours" to surrender to the manipulations of the screen (109–10). Unlike cinema, however, the television apparatus simultaneously transmitted the act of theatrical viewing back to another set of women who remained homebound, opening up a synchronous territory of reception where recreational viewing was held in dispute.

Feminine merriment and the viewer at home

While the networks associated attendance at telecasts with sociable feminine amusement, the industry held starkly different views regarding television, leisure, and the housewife at home. The history of the audience participation show reveals the conflictual way the TV industry understood daytime television's status as an object of recreation for the homemaker, caught as it was between the model of the distracted housewife copied from radio reception and daytime sponsors' growing demands for an attentive TV customer.

Broadcast historians have amply documented early television's obsession with developing programs that would complement the busy housewife's daily routine of work. As Boddy explains, the industry's chief concern during the emergence of television's domestic paradigm was "integrating TV programming into the routines of the housewife's daily chores just as radio had done" (20). Lynn Spigel reiterates this industry preoccupation: "The idea that female spectators were also workers in the home was, by the postwar period, a truism for broadcasting and advertising executives" (75). So entrenched was this belief that Garry Moore articulated the "mission" of his daytime program explicitly in these terms. "I'm convinced," he told *Time* magazine in 1953, that housewives "want to hear the sounds of merriment while they work" ("Moore"). In response to this universal precept, the television industry designed daytime programs they believed conformed to a housewife's ongoing absent-minded state, including segmented formats that could be watched in fits and starts and overdetermined soundtracks, which sustained attention when housewives left the room (Boddy 21; Spigel 78).

As daytime programming advanced, however, this image of interrupted spectatorship in the home had undesirable consequences for the television industry. Concerned that housewives were not paying close enough attention to commercials, sponsors began to balk at television's advertising rates (Bogart 103). A series of studies during the 1950s inflamed this industry squabble about the fair pricing of daytime advertising. In February 1955, Joseph M. Ripley, Jr., conducted a telephone survey of 4,064 housewives in Columbus, Ohio. His results indicated that between the hours of 8 A.M. and 4 P.M., 63 percent of women surveyed whose TV sets were turned on were located "in the same room with the TV set," but only 33.5 percent reported "just watching" (qtd. in Bogart 104).[5] A 1957 survey, this one based upon the viewing diaries of 885 housewives in Tuscaloosa, Alabama, found that only 38.4 percent of the women surveyed reported "doing nothing but watching the program" during daytime hours (Smith 2). Another study in 1957, this one commissioned by Young & Rubicam clients, confirmed that there was "a dissipation of attention due to such factors as answering the telephone, the door bell, sewing, ironing, children's cries, etc. . . . which must be taken into consideration in evaluating the use of television and certainly in the pricing of it." One advertising executive concluded,

"There is no reason, in our opinion, why we should pay television prices for radio listening" (Lindemann). The television industry was trapped between marketing the medium as a work companion for women during the day – and alarming advertisers – or furthering viewing habits that could be criticized as promoting sloth and idleness in homemakers, raising the alarming specter of the "TV-addict housewife" (Spigel 87).

The industry's ambivalence between promoting television as a companion to household chores or as a respite from them was a response to the decade's worry that daytime television would lure housewives into forbidden leisure and disrupt family life. Leo Bogart expresses exactly this apprehension in his summary of Ripley's study, registering surprise "that during most of the day, a third or more of the housewives whose sets are on are seated in front of them with undivided attention" (104–05). Studies like these, which were designed to measure inattention, seemed to discover instead the threatening fact that one in three women was stealing relaxation and pleasure from daytime viewing.

The networks' uncertainty about how to market daytime programming within this climate was telescoped in the rhetoric surrounding NBC's *Matinee Theater*, a daytime live drama widely heralded as "quality television." Debuting in 1956, *Matinee Theater* was the first daytime program promoted as worthy of commanding a housewife's full attention. An NBC internal promotion, prepared for advertisers, pictures an aproned house-wife, her shoes discarded, seated alone in front of her television console. The copy reads, "Women have been writing us the most complimentary letters about the NBC *Matinee Theater* . . . One thing so many of them comment on is the fact that here is a show of quality they can watch in solitary splendor" ("NBC–TV Promotion"). Attached to the promotion is a column written by the *New York Herald Tribune*'s Marie Torre, who praises *Matinee Theater* for "achieving popularity without dislocating American home life." While Torre acknowledges that housewives "squeeze in" a restful hour each day exclusively for TV, she reports that they do so without interfering with the completion of their housework. "[B]read-winners may rest assured," she concludes, "that the washing and ironing will continue, the hearth will be swept and the kiddies will not go neglected." A careful look at NBC's solitary viewer seated before her set reiterates this unease about daytime spectatorship. Though entranced by *Matinee Theater*, she cannot entirely abandon her household labor; she is pictured peeling potatoes as she watches ("NBC-TV Promotion"). NBC executive Thomas E. Coffin stressed this ambivalence regarding recuperative daytime viewing when he warned in a memo that "the major deterrent to watching *Matinee Theater* is the feeling of guilt it arouses."[6]

These unresolved ambiguities attached to feelings of guilt were especially entangled in audience participation shows that could make no claim to quality. In 1958, for example, *Look* magazine characterized *Queen for a Day* as a "housewives' schedule wrecker," a "house-keeping interruption": "Mops are dropped and diapers are ditched from coast to coast" when *Queen* goes on the air ("Queen" 120). Stigmatized as a debased form of feminine entertainment, the daytime audience participation show was not considered worthy of restful viewing in "solitary splendor," yet it elicited the discordant impulse to sit down and watch as predictably as *Matinee Theater*.

The very structure of the audience participation show, which interjected festive studio space into the domestic sphere, unleashed daytime television's pleasure principle, its unresolvable ambiguities for home viewers intact. The genre dared to suggest that women could savor television as a break from household tedium, whether in the studio or at home. Beaming the gemütlichkeit of studio attendance into millions of American homes every day validated women's playful relation to TV and authorized the active pleasures of synchronous home participation. Early television's liveness, immediacy, and ability to collapse space fostered a sense of co-presence in program reception that made active fun possible at home (Stasheff and Bretz 25; Boddy 80). Viewers of audience participation shows were thus caught in a 1950s paradox, torn between rules set for a perpetually laboring housewife, who was permitted to view television only on the run, and the conflicting sanctions of a participatory genre that associated television with relaxation, diversion, and stolen pleasures.

At its core, the audience participation genre was ideally structured to bridge the spatial divide between television's public and private spheres, their contradictions regarding feminine leisure intact, and to mediate mobile and virtual travel between them. The narrative circuit connecting studio and home upon which the audience participation show was premised balanced the bodily presence of the woman traveler in a newly formulated public space with a homemaker's electronic involvement that paradoxically reinforced homebound viewing. A closer look at two of the most successful examples of the audience participation format – *Strike It Rich*, one of television's foremost "sob shows," originating from New York City; and *It Could Be You*, a "show of surprises" produced in Hollywood – helps explain how this narrative circuit worked.

Sob stories and surprises

Like other audience participation shows of the era, *Strike It Rich* offered the home viewer the possibility of free entry into the public space of the live broadcast, either by joining the studio gathering as observer or contestant or by participating from home during the "helping hand" and the "Heart Fund" segments. In this way, the program, like the genre itself, invited both a home viewer's mobile participation as a traveler to the studio and her virtual interplay, relayed across airwaves.

One of the earliest daytime radio programs translated to television, *Strike It Rich* premiered on the CBS TV network in May 1951 (McNeil 796). The show was produced by Walt Framer, the son of a Russian immigrant, who launched the radio version in 1947, a quiz show for money in which contestants explained why they wanted to win. As the radio show evolved, Framer discovered that the public favored contestants whose reasons stirred up feelings of sympathy. By the time *Strike It Rich* landed on television, it was a well-established "misery show" with a do-good "welfare agency" mentality ("Framer"). In 1953, *Newsweek* praised the idealistic and openly patriotic Framer for successfully exploring a "new quiz avenue" ("Winning" 61), and the program was widely regarded as a "quiz show with a heart" (Castleman and Podrazik 85).

Hosted by Warren Hull, a congenial master of ceremonies dubbed "Colgate's ambassador of good will," *Strike It Rich* included several heart-tugging segments, as an episode that aired on 28 November 1956 demonstrates. The first segment, punctuated by melodramatic organ music, features the tale of a married couple determined to win enough money to buy a washing machine; the "helping hand" segment which comes next finds TV actor Paul Ford (of *The Phil Silvers Show*) playing the quiz game on behalf of Edna Austram, whose letter from Baton Rouge, Louisiana (pictured in extreme close-up), explains that she and her invalid husband need cash to build living quarters behind their store; the final segment singles out the next day's contestant from the studio audience in a camera close-up – Michigan native P. G. Glazier, a hard-working itinerant farmer with twenty-six children. Other episodes typically added a concluding "Heart Fund" segment, during which sympathetic viewers made private contributions via an interstudio telephone ("Winning" 61). Within the routine format of *Strike It Rich*, subjects isolated in domestic spaces scattered across the country (like Edna Austram and the "Heart Fund" contributors) were integrated into the program alongside subjects gathered together in the studio space. Through the immediacy of live television, *Strike It Rich* interwove these far-flung reception sites on a daily basis to validate a social world that mixed virtual and physical presence (see Livingstone and Lunt 172–73).

It Could Be You (1956–61), produced by Ralph Edwards and originating from Hollywood, added novel elements to the audience participation format that more completely intermeshed these co-extensive reception sites. The innovative premise of *It Could Be You* was to surprise audience members in the studio and at home with funny and touching stories about themselves and then to reward them with gifts. As emcee Bill Leyden explained in one episode of *It Could Be You*, "we don't ask" people in the audience to talk about themselves, "we tell *them*" (21 May 1957). Posturing as a good-natured surveillance show, *It Could Be You*, according to Leyden, gained information about participants from the show's "spies" and "investigators" (3 April 1956). "Our spies tell us another child is due in August," he says about one woman (21 May 1957), or "Lynn Hamilton, do we know things about you!" (8 November 1956). In this variation, Leyden himself retold participants' private tales – like the amusing story of Mrs. Goodbody's first date (in a hearse) with her mortician husband, Arnold (21 May 1957), or Marjorie Ford's missed rendezvous with a sister headed for a job in New Delhi (8 November 1956). Especially during the program's final "reunion climax," when an audience member is unexpectedly reunited with a long-lost loved one, Leyden is depicted as the guardian of inside information.

Paralleling the espionage in the studio, secrets were collected about members of the viewing audience as well. More than *Strike It Rich*, the narrative strategies of *It Could Be You* amplified literal home participation. Each day two or three home viewers took part in the studio performance as Leyden announced they were receiving prizes at their homes – "right now." "Go to your door," Leyden tells Mr. and Mrs. Charles Moody via camera, because "our spies in Grand Rapids, Michigan, tell us it's your silver anniversary today" (21 May 1957).

The constant repetition of the show's catchphrase – "It could be you!" – furthers the construction of a virtual participants at home by underscoring the program's multiple cross-spatial subjectivity. During the show's opening sequence, as the camera pans an applauding studio audience, the announcer twice declares, "It could be

... YOU!" while a Zoomar camera lens and a roving spotlight isolate unsuspecting audience members in sudden close-up. The announcer's third intonation, "Or . . . it could be . . . YOU!" is pointedly redirected at the home viewer (21 May 1957). Leyden reinforces this rotating referent when he skillfully shifts his gaze from the camera to the studio audience and back again. In a double-directed look during one episode, Leyden, standing on stage, simultaneously tells the studio audience and the viewers at home, "Oh, what we don't know about you!" Then, in a flash, Leyden's address is altered; all at once he is speaking directly through the camera to Mrs. Messer, a mother of ten who lives on a farm in Cincinnati, where "right now" an Amana freezer is being delivered to "your door." Without missing a beat, Leyden then abruptly breaks eye contact with the camera, picks up a hand microphone, and bounds into the audience to joke with a new participant in the studio audience – yet another "you" (8 November 1956). By rhetorically equating the jovial crowd in the studio with the housewife at home, Leyden proposes a subject position that transcends spatial boundaries.

Segues to commercial breaks likewise solicit an attentive and participatory viewer. When Leyden says in one episode, "Maybe our next surprise will be for you. Stay beside that television" (8 November 1956), or "Stay tuned. Because after this break it could be you!" (3 April 1956), he discards the phantom of a distracted housewife glancing furtively at the TV set as she cleans, verifying instead the analogous pleasures made possible within the double world of the audience participation show.

Whether detailing sob stories or secrets, both *Strike It Rich* and *It Could Be You* dictated a relentless interplay between the disparate social realms of public studio space and the private space of the home, all the while postulating free access from one to the other, either in person or through fantasy. In doing so, the audience participation show devised for women of the 1950s what Miriam Hansen has called "a space apart and a space in between" (118). Prefiguring the familiar "cyberspatial neighborhood" produced by the talk show forty years later (Munson 149, 54), the audience participation show transcended spatial duality to conjoin viewers and studio visitors in synchronous time, promising neighborly co-presence within a virtual community that was at the same time securely anchored to the geographic and social world of the visible television studio.

The economic imperatives of the postwar era situated this 1950s virtual/mobile community within the decade's burgeoning structures of consumption. Like all of daytime television, the audience participation show interpellated women viewers as laborers and consumers. As Mary Beth Haralovich has argued, a broad range of powerful capitalist institutions – including the consumer product industry, the housing industry, and television itself – promoted a social subjectivity for the middle-class homemaker after World War II that made her an essential component in a newly emerging consumer culture (61). Historian Elaine Tyler May agrees: "The economic importance of women's role as consumers [in the 1950s] cannot be overstated, for it kept American industry rolling and sustained jobs for the nation's male providers" (167). In keeping with these economic forces, the audience participation show drew women into an imagined community shaped by the prescripts of consumption, the genre's format generating a national market of interchangeable members who bolstered not only product sales but television itself. For the audience participation show did not merely demand home viewers' attention to commercials and the labor of shopping to preserve industry success but also required the corporeal presence of women in the studio to create the television product.

By mandating women's entry into a new version of commercialized public space, the audience participation format also devised a 1950s paradigm not unlike the turn-of-the-century department store, which offered women a new "arena for public female visibility" (McCarthy 281) based upon the consumer principle of free entry, even to "the looker" (Benson 93). If early department stores promulgated "fantasies of escape and luxury" and the aura of a public festival (Leach 139–40) in order to conceal and justify the demand to buy, the television studio likewise covered over a participant's consumption obligations in the festive atmosphere of sorority. Like the department store, the audience participation show sanctioned looking – or being looked at – as a prelude to buying. The housewife's gaze was drawn to the television screen under the pretext of interaction and convivial sisterhood, but her assignation to virtual participation in the domestic sphere also guaranteed the ample supply of "eyeballs" demanded by television advertisers.

While capitalist pressures fortified the success of the audience participation show, other historical forces accounted for the genre's full vitality. Arising during an era of displacement for American women, when "all the Rosies who had riveted" were returning to the daytime routines of homemaking (May 75), the genre confronted the perplexing issue of women's leisure in relation to daytime television, allowing for the interdependence of two incompatible reception spaces and two outlooks regarding permissible television reception. The genre's celebration of television's capacity to entertain women within the confines of a new public space, however commercialized and regulated, countered the contested but grimmer prescriptions for television merely as a companion to daily drudgery. The viewing position mediated by the daytime audience participation show was not restricted to the passive and distracted onlooker at home who dutifully dusted, ironed, and cooked as she watched, denying herself television's guilty pleasures. The genre's ambivalent subject position also embraced the women traveler, the housewife taking a day off, the communal member of a festive new public gathering, and a viewer at home who was a participant, reactor, contestant, and winner. A narrative design that proposed free passage between the newly formed space of the television studio – relegated to the expressivity, amuse-ment, and visibility of women at leisure – and the isolated space of domestic labor interwove these contradictory reception sites into a transcendent world, an electronic "feminine culture" (Brown 204, 206) that extended comfort and recreational susten-ance to the women who spent their days at home. By creating a metaphysic of femi-nine presence, the daytime audience participation show held in balance the opposing tensions between the decade's pull toward home-centered feminine viewing during the day, a conflictual pleasure, and the allurement of television as a new public amusement for women. The audience participation genre bridged the public/private divide not by collapsing public entertainment into the home but by fostering the paradoxical co-existence of studio space and home space and holding in suspension their reception differences.

Notes

I owe special thanks to James Schwoch, Lawrence Lichty, J. Fred MacDonald, and the journal's anonymous reviewer.

1   In her book *Daytime Television Programming*, for example, Marilyn J. Matelski does not separate out "the audience participation show" from other forms, although she notes the popularity of "sob programming" during the 1950s (25) and lists game shows and "talk shows/news magazines" in her review of daytime genres (13–34). Lynn Spigel discusses early television's segmented formatting during the day but does not specifically examine the significance of the audience participation show (75–86); Wayne Munson places Art Linkletter's *House Party, Stand Up and Be Counted*, and *Queen for a Day* within the context of talkshow history (53–55). In *Quiz Craze: America's Infatuation with Game Shows*, Thomas A. DeLong documents the longevity of audience participation formats in game and quiz shows but focuses his research on primetime offerings. Of course, the most extensive scholarship regarding the history of daytime television has addressed the daytime serial, Robert C. Allen's book serving as a key example.

2   Women's daytime audience participation shows also abounded in local markets, but their attachment to more specific geographic communities differentiated them from network versions.

3   *Guiding Light* drew a 12.1; *Search for Tomorrow* a 10.8; *Love of Life* a 10.3; *Valiant Lady* a 9.9; *Arthur Godfrey* a 9.7; and *The Big Payoff* a 9.3.

4   The visibility and participation of African American women requires more research.

5   This summarizes Ripley's table 36 in Bogart.

6   In the same memo, Coffin reiterates the industry's preoccupation with addressing the home viewer's work/leisure dilemma. He worries that CBS's competing shows, including the audience participation show *The Big Payoff*, "require less concentration and less devotion," interfering less with housework, than *Matinee Theater*. The antidote, he suggests, is promotional material that depicts the *Matinee* viewer as "a hard-working woman who deserves an hour of relaxation and rest during the afternoon before she has to plunge into her evening chores. This hour of rest will make her a better wife and mother."

Works cited

Allen, Robert C. *Speaking of Soap Operas*. Chapel Hill: UP of North Carolina, 1985.

Art Linkletter's House Party. CBS. Circa 1959. Videocassette. Collection of Moviecraft, Inc. Orland Park, IL.

"Arthur Godfrey Is TV-Proof but Television May Not Be." *Newsweek* 19 May 1952:62+.

Arthur Godfrey Time. CBS. 22 April 1953. Kinescope. Collection of J. Fred MacDonald & Associates. Chicago, IL.

Barris, Chuck. Memo to Daytime Sales Specialists, 28 August 1956. NBC Archives, Wisconsin Historical Society, Madison, WI. Box 400, Folder 8.

Benson, Susan Porter. *Counter Cultures: Saleswomen, Managers, and Customers in American Department Stores 1890–1949*. Urbana: UP of Illinois, 1986.

Blake, Howard. "An Apologia from the Man Who Produced the Worst Program in TV History." *American Broadcasting: A Source Book on the History of Radio and Television.* Ed. Lawrence W. Lichty and Malachi Topping. New York: Hastings House, 1975. 415–20.

Blum, Daniel. *Pictorial History of Television.* New York: Chilton Company, 1959.

Boddy, William. *Fifties Television: The Industry and Its Critics.* Chicago: UP of Illinois, 1990.

Bogart, Leo. *The Age of Television: A Study of Viewing Habits and the Impact of Television on American Life.* New York: Frederick Ungar Publishing Co., 1956.

Bracker, Milton. "No Question about Quiz Shows." *New York Times Magazine* 26 July 1953: 16+.

Bride and Groom. CBS. 3 February 1953. Kinescope. Collection of J. Fred MacDonald & Associates. Chicago, IL.

Brown, Mary Ellen. "Motley Moments: Soap Operas, Carnival, Gossip, and the Power of the Utterance." *Television and Women's Culture: The Politics of the Popular.* Ed. Mary Ellen Brown. London: Sage, 1990.

Castleman, Harry, and Walter J. Podrazik. *Watching TV: Four Decades of American Television.* New York: McGraw-Hill Book Co., 1982.

"CBS TV City." *Broadcasting and Telecasting* 11 February 1952: 77.

"The Charm Boys." *Time* 15 February 1954: 78.

Coffin, Thomas E. "Attention in Viewing Matinee Theater." Memo to H.M. Beville, Jr., 8 June 1956. NBC Archives, Wisconsin Historical Society, Madison, WI. Box 400, Folder 9.

Cotler, Gordon. "That Strange TV Studio Audience." *New York Times Magazine* 16 May 1954: 19+.

"The Craziest Thing." *Time* 27 September 1954: 71.

DeLong, Thomas A. *Quiz Craze: America's Infatuation with Game Shows.* New York: Praeger, 1991.

"For Richer or Poorer." *Time* 7 April 1952: 55.

"For the Girls at Home." *Newsweek* 15 March 1954: 92–93.

"Framer Strikes a Rich Big Payoff." *Variety* 5 December 1956: 35.

Friedberg, Anne. *Window Shopping: Cinema and the Postmodern.* Los Angeles: UP of California, 1993.

Ganas, Monica, prod. *"Queen for a Day": The Cinderella Story.* Videocassette. U of Kentucky, 1996.

The Garry Moore Show. CBS. 22 April 1952. Kinescope. Collection of J. Fred MacDonald & Associates. Chicago, IL.

"Giveaway-Takeaway." *Newsweek* 15 March 1954: 94.

Hansen, Miriam. *Babel and Babylon: Spectatorship in American Silent Film.* Cambridge: Harvard UP, 1991.

Haralovich, Mary Beth. "Sitcoms and Suburbs: Positioning the 1950s Homemaker." *Quarterly Review of Film and Video* 11 (1989): 61–84.

Herridge, Robert. "TV: The Dramatic Image." *Variety* 9 January 1957: 97.

"In Review: *It Could Be You.*" *Broadcasting and Telecasting* 11 June 1956: 14.

"In Review: *Queen for a Day.*" *Broadcasting and Telecasting* 9 January 1956: 14.

It Could Be You. NBC. 3 April 1956, 8 November 1956, 21 May 1957. Kinescopes. Collection of J. Fred MacDonald & Associates. Chicago, IL.

"Katz Pitches Daytime for Cigarettes." *Broadcasting and Telecasting* 28 May 1956: 46.

La Cossitt, Henry. "They Say He's a Funny Man." *Saturday Evening Post* 17 May 1952: 26+.

Leach, William. *Land of Desire: Merchants, Power, and the Rise of a New American Culture.* New York: Pantheon Books, 1993.

Lichty, Lawrence W. Private Computer Database. Evanston, IL.

Liebman, Max. "Audience Reflexes Can Make or Break a Telecast." *Variety* 5 February 1955: 106.

Lindemann, Carl, Jr. Attachment to memo to Mort Werner, 4 April 1957; text of Rod Erickson's "Speech before the Canadian Association of Radio and Television Broadcasters, March 27, 1957." NBC Archives, Wisconsin Historical Society, Madison, WI. Box 400, Folder 8.

Livingstone, Sonia, and Peter Lunt. *Talk on Television: Audience Participation and Public Debate.* New York: Routledge, 1994.

MacDonald, J. Fred. *One Nation under Television: The Rise and Decline of Network TV.* Chicago: Nelson–Hall Publishers, 1994.

Matelski, Marilyn J. *Daytime Television Programming.* Boston: Focal Press, 1991.

May, Elaine Tyler. *Homeward Bound: American Families in the Cold War Era.* New York: Basic Books, 1988.

McCarthy, Anna. "Outer Spaces: Public Viewing in American Television History." Diss. Northwestern U, 1995.

McNeil, Alex. *Total Television: A Comprehensive Guide to Programming from 1948 to the Present.* 4th ed. New York: Penguin Books, 1996.

"Moore for Housewives." *Time* 2 February 1953: 47.

Munson, Wayne. *All Talk: The Talkshow in Media Culture.* Philadelphia: Temple UP, 1993.

"NBC's $5,000,000 New Tint Studio Bows This Month." *Variety* 5 September 1956: 25+.

NBC-TV Promotion for *Matinee Theater*, January 1956. NBC Archives, Wisconsin Historical Society, Madison, WI. Box 400, Folder 9.

"NBC-TV's Major Daytime Advances; Forge Ahead on Sales, Ratings." *Variety* 6 February 1957: 27+.

O'Meara, Carroll. *Television Program Production.* New York: Ronald Press, 1955.

"On the Happy Occasion of *The Big Payoff*'s Third Anniversary." *Variety* 5 January 1955: 194.

Peiss, Kathy. *Cheap Amusements: Leisure in Turn-of-the-Century New York.* Philadelphia: Temple UP, 1986.

The Price Is Right. NBC. 26 July 1957. Kinescope. Collection of J. Fred MacDonald & Associates. Chicago, IL.

"The Program That Cries." *Newsweek* 2 June 1960: 96+.

Queen for a Day. NBC. 24 February 1956. Kinescope. Collection of J. Fred MacDonald & Associates. Chicago, IL.

Queen for a Day. NBC. March 1956. Videocassette. Museum of Television and Radio. Beverly Hills, CA. T85:0679.

"Queen for a Day: Housewives' Schedule Wrecker." *Look* 1 April 1958: 120–22.

Settel, Irving, and Norman Glenn. *Television Advertising and Production Handbook.* New York: Thomas Y. Crowell, 1953.

Smith, Donald. *Television Program Selection, Liking for Television Programs, and Levels of Attention Given to Television Programs by Housewives in Tuscaloosa, Alabama.* Radio-Television Audience Studies, New Series No. 3. Columbus: Ohio State UP, 1957.

Spigel, Lynn. *Make Room for TV: Television and the Family Ideal in Postwar America.* Chicago: UP of Chicago, 1992.

Stand Up and Be Counted. CBS. June 1956. Videocassette. Museum of Broadcast Communications. Chicago, IL.

Stasheff, Edward, and Rudy Bretz. *The Television Program: Its Writing, Direction, and Production.* New York: A. Wyn, 1956.

Sterling, Christopher H., and John M. Kittross. *Stay Tuned: A Concise History of American Broadcasting.* 2nd ed. Belmont, CA: Wadsworth Publishing Company, 1990.

Strike It Rich. CBS. 28 November 1956. Kinescope. Collection of J. Fred MacDonald & Associates. Chicago, IL.

"Then the House Burned." *Time* 15 February 1954: 78.

Torre, Marie. "NBC Discovers a 'Matinee' Audience." *New York Herald Tribune*, 1956. NBC Archives, Wisconsin Historical Society, Madison, WI. Box 400, Folder 9.

"Troubles & Bubbles." *Time* 15 April 1957: 76.

Truth or Consequences. NBC. 8 January 1957. Kinescope. Collection of J. Fred MacDonald & Associates. Chicago, IL.

"TV Hits the Road." *Newsweek* 2 May 1955: 88.

"Want to See a TV Broadcast?" *Sunset: The Magazine of Western Living* December 1957: 36.

"Winning Ways." *Newsweek* 17 August 1953: 61.

Select Bibliography

This bibliography does not repeat all the references from the main body of the Reader, but provides additional sources to enable the further exploration of feminist television criticism.

Compiled by Abigail Derecho, Elizabeth Nathanson and Jennifer Twyford.

Abu-Lughod, Lila. *Dramas of Nationhood: The Politics of Television in Egypt.* Chicago: University of Chicago Press, 2004.

Acosta-Alzuru, Carolina. " 'I'm Not a Feminist . . . I Only Defend Women as Human Beings': The Production, Representation, and Consumption of Feminism in a *Telenovela.*" *Critical Studies in Media Communication* 20, no. 3 (September 2003): 269–294.

Akass, Kim and Janet, McCabe, eds. *Reading Sex and the City.* London: I.B Tauris, 2004.

—— eds. *Reading the L Word.* London: I.B Tauris, 2007.

Allen, Robert C. *Speaking of Soap Operas.* Chapel Hill, NC: University of North Carolina Press, 1985.

—— ed. *To Be Continued . . .: Soap Operas Around the World.* New York: Routledge, 1995.

—— and Hill, Annette eds. The Television Studies Reader, New York: Routledge, 2004.

Amy-Chinn, Dee. " 'Tis Pity She's A Whore: Postfeminist Prostitution in Joss Whedon's *Firefly.*" *Feminist Media Studies* 6, no. 2 (June 2006): 175–189.

—— and Milly Williamson. "The Vampire Spike in Text and Fandom: Unsettling Oppositions in *Buffy the Vampire Slayer.*" *European Journal of Cultural Studies* 8, no. 3 (August 2005): 275–288.

Andrews, Maggie. "*Butterflies* and Caustic Asides: Housewives, Comedy and the Feminist Movement." In *Because I Tell a Joke or Two: Comedy, Politics and Social Difference*, ed. Stephen Wagg. London: Routledge, 1998, 50–64.

Ang, Ien. *Watching Dallas: Soap Opera and the Melodramatic Imagination.* New York: Methuen, 1985.

—— *Desperately Seeking the Audience.* New York: Routledge, 1991.

—— *Living Room Wars: Rethinking Media Audiences for a Postmodern World.* London: Routledge, 1995.

—— *On Not Speaking Chinese: Living Between Asia and the West.* London: Routledge, 2001.

—— and Hermes, Joke. "Gender and/in Media Consumption." In *Mass Media and Society*, ed. James Curran and Michael Gurevitch. Sevenoaks: Edward Arnold, 1991, 307–328.

Armstrong, Cory L., Michelle L. M. Wood and Michelle R. Nelson. "Female News Professionals in Local and National Broadcast News During the Buildup to the Iraq War." *Journal of Broadcasting & Electronic Media* 50, no. 1 (March 2006): 95–118.

Arthurs, Jane. "Women and Television." In *Behind the Screens: The Structure of British Television in the Nineties*, ed. Stuart Hood. London: Lawrence and Wishart, 1994, 82–101.

—— *Television and Sexuality: Regulation and the Politics of Taste*. Maidenhead: Open University Press, 2004.

Arthurs, Jane and Jean Grimshaw, eds. *Women's Bodies: Discipline and Transgression*. London: Cassell, 1999.

Ashby, Justine. "Postfeminism in the British Frame." *Cinema Journal* 44, no. 2 (Winter 2005): 127–132.

Backstein, Karen. "Soft Love: The Romantic Vision of Sex on the Showtime Network." *Television & New Media* 2, no. 4 (November 2001): 303–317.

Bacon-Smith, Camille. *Enterprising Women: Television, Fandom and the Creation of Popular Myth*. Philadelphia, PA: University of Pennsylvania Press, 1992.

Baehr, Helen. "The 'Liberated Woman' in Television Drama." *Women's Studies International Quarterly* 3, no. 1 (1980): 29–39.

—— and Gillian Dyer, eds. *Boxed-In: Women and Television*. London: Pandora, 1987.

—— and Ann Gray, eds. *Turning It On: A Reader in Women and Media*. London: Arnold, 1996.

Banet-Weiser, Sarah. *The Most Beautiful Girl in the World: Beauty Pageants and National Identity*. Berkeley: University of California Press, 1999.

——, Cynthia Chris and Anthony Frietas, eds. *Cable Visions: Television Beyond Broadcasting*. New York: New York University Press, 2007.

Barker, Chris. "Television and the Reflexive Project of the Self: Soaps, Teenage Talk and Hybrid Identities." *The British Journal of Sociology* 48, no. 4 (December 1997): 611–628.

Barry, Angela. "Black Mythologies: Representations of Black People on British Television." In *The Black and White Media Book*, ed. John Twitchin. Stoke-on-Trent: Trentham Books, 1988, 83–102.

Bathrick, Serafina. "*The Mary Tyler Moore Show*. Women at Home and at Work." In *MTM: "Quality Television"*, ed. Jane Feuer, Paul Kerr, and Tise Vahimagi. London: British Film Institute Publications, 1984.

Battles, Kathleen and Wendy Hilton-Morrow. "Gay Characters in Conventional Spaces: *Will and Grace* and the Situation Comedy Genre." *Critical Studies in Media Communication* 19, no. 1 (March 2002): 87–105.

Baughman, Cynthia, ed. *Women on Ice: Feminist Responses to the Tonya Harding/Nancy Kerrigan Spectacle*. New York: Routledge, 1995.

Bausinger, Hermann. "Media, Technology and Daily Life." *Media, Culture and Society* 6, no. 4 (1984): 343–351.

Becker, Christine. " 'Glamour Girl Classed as TV Show Brain': The Body and Mind of Faye Emerson." *Journal of Popular Culture* 38, no. 2 (November 2004): 242–260.

—— "Televising Film Stardom in the 1950s." *Framework: The Journal of Cinema and Media* 46, no. 2 (Fall 2005): 5–21.

Becker, Ron. *Gay TV and Straight America*. New Brunswick: NJ: Rutgers, 2006.

Bell, David and Joanne Hollows, eds. *Ordinary Lifestyles: Popular Media, Consumption and Taste*. Berkshire: Open University Press, 2005.

Bennett, Jeffrey A. "In Defense of Gaydar: Reality Television and the Politics of the Glance." *Critical Studies in Media Communication* 23, no. 5 (December 2006): 408–425.

Bertrand, Ina. "Australia's *Come In Spinner*. Feminist Ideology as Best Seller (1946) and

Television Mini-series (1990)." *Historical Journal of Film, Radio, and Television* 12, no. 3 (1992): 231–244.

Bielby, Denise D. and C. Lee Harrington. "Opening America?: The Telenovela-ization of U.S. Soap Operas." *Television & New Media* 6, no. 4 (November 2005): 383–399.

Biressi, Anita and Heather Nunn. *Reality TV: Realism and Revelation.* London: Wallflower Press, 2005.

Blackman, Lisa. "Self-Help, Media Cultures and the Production of Female Psychopathology." *European Journal of Cultural Studies* 7, no. 2 (May 2004): 219–236.

Bobo, Jacqueline. *Black Women as Cultural Readers.* New York: Columbia University Press, 1995.

—— and Ellen Seiter. "Black Feminism and Media Criticism: *The Women of Brewster Place.*" *Screen* 32, no. 3 (1991): 286–302.

Boddy, William. *New Media and Popular Imagination: Launching Radio, Television, and Digital Media in the United States.* Oxford: Oxford University Press, 2005.

Bodroghkozy, Aniko. " 'Is This What You Mean By Color TV?': Race, Gender, and Contested Meanings in NBC's *Julia.*" In *Private Screenings: Television and the Female Consumer,* ed. Lynn Spigel and Denise Mann. Minneapolis, MN: University of Minnesota Press, 1992, 143–168.

—— *Groove Tube: Sixties Television and the Youth Rebellion.* Durham, NC: Duke University Press, 2001.

—— "Where Have You Gone, Mary Richards? Feminism's Rise and Fall in Primetime Television." *Iris* (Fall-Winter 2004) 12–20.

Bonner, Frances. *Ordinary Television: Analyzing Popular TV.* London: Sage, 2003.

Boyle, Karen. *Media and Violence: Gendering the Debates.* London: Sage, 2004.

Bragg, Sarah and David Buckingham. "Embarrassment, Education and Erotics: The Sexual Politics of Family Viewing." *European Journal of Cultural Studies* 7, no. 4 (November 2004): 441–459.

Brooks, Dianne. " 'They Dig Her Message': Opera, Television, and the Black Diva." In *Hop on Pop: The Politics and Pleasures of Popular Culture,* ed. Henry Jenkins, Tara McPherson, and Jane Shattuc. Durham, NC: Duke University Press, 2002, 300–315.

Brown, Mary Ellen, ed. *Television and Women's Culture: The Politics of the Popular.* London: Sage, 1990.

—— *Soap Opera and Women's Talk: The Pleasure of Resistance.* Thousand Oaks, CA: Sage, 1994.

Brunsdon, Charlotte. *Screen Tastes: Soap Opera to Satellite Dishes.* London: Routledge, 1997.

—— "Structure of Anxiety: Recent British Television Crime Fiction." *Screen* 39, no. 3 (Autumn 1998): 223–243.

—— *The Feminist, the Housewife, and the Soap Opera.* Oxford: Oxford University Press, 2000.

—— "Feminism, Postfeminism, Martha, Martha, and Nigella." *Cinema Journal* 44, no. 2 (Winter 2005): 110–116.

——, Catherine Johnson, Rachel Moseley and Helen Wheatley. "The Midlands TV Research Group's *8–9 Project.*" *European Journal of Cultural Studies* 4, no. 1, (2001): 29–62.

Buarque de Almeida, Heloisa. "On the Border: Reflections on Ethnography and Gender." In *Global Media Studies: Ethnographic Perspectives,* ed. Patrick D. Murphy and Marwan M. Kraidy. New York and London: Routledge, 2003: 165–183.

Buckingham, David. *Moving Images.* Manchester: Manchester University Press, 1996.

Budd, Mike, Steve Craig, and Clay Steinman. *Consuming Environments: Television and Commercial Culture.* New Brunswick, NJ: Rutgers University Press, 1999.

Burch, Elizabeth. "Media Literacy, Cultural Proximity and TV Aesthetics: Why Indian Soap Operas Work in Nepal and the Hindu Diaspora." *Media, Culture & Society* 24, no. 4 (July 2002): 571–579.

Buttsworth, Sara. " 'Bite Me': Buffy and the Penetration of the Gendered Warrior Hero." *Continuum: Journal of Media and Cultural Studies* 16, no. 2 (2002): 185–199.

Byars, Jackie and Eileen R. Meehan. "Once in a Lifetime: Constructing the 'Working Woman' through Cable Narrowcasting." *Camera Obscura* 33–4 (1994–5): 13–41.

Byers, Michele. "Gender/Sexuality/Desire: Subversion of Difference and Construction of Loss in the Adolescent Drama of *My So-Called Life.*" *Signs* 23, no. 3 (Spring 1998): 711–734.

Cantor, Muriel G. *Prime Time Television: Content and Control.* Beverly Hills, CA: Sage, 1980.

—— and Suzanne Pingree. *The Soap Opera.* Beverly Hills, CA: Sage, 1983.

Carini, Susan M. "Love's Labors Almost Lost: Managing Crisis during the Reign of *I Love Lucy.*" *Cinema Journal* 43, no. 1 (Fall 2003): 44–62.

Carson, Bruce and Margaret Llewellyn-Jones, eds. *Frames and Fiction on Television: The Politics of Identity Within Drama.* Exeter and Oregon: Intellect Books, 2000.

Carter, Cynthia, Gill Branston and Stuart Allan, eds. *News, Gender, and Power.* London and New York: Routledge, 1998.

Carter, Cynthia and Linda Steiner, eds. *Critical Readings: Media and Gender.* Maidenhead: Open University Press, 2004.

Cassidy, Marsha F. *What Women Watched: Daytime Television in the 1950s.* Austin, TX: University of Texas Press, 2005.

—— and Mimi White. "Innovating Women's Television in Local and National Networks: Ruth Lyons and Arlene Francis." *Camera Obscura* 51, 17, no. 3 (2002): 31–69.

Chan, Shun-Hing and Lai-Ching Leung. "Between Viewing and Consuming: How Aging Women in Hong Kong Negotiate Television Advertisements." *Feminist Media Studies* 5, no. 2 (July 2005): 123–140.

Chao, Phoebe Shih. "Gendered Cooking: Television Cook Shows." *Jump Cut* 42 (December 1998), 19–27.

Click, Melissa A. "Untidy: Fan Response to the Soiling of Martha Stewart's Spotless Image." In *Fan Audiences: Identities and Communities in a Mediated World*, ed. Jonathan Gray, C. Lee Harrington and Cornell Sandvoss. New York: New York University Press, 2006, 413–434.

Coleman, Robin R. Means, ed. *Say It Loud!: African-American Audiences, Media, and Identity*, New York: Routledge, 2002.

Creeber, Glen. " 'Taking Our Personal Lives Seriously': Intimacy, Continuity, and Memory in the Television Drama Serial." *Media, Culture & Society* 23, no. 4 (July 2001): 439–455.

Cuklanz, Lisa M. *Rape on Prime Time: Television, Masculinity, and Sexual Violence.* Philadelphia, PA: University of Pennsylvania Press, 1999.

—— and Sujata Moorti. "Television's 'New' Feminism: Prime-Time Representations of Women and Victimization." *Critical Studies in Media Communication* 23, no. 4 (October 2006): 302–321.

Curtin, Michael. "Feminine Desire in the Age of Satellite Television," *Journal of Communication* 49, no. 2, (Spring 1999): 55–70.

—— and Shanti Kumar. "Made in India: In Between Music Television and Patriarchy," *Television and New Media* 3, no. 4 (November 2002): 345–366.

D'Acci, Julie. *Defining Women: Television and the Case of Cagney and Lacey.* Chapel Hill, NC: University of North Carolina Press, 1994.

—— ed. *Lifetime: A Cable Network "For Women"* (Special Issue). *Camera Obscura* 33–4 (1994–5).

—— "Nobody's Woman? *Honey West* and the New Sexuality." In *The Revolution Wasn't Televised: Sixties Television and Social Conflict*, ed. Lynn Spigel and Michael Curtin. New York: Routledge, 1997, 73–94.

Daniels, Therese. "Programmes for Black Audiences." In *Behind the Screens: The Structure of*

British Television in the Nineties, ed. Stuart Hood. London: Lawrence and Wishart, 1994, 65–81.

—— and Jane Gerson, eds. *The Colour Black: Black Images in British Television*. London: British Film Institute, 1989.

Dates, Janette. "From 'Beulah' to 'Under One Roof': African-American Women on Prime-Time Commercial Television." In *Mass Media and Society*, ed. Alan Wells and Ernest A. Hakanen. Greenwich, CT: Ablex Publishing, 1997, 527–541.

—— "Movin' on Up: Black Women Decision Makers in Entertainment Television." *Journal of Popular Film & Television* (Summer 2005): 68–87.

Davis, Glyn and Kay Dickinson, eds. *Teen TV: Genre, Consumption and Identity*. Berkeley, CA: University of California Press, 2004.

Deming, Caren J. "For Television-Centered Television Criticism: Lessons from Feminism." In *Communication Yearbook, 11*, ed. James A. Anderson. Newbury Park: Sage, 1988, 148–176.

Dines, Gail and Jean M. Humez, eds. *Gender, Race and Class in the Media*. Thousand Oaks, CA: Sage, 1995.

Doty, Alexander. "The Cabinet of Lucy Ricardo: Lucille Ball's Star Image." *Cinema Journal* 29, no. 4 (1990): 3–22.

—— *Making Things Perfectly Queer*. Minneapolis: University of Minnesota Press, 1993.

Douglas, Susan. *Where the Girls Are: Growing Up Female with the Mass Media*. New York: Random House, 1994.

Dovey, Jon. *Freakshow: First Person Media and Factual Television* London: Pluto Press, 2000.

Dow, Bonnie J. *Prime-Time Feminism: Television, Media Culture, and the Women's Movement Since 1970*. Philadelphia: University of Pennsylvania Press, 1996.

Drotner, Kirsten. "Girl Meets Boy: Aesthetic Production, Reception, and Gender Identity." *Cultural Studies* 3, no. 2 (1989): 208–225.

Dubrofsky, Rachel. "*The Bachelor*: Whiteness in the Harem." *Critical Studies in Media Communication* 23, no. 1 (March 2006): 39–56.

Dunleavy, Trisha. "*Coronation Street, Neighbors, Shortland Street*: Localness and Universality in the Primetime Soap." *Television & New Media* 6, no. 4 (November 2005): 370–382.

Durham, Meenakshi Gigi. "Constructing the 'New Ethnicities': Media, Sexuality, and Diaspora Identity in the Lives of South Asian Immigrant Girls." *Critical Studies in Media Communication* 21, no. 2 (June 2004): 140–161.

Dyer, Richard, Christine Geraghty, Marion Jordan, Terry Lovell, Richard Paterson and John Stewart. *Coronation Street*. London: British Film Institute, 1980.

Early, Frances and Kathleen Kennedy, eds. *Athena's Daughters: Television's New Woman Warriors*. Syracuse, NY: Syracuse University Press, 2003.

Eaton, Mary. "A Fair Cop? Viewing the Effects of the Canteen Culture in *Prime Suspect* and *Between the Lines*." In *Crime and the Media: The Postmodern Spectacle*, ed. David Kidd-Hewitt and Richard Osborne. London: Pluto Press, 1995, 164–184.

Epstein, Debbie and Deborah Lynn Steinberg. "All Het Up! Rescuing Heterosexuality on *The Oprah Winfrey Show*." *Feminist Review* 54 (Autumn 1996): 88–115.

Feasey, Rebecca. "Watching *Charmed*: Why Teen Television Appeals to Women." *Journal of Popular Film and Television* 34, no. 1 (Spring 2006): 2–9.

Fenton, Natalie. "The Problematics of Postmodernism for Feminist Media Studies." *Media, Culture & Society* 22, no. 6 (November 2000): 723–741.

Feuer, Jane. "Melodrama, Serial Form and Television Today." *Screen* 25, no. 1 (1984): 4–16.

—— *Seeing Through the Eighties: Television and Reaganism*. Durham, NC: Duke University Press, 1995.

——, Paul Kerr, and Tise Vahimagi, eds. *MTM: "Quality Television"*. London: British Film Institute, 1984.

Fisherkeller, JoEllen. "Everyday Learning about Identities among Young Adolescents in Television Culture." *Anthropology & Education Quarterly* 28, no. 4 (December 1997): 467–492.

Fiske, John. *Television Culture*. London: Routledge, 1987.

—— *Media Matters: Everyday Culture and Political Change*. Minneapolis: University of Minnesota Press, 1994.

Franco, Judith. "Cultural Identity in the Community Soap: A Comparative Analysis of *Thuis* (At Home) and *Eastenders*." *European Journal of Cultural Studies* 4, no. 4 (November 2001): 449–472.

Franklin, Sarah, Celia Lury and Jackie Stacey, eds. *Off Centre: Feminism and Cultural Studies*. London: HarperCollins, 1991.

Freedman, Eric. "Public Access/Private Confession: Home Video as (Queer) Community Television." *Television & New Media* 1, no. 2 (May 2000): 179–191.

Gallagher, Margaret. "Shifting Focus: Women and Broadcasting in the European Community." *Studies of Broadcasting 26*, 61–82. Tokyo: NHK Research Institute, 1990.

—— "The Push and Pull of Action and Research in Feminist Media Studies." *Feminist Media Studies* 1, no. 1 (March 2001): 11–15.

Gamman, Lorraine and Margaret Marshment, eds. *The Female Gaze: Women as Viewers of Popular Culture*. London: The Women's Press, 1988.

Garrison, Ednie Kaeh. "U.S. Feminism – Grrrl Style! Youth (Sub)Cultures and the Technologics of the Third Wave." *NWSA Journal* 26, no. 1 (Spring 2000): 141–172.

Geraghty, Christine. *Women and Soap Opera: A Study of Prime Time Soaps*. Oxford: Polity Press, 1991.

—— "British Soaps in the 1980s." In *Come on Down? Popular Culture in Post-War Britain*, ed. Dominic Strinati and Stephen Wagg. London: Routledge, 1992, 133–149.

—— "Feminism and Media Consumption." In *Cultural Studies and Communications*, ed. James Curran, David Morley and Valerie Walkerdine. London: Arnold, 1996, 306–322.

Gerhard, Jane. "*Sex and the City*: Carrie Bradshaw's Queer Postfeminism." *Feminist Media Studies* 5, no. 1 (March 2005): 37–49.

Gill, Rosalind. *Gender and the Media*. Cambridge: Polity, 2007.

Gillespie, Marie. *Television, Ethnicity and Cultural Change*. London: Routledge, 1995.

Giomi, Elisa. " 'It Has to Mean Something . . .': Reading the Success of the Italian Soap Opera *Vivere*." *European Journal of Cultural Studies* 8, no. 4 (November 2005): 465–482.

Givanni, June, ed. *Remote Control: Dilemmas of Black Intervention in British Film and TV*. London: British Film Institute, 1995.

Gledhill, Christine. "Pleasurable Negotiations." In *Female Spectators: Looking at Film and Television*, ed. Deidre E. Pribram. London: Verso, 1988, 64–89.

—— "Speculations on the Relationship Between Soap Opera and Melodrama." *Quarterly Review of Film and Video* 14, no. 1–2 (1992): 103–124.

Gomard, Kirsten. "Political Debates on Danish TV: Negotiation Political Competence and Gender." *Nora: Nordic Journal of Women's Studies* 9, no. 2 (2001): 107–112.

Goodstein, Ethel. "Southern Belles and Southern Buildings: The Built Environment as Text and Context in *Designing Women*." *Critical Studies in Mass Communication* 9, no. 2 (1992): 170–185.

Graham, Helen. "Post-Pleasure: Representations, Ideologies and Affects of a Newly Post-9/11 'Feminist Icon'." *Feminist Media Studies* 7, no. 1 (March 2007): 1–15.

Gray, Ann. *Video Playtime: The Gendering of a Leisure Technology*. London: Routledge, 1992.

Griffen-Foley, Bridget. 'From Tit-Bits to Big Brother: A Century of Audience Participation in the Media'. *Media Culture and Society* 26.4 (2004): 533–548.

Grindstaff, Laura. *The Money Shot: Trash, Class, and the Making of TV Talk Shows*. Chicago: University of Chicago Press, 2002.

Gripsrud, Jostein. *The Dynasty Years: Hollywood Television and Critical Media Studies*. New York: Routledge, 1995.

Gross, Larry. *Up From Invisibility: Lesbians, Gay Men, and the Media in America*. New York: Columbia University Press, 2002.

Gunter, Barrie. *Television and Gender Representation*. London: J. Libbey, 1995.

Haggins, Bambi L. "There's No Place like Home: The American Dream, African-American Identity, and the Situation Comedy." *The Velvet Light Trap* 43 (Spring 1999): 23–36.

Hallam, Julia. *Lynda La Plante*. Manchester: Manchester University Press, 2005.

—— "Remembering *Butterflies*: The Comic Art of Housework." In Jonathan Bignell and Stephen Lacey (eds). *Popular Television Drama: Critical Perspectives*. Manchester and New York: Manchester University Press, 2005, 34–50.

—— and Margaret Marshment. "Framing Experience: Case Studies in the Reception of *Oranges Are Not the Only Fruit*." *Screen* 36, no. 1 (1995): 1–15.

—— and Margaret Marshment. "Questioning the 'Ordinary' Woman: *Oranges Are Not the Only Fruit*, Text and Viewer." In *Feminist Cultural Theory*, ed. Beverley Skeggs, Manchester: Manchester University Press, 1995, 169–189.

Halleck, DeeDee. *Hand-Held Visions: The Impossible Possibilities of Community Media*. New York: Fordham University Press, 2002.

Hamer, Diane and Belinda Budge. *The Good, the Bad, and the Gorgeous: Popular Culture's Romance with Lesbianism*. London: Pandora, 1994.

Hammers, Michele L. "Cautionary Tales of Liberation and Female Professionalism: The Case Against *Ally McBeal*." *Western Journal of Communication* 69, no. 2 (2005): 167–18.

Hamming, Jeanne E. "Whatever Turns You On: Becoming-Lesbian and the Production of Desire in the Xenaverse." *Genders* 34 (2001), <http://www.genders.org/g34/g34_hamming.html>.

Haralovich, Mary Beth. "Suburban Family Sitcoms and Consumer Product Design: Addressing the Social Subjectivity of Homemakers in the 50s." In *Television and Its Audience*, ed. Phillip Drummond and Richard Paterson. London: British Film Institute, 1988, 38–60.

—— "Sitcoms and Suburbs: Positioning the 1950s Homemaker." *Quarterly Review of Film and Video* 11, no. 1 (1989): 61–83.

—— and Lauren Rabinovitz, eds. *Television, History, and American Culture: Feminist Critical Essays*. Durham, NC: Duke University Press, 1999.

Harrington, C. Lee. "Lesbian(s) on Daytime Television: The Bianca Narrative on *All My Children*." *Feminist Media Studies* 3, no. 2 (July 2003): 207–228.

—— and Denise D. Bielby. *Soap Fans: Pursuing Pleasure and Making Meaning in Everyday Life*. Philadelphia, PA: Temple University Press, 1995.

Hartley, John. *Uses of Television*. London: Routledge, 1999.

Hatch, Kristen. "Daytime Politics: Kefauver, McCarthy, and the American Housewife." In *Reality Squared: Televisual Discourse on the Real*, ed. James Friedman. New Brunswick, NJ: Rutgers University Press, 2002, 75–91.

Hayward, Jennifer. *Consuming Pleasures: Active Audiences from Dickens to Soap Opera*. Lexington, KY: University Press of Kentucky, 1997.

Heide, Margaret J. *Television Culture and Women's Lives: thirtysomething and the Contradictions of Gender*. Philadelphia: University of Pennsylvania Press, 1995.

Heinecken, Dawn. *The Warrior Women of Television: A Feminist Cultural Analysis of the New Female Body in Popular Media*. New York: Peter Lang, 2003.

Heller, Dana. "States of Emergency: The Labors of Lesbian Desire in *ER*." *Genders* 39 (2004), <http://genders.org/g39/g39_heller.html>

—— ed. *The Great American Makeover: Television, History, Nation*. New York: Palgrave Macmillan, 2006.

Hendershot, Heather. *Saturday Morning Censors: Television Regulation before the V-Chip*. Durham, NC: Duke University Press, 1998.

—— ed. *Nickelodeon Nation: The History, Politics, and Economics of America's Only TV Channel for Kids*. New York: New York University Press, 2004.

—— "The Good, the Bad, and the Ugly: From *Buffy the Vampire Slayer* to *Dr. 90210*," *Camera Obscura* 61, 21, no. 1 (2006): 47–51.

Henderson, Lisa. "Sexuality, Feminism, Media Studies." *Feminist Media Studies* 1, no. 1 (March 2001): 17–24.

Herman, Didi. " 'I'm Gay': Declarations, Desire, and Coming Out On Prime-Time Television." *Sexualities* 8: 1 (2005): 7–29.

—— " '*Bad Girls* Changed My Life': Homonormativity in a Women's Prison Drama." *Critical Studies in Media Communication*, 20:2 (June 2003), 141–59.

Hermes, Joke. *Re-reading Popular Culture*. Oxford: Blackwell, 2006.

Heyes, Cressida J. "Cosmetic Surgery and the Televisual Makeover: A Foucauldian Feminist Reading." *Feminist Media Studies* 7, no. 1 (March 2007): 17–32.

Hill, Annette. *Reality TV: Factual Entertainment and Television Audiences*. London: Routledge, 2004.

—— *Factual TV: News, Documentary and Reality Television*. London: Routledge, 2006.

Hills, Matt. *Fan Cultures*. London: Routledge, 2002.

Hilmes, Michele, ed. *The Television History Book*. London: BFI, 2003.

—— "Front Line Family: 'Women's Culture' Comes to the BBC." *Media, Culture & Society* 29, no. 1 (January 2007): 5–29.

Hinds, Hilary. "Fruitful Investigations: The Case of the Successful Lesbian Text." *Women: A Cultural Review* 2, no. 2 (1991): 128–133.

—— and Jackie Stacey. "Imaging Feminism, Imaging Femininity: The Bra-Burner, Diana, and the Woman Who Kills." *Feminist Media Studies* 1, no. 2 (July 2001): 153–177.

Ho, Lee-Dong. "Transnational Media Consumption and Cultural Identity: Young Korean Women's Cultural Appropriation of Japanese TV Dramas." *Asian Journal of Women's Studies* 12:2 (2006): 64–87.

Hobson, Dorothy. *Crossroads: The Drama of a Soap Opera*. London: Methuen, 1982.

—— "Housewives and the Mass Media." In *Culture, Media, Language*, ed. Stuart Hall, Dorothy Hobson, Andrew Lowe and Paul Willis. London: Hutchinson, 1980, 105–114.

—— *Soap Opera*. Oxford: Polity Press, 2003.

Hogan, Jackie. "The Construction of Gendered National Identities in the Television Advertisements of Japan and Australia." *Media, Culture & Society* 21 (November 1999): 743–758.

Hole, Anne. "Performing Identity: Dawn French and the Funny Fat Female Body." *Feminist Media Studies* 3, no. 3 (November 2003): 315–328.

Hollows, Joanne. *Feminism, Femininity and Popular Culture*. Manchester: University of Manchester Press, 2000.

—— and Rachel Moseley, eds. *Feminism in Popular Culture*. Oxford and New York: Berg, 2006.

Holmes, Su. " 'As They Really Are, and In Close-Up': Film Stars on 1950s British Television." *Screen* 42, no. 2 (Summer 2001): 167–187.

—— " 'It's a Woman!' The Question of Gender on *Who Wants To Be a Millionaire*." *Screen* 46, no. 2 (2005): 155–173.

—— and Deborah Jermyn. *Understanding Reality TV*. London: Routledge, 2003.

hooks, bell. *Black Looks: Race and Representation*. Boston: South End Press, 1992.

Horowitz, Susan. *Queens of Comedy: Lucille Ball, Phyllis Diller, Carol Burnett, Joan Rivers; and the New Generation of Funny Women.* Amsterdam: Gordon and Breach, 1997.

Houston, Beverle. "Viewing Television: The Metapsychology of Endless Consumption." *Quarterly Review of Film Studies* 9 (1984): 183–195.

Hubert, Susan J. "What's Wrong with this Picture? The Politics of Ellen's Coming Out Party." *Journal of Popular Culture* 33, no. 2 (Fall 1999): 31–36.

Illouz, Eva. *Oprah Winfrey and the Glamour of Misery: An Essay on Popular Culture.* New York: Colombia University Press, 2003.

Inness, Sherrie A. *Tough Girls: Women Warriors and Wonder Women in Popular Culture.* Philadelphia, PA: University of Pennsylvania Press, 1998.

—— ed. *Action Chicks: New Images of Tough Women in Popular Culture.* New York: Palgrave Macmillan, 2004.

Iwabuchi, Koichi, ed. *Feeling Asian Modernities: Transnational Consumption of Japanese TV Dramas.* Aberdeen and Hong Kong: Hong Kong University Press, 2004.

Jackson, Sue. " 'Street Girl': 'New' Sexual Subjectivity in a NZ Soap Drama." *Feminist Media Studies* 6, no. 4 (December, 2006): 469–486.

Jancovich, Mark and James Lyons, eds. *Quality Popular Television: Cult TV, the Industry, and the Fans.* London: BFI, 2003.

Jenkins, III, Henry. *Textual Poachers: Television Fans and Participatory Culture.* New York: Routledge, 1992.

——, Tara McPherson, and Jane Shattuc, eds. *Hop on Pop: The Politics and Pleasures of Popular Culture.* Durham, NC: Duke University Press, 2002.

Jermyn, Deborah. " 'Death of the Girl Next Door': Celebrity, Femininity, and Tragedy in the Murder of Jill Dando." *Feminist Media Studies* 1, no. 3 (November 2001): 343–359.

—— " 'Bringing Out The In You': SJP, Carrie Bradshaw and the Evolution of Television Stardom." In *Framing Celebrity: New Directions in Celebrity Culture*, ed. Su Holmes and Sean Redmond. New York: Routledge, 2006, 67–86.

—— *Crime Watching: Investigating Real Crime TV.* London and New York: I.B. Tauris, 2007.

Johnson, Catherine. *Telefantasy.* London, BFI, 2005.

—— and Turnock, Rob, eds. *ITV Cultures: Independent Television Over Fifty Years.* Berkshire: Open University Press, 2005.

Johnson, Eithne. "Lifetime's Feminine Psychographic Space and the 'Mystery Loves Company' Series." *Camera Obscura* 33–4 (1994–5): 43–74.

Johnson, Fern L. and Karren Young. "Gendered Voices in Children's Television Advertising." *Critical Studies in Media Communication* 19, no. 4 (December 2002): 461–480.

Jones, Sara Gwenllian. "Histories, Fictions, and *Xena: Warrior Princess*." *Television & New Media* 1, no. 4 (November 2000): 403–418.

—— "The Sex Lives of Cult Television Characters." *Screen* 43, no. 1 (Spring 2002): 79–90.

Joyrich, Lynne. "All That Television Allows: TV Melodrama, Postmodernism and Consumer Culture." *Camera Obscura* 16 (1988): 129–154.

—— *Re-Viewing Reception: Television, Gender, and Postmodern Culture.* Bloomington, IN: Indiana University Press, 1996.

Juhasz, Alexandra. *AIDS TV: Identity, Community, and Alternative Videos.* Durham, NC: Duke University Press, 1995.

Kane, Kate. "The Ideology of Freshness in Feminine Hygiene Commercials." *Journal of Communication Inquiry* 14, no. 1 (1990): 82–92.

Kaplan, E. Ann, ed. *Regarding Television: Critical Approaches – An Anthology.* Frederick, MD: University Publications of America, 1983.

—— *Rocking Around the Clock: Music Television, Postmodernism, and Consumer Culture*. London: Methuen, 1987.

—— "Feminist Criticism and Television." In *Channels of Discourse, Reassembled: Television and Contemporary Criticism*, ed. Robert C. Allen. Chapel Hill, NC: University of North Carolina Press, 1992, 211–253.

Karras, Irene. "The Third Wave's Final Girl: *Buffy the Vampire Slayer*." *Thirdspace* 1, no. 2 (March 2002): http://www.thirdspace.ca/articles/karras.htm.

Kaveney, Roz, ed. *Reading the Vampire Slayer: An Unofficial Critical Companion to Buffy and Angel*. London: I.B Tauris, 2002.

Kearney, Mary Celeste. *Girls Make Media*. London: Routledge, 2006.

Kim, L.S. " 'Sex and the Single Girl' and Postfeminism: The F Word on Television." *Television & New Media* 2, no. 4 (November 2001): 319–334.

Kim, Youna. "Experiencing Globalization: Global TV, Reflexivity and the Lives of Young Korean Women." *International Journal of Cultural Studies* 8, no. 4 (December 2005): 445–463.

—— *Woman, Television and Everyday Life in Korea*. London and New York: Routledge, 2005.

—— "How TV Mediates the Husband-Wife Relationship: A Korean Generation/Class/Emotion Analysis." *Feminist Media Studies* 6, no. 2 (June 2006): 129–143.

Kinder, Marsha, ed. *Kids' Media Culture*. Durham, NC: Duke University Press, 1999.

Kooijman, Jaap. "From Elegance to Extravaganza: The Supremes on *The Ed Sullivan Show* as a Presentation of Beauty." *The Velvet Light Trap* 49 (Spring 2002): 4–17.

—— "Outside in America: George Michael's Music Video, Public Sex and Global Pop Culture." *European Journal of Cultural Studies* 7, no. 1 (February 2004): 27–41.

Kreutzner, Gabrielle. *Next Time on Dynasty*. Trier: Wissenschaftlicher Verlag Trier, 1990.

—— and Ellen Seiter, "Not All 'Soaps' are Created Equal: Towards a Crosscultural Criticism of Television Serials." *Screen* 32, no. 2 (1991): 154–172.

Krijnen, Tonny and Irene Costera Meijer. "The Moral Indignation in Primetime Television." *International Journal of Cultural Studies* 8, no.3 (September 2005): 353–374.

Krishnan, Prabha and Anita Dighe. *Affirmation and Denial: Construction of Femininity on Indian Television*. New Delhi: Sage, 1990.

Krzywinska, Tanya. "Dissidence and Authenticity in Dyke Porn and Actuality TV." In *Dissident Voices: The Politics of Television and Cultural Change*, ed. Mike Wayne. London: Pluto Press, 1998, 159–175.

Kuhn, Annette, Rosalind Brunt, Christine Geraghty, Jenny Kitzinger, Beth Edginton, and Roger Silverstone. "Flowers and Tears: The Death of Diana, Princess of Wales." *Screen* 39, no. 1 (Spring 1998): 67–84.

La Pastina, Antonio C. "The Sexual Other in Brazilian Television: Public and Institutional Reception of Sexual Difference." *International Journal of Cultural Studies* 5, no. 1 (March 2002): 83–99.

—— "Telenovela Reception in Rural Brazil: Gendered Readings and Sexual Mores." *Critical Studies in Media Communication* 21, no. 2 (June 2004): 162–181.

Landay, Lori. "Millions 'Love Lucy': Commodification and the Lucy Phenomenon." *NWSA Journal* 11, no. 2 (Summer 1999): 25–47.

Larson, Stephanie Greco. "Black Women on *All My Children*." *Journal of Popular Film & Television* 22, no. 1 (1994): 44–48.

Lavery, David. ed. *This Thing of Ours: Investigating the Sopranos*. New York: Columbia University Press, 2002.

——, Angela Hague, and Maria Cartwright, eds. *Deny All Knowledge: Reading The X-Files*. Syracuse, NY: Syracuse University Press, 1996.

Leal, Ondina Fachel. "Popular Taste and Erudite Repertoire: The Place and Space of Television in Brazil." *Cultural Studies* 4, no. 1 (1990): 19–29.

Lee, Dong-Hoo. "Transnational Media Consumption and Cultural Identity: Young Korean Women's Cultural Appropriation of Japanese TV Dramas." *Asian Journal of Women's Studies* 12, no. 2 (2006): 64–87.

Lee, Janet. "Subversive Sitcoms: *Roseanne* as Inspiration for Feminist Resistance." *Women's Studies* 21, no. 1 (1992): 87–101.

Lee, Minu and Chong Heup Cho. "Women Watching Together: An Ethnographic Study of Korean Soap Opera Fans in the United States." *Cultural Studies* 4, no. 1 (1990): 30–44.

Leibman, Nina. *Living Room Lectures: The Fifties Family in Film and Television.* Austin: University of Texas Press, 1995.

Lentz, Kirsten Marthe. "*Quality* versus *Relevance*: Feminism, Race, and the Politics of the Sign in 1970s Television." *Camera Obscura* 43, 15, no. 1 (2000): 45–93.

Levine, Elana. *Wallowing in Sex: The New Sexual Culture of 1970s American Television.* Durham, NC: Duke University Press, 2007.

Levy, Marie-Françoise. "Television, Family and Society in France 1949–1968." *Historical Journal of Film, Radio and Television* 18, no. 2 (June 1998): 199–133.

Lewis, Lisa A. *Gender Politics and MTV: Voicing the Difference.* Philadelphia, PA: Temple University Press, 1990.

—— ed. *The Adoring Audience: Fan Culture and Popular Media.* New York: Routledge, 1992.

Liebes, Tamar and Sonia Livingstone. "Mothers and Lovers: Managing Women's Role Conflicts in American and British Soap Operas." In *Comparatively Speaking: Communication and Culture Across Space and Time*, ed. Jay G. Blumler, Jack M. McLeod and Karl Erie Rosengren. Newbury Park, CA: Sage, 1992, 94–120.

—— "European Soap Operas: The Diversification of a Genre." *European Journal of Communication* 13, no. 2 (1998): 147–180.

Livingstone, Sonia. *Making Sense of Television: The Psychology of Audience Interpretation.* Oxford: Pergamon Press, 1989.

—— and Peter Lunt. *Talk on Television: Audience Participation and Public Debate.* London: Routledge, 1994.

Lopate, Carol. "Daytime Television: You'll Never Want to Leave Home." *Radical America* 11, no. 1 (1977): 32–51.

Lotz, Amanda D. "Postfeminist Television Criticism: Rehabilitating Critical Terms and Identifying Postfeminist Attributes." *Feminist Media Studies* 1, no. 1 (March 2001): 105–121.

—— *Redesigning Women: Television After the Network Era.* Urbana, IL: University of Illinois Press, 2006.

—— and Sharon Marie Ross. "Bridging Media Specific Approaches: The Value of Feminist Television Criticism's Synthetic Approach." *Feminist Media Studies* 4, no. 2 (2004): 185–202.

Lu, Sheldon H. "Soap Opera in China: The Transnational Politics of Visuality, Sexuality, and Masculinity." *Cinema Journal* 40, no. 1 (Fall 2000): 25–47.

Lubiano, Wahneema. "Black Ladies, Welfare Queens, and State Minstrels: Ideological War by Narrative Means." In *Race-ing Justice, En-Gendering Power: Essays on Anita Hill, Clarence Thomas, and the Construction of Social Reality*, ed. Toni Morrison. New York: Pantheon Books, 1992, 323–363.

Luckett, Moya. "Sensuous Women and Single Girls: Reclaiming the Female Body in 1960s Television," in *Swinging Singles: Representing Sexuality in the 1960s*, ed. Hilary Radner and Moya Luckett. Minneapolis: University of Minnesota Press, 1999, 277–298.

—— "Girl Watchers: Patty Duke and Teen TV," in *The Revolution Wasn't Televised: Sixties Television and Social Conflict*, ed. Lynn Spigel and Michael Curtin. New York: Routledge, 1997, 95–116.

Lury, Karen. *British Youth Television: Cynicism and Enchantment*. Oxford: Oxford University Press, 2001.

—— *Interpreting Television*. London: Hodder Arnold, 2005.

Ly, Anh. "Dispatch from Mali: A Soap Opera Education." *Framework: The Journal of Cinema and Media* 47, no. 2 (Fall 2006): 94–99.

MacDonald, Myra. *Representing Women: Myths of Femininity in the Popular Media*. London: Hodder Arnold, 1995.

—— "Performing Memory on Television: Documentary and the 1960s", *Screen* 47, no. 3 (2006): 327–345.

MacMurraugh-Kavanagh, Madeleine K. " "Drama" into "News": Strategies of Intervention in *The Wednesday Play*." *Screen* 38, no. 3 (1997): 247–259.

—— "The BBC and the Birth of *The Wednesday Play*, 1962–66: Institutional Containment Versus "Agitational Contemporaneity." " *Historical Journal of Film, Radio and Television* 17, no. 3 (1997): 367–381.

—— "Boys on Top: Gender and Authorship on the BBC Wednesday Play, 1964–70." *Media, Culture & Society* 21, no. 3 (May 1999): 409–425.

Madill, Anna and Rebecca Goldmeier. "*EastEnders*: Texts of Female Desire and of Community." *International Journal of Cultural Studies* 6, no. 4 (December 2003): 471–494.

Malik, Sarita. *Representing Black Britain: Black and Asian Images on Television*. London: Sage, 2002.

Manga, Julie Engel. *Talking Trash: The Cultural Politics of Daytime TV Talk Shows*. New York: New York University Press, 2003.

Mankekar, Purnima. "Television Tales and a Woman's Rage: A Nationalist Recasting of Draupadi's "Disrobing" ". *Public Culture* 5, no. 3 (1993), 469–492.

—— *Screening Culture, Viewing Politics: An Ethnography of Television, Womanhood, and Nation in Postcolonial India*. Durham, NC: Duke University Press, 1999.

Manuel, Preethi. "Black Women in British Television Drama–A Case of Marginal Representation." In *Out of Focus: Writings on Women and the Media*, ed. Kath Davies, Julienne Dickey and Teresa Stratford. London: The Women's Press, 1987, 42–44.

Marks, Laura U. "Tie a Yellow Ribbon Around Me: Masochism, Militarism, and the Gulf War on TV." *Camera Obscura* 27 (1991): 55–75.

Mascaro, Thomas A. "Shades of Black on *Homicide: Life on the Street*: Advances and Retreats in Portrayals of African American Women." *Journal of Popular Film & Television* (Summer 2005): 56–67.

Masciarotte, Gloria-Jean. "C'mon Girl: Oprah Winfrey and the Discourse of Feminine Talk." *Genders* 11 (Fall 1991): 81–110.

Mason, Ann, and Marian Meyers. "Living with Martha Stewart Media: Chosen Domesticity in the Experience of Fans." *Journal of Communication* 51, no. 4 (2001): 801–823.

Mato, Daniel. "The Transnationalization of the Telenovela Industry, Territorial References, and the Production of Markets and Representations of Transnational Identities." *Television & New Media* 6, no. 4 (November 2005): 423–444.

Mattelart, Michèle. "Women and the Cultural Industries." *Media, Culture and Society* 4, no. 2 (1982): 133–151.

—— *Women, Media and Crisis: Femininity and Disorder*. London: Comedia, 1986.

Mayer, Vicki, "When the Camera Won't Focus: Tensions in Media Ethnography." *Feminist Media Studies* 1, no. 3 (November 2001): 307–322.

—— *Producing Dreams, Consuming Youth: Mexican Americans and Mass Media*. New Brunswick, NJ: Rutgers University Press, 2003.

—— "Soft-Core in TV Time: The Political Economy of a 'Cultural Trend'." *Critical Studies in Media Communication* 22, no. 4 (October 2005): 302–320.

Mayne, Judith. "*L.A. Law* and Prime-Time Feminism." *Discourse* 10, no. 2 (1988): 30–47.

—— *Framed: Lesbians, Feminists, and Media Culture*. Minneapolis, MN: University of Minnesota Press, 2000.

Mazdon, Lucy. "Contemporary French Television, the Nation, and the Family: Continuity and Change." *Television & New Media* 2, no. 4 (November 2001): 335–349.

McCarthy, Anna. *Ambient Television: Visual Culture and Public Space*. Durham, NC: Duke University Press, 2001.

McCabe, Janet and Kim Akass, eds. *Reading Desperate Housewives: Beyond the White Picket Fence*. New York: Palgrave Macmillan, 2006.

McKee, Alan. " 'Sale of the Century': And the Ladies Look Beautiful Too." In *Australian Television: A Genealogy of Great Moments*, ed. Alan Mckee. Melbourne: Oxford University Press, 2001, 185–198.

McLaughlin, Lisa. "Feminism, the Public Sphere, Media and Democracy." *Media, Culture and Society* 15, no. 4 (1993): 599–620.

McPherson, Tara. "Disregarding Romance and Refashioning Femininity: Getting Down and Dirty with *Designing Women*." *Camera Obscura* 32 (1993–4): 103–123.

McRobbie, Angela. "Post-feminism and Popular Culture." *Feminist Media Studies* 4, no. 3 (November 2004): 255–264.

Meehan, Diane M. *Ladies of the Evening: Women Characters of Prime-Time Television*. Metuchen, NJ: Scarecrow, 1983.

Meehan, Eileen R. "Heads of Household and Ladies of the House: Gender, Genre, and Broadcast Ratings, 1929–1990." In *Ruthless Criticism: New Perspectives in U.S. Communication History*, ed. William S. Solomon and Robert W. McChesney. Minneapolis, MN: University of Minnesota Press, 1993, 204–221.

Meijer, Irene Costera. "The Colour of Soap Opera: An Analysis of Professional Speech on the Representation of Ethnicity." *European Journal of Cultural Studies* 4, no. 2 (May 2001): 207–230.

Mellencamp, Patricia. "Situation Comedy, Feminism, and Freud: Discourses of Gracie and Lucy." In *Studies in Entertainment: Critical Approaches to Mass Culture*, ed. Tania Modleski, 80–95. Bloomington, IN: Indiana University Press, 1986, 80–95.

—— ed. *Logics of Television: Essays in Television Criticism*. Bloomington, IN: Indiana University Press, 1990.

—— *High Anxiety: Catastrophe, Scandal, Age and Comedy*. Bloomington, IN: Indiana University Press, 1992.

Merck, Mandy. *Perversions: Deviant Readings*. New York: Routledge, 1993.

—— ed. *After Diana: Irreverent Elegies*. London and New York: Verso, 1998.

Messner, Michael A., Margaret Carlisle-Duncan and Cheryl Cooky. "Silence, Sports Bras, and Wrestling Porn: Women in Televised Sports News and Highlights Shows." *Journal of Sport and Social Issues*. 27, no. 1 (2003): 38–51.

Meyers, Marian. "African American Women and Violence: Gender, Race, and Class in the News." *Critical Studies in Media Communication* 21, no. 2 (June 2004): 95–118.

Miller, Toby. *The Avengers*. Berkeley, CA: University of California Press, 1998.

Mitchell, Danielle. "Producing Containment: The Rhetorical Containment of Difference in *Will & Grace*." *Journal of Popular Culture* 38, no. 6 (November 2005): 1050–1068.

Modleski, Tania. *Loving with a Vengeance: Mass-Produced Fantasies for Women*. Hamden, CT: Shoestring Press, 1982; London, Methuen 1984.

—— ed. *Studies in Entertainment: Critical Approaches to Mass Culture*. Bloomington, IN: Indiana University Press, 1986.

—— *Feminism without Women*. New York, Routledge, 1991.

Montgomery, Kathryn C. *Target Prime Time: Advocacy Groups and the Struggle over Entertainment Television*. New York: Oxford University Press, 1989.

Moores, Shaun. *Media and Everyday Life in Modern Society*. Edinburgh: Edinburgh University Press, 2000.

Moorti, Sujata. "Cathartic Confessions or Emancipatory Texts? Rape Narratives on *The Oprah Winfrey Show*." *Social Text* 57 (Winter 1998): 83–102.

—— and Karen Ross eds. "Reality Television: Fairy Tale or Feminist Nightmare?" *Feminist Media Studies* 4, no. 2 (July 2004): 203–231.

Moritz, Marguerite J. "American Television Discovers Gay Women: The Changing Context of Programming Decisions at the Networks." *Journal of Communication Inquiry* 13, no. 2 (1989): 62–79.

—— "Old Strategies for New Texts: How American Television Is Creating and Treating Lesbian Characters." In *Queer Words, Queer Images: Communication and the Construction of Homosexuality*, ed. R. Jeffrey Ringer. New York: New York University Press, 1994, 122–142.

Morley, David. *Family Television: Cultural Power and Domestic Leisure*. London: Comedia, 1986.

—— *Television, Audiences and Cultural Studies*. London: Routledge, 1992.

—— *Home Territories: Media, Mobility and Identity*. London: Routledge, 2000.

—— *Media, Modernity and Technology: The Geography of the New*. London and New York: Routledge, 2007.

Morreale, Joanne. "*Xena: Warrior Princess* as Feminist Camp." *Journal of Popular Culture* 32, no. 2 (Fall 1998): 79–86.

—— ed. *Critiquing the Sitcom: A Reader*. Syracuse, NY: Syracuse University Press, 2004.

Morris, Meaghan. *The Pirate's Fiancée: Feminism, Reading, Postmodernism*. London: Verso, 1988.

Morse, Margaret. *Virtualities: Television, Media Art, and Cyberculture*. Bloomington, IN: Indiana University Press, 1998.

Moseley, Rachel. "Makeover Takeover on British Television." *Screen* 41, 3 (2000): 299–314.

—— "Glamorous Witchcraft: Gender and Magic in Teen Film and Television." *Screen* 43, no. 4 (Winter 2002): 403–422.

—— and Jacinda Read. " 'Having It *Ally*': Popular Television and (Post-)Feminism." *Feminist Media Studies* 2, no. 2 (July 2002): 231–249.

Mulvey, Laura. *Visual and Other Pleasures*. New York: Palgrave Macmillan, 1989.

—— "Melodrama In and Out of the Home." In *High Theory/Low Culture: Analyzing Popular Television and Film*, ed. Colin McCabe. Manchester: Manchester University Press, 1986, 80–100.

Mumford, Laura Stempel. "Stripping on the Girl Channel: Lifetime, *thirtysomething*, and Television Form." *Camera Obscura* 33–4 (1994–5): 167–190.

—— *Love and Ideology in the Afternoon: Soap Opera, Women, and Television Genre*. Bloomington, IN: Indiana University Press, 1995.

Munt, Sally R. "A Queer Undertaking: Anxiety and Reparation in the HBO Television Drama Series *Six Feet Under*." *Feminist Media Studies* 6, no. 3 (June 2006): 263–279.

Murray, Susan. *Hitch Your Antenna to the Stars: Early Television and Broadcast Stardom*. New York: Routledge, 2005.

—— and Laurie Ouellette, eds. *Reality TV: Remaking Television Culture*. New York: New York University Press, 2004.

Nash, Ilana. *American Sweethearts: Teenage Girls in Twentieth Century Popular Culture*. Bloomington, IN: Indiana University Press, 2006.

—— " 'Nowhere Else to Go': *Gidget* and the Construction of Adolescent Femininity." *Feminist Media Studies* 2, no. 3 (November 2002): 341–356.

Negra, Diane. "Ethnic Food Fetishism, Whiteness, and Nostalgia in Recent Film and Television." *The Velvet Light Trap* 50 (Fall 2000): 62–76.

—— " 'Quality Postfeminism?' Sex and the Single Girl on HBO." *Genders* 39 (2004), <http://genders.org/g39/g39_negra.html>.

—— and Yvonne Tasker eds. *Interrogating Post-Feminism*. Durham, NC: Duke University Press, 2007.

Nelson, Robin. *TV Drama in Transition* Basingstoke: Macmillan, 1997.

Newcomb, Horace. *Television: The Critical View*, 7th edn. New York: Oxford University Press, 2006.

Nochimson, Martha. *No End to Her: soap Opera and the Female Subject*. Berkeley, CA: University of California Press, 1992.

—— "*Ally McBeal*: Brightness Falls from Air." *Film Quarterly* 53, no. 3 (Spring 2000): 25–32.

Nunn, Heather and Anita Biressi. "*Silent Witness*: Detection, Femininity, and the Post-Mortem Body." *Feminist Media Studies* 3, no. 2 (July 2003): 193–206.

O'Dell, Cary. "A Station of Their Own: An Early TV Station Run by Women." *Television Quarterly* 30, no. 3 (Winter 2000): 58–69.

Opoku-Mensah, Aida. "Marching On: African Feminist Media Studies." *Feminist Media Studies* 1, no. 1 (March 2001): 25–34.

Oren, Tasha G. "Living Room Levantine: Immigration, Ethnicity, and the Border in Early Israeli Television." *The Velvet Light Trap* 44 (Fall 1999): 20–30.

—— and Patrice Petro, eds. *Global Currents: Media and Technology Now*. New Brunswick, NJ: Rutgers University Press, 2004.

Osgerby, Bill and Anna Gough-Yates, eds. *Action TV: Tough-Guys, Smooth Operators and Foxy Chicks*. London: Routledge, 2001.

Oswell, David. *Television, Childhood, and the Home*. Oxford: Oxford University Press, 2002.

Parkins, Wendy. "Oprah Winfrey's Change Your Life TV and the Spiritual Everyday." *Continuum: Journal of Media and Cultural Studies* 15, no. 2 (2001): 145–157.

Parks, Lisa. "Cracking Open the Set: Television Repair and Tinkering with Gender 1949–1955." *Television & New Media* 1, no. 3 (August 2000): 257–278.

—— *Cultures in Orbit: Satellites and the Televisual*. Durham, NC: Duke University Press, 2005.

—— and Shanti Kumar, eds. *Planet TV: A Global Television Reader*. New York: New York University Press, 2002.

Parry-Giles, Shawn J. "Mediating Hillary Rodham Clinton: Television News Practices and Image-Making in the Postmodern Age." *Critical Studies in Media Communication* 17, no. 2 (June 2000): 205–226.

Paterson, Richard. "Planning the Family: The Art of the Television Schedule." *Screen Education* 35 (Summer 1980): 79–85.

Patton, Tracey Owens. "*Ally McBeal* and Her Homilies: The Reification of White Stereotypes of the Other." *Journal of Black Studies* 32, no. 2 (November 2001): 229–260.

Pearson, Rosalind C. "Fact or Fiction?: Narrative and Reality in the Mexican Telenovela." *Television & New Media* 6, no. 4 (November 2005): 400–406.

Pedersen, Vibeke. "Soap, Pin-up and Burlesque: Commercialization and Femininity in Danish Television." *Nordicom Review* 2 (1993), 25–35.

Penley, Constance. *NASA/Trek: Popular Science and Sex in America*. London: Verso, 1997.

Perera, Suvendrini. "Representation Wars: Malaysia, Embassy, and Australia's Corps Diplomatique." In *Australian Cultural Studies: A Reader*, ed. John Frow and Meaghan Morris. Sydney: Allen and Unwin, 1993, 15–29.

Pérez, María de la Luz Casas. "Cultural Identity: Between Reality and Fiction: A Transformation of Genre and Roles in Mexican Telenovelas." *Television & New Media* 6, no. 4 (November 2005): 407–414.

Petro, Patrice. "Mass Culture and the Feminine: The 'Place' of Television in Film Studies." *Cinema Journal* 25, no. 3 (1986): 5–21.

Philips, Deborah. "Transformation Scenes: The Television Interior Makeover." *International Journal of Cultural Studies* 8, no. 2 (June 2005): 213–229.

Piper, Helen. "Reality TV, *Wife Swap* and the Drama of Banality." *Screen* 45, no. 4 (2004): 273–287.

Pitcher, Karen C. "The Staging of Agency in *Girls Gone Wild.*" *Critical Studies in Media Communication* 23, no. 3 (August 2006): 200–218.

Porter, Lorraine. "Tarts, Tampons and Tyrants: Women and Representation in British Comedy." In *Because I Tell a Joke or Two: Comedy, Politics and Social Difference*, ed. Stephen Wagg. London: Routledge, 1998, 65–93.

Press, Andrea L. *Women Watching Television: Gender, Class, and Generation in the American Television Experience*. Philadelphia, PA: University of Pennsylvania Press, 1991.

—— and Elizabeth R. Cole. *Speaking of Abortion: Television and Authority in the Lives of Women*. Chicago: University of Chicago Press, 1999.

—— and Terry Strathman. "Work, Family, and Social Class in Television Images of Women: Prime-Time Television and the Construction of Postfeminism." *Women and Language* 16, no. 2 (1993): 7–15.

Pribram, E. Deidre, ed. *Female Spectators: Looking at Film and Television*. London: Verso, 1988.

Probyn, Elspeth. "TV's Local: The Exigency of Gender in Media Research." *Canadian Journal of Communication* 14, no. 3 (1989): 29–41.

—— "New Traditionalism and Post-Feminism: TV Does the Home." *Screen* 31, no. 2 (1990): 147–159.

—— "Teaching in the Field: Gender and Feminist Media Studies." *Feminist Media Studies* 1, no. 1 (March 2001): 35–39.

Projansky, Sarah. *Watching Rape: Film and Television in Postfeminist Culture*. New York: New York University Press, 2001.

Punwani, Jyoti. "The Portrayal of Women on Indian Television." In *Women in Indian Society: A Reader*, ed. Rehana Ghandially. New Delhi: Sage, 1988, 224–232.

Quimby, Karin. "*Will & Grace*: Negotiating (Gay) Marriage on Prime-Time Television." *Journal of Popular Culture* 38, no. 4 (May 2005): 713–731.

Radner, Hilary. "Quality Television and Feminine Narcissism: The Shrew and the Covergirl." *Genders* 8 (Summer 1990): 110–128.

—— *Shopping Around: Feminine Culture and the Pursuit of Pleasure*. New York: Routledge, 1995.

Radway, Janice. *Reading the Romance: Women, Patriarchy, and Popular Literature*. Chapel Hill, NC: University of North Carolina Press, 1984.

Rajiva, Lila. *The Language of Empire: Abu Ghraib and the American Media*. New York: New York University Press, 2005.

Rakow, Lana F., ed. *Women Making Meaning: New Feminist Directions in Communication*. New York: Routledge, 1992.

—— "Feminists, Media, Freed Speech." *Feminist Media Studies* 1, no. 1 (March 2001): 41–44.

—— and Kimberlie Kranich. "Woman as Sign in Television News." *Journal of Communication* 41, no. 1 (1991): 8–23.

Rao, Leela. "Facets of Media and Gender Studies in India." *Feminist Media Studies* 1, no. 1 (March 2001): 45–48.

Rapping, Elayne. *The Movie of the Week: Private Stories/Public Events.* Minneapolis, MN: University of Minnesota, 1992.

—— *Media-tions: Forays into the Culture and Gender Wars.* Boston: South End Press, 1994.

Reed, Jennifer. "Ellen De Generes: Public Lesbian Number One." *Feminist Media Studies* 5, no. 1 (March 2005): 23–36.

Reid, Evelyn Cauleta. "Viewdata: Television Viewing Habits of Young Black Women in London." *Screen* 30, nos. 1–2 (1989): 114–121.

Rhodes, Jane. "Television's Realist Portrayal of African-American Women and the Case of *L.A. Law*." *Women and Language* 14, no. 1 (1991): 29–34.

—— "Journalism in the New Millennium: What's a Feminist to Do?" *Feminist Media Studies* 1, no. 1 (March 2001): 49–53.

Riegel, Henriette. "Soap Operas and Gossip." *Journal of Popular Culture* 29, no. 4 (Spring 1996): 201–209.

Rivero, Yeidy. *Tuning Out Blackness: Race and Nation in the History of Puerto Rican Television.* Durham, NC: Duke University Press, 2005.

Roberts, Robin. "Music Videos, Performance and Resistance: Feminist Rappers." *Journal of Popular Culture* 25, no. 2 (1991): 141–152.

—— " 'Ladies First': Queen Latifah's Afrocentric Music Video." *African American Review* 28, no. 2 (1994): 245–257.

—— *Sexual Generations: Star Trek: The New Generation and Gender.* Urbana, IL: University of Illinois Press, 1999.

Rofel, Lisa B. "*Yearnings*: Televisual Love and Melodramatic Politics in Contemporary China." *American Ethnologist* 21: 4 (November 1994), 700–722.

Rogers, Deborah D. "Daze of Our Lives: The Soap Opera as Feminist Text." *Journal of American Culture* 14, no. 4 (1991): 29–41.

Roome, Dorothy. "Humour as 'Cultural Revolution' in South African Situation Comedy: Suburban Bliss and Multicultural Female Viewers." *Journal of Film and Television* 51, no. 3–4 (Fall-Winter 1999–2000): 61–87.

Rose, Tricia. "Never Trust a Big Butt and a Smile." *Camera Obscura* 23 (1990): 108–131.

Ross, Karen and Sujata Moorti. "Introduction: War Reporting through a Gendered Lens." *Feminist Media Studies* 5, no. 3 (November 2005): 359–395.

Rothenberg, Molly Anne. "The 'Newer Angels' and the Living Dead: The Ethics of Screening Obsessional Desire." *Camera Obscura* 40–41 (May 1997): 17–42.

Rowe, Kathleen K. *The Unruly Woman: Gender and the Genres of Laughter.* Austin, TX: University of Texas Press, 1995.

Roy, Abhik. "Images of Domesticity and Motherhood in Indian Television Commercials." *Journal of Popular Culture* 32, no. 3 (Winter 1998): 117–134.

Russell, Lorena. "Strangers in Blood: The Queer Intimacies of *Six Feet Under*." In Thomas Richard Fahy, ed. *Considering Alan Ball: Essays on Sexuality, Death, and America in the Television and Film Writings.* Jefferson, NC: McFarland & Co., 2006, 107–123.

Scheiner, Georganne. "Would You Like to Be Queen for a Day? Finding a Working Class Voice in American Television of the 1950s." *Historical Journal of Film, Radio and Television* 23, no. 4 (October 2003): 375–387.

Schlesinger, Philip, Emerson R. Dobash, Russell P. Dobash, and Kay C. Weaver. *Women Viewing Violence.* London: British Film Institute, 1992.

Schulman, Norma Miriam. "Laughing Across the Color Barrier: *In Living Color*." *Journal of Popular Film & Television* 20, no. 1 (1992): 2–7.

Schulze, Laurie. "Getting Physical: Text/Context/Reading and the Made-for-Television Movie." *Cinema Journal* 25, no. 2 (1986): 35–50.

Schwichtenberg, Cathy. "*The Love Boat*: The Packaging and Selling of Love, Heterosexual Romance, and the Family." *Media, Culture and Society* 6, no. 3 (1984): 301–311.

—— ed. *The Madonna Connection: Representational Politics, Subcultural Identities, and Cultural Theory*. Boulder, CO: Westview Press, 1993.

Sconce Jeffrey, *Haunted Media: Electronic Presence from Telegraphy to Television*. Durham, NL: Duke University Press, 2000.

Seiter, Ellen. *Sold Separately: Parents and Children in Consumer Culture*. New Brunswick, NJ: Rutgers University Press, 1993.

—— *Television and New Media Audiences*. Oxford: Oxford University Press, 1999.

—— *The Internet Playground: Children's Access, Entertainment, and Mis-Education*. New York: Peter Lang Publishing, Inc., 2005.

—— and Hans Borchers, Gabrielle Kreutzner, and Eva-Maria Warth. eds. *Remote Control: Television, Audiences, and Cultural Power*. New York: Routledge, 1989.

Sender, Katherine. "Queens for a Day: *Queer Eye for the Straight Guy* and the Neoliberal Project." *Critical Studies in Media Communication* 23, no. 2 (June 2006): 131–151.

Sgroi, Renee M. "*Joe Millionaire* and Women's Positions A Question of Class." *Feminist Media Studies* 6, no. 3 (June 2006): 281–294.

Shattuc, Jane. *The Talking Cure: Women and TV Talk Shows*. New York: Routledge, 1996.

Shaw, Marion and Sabine Vanacker. *Reflecting on Miss Marple*. London: Routledge, 1991.

Shiach, Morag, ed. *Feminism and Cultural Studies*. New York: Oxford, 1999.

Shome, Raka. "White Femininity and the Discourse of the Nation: Re/membering Princess Diana." *Feminist Media Studies* 1, no. 3 (November 2001): 323–342.

Shugart, Helene A., C. Waggoner, and D. Hallstein. "Mediating Third-Wave Feminism: Appropriation as Postmodern Media Practice." *Critical Studies in Media Communication* 18, no. 2 (June 2001): 194–210.

Simpson, Amelia S. *Xuxa: The Megamarketing of Gender, Race, and Modernity*. Philadelphia, PA: Temple University Press, 1993.

Skeggs, Beverley, ed. *Feminist Cultural Theory*. Manchester: Manchester University Press, 1995.

Skirrow, Gillian. "Representations of Women in the Association of Cinematograph, Television and Allied Technicians." *Screen* 22, no. 3 (1981): 94–102.

—— "Hellivision: An Analysis of Video Games." In *High Theory/Low Culture: Analyzing Popular Television and Film*, ed. Colin McCabe. Manchester, UK: Manchester University Press, 1986, 115–142.

Smith-Shomade, Beretta E. *Shaded Lives: African-American Women and Television*. New Brunswick, NJ: Rutgers University Press, 2002.

Spence, Louise. "Life's Little Problems . . . and Pleasures: An Investigation into the Narrative Structures of *The Young and the Restless*." *Quarterly Review of Film Studies* 9, no. 4 (1984): 301–308.

Spigel, Lynn. *Make Room for TV: Television and the Family Ideal in Postwar America*. Chicago: University of Chicago Press, 1992.

—— *Welcome to the Dreamhouse: Popular Media and Postwar Suburbs*. Durham, NC: Duke University Press, 2001.

—— "Designing the Smart House: Posthuman Domesticity and Conspicuous Production." *European Journal of Cultural Studies* 8, no. 4 (November 2005): 403–426.

—— and Denise Mann, eds. *Private Screenings: Television and the Female Consumer*. Minneapolis: University of Minnesota Press, 1992.

—— and Jan Olsson, eds. *Television after TV: Essays on a Medium in Transition*. Durham, NC: Duke University Press, 2004.

Squire, Corinne. "Empowering Women? *The Oprah Winfrey Show*." *Feminism and Psychology* 4, no. 1 (1994): 63–79.

Sreberny, Annabelle. "Gender, Globalization and Communications: Women and the Transnational." *Feminist Media Studies* 1, no. 1 (March 2001): 61–65.

Stabile, Carol. "Getting What She Deserved: The News Media, Martha Stewart, and Masculine Domination." *Feminist Media Studies* 4, no. 3 (November 2004): 315–332.

—— and Deepa Kumar. "Unveiling Imperialism: Media, Gender, and the War on Afghanistan." *Media, Culture & Society* 27, no. 5 (September 2005): 765–782.

Stenger, Josh. "The Clothes Make the Fan: Fashion and Online Fandom when *Buffy The Vampire Slayer Goes* to eBay." *Cinema Journal* 45, no. 4 (Summer 2006): 26–44.

Straayer, Chris. "The She-Man: Postmodern Bi-Sexed Performance in Film and Video." *Screen* 31, no. 3 (1990): 262–280.

Streeter, Thomas and Wendy Wahl. "Audience Theory and Feminism: Property, Gender, and the Televisual Audience." *Camera Obscura* 33–4 (1994–5): 243–261.

Syvertsen, Trine. "Ordinary People in Extraordinary Circumstances: A Study of Participants in Television Dating Games." *Media, Culture & Society* 23, no. 3 (May 2001): 319–337.

Tasker, Yvonne and Diane Negra, eds. "In Focus: Postfeminism and Contemporary Media Studies." *Cinema Journal* 44, no. 2 (Winter 2005): 107–110.

Taylor, Ella. *Prime-Time Families: Television Culture in Postwar America*. Berkeley, CA: University of California Press, 1989.

Taylor, Lisa. "From Ways of Life to Lifestyle: The 'Ordinari-ization' of British Gardening Lifestyle Television." *European Journal of Communication*, 17, no. 4: 479–493.

Thomas, Lyn. *Fans, Feminisms, and "Quality" Media*. London: Routledge, 2002.

Thornham, Sue. "Feminist Interventions: *Prime Suspect I*." *Critical Survey* 6, no. 2 (1994): 226–233.

—— " 'A Good Body': The Case of/for Feminist Media Studies." *European Journal of Cultural Studies* 6, no. 1 (February 2003): 75–94.

—— and Tony Purvis, *Television Drama: Theories and Identities* Basingstoke: Palgrave Macmillan, 2005.

Thornton, Edith. "On the Landing: High Art, Low Art, and *Upstairs, Downstairs*." *Camera Obscura* 31 (1993): 27–46.

Thoveron, Gabriel. "European Televised Women." *European Journal of Communication* 1, no. 3 (1986): 289–300.

Thumin, Janet, ed. *Small Screens, Big Ideas: Television in the 1950s*. London: I.B. Tauris, 2002.

—— *Inventing Television Culture: Men, Women, and the Box*. Oxford, UK: Oxford University Press, 2005.

Thynne, Lizzie. "Women in Television in the Multi-Channel Age." *Feminist Review* 64 (January 2000): 65–82.

Torres, Sasha, ed. *Living Color: Race and Television in the United States*. Durham, NC: Duke University Press, 1998.

Tropiano, Stephen, *The Prime Time Closet: A History of Gays and Lesbians on TV*. New York: Applause, 2002.

Tuchman, Gaye, Arlene Caplan Daniels, and James Benet, eds. *Hearth and Home: Images of Women in the Mass Media*. New York: Oxford University Press, 1978.

Tufte, Thomas. *Living with the Rubbish Queen: Telenovelas, Culture and Modernity in Brazil*. Luton: University of Luton Press, 2000.

Tuladhar, Sumon. "Participatory Video as Post-Literacy Activity for Women in Rural Nepal." *Convergence* 27, nos. 2–3 (1994): 111–117.

Turnbull, Sue. " 'Look at Moiye Kimmie, Look at Moiye!': *Kath and Kim* and the Australian Comedy of Taste." *Media International Australia* 113 (2004): 98–109.

Turner, Graeme. "Cultural Identity, Soap Narrative, and Reality TV." *Television & New Media* 6, no. 4 (2005): 415–422.

Turnock, Robert. *Interpreting Diana: Television Audiences and the Death of a Princess.* London: British Film Institute, 2000.

Tylee, Claire. "The Black Explorer: Female Identity in Black Feminist Drama on British Television in 1992." In *Frames and Fiction on Television: The Politics of Identity Within Drama,* ed. Bruce Carson and Margaret Llewellyn-Jones. Exeter and Oregon: Intellect Books, 2000, 100–112.

Tyler, Carole-Anne. "The Supreme Sacrifice? TV, 'TV', and the Renee Richards Story." *Differences* 1, no. 3 (1989): 160–186.

Unger, Arthur. "Linda Ellerbee: The Newswoman Who Fired the Networks." *Television Quarterly* 31, no. 1 (Spring 2000): 4–18.

Valaskivi, Katja. "Being a Part of the Family? Genre, Gender and Production in a Japanese TV Drama." *Media, Culture & Society* 22, no. 3 (May 2000): 309–325.

Valdivia, Angharad and Ramona Curry. "Xuxa at the Borders of Global TV: The Institutionalisation and Marginalisation of Brazil's Blonde Ambition." *Camera Obscura* 38 (1998): 31–61.

Vavrus, Mary Douglas. "Domesticating Patriarchy: Hegemonic Masculinity and Television's *Mr. Mom.*" *Critical Studies in Media Communication* 19, no. 3 (September 2002): 352–375.

—— "Opting Out Moms in the News: Selling New Traditionalism in the New Millennium." *Feminist Media Studies* 7, no. 1 (March 2006): 47–63.

Vartanian, Carolyn Reed. "Women Next Door to War: *China Beach.*" In *Inventing Vietnam: The War in Film and Television,* ed. Michael Anderegg. Philadelphia, PA: Temple University Press, 1991, 190–203.

Villarejo, Amy. *Lesbian Rule: Cultural Criticism and the Value of Desire.* Durham, NC: Duke University Press, 2003.

Wakefield, Sarah R. " 'Your Sister in Saint Scully': An Electronic Community of Female Fans of *The X Files.*" *Journal of Popular Film and Television* 29, no. 3 (2001): 130–137.

Walker, Alexis J. "Couples Watching Television: Gender, Power, and the Remote Control." *Journal of Marriage and the Family* 58, no. 4 (November 1996): 813–823.

Walkerdine, Valerie. *Schoolgirl Fictions.* London: Verso, 1990.

—— *Daddy's Girl: Young Girls and Popular Culture.* Cambridge, MA: Harvard University Press, 1997.

—— *Children, Gender, Video Games: Towards a Relational Approach to Multimedia.* London: Palgrave: Macmillan, 2007.

Walkowitz, Rebecca L. "Reproducing Reality: Murphy Brown and Illegitimate Politics." In *Media Spectacles,* ed. Marge Garber, Jann Matlock, and Rebecca L. Walkowitz. New York: Routledge, 1993, 40–56.

Wallace, Michele. *Invisibility Blues: From Pop to Theory.* London: Verso, 1990.

Walters, Suzanna Danuta. *Material Girls: Making Sense of Feminist Cultural Theory.* Berkeley: University of California Press, 1995.

—— *All the Rage: The Story of Gay Visibility in America.* Chicago: University of Chicago Press, 2003.

Wang, Jennifer Hyland. " 'Everything's Coming Up *Rosie*': Empower America, Rosie

O'Donnell, and the Construction of Daytime Reality." *The Velvet Light Trap* 45 (Spring 2000): 20–35.

Wayne, Mike, ed. *Dissident Voices: The Politics of Television and Cultural Change.* London: Pluto Press, 1998.

Weber, Brenda R. "Beauty, Desire, and Anxiety: The Economy of Sameness in ABC's *Extreme Makeover.*" *Genders* 41 (2005), <http://genders.org/g41/g41_weber.html>.

Wheatley, Helen. *Gothic Television.* Manchester: Manchester University Press, 2005.

—— "Rooms Within Rooms: *Upstairs Downstairs* and the Studio Costume Drama of the 1970s." In *ITV Cultures: Independent Television Over Fifty Years,* ed. Catherine Johnson and Robert Turnock. Berkshire: Open University Press, 2005, 143–158.

Whelehan, Imelda. *The Feminist Bestseller: From Sex and the Single Girl to Sex and the City.* London: Palgrave Macmillan, 2004.

White, Mimi. *Tele-Advising: Therapeutic Discourse in American Television.* Chapel Hill, NC: University of North Carolina Press, 1992.

—— "Women, Memory and Serial Melodrama: Anecdotes in Television Soap Opera." *Screen* 35, no. 4 (1994): 336–353.

White, Susan. "*Veronica Clare* and the New *Film Noir* Heroine." *Camera Obscura* 33–4 (1994–5): 77–100.

Wilcox, Rhonda V. and David Lavery, eds. *Fighting the Forces: What's at Stake in Buffy the Vampire Slayer?* Lanham, MD: Rowman & Littlefield, 2002.

Williamson, Milly. *The Lure of the Vampire: Gender, Fiction and Fandom from Bram Stoker to Buffy.* London and New York: Wallflower Press, 2005.

Wilson, Pamela. "Upscale Feminine Angst: *Molly Dodd,* the Lifetime Cable Network and Gender Marketing." *Camera Obscura* 33–34 (1994–5): 103–130.

Wood, Helen. "Texting the Subject: Women, Television, and Modern Self-Reflexivity." *Communication Review* 8, no. 2 (2005): 115–135.

Woodward, Kathleen. "Traumatic Shame, Televisual Culture, and the Cultural Politics of the Emotions." *Cultural Critique* 46 (Autumn 2000): 210–240.

Young, John. "Toni Morrison, Oprah Winfrey, and Postmodern Popular Audiences." *African American Review* 35, no. 2 (Summer 2001): 181–204.

Zacharias, Usha. "The Smile of Mona Lisa: Postcolonial Desires, Nationalist Families, and the Birth of Consumer Television in India." *Critical Studies in Media Communication* 20, no. 4 (December 2003): 388–406.

Zeynep, Alat. "News Coverage of Violence Against Women: The Turkish Case." *Feminist Media Studies* 6, no. 3 (September 2006): 295–314.

Zimmerman, Patricia R. "Good Girls, Bad Women: The Role of Older Women on *Dynasty.*" *Journal of Film and Video* 37 (Spring 1985): 66–74.

Zook, Kristal Brent. *Color by Fox: The Fox Network and the Revolution in Black Television.* Oxford: Oxford University Press, 2005.

Zoonen, Liesbet van. "A Tyranny of Intimacy? Women, Femininity and Television News." In *Communication and Citizenship: Journalism and the Public Sphere in the New Media Age,* ed. Peter Dahlgren and Colin Sparks. London: Routledge, 1991, 217–235.

—— *Feminist Media Studies.* London: Sage, 1994.

—— *Entertaining the Citizen: When Politics and Popular Culture Converge.* Boulder, CO: Rowman and Littlefield, 2004.

Index

CONTEMPORARY AMERICAN CINEMA

Linda Ruth Williams and Michael Hammond (eds)
Both at University of Southampton, UK

Contemporary American Cinema is the first comprehensive introduction to post-classical American film. Covering American cinema since 1960, the book is unique in its treatment of both Hollywood and non-mainstream cinema. Critical essays from leading film scholars are supplemented by boxed profiles of key directors, producers and actors; key films and key genres; statistics from the cinema industry.

Lavishly illustrated with over fifty film stills in black and white, and colour, the book has two tables of contents allowing students to use the book chronologically, decade-by-decade, or thematically by subject. Designed especially for courses in film, cultural studies and American studies, *Contemporary American Cinema* features a glossary of key terms, fully referenced resources and suggestions for further reading, sample essay questions, suggestions for class work and a filmography.

Contents

The Sixties: *1: Introduction: Endgames and Challenges: Key movements in American Cinema in the 1960s – 2: Debts, disasters and mega-musicals: The decline of the studio system – 3: The American New Wave, Part 1: 1967–1970 – 4. Popular Mainstream Films,1967–1970 – 5: Other Americas: The underground, exploitation and the avant garde – 6: Documentary Cinema in the 1960s –* **The Seventies:** *1: Introduction: Key Movements in 1970s Cinema – 2: The American New Wave, Part 2: 1970–1975 – 3. Popular Mainstream Films, 1970–1975 – 4: New Hollywood and the Rise of the Blockbuster – 5: Blaxploitation –* **The Eighties:** *1: Introduction: Key Movements in 1980s Cinema – 2: Film in the age of Reagan: action cinema and reactionary politics – 3: The Rise of Independent Cinema – 4: Disney and the Family Adventure movie since the 1970s – 5: Vietnam at the movies – 6: New Queer Cinema –* **The Nineties:** *1: Introduction: Key Movements in 1990s Cinema – 2: Cameron and Co.: The Nineties Blockbuster – 3: New Black Cinema – 4: Female Directors and Women in Production – 5: Action Women and Muscle Men – 6: Home Viewing: Video and DVD – Suggested Further Reading – Essay Questions – Bibliography – Filmography – Index*

Contributors include:

Michele Aaron, Jose Arroyo, Tim Bergfelder, Leslie Felperin, Lee Grieveson, Sheldon Hall, Michael Hammond, Jim Hillier, Susan Jeffords, Barbara Klinger, Peter Kramer, Richard Maltby, Jonathan Munby, Steve Neale, Stephen Prince, Eithne Quinn, Mark Shiel, Yvonne Tasker, Linda Ruth Williams, Jim Russell, Mark Jancovich, Cathy Fowler, Brian Winston, Patricia Zimmerman, Carl Plantinga, Geoff King, Jeffrey Sconce.

440pp   0 335 21831 8 (Paperback)   0 335 21832 6 (Hardback)

The **McGraw-Hill** Companies

What's new from Open University Press?

Education... Media, Film & Cultural Studies

Health, Nursing & Social Welfare... Higher Education

Psychology, Counselling & Psychotherapy... Study Skills

Keep up with what's buzzing
at Open University Press
by signing up to receive
regular title information at
www.openup.co.uk/elert

Sociology

OPEN UNIVERSITY PRESS

McGraw - Hill Education